Religion and the American Revolution

Religion *and the* American Revolution

AN IMPERIAL HISTORY

Katherine Carté

Published by the
OMOHUNDRO INSTITUTE OF
EARLY AMERICAN HISTORY AND CULTURE,
Williamsburg, Virginia,
and the
UNIVERSITY OF NORTH CAROLINA PRESS,
Chapel Hill

The Omohundro Institute of Early American History and Culture is sponsored by the College of William and Mary. On November 15, 1996, the Institute adopted the present name in honor of a bequest from Malvern H. Omohundro, Jr.

Manufactured in the United States of America

Cover illustrations: (background) © Shutterstock.com/Vadim Georgiev; (foreground) from the British satirical print *Spectatum admissi, risum teneatis, amici?*

Library of Congress Cataloging-in-Publication Data
Names: Carté, Katherine, author.
Title: Religion and the American Revolution : an imperial history / Katherine Carté.
Description: Williamsburg, Virginia : Omohundro Institute of Early American History and Culture ; Chapel Hill : University of North Carolina Press, [2021] | Includes bibliographical references and index.
Identifiers: LCCN 2020055721 | ISBN 9781469662640 (cloth ; alk. paper) | ISBN 9781469662657 (ebook)
Subjects: LCSH: Church and state—United States—History. | Protestantism—Political aspects—Great Britain. | Protestantism—Political aspects—United States. | Religion and politics—United States—History. | Church and state—Great Britain—History. | United States—History—Revolution, 1775–1783—Religious aspects. | Great Britain—Colonies—America—History—17th century.
Classification: LCC E209 .C3625 2021 | DDC 322/.10973—dc23
LC record available at https://lccn.loc.gov/2020055721

The University of North Carolina Press has been a member of the Green Press Initiative since 2003.

For Marshall and Elaine

Acknowledgments

When I first began to think about the questions at the heart of this project, more than twelve years ago, I had a toddler on my lap and another child on the way. I thought I could satisfy my curiosity about the nature of international protestant community efficiently through research that would be mostly digital. I could not have been more wrong. Instead, as the research question ballooned, it transformed into something that has required years of travel, archival work, and writing and rewriting. More than a decade has passed, and the little ones are now nearly grown. This book is dedicated to them.

I am deeply grateful to the institutions and organizations that have made this journey possible. Support from an American Council of Learned Societies Charles A. Ryskamp Fellowship enabled a year at Princeton University's Center for the Study of Religion, where thanks are especially due to Anita Kline and Jenny Wiley Legath. That year was supremely generative, and I am grateful to everyone in the CSR community. Further support came from the Library Company of Philadelphia, the Historical Society of Pennsylvania, the American Philosophical Society, the Society of Antiquaries of Scotland, and a Sam Taylor Fellowship. The institutions at which I worked, Texas A&M University and Southern Methodist University, were also generous in their support, and I would like to thank the deans and provosts at these universities for valuing research in the humanities. In the project's later stages, I had the pleasure of being the Sons of the American Revolution Visiting Professor at King's College London for the Georgian Papers Project, an opportunity that provided both essential time and access to incredible resources. Portions of Chapter 1 were previously published in the *William and Mary Quarterly,* 3d Ser., LXXV (2018), 37–70. They are reprinted here with permission.

Many of the most enjoyable moments along the way have been in the more than forty archives across five countries that I visited to complete this study. There is no way to list each archivist and librarian who shared their time and expertise, but a few deserve special thanks. Jim Green and Cornelia King at the Library Company of Philadelphia, Helen Weller at Westminster College

Library, Rebecca Jackson at the Staffordshire Record Office, and Oliver Walton at the Royal Archives were all generous with their time and energy, as was everyone at Lambeth Palace Library. Someday I will make a list of archives by reading-room temperature, but for now I will thank the Beinecke Library for including sufficient heat to its already long list of resources. Thanks also go to Megan Corley, Grace Vargas, and Arnaud Zimmern for their research assistance.

I have been privileged to share this work with several audiences. I very much appreciate their questions and comments, many of which shaped the project in profound ways. Thank you to the communities supported by Mike Zuckerman's incredible Salon, the Omohundro Institute of Early American History and Culture's colloquium series, the WMQ-EMSI Workshop on "The Age of Revolutions," the Rocky Mountain Seminar in Early American History, the Cambridge American History Seminar, the Colloquium on Religion and History at Notre Dame, and the Vanderbilt History Seminar for their time and for their suggestions. The Center for Presidential History and the Clements Center for Southwest Studies at SMU generously sponsored a manuscript workshop for this project in 2017. Andrew O'Shaughnessy and Mark Valeri offered thorough and thoughtful feedback, as did everyone else present. Mark Noll did the same at a later date, and I am deeply grateful for his feedback and suggestions as well.

Numerous conversations with friends and colleagues have also been important for finding sources, developing half-formed ideas, fixing mistakes, locating good coffee near archives, and generally sharing joy and misery. I have appreciated insights and help from Craig Atwood, Shelby Balik, Kristen Beales, Troy Bickham, Cyndy Bouton, Arthur Burns, Ted Campbell, Mark Chancey, Lindsay Chervinsky, Rick Cogley, Emily Conroy-Krutz, Ed Countryman, Heather Curtis, Camille Davis, Jessica Delgado, Grayson Dickson, Joe Dooley, Margi Evans, John Fea, Susan Ferber, Linford Fisher, Aaron Fogleman, Brian Franklin, Craig Gallagher, Jen Graber, Keith Grant, Christopher Grasso, Andy Graybill, Emma Hart, April Hatfield, Ben Irvin, Christopher Jones, Hillary Kaell, MaryKate Kenney, Andrew Klumpp, Tom Knock, Sarah Knott, Courtney Lacy, Ned Landsman, Kathryn Gin Lum, Spencer McBride, Brendan McConville, Christopher Minty, Amanda Moniz, Angel-Luke O'Donnell, Ben Park, Sarah Pearsall, Seth Perry, Carla Gardina Pestana, Paul Peucker, Andrew Preston, Ashton Reynolds, Dan Richter, Brett Rushforth, Owen Stanwood, Tom Tweed, Peter Walker, Oliver Walton, Molly Warsh, Adrian Chastain Weimer, Ben Wright, and Karin Wulf. Very early in this project I had the pleasure to be included in an exceptionally wonderful cohort with the Young Scholars of American Religion at IUPUI. More than a decade later, their friendship continues to be a wonderful part of my academic life. Thanks to Ed Blum, Darren Dochuk, Spencer Fluhman, Becky Goetz, Paul Harvey, Charles Irons, Katie Lofton, Amanda Porterfield, Randall Stephens, Matt Sutton, and Tisa Wenger, and to Phillip Goff for making the program possible.

In recent years I've been blessed with the very best of writing groups. Sharing work with and benefiting from the wisdom of Elesha Coffman, Nicole Kirk, Jenny Wiley Legath, Rachel Lindsey, Jessica Parr, Tisa Wenger, and Rachel Wheeler has been productive, sustaining, and fun. Elesha, in particular, has found a way to bring fresh eyes—and sharp wit—to work she has read in more than eight years of iterations. Rachel Wheeler's thoughtful engagement with history and its meaning has been making me a better historian since we took the German Script Course in the Moravian Archives twenty years ago. Shelby Balik read and commented on key sections, and Travis Glasson provided a thorough and helpful read of the whole manuscript. Working with all the folks at the Omohundro Institute has been a joy. Nadine Zimmerli oversaw this project for almost all of its gestation. Her thoughtful, informed, perceptive, and yet always kind suggestions were an essential support without which, on some dark days, I would surely have given up. Cathy Kelly, Ginny Chew, and Kathy Burdette have made its final steps a breeze, and I am grateful for their excellent editorial insights and experienced hand. Joseph Stuart provided essential assistance with the index. I'd also like to thank the outside readers, whose comments and engagement improved the project immeasurably.

Researching and writing this book has overlapped with half my thirties and most of my forties, years during which I was also—constantly and urgently—a mother, spouse, and professor. Essential to this journey has been the guidance and mentorship of senior women who have mastered the combination of academic brilliance and human decency to which we all ought to aspire. Thank you to them, especially, for not pretending it is easy. I could not be more grateful to Cathy Matson, Amanda Porterfield, Judith Weisenfeld, and, above all, Sylvia Hoffert for their kindness, generosity, and advice. The community of writers that Sylvia fostered around her table, with a plate of cheese and a glass of wine, is something I will treasure forever. Her guidance in the years since has been just as important.

For the many hours of laughter, relaxation, and friendship that we've shared while this book slowly marched on, I thank the Leybovich-Glikins, the Rosens, and the Simaneks. To Lynn Dickinson, and to the PCDWA and HPUD clans, thank you for the friendship and the hopeful path forward you all have offered for our wounded world. Chelsea Brown, Pam Corley, Kacy Hollenback, and

Sheri Kunovich provide the best escapes. Sheela Athreya, Connie Kim-Gervey, Jenny Turner, and Janeen Wood are my always people, the ones who have been there through thick and thin, and especially through mile twenty-fives and Sunday witching hours. My family—Kimberly Bowron, Carly Carte, Lane Carte, the Feinsteins, Trish Fiedler, the Huddells, all the Sato Johnsons, and the Websters—have been lovingly patient and even interested in the progress of this project. My grandmother, Doris Huddell, is the loving center of all of our family. I treasure every conversation I've ever had with her, especially the ones where she shared our family's rich history with me. Toby and Lory Engel have been loving and supportive every step of the way. We are blessed to have them here with us in Texas, and it is hard to imagine this getting done without their assistance. Thanks, too, to all the extended Engel-Rodney-Bienstock clan, especially Mark Burlet, Ben Engel, Evie Engel, Ivy Engel, Jocelyn Engel, Josh Engel, Sarah Engel, Marni Karlin, and Laura Struve. Adam Carte, more than anyone else, knows why this book is autobiographical, and I thank him for a lifetime of discussions, shared experiences, and kindness. I could never publish a book without putting in the names of my parents, Elaine Huddell Carte and Gene Carte. I will never stop missing them; their examples and passions continue to shape all I do.

I have read many acknowledgements where the author thanks her children for their grace in sharing their parent with the book. I always imagined a happy toddler playing outside the door of a home office (never on a screen) while the parent cheerfully typed away inside. That has not been my experience. My vibrant children would probably have preferred not to share their mother with this book, but they have grown up with this project, and with their parents' work more generally, as an intractable reality in their lives. Marshall attended three schools in three years on account of his peripatetic academic parents. Elaine, at five or six years old, counted how many pictures of documents competed with pictures of her on my phone, a quantifiable measure of my attention. I missed Halloweens, concerts, and so many ordinary moments. That they've adapted to these aspects of their lives so nimbly makes me appreciate them all the more. I've also had the joy of watching them grow into compassionate and interesting people. They have brought good humor, generosity, curiosity, and a sense of adventure to every part of this process and to our lives. I could not be prouder of each of them. Every trip we were on was better because they were there; every chapter is better because of what they contribute to my life. They are under no obligation ever to read a word of what follows, because they've lived it. I am profoundly grateful that now, all these years later, they understand why writing this book has been important for me to do and that they are excited for it with me. Jeffrey Engel is that other academic parent. In addition to being a wonderful co-parent and historian, he is also my husband and a true partner (lifestyle associate?) in everything I do. He has talked through nearly every paragraph of this book and read many more chapters than ever made it into the final product. And he's the kind of husband who understands why a still happily married woman might need to go back to using her birth name after nearly twenty years. What more needs to be added?

Contents

Acknowledgments vii

List of Illustrations xv

List of Abbreviations and Short Titles xvii

Note on Capitalization xix

Introduction 1

1 Britain's Imperial Protestantism 23

2 Stamps, Bishops, and Missions: Continuity in the 1760s 83

3 Bending Apart, 1773–1774 126

4 National Wars: Public Religion in the First Years of the Revolution 169

5 The War's Consequences for Protestant Communities 207

6 Antipopery and the End of the Protestant State 246

7 The New Protestant Order 287

8 Transforming Religious Establishments 335

Conclusion 376

Index 381

Illustrations

FIGURE 1 *England's Memorial* 29

FIGURE 2 *Council of Ministers* 51

FIGURE 3 Seal of the Society for the Propagation of the Gospel in Foreign Parts 80

FIGURE 4 *The Repeal; Or the Funeral of Miss Ame-Stamp* 91

FIGURE 5 "The Reverend Mr. Samson Occom" 118

FIGURE 6 *The Mitred Minuet* 145

FIGURE 7 *Fame's Rewards* 146

FIGURE 8 *The First Prayer in Congress* 159

FIGURE 9 John Newton's Hymn 184

FIGURE 10 "Second Page of Draft of the Articles of Confederation by John Dickinson, 1776" 202

FIGURE 11 *"General Pete" Muhlenberg* 220

FIGURE 12 *An East Prospect of the City of Philadelphia* 224

FIGURE 13 *Death of General Mercer* 229

FIGURE 14 *A Representation of the Figures Exhibited and Paraded through the Streets of Philadelphia* 257

FIGURE 15 "Proclamation," Feb. 3, 1779 273

FIGURE 16 *No Popery or Newgate Reformer* 280

FIGURE 17 *Fanat[i]cism Revived* 283

FIGURE 18 *The Right Reverend Samuel Seabury* 312

FIGURE 19 *Doctor Phlogiston* 358

FIGURE 20 *By the President of the United States of America: A Proclamation* 373

Abbreviations and Short Titles

BAR	John Rippon, *The Baptist Annual Register, for 1790, 1791, 1792, and Part of 1793; Including Sketches of the State of Religion among Different Denominations of Good Men at Home and Abroad* [London, 1793?]
CUL	Cambridge University Library
Dartmouth Papers	Papers of the Legge Family, Earls of Dartmouth, Staffordshire Record Office, U.K.
DWL	Dr. Williams Library, London
HSP	Historical Society of Pennsylvania, Philadelphia
JRL	John Rylands Library, University of Manchester, U.K.
LMA	London Metropolitan Archives
LPL	Lambeth Palace Library, London
MHS	Massachusetts Historical Society, Boston
NEC	New England Company
NRS	National Records of Scotland, Edinburgh
PDD, Minutes	Protestant Dissenting Deputies, General and Committee Meeting Minutes, London Metropolitan Archives
SPCK	Society for Promoting Christian Knowledge
SPCKNA	Society for Propagating Christian Knowledge among the Indians in North-America
SPG	Society for the Propagation of the Gospel in Foreign Parts
SPRKP	Society for Promoting Religious Knowledge among the Poor
SRO	Staffordshire Record Office, U.K.

SSPCK	Society in Scotland for Propagating Christian Knowledge
TNA	The National Archives, Kew, U.K.
WMQ	*William and Mary Quarterly*

Note on Capitalization

Many names for modern denominations originate in styles of church governance or distinctions in theology. Churches with bishops are known as *episcopal;* churches governed by presbyteries (regional councils of clergy and laity) are *presbyterian;* churches governed at the congregational level are *congregationalist* or *independent;* and the term *baptist* generally refers to congregations that embrace adult baptism as well as a congregational form of government.

It should not be assumed that all those who embraced a particular style of church governance or theology shared formal institutional ties. For this reason, these terms, as well as the word *protestant,* are lowercased. In contrast, particular ecclesiastical organizations, such as the Church of England (Anglicans), Church of Scotland, or the Synod of New York and Philadelphia are capitalized as usual, as are the cohesive Quakers and Moravians.

Religion and the American Revolution

Introduction

In August 1772, Britain's secretary of state for American affairs, Lord Hillsborough, resigned from his office over a dispute about selling off land in the Ohio Valley to speculators. Amid fears that his government would fall, the prime minister, Lord North, turned to his stepbrother, William Legge, earl of Dartmouth, to fill Hillsborough's position. Dartmouth was experienced in American matters; he had been the president of the Board of Trade overseeing colonial policy during the Stamp Act crisis in 1765. But North reached out to him primarily on personal grounds. "You can not, I think," North wrote, "doubt of my earnest wish to have you within the service of the Crown, . . . and you must be sensible how much I stand in need of your friendship and assistance upon the present occasion." Dartmouth acquiesced, though his own inclinations were more for religion than for politics, and he placed himself at the eye of a storm that would only worsen over the three years he served in the role. He stepped down not long after ordering a military buildup in Massachusetts that triggered the "shot heard round the world" in Lexington in 1775.[1]

In 1772, however, many religious leaders rejoiced at his appointment. British philanthropist John Thornton wrote to his friend John Newton, clergyman and author of the words to the hymn "Amazing Grace," that he "hope[d] . . . Dartmouths appointm[en]t will be of service to religion." Dartmouth was widely known on both sides of the Atlantic for his piety. A member of the Church of England, he was also deeply involved in the cross-denominational protestant awakening movement that had sparked waves of revivals in the 1730s and 1740s. He was a close collaborator of Selina Hastings, the countess of Huntingdon, who was herself the longtime patron of George Whitefield, the century's greatest itinerant evangelist. Dartmouth was a member of the London-based Society for Promoting Christian Knowledge, and he was a trustee of the funds raised to support Eleazar Wheelock's college in New Hampshire, a school that had been named after him. He regularly met with Anglican missionaries destined

1. Lord North, quoted in B. D. Bargar, *Lord Dartmouth and the American Revolution* (Columbia, S.C., 1965), 56. See also Nick Bunker, *An Empire on the Edge: How Britain Came to Fight America* (New York, 2014), 194–195.

for America, and he corresponded with many of them after they crossed the ocean. On his appointment, he received a letter from a Scottish minister saying that it was "by a Special particular providence of God that you are entrusted with the concerns of America." He received another such letter from a congregationalist minister who had recently emigrated to Boston. Its writer said he was "persuaded that your Lordship, in becoming a part of administration, acts upon nobler motives, than what influence the generality; and that you mean the glory of God, in the prosperity of the whole British Empire, and more particularly of the Mother Country and its Colonies." The poet Phillis Wheatley, who met Dartmouth while she was in England, penned a work to him, expressing her hopes that he would aid the cause of abolition. Religious leaders on both sides of the Atlantic believed they had an advocate for their causes in Dartmouth.[2]

With hindsight it is clear that having a pious man at the head of American affairs in the 1770s did little to heal the rifts that were separating Parliament from the colonies. But neither that fact nor the reality that the vast majority of religious leaders on either side of the Atlantic would take up the cause of their local governments in the war that soon followed should obscure the world made visible by Dartmouth's extensive connections to myriad religious communities across the British Empire. That world surrounded and depended on the empire and its government. It united religious institutions in common purpose, and it provided a mechanism through which internal differences and disagreements could be balanced by what was shared.

Before the American Revolution divided it, an interlocking system of religious networks, societies, and communities connected distant protestants to one another across the British Empire. They advocated for the cause of religion within its bounds. Through their labors, and with the support of those in government, the participants in these protestant institutions aimed to "[advance] the Knowledge of our Lord Jesus Christ to thousands of poor, neglected souls," in the words of the countess of Huntingdon. Similar sentiments reverberated between American clergymen when they organized missions to Indigenous

2. John Thornton to John Newton, Sept. 10, 1772, John Newton: Correspondence with John Thornton, Add. MS 7826/1/B, Special Collections, Cambridge University Library; James Alice to Lord Dartmouth, Nov. 5, 1772, Papers of the Legge Family, Earls of Dartmouth (hereafter cited as Dartmouth Papers), D(W) 1778/II/453, Staffordshire Record Office, U.K. ("particular providence"); William Gordon to Lord Dartmouth, Oct. 24, 1772, ibid., D(W) 1778/II/442 ("persuaded"); Gordon to Joseph Bellamy, Sept. 9, 1766, Joseph Bellamy Papers, box 190, folder 2959, item 81621, Hartford Seminary Library, Conn. For Dartmouth's activities, see William Giberne to Dartmouth, 1765, Dartmouth Papers, D(W) 1778/II/127; Bernard Page to Dartmouth, July 22, 1772, and Oct. 19, 1772, ibid., D(W) 1778/II/4360; Richard Terrick, bishop of London to Dartmouth, Apr. 18, 1766, ibid., D(W) 1778/II/192. Dartmouth's appointment as secretary of state is also discussed in Benjamin Woods Labaree, *The Boston Tea Party* (1964; rpt. Boston, 1979), 83–84.

peoples, often combining support from an alphabet soup of British protestant groups. Religious leaders communicated with one another about the best way to promote religion, and they did so with the conscious understanding that they worked underneath the umbrella of the British Empire. They gave institutional life to assertions that as a people *"Britons"* were "Protestants and free," ready to "appear in the Defence of the Protestant Religion, and our National Privileges," as leaders of the Church of Scotland phrased it for a national fast day in 1756. They did so by staffing and sustaining congregations and missions in disparate British territories, and they did it by providing public worship for the pious people who stood behind their righteous government.[3] After 1775, the American Revolution severed those connections among protestants that had been nurtured and built across Britain's eighteenth-century empire. It also transformed the system of denominations that had organized protestants for nearly a century, the relationships that linked Anglo-American religious leaders, and the ways that religious communities on both sides of the Atlantic related to their governments. This book tells that story.[4]

3. Countess of Huntingdon to Dartmouth, Sept. 21, 1772, D(W) 1778/II/436, Dartmouth Papers ("Knowledge"). See also Samuel Davies to Joseph Bellamy, Feb. 23, 1757, Gratz University Presidents Case 7, box 12, Historical Society of Pennsylvania, Philadelphia. For *"Britons,"* see "Act of the General Assembly" of the Church of Scotland, May 31, 1756, in Philip Williamson et al., eds., *National Prayers: Special Worship since the Reformation* (Woodbridge, U.K., 2013), 494–495. As an investigation of religion, political power, and empire, this book is informed by interdisciplinary perspectives on the intertwining of those forces. Particularly helpful in this context have been Sylvester A. Johnson, *African American Religions, 1500–2000: Colonialism, Democracy, and Freedom* (New York, 2015); Linda Gregerson and Susan Juster, eds., *Empires of God: Religious Encounters in the Early Modern Atlantic* (Philadelphia, 2011); Tisa Wenger, *We Have a Religion: The 1920s Pueblo Indian Dance Controversy and American Religious Freedom* (Chapel Hill, N.C., 2009); Tomoko Masuzawa, *The Invention of World Religions; or, How European Universalism Was Preserved in the Language of Pluralism* (Chicago, 2005); Jonathan Z. Smith, "Religion, Religions, Religious," in Mark C. Taylor, ed., *Critical Terms for Religious Studies* (Chicago, 1998), 269–284; and David Chidester, *Savage Systems: Colonialism and Comparative Religion in Southern Africa* (Charlottesville, Va., 1996).

4. For histories of religion and the American Revolution, see Spencer W. McBride, *Pulpit and Nation: Clergymen and the Politics of Revolutionary America* (Charlottesville, Va., 2016); John Fea, *Was America Founded as a Christian Nation? A Historical Introduction* (Louisville, Ky., 2011); Susan Juster, "The Evangelical Ascendency in Revolutionary America," in Edward G. Gray and Jane Kamensky, eds., *The Oxford Handbook of the American Revolution* (Oxford, 2013), 407–426; James P. Byrd, *Sacred Scripture, Sacred War: The Bible and the American Revolution* (Oxford, 2013); Thomas S. Kidd, *God of Liberty: A Religious History of the American Revolution* (New York, 2010); James B. Bell, *A War of Religion: Dissenters, Anglicans, and the American Revolution* (Basingstoke, U.K., 2008); Frank Lambert, *The Founding Fathers and the Place of Religion in America* (Princeton, N.J., 2003); Ruth Bloch, *Visionary Republic: Millennial Themes in American Thought, 1756–1800* (Cambridge, 1985); Nathan O. Hatch, *The Sacred Cause of Liberty: Republican Thought and the Millennium in Revolutionary New England* (New Haven, Conn., 1977); and Mark A. Noll, *Christians in the American Revolution* (Grand Rapids, Mich., 1977). For influential studies of early American religion that include the Revolution as an important subject, see Mark A. Noll, *America's God: From Jonathan Edwards to Abraham Lincoln* (Oxford, 2002); Jon Butler, *Awash in*

Because late colonial protestants lived in a world governed by the British Empire, understanding how the American Revolution changed religion requires an imperial approach. Imperial—rather than simply transatlantic—because, as the pages that follow will demonstrate, connections between protestant groups and governments, local, national, and imperial, were at the heart of imperial protestantism.[5] Government support came in the form of public money for established churches, but it came in many other forms as well. Governments adjudicated which religious groups qualified for toleration and which represented civil disorder. They balanced competing claims for resources, and they gave protestant leaders a powerful platform, the public pulpit, from which to claim authority. Official charters and royal approval also legitimized protestant institutions, such as missionary societies, colleges, and universities. When the Church of England's missionary arm, the Society for the Propagation of the Gospel in Foreign Parts, performed its labors, it did so with a royal charter directing it to serve British "Plantations, Colonies, and Factories beyond the Seas" that lacked "publick Worship of God" and were thus abandoned to "Atheism" and "Infidelity," not to mention "Popish Superstition and Idolatry." The reference to Catholic "popery" was not incidental; Britain's protestant empire was

---

a Sea of Faith: Christianizing the American People (Cambridge, Mass., 1990); Patricia U. Bonomi, *Under the Cope of Heaven: Religion, Society, and Politics in Colonial America*, 2d ed. (1986; rpt. New York, 2003); and Rhys Isaac, *The Transformation of Virginia, 1740–1790* (Williamsburg, Va., and Chapel Hill, N.C., 1982).

5. The most significant survey of religion in the British Empire is Carla Gardina Pestana, *Protestant Empire: Religion and the Making of the British Atlantic World* (Philadelphia, 2009). J. C. D. Clark, *The Language of Liberty, 1660–1832: Political Discourse and Social Dynamics in the Anglo-American World* (Cambridge, 1994) offered an intellectual historical interpretation of the empire's dynamics. See also Edward E. Andrews, "Tranquebar: Charting the Protestant International in the British Atlantic and Beyond," *WMQ*, 3d Ser., LXXIV (2017), 3–34; Nancy L. Rhoden, "Anglicanism, Dissent, and Toleration in Eighteenth-Century British Colonies," in Ignacio Gallup-Diaz, Andrew Shankman, and David J. Silverman, eds., *Anglicizing America: Empire, Revolution, Republic* (Philadelphia, 2015), 125–152; Evan Haefeli, "Toleration and Empire: The Origins of American Religious Pluralism," 103–135, and Jeremy Gregory, "'Establishment' and 'Dissent' in British North America: Organizing Religion in the New World," 136–169, both in Stephen Foster, ed., *British North America in the Seventeenth and Eighteenth Centuries* (Oxford, 2013); P. J. Marshall, "Transatlantic Protestantism and American Independence," *Journal of Imperial and Commonwealth History*, XXXVI (2008), 345–362; Nicholas Guyatt, *Providence and the Invention of the United States, 1607–1876* (Cambridge, 2007); and David L. Jacobson, "The King's Four Churches: The Established Churches of America, England, Ireland, and Scotland in the Early Years of George III," *Anglican and Episcopal History*, LIX (1990), 181–201. For international protestantism, a related but distinct topic, see, for example, Katherine Carté Engel, "The SPCK and the American Revolution: The Limits of International Protestantism," *Church History*, LXXXI (2012), 77–103; Stephen Conway, "Christians, Catholics, Protestants: The Religious Links of Britain and Ireland with Continental Europe, 1689–1800," *English Historical Review*, CXXIV (2009), 833–862; and Daniel L. Brunner, *Halle Pietists in England: Anthony William Boehm and the Society for Promoting Christian Knowledge* (Göttingen, Ger., 1993).

The historiography of transatlantic religious history is vast. For the awakening movement, see, for example, Mark A. Noll, *The Rise of Evangelicalism: The Age of Edwards, Whitefield, and the*

usually in a state of ideological and theological opposition, and often in literal military conflict, with what Britons viewed as the corrupted and evil forces of the papacy, embodied by the Catholic powers of Spain and France. Connections among protestants within Britain's empire, as well as the strength of its protestant churches within each region, thus carried significant geopolitical meaning. The collaborations built through these connections furthered Britain's transcendent historic mission, supported by God's providential favor for protestants. Seen in this light, Dartmouth's wide network with its connections that cut across religious communities was no accident. An influential aristocrat who was also very devout, he was a point of contact between the religious and the governmental worlds. Governments, and power, were at the center of Britain's imperial protestantism; governments ruptured it and put different structures in its place through the American Revolution.[6]

Imperial protestantism was thus the system of government privilege, protestant institutions, and social networks that made Britain's empire and its religion protestant. That system is described here as a *scaffolding,* made up of pillars in each of the empire's many disparate polities and planks that bridged the distances between them. The pillars were the empire's various systems of

---

Wesleys (Downers Grove, Ill, 2003); Frank Lambert, *Inventing the "Great Awakening"* (Princeton, N.J., 1999); W. R. Ward, *The Protestant Evangelical Awakening* (Cambridge, 1992); and Leigh Eric Schmidt, *Holy Fairs: Scotland and the Making of American Revivalism,* 2d ed. (1989; rpt. Grand Rapids, Mich., 2001). See also John W. Catron, *Embracing Protestantism: Black Identities in the Atlantic World* (Gainesville, Fla., 2016); Sarah Crabtree, *Holy Nation: The Transatlantic Quaker Ministry in an Age of Revolution* (Chicago, 2015); Anna M. Lawrence, *One Family under God: Love, Belonging, and Authority in Early Transatlantic Methodism* (Philadelphia, 2011); Bertrand Van Ruymbeke, *From New Babylon to Eden: The Huguenots and Their Migration to Colonial South Carolina* (Columbia, S.C., 2006); and Jon F. Sensbach, *Rebecca's Revival: Creating Black Christianity in the Atlantic World* (Cambridge, Mass., 2005). Seventeenth-century puritan studies have long been done in a transatlantic vein. See, for example, David D. Hall, *The Puritans: A Transatlantic History* (Princeton, N.J., 2019); Michael P. Winship, *Hot Protestants: A History of Puritanism in England and America* (New Haven, Conn., 2018); and Stephen Foster, *The Long Argument: English Puritanism and the Shaping of New England Culture, 1570–1700* (Williamsburg, Va., and Chapel Hill, N.C., 1991). For the Revolutionary era, see Gideon Mailer, *John Witherspoon's American Revolution* (Williamsburg, Va., and Chapel Hill, N.C., 2017); Christopher Cannon Jones, "Methodism, Slavery, and Freedom in the Revolutionary Atlantic, 1770–1820" (Ph.D. diss., College of William and Mary, 2016); and Peter W. Walker, "The Church Militant: The American Loyalist Clergy and the Making of the British Counterrevolution, 1701–92" (Ph.D. diss., Columbia University, 2016).

6. This investigation of the parameters of establishment mirrors what has been done looking for "informal" establishment in the nineteenth and twentieth centuries. See, for example, Tisa Wenger, *Religious Freedom: The Contested History of an American Ideal* (Chapel Hill, N.C., 2017); David Sehat, *The Myth of American Religious Freedom* (New York, 2011); and Tracy Fessenden, *Culture and Redemption: Religion, the Secular, and American Literature* (Princeton, N.J, 2007). For the SPG's charter, see Richard Terrick, *A Sermon Preached before the Incorporated Society for the Propagation of the Gospel in Foreign Parts . . .* (London, 1764), 37–38. The perspective of establishment advanced here is similar to, but also very different from, that given by J. C. D. Clark, *English Society, 1660–1832: Religion, Ideology, and Politics during the Ancien Regime* (Cambridge, 1985). Clark's version of a confessional state emphasizes social hierarchy within England, while

establishment and toleration. England, Scotland, Massachusetts, New York, and Virginia—to name only some of these many places—each had distinctive religious histories. After the Glorious Revolution, however, these diverse systems began to converge, and a few denominations emerged as privileged across the empire, particularly Anglicans, presbyterians, and congregationalists. In nearly every part of the empire, one of those three groups enjoyed the privileges of establishment. Largely parallel after the 1730s, the separate colonial and national establishments functioned in overlapping and reinforcing ways as the empire's single, mixed establishment: the pillars of the imperial protestant scaffold. Societies, organizations, and networks of religious leaders bridged the distinct establishments. For much of the eighteenth century, three networks—Anglicans, dissenters, and awakened protestants—dominated this system. They, and the institutions they supported, functioned as the scaffolding's planks. They structured communication between distant protestants within the empire. Over the course of the imperial crisis and the war that followed, Revolutionary leaders and their imperial counterparts, those in government and those in protestant institutions, made choices that bent, divided, and restructured that scaffold, transforming Anglo-American religious communities and their connections to government.[7]

The imperial perspective that lies at the heart of this work distinguishes it from what many readers expect from a book on religion and the American

---

I argue for an imperial religious establishment as a meeting ground of multiple denominations. For discussion of Clark's thesis that Britain was a "confessional state," particularly as it relates to Anglicanism, see Andrew C. Thompson, "Toleration, Dissent, and the State in Britain," in Thompson, ed., *The Oxford History of Protestant Dissenting Traditions*, II, *The Long Eighteenth Century, c. 1689–c. 1828* (Oxford, 2018), 263–283; Brent S. Sirota, *The Christian Monitors: The Church of England and the Age of Benevolence, 1680–1730* (New Haven, Conn., 2014), 9–12; Jeremy Gregory, "Introduction," in Gregory, ed., *The Oxford History of Anglicanism*, II, *Establishment and Empire, 1662–1829* (Oxford, 2017), 3–12; Andrew C. Thompson, "Early Eighteenth-Century Britain as a Confessional State," in Hamish Scott and Brendan Simms, eds., *Cultures of Power in Europe during the Long Eighteenth Century* (Cambridge, 2007), 86–109; Jeremy Black, "Confessional State or Elect Nation? Religion and Identity in Eighteenth-Century England," in Tony Claydon and Ian McBride, eds., *Protestantism and National Identity: Britain and Ireland, c. 1650–c. 1850* (Cambridge, 1998), 53–74; and Richard W. Davis, "The Politics of the Confessional State, 1760–1832," *Parliamentary History*, IX (1990), 38–49. The present study posits a far more theologically limited, though at the same time more geographically and denominationally extensive, role for the relationship between religious institutions and government in how historians interpret eighteenth-century Anglo-American religion.

7. For elaboration of what is meant here by networks, see Chapter 1, below. I use the term *awakened protestants* to refer to those groups who have customarily been called *evangelicals*. For discussions of that term, see Douglas L. Winiarski, *Darkness Falls on the Land of Light: Experiencing Religious Awakenings in Eighteenth-Century New England* (Williamsburg, Va., and Chapel Hill, N.C., 2017), 13–16.; Linford D. Fisher, "Evangelicals and Unevangelicals: The Contested History of a Word, 1500–1950," *Religion and American Culture*, XXVI (2016), 184–226; and Sam Haselby, *The Origins of American Religious Nationalism* (New York, 2015), 24. I have chosen here to use the term *awakened protestants* because it mimics the language of "awakening" used by both English and

Revolution. It sets aside a nationalist American framing that tends to underestimate the depth of American integration in the British Empire before 1775, and in so doing it disregards a deceptively erroneous and yet popular narrative that every history teacher and professor hears from their students. As that story runs, English puritans, fleeing religious persecution at home, settled in New England. Some indefinite number of years later, residents of those colonies fought England for their freedom, and, having once fled religious persecution, they enshrined freedom of religion in the Federal Constitution. American unity and a devotion to religious liberty, construed here as mutually reinforcing, are taken for granted. Even those who quickly acknowledge that the puritans did not promote religious freedom in their own lands will often still accept some version of this story that combines political action motivated by protestant faith, constitutionalism, and religious freedom in a mysterious alchemy destined to produce the distinctive American religious tradition.[8]

The most problematic part of this myth is not its reductionism or its inaccuracy; rather, it presumes an identifiable "American" religious people predated the Revolutionary era. In that version of history, when Parliament tried to impose new taxes, religious leaders—men like New England's Jonathan Mayhew or Charles Chauncy—merely had to recognize and articulate the threats to liberty posed by a distant, tyrannical Britain. They urged the colonists on in their protests, joining religious rationales for revolution to the political arguments

German speakers during the period. For example, in 1756 John Erskine wrote to Joseph Bellamy of "One Mr. Brown a young curate [who] was awakened Octr. 1754 by occasionally conversing [with] Mr. Williams a pious Dissenting Merch[ant]." See Erskine to Bellamy, Apr. 20, 1756, Bellamy Papers, box 188, folder 2932, item 81241.

8. Several previous scholars have emphasized imperial dynamics in the conflict, though their numbers are far smaller than those who treat the American Revolution within an American national context. Most significant among these is Clark, *Language of Liberty*, and others who have emphasized the significance of divisions between dissenters and Anglicans. See also Bell, *War of Religion*; and Carl Bridenbaugh, *Mitre and Sceptre: Transatlantic Faiths, Ideas, Personalities, and Politics, 1689–1775* (New York, 1962). Particularly useful for the present project has been Ned C. Landsman, "British Union and American Revolution: Imperial Authority and the Multinational State," in Patrick Spero and Michael Zuckerman, ed., *The American Revolution Reborn* (Philadelphia, 2016), 107–131; and Landsman, "The Episcopate, the British Union, and the Failure of Religious Settlement in Colonial British America," in Chris Beneke and Christopher S. Grenda, eds., *The First Prejudice, Religious Tolerance and Intolerance in Early America* (Philadelphia, 2011), 75–97. For the war in a shared Anglo-American religious context, see Susan Juster, *Doomsayers: Anglo-American Prophecy in the Age of Revolution* (Philadelphia, 2003). For America's dual founding, see Sarah Rivett, "Early American Religion in a Postsecular Age," *Proceedings of the Modern Language Association*, CXXVIII (2013), 989–995. Fea's *Was America Founded as a Christian Nation* serves as a guide to the critical engagement of the Christian version of this narrative for general audiences. For twenty-first-century conservative Christian readings of the Revolutionary era, see Kate Carté Engel, "The Founding Fathers in Modern America," in Matthew Avery Sutton and Darren Dochuk, eds., *Faith in the New Millennium: The Future of Religion and American Politics* (New York, 2016), 7–24.

made in other quarters. Building on this historical narrative, Americans for generations have argued vigorously about whether the outcome of the Revolution was to establish a Christian nation or to finally and righteously build a wall between church and state. Scholars entering that fray have often, if sometimes inadvertently, reiterated the importance of this essentially nationalistic framing for the subject of religion and the American Revolution.[9]

Overlooked in these discussions is the most salient fact about the formation of the United States in terms of religion. It was formed—abruptly and violently—out of another empire that was also coded as religious, that was also seen by its leaders, religious and political, as promoting God's plan in a sacred history. By setting this subject in its imperial context, this study resurrects the political and religious world in which colonial protestants oriented their religious lives around the British Empire. That starting point is essential to understanding how the Revolution challenged and changed religious communities.

Academic historians, of course, are well aware that Britain's North American colonies were integrated in myriad ways into Britain's empire, and the story of the American Revolution told in academic studies is far more complex than the popular narrative. Historians do not presume any proto-nationalist American sensibility rooted in seventeenth-century puritanism. Yet they, too, have underestimated the importance of connections across, and investment in, the British Empire as an organizational factor in transatlantic British protestantism, although such connections are essential to understanding how religious leaders acted in the Revolutionary era. One reason for the oversight is the ongoing division between American and British religious historiographies. Historians of eighteenth-century British religion have paid quite limited attention to the influence of the American colonies on religion within Britain. More important, however, has been the tendency for early Americanists to see religion as a source of division and conflict in colonial society at the expense of attention to what was shared across colonies and regions. They have emphasized the regional distinctions between New England's densely churched landscapes and the tenuous position of the legally established Church of England in many parts

9. Historians engaging in the popular discussions over whether the United States was founded as a Christian nation work within this narrative of necessity. See, for example, Mark David Hall, *Did America Have a Christian Founding? Separating Modern Myth from Historical Truth* (Nashville, Tenn., 2019); Steven K. Green, *Inventing a Christian America: The Myth of the Religious Founding* (New York, 2015); Isaac Kramnick and R. Laurence Moore, *The Godless Constitution: A Moral Defense of the Secular State* (New York, 2005); Frank Lambert, *The Founding Fathers and the Place of Religion in America* (Princeton, N.J., 2003); and Derek H. Davis, *Religion and the Continental Congress, 1774–1789: Contributions to Original Intent* (New York, 2000). For an interesting counterexample, see James H. Hutson, *Church and State in America: The First Two Centuries* (Cambridge, 2008).

of the South. They note the diversity of congregations and of ethnicities in the mid-Atlantic colonies and the linkages between denominational competitions and the development of local politics. Many of these studies have also explored the role that waves of revivals in the mid-eighteenth century played in bringing new conflicts to settled religious communities.[10]

This attention to struggle and division has created the sense among historians that colonial protestants shared little and quarreled more, obscuring the collective privilege and functional collaboration that dominant protestants enjoyed and exercised across colonies and, indeed, across the empire. Though a growing number of scholars have noted an imperial orientation within colonial protestant communities in the mid-eighteenth century, the implications

10. Catherine A. Brekus noted this trend in the field in 2018: "Impressed by the diversity of Protestants in early America, some [scholars] seem to assume that they were too fractured to have united in pursuit of a common goal. Yet, despite their competition for converts . . . Protestants not only dominated colonial governments but also influenced everything from attitudes toward the body to the rise of capitalism." See Brekus, "Contested Words: History, America, Religion," *WMQ*, 3d Ser., LXXV (2018), 3–36 (quotation on 32). For British religious historiography of the period, see Thompson, ed., *Oxford History of Protestant Dissenting Traditions*, II; and Gregory, ed., *Oxford History of Anglicanism*, II. See also John Walsh, Colin Haydon, and Stephen Taylor, eds., *The Church of England, c. 1689—c. 1833: From Toleration to Tractarianism* (Cambridge, 1993). Studies of Anglicanism that are transnational emphasize missions. See Norman Etherington, ed., *Missions and Empire* (Oxford, 2005), esp. Eliga Gould, "Prelude: The Christianizing of British America," 19–39; Rowan Strong, *Anglicanism and the British Empire, c. 1700–1850* (Oxford, 2007); and Andrew Porter, *Religion versus Empire? British Protestant Missionaries and Overseas Expansion, 1700–1914* (Manchester, U.K., 2004). For influential works that emphasize religious conflict in the colonies, see, for example, Bonomi, *Under the Cope of Heaven*; and Butler, *Awash in a Sea of Faith*, 55. Within specific regions, conflict has also been a dominant narrative. For New England, see Winiarski, *Darkness Falls on the Land of Light*; and C. C. Goen, *Revivalism and Separatism in New England, 1740–1800: Strict Congregationalists and Separate Baptists in the Great Awakening* (New Haven, Conn., 1962). For divisions between Anglicans and dissenters, see Bell, *War of Religion*; and Bridenbaugh, *Mitre and Sceptre*. For the South, see Thomas J. Little, *The Origins of Southern Evangelicalism: Religious Revivalism in the South Carolina Lowcountry, 1670–1760* (Columbia, S.C., 2013); John A. Ragosta, *Wellspring of Liberty: How Virginia's Religious Dissenters Helped Win the American Revolution and Secured Religious Liberty* (New York, 2010); Monica Najar, *Evangelizing the South: A Social History of Church and State in Early America* (New York, 2008); Philip N. Mulder, *A Controversial Spirit: Evangelical Awakenings in the South* (Oxford, 2002); Marjoleine Kars, *Breaking Loose Together: The Regulator Rebellion in Pre-Revolutionary North Carolina* (Chapel Hill, N.C., 2002); and Isaac, *Transformation of Virginia*. For a counternarrative in Virginia, see Lauren F. Winner, *A Cheerful and Comfortable Faith: Anglican Religious Practice in the Elite Households of Eighteenth-Century Virginia* (New Haven, Conn., 2010); John K. Nelson, *A Blessed Company: Parishes, Parsons, and Parishioners in Anglican Virginia, 1690–1776* (Chapel Hill, N.C., 2001); Edward L. Bond, *Damned Souls in a Tobacco Colony: Religion in Seventeenth-Century Virginia* (Macon, Ga., 2000); and Joan R. Gundersen, *The Anglican Ministry in Virginia, 1723–1776: A Study of a Social Class* (New York, 1989). For the Middle Colonies, see John Smolenski, *Friends and Strangers: The Making of a Creole Culture in Colonial Pennsylvania* (Philadelphia, 2012); Peter Silver, *Our Savage Neighbors: How Indian War Transformed Early America* (New York, 2008); and Sally Schwartz, *"A Mixed Multitude": The Struggle for Toleration in Colonial Pennsylvania* (New York, 1987). For the parallel story in New York, see Randall Balmer, *A Perfect Babel of Confusion: Dutch Religion and English Culture in the Middle Colonies* (New York, 1989); and Richard W. Pointer, *Protestant Pluralism and the New York Experience: A Study of Eighteenth-Century Religious Diversity* (Bloomington, Ind., 1988).

of that perspective for the American Revolution, as well as the nature of the institutions that structured that orientation, have not yet been plumbed. More generally, Americanists have assumed a macronarrative of early American religion in which religious conflict in the late colonial period functions to explain the organization of colonial politics, the coming of the American Revolution, and why Americans of the Revolutionary era welcomed the disestablishment of religion as a means of relief from internal strife. When religious divisions are so foundational in so many overlapping narratives, it becomes very difficult to see what was shared. When what was shared by colonists and Britons is overlooked, it is difficult to see what changed when Americans and Britons went to war against each another. Restoring that history is this book's first project.[11]

It thus starts with a protestant empire. By tracing the intersections between religious institutions and governments, the scaffolding of imperial protestantism, it becomes possible to see with more clarity how that scaffolding made the British empire protestant. It did so in two ways. First and most directly, it enmeshed government bodies and religious institutions so that those in government could claim to speak for "protestant" causes and spread their policies through protestant leaders. But, second, imperial protestantism made the empire protestant *as opposed to* Anglican, presbyterian, or some other more specific designation. In other words, imperial protestantism was the meeting point of multiple denominations, those dominant groups across much of the empire that enjoyed official legitimacy. It was the intersection of those groups with systems of establishment and government legitimacy. In the colonial period, imperial protestantism promoted Britain's empire; during the American Revolution, its leaders had to make complicated choices about whether those same structures would support either rebellion against imperial policy or fratricidal war.

Defining imperial protestantism as the empire's intertwining religious institutions and establishments provides a means to integrate the divergent ways historians have considered eighteenth-century British protestantism. Indeed, the word *protestant* inhabits two quite separate areas of historical inquiry. Scholars of British and colonial political culture have argued persuasively since the 1990s that protestantism was a powerful force in public life. They have asserted, and

11. For works that emphasize imperial dynamics, see Mark A. Noll, *In the Beginning Was the Word: The Bible in American Public Life, 1492–1783* (New York, 2016), 150–177; Mark Valeri, *Heavenly Merchandize: How Religion Shaped Commerce in Puritan America* (Princeton, N.J., 2010), 122–134; Guyatt, *Providence and the Invention of the United States;* and Thomas S. Kidd, *The Protestant Interest: New England after Puritanism* (New Haven, Conn., 2004). An imperial perspective is also central to several works focused on the Revolution itself, including Bloch, *Visionary Republic;* Hatch, *Sacred Cause of Liberty;* and Bridenbaugh, *Mitre and Sceptre.*

also disputed, that it was a source of shared political identity. They have tracked its influence and ascribed to it power in political controversies. Moreover, the competitions between protestant and Catholic empires are seen to have driven European expansion in the early modern era. This is protestantism as political glue in a sort of sanctified state. Yet, at the same time, protestantism also refers to a broad religious movement, that which was born of Martin Luther's 1517 Reformation, named for the "protesting" princes at the Diet of Speyer in 1529, and organized in the life of eighteenth-century Europeans and Americans through a variety of denominations. Historians of religion use the term *protestantism* to refer to the characteristics of this movement, quite separate from politics. They trace, rather, the evolution and influence of protestant theology, practice, schism, and community through time and across nations. Imperial protestantism, understood as a series of religious institutions tethered to the British government, makes it possible to bring the political and the religious versions of protestantism into a single conversation. It demonstrates that the history of protestantism as a political force is inextricably bound up with the history of protestant institutions.[12]

An architectural metaphor—scaffolding—provides the means to investigate religion not only as a matter of belief but also as a system of institutions

12. The study of protestantism as part of British political life is most closely associated with Linda Colley, *Britons: Forging the Nation, 1707–1837* (New Haven, Conn., 1992); and Kathleen Wilson, *The Sense of the People: Politics, Culture, and Imperialism in England, 1715–1785* (Cambridge, 1995). The topic has taken on many forms. For protestantism and England, culturally and politically, see Tony Claydon, *Europe and the Making of England, 1660–1760* (Cambridge, 2007). For religion as part of national identity, see the essays in Claydon and McBride, eds., *Protestantism and National Identity;* and J. C. D. Clark, "Protestantism, Nationalism, and National Identity, 1660–1832," *Historical Journal,* XLIII (2000), 249–276. For religion and the formation of the English Empire, see Alexander B. Haskell, *For God, King, and People: Forging Commonwealth Bonds in Renaissance Virginia* (Williamsburg, Va., and Chapel Hill, N.C., 2017); and David Armitage, *The Ideological Origins of the British Empire* (Cambridge, 2000). For protestantism and foreign policy, see Andrew C. Thompson, *Britain, Hanover, and the Protestant Interest, 1688–1756* (Woodbridge, U.K., 2006); Laurence Huey Boles, Jr., *The Huguenots, the Protestant Interest, and the War of the Spanish Succession, 1702–1714* (New York, 1997); and Steven C. A. Pincus, *Protestantism and Patriotism: Ideologies and the Making of English Foreign Policy, 1650–1668* (Cambridge, 1996). For protestantism in North America, see Craig Gallagher, "Covenants and Commerce: Scottish Networks and the Making of the British Atlantic World" (Ph.D. diss., Boston College, 2017); Daniel Robinson, "Giving Peace to Europe: European Geopolitics, Colonial Political Culture, and the Hanoverian Monarchy in British North America, ca. 1740–63," *WMQ,* 3d Ser., LXXIII (2016), 291–332; Samuel Fisher, "Fit Instruments in a Howling Wilderness: Colonists, Indians, and the Origins of the American Revolution," ibid., 647–680; Owen Stanwood, *The Empire Reformed: English America in the Age of the Glorious Revolution* (Philadelphia, 2011); Brendan McConville, *The King's Three Faces: The Rise and Fall of Royal America, 1688–1776* (Williamsburg, Va., and Chapel Hill, N.C., 2006); and Kidd, *The Protestant Interest.* For treatments of British protestantism in this vein, see, for example, Noll, *In the Beginning Was the Word;* and Ward, *Protestant Evangelical Awakening.* Neither of these works ignores political contexts, but neither do they foreground political constructions of protestantism.

through which power and influence flowed. This metaphor builds on studies of the role of religion in colonization that have emphasized the interweaving of Christianity with the most destructive aspects of empire, particularly the seizure of Indigenous land and the enslavement of both Indigenous and African peoples. These textured stories of religion in colonial encounters have a centralized, imperial counterpart, one explored in full here for the first time. A comprehensive picture of the role of religion in the colonial process requires attention to the ways that powerful and normative religious and governmental institutions reinforced one another. The scaffolding of imperial protestantism surrounded the empire and depended on it. Religious and political leaders drew strength from one another, buttressing their collective authority and providing protestants with reasons for why the British Empire was the best vessel for fulfilling God's plan for humanity.[13]

Because this narrative focuses on that history of governmental and institutional cooperation, it is profoundly whiter and more male than any study of eighteenth-century Anglo-American religious history should be if it makes any pretense of being comprehensive of lived protestant experience. This study, instead, focuses on religious leaders, clergy, and a few allied laypeople and their partners in government. Its imperial nature only reinforces its demographic imbalance, as educated, privileged, white, and male clergy dominated the networks and institutions that had a transatlantic footprint in Britain's eighteenth-century empire. But the homogeneity of the cadre of protestant leaders is not an incidental part of this history. It was a result of those institutions' connections to power, government, and empire. Seeing these connections, ensuring that attention to institutional positioning is central to how we understand the

13. For religion in the process of empire in the early modern period, see Katharine Gerbner, *Christian Slavery: Conversion and Race in the Protestant Atlantic World* (Philadelphia, 2018); Heather Miyano Kopelson, *Faithful Bodies: Performing Religion and Race in the Puritan Atlantic* (New York, 2016); Sylvester A. Johnson, *African American Religions, 1500–2000: Colonialism, Democracy, and Freedom* (New York, 2015); Travis Glasson, *Mastering Christianity: Missionary Anglicanism and Slavery in the Atlantic World* (New York, 2012); Rebecca Anne Goetz, *The Baptism of Early Virginia: How Christianity Created Race* (Baltimore, 2012); Kristen Block, *Ordinary Lives in the Early Caribbean: Religion, Colonial Competition, and the Politics of Profit* (Athens, Ga., 2012); and Sylvia R. Frey, *Water from the Rock: Black Resistance in a Revolutionary Age* (Princeton, N.J., 1991), esp. 21–26. For Indigenous and African Christians and interactions with protestant missionaries, see, for example, Edward E. Andrews, *Native Apostles: Black and Indian Missionaries in the British Atlantic World* (Cambridge, Mass., 2013); Linford D. Fisher, *The Indian Great Awakening: Religion and the Shaping of Native Cultures in Early America* (New York, 2012); Rachel Wheeler, *To Live upon Hope: Mohicans and Missionaries in the Eighteenth-Century Northeast* (Ithaca, N.Y., 2008). A related discussion, mostly concerned with the nineteenth century, can be found in Hilary M. Carey, *God's Empire: Religion and Colonialism in the British World, c. 1801–1908* (Cambridge, 2011); Strong, *Anglicanism and the British Empire*; and Porter, *Religion versus Empire?*

religion of the empire's dominant protestants, is an essential piece of the larger story of religion and empire in the Age of Revolution.[14]

As an institutional history, this study is also far less concerned with religion as belief—be they the beliefs of soldiers, clergy, politicians, or polemicists—than is usual for histories of religion. Similarly, there is little that could be considered "lived religion," or the religious experience of individuals. It does not exclude these topics as a way to dismiss the sincerity of the beliefs of the people it describes; rather, it turns its attention to the pivotal role that governments, power, and politics played in defining the terms of religious communities and also in setting the rules for protestant institutions when it came to public life. It also reflects that religious beliefs and experiences are inherently individual, localized, and diverse. The geographic scale of the present project militates against discussing those facets of religion. Yet, at the same time, it reveals the common dynamics of protestant institutions, governments, and public events.

This institutional perspective makes it possible to see the structures that organized dominant protestant institutions and public religion in coordinated ways across the empire, precisely the structures that were most implicated in and vulnerable to the imperial rupture. It does not, however, suggest that protestants across the empire, or even just across the colonies, cooperated without strife. On the contrary, conflicts and competitions between religious groups were intrinsic to imperial protestantism, and those struggles played into the politics of the Revolution in many ways. Political rivalries often matched de-

14. Spencer McBride examines the history of American clergy during the Revolutionary period in *Pulpit and Nation*. For more specific studies, see Walker, "The Church Militant"; William Pencak, "Out of Many, One: Pennsylvania's Anglican Loyalist Clergy in the American Revolution," in Pencak, ed., *Pennsylvania's Revolution* (University Park, Pa., 2010), 97–120; Bell, *War of Religion*, esp. 222–245; James B. Bell, "The Making of an Eighteenth-Century American Anglican Clergyman," Massachusetts Historical Society, *Proceedings*, CVI (1994), 82–111; Jonathan D. Sassi, *A Republic of Righteousness: The Public Christianity of the Post-Revolutionary New England Clergy* (New York, 2001); Nancy L. Rhoden, *Revolutionary Anglicanism: The Colonial Church of England Clergy during the American Revolution* (Hampshire, U.K., 1999); Joan R. Gundersen, *The Anglican Ministry in Virginia, 1723–1776: A Study of a Social Class* (New York, 1989); Carol Van Voorst, *The Anglican Clergy in Maryland, 1692–1776* (New York, 1989); and Alice M. Baldwin, *The New England Clergy and the American Revolution* (Durham, N.C., 1928). For Britain and its clergy, see Sara Slinn, *The Education of the Anglican Clergy, 1780–1839* (Woodbridge, U.K., 2017); W. M. Jacob, *The Clerical Profession in the Long Eighteenth Century, 1680–1840* (Oxford, 2007); and Paul Langford, "The English Clergy and the American Revolution," in Eckhart Hellmuth, ed., *The Transformation of Political Culture: England and Germany in the Late Eighteenth Century* (New York, 1990), 275–307. Of course, not all religious leaders were white or male, though those who were not faced very different challenges to their authority than those who were. See, for example, Paul B. Moyer, *The Public Universal Friend: Jemima Wilkinson and Religious Enthusiasm in Revolutionary America* (Ithaca, N.Y., 2015); Andrews, *Native Apostles;* and Catherine A. Brekus, *Strangers and Pilgrims: Female Preaching in America, 1740–1845* (Chapel Hill, N.C., 1998). Religious challenges to the "gender order" are investigated by Aaron Spencer Fogleman, *Jesus Is Female: Moravians and the Challenge of Radical Religion in Early America* (Philadelphia, 2007).

nominational distinctions, and those allegiances played a significant role in the chaos of civil war in the 1770s. But tracing the macro-level rules by which those conflicts functioned before the war—in effect, seeing what was shared by protestants as well as what divided them across the empire—brings an imperial religious politics into view, a system for organizing the relationship among powerful religious institutions and governments. That religious politics defined which forms of religious expression were recognized as legitimate or valid at the centers of power and what forms of religious life were left unacknowledged, often unrecorded. It determined who could participate in the body politic and who was left on its fringes. The American Revolution disrupted that religious politics because it cleared away the institutions that had organized religious power within the British Empire.[15]

One further caveat is warranted before turning to the specific story told in these pages. If an imperial perspective on religion and the American Revolution demands a wider geographic context than is usually employed by either the American public or academic historians, it requires a narrower geographic perspective than historians of the British Empire generally use. Imperial protestantism did not bind every part of the empire together. Mapping the ties that connected distant British protestants, the archival endeavor at the heart of this project, uncovered a geography for imperial protestantism that joined Britain to those American colonies founded in the seventeenth and early eighteenth centuries. Its heart lay in Britain and in the North American colonies that stretched from Nova Scotia to Georgia, and it included, though less vigorously, the British West Indies. Yet significant portions of the empire remained outside its bonds. The most notable example is Ireland, which was at most marginal to the eighteenth-century protestant system discussed here. Although that island was without question central to British imperial history during this period, its distinctive laws respecting religion and its majority Roman Catholic population largely pushed it to the edge of an otherwise robust system connecting the protestant-dominated American colonies to Britain. Similarly, Britain's engagements in India and in the territories gained after 1763 remained separate from the scaffolding. In all these cases, there are complex stories that deserve telling, but they are beyond the scope of this book.[16]

15. For works on Americans' loyalties and loyalism, see Virginia DeJohn Anderson, *The Martyr and the Traitor: Nathan Hale, Moses Dunbar, and the American Revolution* (New York, 2017), 94–96; Michael A. McDonnell, "War Stories: Remembering and Forgetting the American Revolution," in Spero and Zuckerman, eds., *American Revolution Reborn*, 9–28; and Maya Jasanoff, *Liberty's Exiles: American Loyalists in the Revolutionary World* (New York, 2011).

16. Pestana includes Ireland in her *Protestant Empire*. See also Charles Ivar McGrath, *Ireland and Empire, 1692–1770* (London, 2007), 13–35; T. C. Barnard, *A New Anatomy of Ireland: The*

By tracing the origins, progress, and consequences of the American Revolution through the lens of imperial protestantism—through the destruction of the scaffolding that bound distant protestants to one another and to the empire—new perspectives on religion and the American Revolution come into view. First, by looking carefully at the connections between protestant institutions and government, it is possible to shed fresh light on the place of religion in the imperial conflict and to understand why the scaffolding of imperial protestantism functioned to prevent religious institutions and issues from fracturing the empire. This subject needs renewed attention. In the late twentieth century, scholars of the founding era emphasized the place of political ideology in causing the American Revolution. Their depiction of the colonial struggle with Parliament gave an important voice to religious leaders who articulated political philosophy in a form—the sermon—that historians have assumed shaped the attitudes of ordinary Americans. This largely intellectual approach to the broad subject of the American Revolution elevated New England's religious leaders, and their counterparts among British dissenters and radicals, in shaping the United States' political trajectory. It also gave prominent roles to the era's most clearly religious issues—the fight over the placement of an American bishop in the colonies and the panic about popery associated with the Quebec Act—because they coincided with that ideological paradigm. From the perspective of this school of thought, religion and religious divisions were crucial to the empire's fracture.[17]

Irish Protestants, 1649–1770 (New Haven, Conn., 2003); Barnard, "Protestantism, Ethnicity, and Irish Identities, 1660–1760," in Claydon and McBride, eds., *Protestantism and National Identity,* 207–235; and Ian McBride, "'The Common Name of Irishman': Protestantism and Patriotism in Eighteenth-Century Ireland," ibid., 236–261. For Ireland and the American Revolution, see Vincent Morley, *Irish Opinion and the American Revolution, 1760–1783* (Cambridge, 2002). For India, see Andrews, "Tranquebar," *WMQ,* 3d Ser., LXXIV (2017), 3–34; Penelope Carson, *The East India Company and Religion, 1698–1858* (Woodbridge, U.K., 2012); Robert Eric Frykenberg, "Christian Missions and the Raj," in Etherington, ed., *Missions and Empire,* 107–130; and Strong, *Anglicanism and the British Empire,* 120–122. For the territories ceded in 1763, see Jessica L. Harland-Jacobs, "Incorporating the King's New Subjects: Accommodation and Anti-Catholicism in the British Empire, 1763–1815," *Journal of Religious History,* XXXXIX (2015), 203–223; Aaron Willis, "The Standing of New Subjects: Grenada and the Protestant Constitution after the Treaty of Paris (1763)," *Journal of Imperial and Commonwealth History,* XLII (2014), 1–21; and David Milobar, "Quebec Reform, the British Constitution, and the Atlantic Empire, 1774–1775," *Parliamentary History,* XIV (1995), 65–88.

17. For religion within Revolutionary political ideology, see Edmund S. Morgan, "The Puritan Ethic and the American Revolution," *WMQ,* 3d Ser., XXIV (1967), 3–43; Bernard Bailyn, *The Ideological Origins of the American Revolution,* enl. ed. (Cambridge, Mass., 1992), 32–47; James T. Kloppenberg, "The Virtues of Liberalism: Christianity, Republicanism, and Ethics in Early American Political Discourse," *Journal of American History,* LXXIV (1987), 9–33; Melvin B. Endy, Jr., "Just War, Holy War, and Millennialism in Revolutionary America," *WMQ,* 3d Ser., XLII (1985), 3–25; Colin Bonwick, *English Radicals and the American Revolution* (Chapel Hill, N.C., 1977); and Ruth Bloch, "Religion, Literary Sentimentalism, and Popular Revolutionary Ideology,"

In more recent decades, historians' explanations for the Revolution's origins have moved away from political ideology. That shift has simultaneously discounted the importance of the religious perspectives that were nested within that ideological narrative. Informed by both transcontinental and international historiographical trends, scholars now stress the significance of tensions over the preservation of slavery and access to Indigenous lands for explaining the fight between Parliament and colonists. (Not coincidentally, Lord Dartmouth was an acceptable choice for his post as head of American affairs because he was personally involved in speculation and the crisis that led to his appointment had to do with the Ohio Company.) At the same time, renewed attention to the precipitousness of the descent into war after 1774, a narrative with which the present study concurs, has also limited consideration of the ideological struggles of the 1760s, including the oft-discussed controversy over placing an Anglican bishop in North America. In other words, having justified the study of religion and the American Revolution through religion's influence on political ideology, many historians left religion behind when they turned away from ideology and from the earlier years of the imperial crisis.[18]

---

in Ronald Hoffman and Peter J. Albert, eds., *Religion in a Revolutionary Age* (Charlottesville, Va., 1994), 308–330. For the definitive historiographical treatment of these arguments, see Daniel T. Rodgers, "Republicanism: The Career of a Concept," *Journal of American History,* LXXIX (1992), 11–38, esp. 17. The fullest elaboration of the thesis that religion formed a primary part of the political ideology of the Revolutionary era can be found in Clark, *Language of Liberty;* and Bell, *A War of Religion*. The persuasiveness of these arguments has faded, as historians have turned away from ideological explanations for the Revolution, but there are echoes in more recent treatments. See, for example, Benjamin L. Carp, *Rebels Rising: Cities and the American Revolution* (Oxford, 2007). Carp argued for the primacy of congregationalists in the imperial crisis in New England, but more as "networks of mobilization" rather than "solely on theological or ideological abstractions" (133); see also 121–124. In 1997, Gordon S. Wood expressed a not-infrequent assumption that sermons popularized political thought when he wrote: "Despite the growth of Enlightenment among elites in eighteenth-century America, Protestantism in one form or another still remained the principal means by which most common people ordered and explained the world and made it meaningful." See Wood, "Religion and the American Revolution," in Harry S. Stout and D. G. Hart, eds., *New Directions in American Religious History* (New York, 1997), 173–205 (quotation on 175). For works that situate the bishop controversy and Quebec Act in the imperial crisis, see Bridenbaugh, *Mitre and Sceptre;* Bloch, *Visionary Republic;* James West Davidson, *The Logic of Millennial Thought: Eighteenth-Century New England* (New Haven, Conn., 1977); and Hatch, *Sacred Cause of Liberty*. See also Nicholas Guyatt, *Providence and the Invention of the United States, 1607–1876* (Cambridge, 2007). More recent interpretations of the bishop controversy have emphasized its role within the development of transatlantic Anglicanism. See Peter M. Doll, *Revolution, Religion, and National Identity: Imperial Anglicanism in British North America, 1745–1795* (Madison, N.J., 2000); and Peter W. Walker, "The Bishop Controversy, the Imperial Crisis, and Religious Radicalism in New England, 1763–74," *New England Quarterly,* XL (2017), 306–343. For an imperial perspective similar to the one taken here, see Landsman, "The Episcopate," in Beneke and Grenda, eds., *First Prejudice,* 75–97.

18. S. Max Edelson, *The New Map of Empire: How Britain Imagined America before Independence* (Cambridge, Mass., 2017); Kathleen DuVal, *Independence Lost: Lives on the Edge of the American Revolution* (New York, 2015); Claudio Saunt, *West of the Revolution: An Uncommon History of*

Religion and the American Revolution reopens questions about the place of religion in the imperial crisis and the war that followed, but it does not attempt to resurrect arguments that religion can explain why colonists did or did not rebel. Quite the contrary. By attending to the structures and relationships of imperial protestantism, and by noting the durability of the connections built though that scaffolding, it recasts the issue. Why did religious voices figure prominently in some moments of the imperial crisis and disappear in others? Why did religious leaders celebrate the Stamp Act's repeal with so much more vigor than they had protested its passage? Why were fights over issues like an Anglican bishop for the colonies so intense and yet simultaneously so limited? Why did American religious leaders accept so readily the Treaty of Alliance with France (1778)? The answers to these questions are found in the nature of the connections among protestants across the empire and in their relationships to government authorities—in short, in imperial protestantism.

Further questions also come to light. Reconfiguring how we understand protestant leaders' relationship to the British Empire focuses attention on their role as apologists for what all participants knew was a fratricidal war among coreligionists. Sermons preached from the public pulpit, as well as other statements by religious leaders, have often been used to represent public sentiment. On the American side, they have illustrated growing American support for rebellion and a nascent religious nationalism, while on the British side they have been used to measure religious partisanship. From the vantage point of imperial protestantism, a different lesson can be drawn from this evidence, one that places the close connections between protestant institutions and government at the heart of religious discussions about the war. It becomes clear that the American Continental Congress actively repurposed the tools of imperial protestantism to shore up its own legitimacy, despite its awareness that the

---

1776 (New York, 2014); Alan Taylor, *American Revolutions: A Continental History, 1750–1804* (New York, 2016); Eliga H. Gould, *Among the Powers of the Earth: The American Revolution and the Making of a New World Empire* (Cambridge, Mass., 2012). For the preservation of slavery as an engine of revolution, see Christopher Leslie Brown, *Moral Capital: Foundations of British Abolitionism* (Williamsburg, Va., and Chapel Hill, N.C., 2006); and Woody Holton, *Forced Founders: Indians, Debtors, Slaves, and the Making of the American Revolution in Virginia* (Williamsburg, Va., and Chapel Hill, N.C., 1999). For Dartmouth, see Bargar, *Lord Dartmouth*, 68–69; Edelson, *New Map of Empire*, 312–313. For treatments of the Revolution that begin in 1774 and 1775, see Robert G. Parkinson, *The Common Cause: Creating Race and Nation in the American Revolution* (Williamsburg, Va., and Chapel Hill, N.C., 2016). See also Michael A. McDonnell and David Waldstreicher, "Revolution in the *Quarterly?* A Historiographical Analysis," *WMQ*, 3d Ser., LXXIV (2017), 633–666, esp. 654. Within the realm of religion and the Revolution, see McBride, *Pulpit and Nation*. Exceptions to this trend include studies on specific crises, including Eric Hinderaker, *Boston's Massacre* (Cambridge, Mass., 2017); and Benjamin L. Carp, *Defiance of the Patriots: The Boston Tea Party and the Making of America* (New Haven, Conn., 2010).

United States did not command the kind of institutional religious infrastructure that the British Empire had been able to master. In Britain, the delayed but powerful invocation of public protestantism in late 1776 by central authorities gave witness to the difficulty of waging civil war in religious terms. As governments deployed public religion, religious leaders responded by creating rhetorically separate religious nations, albeit ones that were inherently unequal. British government leaders could count on continuing ties between themselves and protestant institutions in their nation, while the Continental Congress knew all too well that it had no formal connections to American protestant institutions.[19]

The Revolutionary War—the years of fighting that followed 1775—transformed not just those connections to government but also the protestant communities that had bound the empire together, the planks in the imperial protestant scaffold. These effects were far greater than is generally assumed. The networks that had structured transatlantic ties before the war fractured under its strains. Their destruction created room for new, nationally bounded protes-

19. In this approach, this work thus takes a similar strategy to reassessments of the development of the United States federal government. For a summary of this literature, see Gautham Rao, "The New Historiography of the Early Federal Government: Institutions, Contexts, and the Imperial State," *WMQ*, 3d Ser., LXXVII (2020), 97–128, esp. 101. Critical attention to the public pulpit is more common in the British context than in the American. See Pasi Ihalainen, *Protestant Nations Redefined: Changing Perceptions of National Identity in the Rhetoric of the English, Dutch, and Swedish Public Churches, 1685–1772* (Leiden, 2005); Robert Hole, *Pulpits, Politics, and Public Order in England, 1760–1832* (Cambridge, 1989); and Jennifer Farooq, *Preaching in Eighteenth-Century London* (Woodbridge, U.K., 2013). The fullest treatment of American sermons in the context of the Revolution is James P. Byrd, *Sacred Scripture, Sacred War: The Bible and the American Revolution* (New York, 2013). Public sermons form an important basis for Harry S. Stout, *The New England Soul: Preaching and Religious Culture in Colonial New England* (New York, 1986), in his analysis of New England's path through the Revolution, and he argues, generally, that religious leaders were particularly important; see, esp., 281–311. For British sermons and the American Revolution, see Henry P. Ippel, "Blow the Trumpet, Sanctify the Fast," *Huntington Library Quarterly*, XLIV (1980), 43–60; and Ippel, "British Sermons and the American Revolution," *Journal of Religious History*, XII (1982), 191–205. For sermons and other religious sources as evidence of American political sentiment, see, for example, Bloch, *Visionary Republic*; Hatch, *Sacred Cause of Liberty*; and T. H. Breen, *The Marketplace of Revolution: How Consumer Politics Shaped American Independence* (New York, 2004), 14–15. For religion in British politics surrounding the American Revolution, the work of James E. Bradley has been particularly important. See his *Popular Politics and the American Revolution in England: Petitions, the Crown, and Public Opinion* (Macon, Ga., 1986); Bradley, *Religion, Revolution, and English Radicalism: Nonconformity in Eighteenth-Century Politics and Society* (Cambridge, 1990); and Bradley, "The Anglican Pulpit, the Social Order, and the Resurgence of Toryism during the American Revolution," *Albion*, XXI (1989), 361–388. See also Nigel Aston, "Archbishop Markham and Political Preaching in Wartime England, 1776–77," in Robert D. Cornwall and William Gibson, eds., *Religion, Politics, and Dissent, 1660–1832: Essays in Honour of James E. Bradley* (Farnham, U.K., 2010), 185–217; and C. C. Bonwick, "English Dissenters and the American Revolution," in H. C. Allen and Roger Thompson, eds., *Contrast and Connection: Bicentennial Essays in Anglo-American History* (Athens, Ohio, 1976), 88–112. For an overall survey of religion and the American war in Britain, see Stephen Conway, *The British Isles and the War of American Independence* (Oxford, 2000), chap. 7. These questions are taken up more fully in Chapter 4, below.

tant institutions. In the United States, the war also brought havoc to the physical infrastructure of religious institutions wherever armies moved. Churches burned, missions collapsed, ministers fled, universities and their libraries were scattered. Meanwhile, the societies that had sustained transatlantic projects, almost all based in Britain, withdrew their support from the rebelling colonies, forcing Americans to find new forms of finance and Britons to seek new outlets for religious activism. Though Anglo-American religious ties would eventually flourish in the decades after the war, those new connections differed in form and nature from their colonial predecessors.[20]

As mentioned above, the word *protestant* is important here, as the end of political protestantism is a crucial aspect of the war. Historians have found that the national and international rhetoric of protestantism peaked after the Seven Years' War, arguing that religion generally became a less significant influence on political matters after that point. Political protestantism lived on in the empire's religious institutions, however, and it became an issue for both Americans and Britons during the Revolutionary War. It thus continues to be relevant to the history of religion, even after the period when heads of state evidently made political choices with little concern for their divine implications. When the American Revolution disrupted imperial protestantism, the last remnants of the confessional era fell away, evidenced by the United States' alliance with Catholic France and by British reactions to the dramatic Gordon Riots, led by the self-styled "Protestant Association" in 1780. These events forced the leaders of protestant institutions to reexamine, and then abandon, their commitment to a political version of protestantism that no longer served the interests of government.[21]

20. Pestana's *Protestant Empire* discusses the disruptions of the Revolutionary period, but because she does not trace a shared protestantism, the scope of the ruptures it caused are not part of her study. See also Noll, *Rise of Evangelicalism,* 194–232. Scholarship connecting transatlantic projects in the postwar period with those in the colonial period has oversimplified the consequences of the American Revolution. See, for example, Emily Conroy-Krutz, *Christian Imperialism: Converting the World in the Early American Republic* (Ithaca, N.Y., 2015), 7–8; Kariann Akemi Yokota, *Unbecoming British: How Revolutionary America Became a Postcolonial Nation* (New York, 2011), 159–161; and Gordon S. Wood, *Empire of Liberty: A History of the Early Republic, 1789–1815* (New York, 2009), 490–491.

21. For the decline of religion in politics after 1763, see Black, "Confessional State or Elect Nation?" in Claydon and McBride, eds., *Protestantism and National Identity,* 71; Ihalainen, *Protestant Nations Redefined,* 594–595; Thompson, *Britain, Hanover, and the Protestant Interest,* 216–221; Claydon, *Europe and the Making of England,* 360–361. McConville, *The King's Three Faces,* and Silver, *Our Savage Neighbors,* argue for the persistent importance of political protestantism and antipopery in the colonies in the later days of the colonial crisis, as does Ruth Bloch, *Visionary Republic.* In contrast, Parkinson, *Common Cause,* argues for the importance of racial distinctions in forming American unity during the war. The present project finds the link between these two perspectives, without minimizing the persistence of either popular or theological anti-Catholicism, which certainly persisted.

As the war drew to a close, its consequences for protestant institutions across the empire and in the new United States became clear. Most prominent among them was the transformation of the Anglo-American denominational order, the remaking of the system by which protestants had organized their religious lives for nearly a century. Since the Glorious Revolution, a few denominations had dominated protestant life across the empire. They were accompanied by smaller numbers of fellow travelers, those protestant groups defined by immigration, such as German Lutherans or Dutch Reformed, or the sectarian Moravians and Quakers. The damage the Revolution caused within the scaffolding of imperial protestantism opened the way for dramatic and rapid change to that system, through which Anglicans, presbyterians, and congregationalists had dominated. The Church of England, the empire's largest protestant institution, fractured and restructured. But the greatest changes came because the dynamic forces of revival and awakening, which had remained within the dominant denominations for decades, started to move in large numbers to the outside of older, established institutions. John Wesley's followers, who had been within the Church of England, now founded new denominations, called Methodists, on both sides of the Atlantic. A rapidly growing list of other awakened groups—and even more diverse denominations—formed as well. The nineteenth-century's institutional religious dynamism was predicated, in both Britain and America, on the destruction of the colonial protestant order.[22]

Finally, an imperial perspective allows for a reexamination of postwar realignments in matters of church and state. The term *disestablishment* is associated with the weakening and ending of state support for specific protestant bodies. Historians agree that it was the most direct and lasting outcome of the American Revolution for religion in the United States. The complexities of the period become more evident, however, after having traced imperial protestantism through the era of the Revolution. At the level of the new states (former colonies) in America, those at the helm of government, without the guardrails of Britain's mixed establishment, chose to eliminate boundaries around religious groups that had ensured protestant institutions would be orderly and

22. The rapid growth of awakened denominations is central to the historiography of religion in the early Republic. See Shelby M. Balik, *Rally the Scattered Believers: Northern New England's Religious Geography* (Bloomington, Ind., 2014); Jewel L. Spangler, *Virginians Reborn: Anglican Monopoly, Evangelical Dissent, and the Rise of the Baptists in the Late Eighteenth Century* (Charlottesville, Va., 2008); Dee E. Andrews, *The Methodists and Revolutionary America, 1760–1800: The Shaping of an Evangelical Culture* (Princeton, N.J., 2000); Cynthia L. Lyerly, *Methodism and the Southern Mind, 1770–1810* (New York, 1998); Christine Leigh Heyrman, *Southern Cross: The Beginnings of the Bible Belt* (New York, 1997); Butler, *Awash in a Sea of Faith;* Nathan O. Hatch, *The Democratization of American Christianity* (New Haven, Conn., 1989); and Stephen A. Marini, *Radical Sects of Revolutionary New England* (Cambridge, 1982).

loyal. The loss of former ties to colonies reshaped British protestantism, too, as some voices yearned to believe they were in a new era of religious liberty and others doubled down to secure the remaining empire. A very different phenomenon occurred at the American national level, however. There had never been a united American institutional religion, and the Constitution's framers did not create one. Instead, they built a nation that was independent of religious institutions, even though American religious leaders continued to embrace and articulate the kind of religious nationalism they had inherited from imperial protestantism. American national religion became a conflict between these two factors.[23]

This imperial history of religion and the American Revolution forces the structures that connected protestant institutions and governments in the late colonial period into the conversation about religion and the American Revolution. It demands that we think of the Revolution not just as the rise of something new, the American nation and freedom of religion, but also as the destruction of something old, an imperial system in which religious affiliation was a fundamental building block of civic participation and interwoven into the structures of power and politics at the highest levels. The American Revolution disrupted that system—that form of religious politics—on both sides of the Atlantic, with specific consequences for the organization of religious communities and for how religious leaders engaged the governments within which they worked. Though the shifts were naturally much greater in the United States than in Britain, the loss of a shared system nonetheless mattered to both because it disrupted the bonds that had connected the disparate parts of the British Empire, redirected once-shared energies in divergent directions, and challenged everyone to reassess the role of religion in public life.

23. There is a rich historiography on the subject of American disestablishment, much of it focused on Virginia. See John Ragosta, *Religious Freedom: Jefferson's Legacy, America's Creed* (Charlottesville, Va., 2013); Thomas E. Buckley, *Establishing Religious Freedom: Jefferson's Statute in Virginia* (Charlottesville, Va., 2013); Ragosta, *Wellspring of Liberty;* and Merrill D. Peterson and Robert C. Vaughan, eds., *The Virginia Statute for Religious Freedom: Its Evolution and Consequences in American History* (Cambridge, 1988). For New England, see William G. McLoughlin, *New England Dissent, 1630–1833: The Baptists and the Separation of Church and State,* 2 vols. (Cambridge, Mass., 1971). The best survey of the national picture is Carl H. Esbeck and Jonathan J. Den Hartog, eds., *Disestablishment and Religious Dissent: Church-State Relations in the New American States, 1776–1833* (Columbia, Mo., 2019). For works that trace issues around religious freedom, see Beneke and Grenda, eds., *First Prejudice;* and Chris Beneke, *Beyond Toleration: The Religious Origins of American Pluralism* (New York, 2006). For reform in Britain triggered by the American Revolution, see Jasanoff, *Liberty's Exiles;* Brown, *Moral Capital;* Eliga H. Gould, *The Persistence of Empire: British Political Culture in the Age of the American Revolution* (Williamsburg, Va., and Chapel Hill, N.C., 2000); Wilson, *Sense of the People;* and Colley, *Britons.* For religious politics in the 1780s, see Arthur Burns and Joanna Innes, eds., *Rethinking the Age of Reform: Britain, 1780–1850* (Cambridge, 2003); and G. M. Ditchfield, "The Parliamentary Struggle over the Repeal of the Test and Corporation Acts, 1787–1790," *English Historical Review,* LXXXIX (1974), 551–577.

The institutional perspective taken in these pages makes it possible to reconstruct the religious world into which the American Revolution intruded. It is a history of how those institutions related to governments and how they were reshaped by the transformation of the British Empire and the foundation of the United States. The focus is thus on the politics of religion, not merely because it relates to events we normally consider political but because all of its actors, religious leaders and those in government, behaved politically. Their actions should not be read cynically. They used the structures of power to further the goals that they held close to their hearts, be that spreading the true Christian faith, promoting stability, protecting the empire, or freeing Americans from tyranny. All of these impulses remade the Anglo-American religious world. Lord Dartmouth resigned his position at the head of American affairs before the end of 1775; he had no stomach for the fight that followed. But the traces of his labors on behalf of imperial protestantism lingered on in the United States in the college that still bears his name. It is not the only such residue. Imperial protestantism, the connections it fostered and the means of its destruction, lie at the heart of American religion.

1
Britain's Imperial Protestantism

In 1762, Archbishop of Canterbury Thomas Secker used backroom politicking to get Britain's Privy Council to block an act of the Massachusetts General Assembly authorizing a new missionary society. The archbishop's objections were not related to the purpose or nature of the new Society for Propagating Christian Knowledge among the Indians in North-America (SPCKNA). After all, it looked and sounded a lot like the Church of England's Society for the Propagation of the Gospel in Foreign Parts (SPG), of which Secker was the head. The SPCKNA had been created by a government act, like the Anglican SPG, and its leaders were part of the established church in Massachusetts, just as the SPG's were in England. Rather, Secker's objections lay in denominational competition. The Massachusetts project was sponsored by New England congregationalists, whom Secker thought of as "dissenters," members of a transatlantic community that included English presbyterians, congregationalists, and baptists—denominations that refused to conform to the Church of England. A deep and lasting antagonism existed between the dissenting and Anglican communities on both sides of the Atlantic, even though both groups were protestant, enjoyed the privileges of establishment where they could, and agreed on the value of building organized protestant Christianity.[1]

That the Anglican Secker would thwart a dissenting missionary group was hardly surprising. The tensions between Anglicans and dissenters in Britain's eighteenth-century empire are well known. What is more striking in this story is what the two groups had in common. First, both sides assumed that missionary

1. As explained in more detail below, the term *dissenter* generally referred to these groups, though there were other protestant denominations who also refused to conform to the Church of England. For the SPCKNA, see Jonathan Mayhew to Thomas Hollis, Apr. 6, 1762, in Bernhard Knollenberg, ed., "Thomas Hollis and Jonathan Mayhew: Their Correspondence, 1759–1766," Massachusetts Historical Society (MHS), *Proceedings,* 3d Ser., LX (October 1947–May 1950), 127–131; Samuel Cooper, "At a Meeting of the Society," May 6, 1762, Records of the New England Company, Family History Library microfilm, reel 1786590; Thomas Secker: Papers Relating to the Church in the American Colonies (hereafter cited as Secker Papers), MS 1123/3, items 269, 271, 276, 277, 278, 279, Lambeth Palace Library, London (LPL). See also Linford D. Fisher, "'Not in Our Neighborhood': The SPGNA, American Indians, and the Turn to Foreign Missions in the Early Republic," *Commonplace: The Journal of Early American Life,* http://commonplace.online/article/not-in-our-neighborhood.

work should be carried out by government-sanctioned voluntary societies and led by members of the established church. Second, Anglicans and dissenters acted on the presumption that government authorities in London would treat their separate projects as roughly equivalent because both promoted an authentic protestant faith. Secker did not openly condemn the SPCKNA because it was unseemly for one legitimate denomination of protestants to oppose the good work of another legitimate denomination. "Our Society for propagating the Gospel cannot with a very good Grace make any opposition," he wrote to the bishop of London. The archbishop knew that "no serious man can object against the Intention" the New Englanders had expressed. To make his case, Secker had to pivot away from discussion of religion. He argued to the Privy Council that the new society could damage Britain's policy with Indigenous Americans, and on those nonreligious grounds the Council vetoed the Massachusetts act.[2]

At this juncture, the Massachusetts leaders gave up their effort because respectable missionary organizations worked arm in arm with authorities, not against them. Secker's choice of political strategy and the dissenters' acquiescence in the face of their loss were two sides of the same coin; government bodies set the rules for protestant institutions. Dissenters conveyed the news of the veto from London to Boston, and they howled with anger, reflecting, too, that the two sides in the conflict shared strong networks that facilitated transatlantic communication among religious leaders in Britain's far-flung territories. But the dissenters' anger changed little about the outcome. Only when the United States was free of the constraints of the British Empire, when its religious communities ceased to recognize the shared authority of the Privy Council, did New Englanders form their own, independent missionary society.[3]

The American Revolution destroyed the habits and mechanisms of connection, competition, and legitimation between protestant institutions that were evident in the SPCKNA incident. It also transformed the networks of connection that linked protestants on one side of the ocean to the other. Recovering that system, a protestant scaffolding that surrounded the empire, is essential

2. Thomas Secker to Richard Osbaldeston, Oct. 5, 1762, Secker Papers, MS 1123/3, item 276; "Extract from the Records of the Privy Council," May 11, 1763, ibid., MS 1123/3, item 308. There is an extensive literature describing tensions between Anglicans and dissenters in North America and in England. For the SPCKNA specifically, see Carl Bridenbaugh, *Mitre and Sceptre: Transatlantic Faiths, Ideas, Personalities, and Politics, 1689–1775* (New York, 1962), 209–211; and James B. Bell, *A War of Religion: Dissenters, Anglicans, and the American Revolution* (Basingstoke, U.K., 2008), 68. J. C. D. Clark placed these competitions at the center of the story of the American Revolution in *The Language of Liberty, 1660–1832: Political Discourse and Social Dynamics in the Anglo-American World* (Cambridge, 1994). By focusing on the very real tensions between these two groups, these arguments obscure their commonalities.

3. The Massachusetts projectors turned some of their zeal toward the Society in Scotland for Propagating Christian Knowledge, an existing transatlantic organization. See Henry Caner

to understanding how the American Revolution reformed Anglo-American religion into a new shape. Doing so reveals a colonial-era system in which protestant groups competed by a shared set of rules and worked to common ends. That shared system was remarkably robust, and it was rooted in the political circumstances of the late seventeenth and early eighteenth centuries. More precisely, it resulted from political choices made in the era of the Glorious Revolution and the Act of Union, when Britain's imperial governors defined their conglomerated polity in religious terms, through its protestantism. That political stratagem had direct consequences for protestant institutions, which benefited from government legitimization and support. It also had consequences for Anglo-American religious community, as it provided a framework within which transatlantic protestant networks and projects developed. The dynamics of eighteenth-century protestantism, including fights between Anglicans and dissenters, as well as the fractures around the growing awakening movement, must be understood within that framework. It steered the empire's protestants toward a common purpose, even when they struggled with one another.

When imperial protestantism comes into view, it is possible to see how central policies forged diverse church establishments into a roughly common shape, why transatlantic religious institutions connected particular protestant communities to one another, and the way both communities and policies intertwined protestants' plans to build their faith with the goals of the state. Yet historians of eighteenth-century Anglo-American religion have long overlooked these common structures of eighteenth-century imperial protestantism, focusing instead on regional and national protestant cultures. It is an oversight that has had direct consequences for interpreting the place of religion in the imperial crisis and war. By stressing local variation and overlooking the broad patterns that were evident across the empire, scholars have also underestimated the extent to which imperial policy determined the shape and focus of protestant community. As a result, it has been hard to see the myriad ways that the American Revolution—at its core a rupture in the British Empire—transformed religious communities and institutions.[4]

---

to Secker, Aug. 16, 1763, Secker Papers, MS 1123/3, item 317. For dissenting discussions of the event, see Jasper Mauduit to James Bowdoin, Apr. 7, 1763, in "The Bowdoin and Temple Papers," MHS, *Collections,* 6th Ser., IX (1897), 14–16; Andrew Eliot to Jasper Mauduit, June 1, 1763, Jasper Mauduit Papers, MHS, Boston; Charles Chauncy to Mauduit, May 4, 1763, and May 6, 1763, ibid. For the eventual reforming of the society, see Fisher, "'Not in Our Neighborhood,'" *Commonplace,* http://commonplace.online/article/not-in-our-neighborhood.

4. For studies that take a transatlantic approach to Anglo-American religion, see, especially, Carla Gardina Pestana, *Protestant Empire: Religion and the Making of the British Atlantic World* (Philadelphia, 2009). For transatlantic awakenings within the British Empire, see, for example,

Britain's imperial protestantism surrounded the empire. Acting as a scaffold, imperial protestantism bound the empire together and depended on it at the same time. The pillars holding up this scaffolding were the various church establishments around the empire, each unique to a specific jurisdiction but nonetheless united into a common outline that was determined by shared pressures of central policy. Between these parallel establishments, communities flourished. When protestants wanted to spread the gospel, to communicate with distant fellows, or needed support in a local conflict, they relied upon the denominations, religious societies, and personal relationships that linked the empire's distant religious communities. These were the scaffolding's planks. They bridged regions and crossed the ocean, but they followed the boundaries of the empire, and they functioned under its protection and by its rules. As a whole, the scaffolding did not prevent the kinds of competitions that were

---

Mark A. Noll, *The Rise of Evangelicalism: The Age of Edwards, Whitefield, and the Wesleys* (Downers Grove, Ill., 2003); Frank Lambert, *Inventing the "Great Awakening"* (Princeton, N.J., 1999); W. R. Ward, *The Protestant Evangelical Awakening* (Cambridge, 1992); Michael J. Crawford, *Seasons of Grace: Colonial New England's Revival Tradition in Its British Context* (New York, 1991); and Leigh Eric Schmidt, *Holy Fairs: Scotland and the Making of American Revivalism,* 2d ed. (Grand Rapids, Mich., 2001). In addition, there are a significant number of transatlantic denominational studies. See, for example, Sarah Crabtree, *Holy Nation: The Transatlantic Quaker Ministry in an Age of Revolution* (Chicago, 2015); Anna M. Lawrence, *One Family under God: Love, Belonging, and Authority in Early Transatlantic Methodism* (Philadelphia, 2011); Katherine Carté Engel, *Religion and Profit: Moravians in Early America* (Philadelphia, 2009); Renate Wilson, *Pious Traders in Medicine: A German Pharmaceutical Network in Eighteenth-Century North America* (University Park, Pa., 2000); Hywel M. Davies, *Transatlantic Brethren: Rev. Samuel Jones (1735–1814) and His Friends: Baptists in Wales, Pennsylvania, and Beyond* (Bethlehem, Pa., 1995); Stephen Foster, *The Long Argument: English Puritanism and the Shaping of New England Culture, 1570–1700* (Williamsburg, Va., and Chapel Hill, N.C., 1991); and Marilyn J. Westerkamp, *Triumph of the Laity: Scots-Irish Piety and the Great Awakening, 1625–1760* (New York, 1988). These studies have not, however, been integrated into a broader picture of a shared Anglo-American protestantism. Early American religious history continues to be a distinct field. For influential surveys of it, see Catherine A. Brekus, "Contested Words: History, America, Religion," *William and Mary Quarterly,* 3d Ser., LXXV (2018), 3–36; Charles L. Cohen, "The Post-Puritan Paradigm of Early American Religious History," *WMQ,* 3d Ser., LIV (1997), 695–722; Patricia U. Bonomi, *Under the Cope of Heaven: Religion, Society, and Politics in Colonial America,* updated ed. (Oxford, 2003); and Jon Butler, *Awash in a Sea of Faith: Christianizing the American People* (Cambridge, Mass., 1990). Moreover, studies of religion within the colonies are almost always regionally based, differentiating puritan and post-puritan New England from the diverse Middle Colonies and the Anglican-dominated South. English and Scottish religious historiography is also generally bounded by nation. See, for example, Brent S. Sirota, *The Christian Monitors: The Church of England and the Age of Benevolence, 1680–1730* (New Haven, Conn., 2014); John Walsh, Colin Haydon, and Stephen Taylor, eds., *The Church of England, c. 1689–c. 1833: From Toleration to Tractarianism* (Cambridge, 1993); J. C. D. Clark, *English Society, 1660–1832: Religion, Ideology, and Politics during the Ancien Regime* (Cambridge, 2000). For Scotland, see, for example, John R. McIntosh, *Church and Theology in Enlightenment Scotland: The Popular Party, 1740–1800* (East Linton, U.K., 1998); and Richard B. Sher, *Church and University in the Scottish Enlightenment: The Moderate Literati of Edinburgh* (Princeton, N.J., 1985). Surveys of Anglicanism and dissent have also taken regionally bounded approaches. See Jeremy Gregory, ed., *The Oxford History of Anglicanism,* II, *Establishment and Empire, 1662–1829* (Oxford, 2017); and Andrew C. Thompson, ed., *The Oxford History of Protestant Dissenting Traditions,* II, *The Long Eighteenth Century, c. 1689–c. 1828* (Oxford, 2018).

evident between Archbishop Secker and the Massachusetts dissenters, but it kept them from spiraling into major political conflicts, and it pushed protestant institutions into a form through which they supported and strengthened the bonds of empire.

THE BRITISH EMPIRE'S PROTESTANT ESTABLISHMENT

Britain's protestant scaffolding bound together groups that had, before the eighteenth century, been hostile, even at war. Indeed, there was no British Empire before 1707, and the various polities that eventually constituted that empire—England, Scotland, Wales, and a variety of colonies founded under diverse arrangements—were more divided by faith than joined by it. Those divisions were rooted in the sixteenth century. After its split from Rome in the Reformation, the Church of England, with its daughter church in Wales, developed as an *episcopal* church, meaning that it had bishops. Those bishops sat in the House of Lords and thus played a direct role in the national government. Scotland, on the other hand, had embraced a *presbyterian* form of protestantism, in which the established church received funds and support from the government but in place of bishops the church was run by presbyteries, bodies made up of clergy and laity. When Scotland's James VI became England's James I in 1603, bishops were gradually instituted in Scotland, only to be swept away from both countries during the puritan ascendency in the 1640s and 1650s. The same era saw the establishment of puritan colonies in New England, which developed a congregationally based church establishment. Congregationalists, also known as independents, followed a model of church organization in which each congregation chose its own leaders and acted independently of any governing body. The distinctions between denominations, in other words, were also in part distinctions between systems of church government, raising issues that then overlapped with the way the state governed religious institutions. When the Stuart dynasty was restored to the throne in 1660, bishops were reinstated across Great Britain, much to the distress of many Scots, who still adhered to presbyterianism. New England's congregationalists were greatly relieved to see their establishments survive intact. Meanwhile, most of England's other seventeenth-century American colonies gave government support to local versions of the Church of England, though no Anglican bishop was ever placed in the colonies, so they remained dependent on the bishop of London.[5]

5. For an excellent study of the interplay between religion and the formation of colonies, see Alexander B. Haskell, *For God, King, and People: Forging Commonwealth Bonds in Renaissance Virginia* (Williamsburg, Va., and Chapel Hill, N.C., 2017). David Armitage contextualizes religion

The Restoration kings led an empire in which dominant attitudes about the correct organization of the established church—episcopal, presbyterian, or congregational—could be categorized geographically. Anglicans, supporting episcopalianism, dominated England, Wales, and the colonies where Anglicanism had been established, in the Caribbean and in the southern colonies on the North American mainland. Presbyterian sentiment prevailed in Scotland. Congregationalists predominated in New England and had notable minority communities in England. The North American Middle Colonies, particularly New York and Pennsylvania, contained a cacophony of competing voices, including important groups of baptists, Quakers, and Dutch Reformed. At the end of nearly a century of religious warfare, most protestant leaders across the empire agreed on the importance of religious establishment as part of a stable state, but they were sharply divided on the organization of such establishments. Even in those places, such as Rhode Island and Pennsylvania, where there was no religious establishment, protestant groups largely held sway.[6]

The idea of *protestantism*—an overarching religious identity—served to unite divergent ideas about establishment when these disparate polities were consolidated into Britain's eighteenth-century empire. The events of the Glorious Revolution ushered that idea to the fore of British politics. In 1689, the Catholic king James II was ousted when the English political classes rejected their "popish

---

alongside other motives for imperial expansion in Armitage, *The Ideological Origins of the British Empire* (Cambridge, 2000). For discussions of the Restoration, see Carla Gardina Pestana, *The English Atlantic in an Age of Revolution, 1640–1661* (Cambridge, Mass., 2007), 215–220; and Pestana, *Protestant Empire*, 112–114. For the Church of England in the seventeenth-century empire, see James B. Bell, *The Imperial Origins of the King's Church in Early America, 1607–1783* (Basingstoke, U.K., 2004), 3–9; and Katharine Gerbner, *Christian Slavery: Conversion and Race in the Protestant Atlantic World* (Philadelphia, 2018), 28–29.

6. There were about one hundred thousand "non-conformists" in England and Wales according to a 1676 census. See Stephen Orchard, "Congregationalists," in Thompson, ed., *Oxford History of Protestant Dissenting Traditions*, II, 33. A smaller portion of these were congregationalists. For religious diversity and establishment in the Restoration period, see Peter N. Miller, *Defining the Common Good: Empire, Religion, and Philosophy in Eighteenth-Century Britain* (Cambridge, 1994), esp. 28–29; Andrew R. Murphy, *Conscience and Community: Revisiting Toleration and Religious Dissent in Early Modern England and America* (University Park, Pa., 2001); Alexandra Walsham, *Charitable Hatred: Tolerance and Intolerance in England, 1500–1700* (Manchester, U.K., 2006), esp. 49–56; and Andrew C. Thompson, "Toleration, Dissent, and the State in Britain," in Thompson, ed., *Oxford History of Protestant Dissenting Traditions*, II, 267–269. For British North America, See Chris Beneke, *Beyond Toleration: The Religious Origins of American Pluralism* (New York, 2006); and Chris Beneke and Christopher S. Grenda, eds., *The First Prejudice: Religious Tolerance and Intolerance in Early America* (Philadelphia, 2011). For increasing religious diversity because of the conflicts of the 1640s and 1650s, see Pestana, *Protestant Empire*, 106–112. See also Evan Haefeli, *New Netherland and the Dutch Origins of American Religious Liberty* (Philadelphia, 2012); and John Smolenski, *Friends and Strangers: The Making of a Creole Culture in Colonial Pennsylvania* (Philadelphia, 2010). For commitments to establishment more generally, see Scott Sowerby, *Making Toleration: The Repealers and the Glorious Revolution* (Cambridge, Mass., 2013); and Walsham, *Charitable Hatred*.

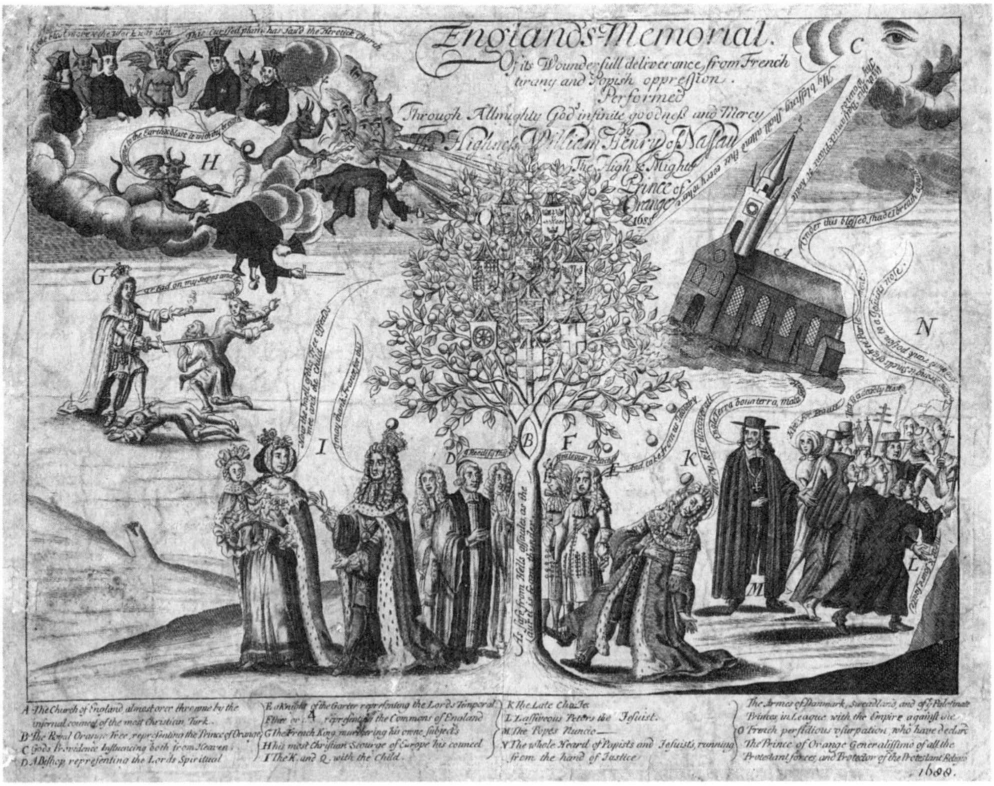

FIGURE 1 *England's Memorial.* . . . Circa 1688. Anonymous print showing William and Mary's ascension, the divine protection of the Church of England, and the vanquishing of papist forces. 1868,0808.3311.

prince" on the grounds that such a leader could not rule a "Protestant kingdom," to use the words of the English Bill of Rights. When William and Mary took over the English throne, they did so as protestant rulers (see Figure 1). The new sovereigns charted a protestant political strategy at both the domestic and international levels. They spearheaded the politics of the "protestant interest" in war against the Catholic French. In 1689, they enacted the Act of Toleration, which extended the sphere of legitimate religion within England to include not just the Church of England but also "protestant dissenters," the term for those who scrupled to join the church but were willing to swear the requisite loyalty oaths and were also otherwise orthodox according to the Thirty Nine Articles, the Church of England's list of theological statements, with minor exceptions. Protestantism, rather than membership in a specific state church, became a vehicle for the political unity of England and Wales. Competing factions—

Anglicans and dissenters, for example—did not have to embrace one another, but they did have to accept one another's civic legitimacy.[7]

The union of England and Scotland into protestant Britain was the most important step in this process because it created a *bi-confessional* state, one that had two separate established churches. Importantly, that did not mean mere toleration of Scottish presbyterianism within an Anglican (that is, episcopal) Britain; rather, it meant the monarchy offered official protection to two separate versions of church establishment in two parts of a united realm. Scotland regained its presbyterian system as part of its acceptance of the revolutionary settlement. The astute move allowed William to solidify control of Scotland, but it also embedded institutional complexity into the heart of the British religious system; England would remain episcopal, with the monarch as the head of the Church of England, while Scots saw protection of their presbyterian church as a basic condition of their allegiance to the crown. Protestantism united the two churches. In 1701, the importance of protestantism only increased when Parliament passed the Act of Settlement naming the protestant (and Lutheran) Electress Sophia of Hanover and her heirs as the next monarchs. The act leapt over more than fifty intervening claimants, including those of the exiled Catholic Stuart family. Scots resisted the idea that their crown too would be disposed of in this way, but in 1707 the Act of Union formally joined England and Scot-

7. "English Bill of Rights 1689: An Act Declaring the Rights and Liberties of the Subject and Settling the Succession of the Crown," Avalon Project: Documents in Law, History, and Diplomacy, https://avalon.law.yale.edu/17th_century/england.asp. The consolidation of British authority after the Glorious Revolution was broad and uneven and far beyond the scope of this work. For religious issues in the period, see Sirota, *Christian Monitors*, esp. 55–65; Sowerby, *Making Toleration;* Steve Pincus, *1688: The First Modern Revolution* (New Haven, Conn., 2009), esp. 5–7, 400–434, 450–458; Pincus, "'To Protect English Liberties': The English Nationalist Revolution of 1688–1689," in Tony Claydon and Ian McBride, eds., *Protestantism and National Identity: Britain and Ireland, c. 1650–c. 1850* (Cambridge, 1998), 75–104; and Claydon, *William III and the Godly Revolution* (Cambridge, 1996). For William III's foreign policies and protestantism, see Claydon, *Europe and the Making of England, 1660–1760* (Cambridge, 2007), 164–168; Owen Stanwood, *The Empire Reformed: English America in the Age of the Glorious Revolution* (Philadelphia, 2011), 125–126; and Pincus, *1688*, 269–274. See also Laurence Huey Boles, Jr., *The Huguenots, the Protestant Interest, and the War of the Spanish Succession, 1702–1714* (New York, 1997); and Andrew C. Thompson, *Britain, Hanover, and the Protestant Interest, 1688–1756* (Woodbridge, U.K., 2006). For the politics of religious and political union, see Claydon, *William III*, 150–190. See also John Spurr, "The Church of England, Comprehension, and the Toleration Act of 1689," *English Historical Review*, CIV (1989), 927–946; Jonathan I. Israel, "William III and Toleration," in Ole Peter Grell, Jonathan I. Israel, and Nicholas Tyacke, eds., *From Persecution to Toleration: The Glorious Revolution and Religion in England* (Oxford, 1991), 129–170; W. M. Spellman, *The Latitudinarians and the Church of England, 1660–1700* (Athens, Ga., 1993), 135–138; William L. Sachs, *The Transformation of Anglicanism: From State Church to Global Communion* (Cambridge, 1993), 11–21; Linda Colley, *Britons: Forging the Nation, 1707–1837* (New Haven, Conn., 1992), 19–20; Walsham, *Charitable Hatred*, 267–269; Pincus, *1688*, 425–434; and Sirota, *Christian Monitors*, 73–79. For ongoing tensions, see, for example, Carys Brown, "Politeness, Hypocrisy, and Protestant Dissent in England after the Toleration Act, *c.* 1689–*c.* 1750," *Journal for Eighteenth-Century Studies*, XLI (2018), 61–80.

land into one polity with one Parliament. Importantly, the new union preserved the rights and privileges of the presbyterian Church of Scotland and its General Assembly. Henceforth, Britain's mixed establishment embraced two divergent church systems and a certain degree of legalized toleration, all governed by a monarchy justified through its protestantism. It certainly did not mean the end of religious conflict, but it did have lasting effects for which protestant institutions could claim public legitimacy.[8]

The British bi-confessional state was the center of an empire with a mixed establishment. It included three established denominations, Anglican, presbyterian, and congregationalist, all collectively protestant. The specifics of church establishment were determined at the national or colonial level, but they were gradually pushed into a common shape by central pressures. Those pressures limited the ability of local establishments to persecute those who were considered loyal protestants in some other part of the empire. Anglican, presbyterian, and congregationalist establishments were forced to accept, at minimum, public worship by other loyal protestants. In practice, this meant tolerating Anglicans and those denominations covered by the Act of Toleration. In 1711, for example, Parliament passed an act protecting loyal Scottish episcopalians "in the Exercise of their Religious Worship, and in the Use of the Liturgy of the Church of England," provided they swore the necessary oaths. Additionally, in a move

8. The idea of a bi-confessional state is explored in James J. Caudle, "James Boswell and the Bi-Confessional State," in William Gibson and Robert G. Ingram, eds., *Religious Identities in Britain, 1660–1832* (Aldershot, U.K., 2005), 119–146. See also Ned C. Landsman, "British Union and American Revolution: Imperial Authority and the Multinational State," in Patrick Spero and Michael Zuckerman, eds., *The American Revolution Reborn* (Philadelphia, 2016), 107–131; and David L. Jacobson, "The King's Four Churches: The Established Churches of America, England, Ireland, and Scotland in the Early Years of George III," *Anglican and Episcopal History*, LIX (1990), 181–201. For Scotland in this period, see Andrew L. Drummond and James Bulloch, *The Scottish Church, 1688–1843: The Age of the Moderates* (Edinburgh, 1973), 3–6, 15–18; Bruce P. Lenman, "The Scottish Nobility and the Revolution of 1688–1690," in Robert Beddard, ed., *The Revolutions of 1688: The Andrew Browning Lectures 1988* (Oxford, 1991), 159–160; Clare Jackson, *Restoration Scotland, 1660–1690: Royalist Politics, Religion, and Ideas* (Woodbridge, U.K., 2003), 191–215; Jeffrey Stephen, *Scottish Presbyterians and the Act of Union 1707* (Edinburgh, 2007); Ryan K. Frace, "Religious Toleration in the Wake of Revolution: Scotland on the Eve of Enlightenment (1688–1710s)," *History*, XCIII (2008), 355–375; and Jeffrey Stephen, *Defending the Revolution: The Church of Scotland, 1689–1716* (Farnham, U.K., 2013). For the Act of Settlement and Act of Union in Scotland, see Colin Kidd, *Subverting Scotland's Past: Scottish Whig Historians and the Creation of an Anglo-British Identity, 1689c.–1830* (Cambridge, 1993). Historians have extensively debated how effective shared protestantism, and these events in particular, were in uniting the various realms of Britain. See, for example, Tony Claydon and Ian McBride, "The Trials of the Chosen Peoples: Recent Interpretations of Protestantism and National Identity in Britain and Ireland," in Claydon and McBride, eds., *Protestantism and National Identity*, 18–20; Pasi Ihalainen, *Protestant Nations Redefined: Changing Perceptions in the Rhetoric of the English, Dutch, and Swedish Public Churches, 1685–1772* (Leiden, 2005), 187–195. The present argument is less concerned with the construction of a shared political identity than with the impact of these legal transitions on religious institutions, which were forced to cohabitate politically after the early eighteenth century.

that angered the General Assembly of the Church of Scotland, Parliament prevented civil penalties from being attached to religious excommunication, essentially limiting the scope of the General Assembly's jurisdiction to its own adherents. In effect, this meant that in Scotland, as in England, no single church could eliminate loyal protestant dissenters. In England, laws that made it difficult for protestants who did not conform to the Church of England to enter civic life were passed in the 1710s, but then then they were quickly repealed, although the older Test and Corporation Acts, which excluded dissenters from some professions, from English universities, and from government positions remained in place. Protestant dissenters (including presbyterians, who embraced establishment in Scotland, and congregationalists, who were similarly establishmentarian in New England) became an accepted part of England's religious landscape. Religious leaders had to make space—in their work, in their public pronouncements, in their sense of legitimate establishment—for the reality of a variety of loyal protestant denominations.[9]

In the early decades of the eighteenth century, colonial regimes fell into line with those in Britain, bringing a form of imperial unity—protestant establishment with limited toleration—to what had been disparate seventeenth-century arrangements. It was a flexible, if centralizing, system.[10] Parliament did not legislate religious matters directly for the American colonies, but provincial authorities and their counterparts in London furthered policies that prevented

9. For Scotland, see Drummond and Bulloch, *The Scottish Church*, 17–20; "An Act to Prevent the Disturbing Those of the Episcopal Communion in That Part of Great Britain Called Scotland, in the Exercise of Their Religious Worship, and in the Use of the Liturgy of the Church of England; and for Repealing the Act Passed in the Parliament of Scotland, Intituled, 'An Act against Irregular Baptisms and Marriages,'" 1711, in Archibald John Stevens, *The Statutes Relating to the Ecclesiastical and Eleemosynary Institutions of England, Wales, Ireland, India, and the Colonies; with the Decisions Thereon* (London, 1845), I, 698. Ireland's path diverged from the rest of the empire, including in its legal limitations on dissenting protestants. See Pestana, *Protestant Empire*, 167–168. For occasional conformity, see Brent S. Sirota, "The Occasional Conformity Controversy, Moderation, and the Anglican Critique of Modernity, 1700–1714," *Historical Journal*, LVII (2014), 81–105; Sachs, *The Transformation of Anglicanism*, 18; Michael R. Watts, *The Dissenters*, I, *From the Reformation to the French Revolution* (Oxford, 1978), 266–267; David L. Wykes, "Religious Dissent, the Church, and the Repeal of the Occasional Conformity and Schism Acts, 1714–1719," in Robert D. Cornwall and William Gibson, eds., *Religion, Politics, and Dissent, 1660–1832: Essays in Honor of James E. Bradley* (Farnham, U.K., 2010), 165–184; John Walsh and Stephen Taylor, "Introduction: The Church and Anglicanism in the 'Long' Eighteenth Century," in Walsh, Haydon, and Taylor, eds., *The Church of England*, 33; and Linda Colley, *In Defiance of Oligarchy: The Tory Party, 1714–60* (Cambridge, 1982), 13. David Parrish, *Jacobitism and Anti-Jacobitism in the British Atlantic World, 1688–1727* (Woodbridge, U.K., 2017), interprets these conflicts, and parallel ones in the colonies, as a single imperial phenomenon.

10. J. H. Elliot has described such flexibility as "composite monarchy." See Elliott, *Spain, Europe, and the Wider World, 1500–1800* (New Haven, Conn., 2009), 3–24. See also Jack P. Greene, *Peripheries and Center: Constitutional Development in the Extended Polities of the British Empire and the United States, 1607–1788* (1986; rpt. New York, 1990).

any single church from dominating a colonial jurisdiction, despite the efforts of those who wished otherwise. South Carolina's legislature passed strict laws supporting an Anglican establishment in 1704, for example, but they were struck down by Queen Anne's government with the support of Parliament. After some wrangling, South Carolina passed a new, slightly less stringent law establishing the Church of England, but the colony possessed a large dissenting population nonetheless. In New York, in 1707, presbyterian Francis Makemie appealed to both the Act of Toleration and, subsequently, the Act of Union and the new position of the Church of Scotland in a united Britain to argue for his freedom after being arrested for preaching without a license. He argued that his license to preach, granted in Barbados but already recognized in Virginia and Maryland, ought to assure his standing throughout the empire, and the court agreed. Farther to the north, Massachusetts's congregationalist establishment was softened by the addition of protections based in "liberty of Conscience" to its 1691 charter. The move permitted Anglicans to gain space in the old puritan stronghold. At the same time, Massachusetts's congregationalist establishment also received protection from metropolitan authorities. In 1732, the solicitor general in London ruled that the 1691 Charter did not forbid a congregationalist establishment, dashing the hopes of Anglicans who wished for a supreme Church of England across the empire. Two common threads ran through these various cases: religious establishments remained a vital part of local governments, and yet the legal privileges granted to those establishments never extended to the point where they could eliminate members of other loyal protestant denominations.[11]

11. Butler, *Awash in a Sea of Faith*, 98–116, influentially argued this period was one of increasing religious institutionalism across the colonies. Most works on colonial religious establishments emphasize a particular region or colony, thus obscuring commonalities structured by a shared imperial relationship. See, for example, William G. McLoughlin, *Soul Liberty: The Baptists' Struggle in New England, 1630–1833* (Hanover, N.H., 1991); or John A. Ragosta, *Wellspring of Liberty: How Virginia's Religious Dissenters Helped Win the American Revolution and Secured Religious Liberty* (Oxford, 2010). For an overview of each different religious establishment in the colonies that became the United States, see Thomas J. Curry, *The First Freedoms: Church and State in America to the Passage of the First Amendment* (New York, 1986). For South Carolina, see Parrish, *Jacobitism and Anti-Jacobitism*, 98–108; James Lowell Underwood, "'Without Discrimination or Preference': Equality for Catholics and Jews under the South Carolina Constitution of 1790," in Underwood and W. Lewis Burke, eds., *The Dawn of Religious Freedom in South Carolina* (Columbia, S.C., 2006), 17–21. For the New York case, see Francis Makemie, *A Narrative of a New and Unusual American Imprisonment of Two Protestant Ministers . . .* (New York, 1707), 3, 16, 32, 41; David S. Lovejoy, *The Glorious Revolution in America* (New York, 1972), 346–348; Ned Landsman, "The Episcopate, the British Union, and the Failure of Religious Settlement in Colonial British America," in Beneke and Grenda, eds., *The First Prejudice*, 75–98; and William E. Nelson, *The Common Law in Colonial America*, II, *The Middle Colonies and the Carolinas, 1660–1730* (Oxford, 2013), 56. For Massachusetts, see "The Charter of Massachusetts Bay—1691," Avalon Project, http://avalon.law.yale.edu/17th_century/mass07.asp; and Foster, *The Long Argument*, 231–285.

By the 1730s, Britain's mixed establishment spanned a vast empire, the result of centralizing forces and the widespread presumption that government should structure institutional religious life. In nearly every region, taxes supported one of three churches. In England, Wales, New Hampshire, the mainland colonies from the Chesapeake southward, and the Caribbean, that was the Church of England. Anglican congregations, often supported by the church's missionary arm, the SPG, existed nearly everywhere else as well. Presbyterians enjoyed establishment in Scotland, and they were a substantial and influential group in much of the denominationally diverse Middle Colonies in British North America, including in Pennsylvania, one of the few places without a formal establishment. Congregationalists were established in most of New England, but even Massachusetts's charter guaranteed "liberty of Conscience . . . in the Worshipp of God to all Christians (Except Papists)." After 1727, it also permitted those outside the established church to pay to maintain their own ministers. A few places had more complex arrangements. New York's seventeenth-century heritage of allowing communities to use taxes to support whatever minister they chose, including presbyterians and Dutch Reformed, ran afoul of eighteenth-century royal governors who sought to privilege the Church of England, as Francis Makemie found. The resulting stalemate made for decades of legal and political squabbles, but these were fights over access to establishment, not efforts to end it. All those involved concurred in the belief that the province of New York ought to support "good sufficient Protestant Minister[s]" and churches as part of the public welfare. Across all of these territories, those three denominations dominated the religious sphere in public life. They vied for privileges, but they did not seek to alter the imperial structures that differentiated them from such dangers as popery and irreligion, and they supported the idea that true protestants were loyal to the British Empire.[12]

For increasing Anglican presence in New England, see Parrish, *Jacobitism and Anti-Jacobitism*, 150–164; Bell, *War of Religion*, 130–141; Richard L. Bushman, *From Puritan to Yankee: Character and the Social Order in Connecticut, 1690–1765* (Cambridge, Mass., 1967), 166–167; Curry, *First Freedoms*, 106–110; and Peter W. Walker, "The Church Militant: The American Loyalist Clergy and the Making of the British Counterrevolution, 1701–92" (Ph.D. diss., Columbia University, 2016), 59–65. Curry, *First Freedoms*, 111–112, discusses the legal disputes over Massachusetts's establishment. For the consequences of these developments on practices of toleration, see Beneke, *Beyond Toleration*, 8. See also Jeremy Gregory, "'Establishment' and 'Dissent' in British North America: Organizing Religion in the New World," in Stephen Foster, eds., *British North America in the Seventeenth and Eighteenth Centuries* (Oxford, 2013), 136–169, for a related argument on the rise of a mixed establishment.

12. "The Charter of Massachusetts Bay—1691," Avalon Project, http://avalon.law.yale.edu/17th_century/mass07.asp. For New York's act, see R. Townsend Henshaw, "The New York Ministry Act of 1693," *Historical Magazine of the Protestant Episcopal Church*, II (1933), 199–204 (quotation on 202). For the Church of England in its various locations, see the essays in Gregory, ed., *Oxford*

Pennsylvania and Rhode Island provide instructive exceptions to the terms of the empire's mixed establishment. In each case, though for different reasons, colonial leaders chose not to establish a state church. The patterns of religious diversity that developed in each case have been seen as harbingers of future American disestablishment. Yet these experiments existed within the structures of the imperial establishment, just as their fellows did. Pennsylvania, where Quakers dominated, did not provide tax privileges to any denomination, and it permitted a far wider range of religious diversity than other colonies, but its founders still assumed that laws and governance would stem from Quaker principles. In addition, it restricted officeholding to Christians, and pressure from imperial authorities led to a law in 1705 that banned Catholics from office. Rhode Island, founded by baptist Roger Williams as a safe haven from puritan Massachusetts's strict establishment, had anti-Catholic laws that dated from 1719. Moreover, its 1663 royal charter couched its bold statement of religious freedom in the assurance that it would "bee noe breach of the unitie and uniformitie established in this nation." The empire's mixed establishment, in other words, was flexible and strong enough to contain a few spaces where the more typical dynamics of establishment and toleration did not hold sway. Moreover,

---

History of Anglicanism, II, which are organized by region. For presbyterians, see Westerkamp, *Triumph of the Laity;* Ned C. Landsman, *Crossroads of Empire: The Middle Colonies in British North America* (Baltimore, 2010), 129–140; and Bonomi, *Under the Cope of Heaven,* 171–176. The colonies of Pennsylvania and Rhode Island diverged significantly in their establishments, although, as will be argued below, they were integrated into the empire's protestant system through its denominations and other practices. For Rhode Island's founding, see John M. Barry, *Roger Williams and the Creation of the American Soul: Church, State, and the Birth of Liberty* (New York, 2012). For excellent treatments of Pennsylvania's religio-political culture, see Patrick M. Erben, *A Harmony of the Spirits: Translation and the Language of Community in Early Pennsylvania* (Williamsburg, Va., and Chapel Hill, N.C., 2012); and Smolenski, *Friends and Strangers.* Historians agree that in the Middle Colonies, denominational affiliation inflected local politics, particularly in the middle decades of the eighteenth century. See Sally Schwartz, *"A Mixed Multitude": The Struggle for Toleration in Colonial Pennsylvania* (New York, 1988); Bonomi, *Under the Cope of Heaven,* 61–66, 168–181; Peter Silver, *Our Savage Neighbors: How Indian War Transformed Early America* (New York, 2008); and Catherine A. Brekus, "Dissent in the America Colonies before the First Amendment," in Thompson, ed., *Oxford History of Protestant Dissenting Traditions,* II, 190. For New York, see Richard W. Pointer, *Protestant Pluralism and the New York Experience: A Study of Eighteenth-Century Religious Diversity* (Bloomington, Ind., 1988); Randall Balmer, *A Perfect Babel of Confusion: Dutch Religion and English Culture in the Middle Colonies* (Oxford, 1989); Landsman, *Crossroads of Empire,* 117–124; and Haefeli, *New Netherland and the Dutch Origins of American Religious Liberty.* Anti-Jacobitism and antipopery presented the ongoing political threats, internal and external, against which this constellation of institutions and ideas was formed. For their influence in colonial America, see Parrish, *Jacobitism and Anti-Jacobitism;* Stanwood, *Empire Reformed;* Brendan McConville, *The King's Three Faces: The Rise and Fall of Royal America, 1688–1776* (Williamsburg, Va., and Chapel Hill, N.C., 2006). Conflicts between denominations play an important role in Anglo-American religious historiography, including explaining the Revolution itself, an interpretation with which the present study differs. See, for Virginia, Rhys Isaac, *The Transformation of Virginia, 1740–1790* (Williamsburg, Va., and Chapel Hill, N.C., 1982); and Bell, *War of Religion.*

by the mid-eighteenth century the same mix of denominations that prevailed elsewhere were demographically dominant in those spaces as well.[13]

At the heart of that mixed establishment was the king. He secured the official status of the empire's established churches, and he defined the range of tolerated protestant institutions as well. The monarch was the head of the Church of England, but he was also protector of the Church of Scotland. The accession oaths taken by the Hanoverians required them to "inviolably maintain and preserve" the "Settlement of the true Protestant Religion with the Government Worship Discipline right and Privileges" of the Church of Scotland. They took this duty seriously. Frederick, Prince of Wales (George III's father), had presbyterian chaplains, and George III declined to hear a petition from presbyterian "Seceders," a schismatic group in Scotland, on the grounds that they were not the established church. A formal representative of the monarch attended Scotland's General Assembly each year, reinforcing its importance. In addition, the Georgian kings annually supplied the *regium donum,* a grant that supported indigent dissenting clergy, elevating and legitimating the position of English dissent. The court maintained German and French royal chapels, giving even wider meaning to the official toleration of diverse protestant denominations. In a similar vein, the 1749 passage by Parliament of an act giving formal recognition to the Moravians as "an antient Protestant" group protected a degree of diversity among loyal protestant outsiders. Protestant congregations, near and far, regularly sent letters of congratulations and petitions to the king, and he responded to their loyal addresses. The monarch, by law a protestant, was in practice the point of intersection for Britain's legitimate protestant bodies, established and tolerated.[14]

13. For Rhode Island's charter, see "Charter of Rhode Island and Providence Plantations—July 15, 1663," Avalon Project, https://avalon.law.yale.edu/17th_century/ri04.asp. For Pennsylvania, see David Little, "The Pennsylvania Experiment with Freedom of Conscience and Church-State Relations," in Carl H. Esbeck and Jonathan J. Den Hartog, eds., *Disestablishment and Religious Dissent: Church-State Relations in the New American States, 1776–1833* (Columbia, Mo., 2019), 71–95; Smolenski, *Friends and Strangers;* and Erben, *Harmony of the Spirits.* For Rhode Island, see James S. Kabala, "Church and State in Rhode Island," in Esbeck and Hartog, eds., *Disestablishment and Religious Dissent,* 55–70.

14. "Union with Scotland Act 1706," Article XXV, http://www.legislation.gov.uk/aep/Ann/6/11/part/18 ("inviolably"). For the role of the crown as an intermediary with various denominations around the empire, see K. R. M. Short, "The English Regium Donum," *English Historical Review,* LXXXIV (1969), 59–78; Jacobson, "The King's Four Churches," *Anglican and Episcopal History,* LIX (1990), 181–201; Stephen, *Scottish Presbyterians,* 53–54, 64; and J. C. Lees, "The Religious Retinue of Leicester House: Chaplains of Frederick Louis, Prince of Wales, 1729–51," *Journal for Eighteenth-Century Studies,* XL (2017), 89–109. For the Seceders' petition, see Lord Rochford to Sir John Pringle, June 2, 1769, in Joseph Redington, ed., *Calendar of Home Office Papers of the Reign of George III, 1766–1769, Preserved in Her Majesty's Public Record Office* (London, 1879), 474. The Hanoverian court was a key node in connections with Continental protestants, including the Halle Pietists. See Daniel L. Brunner, *Halle Pietists in England: Anthony William Boehm and the*

Across the empire, governments protected the religion promoted by legitimate protestant bodies, those which were loyal and also possessed a "sufficient Protestant Minister," in the words of the New York statute. Many colonial jurisdictions required a license for a minister to preach, and local governments were unlikely to license anyone who did not conform to their sense of what a minister should look like. He (almost invariably, *he*) was likely educated, white, and recognized by a denomination that local, often county-level, authorities thought trustworthy. This was a profoundly conservative standard; religious upstarts faced skepticism and hostility. Widespread laws against blasphemy and Sabbath breaking also had the effect of shoring up the authority of protestant churches, as did at least formal requirements to attend established churches for those who did not dissent. Although significant diversity existed across the empire, in general these laws distanced questions of legitimate or appropriate religion from issues of theology or ecclesiastical organization, about which there was accepted diversity among protestants. Rather, crimes such as heresy, blasphemy, and Sabbath breaking were committed by individuals (whether lay or clerical) who represented disorder to the state. Thus, the French Prophets, a group of enthusiastic Huguenots who caused a stir in London in the early eighteenth century, were tried for "Impostures in Religion" and sedition. These were crimes of individuals against a state that took as part of its mission the protection of religion. Likewise, Connecticut's Rogerenes, who followed a Saturday Sabbath observance, were denied the right to gather on their holy day by that province's General Assembly. Even the Act of Toleration required dissenting religious gatherings to be public so the state could oversee potentially dangerous

---

Society for Promoting Christian Knowledge (Göttingen, Ger., 1993). For the monarchy's financial support of non-Anglican clergy, particularly foreign protestants, see George III's establishment book, "The Establishment of the Yearly Charge of the Salaries to the Officers and Servants of His Majesty's House to Commence the First Day of July 1761," July 1, 1761, fol. 4, Royal Archives (RA) EB/EB/39, Windsor, U.K. For communications with the Church of Scotland, see the 1766 Register of the Actings and Proceedings of the General Assembly of the Church of Scotland, Records of the General Assembly of the Church of Scotland (CH1) 1/58, National Records of Scotland, Edinburgh (NRS). For the 1749 Moravian Act, see Colin Podmore, *The Moravian Church in England, 1728–1760* (Oxford, 1998), 228 ("antient"). For petitions and correspondence to the king from various denominations, see, for example, Protestant Dissenting Deputies, General and Committee Meeting Minutes, Oct. 23, 1751, CLC/181/MS03083/001, London Metropolitan Archives (LMA); Minutes of the Body of Protestant Dissenting Ministers of the Three Denominations (hereafter cited as Minutes of the Three Denominations), II, part 1, Sept. 14, 1762, Dr. Williams Library, London (DWL). See also Caleb Ashworth to Mercy Doddridge, Mar. 29, 1765, L. 1/4/8, DWL; Petition from New York Presbyterians to King George III, Fulham Papers, XLI, fols. 287–295, LPL; Ezra Stiles to Joseph Jennings, Nov. 17, 1766, Ezra Stiles Papers, Beinecke Rare Book and Manuscript Library, Yale University, New Haven, Conn.; First Presbyterian Church in the City of New York, Minutes, July 13, 1771, Record Group 413, Series 1, box 1, Presbyterian Historical Society, Philadelphia. Brendan McConville argues for substantial individual investment in the king among those in British North America, in *The King's Three Faces*.

or seditious behavior. The specifics of the relationship between magistrates and the church varied from place to place, but in general those groups that gained status as legitimate protestants enjoyed collective privileges from the state that were denied to those deemed, more simply, troublemakers.[15]

When that protestant establishment is in full view as a series of local variations overseen by centralizing authorities, it becomes clear that religious legitimacy was a status one could carry from one part of the empire to another, a significant fact in the mobile eighteenth-century Atlantic world. The peripatetic Francis Makemie, as noted above, was licensed to preach in both Virginia and Maryland. At the county court in Accomack, Virginia, in 1699, Makemie made his case based on both taking the oaths required in the Act of Toleration and his license from Barbados. As a presbyterian, he had a powerful case in each jurisdiction. His petitions for a license should also highlight the privilege he carried with him as a presbyterian. It is nearly impossible to imagine that any of those local courts who evaluated his application for a license would have granted one to someone who was not ordained by a recognized denomination or to a religious community that did not have recognized clergy. Legitimacy in part of the empire rested on legitimacy in a different part of the empire. The empire's mixed establishment, even though it was adjudicated at the local level, had the effect of defining a relatively uniform, legitimate—that is, recognized by those with political authority—religious community. Indeed, focusing on well-known

15. For struggles to be recognized as a legitimate minister, see Catherine A. Brekus, *Strangers and Pilgrims: Female Preaching in America, 1740–1845* (Chapel Hill, N.C., 1998), 27–29; Thomas Kidd, "Passing as a Pastor: Clerical Imposture in the Colonial Atlantic World," *Religion and American Culture*, XIV (2004), 149–174; and Linford D. Fisher, *The Indian Great Awakening: Religion and the Shaping of Native Cultures in Early America* (Oxford, 2014), 114–117. Certainly, nonwhite religious leaders existed, often beyond the boundaries of institutional protestant records. See Edward E. Andrews, *Native Apostles: Black and Indian Missionaries in the British Atlantic World* (Cambridge, Mass., 2013). For laws regarding religious matters, see John K. Nelson, *A Blessed Company: Parishes, Parsons, and Parishioners in Anglican Virginia, 1690–1776* (Chapel Hill, N.C., 2001), 244–249; Susan Juster, "Heretics, Blasphemers, and Sabbath Breakers: The Prosecution of Religious Crime in Early America," in Beneke and Grenda, eds., *The First Prejudice*, 123–142; David Nash, "Analyzing the History of Religious Crime: Models of 'Passive' and 'Active' Blasphemy since the Medieval Period," *Journal of Social History*, XLI (2007), 5–29; Nelson, *Common Law in Colonial America*, II, 75, 91; and M. Louise Greene, *The Development of Religious Liberty in Connecticut* (Boston, 1905), 187. For New England, see C. C. Goen, *Revivalism and Separatism in New England, 1740–1800: Strict Congregationalists and Separate Baptists in the Great Awakening* (New Haven, Conn., 1962), 267–268. For the French prophets, see Lionel Laborie, *Enlightening Enthusiasm: Prophecy and Religious Experience in Early Eighteenth-Century England* (Manchester, U.K., 2015), 176–180; and Susan Juster, *Doomsayers: Anglo-American Prophecy in the Age of Revolution* (Philadelphia, 2003), 24–33. For prosecutions of religious disorder, see Bushman, *From Puritan to Yankee*, 166; Sirota, *Christian Monitors*, 175, 208–209. In North American colonies where Anglicanism was established, the vestry system placed authority for policing religion in the hands of lay Anglicans. See Bell, *Imperial Origins*, 125–136. Licensing preachers played a key role in defining "legitimate" religion in the colonies. For a detailed list of legal cases involving religion in Virginia after 1763, see Ragosta, *Wellspring of Liberty*, 171–180.

cases of persecution, including Makemie's in New York, can distract from a more fundamental rule at play: only those groups who could be recognized as possessing "a good sufficient Protestant Minister" could hope to participate.[16]

Britain's mixed establishment preserved important room for toleration, and protestant groups who were outside establishment in a given place—especially English dissenters—championed its virtues. Anglicans, presbyterians, and congregationalists all advocated for limits on establishment when they did not enjoy it. This generalized embrace of religious liberty created space for what can be considered the unintended beneficiaries of Britain's mixed establishment, sectarian groups like the Quakers, Moravians, and to a lesser extent even the baptists, who did not advocate for religious establishments anywhere but who nonetheless benefited from being members of protestant institutions in an empire that valued just that form of religious organization. Generally, they were quiescent and orthodox enough not to be considered a widespread threat to social order, and they were therefore able to thrive within their limits. Controversies over the Moravians' agitations around midcentury were the exception that proved the rule. In the face of significant opposition, they gained official approval from Parliament and tacked toward the center. Those moves largely protected them from persecution but did not gain them respectability. The presence of such groups complicated the religious landscape, but they presented no challenge to Britain's mixed establishment.[17]

The same principles can be used to understand the place in the empire of "foreign protestants," those who immigrated from the Continent but did not wish to conform to the established churches in the places they settled. Most, including German Lutherans, German Reformed, and Dutch Reformed, were members of established churches in their home territories and were thus not considered schismatic (or guilty of dividing the church). They earned comparatively easy acceptance in Britain's protestant world. Those persecuted for their protestantism by Catholic authorities were also welcome. Indeed, because

16. Henry C. McCook, "Records of Accomack County, Virginia, Relating to the Rev. Francis Makemie," part 2, *Journal of the Presbyterian Historical Society,* IV (1907), 74–75. For Virginia, see William Henry Foote, *Sketches of Virginia, Historical and Biographical* (Philadelphia, 1850), 131–140; and Petition of Clergy of Virginia to the House of Burgesses, Fulham Papers, XIV, fols. 269–270. New York's Ministry Act, the basis of the controversy, contains the phrase "a good sufficient Protestant Minister" and can be found in "The Ministry Act, 1693," *Ecclesiastical Records: State of New York,* II (Albany, 1901), 1077.

17. I am grateful for the insights of Travis Glasson in helping me formulate this argument about "unintended beneficiaries." For the Moravians, see Paul Peucker, *A Time of Sifting: Mystical Marriage and the Crisis of Moravian Piety in the Eighteenth Century* (University Park, Pa., 2015); Podmore, *Moravian Church in England;* Engel, *Religion and Profit;* and Aaron Spencer Fogleman, *Jesus Is Female: Moravians and the Challenge of Radical Religion in Early America* (Philadelphia, 2007). The positions of the Quakers and the baptists are explored more fully below.

of Britain's pro-protestant policies, the empire became home to large numbers of protestant refugees. Huguenots, exiled French protestants, were an international cause célèbre in the early years of the eighteenth century, for example, and a substantial French-speaking protestant population settled in both Britain and South Carolina. German immigrants led to a notable Lutheran and Reformed presence, particularly in the Middle Colonies. Efforts to support the persecuted Salzburger protestants from Austria became a part of the colonial project in Georgia. German and French protestant communities also found homes in Nova Scotia. In 1740, Parliament codified naturalization policies for the empire and granted naturalization to any protestant who had lived in the empire for seven years, could subscribe to oaths of allegiance and protestant belief, and could provide evidence of communion from a protestant church. That final requirement reinforced the need for recognized protestant clergy, even as it also eschewed any obligation for immigrants to conform to legally established churches. Over time, these policies created enduring protestant minority communities that were neither dissenting nor Anglican. Although foreign protestants had no expectation that they could gain the establishment privileges that the dominant British denominations enjoyed, they did not face persecution, and their leaders usually found easy acceptance from their Anglophone fellows.[18]

By the mid-eighteenth century, the terms of the imperial protestant establishment were fairly uniform. Nova Scotia provides a good example. Governor Edward Cornwallis brought a group of British settlers when he founded Halifax

18. For foreign protestants in the British Empire, see Brunner, *Halle Pietists in England,* 58; Owen Stanwood, *Global Refuge: Huguenots in an Age of Empire* (New York, 2020); Stanwood, "From the Desert to the Refuge: The Saga of New Bordeaux," *French Historical Studies,* XL (2017), 5–32; Stanwood, "Between Eden and Empire: Huguenot Refugees and the Promise of New Worlds," *American Historical Review,* CXVIII (2013), 1319–1344; Bertrand Van Ruymbeke, *From New Babylon to Eden: The Huguenots and Their Migration to Colonial South Carolina* (Columbia, S.C., 2006); Sugiko Nishikawa, "The SPCK in Defence of Protestant Minorities in Early Eighteenth-Century Europe," *Journal of Ecclesiastical History,* LVIII (2005), 730–748; Bernard Cottret, *The Huguenots in England: Immigration and Settlement, 1550–1770* (Cambridge, 1991), 188–190; Jeremy Black, "Confessional State or Elect Nation? Religion and Identity in Eighteenth-Century England," in Claydon and McBride, eds., *Protestantism and National Identity,* 67–69; Ward, *Protestant Evangelical Awakening,* 103–107; Winthrop Pickard Bell, *The "Foreign Protestants" and the Settlement of Nova Scotia: The History of a Piece of Arrested British Colonial Policy in the Eighteenth Century* ([Toronto], 1961); and Renate Wilson, "Halle Pietism in Colonial Georgia," *Lutheran Quarterly,* XII (1998), 271–301. The flood of German-speaking immigrants to the North American colonies, particularly Pennsylvania, is chronicled in Aaron Spencer Fogleman, *Hopeful Journeys: German Immigration, Settlement, and Political Culture in Colonial America, 1717–1775* (Philadelphia, 1996). See also Schwartz, *"A Mixed Multitude,"* 81–119. For the Naturalization Act, see ibid., 160–164. See also Ned C. Landsman, "Roots, Routes, and Rootedness: Diversity, Migration, and Toleration in Mid-Atlantic Pluralism," *Early American Studies,* II (2004), 267–309. Jews also received a route to naturalization at the same time, with mixed results. See William Pencak, *Jews and Gentiles in Early America, 1654–1800* (Ann Arbor, Mich., 2005), 100–105.

in 1749, and he almost immediately began requesting foreign protestants to build up the colony, even as the British expelled the area's Acadian Catholic population. German and French protestants began arriving soon afterward. Significant numbers of New England congregationalists also moved into the region. In 1767, more than half of Nova Scotia's population stemmed from older colonies to the south, largely dissenters. Another nearly 15 percent of the population were foreign protestants, and about 25 percent came from Britain and Ireland. By then, protestant institutions were already on a firm footing. Two Anglican missionaries, sponsored by the Board of Trade, had arrived with the first settlers destined for Halifax in 1749. The first Anglican Church, Saint Paul's, was established by royal proclamation in the same year. Halifax's first dissenting congregation, Saint Matthews, was founded then also, and its first Lutheran church came soon after. This diverse arrangement was then enshrined in law by the provincial assembly with a law that decreed "the fixed form of worship amongst us" as Anglican but then immediately qualified that primacy by adding that it was "the true intent and meaning of this act, that Protestants, dissenting from the Church of England, whether they be Calvinists, Lutherans, Quakers, or under what denomination soever, shall have free liberty of conscience." These protestants could "erect and build meeting houses" and employ ministers under contractual terms that would be enforced by the Nova Scotian government. Moreover, they did not have to pay taxes to the Church of England. Legal establishment and toleration in Nova Scotia coexisted along roughly the same terms as in the rest of the empire.[19]

The effect of the imperial establishment was to create parallel religious systems across the empire's different polities. The dominant denominations—Anglicans, presbyterians, and congregationalists—enjoyed the gravitas of legal establishment in part of the empire and could assume they were eligible for at least toleration everywhere. Where they could, they jealously guarded their privileges. And yet, other recognized protestant groups also benefited from the mixed establishment and from the protection governments provided to protestant institutions generally. Struggles to determine what the terms of toleration

19. "An Act for the Establishment of Religious Public Worship in this Province, and for Suppressing Popery," in Richard John Uniacke, *The Statutes at Large, Passed in the Several General Assemblies Held in His Majesty's Province of Nova Scotia . . .*, I (Halifax, 1805), 7. For the Acadian expulsion and the British settlement of Nova Scotia, see Christopher Hodson, *The Acadian Diaspora: An Eighteenth-Century History* (Oxford, 2012), 15–46; and Peter M. Doll, *Revolution, Religion, and National Identity: Imperial Anglicanism in British North America, 1745–1795* (Madison, N.J., 2000), 38–46. For Cornwallis, the recruitment of foreign protestants, and the founding of Halifax's churches, see Bell, *The "Foreign Protestants,"* 9, 317–318, 338. For the population in 1767, see Elizabeth Mancke, *The Fault Lines of Empire: Political Differentiation in Massachusetts and Nova Scotia, ca. 1760–1830* (New York, 2005), 10, 35–36. Some of the Irish immigrants were also Catholic.

were in any given place played out in local courts, councils, and assemblies, making governmental—rather than ecclesiastical—leaders the principal authorities on what constituted loyal or legitimate protestantism.

Not incidentally, shared protestantism also facilitated an enormous amount of mobility within the empire. Fear of religious persecution did not prevent Scots-Irish migrants from moving to Virginia or North Carolina, nor did it prevent congregationalists from moving to Nova Scotia. Boston merchants traveled to London with the knowledge that they would be able to find a welcoming dissenting community. Anglicans could trust that they would find co-religionists anywhere in the empire, even if they enjoyed establishment only in most of that empire. More marginal denominations that could claim to be protestant could assume relative freedom from government persecution, though not necessarily from scorn or prejudice. To be a participant in an organized protestant community was thus to be one of the empire's religious insiders. Forms of religious expression not recognized by such authorities often met insurmountable hurdles. And, of course, all Catholics faced explicit legal barriers in an empire where civil life was defined by shared protestantism. As the empire's separate establishments converged in basic outline, and as people moved between them expecting to be able to carry with them at least most of the privileges they had enjoyed in other parts of the empire, they created a collective imperial protestantism.[20]

The British Empire's mixed establishment was not an establishment in the traditional sense, in which a particular church receives a sort of religious monopoly, a source of irritation to those, particularly Anglicans, who believed the empire should have a single church. But the mixed system was a structure nonetheless, one in which claiming status as a protestant carried with it certain benefits that were enforced by law and in which protestant churches and their leaders continued to advocate for the importance of a close connection between church and state. This interweaving of local and imperial government with protestant privilege did not ensure religious harmony. Protestants continued to squabble, as they long had. But religious uniformity—either through a single denomination or a single theology—had never been the goal of imperial

20. The Moravians, for example, suffered localized legal persecution and a great deal of scorn but could move around the empire with freedom nonetheless because they enjoyed protection under a specific 1749 act of Parliament. See Rachel Wheeler, *To Live upon Hope: Mohicans and Missionaries in the Eighteenth-Century Northeast* (Ithaca, N.Y., 2008), 201–206; and Podmore, *Moravian Church in England,* 228–265. For legal restrictions on Catholics in England, see Colin Haydon, *Anti-Catholicism in Eighteenth-Century England, c. 1714–80: A Political and Social Study* (Manchester, U.K., 1993), 14–15; for the North American colonies, see Curry, *First Freedoms,* 80. For Catholic life in British North America, see Maura Jane Farrelly, *Papist Patriots: The Making of an American Catholic Identity* (Oxford, 2012).

coalescence at the root of the mixed establishment. Its pragmatic origins lay rather in deflecting religious conflict away from the state, in containing the religio-political differences of the seventeenth century. The rapid diffusing of the SPCKNA controversy is a case in point. The frustrations it generated, though real, were limited by shared deference to imperial authorities. The empire's mixed establishment created the territory upon which protestant institutions competed without challenging one another's status as part of a wider system that supported them all.

THE THREE NETWORKS OF IMPERIAL PROTESTANTISM

Transatlantic religious communities bridged the distance between the empire's different colonies and regions, connecting protestants within its various church establishments to one another. They did so for a variety of organic reasons. Protestants moved across the ocean, and they took their religious communities with them. Congregations sought clergy from distant ordaining bodies, revivalists traveled from place to place, missionaries sought out unconverted communities, and immigrants settled in new regions without abandoning the religious communities of their birthplaces. Clergy and dedicated lay people reached out to one another in order to build and sustain institutional religious life within the empire. A shared imperial protestantism came to life through these connections. Transatlantic phenomenon have received much attention because of the flourishing of transnational and global history approaches. But, within the field of religious history, these investigations have tended to examine connections in segments, by looking at individual denominations or at particular movements. Those strategies obscure, however, the connections between communities and the central role played by political boundaries in shaping protestant community. A thorough reconstruction of the ways protestants communicated with one another finds a system that functioned through networks rather than through the denominational categories most frequently used to understand protestant community. Extended but overlapping networks of Anglicans, dissenters, and awakened protestants circled the British Empire. Although these groups are not unfamiliar to historians, their position as the planks in the scaffolding of imperial protestantism is only visible when they are traced together.[21]

21. For denominational or community approaches to transatlantic protestantism, see, for example, Crabtree, *Holy Nation;* Jonathan Strom, Hartmut Lehmann, and James Van Horn Melton, eds., *Pietism in Germany and North America, 1680–1820* (Farnham, U.K., 2009); and Westerkamp, *Triumph of the Laity*. For transatlantic Anglicanism, see, for example, Bell, *Imperial Origins;* and Nancy L. Rhoden, *Revolutionary Anglicanism: The Colonial Church of England Clergy during the American Revolution* (Basingstoke, U.K., 1999). For dissenters, see Bartholomew P. Schiavo, "The

Just as with the empire's mixed establishment, looking at the overlapping strands of religious community that bound the empire together, and thus seeing its networks emerge clearly, requires attention to both differences and commonalities. Those who built such connections used a common set of tools to bind one place to another. The three networks were constructed through correspondence among religious leaders, shared projects promoting religious institutions, and voluntary societies. Many of these connections traced their origins to before the Glorious Revolution, but the shape the networks took in the eighteenth century depended on the mixed establishment that grew out of that era. All worked within the bounds of that system, which enabled them to act as proponents of the empire's normative protestant religion. That they used similar methods did not mean they always worked in concert, however. Each of the networks created its own separate—yet overlapping and also competing—ties between the empire's dispersed religious establishments. Their dynamics structured most long-distance communication among British protestants. Together these three networks encircled the empire, linking distant Britons to a shared protestantism.[22]

The largest of these networks, the Church of England, was unique in that it was the only formal ecclesiastical institution that linked distant protestants to one

---

Dissenter Connection: English Dissenters and Massachusetts Political Culture: 1630–1774" (Ph.D. diss., Brandeis University, 1976); and Bridenbaugh, *Mitre and Sceptre*. Connections between New England's dissenters and their English counterparts originated in transatlantic puritanism, a subject with its own literature. See, for example, Foster, *The Long Argument*. For awakened protestantism, see, for example, Noll, *Rise of Evangelicalism;* Lambert, *Inventing the "Great Awakening";* Ward, *Protestant Evangelical Awakening;* Crawford, *Seasons of Grace;* and Schmidt, *Holy Fairs*. For introductions to British Atlantic history, see Bernard Bailyn and Patricia L. Denault, eds., *Soundings in Atlantic History: Latent Structures and Intellectual Currents, 1500–1830* (Cambridge, Mass., 2009); and David Armitage and Michael J. Braddick, eds., *The British Atlantic World, 1500–1800* (Basingstoke, U.K., 2002).

22. Treatments of transatlantic religious correspondence include Susan O'Brien, "A Transatlantic Community of Saints: The Great Awakening and the First Evangelical Network, 1735–1755," *AHR*, XCI (1986), 811–832; and Lambert, *Inventing the "Great Awakening."* John Fea used a similar approach for investigating Eleazar Wheelock's community; see Fea, "Wheelock's World: Letters and the Communication of Revival in Great Awakening New England," American Antiquarian Society, *Proceedings*, CIX (2001), 99–144. For the study of networks in the transatlantic system, see Lindsay O'Neill, *The Opened Letter: Networking in the Early Modern British World* (Philadelphia, 2015), 5–6. For voluntary societies, see Laura M. Stevens, *The Poor Indians: British Missionaries, Native Americans, and Colonial Sensibility* (Philadelphia, 2004); Travis Glasson, *Mastering Christianity: Missionary Anglicanism and Slavery in the Atlantic World* (New York, 2012); Margaret Connell Szasz, *Scottish Highlanders and Native Americans: Indigenous Education in the Eighteenth-Century Atlantic World* (Norman, Okla., 2007); John C. Van Horne, ed., *Religious Philanthropy and Colonial Slavery: The American Correspondence of the Associates of Dr. Bray, 1717–1777* (Urbana, Ill., 1985); Isabel Rivers, "The First Evangelical Tract Society," *Historical Journal*, L (2007), 1–22; and William Kellaway, *The New England Company, 1649–1776: Missionary Society to the American Indians* (New York, 1961). Sirota, *Christian Monitors*, explores Anglican revival as a key thread within the movement to found religious voluntary societies in the early eighteenth century.

another through a reliable hierarchy with relatively clear lines of communication. The system reflected the church's territorial nature; and there were voices within Anglicanism that wanted the church's reach to be coterminus with the British government's authority. That vision was impossible under the terms of the Act of Union, but a more realistic goal in the eighteenth century was extending its episcopal structure to the colonies. A persistent irritant in Anglican circles was that some of those colonies had congregationalist establishments—and that even some of the Anglican colonies resisted the imposition of a bishop. But, despite differences of opinion about what legal status it ought to have in the colonies, within the Anglican community channels for communication were fairly clear in the eighteenth century. Though no diocese had been created with authority specifically for the colonies, beginning in the 1670s the bishop of London had assumed some responsibilities for colonial clergy, particularly in those places—such as Virginia and Maryland—where Anglican establishments were in place.[23]

A second—and far larger—chain of communication ran through the SPG, a semi-private missionary body founded in 1701. It developed as part of a wave of Anglican energy in the early part of the eighteenth century, itself a reaction against the threat posed to Anglican hegemony by Britain's developing mixed establishment. The archbishop of Canterbury was generally the head of the SPG, and it had a royal charter; both these factors linked it closely to religious and governmental authority in London. In terms of communication, however, its secretaries were more important. The many missionaries sent by the SPG to serve in colonial churches over the course of the eighteenth century reported back regularly to the "Venerable Society" via its secretaries. Huge volumes of correspondence traveled between colonies and metropole under the aegis of the SPG, and missionaries often corresponded with one another as well. Those within the Church of England therefore had a clear mechanism through which to communicate with distant Anglicans.[24]

Communications within the Anglican network tended to focus on practical matters of clerical postings, public worship, and the administration of the

23. Bell, *Imperial Origins,* 17; James B. Bell, "North America," in Gregory, ed., *Oxford History of Anglicanism,* II, *Establishment and Empire,* 160–188. For colonial Anglicanism more generally, see Rhoden, *Revolutionary Anglicanism*. Virginia's Anglicanism has come in for particular attention. See Lauren F. Winner, *A Cheerful and Comfortable Faith: Anglican Religious Practice in the Elite Households of Eighteenth-Century Virginia* (New Haven, Conn., 2010); Nelson, *A Blessed Company;* Edward L. Bond, *Damned Souls in a Tobacco Colony: Religion in Seventeenth-Century Virginia* (Macon, Ga., 2000); Joan R. Gundersen, *The Anglican Ministry in Virginia, 1723–1766: A Study of a Social Class* (New York, 1989).

24. For conservative Anglicanism and voluntary reform movements of the early eighteenth century, see Sirota, *Christian Monitors,* esp. chap. 2 and 230–233. For the founding of the SPG and its structure, see Glasson, *Mastering Christianity,* 18–26, 35, 291 (quotation). See also Rowan Strong, *Anglicanism and the British Empire, c. 1700–1850* (Oxford, 2007).

sacraments, in part because those subjects appeared in the requirements the SPG placed on its regular reporting. In 1729, George Ross, a missionary in New Castle, Delaware, wrote that "religion never appeared in this place in so shineing and lively a State, as it does at present." As evidence, he noted that his flock now included "a Sett of very honest zealous Churchmen, whose lives adorn their profession, and cool the heat of those [presumably non-Anglicans], who are prejudiced against our grave and manly worship." Another writer, this one from Boston, had more dismal news when he wrote in 1738, following a convention of the Anglican missionaries in New England. Among the complaints: the congregation in Scituate, Massachusetts, was dissatisfied with its missionary; the schoolmaster stationed in Boston had vacated his post; and there were good reasons to place a missionary in Hopkinton, which was "destitute of any regular Publick worship." By sending back such practical information, missionaries in the field helped Anglicans in London direct their efforts.[25]

Anglican missionaries gave statistics as well, reporting the number baptized by demographic category and the numbers that attended Holy Communion. A Boston missionary, for example, reported school attendance in Providence and also that "in my own Parish since my last I have baptized 28 Persons, where of Ten are Adults, and received three to the Holy Communion." Though the populations involved were quite different, a similar report came from New Providence, in the Bahamas. There the missionary "baptiz'd Eight White Children and also Two Negro Children, as also Two Adult Negro Slaves, whom I found desirous and dispos'd to receive the Holy Sacrament of Baptism." The labors of these missionaries spreading the gospel, which they summarized in statistical form, marked the expansion of Anglicanism, and of the protestant faith, to the empire's edges. When they were reported back up the chain of command, digested into regular reports, and circulated to interested protestants across the empire, they integrated the transatlantic protestant community and integrated the work of missionizing into its sense of religious work. Moreover, through this constant stream of basic information, Anglicans maintained clear and comparatively durable lines of communication.[26]

25. George Ross to David Humphries, Oct. 4, 1729, Records of the Society for the Propagation of the Gospel in Foreign Parts (SPG), Series B, VI, item 252, British Online Archives, https://microform.digital/boa; Roger Price to SPG, Nov. 16, 1738, ibid., Series B, VII, item 1. Ross did not remain so optimistic; see ibid., Nov. 7, 1732, item 275. For conventions among Anglican clergy in North America, see Bell, *Imperial Origins*, 110–113.

26. James Macsparran to SPG, Sept. 21, 1738, Records of the SPG, Series B, VII, item 33; Robert Carter to SPG, July 16, 1763, ibid., Series B, VI, item 15. For the SPG's approaches to converting slaves, see Glasson, *Mastering Christianity*. For transatlantic print culture and the impact of such reports, see Stevens, *Poor Indians*.

More spontaneous and personal communications also circulated in Anglican circles, though such missives tended to follow the same lines of hierarchy that characterized the SPG's correspondence. They also reinforced the institutional aspects of Anglican religious life in that they were often the site of complaints about the American colonies' lack of a bishop. The effect of this strand of correspondence within the network was to strengthen the centralized and highly structured nature of the Anglican system as a whole. New York's Anglicans appealed to Richard Terrick, when he was bishop of London, in their efforts to promote an episcopal seat in America, for example. Similarly, Boston's Henry Caner maintained a regular correspondence with Thomas Secker, when Secker was the archbishop of Canterbury, as did a number of other American Anglicans. Such an orderly system was easy to navigate. Those in Britain who wished to learn more about the colonies need only turn to the SPG, which published regular reports. Those in the colonies who needed assistance could petition the bishop of London or the society itself. Although participants complained about the frustrations of competing with dissenters—a missionary in Delaware remarked that, "in Baptizing white Children, I am oblig'd, to take the parents sometimes as Surties, or otherwise they go to the presbiteran meeting Houses and initiate their Children"—they spent little time discussing the content of Christian spiritual experience when they wrote back to London. They emphasized instead their diligent labors to promote the proliferation of public worship and access to the church's sacraments.[27]

Connecting Anglicans to distant protestants was also the work of two additional voluntary societies. The Society for Promoting Christian Knowledge (SPCK), founded in 1698, maintained an overwhelmingly English membership, but it promoted ties to foreign protestants, shared missionary work with Halle pietists in India under the authority of the Danish crown, and, in keeping with its mission as a tract society, sent large quantities of devotional materials wherever they were needed, including North America and the Caribbean. The Associates of Dr. Bray (founded in 1724), another Anglican body, focused on education for enslaved Africans and on supporting libraries for the clergy. Between these smaller societies, the work of the SPG, and the Church of England's far reaching establishment, Anglican religious leaders across the empire had consistent ways to communicate with one another, and those who wished

27. W. Hacket to SPG, Aug. 2, 1731, Records of the SPG, Series B, VI, item 241; Clergy of the Church of England in New York to the bishop of London, September 1762, Fulham Papers, XLI, 271. The communication between North American clergy and the bishop of London are calendared in William Wilson Manross, comp., *The Fulham Papers in the Lambeth Palace Library: American Colonial Section Calendar and Indexes* (Oxford, 1965); see, for example, 62–76.

to further "the State of Religion" in a distant place, or to receive news about such work, had a variety of ways to do so. Those in North America knew they were doing work that had the support of the church's hierarchy in Britain, and those in Britain could be confident that the important project of promoting religion was being undertaken in those regions that the spread of the empire had brought within their reach.[28]

The dissenting community supplied the second network in the imperial protestant system. Smaller than the Anglican network, it was nonetheless robust. Although it stemmed from the strong ties maintained by the transatlantic puritan community in the early seventeenth century, its eighteenth-century structure depended on organizations founded after the empire's mixed establishment took its full form. It expanded from the collaboration of the "Three Denominations" of congregationalists, presbyterians, and baptists in England. Leaders of those three groups worked together locally for political and legal purposes in London. The organizations they started—in particular the Protestant Dissenting Ministers of the Three Denominations, founded in 1727, and the Protestant Dissenting Deputies, founded in 1732—formed the institutional center of dissent at a broader geographic level. As the eighteenth century progressed, English dissenters built connections to coreligionists in other parts of the empire, particularly in New England. That New Englanders adopted the label *dissenter* to describe their own community, even though their American colonies had been largely populated before the word came into regular use to describe nonconformists, is indicative of the community's affective strength. The "dissenting interest," as it was sometimes termed, blended legally established churches (in New England and Scotland) and tolerated ones (in England and some other jurisdictions) that felt a sense of commonality. Dissenters worked together to support one another across those borders. For example, Nova Scotia's dissenters sent petitions to the Protestant Dissenting Deputies in London, the General Assembly of the Church of Scotland, and the Associated Pastors of the Churches of Boston to raise funds for ministers. This was a fair

28. The SPCK, which was predominantly but not exclusively Anglican, also connected Anglicans with distant protestants outside the empire. See Edward E. Andrews, "Tranquebar: Charting the Protestant International in the British Atlantic and Beyond," *WMQ*, 3d Ser., LXXIV (2017), 3–34; Sirota, *Christian Monitors*, chap. 2; and Katherine Carté Engel, "The SPCK and the American Revolution: The Limits of International Protestantism," *Church History*, VIII (2012), 77–103. For the Associates of Dr. Bray, see Van Horne, ed., *Religious Philanthropy and Colonial Slavery*. For the SPCK's role in connecting English protestants to those on the Continent, see Eamon Duffy, "*Correspondence Fraternelle;* The SPCK, the SPG, and the Churches of Switzerland in the War of the Spanish Succession," in Derek Baker, ed., *Reform and Reformation: England and the Continent, c. 1500–1750* (Oxford, 1979), 251–280; and Nishikawa, "The SPCK in Defence of Protestant Minorities," *Journal of Ecclesiastical History*, LVIII (2005), 730–748. For the circulation and impact of missionary societies' reports, see Stevens, *Poor Indians*.

representation of the geography of dissent: headquartered in London, closely tied to New England, and loosely connected to outposts in other parts of the empire and Protestant Europe.[29]

The Protestant Dissenting Deputies, in London, paid particular attention to dissenters in the colonies in the 1740s and 1750s, under the leadership of Dr. Benjamin Avery. Avery, a presbyterian minister turned doctor, led the deputies for more than twenty-five years. He cultivated connections with Americans, and he considered colonial dissenters a part of the dissenting interest. In 1749, he advocated on behalf of Massachusetts against the creation of a bishop, lobbying in that case with the dukes of Bedford and Newcastle. The Deputies developed into an institution that Americans looked to as their representatives to the English government. A Boston "committee of ministers" sought ongoing communication with the Deputies, and in 1751 Avery received a request for assistance "from the Churches in new Hampshire," where officials were "endeavoring to Discountenance the Dissenting Interest there." The Deputies became an important point of connection between dissenters in North America and in England, but maintaining those ties took continual effort, as there was no self-perpetuating structure to fall back on. After Avery died in 1764, the links between the Deputies and North America grew less frequent.[30]

Though the Protestant Dissenting Deputies were important, the most significant connections binding together the dissenting community were personal. Delineating the correspondence of two New England congregationalists, Newport's Ezra Stiles and Boston's Jonathan Mayhew, sketches the parameters of the dissenting network more thoroughly and points to the strength of an England–New England link. Mayhew's success as a writer brought him notice in England, in particular through the efforts of his longtime London correspondent, the radical political activist Thomas Hollis. Mayhew's other English connections included presbyterian theologian Nathaniel Lardner, Exeter's dis-

29. Records of the General Assembly of the Church of Scotland, Case of the Protestant Dissenters, 1771, Ch1/2/113, fol. 377, NRS; Minutes of the Boston Association of Ministers, Apr. 8, 1769, BMS 71/1, Harvard Divinity School Library, Cambridge, Mass.; Samuel Stennett to James Manning, Aug. 10, 1770, James Manning Papers, MS-1C-1, box 1, folder 55, John Hay Library, Providence, R.I.; Protestant Dissenting Deputies, General and Committee Meeting Minutes (hereafter cited as PDD, Minutes), Sept. 25, 1751, CLC/181/MS03083/001, LMA. For the institutions of dissent, see Watts, *The Dissenters,* I, 290–292, 485–486; Alison Gilbert Olson, *Making the Empire Work: London and American Interest Groups, 1690–1790* (Cambridge, Mass., 1992), 99–102; and Bernard Lord Manning, *The Protestant Dissenting Deputies,* ed. Ormerod Greenwood (Cambridge, 1952), 1–7. For the transatlantic dimensions of the dissenting community, see Bridenbaugh, *Mitre and Sceptre;* Schiavo, "The Dissenter Connection"; and Alison G. Olson, "The Eighteenth Century Empire: The London Dissenters' Lobbies and the American Colonies," *Journal of American Studies,* XXVI (1992), 41–58.

30. PDD, Minutes, Apr. 5, May 5, Sept. 27, 1749, Oct. 10, 1750, Sept. 25, 1751, 314–315, 328, 342, CLC/181/MS03083/001, LMA; Bridenbaugh, *Mitre and Septre,* 40, 51–53.

senting minister Micaiah Towgood, and the London lawyer brothers Jasper and Israel Mauduit. While English dissenters came to Mayhew, Stiles built his own networks. He actively sought out connections with dissenters in England and other parts of the Reformed world. He maintained correspondence with Lardner, as Mayhew did, with Lardner's nephew Joseph Jennings, and with London dissenter Philip Furneaux. The networks of connection widened on both sides of the Atlantic. Furneaux and several of Stiles's other correspondents were acquainted through London's dissenting circles with baptists John Gill and Samuel Stennett, men who corresponded with New England coreligionists Isaac Backus and James Manning. Dissenters used these channels to send news between England and New England. These personal connections, by men who self-identified as dissenters and communicated on those terms, reinforced the dissenting network's structure, even in the absence of the kind of dense organization maintained by Anglicans' hierarchical organization (see Figure 2). It also smoothed over the denominational boundaries that might otherwise have separated dissenters, as well as the distinctions in legal status that separated English dissenters, who relied on the Act of Toleration for protection, from those in New England, where dissenters were the establishment.[31]

Dissenters moved easily between their community's various locations. A good illustration of the network can be seen in the record of a journey taken in 1754 and 1755, when American presbyterian ministers Samuel Davies and William Tennent traveled to England to raise funds for the College of New Jersey (later Princeton University). English dissenters embraced the travelers as one of their fellowship. Wealthy layman Dennys De Berdt, despite some less than flattering words about the college, arranged for the men's housing in London. The welcome continued; Davies and Tennent soon received social calls from other dissenting ministers, including congregationalist Thomas Gibbons, whom Davies called his "dear Correspondent." Fellowship extended to

31. For examples of the dissenting network, see letters from Richard Price, George Benson, Jasper and Israel Mauduit, and Micaiah Towgood, Jonathan Mayhew Papers, Howard Gottlieb Research Center, Boston University; Theophilus Lindsey to William Harris, n.d. [editor suggests late 1763], in G. M. Ditchfield, ed., *The Letters of Theophilus Lindsey (1723–1808)*, I, *1747–1788*, Church of England Record Society, XV (Woodbridge, U.K., 2007), 91; Nathaniel Lardner to John Wiche, Jan. 21, 1768, 12.45, letter 33, DWL; Knollenberg, ed., "Thomas Hollis and Jonathan Mayhew," MHS, *Procs.*, 3d Ser., LXIX (October 1947–May 1950), 102–193. For Samuel Mather, see Mather to Thomas Hollis, Dec. 11, 1762, ibid., 133–135. The outlines of Stiles's correspondence can be reconstructed from Harold E. Selesky, ed., *A Guide to the Microfilm Edition of the Ezra Stiles Papers at Yale University* (New Haven, Conn., 1978). Institutional records of the dissenting network are PDD, Minutes, CLC/181/MS03083/001–002, LMA; Minutes of the Three Denominations, II, 1761–1797, DWL. For baptist communications within the dissenting network, see Manning Papers, MS-1C-1; John Gill to Isaac Backus, Mar. 17, 1764, Isaac Backus Papers, RG 280, Yale University Divinity School Library, New Haven, Conn.

FIGURE 2 *Council of Ministers*. Oil on wood panel, circa 1744. Painted in the home of Newburyport, Massachusetts, minister John Lowell by an unidentified artist. 1964.27. Harvard Art Museums / Fogg Museum, Gift of Dr. Francis L. Burnett and Mrs. Esther Lowell Cunningham

the sharing of pulpits as well. Davies "preached in many of the Pulpits of the 3 Denominations," according to his diary, and he received "the warm Approbation of a Number." He also sought to learn the internal dynamics of London dissent. He recorded that baptist Samuel Stennett "has [the] most influence in Court, of any of the Dissenting ministers," and lawyer Jasper Mauduit was "the hearty Friend of the Dissenters in Virginia" and "one of the Committee that has the Management of the secular Affairs of the Dissenters in Court." The Americans were treated as respected colleagues as they moved about London, and their assumption that the English dissenting community would welcome them was borne out with friendliness.[32]

32. George William Pilcher, ed., *The Reverend Samuel Davies Abroad: The Diary of a Journey to England and Scotland, 1753–55* (Urbana, Ill., 1967), xi, 13, 43, 45, 49, 134; Craig Gilborn, "The Reverend Samuel Davies in Great Britain," *Winterthur Portfolio*, VIII (1973), 45–62.

The dissenting network, like its Anglican fellow, also maintained missionary organizations. Its largest, the Society for the Propagation of the Gospel in New England, commonly known as the New England Company (NEC), was founded in 1649, during the puritan ascendency. Its charter was confirmed by Charles II after the Restoration, and it carried out work in New England, including through its support of missionary John Eliot throughout the second half of the seventeenth century. Later, in the eighteenth century, its projects included the mission at Stockbridge, Massachusetts, where both John Sargeant and Jonathan Edwards labored. The NEC, though based in and administered from London, functioned in North America through a committee in Boston, made up of leading dissenters—clerical and lay—from that city. It also collaborated at times with a second body, the Society in Scotland for Propagating Christian Knowledge (SSPCK), founded in 1709. It, too, had a commission organizing its labors in New England as well as one in London. The overlap in North America between these bodies points to the complexities, and the integrity, of the dissenting network. Both Scottish presbyterians and New England's congregationalists were in positions of establishment in their home territories, whereas the English core of the network was not. Nonetheless, their connections to the world of dissent grew from their shared Calvinist sensibilities and their intrinsic sense of separation from Anglicanism.[33]

Discussions within the dissenting network emphasized particularly the nature of civil and religious establishments, and many dissenters saw themselves as advocates of "civil and religious liberty." This belief was no doubt in part because the institutions that helped mediate much communication—particularly the Protestant Dissenting Deputies—considered legal advocacy of dissenting issues as its core mission. When Samuel Davies pleaded the cause of the Virginia dissenters to his fellows in London, they came to agreement on it as a "Cause of Liberty." When London presbyterian Richard Price sent a letter of endorsement for a particular candidate to be the agent for Massachusetts to Jonathan Mayhew, he wrote that the merchant was "a Friend to civil and religious Liberty," and he wished well to Mayhew's "Endeavours to promote the Cause of Liberty and rational Religion." The Protestant Dissenting Ministers of the Three Denominations gave thanks to the esteemed Dr. Furneaux "for the great Service he has done to the Cause of religious liberty in general, and

33. For the NEC, see Kellaway, *The New England Company*. For the SSPCK, see Szasz, *Scottish Highlanders and Native Americans*, 122–124; Frederick V. Mills, Sr., "The Society in Scotland for Propagating Christian Knowledge in British North America, 1730–1775," *Church History*, LXIII (1994), 15–30; and Donald E. Meek, "Scottish Highlanders, North American Indians, and the SSPCK: Some Cultural Perspectives," *Records of the Scottish Church History Society*, XXIII (1989), 378–396.

for his able Defence of the Rights and Privileges of the Protestant Dissenters in Particular." A Bristol minister, Thomas Wright, summed up the relationship by saying that the "Dissenters in England bear hearty good will to their Brethren in America, and have been ready upon many occasions to assist them with their fortune." Though Americans now seemed ready to shoulder more burdens themselves, Wright thought that many among his fellow dissenters "will, I dare say, be ready to assist [their American counterparts] to the utmost of their power" to protect the colonies from the imposition of "ecclesiastical projects" [from Anglicans] that "might be hurtfull to their religious liberty and purity." Although such professions of commitment to religious liberty were a hallmark of British political discourse generally, they played an outsized role in the communications within the dissenting network.[34]

Imperial protestantism's third network linked awakened protestants to one another.[35] That movement's roots stretched into central Europe and to Scotland's great communion fairs, and it spread throughout the British Empire via the actions of energetic itinerants, including the efforts of Anglicans George Whitefield and John Wesley, as well as the more radical Moravians, who played a catalytic role in the movement's early days but were then relegated to the fringes of legitimate British protestantism. Widespread revivals flourished in the 1730s and 1740s through the work of these itinerants and through a flood of publications. As a group, awakened protestants collaborated loosely and downplayed their quite significant theological differences so that their drive to nurture a personal, vital protestant piety took shape in diverse communities.[36]

34. Pilcher, ed., *Reverend Samuel Davies Abroad*, 134; Richard Price to Jonathan Mayhew, Jan. 4, 1764, Mayhew Papers, item 56; Minutes of the Three Denominations, II, Apr. 16, 1771, 89, DWL; Thomas Wright to Ezra Stiles, July, 24, 1766, Stiles Papers.

35. This study defines awakened protestantism by building outward from the networks of the movement's widely recognized leaders such as Jonathan Edwards, Samuel Hopkins, Joseph Bellamy, George Whitefield, John Erskine, John Newton, Selina Hastings, and the Wesley brothers, John and Charles. Describing the group that I call *awakened protestants* has presented persistent challenges to historians. *Evangelical*, until recently the term used most often by scholars, was not used as a descriptor for this specific grouping in the eighteenth century and has increasingly fallen from favor because of associations it has accrued in twenty-first-century contexts. For discussions of the term, see Linford D. Fisher, "Evangelicals and Unevangelicals: The Contested History of a Word, 1500–1950," *Religion and American Culture*, XXVI (2016), 184–226; Douglas L. Winiarski, *Darkness Falls on the Land of Light: Experiencing Religious Awakenings in Eighteenth-Century New England* (Williamsburg, Va., and Chapel Hill, N.C., 2017), 13–16; D. Bruce Hindmarsh, *The Spirit of Early Evangelicalism: True Religion in a Modern World* (New York, 2018), 9.

36. The role of the Moravians in the early days of the awakening movement is undeniable, but by the 1750s they were seen as too radical by more mainstream leaders, including Gilbert Tennent. Anti-Moravian sentiment hit a high point in the early 1750s, in both England and Germany, and after that the group faced significant social ostracization in both Britain and North America. See Milton J. Coalter, Jr., "The Radical Pietism of Count Nicholas Zinzendorf as a Conservative Influence on the Awakener, Gilbert Tennent," *Church History*, XLIX (1980), 35–46; Podmore, *The Moravian Church in England*; Fogleman, *Jesus Is Female*; Wheeler, *To Live upon Hope*, 188–189.

Awakened protestants drew their great strength as a network from their ability to work within many quarters of Britain's protestant establishment. This nimble organization was accomplished by the collaboration of a number of key individuals who maintained an extensive correspondence. Most of them were within one of British protestantism's dominant denominations, and this fact was important because it meant that core leaders retained connections to the Church of England, the Church of Scotland, and to dissenting circles. Anglicans John Wesley and Selina Hastings, each at the head of what would eventually become a denomination, maintained extensive correspondence within their own networks. George Whitefield, too, communicated with and visited protestant leaders throughout the empire. August Gottlieb Francke, the leader of the pietist institutions in Halle, Germany, was likewise a member of an established church and head of an expansive international network that included London and a cadre of ministers in North America. John Erskine was a leader within the Church of Scotland and consistently sought out contacts with leading protestants overseas, not only within presbyterianism. The most well-known American voices within the movement, Jonathan Edwards, Joseph Bellamy, and Samuel Hopkins—New Englanders all—were not particularly active in dissenting networks; instead, each of these individuals maintained correspondence with Erskine. At the same time, their cultural location within the dissenting world was evidence of the awakening's flowering within dissent more generally.[37]

Like dissenters and Anglicans, awakened protestants, too, maintained missions. In one sense, the entire movement was a mission. The effort to bring fellow protestants to an awakened spiritual life required the same kinds of outreach, coordination, and funding as missions to Indigenous peoples or Africans did. But awakened protestants engaged in that latter form of religious work as well. In 1740, evangelist George Whitefield purchased a large tract of land in

---

For the rise of awakened protestantism as a transatlantic movement, see Noll, *Rise of Evangelicalism;* Ward, *Protestant Evangelical Awakening;* Schmidt, *Holy Fairs;* Crawford, *Seasons of Grace.* For awakened print culture, see Jennifer Snead, "Print, Predestination, and the Public Sphere: Transatlantic Evangelical Periodicals, 1740–1745," *Early American Literature,* XLV (2010), 93–118; Rivers, "The First Evangelical Tract Society," *Historical Journal,* L (2007), 1–22; Lambert, *Inventing the "Great Awakening."*

37. Wesley, Hastings, and Whitefield are each the subject of significant literatures. For collections of their correspondence, see, for example, John Telford, ed., *The Letters of the Rev. John Wesley, A.M.: Sometime Fellow of Lincoln College, Oxford,* IV, *January 16, 1758, to February 27, 1766* (London, 1931); and John R. Tyson with Boyd S. Schlenther, eds., *In the Midst of Early Methodism: Lady Huntingdon and Her Correspondence* (Lanham, Md., 2006), esp. 211–243. See also Peter Y. Choi, *George Whitefield: Evangelist for God and Empire* (Grand Rapids, Mich., 2018); Thomas S. Kidd, *George Whitefield: America's Spiritual Founding Father* (New Haven, Conn., 2014). For connections between Halle and North America, see Hermann Wellenreuther, *Heinrich Melchior*

Pennsylvania where he planned to build a school for African Americans. (It was soon sold to the Moravians, who planted Nazareth, Pennsylvania, there.) His project for an orphan house for Africans in Bethesada, Georgia, lasted throughout his lifetime. Awakened leader Jonathan Edwards was himself a missionary in Stockbridge, Massachusetts, and he published the influential biography of missionary David Brainerd. Scot John Erskine was active in the SSPCK, a vantage point from which he, too, promoted missionary work. As Erskine's activities suggest, awakened protestants had fewer missionary societies of their own because they supported networks of ministers and worked through the societies of the denominations they were otherwise members of, but they did found in 1750 the Society for Promoting Religious Knowledge among the Poor (SPRKP), and it also focused some of its energies on North America. Such societies were a tried-and-true method for spreading and supporting religion across the empire, and awakened protestants did not leave it behind.[38]

Letters exchanged by awakened protestants focused more on the spiritual and divine nature of religious work (as opposed to the logistical or institutional) than the discussions that characterized either of the other two networks. Explicit and emotional references to God, Jesus, and the work of the Holy Spirit, often termed as emphatic exclamations, were pervasive. When Jonathan Edwards invited Whitefield to visit Northampton in 1740, for example, he wrote to the itinerant, describing him as "One that has the Blessing of Heaven attending you wherever you go." Then, writing of an Anglican who had been awakened, Edwards exclaimed, "Blessed be God that hath done it! who is with you, and helps you, and makes the weapons of your warfare mighty." Whitefield, when writing to the countess of Huntingdon about the best way to preach to England's elite, wrote: "O that I may be enabled, when called to preach to any of them, so to preach as to win their souls to the blessed JESUS!" Reports about revivals talked of the work in spiritual terms. John Erskine wrote from Scot-

---

Mühlenberg und die deutschen Lutheraner in Nordamerika, 1742—1787: Wissentransfer und Wandel eines atlantischen zu einem amerikanischen Netzwerk (Berlin, 2013), 287–311. For connections between Halle and London, see Christina Jetter-Staib, "'Da sie keinen Scrupel machen, mit uns in guter gemeinshaft zur beforderung des Reiches christi zu leben . . .': Der Londoner Hofprediger Friedrich Michael Ziegenhagen (1694–1776) als Mittler zwischen Halle und England," in Holger Zaunstöck, Andreas Gestrich, and Thomas Müller-Bahlkeet, eds., *London und das Hallesche Waisenhaus: Eine transnationale Kommunikationsgeschichte im 18. Jahrhundert* (Wiesbaden, Ger., 2014), 139–160. For Erskine and North American awakened leaders, see Hindmarsh, *Spirit of Early Evangelicalism,* 82–83; Jonathan M. Yeager, *Enlightened Evangelicalism: The Life and Thought of John Erskine* (Oxford, 2011), esp. 141–163; and O'Brien, "A Transatlantic Community of Saints," *AHR,* XCI (1986), 811–832.

38. For Whitefield's Pennsylvania purchase, see Choi, *George Whitefield,* 146–147. For Edwards as a missionary, see Wheeler, *To Live upon Hope,* 180–186. For the SPRKP, see Rivers, "The First Evangelical Tract Society, " *Historical Journal,* L (2007), 1–22.

land to Joseph Bellamy in Connecticut about an Anglican rector who had "met [with] much reproach and opposition for preaching the doctrines of grace." Fortunately, despite those obstacles, his "labours have been blessed to rouze many from their security." Such explicitly Christian references were not absent from the Anglican and dissenting correspondence, but they were remarkably present in awakened circles, where ministers attested to the strength of their faith and their commitment through such descriptions. The same tone characterized writing by awakened protestants in the public sphere as well, and it made their spiritual community, and their correspondence networks, distinctive.[39]

Awakened leaders often used the phrase "vital religion" in their correspondence to describe the version of religion they sought to nurture, separating it from what they saw as a stale or institutional version of the concept. Here again, the term was not exclusive to the awakened community, but its participants used it in a way that denoted an internal understanding of their project as specific and in opposition to something lacking or amiss in the religion of other protestants. Presbyterian minister Gilbert Tennent, in a 1735 printed work, declared, in opposition to the assertion that prayer could "be *formal,*" that "praying frequently, if with necessary Caution and Solemnity[,] is the appointed Way and Mean to obtain vital Religion." The phrase was common in correspondence as well. Jonathan Edwards wrote to Thomas Gillespie in Scotland of overconfident believers with "bold, proud and stupid Confidence" who had "given the greatest wound to the Cause of Truth and vital Religion that ever it suffered in America." Erskine mused to Bellamy that "what you say of the decline of vital religion, the w[ith]draw of divine influences and the growth of Arminian and Socinian tenets in your parts, is equally true of Britain." English layman Dennys De Berdt wrote to awakened Anglican and leading politician William Legge, Lord Dartmouth, that the college in Princeton was the "only Colledge where Vital Religion is Regarded." In dealing with George Whitefield's literary estate, Robert Keen, the countess of Huntingdon's agent, "grieved to think Mr Whitefield's memory should be thus hurt" by a poor edition of his sermons, so that "vital Religion [would] be unnecessarily brought into contempt."

39. Jonathan Edwards to George Whitefield, Feb. 12, 1739, item A23, *Works of Jonathan Edwards Online* (hereafter cited as *WJE Online*), XXXII, *Correspondence by, to, and about Edwards and His Family,* http://edwards.yale.edu; Whitefield to Lady Huntingdon, Aug. 21, 1748, in Tyson with Schlenther, eds., *In the Midst of Early Methodism,* 74; John Erskine to Joseph Bellamy, Apr. 20, 1756, Joseph Bellamy Papers, box 188, folder 2932, item 81241, Hartford Seminary Library, Conn.; L[uke] Tyerman, *The Life of the Rev. George Whitefield, B.A., of Pembroke College, Oxford,* II (London, 1877), 193. For Whitefield's letters, see Hindmarsh, *Spirit of Early Evangelicalism,* 36–40. Defining what characterized the awakening movement is difficult, as awakened protestants were not, before the American Revolution, in distinct denominations. For the best treatment of the subject, see Hindmarsh, *Spirit of Early Evangelicalism.*

All told, awakened leaders had a strong sense of their own shared project and its differentiation from that promoted by other religious leaders, despite usually being rooted in the established churches where they lived.[40]

Many of the connections between dissenters or between awakened protestants crossed denominational lines. Seeing that networks, rather than denominations, were the organizing structures of Anglo-American protestantism is thus crucial because it helps explain why so many long-distance connections among religious leaders ignored denominational boundaries. Denominations were important, particularly at the local level, because they were intrinsic to the terms of legal establishment, and certainly eighteenth-century Britons used them continually. But denomination was not a defining characteristic for either the dissenting or the awakened network. (The Anglican network, of course, was inherently denominational.) In England, the dissenting network was dominated by the three traditional denominations, but dissenting circles included a few liberal Anglicans, particularly those who tended toward unitarianism. Anglican archdeacon Francis Blackburne was known widely in British and colonial dissenting circles, for example. On the other hand, presbyterian members of the Church of Scotland were only occasionally connected to the dissenting network as the century wore on, suggesting that the idea of being a presbyterian did not specifically attach someone to the transatlantic community of dissent. The awakened community crossed denominational lines in much the same way. Anglicans dominated the leadership of the transatlantic awakening movement, but the prominent roles played by Scottish presbyterian John Erskine and by New England congregationalists Jonathan Edwards and Joseph Bellamy point to the network's denominational diversity.[41]

Recognizing that denominational categories were comparatively unimportant in the empire's long-distance religious networks, in the planks that bound the empire's protestant scaffold together, has further implications. It should be noted, for example, that the major denominations—with the important exception of the Church of England—did not maintain systematic transatlantic com-

40. "Experimental religion" operated in a similar way. See Edwards to Thomas Gillespie, Apr. 1750, *WJE Online,* XXXII; Gilbert Tennent, *A Solemn Warning to the Secure World, from the God of Terrible Majesty . . .* (Boston, [1735]), 69; Erskine to Bellamy, Mar. 24, 1755, Bellamy Papers, box 188, folder 2932, item 81234; Dennys De Berdt to William Legge, Aug. 22, 1766, Papers of the Legge Family, Earls of Dartmouth (hereafter cited as Dartmouth Papers), D(W) 1778/II/229, Staffordshire Record Office, Stafford, U.K.; and Robert Keen to Selina Hastings, Sept. 14, 1771, A1/3/2, Cheshunt College Archives, Westminster College, Cambridge.

41. Thomas Wright to Ezra Stiles, Mar. 24, 1768, Stiles Papers. See Stiles to Charles Chauncy, March 1770, Andrews-Eliot Correspondence, 104/3, MHS. See also Ditchfield, ed., *The Letters of Theophilus Lindsey,* I, xli–xlii, particularly relating to attempts to repeal subscription requirements in England.

munications as denominations. Even the presbyterians, whose stronghold in Scotland allowed them to argue for a formal position in the British Empire, did not develop a comprehensive denominational structure. There were theological reasons for their reluctance to do so. Presbyterians embraced a regional understanding of ecclesiastical authority. But, just as important, different groups of presbyterians apparently did not feel the need to communicate *as presbyterians*. Cultural and ethnic habits meant that English presbyterians outside England looked to that country for leadership, while mid-Atlantic presbyterians looked to the Church of Scotland. The substantial British ex-patriot community in Rotterdam possessed both an English presbyterian and a Scottish church. As a transatlantic community, presbyterianism was organizationally weak, and congregationalists and baptists doubly so. Efforts at denominational correspondence were slow, halting, and unsystematic.[42]

At the same time, it is also striking that all three of these networks were almost exclusively made up of Anglicans, presbyterians, congregationalists, and baptists as well as a meaningful number of foreign protestants. Largely absent were Quakers and Moravians, transatlantic protestant groups who held themselves apart from—and often were not welcome in—the community of protestants. These groups enjoyed toleration in most places and were generally recognized by provincial and national governments as dissenters. But they also downplayed shared protestantism in favor of distinctive conceptions of group identity. Quakers saw themselves as a "nation of Zion," and the Moravians tried to organize and place themselves at the head of all Christians according to what they called the "Tropus" concept, in which all Christians could be united while maintaining their unique heritages. Indeed, Quakers dominated a colony that did not participate directly in the empire's mixed establishment, which made them more suspect. Quakers in England, though protected by the Act of Toleration, did not join the principal dissenting organizations, and in Massachusetts they could not receive exemption from paying taxes to support the establishment. When, in the 1760s, congregationalists and presbyterians in North America organized as "dissenters" to resist Anglican encroachment, Quakers were not included in their new society. The Moravians, despite enjoying a special legal status in the British Empire after 1749, remained on the radical fringe of German pietism, a movement dominated by Halle pietists who had strong connections with the Hanoverian court and the Anglican establishment.

42. Guy S. Klett, ed., *Minutes of the Presbyterian Church in America, 1706–1788* (Philadelphia, 1976), 415, 456; Consistory Records of the English Presbyterian Church in Rotterdam, 993/2, and Minutes of the Scots Church in Rotterdam, 962.01/7, both in Gemeentearchief Rotterdam, Netherlands.

When awakened presbyterian Gilbert Tennent sought respectability, he did it by excoriating his Moravian peers, despite their shared commitment to protestant awakening. After the early 1750s, the Moravians were generally excluded from respectable protestant circles. From the perspective of the leaders of imperial protestantism, Quakers and Moravians were not really full members, even if governments permitted their presence.[43]

Looking at the three networks of imperial protestantism together, the centripetal force exerted by their common relationship to the structures of government and to the empire's mixed establishment stands out. It becomes possible to see the scaffolding of imperial protestantism at work. The vast majority of religious leaders across all three networks worked as part of established denominations, a fact that cannot be underestimated. Moreover, even those who did not, like England's dissenters or missionaries supported by the SPG in New England, were part of networks in which establishments were strong. From this base, and from the constant attention to government-determined legitimacy that it demanded, numerous other points of connection between religious leaders and government grew. The loftiest point of connection was the king, who heard petitions from and gave patronage to all legitimate protestant groups and causes. Lesser government figures could also be important. Lord Dartmouth was known for his piety. As a high-ranking government official, he received letters from many different religious leaders who wished him to intervene in one way or another. The dispute over the new missionary society for New England, thwarted by Archbishop Thomas Secker, provides another example of competing religious networks engaging one another through political mechanisms. Though Anglicans defeated the SPCKNA, both sides had agreed on the basic form of missionary work, and both understood that legiti-

43. For Quakers, see Crabtree, *Holy Nation,* esp. 2–9, 35. For the Moravians, see Peter Vogt, "Brüdergemeine—das theologische Programm eines Namens," *Unitas Fratrum,* XLVIII (2001), 81–105; Vogt, "Zinzendorf und die Pennsylvanischen Synoden 1742," ibid., XXXVI (1994), 5–62; and Podmore, *Moravian Church in England,* 164–165. Anti-Moravian sentiment is explored by Fogleman in *Jesus Is Female.* For anti-Quaker sentiment, see Silver, *Our Savage Neighbors,* 194–199. See Smolenski, *Friends and Strangers,* for discussion of how Quakers sought to create a distinctive religious culture. For the Quakers on the outside of dissenting bodies, see Manning, *Protestant Dissenting Deputies,* 20; Watts, *The Dissenters,* I, 389. For presbyterian-congregational coordination, see David D. Field, Stephen Dodd, and Eleazar T. Fitch, *Minutes of the Convention of Delegates from the Synod of New York and Philadelphia and from the Associations of Connecticut; Held Annually from 1766 to 1775, Inclusive* (Hartford, Conn., 1843); and the discussion in Edmund S. Morgan, *The Gentle Puritan: A Life of Ezra Stiles, 1727–1795* (Williamsburg, Va., and Chapel Hill, N.C., 1962), 237–254. For Tennent and the Moravians, see Coalter, "The Radical Pietism of Count Nicholas Zinzendorf," *Church History,* XLIX (1980), 35–46. The Moravians also suffered because of their situation as outsiders in Saxony, where the Halle pietists, with whom the Moravians had fallen out, remained within the realm of respectability. For the Halle-London connection, see Brunner, *Halle Pietists in England;* and Wellenreuther, *Heinrich Melchior Mühlenberg.*

mate missionary work required government approval. A similar analysis can be made of conflicts related to the founding of King's College, in New York. That struggle brought Anglican, presbyterian, and Dutch Reformed religious leaders into contention precisely because they all felt entitled to claim public religious space as legitimate protestants. Scholars have interpreted such conflicts as evidence of religion's role in fracturing local community. Situating those dynamics in an empire-wide perspective suggests that, although local divisions were significant, those religious communities remained collectively integrated into the empire's fabric. The competing networks of imperial protestantism shared a common relationship to government authority. In the colonial period, they reinforced the bonds of empire and made religious community dependent on imperial structures. In the era of the Revolution, they would leave protestants exposed to shifting political winds.[44]

A closer look at the scaffolding's functioning reveals something further. Although dissenters and Anglicans remained in a fairly steady state of opposition to one another throughout the eighteenth century, the awakened network, which originated in the revival movements of the 1720s through 1740s, bridged them in important ways during the century's middle decades. That movement developed within each of the major denominations as well as among Continental protestants. Yet, as mentioned above, most of the movement's leaders remained within those privileged denominations that made up the British protestant system, and those individuals also maintained ties to their local denominational organizations. This situation created overlap between the two networks of awakened protestants and dissenters, and also between awakened protestants and Anglicans. Thus, although awakened protestants maintained an identifiable network, they also ran nimbly along the scaffold on the planks built by their fellows.[45]

44. For admiration of Legge, see, for example, James Alice to Legge, Nov. 5, 1772, Dartmouth Papers, D(W) 1778/II/453; Erskine to Legge, Oct. 20, 1775, ibid., D(W) 1778/II/1562; John Ewing to Legge, July 3, 1775, ibid., D(W) 1778/II/1349; Richard Jackson to Lord Dartmouth, Mar. 26, 1772, ibid., D(W) 1778/I/585. For the controversy over King's College, see Milton M. Klein, "Introduction," in Klein, ed., *The Independent Reflector; or, Weekly Essays on Sundry Important Subjects, More Particularly Adapted to the Province of New-York by William Livingston and Others* (Cambridge, Mass., 1963), 31–39; and Donald F. M. Gerardi, "The King's College Controversy, 1753–1756, and the Ideological Roots of Toryism in New York," *Perspectives in American History,* XI (1977–1978), 145–196. For the struggle to control King's College, see also "Church of New York: Petition of the Collegiate Church, of New York City, to the Assembly, for a Professorship of Divinity in Kings College, Oct. 25, 1754," 3505–3506, "Draft of a Charter for a College in the City of New York Presented, October 31, 1754," 3506, and "Royal Charter of Kings College, New York, October 31, 1754," 3506–3515, in *Ecclesiastical Records: State of New York,* V (Albany, N.Y., 1905); Pointer, *Protestant Pluralism,* 55–59; and Don R. Gerlach and George E. DeMille, "Samuel Johnson and the Founding of King's College, 1751–1755," *Historical Magazine of the Protestant Episcopal Church,* XLIV (1975), 335–352.

45. An important caveat must be made here. A significant number of what historians would identify as awakened protestants (though they themselves would not have used that term)

Coordinating between awakened protestants and their fellows took conscious effort, a fact that was evident when awakened presbyterians Samuel Davies and William Tennent went to England in the early 1750s to raise money for Princeton. Although the pair made direct use of the dissenting network on their journey, they were also conscious that, as awakened protestants, their views did not align precisely with all dissenters. Davies was pleased when he met with fellow presbyterian Samuel Chandler and found the well-known divine to be one "of uncommon Sagacity and Readiness." He was relieved, as Chandler had "been formerly suspected of Arminianism and Socinianism," tendencies that were rejected by Davies and his fellows in the awakening movement. Tennent, on the other hand, had to quell the concerns of dissenting lawyer Israel Mauduit, an important figure in London's dissenting organizations and their legal efforts. Tennent had mentioned that Calvinists led the College of New Jersey, almost prompting "an unseasonable Dispute." The American then produced the college's charter and showed that it suited the Mauduit brothers' desire for a school that would not be religiously divisive, and that ended the affair. Davies and Tennent were engaged in both the dissenting and the awakened protestant networks; they had to be careful how they presented to each.[46]

Most negotiations between dissenters, Anglicans, and proponents of the awakening were more indirect than those engaged in by Davies and Tennent, and the overlap between the networks can be seen principally in the fact that the same individuals appear in both. John Witherspoon, the awakened Scot who became president of the College of New Jersey and a signer of the Declaration of Independence, is a good example. He corresponded with leading awakened protestants, including his Scottish colleague John Erskine, before and after his migration to North America. Yet he also participated with Ezra Stiles—who could not be considered a part of the awakening movement—in an effort to unite North American dissenters in the 1760s, and in that context

remained outside the dominant denominations and their transatlantic hierarchies because those denominations were defined in large part by the structures of racial and social hierarchy. Large numbers of African American and Indigenous protestants, as well as poorer whites, were brought to the awakening movement by preachers outside or on the fringes of the dominant denominations, including the Moravians and some baptist groups. Thus, the reach of the awakening as a style of faith outpaced the organization of a transatlantic awakened community described in these pages. During the colonial period, however, these groups had little or no presence in the transatlantic and intercolonial networks of protestantism. See Fisher, *Indian Great Awakening,* 108–109; Wheeler, *To Live upon Hope,* 201; John Howard Smith, *The First Great Awakening: Redefining Religion in British America, 1725–1775* (Madison, N.J., 2015), 199–223, 247–269; and Charles F. Irons, *The Origins of Proslavery Christianity: White and Black Evangelicals in Colonial and Antebellum Virginia* (Chapel Hill, N.C., 2008), 40–44.

46. Pilcher, ed., *Reverend Samuel Davies Abroad,* 47, 48, 49; Gilborn, "The Reverend Samuel Davies," *Winterthur Portfolio,* VIII (1973), 45–62.

Witherspoon submitted an appeal to the Protestant Dissenting Deputies in London for assistance in the struggle against a colonial bishop. William Gordon, a London-based independent minister, corresponded with Joseph Bellamy in Connecticut, but he was also a delegate to the Protestant Dissenting Ministers of the Three Denominations in and around London. George Whitefield provides an extreme example of interdenominational connections, but the difference between his network and those of his peers was one of degree, not nature. Awakened protestants, although a distinctive group within the culture of transatlantic protestantism, were also deeply embedded within it.[47]

Britain's mixed protestant establishment developed as a response to shared pressures of imperial policy. Within that system, three overlapping networks of protestants joined distant Britons to one another. Though each had a distinctive character, their shared methods—and overlapping personnel—created a common set of practices about the proper way to promote religion within the empire. When those structures and habits, rather than the distinctions that divided Anglicans, dissenters, and awakened protestants, become the focus of attention, the collaborations and common goals that joined British protestants into a single whole come into view. They were not based in a single denomination or in agreement on theological issues. Instead, imperial protestantism relied on a dense web of transatlantic connections, on common practices, and on the agreement among most dominant protestants that religious projects functioned to promote religion across the empire with the approval of government authorities. Within that system, religious leaders could nurture grudges and competitions, gripes they were often eager to share with distant correspondents. Yet that does not mean that the various networks always worked at cross purposes or sought one another's elimination. To return to the metaphor of scaffolding, the planks built by the three networks were distinct and yet mutually reinforcing. Together they strengthened the ties between distant British places with distinct church establishments. Their fundamental dependence on government authority kept them within the bounds of legitimate religion, in an

47. Pilcher, ed., *Reverend Samuel Davies Abroad*, 43–44, 66. Gideon Mailer, *John Witherspoon's American Revolution* (Williamsburg, Va., and Chapel Hill, N.C., 2017), 124–139, places Witherspoon in Scottish and North American evangelical networks. See also Erskine to John Ryland, Oct. 18, 1790, John Erskine Papers, Edinburgh University Library; PDD, Minutes, Sept. 1, 1774, CLC/181/MS03083/002, 179, LMA. William Gordon and Joseph Bellamy corresponded throughout the 1760s. See, for example, Gordon to Bellamy, July 23, 1760, Bellamy Papers, box 188, folder 2933, item 81271; and Gordon to Bellamy, Sept. 9, 1766, ibid., box 190, folder 2959, item 81621. For Gordon's activities in London, see Minutes of the Three Denominations, II, part 1, 1761–1791, DWL. The weakest connections, conversely, were between dissenters and Anglicans who were distant from one another, as they had no local reasons to communicate and would find it difficult to connect via others within the broader community.

imperial if not always in a local sense. Interpretations of British protestantism that stress local divisions, whether over the disruptive influence of revivalism or the lasting tensions between Anglicans and dissenters, underestimate the extent to which religious leaders, of all the networks, worked to the same ends. The ways that they did so reinforced, rather than challenged, the authority of imperial officials and the connections that existed between the empire's distant reaches. The scaffolding of imperial protestantism was well equipped to manage the competitions between its networks.

THE FISSURES AND CONNECTIONS OF THE AWAKENING MOVEMENT

Recognizing the suppleness and strength of imperial protestantism prompts a reassessment of some of the more prominent moments of religious conflict during the late colonial period, particularly those that developed because of the awakening movement that increased in strength over the second half of the eighteenth century. Doing so points to why major change—the formation of new denominations and the refashioning of church establishments—did not come until after the American Revolution disrupted imperial protestantism. Virginia's tensions between Anglicans and presbyterians provide a good example. That colony's religious establishment, like those in many parts of the empire, privileged the Church of England while tolerating other protestant denominations. Presbyterian immigrants—Francis Makemie among them—had long been a part of the colony's landscape, though for the most part Anglicans monopolized religious life. A new challenge to Anglican authority arose after itinerant minister George Whitefield traveled through Virginia in 1739. Laypeople inspired by him in Hanover County constituted themselves into an informal group, then they founded a congregation and sought ordained leadership. They reached out to presbyterians to their north—a reflection of their sense that they needed a recognizable protestant minister from a denomination with sufficient authority to lead them. The Philadelphia Synod responded by sending a newly ordained minister, Samuel Davies, to Virginia. Over the next decade, Davies became an eager and effective advocate for both the awakening movement and religious toleration in Virginia, but to do so he relied heavily on knowledge of how Britain's mixed establishment functioned and also on connections to distant coreligionists.[48]

48. Influential arguments have posited that awakened protestants had both divisive and democratizing impacts on American colonial religion. Most important among these are Isaac, *The Transformation of Virginia;* and Bonomi, *Under the Cope of Heaven.* John Ragosta has updated

The Virginia controversies of which Davies was a part started as a contest over access to toleration within the empire's mixed establishment by one of its dominant denominations, presbyterians. Davies believed that, as members of that group, with a duly ordained minister (himself), his congregants were entitled to toleration in Virginia, as long as they followed the regular protocols asserting loyalty to Britain's protestant king. In 1747, he petitioned the colony's lieutenant governor and council for a license to preach, and he was granted one after taking "the usual oaths to his Majesty's person and government, and subscrib[ing] the Test." He was permitted "to assemble and meet any congregations of Dissenters," only if those dissenters were "peaceable . . . and conform themselves according to the directions of the acts of parliament in that behalf made." Unfortunately for Davies and his colleagues, they preached vigorously enough, and attracted enough attention, that local Anglican elites felt the presbyterians had moved beyond the role of legitimate dissent.[49]

Virginia's Anglican clergy knew that they were not alone in their resistance to the awakening movement—it was disruptive across all of the protestant world. Awakened Anglicans in England strained against regulations governing itinerant preaching and found shelter in the chapels of titled laypeople. In Scotland, the popular and moderate wings of the Church of Scotland vied for control of

---

and restrained the excesses of Isaac's argument for Virginia, including exploration of the ways that dissenters depended on British protections of their liberty. See Ragosta, *Wellspring of Liberty*, 40–42. He also tracks the timing and influence of the war in the growth of new denominations and their arguments for religious liberty, a method the present study also embraces. See also Jewel L. Spangler, *Virginians Reborn: Anglican Monopoly, Evangelical Dissent, and the Rise of the Baptists in the Late Eighteenth Century* (Charlottesville, Va., 2008), for an argument that emphasizes the colony's baptists. Related arguments that awakened protestants represented a democratic impulse can be found in Noll, *Rise of Evangelicalism*, esp. 186–187. Scholars of New England revivals have noted the timing of denominational shifts, but with minimal attention to the chronology of the war and its attendant shifts in political structure. See, for example, Goen, *Revivalism and Separatism*, 155–157, 204; and Winiarski, *Darkness Falls on the Land of Light*, 43, 426–427. For Virginia's Anglicans, see Ragosta, *Wellspring of Liberty*, 36–40; Winner, *A Cheerful and Comfortable Faith*; and Nelson, *A Blessed Company*. For the Hanover Presbyterians and Davies's arrival, see George William Pilcher, *Samuel Davies: Apostle of Dissent in Colonial Virginia* (Knoxville, Tenn., 1971); Rodger M. Payne, "New Lights in Hanover County: Evangelical Dissent in Piedmont Virginia, 1740–1755," *Journal of Southern History*, LXI (1995), 665–694; Philip N. Mulder, "Converting the New Light: Presbyterian Evangelicalism in Hanover, Virginia," *Journal of Presbyterian History*, LXXV (1997), 141–151; Ragosta, *Wellspring of Liberty*, 15–42.

49. Foote, *Sketches of Virginia*, 160 (quotations). Davies's role in advocating for presbyterians' religious liberties and spreading awakening in Virginia is discussed in Pilcher, ed., *Samuel Davies*; Isaac, *The Transformation of Virginia*, 150–154; John B. Boles, *The Great Revival: Beginnings of the Bible Belt* (Lexington, Ky., 1996), 1–2; Noll, *Rise of Evangelicalism*, 35, 175, 184–185; Spangler, *Virginians Reborn*, 56–75; Philip N. Mulder, *A Controversial Spirit: Evangelical Awakenings in the South* (Oxford, 2002), 11, 31–33; Thomas S. Kidd, *The Great Awakening: The Roots of Evangelical Christianity in Colonial America* (New Haven, Conn., 2007), 238; Kidd, *God of Liberty: A Religious History of the American Revolution* (New York, 2010), 50–52; Ragosta, *Wellspring of Liberty*, 18, 22, 40; and Smith, *First Great Awakening*, 274–276.

the denomination's apparatus. Mid-Atlantic presbyterianism ruptured over the proper qualifications of the clergy, with the New Side–Old Side schism stretching from 1741 to 1758. In New England, those ministers who opposed the awakening movement used local governments to try to limit the ability of itinerants to preach, a practice that continued for decades in the southern colonies. Awakened ministers who transgressed too far over the boundaries, such as New England's James Davenport, faced criminal penalties. Revivals and the techniques used to spread them threatened established ministers in all parts of the empire.[50]

When Virginia's Anglicans and presbyterians squared off, both sides viewed the conflict through the lens of their connections to imperial protestantism. Anglicans acted first. Their first line of defense against Davies and his fellows was to try to exclude them from the structures that bounded legitimate protestantism across the empire. They corresponded with the Old Side Synod of Philadelphia and received assurance that "the Ring-leaders" of Davies's crew had been "excluded" from the synod "for their erroneous Doctrines, and Practices" in 1741. When the Anglicans reported this information to the House of Burgesses, they asserted that their information was from legitimate British protestants, as the Old Side body had never been "reprehended for Errors in Doctrine, Discipline or Government, either by the establish'd Kirk of Scotland, the Presbyterian Dissenters in England, or any other Body of Presbyterians whatsoever." The list of British protestant institutions served here to distinguish between those who deserved protection and those who did not. The terms of distinction were not theological, or even related to details of local establishment, but grew from the unique configurations of imperial protestantism.[51]

Correspondence within the networks of transatlantic protestantism came next, and both sides in the squabble resorted to it. Virginia's Anglicans reached out to the bishop of London, hoping for his intervention to support their authority in the colony's religious life. But, even as Anglicans appealed to London, so, too, did Davies. Moreover, in this moment he shrewdly knew that it was more effective to appeal to his credentials as a dissenter than to his status as an awakened protestant. Accordingly, he reached out across the Atlantic to English dissenters, albeit to those who were sympathetic to the awakening movement.

50. Winiarski, *Darkness Falls on the Land of Light,* 379–380; Westerkamp, *Triumph of the Laity,* 165–194; Timothy D. Hall, *Contested Boundaries: Itinerancy and the Reshaping of the Colonial American Religious World* (Durham, N.C., 1994); McIntosh, *Church and Theology,* 20–27; Lambert, *Inventing the "Great Awakening,"* 185–221; Mulder, *A Controversial Spirit,* 12–13; Bonomi, *Under the Cope of Heaven,* 163; Kidd, *Great Awakening,* 139–146, 153–154; Ragosta, *Wellspring of Liberty,* 22–36; Bradley J. Longfield, *Presbyterians and American Culture: A History* (Louisville, Ky., 2013), 14–17, 25–27.

51. Petition of the Clergy of Virginia to the House of Burgesses, Fulham Papers, XIV, fols. 269–270.

He chose Philip Doddridge, a prominent congregationalist minister and teacher in Northampton, England, for help. He described his labors but confessed that it was "an unhappiness to be under the Odium of the Government and Clergy, as incendiaries and Promoters of Schism." Because of that suspicion, "Sundry Measures have been and still are pursued to restrain and suppress us," he reported, and some had even been "indicted and fined," even "tho we are equally willing to comply with the Act of Toleration (as I have actually done.)" Davies, like his Anglican counterparts, moved up the chain of command that ran to London. He could not control the Anglican-dominated Virginia government, but he could appeal to the terms of the empire's mixed establishment. The Virginia fight thus unfolded through the networks of imperial protestantism.[52]

But the networks of imperial protestantism overlapped in interesting ways, and they could loop back on themselves. English religious leaders, both dissenters and Anglicans, looked at the colonial incident as one that needed to be—and would be—resolved without any significant disturbance to the wider system. Doddridge accordingly decided to reach out directly to the bishop of London, Thomas Sherlock. That Sherlock had already been made aware of the Virginia conflict through the Anglican clerical network was immaterial; Doddridge had his own claim to the bishop's ear as an esteemed ministerial colleague. The dissenter and the bishop discussed the practical functioning of dissenting congregations in England, and they both expressed their frustration at the difficulties facing their own coreligionists in the colonies. They shared news of their conversations freely back through their networks, so freely, in fact, that one of Sherlock's Anglican subordinates was "surprized" when Davies himself pulled out "Extracts of a Letter f[ro]m your Lordship to me, and of mine to your Lordship, relating to himself." The lines of communication between London and Virginia ran in all directions. Rather than reinforcing the local boundaries between presbyterians and Anglicans, this correspondence reconfigured the tension as one between awakened dissenters and Anglicans that percolated in many places, and in that context Virginia's events were not a cause for particular alarm to the Londoners. As the opposing Virginians brought powerful English advocates into the case, the result was to make it more difficult for the Virginians to interpret either their establishment or its toleration in ways that diverged significantly from what were effectively imperial norms.[53]

52. Thomas Lee to Thomas Sherlock, May 11, 1750, Fulham Papers, XIII, fols. 35–36; William Dawson to Sherlock, July 27, 1750, ibid., fols. 37–38; Samuel Davies to Philip Doddridge, Oct. 2, 1750, ibid., fols. 39–40.

53. Dawson to Sherlock, Feb. 10, 1752, Fulham Papers, XIII, fol. 49. For correspondence between Sherlock, Doddridge, Davies, and the other players in this story, see Fulham Papers, XIII, fols. 35–48. Davies also made his case in print. See Samuel Davies, *The Impartial Trial, Impartially*

Those norms dictated that, although religious leaders from the three networks could advocate and lobby, their counterparts in government would decide. London officials replied to their counterparts in Virginia urging moderation. Their disinclination to support either an enhancement of the Anglican establishment at the expense of presbyterians or to support a radical version of toleration reinforced the empire's mixed establishment. The Board of Trade directed the Council in Virginia to take care of "Toleration and a free Exercise of Religion," which they saw as "so valuable to a Branch of true Liberty, and so essential to the enriching and improving of a Trading Nation, it sh[oul]d ever be held sacred in His Majesty's Colonies." In the same breath, the Board also "admonish[ed]" Davies to "make a proper Use of that Indulgence." The non-answer said little directly, but a great deal indirectly. Religious matters were salient, but secondary. Toleration was an important value, but it also served the empire's health and economy. The Board of Trade was saying, albeit in uncertain terms, that Virginia's Anglicans should not torment dissenters, but neither should dissenters disturb the public peace. Virginia's Anglicans relented, a bit. Davies stayed in Virginia, and awakened presbyterianism continued to grow there in the 1750s and 1760s. Anglican elites continued their efforts to restrain the growth of the awakening movement, particularly—and sometimes brutally—in the late 1760s when baptists, who often resisted and skirted the structures of imperial protestantism, began to increase in numbers. But one should be careful not to draw a clean line from Davies's battle to theirs. For fifteen years in between, awakened presbyterianism gained ground in Virginia. Moreover, and most important for the health of imperial protestantism and the empire's peace, the immediate crisis had dissipated and did not become a source of political conflict between Virginia and London.[54]

In the 1750s and 1760s, imperial protestantism functioned to quell, if not necessarily eliminate, tensions caused by the awakening movement when it came to local establishments. The revivals led to fractures within local congregations, but those new churches largely stayed within the patterns of legitimacy set by imperial protestantism. It was most disruptive of settled religious institutions in New England, but even there the fracturing primarily led to a multiplication

Tried, and Convicted of Partiality: In Remarks on Mr. Caldwell's, Alias Thornton's Sermon, Intituled, an Impartial Trial of the Spirit, etc. and the Preface of the Publisher in Virginia, to Which Is Added, a Short Appendix, Proving the Right of the Synod of New-York to the Liberties Allowed to Protestant Dissenters, by the Act of Toleration (Williamsburg, Va., 1748); he later traveled to London to make his case in person. See also Olson, "The Eighteenth Century Empire," *Journal of American Studies,* XXVI (1992), 41–58.

54. Dawson to Sherlock, Aug. 6, 1751, Fulham Papers, XIII, fols. 47–48; Olson, "The Eighteenth Century Empire," *Journal of American Studies,* XXVI (1992), 53; Mulder, *A Controversial Spirit,* 32–33, 37–38. For persecution of baptists, see Ragosta, *Wellspring of Liberty,* 26–36.

of institutions within the protestant system while the imperial establishment was still in place. Revivalist and separatist protestants gravitated toward baptist congregations in New England. They were thus outside the region's congregationalist establishment, but not outside the community of religious leaders or the wider systems of British protestantism. Isaac Backus, a congregationalist turned baptist minister, was swept up in the revivals of the early 1740s. He became a separate congregationalist minister and then, in 1756, a baptist. At that point, he halted and drew a line between what he deemed acceptable religious expressions and what went too far. Within a few years, Backus became a significant figure in transatlantic baptist circles. In 1764, he wrote to London's Benjamin Wallin, a prominent minister who was not himself a proponent of revival, reporting on the state of religion in New England, describing the problems of dealing with an established church as well as the progress of revival. Proponents of awakening contended with their opponents for control of the apparatus of local religious institutions, but they also claimed a place within Britain's protestant community. The communities of imperial protestantism were flexible enough, and membership within them valuable enough to participants, to contain much of the revivals' energies.[55]

Put another way, awakened protestants stayed within Britain's dominant institutional systems during the colonial period because most of them wished to do so. They did not want to cause schism but worked instead to revitalize piety within existing churches. Preparing for the 1747 Concert for Prayer, publicized by Jonathan Edwards, awakened protestants conjured a world in which protestants would "be *united* in thus seeking the Lord of Hosts." These souls would be "the *Inhabitants of many Cities,* and of many Countries, *yea, many People, and strong Nations;* great Multitudes in different Parts of the World" would share in the "Business." John Wesley worked to stave off rupture within the Church of England, even as his own activities and that of many of his itinerant preachers tended to move in that direction. In 1760, he published his *Reasons against*

55. Backus to Benjamin Wallin, Nov. 16, 1764, transcription by Alval Hovey, Isaac Backus Papers. Jon Butler makes a similar argument about revivals strengthening traditional institutions with regard to North America in *Awash in a Sea of Faith,* 178–181. William Harrison Taylor goes a step further and argues for presbyterian investment in Christian unity, a perspective with which the present project concurs. See Taylor, *Unity in Christ and Country: American Presbyterians in the Revolutionary Era, 1758–1801* (Tuscaloosa, Ala., 2017). Douglas L. Winiarski argues that New England's congregational clergy engaged in a protracted internal battle between 1745 and 1780 (*Darkness Falls on the Land of Light,*19, 367–506, esp. 372, 402). See also Goen, *Revivalism and Separatism,* 193–199. For Backus, see Winiarski, *Darkness Falls on the Land of Light,* 389–390, 401–402, 406–407. For arguments demonstrating the increasing strength of religious institutions and ecclesiastical conformity before the outbreak of Revolution, see, for example, Butler, *Awash in a Sea of Faith,* 128; Noll, *Rise of Evangelicalism,* 178–187; and Pestana, *Protestant Empire,* 197–215. The present interpretation supports those findings.

Separation, originally written several years earlier, itemizing a long list of reasons why schism would be bad. His reasons ranged from the practical—"BECAUSE it would hinder Multitudes of those who neither love nor fear God, from hearing us at all"—to the fundamental, separating would "banish Peace from among us, and that without Hope of its Return." Such an act would be wrong on its own terms, as division ran contrary to the goals of Christian unity. In addition, it was ineffective with regard to the spread of vital religion. That had been the lesson of the centuries since the Reformation, he continued, when "Witnesses of pure Religion," who "lived and died (like [German pietist] *John Arndt,* [English puritan] *Robert Bolton,* and many others) in the Churches to which they belonged," "spread the Leaven of true Religion far and wide." Those who divided, Wesley continued, "lost the Spirit of Religion themselves in the Spirit of Controversy." Awakened protestant leaders considered themselves at the head of "connexions," networks of protestants within and across denominations. By choosing a mode of relation that was not explicitly or historically ecclesiastical, they hoped to sidestep schism, and they became instead the connective tissue between protestant communities across the empire.[56]

Ultimately, then, the struggles between those who advocated awakening and their foes led to the strengthening, rather than the weakening, of British protestantism in the middle decades of the eighteenth century. Most of the movement's leaders brought or kept their followers inside the empire's dominant denominations, just as Davies had done with the congregations forming in Whitefield's wake. Few awakened clergy were willing to risk the stain of radicalism and division that attached to the Moravians after the early 1750s. Quite the contrary, many awakened protestant leaders, men like Isaac Backus and Samuel Davies, sought respectability through ordination and congregational authority. They founded schools and universities to train ministers, replicating the institutional structures of imperial protestantism. Awakened leaders pursued these strategies for attaining legitimacy even as they also sought to create a new understanding of Christian experience. The movement's most prominent voices—the itinerant George Whitefield, Anglicans John and Charles Wesley and Selina Hastings, Scottish presbyterian John Erskine, and New Englanders Jonathan Edwards and Joseph Bellamy—remained within state-funded denominations

56. Jonathan Edwards, *An Humble Attempt to Promote Explicit Agreement and Visible Union of God's People in Extraordinary Prayer . . .* (Boston, 1747 [1748]), 9 (quotations) (the italicized sections are quotations from the Scottish memorial promoting the concert, which referred to Zechariah 8:20–22); John Wesley, *Reasons against a Separation from the Church of England* (London, 1760), 3, 4, 5. See also Lambert, *Inventing the "Great Awakening,"* 164–165; Frank Baker, *John Wesley and the Church of England* (London, 1970), 160–179; Hindmarsh, *Spirit of Early Evangelicalism,* 56–57.

through most or all of their careers. As the major waves of revivals ebbed in the 1750s, New Light and Old Light communities came to resemble each other in many places. North American presbyterians reunited in 1758 in the Synod of New York and Philadelphia, seeing their shared interests as a denomination as more significant than their differences. Similarly, the awakening-aligned Anglican Saint Paul's Church in Philadelphia, which prominent minister William Smith described by saying that "their Principles lead them to an *independent Church of England,*" ultimately came back into the Anglican fold through the agency of Whitefield in London. While its major leaders remained committed to the dominant denominations, and while those denominations were committed to combatting divisions rather than falling into schism, the dominance of the major protestant denominations across the British Empire held.[57]

The transatlantic awakened network was an important factor keeping awakened protestants within the protestant fold. Davies's connections to the awakened network in Britain, with its many Anglican members, led him to take a comparatively conciliatory stance toward the Church of England in matters that did not relate to establishment. In 1757, Davies published a tract in London singing the praises of the SPRKP, a group that had supported his work and sent large numbers of books to Virginia. He wrote that he knew "of hardly any modern institution, which bears so favourable an aspect upon the declining interests of Religion and Virtue in our degenerate world, as that *generous* [London] SOCIETY." He took pains, even with his largely dissenting audience in the SPRKP, to point out that he had no objections to Anglicans generally. No doubt that reflected his knowledge that the group included the likes of the countess of Huntingdon and George Whitefield, loyal Anglicans both. He asserted that his motives were untainted by any effort to divide the protestant community. When Davies wrote about the increasing numbers of dissenters in Virginia for an English audience, for example, he protested that the defections from the established church "were not against the peculiar *Rites* and *Ceremonies* of that Church, much less against her excellent *Articles*." Whatever reasons

57. William Smith to Richard Terrick, Nov. 12, 1766, William Smith Papers, III, item 66, Hawks Collection, Archives of the Episcopal Church, Austin, Tex. (quotation); Noll, *Rise of Evangelicalism,* 156–185; McConville, *The King's Three Faces,* 166–167; Pestana, *Protestant Empire,* 216–217. For schools and universities, see Neil J. O'Connell, "George Whitefield and Bethesda Orphan-House," *Georgia Historical Quarterly,* LIV (1970), 41–62; McLoughlin, *Soul Liberty,* 7–8; Boyd Stanley Schlenther, *Queen of the Methodists: The Countess of Huntingdon and the Eighteenth-Century Crisis of Faith and Society* (Durham, U.K., 1997), 75–79; Longfield, *Presbyterians and American Culture,* 19–23; and Deborah Mathias Gough, *Christ Church, Philadelphia: The Nation's Church in a Changing City* (Philadelphia, 1995), 78–82. See also Susan Juster, *Disorderly Women: Sexual Politics and Evangelicalism in Revolutionary New England* (Ithaca, N.Y., 1994), 75–107; and Christopher Grasso, *A Speaking Aristocracy: Transforming Public Discourse in Eighteenth-Century Connecticut* (Williamsburg, Va., and Chapel Hill, N.C., 1999), 342.

there were for Virginia's laypeople to prefer his church, in other words, it was not because of prejudice against Anglicanism per se, and the fault must be local. When he asked to have one of his own sermons printed, he urged that "the Names of the London Ministers" be used because they would "have great weight in Virginia." He pressed his case: "As the design is most Catholic, and all Christians agree in it, I should be glad the recommendations might be signed by some of all Parties." A shared endorsement, he thought, could "render it acceptable to the Church People in Virginia." As a practical matter, seeking funds and support from London, he could not, did not, treat the Church of England as an enemy. The collaboration he hoped he could win—through transatlantic connections—required local moderation. Davies was active as an awakened protestant and as a dissenter. His status as a dissenter brought him into conflict with Anglicans, but his position in the awakening movement gave him reason to set those prejudices aside.[58]

The scaffolding that bound Britain's empire together did not eliminate conflict over the terms of church establishments or between the three religious networks, and it did not prevent conflicts over the awakening movement. But it did provide a mechanism to address those conflicts and a reason for awakened protestants to work within, rather than against, the protestant institutions that dominated across the empire. Anglicans, dissenters, and awakened protestants clashed and competed. Local leaders tried to sway religious establishments to serve their ends, whether that be to limit Anglicanism in New England or presbyterians and baptists in Virginia. In all these situations, interregional connections and shared ties to metropolitan authorities provided mechanisms for those conflicts to be aired and overcome, if not exactly resolved. The desire on the part of historians to see such conflicts within the framework of the coming American Revolution has obscured the fact that the structures of imperial

58. Samuel Davies, *Letters from the Rev. Samuel Davies: etc. Shewing the State of Religion in Virginia, Particularly among the Negroes; Likewise an Extract of a Letter from a Gentleman in London to His Friend in the Country, Containing Some Observations on the Same*, 2d ed. (London, 1757), 8–13 ("hardly any," 12); Davies, *The State of Religion among the Protestant Dissenters in Virginia; in a Letter to the Rev. Mr. Joseph Bellamy, of Bethlem, in New-England: From the Reverend Mr. Samuel Davies, V.D.M. in Hanover County, Virginia* (Boston, 1751), 6 ("peculiar *Rites*"); Davies, *Letters from the Rev. Samuel Davies, etc. Shewing the State of Religion (Particularly among the Negroes) in Virginia . . .* (London, 1757), 22; Thomas Gibbons, *The Excellency of the Gospel, and the Happiness of an Interest in It . . .* (London, 1752), 37; *An Account of the Society for Promoting Religious Knowledge among the Poor* (London, 1759). See also Rivers, "The First Evangelical Tract Society," *Historical Journal*, L (2007), 1–22, esp. 6; F. W. B. Bullock, *Voluntary Religious Societies, 1520–1799* (St. Leonards-on-Sea, 1963), 237; Amanda B. Moniz, *From Empire to Humanity: The American Revolution and the Origins of Humanitarianism* (New York, 2016), 53–57. The sermon printed is Davies, *The Duty of Christians to Propagate Their Religion among Heathens, Earnestly Recommended to the Masters of Negroes Slaves in Virginia: A Sermon Preached in Hanover, January 8, 1757* (London, 1758).

protestantism, both Britain's mixed establishment and the organizational ties that protestants built between disparate places, endured for decades and absorbed much of the energy of the awakening movement, despite those periodic controversies. Though it was not a system with a specific designer or architect, the nexus of religious and governmental power, with the legitimacy it brought, was difficult to resist. Its strength reflected the understanding by political and religious leaders across the empire that Britain's mixed imperial establishment, and also their connections to one another, benefited them more than they constricted opportunities. Moreover, it reflected the widespread belief that the British Empire, as a large and diverse polity, promoted protestantism in line with God's will. Those commitments continued as long as the empire, and its religious policies, persisted as the core around which the whole was built.

PROTESTANTISM AND EMPIRE

The scaffolding of British protestantism followed the empire's outlines, but that fact alone is not enough to call Britain's protestantism *imperial,* that is, to say that the empire's dominant protestant denominations were tethered to the empire itself. Rather, imperial protestantism existed because protestant leaders embraced ideas and projects that were in line with imperatives in the control of the empire's political leaders. They did so from the public pulpit, a crucial merging of religious and governmental authority, and they did so through their energetic promotion of efforts to extend protestantism to new populations. In these ways, Britain's protestants, those who participated in the networks and institutions that spanned the empire, supported the empire's policies in matters of crucial importance to its preservation: war, expansion into Indigenous lands, and slavery. Historians have long explored the ways that political factions grew out of denominational differences, particularly those between Anglicans and dissenters. But, as with the parallel nature of establishments across the empire or the overlapping character of protestantism's networks, internal division should not be used to dismiss either common commitments or the ways that imperial protestantism, as expressed by religious leaders from all its networks, supported the goals of empire.[59]

59. The question of religion and protestant empire has two permutations. First, there is an extensive literature on protestantism as a political unifier in the eighteenth-century British Empire. See note 8, above. Second, British historians have debated the role of religion in serving their empire, though these discussions privilege the nineteenth-century empire. See Strong, *Anglicanism and the British Empire;* Andrew Porter, *Religion versus Empire? British Protestant Missionaries and Overseas Expansion, 1700–1914* (Manchester, U.K., 2004); and Hilary M. Carey, *God's Empire: Religion and Colonialism in the British World, c. 1801–1908* (Cambridge, 2011). Scholarship rooting

The empire's politics and its public religion intersected in several significant ways. The first was ideological and theological. All three branches of British protestantism embraced the idea that Britain's imperial wars were a fight against a Catholic menace, presenting a common front of religious and political ends. There is no reason to view such positions as cynical, inauthentic, or merely as an expression of "civil religion."[60] For British subjects on both sides of the Atlantic, being a protestant meant both spiritual and temporal freedom from the pope's tyranny. It meant being a part of the true faith of Christianity, and, simultaneously, fighting against the very real political and military threats posed by earthly Catholic power, whether in the form of the pope, the Jesuits, or the military might of the Spanish and French empires and their Indigenous American allies. Both the Anglican SPG and the presbyterian SSPCK included negative references to popery in their foundational documents. The former compared the gentle practices of protestant colonists, where "no one Instance was given of hunting poor Souls into a forc'd Conversion," to those of their French and Spanish counterparts. The SSPCK sought to protect those in the "Highlands and Islands" of Scotland from "Popish error and superstition," and the Church of Scotland regularly collected statistics on Catholics around the country. Every four years, Harvard College's Dudleian Lecture (invariably preached by a dissenter) was "against popery," an opportunity that prominent ministers used to convince hearers of the heretical nature of Catholicism. Anti-Catholicism created easy grounds for collaboration between political leaders and their clerical counterparts.[61]

political perspectives in denominational differences is particularly notable in English historiography. See, for example, Colin Bonwick, *English Radicals and the American Revolution* (Chapel Hill, N.C., 1977); James E. Bradley, *Religion, Revolution, and English Radicalism: Nonconformity in Eighteenth-Century Politics and Society* (Cambridge, 1990); and Clark, *Language of Liberty.*

60. The concept of "civil religion" is most closely associated with Robert N. Bellah, "Civil Religion in America," *Daedelus,* CXXXIV, no. 4 (Fall 2005; orig. pub. Winter 1967), 40–55. It is not used in the present project because it has been more fully articulated within a post-Revolutionary context of nation rather than an early modern context of empire and international confessional rivalry. See, for example, Philip Gorski, *American Covenant: A History of Civil Religion from the Puritans to the Present* (Princeton, N.J., 2017).

61. *An Account of the Society for Propagating the Gospel in Foreign Parts* (London, 1706), 2–3 (quotation on 3). For the Church of Scotland, see, for example, "Assembly Papers of the General Assembly of the Church of Scotland," 1771, Ch1/2/113, NRS. For American antipopery, see Brendan McConville, "Pope's Day Revisited: 'Popular' Culture Reconsidered," *Explorations in Early American Culture,* IV (2000), 265; Owen Stanwood, "Catholics, Protestants, and the Clash of Civilizations in Early America," in Beneke and Grenda, eds., *The First Prejudice,* 218–240, esp. 231; Pauline Maier, "The Pope at Harvard: The Dudleian Lectures, Anti-Catholicism, and the Politics of Protestantism," MHS, *Procs.,* 3d Ser., XCVII (1985), 16–41 (quotation on 16). For British anti-Catholicism in this period, see Haydon, *Anti-Catholicism in Eighteenth-Century England;* and Choi, *George Whitefield,* 172–181.

Wartime anti-Catholicism resonated in the American colonies, and it brought together religious leaders from all three protestant networks. During the Seven Years' War, the 1757 Dudleian Lecture by Massachusetts congregationalist (and dissenter) Edward Wigglesworth warned that "the Church of *Rome*" was "a restless, incroaching and implacable Enemy to *Protestants* of every Denomination." The threat of Catholic France made distinctions between protestants far less important than the chasm between the true "Doctrines of Religion" and Catholicism. He asked Harvard's students to "consider, how much the *Protestant* Interest, both in *Europe* and *America,* is at this Day threatened, by the Sword of its *Popish* Enemies; this is the Controversy in which it seems most likely that we may be bro't to the Trial." In a similar vein, Pennsylvania's Anglican preacher Thomas Barton called for unity among protestants because "the chief and greatest" disaster they faced if Britain lost the war was "being obliged to exchange our holy Protestant Religion for Popish Error and Delusion." To prevent this terrible fate, colonists had to "lay aside every idle Divide and Distinction" among them and "be heartily united for the future." In the face of this danger, "the MEMBERS of the CHURCH of ENGLAND, and PROTESTANT DISSENTERS *of all Denominations,* may now plainly perceive that they have but one common Interest, as they have one common Danger." State sermons in England followed similar lines. Religious leaders organized loyal protestants to protect the empire, and the souls of its inhabitants, from the Catholic menace. Awakened protestant Samuel Davies, too, preached in this vein several times, proving his loyalty to empire and instilling it in his hearers as well. Anti-Catholic rhetoric was comprehensible in both political and religious terms, and it pulled Britons toward a common center.[62]

It is notable that many of the sermons through which protestant leaders addressed such matters were preached from the public pulpit, occasions such

62. For the protestant interest in European politics, see Thompson, *Britain, Hanover, and the Protestant Interest;* Edward Wigglesworth, *Some Thoughts upon the Spirit of Infallibility, Claimed by the Church of Rome: Offer'd at the Anniversary Dudleian-Lecture, at Harvard-College in Cambridge, May 11. 1757* (Boston, 1757), 24, 31; and Thomas Barton, *Unanimity and Public Spirit: A Sermon, Preached at Carlisle, and Some Other Episcopal Churches, in the Counties of York and Cumberland, from after General Braddock's Defeat* . . . (Philadelphia, 1755), 9, 13–14. See also Samuel Davies, *Religion and Patriotism the Constituents of a Good Soldier: A Sermon Preached to Captain Overton's Independent Company of Volunteers, Raised in Hanover County, Virginia, August 17, 1755* (Philadelphia, 1755). Davies preached a series of patriotic sermons during the Seven Years' War, including Davies, *The Crisis; or, The Uncertain Doom of Kingdoms at Particular Times: Considered with Reference to Great-Britain and Her Colonies in Their Present Circumstances; a Sermon, Preached in Hanover, Virginia, October 28, 1756; a Day Appointed by the Synod of New-York, to Be Observed as a General Fast, on Account of the Present War with France* . . . (London, 1757); and Davies, *Virginia's Danger and Remedy: Two Discourses, Occasioned by the Severe Drought in Sundry Parts of the Country; and the Defeat of General Braddock* (Williamsburg, Va., 1756). Several historians have explored the religious themes of American preaching during the Seven Years' War, often

as days of fast and thanksgiving and important moments of government ceremony or commemoration, when government officials requested that leaders of protestant institutions preach. These moments provided a second way that religious leaders from Britain's dominant denominations supported the goals of empire. It was a unique collaboration between protestant leaders and governments at many levels and a useful way for local religious leaders to remind their communities of their membership in a wider empire. At the same time, those who preached on such days—almost exclusively representatives of one of the empire's dominant denominations—could claim a mantle of authority given by the state, and the state, in return, could rely on ministers to validate its decisions. Following the practices of the mixed establishment, days of fast and thanksgiving were usually declared locally. They celebrated imperial events and occurred in many places; they tied the ends of the empire together. A good example is the series of celebrations declared after the British army took the French stronghold of Quebec on September 18, 1759, the turning point of the Seven Years' War. Nearby New Englanders commemorated the triumph with days of thanksgiving proclaimed by governors and the Massachusetts General Assembly, events held from late October to late November. The Bay Colony's Samuel Cooper preached before the province's governor. "WHAT but the divine Arm has supported and defended the Protestant Religion, so wonderful in it's Rise, so small and tender in it's Infancy, and so constantly opposed and persecuted by a formidable Power." Yet he had seen the righteous cause triumph, and he hoped to see it continue. "MAY God Still bless the *British* Arms wherever they are employed! Still may He advance the Cause of Liberty, and pure Religion, till every Nation shall be happy." Protestant religion, then, was furthered not just by ministers but also by the success of the British state.[63]

---

in New England. See Nathan O Hatch, *The Sacred Cause of Liberty: Republican Thought and the Millennium in Revolutionary New England* (New Haven, Conn., 1977), 21–54; Ruth Bloch, *Visionary Republic: Millennial Themes in American Thought, 1756–1800* (Cambridge, 1985), 37–45; Harry S. Stout, *The New England Soul: Preaching and Religious Culture in Colonial New England* (New York, 1986), 233–255; Nicholas Guyatt, *Providence and the Invention of the United States, 1607–1876* (Cambridge, 2007), 53–69; James P. Byrd, *Sacred Scripture, Sacred War: The Bible and the American Revolution* (Oxford, 2013), 23–27; and John F. Berens, *Providence and Patriotism in Early America, 1640–1815* (Charlottesville, Va., 1978), 32–50. Mark Noll has argued for the integration of the British Empire in American colonial religion during this period; see Noll, *In the Beginning Was the Word: The Bible in American Public Life, 1492–1783* (Oxford, 2016), 150–176; and Choi, *George Whitefield*, 181–186.

63. Samuel Cooper, *A Sermon Preached before His Excellency Thomas Pownall*, Esq.... (Boston, [1759]), 21, 53. For investigations of the public pulpit, see Ihalainen, *Protestant Nations Redefined;* and W[illiam] DeLoss Love, Jr., *The Fast and Thanksgiving Days of New England* (Boston, 1895). For a broad survey of religio-political preaching in New England between 1750 and 1785, see Grasso, *A Speaking Aristocracy*, 66–85.

This thanksgiving ritual was repeated across the empire, reiterated in the different jurisdictions of the imperial establishment. After learning of the army's success at Quebec, George II issued a proclamation "appointing and commanding, That a General Thanksgiving to Almighty God, for these His Mercies, be observed throughout Our Kingdom of England, Dominion of Wales, and Town of Berwick upon Tweed." Similar proclamations were issued for Scotland and Ireland to observe a thanksgiving on the same date, November 29, 1759. The Board of Trade sent a letter, dated November 13, 1759, to the colonial governors to "signify to you His Majesty's Commands, that you do, as soon as possible after the Receipt hereof, appoint a proper day" for "publick Thanksgiving." Perhaps news of the order spread ahead of the official word, or maybe colonial governors merely knew that they ought to celebrate in such a way. Both Pennsylvania and New York declared days of thanksgiving, the former on October 31 and the latter on November 22. In New Germantown, Pennsylvania, German Lutheran Henry Melchior Mühlenberg preached "a solemn service of thanksgiving for the glorious acts of God which the most gracious and omnipotent Lord of Sabaoth has done, in short succession, to the unspeakable consolation of His Protestant Church that was sitting in ashes," by which he meant victories in both central Europe and Quebec.[64]

The public ritual was shared not just across space but also across the various parts of imperial protestantism, unifying the protestants who participated in a shared ritual and giving all of them access to the same institutional authority regardless of whether they were privileged by the terms of establishment in a particular place. Lest any miss the point that all protestants were supposed to participate in the day of thanksgiving declared in 1759, the king issued his orders to "all Our loving Subjects" and ordered that they comply "upon Pain of suffering such punishment as We may justly inflict upon all such as shall condemn or neglect the Performance of so religious and necessary a Duty." Governor James

64. *Journal of the Commissioners for Trade and Plantations*, XI, *From January 1759 to December 1763: Preserved in the Public Record Office* (London, 1935), Nov. 10, 13, 1759, 58–59, outlines the course of events from the king's general fast to the orders to "all His Majesty's colonies in America" (58). See also Lords of Trade to Gov. [James] Hamilton, Nov. 13, 1759, and "Proclamation for a Thanksgiving Day, 1759," in Samuel Hazard, ed., *Pennsylvania Archives . . .*, 1st Ser., III, *Commencing 1756* (Philadelphia, 1853), 690–691. The royal proclamation, dated Oct. 23, 1759, was printed in the *London Gazette*, Oct. 23–27, 1759, [1]; and the *London Evening-Post*, Oct. 27–30, 1759, [1]. For Mühlenberg's sermon, see *The Journals of Henry Melchior Muhlenberg*, trans. Theodore G. Tappert and John W. Doberstein, 3 vols. (Philadelphia, 1942–1958), I, 419. Numerous accounts of New England thanksgivings also appeared in the newspapers, as well as mentions of the English events. See, for example, *Boston Evening-Post*, Feb. 4, 1760, [3]. For an overall account of the day and celebration, see Love, *Fast and Thanksgiving Days of New England*, 310–312; and Fred Anderson, *Crucible of War: The Seven Years' War and the Fate of Empire in British North America, 1754–1766* (New York, 2000), 365–368, 373–376.

De Lancey in New York ordered that the thanksgiving be held "in all Churches and Chapels and other Places of publick Worship," and Governor William Denny in Pennsylvania, where there was no established church, said that he "recommend[ed]" the practice "to the Ministers and Preachers of the Gospel of all Denominations." Religious leaders from across the system responded. The published sermons alone included New England congregationalists, bishops of the Church of England, Scottish presbyterians, and a host of rural English ministers. London dissenter Richard Price and English baptist Benjamin Wallin preached, as did revivalist George Whitefield, known as the Grand Itinerant, who was likewise in London. Whitefield's biographer recorded that he was "too impulsive to wait for royal proclamations" and thus preached his thanksgiving sermons on October 19, arousing the ire of those who opposed his freewheeling patriotism. Awakened Anglican Charles Wesley published a series of hymns for the event. Though protestant leaders differed on any number of theological issues, and also on matters of specific policy, they collectively lent the moral authority of religion to the king and his subordinates when he asked, and the rituals of public religion reinforced their authority in turn.[65]

The public pulpit anchored the voices that clergy used when they preached, even on ordinary days, to the ship of state. Although the vast majority of sermons were not given on days of fast or thanksgiving, the public pulpit enhanced the position of clergy as leaders in the public sphere; it gave their voices a sense of authority and legitimation that linked protestantism to political authority. Sermons were often published, and a disproportionate number of those published were "occasional" sermons, those preached from the public pulpit or at other special moments. Because influential scholars have argued for a decline of religious authority in the eighteenth century, historians have often examined

65. "By the King, a Proclamation," *London Gazette,* Oct. 23–27, 1759, [1]. Denny's proclamation ran in the *Pennsylvania Gazette* (Philadelphia), Oct. 18, 1759, [3]; De Lancey's appeared in the *New-York Gazette,* Nov. 5, 1759, [3]. The English Short Title Catalogue lists at least forty sermons preached on that day that were subsequently published. See, for example, James [Johnson], *A Sermon Preached before the Right Honourable the Lords Spiritual and Temporal in Parliament Assembled* . . . (London, 1759); Richard Price, *Britain's Happiness, and the Proper Improvement of It, Represented in Sermon, Preach'd at Newington-Green, Middlesex, on Nov. 29, 1759* . . . (London, 1759); John Wesley and Charles Wesley, *Hymns to Be Used on the Thanksgiving-Day, Nov. 29, 1759; and After It* ([London, 1759]); Benjamin Wallin, *The Joyful Sacrifice of a Prosperous Nation* . . . (London, 1760); and Alexander Gerard, *National Blessings an Argument for Reformation; a Sermon, Preached at Aberdeen, November 29, 1759* . . . (Aberdeen, U.K., 1759). They were published in England, Scotland, Ireland, and New England, though the observations took place in a wider range of places. For Whitefield, see Tyerman, *Life of the Rev. George Whitefield,* II, 422. Whitefield's preaching on the event was also reported in Boston ("London," *Boston-Gazette, and Country Journal,* Jan. 28, 1760, [3]). See also Philip Williamson et al., eds., *National Prayers: Special Worship since the Reformation,* II, *General Fasts, Thanksgivings, and Special Prayers in the British Isles, 1689–1870* (Woodbridge, U.K., 2013), 516–538.

public preaching for its importance relative to other forms of cultural authority in the era. Although it is true that clergy increasingly competed for attention with scientists, satirists, and pamphleteers of all genres, this reality does not change that, from the perspective of religious institutions, those clergy who represented the empire's dominant denominations, and who therefore had access to the public pulpit, tended to hew the party line on matters that were essential for the empire's stability. They were reliable allies when it came to knowing whom to oppose in times of war, promoting the belief that British victories should be interpreted as beneficial to Indigenous peoples, or sustaining the idea that the enslavement of Africans provided an opportunity to spread protestantism.[66]

This anchoring effect was visible even at moments when clergy voiced opinions that justified opposition to government. Jonathan Mayhew preached his famous *Discourse concerning Unlimited Submission* on January 30, 1750, the anniversary of Charles I's execution. The sermon has been seen as an original moment in the American resistance to Parliament and as a link between puritans who resisted tyranny in the seventeenth century and Americans who did the same in the late eighteenth. An elderly John Adams repeatedly referred to Mayhew as a key figure in inspiring the American Revolution, though the clergyman died in 1766. One historian described Mayhew's 1750 *Discourse* as having "established the tone and justification for opposition to an Anglican bishop and resistance to British religious and political power." Yet without dismissing the significance of Mayhew's ideas, it is important not to overlook the format of his sermon and the framing through which he articulated these ideas. The anniversary Mayhew chose to deliver his discourse referenced, of course, a moment in English history. Religious voices on both sides of the Atlantic disputed the meaning of Charles's execution, so Mayhew was participating in a transatlantic discourse rather than fundamentally reshaping it. (Not to mention that he copied portions of his *Discourse* from the liberal English Anglican Benjamin Hoadley.) The text itself also reinforced the legitimacy of the Hanoverian monarchy. Mayhew noted the justice of the Glorious Revolution, for example, and

66. Several scholars of the "public sphere," an idea most associated with Jürgen Habermas, *The Structural Transformation of the Public Sphere: An Inquiry into a Category of Bourgeois Society*, trans. Thomas Burger with Frederick Lawrence (Cambridge, Mass., 1989), have argued for the decline of religion and clerical authority over the course of the eighteenth century. Michael Warner argues that religion functioned as a force of unity in the printed public sphere, only becoming a meaningful site for division after the separation of church and state (Warner, *The Letters of the Republic: Publication and the Public Sphere in Eighteenth-Century America* [Cambridge, Mass., 1990], 34–35, 57–58). Christopher Grasso argues for a central role for the midcentury revivals in a parallel decline. See Grasso, *A Speaking Aristocracy*, 136–143. See also Robert Hole, *Pulpits, Politics, and Public Order in England, 1760–1832* (Cambridge, 1989); and Ihalainen, *Protestant Nations Redefined*; Stout, *New England Soul*.

the despicable nature of the Jacobite uprisings. It was an important sermon of resistance, and its ideas were undoubtedly influential in that context, but it also couched political discontent within the structures of imperial protestantism, making it conservative even as it was provocative.[67]

Mayhew lent his voice to a transatlantic discussion of political dissent, and clergy were active participants in those conversations, but the authority he (and his clerical peers) claimed to make such statements derived from his position in the structures of imperial protestantism: his position as part of the established church of Massachusetts and his use of the rituals of public religion. In that sense, Mayhew's use of the pulpit to justify resistance to imperial authorities, while still upholding the regime's legitimacy, is the exception that proves the rule. For the most part, the messages protestant leaders preached about the Hanoverians, the British Empire, and its role in God's plan at times of peace and war reinforced the connection between protestantism and the goals of empire.

The desire to spread Christianity to new souls, in the hands of Britain's dominant denominations, also supported the goals of empire. Missions formed a major theme in the publications and projects of British protestantism because expanding the faith to new peoples was the central opportunity offered to Christians by colonization and conquest. As Anglican bishop Joseph Butler preached before the SPG in 1739, "No one [had] a Right to be called a Christian" who did not support Christianity at home and, in "an Obligation but little more remote," help to spread it abroad. This duty required them to minister to the enslaved, and "the like Charity we owe to the Natives." In other words, the expansion of the British Empire enabled protestants to fulfill their duties as Christians, to spread the faith to those who needed it most. The Anglican SPG, presbyterian SSPCK, and dissenting NEC all sponsored missionaries in North America. The NEC and SPG each included images of Indians imploring for help on their seals (see Figure 3). For the SPG, work among Indigenous peoples was one of "three great Branches" of the society's labors, alongside

67. Kidd, *God of Liberty,* 60 (quotation); Jonathan Mayhew, *A Discourse concerning Unlimited Submission and Non-Resistance to the Higher Powers: With Some Reflections on the Resistance Made to King Charles I. and on the Anniversary of His Death . . .* (Boston, 1750). For historians' use of Mayhew, see J. Patrick Mullins, *Father of Liberty: Jonathan Mayhew and the Principles of the American Revolution* (Lawrence, Kans., 2017), 3. For discussions of the sermon that emphasize, as I do here, its chronological context (including ongoing tensions between Anglicans and dissenters) and its non-Revolutionary character, while also tracing the arguments to which it has been put, see Chris Beneke, "The Critical Turn: Jonathan Mayhew, the British Empire, and the Idea of Resistance in Mid-Eighteenth-Century Boston," *Massachusetts Historical Review,* X (2008), 23–56; Mullins, *Father of Liberty,* 44–65. For transatlantic discussions of the importance of Charles I's execution, see McConville, *The King's Three Faces,* 98–100; Guyatt, *Providence and the Invention of the United States,* 69–76. See also Clark, *Language of Liberty,* 116.

FIGURE 3 Seal of the Society for the Propagation of the Gospel in Foreign Parts. From C. F. Pascoe, *Two Hundred Years of the S.P.G.: An Historical Account of the Society for the Propagation of the Gospel in Foreign Parts, 1701–1900* . . . (London, 1901), iv.

"the Care and Instruction of our own People, settled in the Colonies," and "the Conversion of the Negroes." Its regularly collected *notitia*—a semiannual census of missionary work—counted the "N[umber] of Heathens and Infidels" converted. The society sent missionaries to the Haudenosaunee in 1710 and also to work among Indigenous communities in South Carolina. This type of missionary work, and the idea that Indigenous peoples presented an obstacle to the progress of religion, also appeared in society publications. Missionary work, called for by British conquest of Indigenous peoples and enslavement of Africans, thus provided the immediate occasion for many protestants in Britain to act on a core Christian teaching, and in doing so to engage with and collaborate with their fellow imperial subjects in America.[68]

Religious leaders also justified slavery through missionary work. As that institution played a larger and larger role in the empire's economy, religious leaders painted it as an occasion to bring more souls to Christianity. Missionary outreach to the enslaved thus allowed religious leaders to define their relationship to slavery, and the relationship of protestantism to slavery more generally, in positive terms. When planters resisted the efforts of missionaries, religious leaders developed a form of protestantism that was compatible with slavery. Indeed, British protestant leaders, particularly Anglicans, spent much of the eighteenth century appeasing slaveholders and, eventually, justifying slavery. In 1727, Bishop of London Edmund Gibson published a letter that urged planters to "promote the Instruction of their Negroes in the Christian Faith" and sought

68. Joseph [Butler], *A Sermon Preached before the Incorporated Society for the Propagation of the Gospel in Foreign Parts* . . . (London, 1739), 12–13; David Humphreys, *An Historical Account of the Incorporated Society for the Propagation of the Gospel in Foreign Parts* . . . (London, 1730), 22–23 (quotation), 50, 84, 91, 93, 96; Glasson, *Mastering Christianity*, 32–36; Andrews, *Native Apostles*, 66–79; Stevens, *Poor Indians*, 111–137.

to set aside thoughts that the work was too hard or that it would result in the freeing of those enslaved. As to the second issue, Gibson wrote, "It may be very truly reply'd, that Christianity, and the embracing of the Gospel, does not make the least Alteration in Civil Property, or in any of the Duties which belong to Civil Relations." Protestant religious work among the enslaved extended the apparatus of institutional Christianity among those who did not have it, and it also provided a script for those within protestant communities to respond to the existence of slavery. Missionary work, in other words, provided white protestants with a way to interpret their own relationships to slavery and to enslaved Africans as one of benevolence. It was an answer that also served the needs of the empire's most powerful political forces.[69]

It may at first glance appear to be a thin case to say that British protestantism was imperial because of wartime rhetoric, the existence of the public pulpit, and the apologetics religious leaders offered for slavery and the displacement of Indigenous peoples. To understand the implications of this argument, however, one must remember that the question at hand is not whether the British empire was protestant, in the sense that imperial leaders based their policies on religious goals. Rather, the key point here is that Britain's religious leaders, those who guided its protestant institutions, societies, and networks, embraced the stability and expansion of the empire as the best vessel through which to ensure a thriving protestant world. This core belief was evident across all three of the networks that bridged the empire's distances and among the leaders of all its established churches. Room remained for significant differences in political philosophy and theology within the scaffolding of the protestant empire. But protestant leaders, as representatives of the empire's dominant denominations, believed protestantism was best served by being British. That conviction, and their actions, wove the imperatives of empire through the scaffolding of imperial protestantism, further binding its various networks and societies to the imperial state around which they revolved.

69. Edm[und] Gibson, *A Letter of the Lord Bishop of London to the Masters and Mistresses of Families in the English Plantations Abroad; Exhorting Them to Encourage and Promote the Instruction of Their Negroes in the Christian Faith* (London, 1727), 3, 11. Discussions of proslavery Christianity can be found in Gerbner, *Christian Slavery*, 112–136; Sylvester A. Johnson, *African American Religions, 1500–2000: Colonialism, Democracy, and Freedom* (New York, 2015); Rebecca Anne Goetz, *The Baptism of Early Virginia: How Christianity Created Race* (Baltimore, 2012), 144–161; Glasson, *Mastering Christianity*, 75–110; and Christopher Leslie Brown, *Moral Capital: Foundations of British Abolitionism* (Williamsburg, Va., and Chapel Hill, N.C., 2006), 63–73. For George Whitefield's engagement with slavery, see Choi, *George Whitefield*, 127–168; Jessica M. Parr, *Inventing George Whitefield: Race, Revivalism, and the Making of a Religious Icon* (Jackson, Miss., 2015); and Travis Glasson, "'Baptism Doth Not Bestow Freedom': Missionary Anglicanism, Slavery, and the Yorke-Talbot Opinion, 1701–30," *WMQ*, 3d Ser., LXVII (2010), 279–318.

Britain's imperial protestantism was more than the sum of its disparate parts. Policies that built on shared protestantism to unify the empire and that simultaneously embraced a series of mixed establishments ensured that more than one denomination would thrive in most British places. During the middle decades of the eighteenth century, transatlantic links built from mobility, missionary impulses, and the desire to promote the empire's religion connected religious leaders of distant places to one another. Parallel establishments were bridged by overlapping networks of protestants who differed in perspective but not in method. Their competitions were durable and sometimes fierce, but while they remained within the structures of imperial protestantism, those struggles did not result in serious change to the terms of the protestant establishment or provide any meaningful threat to the empire itself. Instead, the voices of protestant leaders joined together to support the empire that privileged their voices as religious leaders.

2
Stamps, Bishops, and Missions
Continuity in the 1760s

In April 1766, English dissenter Micaiah Towgood wrote to congregationalist Jonathan Mayhew in Boston. Both men were well-known polemicists, and they enjoyed a warm correspondence. Towgood congratulated his American colleague "most heartily" on a recent publication protesting the idea of an Anglican bishop for the colonies, but he worried that championing religious liberty might have had deleterious effects. "Perhaps the Reluctance you have shewn to have the *Episcopal* Bit put in your Mouth," he wrote, "may have hasten'd your being saddled with that disagreable Tax." Towgood referred to the Stamp Act, a measure so hated in the colonies that protests had led to its repeal in March 1766. His linkage of the tensions over an Anglican bishop to disputes about colonial taxation strikes a familiar chord when it comes to the 1760s, a period historians have long scavenged for seeds of the coming American Revolution.[1]

Religion—specifically New England religion—has been seen as one of those seeds. It is used to explain the ideological division between democratic-leaning Americans, represented by dissenters, and more authoritarian Britons, a stance articulated by Anglicans. It is an argument with a distinguished lineage. Even contemporaries explained American stubbornness (or love of liberty, depending on one's position) as related to New England's puritan past. Two hundred years later, pieces of that narrative still resonated. In the second half of the twentieth century, historians argued that the ideological contests between colonists and Parliament in the 1760s and 1770s were the anvils on which American thought and institutions were formed, and they often reserved a crucial role for dissenting thought, particularly through the bishop controversy. Though for most historians religious struggles were ancillary to the more important political fights, for a few scholars religion became the driving force of what was eventually called, by James B. Bell, a "war of religion." But even for those less

1. Michaiah Towgood to Jonathan Mayhew, Apr. 6, 1766, Jonathan Mayhew Papers, item 94, Howard Gottlieb Research Center, Boston University.

given to hyperbole, when the American Revolution was conceived as a struggle over Anglo-American political ideology, the fights Towgood and Mayhew described mattered a great deal.[2]

But how important were they? The answer to that question does not turn on the importance of religion to politics in some abstract calculus but rather on what the American Revolution is meant to encompass. By the turn of the twentieth-first century, the ideological framing for the American Revolution became less compelling to scholars as more attention turned to the significance of transcontinental dynamics in North America, to white colonists' investment in perpetuating slavery, to the violence and disruption of the war years across the continent, and to the significant number of American colonists who were ambivalent at best about the course of Revolution. Viewed in this way, the Revolution was, in the words of Jane Kamensky and Edward Gray, not so much "a series of discreet, momentous turning points," like those represented by the Stamp Act or the bishop controversy, but more something to be studied in "the *longue durée*." When the American Revolution is seen as a contest that unfolded over a continent, involving multiple Indigenous and European empires—in

2. For a contemporary version of the argument that New Englanders' puritan past shaped the crisis, see John Erskine, *Shall I Go to War with My American Brethren?* . . . (London, 1769). Though scholars of republicanism in the late twentieth century placed less emphasis on religion than on political theory, they generally reserved an important role for dissenters in the articulation of political philosophy, and thus religion continued to play a significant role in the discussion. See, for example, Bernard Bailyn, *The Ideological Origins of the American Revolution* (Cambridge, Mass., 1992), 32–47; Mark A. Noll, *America's God: From Jonathan Edwards to Abraham Lincoln* (New York, 2002), 61–63; and J. C. D. Clark, *The Language of Liberty, 1660–1832: Political Discourse and Social Dynamics in the Anglo-American World* (Cambridge, 1994). For the definitive historiographical treatment of these arguments, see Daniel T. Rodgers, "Republicanism: The Career of a Concept," *Journal of American History,* LXXIX (1992), 11–38. Rodgers notes that the republicanism literature both secularized political ideology and sidelined religion. The persuasiveness of these arguments has faded, as historians have turned away from ideological explanations for the Revolution. A more nuanced position can be found in Benjamin L. Carp, *Rebels Rising: Cities and the American Revolution* (New York, 2007). Carp argued for the primacy of congregationalists in the imperial crisis in New England, but more as "networks of mobilization" rather than "solely on theological or ideological abstractions" (121–124, 133 [quotation]). During the same general era, a second set of scholars also placed religion at the heart of the changes that caused the Revolution, arguing for the democratizing influence of awakened groups rather than dissenting ideology. Most influential in these works are Alan Heimert, *Religion and the American Mind: From the Great Awakening to the Revolution* (Cambridge, Mass., 1966); and Rhys Isaac, *The Transformation of Virginia, 1740–1790* (Williamsburg, Va., and Chapel Hill, N.C., 1982). For works that emphasize religion as a cause of the American Revolution, see, for example, James B. Bell, *A War of Religion: Dissenters, Anglicans, and the American Revolution* (Basingstoke, U.K., 2008), which argues that "the debate over the prospect of the appointment of an Anglican prelate was joined with colonial fears and objections to the authority of Parliament" (x–xi); see also 211–221 for a full statement of the argument that the Revolution was a "war of religion." This argument follows the lines laid out by Clark, *Language of Liberty*. Also important in establishing the significance of the bishop controversy to the Revolutionary struggle was Carl Bridenbaugh, *Mitre and Sceptre: Transatlantic Faiths, Ideas, Personalities, and Politics, 1689–1775* (New York, 1962).

short, when it is seen as an event in the history of early modern empire—the ideological contests between Anglicans and dissenters take on a more limited significance, despite their intertwining with the era's political thought. Indeed, looked at from the perspective of the empire's religious dynamics over the course of the eighteenth century, they were yet another example of friction in a creaky system.[3]

That broader geographic and chronological framing is well suited to investigating how imperial protestantism—Britain's mixed establishment, religious institutions, and transatlantic networks—fared during the 1760s. Freed of the burden of explaining why Americans committed to resisting British authority, the frictions between protestants during these years tell a new and important tale. That tale shows more evidence of continuity with the colonial era than it

3. Edward G. Gray and Jane Kamensky, "Introduction: American Revolutions," in Gray and Kamensky, eds., *Oxford Handbook of the American Revolution* (New York, 2013), 6. Michael A. McDonnell and David Waldstreicher also noted a shift away from ideological topics. "In the last generation or two," they wrote about articles in the *William and Mary Quarterly,* "few authors have dealt with the period 1763–75, leading to a dearth of articles on topics such as paranoia, republicanism, ideology, and the coming of the revolution." In addition, "articles tying religion, colonial economics, and social movements to the origins of the revolution are also noticeably absent." See McDonnell and Waldstreicher, "Revolution in the Quarterly? A Historiographical Analysis," *William and Mary Quarterly,* 3d Ser., LXXIV (2017), 633–666 (quotation on 654). For scholarship on the Revolution that prefers a continental and imperial perspective on the Revolution over an ideological one, see, for example, S. Max Edelson, *The New Map of Empire: How Britain Imagined America before Independence* (Cambridge, Mass., 2017); Alan Taylor, *American Revolutions: A Continental History, 1750–1804* (New York, 2016); Claudio Saunt, *West of the Revolution: An Uncommon History of 1776* (New York, 2014); Kathleen DuVal, *Independence Lost: Lives on the Edge of the American Revolution* (New York, 2015); Eliga H. Gould, *Among the Powers of the Earth: The American Revolution and the Making of a New World Empire* (Cambridge, Mass., 2012); and François Furstenberg, "The Significance of the Trans-Appalachian Frontier in Atlantic History," *American Historical Review,* CXIII (2008), 647–677. For works emphasizing the diversity of American public opinion and the difficulty of harnessing it to the Revolutionary movement, see Maya Jasanoff, *Liberty's Exiles: American Loyalists in the Revolutionary World* (New York, 2011); Robert G. Parkinson, *The Common Cause: Creating Race and Nation in the American Revolution* (Williamsburg, Va., and Chapel Hill, N.C., 2016); and Patrick Spero and Michael Zuckerman, eds., *The American Revolution Reborn* (Philadelphia, 2016). For slavery at the heart of the conflict, see Woody Holton, *Forced Founders: Indians, Debtors, Slaves, and the Making of the American Revolution in Virginia* (Williamsburg, Va., and Chapel Hill, N.C., 1999); and Christopher Leslie Brown, *Moral Capital: Foundations of British Abolitionism* (Williamsburg, Va., and Chapel Hill, N.C., 2006). In keeping with this trend, more recent works on religion and the American Revolution have strongly emphasized the war years and a wider scope of "religion" than New England dissenters, as this work does. See James P. Byrd, *Sacred Scripture, Sacred War: The Bible and the American Revolution* (New York, 2013); and Spencer W. McBride, *Pulpit and Nation: Clergymen and the Politics of Revolutionary America* (Charlottesville, Va., 2016). For more recent works that do emphasize the series of tax bills over which colonists and Parliament quarreled but do not see a major role for religion, see, for example, Thomas P. Slaughter, *Independence: The Tangled Roots of the American Revolution* (New York, 2014); and Justin du Rivage, *Revolution against Empire: Taxes, Politics, and the Origins of American Independence* (New Haven, Conn., 2017). The present argument also aligns with the consensus that the period after 1770 marked a general lull in imperial relations, placing the explanation for imperial collapse after 1773. See Slaughter, *Independence,* 311–312.

does evidence of growing change. Both the well-known events of the period, such as the Stamp Act and the bishop controversy, and less frequently remembered incidents, like George Whitefield's attempt to found a college in Georgia, reveal how imperial protestantism weathered and deflected conflict, even as tensions rose between colonists and the British government. Despite the struggles over Parliament's authority to legislate for the colonies, government and religious leaders remained committed to their shared imperial protestantism. American religious leaders were cautious when it came to protesting Parliament, and the habits of protestant leadership constrained the ways they used their voices. Parliament, for its part, showed no interest in altering the imperial establishment within the regions bounded by its scaffold, a crucial stance that prevented the long-simmering fights between Anglicans and dissenters from boiling over, even as they roiled, became increasingly political, and produced frustration. But Parliament was not the only thing binding together protestants across the empire. Awakened protestants continued to bridge the gaps between different parts of British protestantism with energy and purpose in the 1760s, even when they bristled at the restrictions placed on them. As creaky as the empire it surrounded, the scaffolding of protestantism still tied distant British places to one another as the decade came to a close.

POLITICAL CRISIS, RELIGIOUS RESPONSE

In Britain's eighteenth-century empire, government and people alike expected religious leaders to provide moral authority at moments of public worry and transition. These expectations were the basis of the public pulpit, and they guided the way that protestant leaders responded to political events. The controversies between Parliament and colonies over taxation in the 1760s—the Stamp Act most important among them—were examples of such crises for Americans. In those moments, American religious leaders, regardless of their placement in the typology of protestant networks, were in a difficult position. For much of the eighteenth century, the most serious crises had come in the form of wars against Catholic Spain and France, and, in those moments, protestant leaders helped remind their congregants that—as protestants, as residents of a colony, and as part of an empire that fought for protestantism—they needed to rally to the cause. This comfortable connection between empire, colony, and congregation was disrupted for American religious leaders in 1765. The political fights that started with the Stamp Act crisis took on a different character because they pitted colonists, from many of Britain's North American colonies, against Parliament over an issue that had no obvious religious resonance.

American religious leaders, accustomed to treating the British Empire as a vessel for championing their religion and more used to seeing themselves as Anglicans, dissenters, or awakened protestants than they were to seeing themselves as Americans, fell back on the structures of imperial protestantism to transmit their opposition and then to rejoice when political affairs seemed to relax. The Stamp Act crisis thus exposed—and then quickly reaffirmed—the mechanisms of imperial protestantism.[4]

The Stamp Act had its origins in the Seven Years' War, a conflict that protestant leaders had supported as a contest against the forces of popery. In its aftermath, George Grenville, the first lord of the treasury, decided to raise revenue and tighten enforcement of colonial trade laws. He also wanted to bring the colonies under the control of Parliament in a more orderly and (from a British perspective) more productive manner. American colonists resisted. The 1764 Sugar Act inspired angry outcries from colonial merchants and politicians, who argued against Parliament's right to tax the colonists. A year later, in March 1765, Grenville followed with a Stamp Act, a direct tax on colonial consumers that required them to put official stamps on certain kinds of papers and documents. Colonists throughout the empire were outraged. Spurred to action by the measure, they organized and protested. In Virginia, at Patrick Henry's urging, the House of Burgesses passed a series of resolutions insisting that Virginians had "all the Liberties, Privileges, Franchises, and Immunities, that have at any Time been held, enjoyed, and possessed, by the people of *Great Britain*," privileges that certainly included "the Taxation of the People by themselves, or by Persons chosen by themselves to represent them." This sentiment, in its more memorable form, "no taxation without representation," became a rallying cry for colonial resistance. The protests swelled to include riots, destruction of the hated stamps, and an intercolonial Stamp Act Congress. British merchants worried about their trade joined the calls for the act's repeal, which came in March 1766.[5]

American religious leaders across the three networks thought the measure

4. For a survey of the taxation crises, see Craig B. Yirush, "The Imperial Crisis," in Gray and Kamensky, eds., *Oxford Handbook of the American Revolution*, 85–102. See also Slaughter, *Independence;* and Rivage, *Revolution against Empire.*

5. For the Stamp Act and its evolution, see Edmund S. Morgan and Helen M. Morgan, *The Stamp Act Crisis: Prologue to Revolution* (1953; rpt. Williamsburg, Va., and Chapel Hill, N.C., 1995), esp. 72, 93–95 (quotation on 93). Although Morgan and Morgan remains the standard treatment, the period received a more recent revaluation in Zachary McLeod Hutchins, ed., *Community without Consent: New Perspectives on the Stamp Act* (Hanover, N.H., 2016), especially, in the present context, J. Patrick Mullins, "The Sermon That Didn't Start the Revolution: Jonathan Mayhew's Role in the Boston Stamp Act Riots," 3–35. For Stamp Act politics on both sides of the Atlantic, see Du Rivage, *Revolution against Empire,* 101–146. Brendan McConville, *The King's Three Faces: The Rise and Fall of Royal America, 1688–1776* (Williamsburg, Va., and Chapel Hill, N.C., 2006), 261–264, discusses political-religious panic in the context of the Stamp Act. For a

was bad policy that brought unfortunate consequences. Philadelphia's Francis Alison wrote to Ezra Stiles in Rhode Island that he was "amazed that the English Parliament has given their own Constitution such a blow, as to tax men without their consent, given by themselves or by their proxies." Anglicans, though often less vociferous in their protests, agreed with the assessments of their dissenting colleagues. Massachusetts's Henry Caner noted in a letter to Archbishop Thomas Secker that the policies behind the Stamp Act had put the Americans in a terrible economic position, even if he deplored their response. Jonathan Boucher, an Anglican in Saint Mary's Parish, Maryland, who would have no sympathy for the Americans a decade later, wrote to a correspondent in England that the "poor Americans, you will own, are truly to be pitied: their best and dearest Rights, w'c, ever like Britons They are anxiously jealous of, have been mercilessly invaded by Parliament, who till now, never pretended to any such Privileges." Parliament, he continued, "even supposing They had a Right to impose upon us an internal Tax, are as ignorant of the Means of doing it w'th the Ease to the People, and Profit to the State, as They w'd be to prescribe an Assessm't for the Inhabitants of Kamschatka." Awakened layman and Georgia politician James Habersham wrote to Anglican evangelist George Whitefield that his "very Flesh tremble[d]" at the consequences of a measure that had been "passed with too much Precipitation." Whitefield lent his moral support to the bill's opposition by attending Parliament when his friend, Benjamin Franklin, testified against it, though the evangelist made no explicit public statement. Heinrich Melchior Mühlenberg, writing from Philadelphia to Gotthilf August Francke in Halle, compared the tumult to a bloodletting. The British, he said, had "unawares cut into a nerve, through which the limbs were lamed, and the nerve fluid, or the body's fluid, flowed out, and a consumption followed." "And immediately afterwards, the poor lame animal was to be stamped, and is because of it fallen into mania and convulsions." The Stamp Act crisis presented a challenge to American religious leaders; British policy was bad, but so, too, was overreaction.[6]

Despite relatively uniform opposition to the Stamp Act from American protestant leaders, religious arguments did not play a major part in the resistance

---

contemporary survey of the pamphlets published, see *A Collection of the Most Interesting Tracts, Lately Published in England and America, on the Subjects of Taxing the American Colonies . . .* (London, 1766). Although most of the attention to the Stamp Act protests focuses on those colonies that became the United States, protests extended to other colonies as well, including Nova Scotia and the Leeward Islands. See Molly Perry, "Buried Liberties and Hanging Effigies: Imperial Persuasion, Intimidation, and Performance during the Stamp Act Crisis," in Hutchins, ed., *Community without Consent*, 56–57; and Andrew Jackson O'Shaughnessy, *An Empire Divided: The American Revolution and the British Caribbean* (Philadelphia, 2000), 81–82.

6. Frances Alison to Ezra Stiles, June 13, 1765, Ezra Stiles Papers, Beinecke Rare Book and Manuscript Library, Yale University, New Haven, Conn.; Henry Caner to Thomas Secker, Sept. 5, 1765,

movement—which emphasized whether Parliament had the right to tax colonists—and only a few clergy become prominently associated with the resistance. That lack of entanglement is worth pondering. Though most American clergy did not articulate why they did not choose to speak out publicly on the Stamp Act, their positions within the imperial establishment suggest explanations. Most clergy were part of dominant and privileged local denominations so that habits of sympathy connected religious leaders and government authorities, even in places like Scotland and New England, where the established church was not the Church of England. Protestant clergy from all three networks supported obedience to civil authorities, an uncontroversial protestant doctrine. Moreover, it was unseemly for one occupying a post of such dignity to engage too explicitly in politics. As John Tucker told a convention of fellow Massachusetts congregationalists in 1768, "We have little to do with politicks, farther than to exhort our people." And yet it was unavoidably true that this was a sensibility that could be honored in the breech. That tension, never resolved, served to heighten attention to the political actions of religious leaders. When they acted with clear political intent, they often defended their choices explicitly. Rather than assuming that religious leaders led their congregants, it is more appropriate to ask under what circumstances religious leaders were willing to take the chance to speak out in protest.[7]

There were ample reasons not to speak up when it came to the Stamp Act. Many of the protests were destructive and a clear threat to public order. In addi-

---

The Letterbook for the Rev. Henry Caner, 1728–1778, microfilm edition; Jonathan Boucher to John James, Dec. 9, 1765, in "Letters of Rev. Jonathan Boucher," *Maryland Historical Magazine,* VII, no. 1 (March 1912), 295–296; James Habersham to George Whitefield, Jan. 27, 1766, in Habersham, *The Letters of Hon. James Habersham, 1756–1775,* Georgia Historical Society, *Collections,* VI (Savannah, Ga., 1904), 54–55; Heinrich Melchior Mühlenberg to Gotthilf August Francke, Nov. 23, 1765, in Kurt Aland, ed., *Die Korrespondenz Heinrich Melchior Mühlenbergs: Aus der Anfangszeit des Deutschen Luthertums in Nordamerika,* IV, *1763–1768* (Berlin, 1990), 336–338 ("unawares" on 338) (translation by the author). For Whitefield, see also Thomas S. Kidd, *George Whitefield: America's Spiritual Founding Father* (New Haven, Conn., 2014), 241–242. Whitefield heard a similar account from New York's William Smith. The letter ended up in the collections of William Legge, Lord Dartmouth, an influential awakened Anglican. See William Smith to George Whitefield, Dec. 6, 1765, in Papers of the Legge Family, Earls of Dartmouth (hereafter cited as Dartmouth Papers), D(W) 1778/II/820, Staffordshire Record Office, Stafford, U.K. Some preached obedience to their congregants and pled their loyalty to their superiors in England. Edward Winslow, in Massachusetts, wrote that he had "endeavoured to urge upon the people of this Mission a special regard to the duties of loyalty to His Majesty," and he did "not know that any of the people of my charge have acted any part." Winslow saw the repeal as restoring order and loyalty. See Mr. Winslow to the Secretary, Jan. 8, 1766, in Williams Stevens Perry, ed., *Historical Collections Relating to the American Colonial Church,* III (Hartford, Conn., 1878), 521 (quotations), 525.

7. John Tucker, *Ministers Considered as Fellow-Workers . . .* (Boston, 1768), 24. Clergy often protested that they engaged in politics only when they had to as it was not a natural position for the office. Such statements must be read with a grain of salt—they tended to come in political pronouncements—but the statements also reflected beliefs that clergy should confine their political

tion, the act itself touched on religious institutions only in a glancing fashion—a minor provision in the act included documents in courts "exercising ecclesiastical jurisdiction," but there were no ecclesiastical courts in North America, and the act contained no provisions to create them—and it did not concern the structures of the imperial establishment at all. With these reasons to be cautious, religious leaders did not seek to turn the Stamp Act into a religious issue for the American public. Although it is circular reasoning to say something did not become religious because it was not religious, the important point is to note that religious leaders could have made different choices that might have determined a different outcome. The Stamp Act crisis did not become religious because religious leaders largely accepted that it ought not be so.[8]

In light of the relatively small part played by religious leaders and arguments in the crisis, the outsized attention received by those who did speak up—or were perceived to do so—is all the more striking. As the moral representatives of legitimate protestantism, their voices had particular gravitas. Rumors that clergy (most notably what loyalist Peter Oliver called Boston's "Black Regiment") organized and inspired rebellion invoked anticlerical suspicions that such men wielded an influence that could be insidious. The expectation that clerical voices mattered came home to Boston congregationalist Jonathan Mayhew, one who did venture into the fray. On August 25, 1765, he preached a now-lost sermon that contemporaries connected to the destruction of Lieutenant Governor Thomas Hutchinson's house the following day. Mayhew was aghast; he believed his sermon had advocated thoughtful resistance, not violent destruction. He wrote to Hutchinson protesting that he had "cautioned my Hearers very particularly against the abuses of liberty." Connecticut's Stephen Johnson, in contrast, wrote about the Stamp Act for newspapers, but he did so anonymously. On the other side of the Atlantic, Anglican James Scott, a chaplain to the earl of Sandwich, published a series of newspaper articles under the pseudonym "Anti-Sejanus," supporting the government's desire to bring order to the unruly empire, a stance that earned him a leading position in one

---

speech within appropriate bounds. See, for example, W[illiam] Smith's preface to Thomas Barton's *Unanimity and Public Spirit*... (Philadelphia, 1755). For discussions of religion and the Stamp Act, see John Fea, *Was America Founded as a Christian Nation? A Historical Introduction* (Louisville, Ky., 2011), 99–100; McBride, *Pulpit and Nation*, 91–92; Byrd, *Sacred Scripture*, 27–32; Thomas S. Kidd, *God of Liberty: A Religious History of the American Revolution* (New York, 2010), 33–34. Morgan and Morgan, *Stamp Act Crisis*, frames the protests against stamps in Connecticut in terms of the tensions between awakened protestants and their foes (230–247); as did Alan Heimert in *Religion and the American Mind*, 239–293. For the relatively small reaction to the Stamp Act in British dissenting circles, see Colin Bonwick, *English Radicals and the American Revolution* (Chapel Hill, N.C., 1977), 58–60.

8. Bridenbaugh, *Mitre and Sceptre*, 234–259.

FIGURE 4 *The Repeal; Or the Funeral of Miss Ame-Stamp*. By Benjamin Wilson. Engraving, 1766. James Scott, "Anti-Sejanus," leads the ignominious procession burying the Stamp Act. Two unnamed bishops bring up the group's tail. In this depiction, religious leaders symbolically embrace the government's policy, bringing no honor to religion. This satiric overestimation of the influence of clergy parallels Peter Oliver's more serious description of the "Black Regiment" of New England clergy fomenting protests against Britain. Most protestant leaders took no public stance on the Stamp Act, regardless of their private sentiments. Courtesy of the Library of Congress Prints and Photographs Division, Washington, D.C.

of the most widely circulated satirical prints of the era (see Figure 4). Though the Stamp Act was not a measure with direct ties to religious institutions or establishment, three of the eleven figures in the cartoon wore clerical robes. The intense attention turned onto the political positions taken by protestant leaders raised the stakes for those who thought to voice their opinions.[9]

Given the pressures on clergy not to speak up politically, it is noteworthy that many of the religious leaders who chose to protest Parliament's actions did so from the public pulpit. In the Stamp Act crisis, and in the years that followed, that crucial intersection between institutional religion and government became a site of conflict because all sides assumed it to be influential and sought to control it when possible. As Americans became more united in their opposition to the Stamp Act, the public pulpit was a natural way to publicize and legitimize their resistance. But declaring a special day of fasting to mark the passage of the act (and consequently to name it as bad) required the assent of colonial governors, most of whom were appointed by the crown. Some royal officials flatly refused. New Hampshire's governor would not give his assent to a fast day to lament the act's passage, and neither would Massachusetts's. Nevertheless, Boston's Andrew Eliot felt confident enough in the support he had from the population around him that he used another opportunity, an election day sermon, to voice his resistance. Speaking directly to royal officials, he stressed the importance of local assemblies, constitutional traditions, and occasional revolution. It was a clear statement of resistance in a heated moment, even if Eliot cushioned his words with praise for the glorious British constitution and the importance of a hereditary monarchy. The performance placed Eliot, in his role as a minister, in a prominent place in the protests, and it made the public pulpit itself a zone of contest and political control. There was little occasion for others in Massachusetts to follow his example, however, as no fast day

9. For the "Black Regiment," see Douglass Adair and John A. Schutz, eds., *Peter Oliver's Origin and Progress of the American Revolution, a Tory View* (San Marino, Calif., 1961), 29, 41–45. For Jonathan Mayhew to Thomas Hutchinson, Aug. 27, 1765, see J. Patrick Mullins, *Father of Liberty: Jonathan Mayhew and the Principles of the American Revolution* (Lawrence, Kans., 2017), 163. For a fuller assessment of the sermon, which was preached on a Wednesday afternoon to his congregation and thus not from the public pulpit, see Mullins, "The Sermon That Didn't Start the Revolution," in Hutchins, ed., *Community without Consent*, 3–35. See also Mullins, *Father of Liberty*, 1–2, 158–165; and Byrd, *Sacred Scripture*, 29–30. Mullins describes Mayhew as the "only New England clergyman to take an explicit and public stand against the Stamp Act" (Mullins, *Father of Liberty*, 160). For Stephen Johnson, see Bernard Bailyn, "Religion and Revolution: Three Biographical Studies," *Perspectives in American History*, IV (1970), 125. For James Scott, see Du Rivage, *Revolution against Empire*, 132–134. Other notable participants in the protests were Connecticut's Ebenezer Devotion and Samuel Johnson. See Harry S. Stout, *The New England Soul: Preaching and Religious Culture in Colonial New England* (New York, 1986), 263–266.

was declared there on account of the Stamp Act turmoil. Government leaders controlled access to the public pulpit, making it a difficult place from which to agitate for revolution.[10]

In those places where political will and government permission coincided, religious leaders provided a strong defense of the American protests. It was a pattern that would repeat itself in the crises of the 1770s; when a consensus emerged between those who controlled the apparatus of government and those who were governed, religious leaders spoke clearly from the public pulpit. During the Stamp Act crisis, such a coalescence of forces was most visible in the colonies that lacked royal governors. In November 1765, Rhode Island, which did not consistently hold fall thanksgivings in uneventful years, held a thanksgiving "for the Preservation of our invaluable Liberties and Privileges." The governor's text embedded the colony in a British imperial context, asking for prayers for the king and his newborn son and for God's "continue[d] . . . Regard to the Kingdoms of *Great-Britain* and *Ireland,* and their Dependencies, to the *British* Plantations in general, and this Colony in particular." But it also asked that God would "frustrate every Attempt to deprive" the colonies of those "invaluable Rights, Liberties, and Privileges, civil and religious." In Connecticut, the Stamp Act protests led to a revolt of the assembly against the governor. During a special session, the assembly asked for a proclamation for a fast day to lament "the dark aspects of Divine Providence with regard to our most dear and valuable rights and privileges" and to "implore divine aid, direction and wisdom, as the melancholy state of affairs require." Even more surprising, they received one from the embattled governor, Thomas Fitch. These were collective acts of protest through which clergy of the imperial establishment articulated the complaints of their colonies.[11]

The sermons preached from the public pulpits of Rhode Island and Con-

10. W. DeLoss Love, Jr., *The Fast and Thanksgiving Days of New England* (Boston, 1895), 329–330; Andrew Eliot, *A Sermon Preached before His Excellency Francis Bernard . . .* (Boston, 1765); Mullins, *Father of Liberty,* 156–157; Charles W. Akers, *The Divine Politician: Samuel Cooper and the American Revolution in Boston* (Boston, 1982), 64–65.

11. Samuel Ward, "A Proclamation," *Newport Mercury* (R.I.), Nov. 18, 1765, [1]; Love, *Fast and Thanksgiving Days,* 329–330, 500; *The Public Records of the Colony of Connecticut, from May, 1762, to October, 1767, Inclusive; Transcribed and Edited in Accordance with a Resolution of the General Assembly,* XII (Hartford, Conn., 1881), 447. Governor Thomas Fitch followed the assembly's instructions and declared a fast day, but his text was far less supportive of the protests than the Rhode Island proclamation had been. See Fitch, *By the Honorable Thomas Fitch, Esq; Governor of His Majesty's English Colony of Connecticut, in New-England in America; a Proclamation for a Day of Public Fasting and Prayer* (New London, Conn., 1765). For a passionate argument against the Stamp Act preached on Connecticut's fast day, see Stephen Johnson, *Some Important Observations, Occasioned by, and Adapted to, the Publick Fast . . .* (Newport, R.I., 1766).

necticut attested to populations that were protective of their civil and religious liberties. Newport's Ezra Stiles, in a fast-day speech, lamented the Parliament's "stripping us of one of those Immunities which heretofore distinguished an Englishman. Tax without our Consent." Stephen Johnson, an awakened protestant minister from Lyme, Connecticut, declared the "unhappy fate of all America" was to be oppressed by a corrupt Britain, and he argued that resistance to the act was biblically justified. Compliance with such an oppressive measure as the Stamp Act "cannot comport with the will of God, but seems highly injurious to the honour of God, to the interest of religion, and the good of mankind, and particularly to all the members of such a free state." For Johnson, and some others who would write in the same vein, political tyranny was a threat to civil and religious liberty, if not directly to institutional protestant life. In Bethlehem, Connecticut, Joseph Bellamy, a prominent awakened protestant, preached often from his own pulpit protesting what he saw as British injustices, as did other Connecticut ministers who were confident of public support.[12]

Without doubt, on these occasions the clergy of New England communicated deeply held beliefs about the injustice of Parliament's actions and the righteousness of colonial protests. The themes in these sermons harked back to traditions of political resistance and liberty that flourished in New England, and indeed that Jonathan Mayhew had expressed more than a decade earlier in his *Discourse concerning Unlimited Submission*. In this sense, the political theology nurtured by dissenters on both sides of the Atlantic can be linked to the ideology of the Revolutionary movement, particularly in New England. Yet it is equally important that religious leaders largely did not shepherd, in a political sense, the activism that some in their ranks encouraged, leaving that task instead to an emerging cadre of political actors, men such as John Adams and James Otis, who developed and pushed such arguments to new intent over the years that followed. As a source and mark of political ideology, such sermons

12. Ezra Stiles quoted in Edmund S. Morgan, *The Gentle Puritan: A Life of Ezra Stiles, 1727–1795* (Williamsburg, Va., and Chapel Hill, N.C., 1962), 226; Johnson, *Some Important Observations*, 4, 21. For Connecticut's Stamp Act politics, see also Richard L. Bushman, *From Puritan to Yankee: Character and the Social Order in Connecticut, 1690–1765* (Cambridge, 1967); and Morgan and Morgan, *Stamp Act Crisis*, 242–247. For the Stamp Act sermons more generally, see Byrd, *Sacred Scripture*, 30–31; Love, *Fast and Thanksgiving Days*, 329–331; Mullins, *Father of Liberty*, 156–157; Akers, *Divine Politician*, 64–65; Nathan O. Hatch, *The Sacred Cause of Liberty: Republican Thought and the Millennium in Revolutionary New England* (New Haven, Conn., 1977), 82–83. For Bellamy, see Mark Valeri, *Law and Providence in Joseph Bellamy's New England: The Origins of the New Divinity in Revolutionary America* (New York, 1994), 150. See also Mark A. Noll, "Ebenezer Devotion: Religion and Society in Revolutionary Connecticut," *Church History*, XLV (1976), 303–305. There were a few mentions to New England fast days in newspapers outside the region, spreading the influence of those events beyond their region. See, for example, the *Georgia Gazette* (Savannah), Aug. 6, 1766.

were certainly significant. Yet, from the vantage point of 1765 and the scaffolding of imperial protestantism, the more striking fact is their comparative infrequency.[13]

In the context of the Stamp Act, the strong voices that emerged from New England's public pulpit were the exceptions. Despite their influence in the developing political discourse, the infrequency of such sermons across the colonies as a whole resulted from ingrained habits of imperial protestantism that militated against the parliamentary controversy becoming "religious," and it attests to the essential difficulties in turning the apparatus of imperial protestantism into a means of protest against government. The paucity of fast days (a consequence of the royal governors' objecting to the protests) permitted most religious leaders to stay out of the fray or to encourage their congregants in more limited contexts. In those places where no sympathetic governor declared a fast day or where clergy and congregants were less sure of one another's sentiments—a situation that was particularly likely in the Anglican-dominated southern colonies—the pulpit was a difficult tool at best.

If the structures of the imperial establishment limited protests, so, too, did the habits of the transatlantic protestant community. Religious leaders who wrote to their peers were often corresponding across the ocean, where opinions differed substantially. Even though dissenter Micaiah Towgood eagerly supported his Boston colleague Jonathan Mayhew, the Londoner still mused that Britons were far more highly taxed than their American counterparts. He noted the "immense and tremendous Debt under which the Mother Country groans, and the Height to which almost every Thing is taxed amongst us, beyond what it is with you," and he thought there might be other ways the colonies might "lighten" Britons' "heavy load." Imperial protestantism, with its deep connections to state authority and tendency to organize religious community through transatlantic networks rather than among Americans, worked against its structures rapidly being turned into a voice of direct and specific protest.[14]

After the Stamp Act's repeal in 1766, the structural imperatives of imperial protestantism and the sentiments of American religious leaders fell back together. At that moment, a chorus of religious leaders spoke out in near unison. The empire had righted itself, and Parliament had protected the liberties of British subjects. The largest quantity—and the most prominent—sermons preached in relation to the entire Stamp Act crisis came at this moment. They

13. For the influence of dissenting political thought on the development of political resistance, see, for example, Bridenbaugh, *Mitre and Sceptre;* Bailyn, *Ideological Origins,* 44–60; Clark, *Language of Liberty,* esp. 362–372; and Noll, *America's God,* 78–82.

14. Towgood to Mayhew, Apr. 6, 1766, Mayhew Papers, item 94.

were celebrations of repeal rather than acts of protest. Jonathan Mayhew once again led the way. His "Snare Broken" sermon, preached on a thanksgiving day called in Massachusetts to commemorate the repeal, was printed on both sides of the Atlantic. Mayhew dedicated his printed text to William Pitt, whom he credited with saving the colonies not only in the recently concluded war with France but also in the case of the Stamp Act. Although he framed the sermon itself as a call for gratitude to God for deliverance, his primary goal was to proclaim that the Americans' points had been fully achieved, that their sufferings had been extreme, and that they were willing to endure more if need be. He referenced the issue of an Anglican bishop for the colonies but in phrasing that put distance between himself and those who worried about it, even as he also must have had tongue firmly planted in cheek. "Some suspected," he wrote, "that this money was partly intended to maintain a standing army of bishops, and other ecclesiastics. . . . These *strange* notions and fears prevailed very much among certain odd people, who liked their old religion, and were not able to see the reasonableness of their paying for the support of any other." The teasing tone hinted that Mayhew was reserving judgment where his loyalties lay within the empire.[15]

But most repeal sermons took a more comfortable and familiar line of argument, rejoicing in the Americans' success but also reinforcing loyalty to the empire. Johan Joachim Zubly, a German Calvinist minister in Georgia who served a presbyterian congregation, preached and published a sermon that celebrated the end of strife, and, in the traditional fashion of the genre, called on his hearers to eschew sin, as "temporal happiness cannot be more surely promoted, nor our civil and religious liberties be better secured, than by a life suitable to the dignity of our christian profession. . . . We cannot be good christians unless we

15. Jonathan Mayhew, *The Snare Broken: A Thanksgiving Discourse . . .* (Boston, 1766), 17–18. Prominent sermons preached for the Stamp Act repeal also include J. J. Zubly, "The Stamp-Act Repealed; a Sermon, Preached in the Meeting at Savannah in Georgia, June 25th, 1776," in Randall M. Miller, ed., *"A Warm and Zealous Spirit": John J. Zubly and the American Revolution, a Selection of His Writings* (Macon, Ga., 1982); Joseph Emerson, *A Thanksgiving-Sermon Preach'd at Pepperell, July 24th 1766; a Day Set Apart by Public Authority as a Day of Thanksgiving on the Account of the Repeal of the Stamp-Act* (Boston, 1766); Charles Chauncy, *A Discourse on "The Good News from a Far Country" . . .* (Boston, 1766); and David S. Rowland, *Divine Providence Illustrated and Improved; a Thanksgiving-Discourse, Preached (by Desire) in the Presbyterian, or Congregational Church in Providence, N.E. Wednesday June 4, 1766; Being His Majesty's Birth Day, and Day of Rejoicing, Occasioned by the Repeal of the Stamp-Act* (Providence, [R.I.], 1766). See also Stout, *New England Soul,* 266–268; and Nicholas Guyatt, *Providence and the Invention of the United States, 1607–1876* (New York, 2007), 84–86. See also Mullins, "The Sermon That Didn't Start the Revolution," in Hutchins, ed., *Community without Consent,* 18–19; and Pauline Maier, *From Resistance to Revolution: Colonial Radicals and the Development of American Opposition to Britain, 1765–1776* (New York, 1991), 64–65. According to the English Short Title Catalogue, Mayhew's sermon was reprinted at least once in Boston and once in London. Compare also Charles Chauncy's *Discourse on "The Good News from a Far Country."*

are also good subjects and good members of the community." Joseph Emerson, in Massachusetts, preached an overheated sermon about the threat the Stamp Act had posed, but he framed the colonies' redemption from the hated legislation within the history of great protestant deliverances of Britain, including the failure of the Spanish Armada, the failure of the Gunpowder Plot, and the successful Glorious Revolution. In this, he drew on a hymn by Isaac Watts, a key writer in the print culture of transatlantic protestantism. Samuel Cooper of Boston, who had never formally taken a stand on the Stamp Act issue, recycled a sermon he had first preached in front of Governor Thomas Pownall in 1759 to celebrate the British military victory in Quebec. The original version recounted the glorious and providential success of the "Protestant interest" around the globe. The revised version was merely amended for the new context, suggesting that Cooper did not see the Stamp Act as causing a complete upheaval of the colonial position in the world. The presbyterian Synod of New York and Philadelphia issued a pastoral letter in 1766 recounting the terrible crisis that had passed, and they "[shuddered] at the very Thoughts of the Consequences" if the British leadership "instead of yielding to a Spirit of Moderation, [had] unhappily recurred to Force." They called on their members to repent their sins and to "honour your King, and pay a due Submission to his august Parliament." The sermons were strewn with references to a shared British and American people, to the wisdom of Parliament and king, to Magna Carta, and to the Glorious Revolution; they must have felt reassuring in 1766.[16]

On balance, the repeal sermons reaffirming the empire's righteousness outweighed the moments in which religious leaders aided American protests. Religious institutions did not become a site of political protest during the 1760s. Protestant leaders' most important tool for speaking out on political topics, the public pulpit, was ill-suited for resistance, and the networks of transatlantic protestantism could not easily create lines of connection between New England dissenters and southern Anglicans for the start of a proto-American religious community. Subsequent pieces of legislation through which Parliament asserted its authority, much to the distress of those colonists who increasingly believed that they could never be fairly represented across the ocean, did not result in waves of fast days either. American religious leaders largely stayed

16. Zubly, "The Stamp-Act Repealed," in Miller, ed., *"A Warm and Zealous Spirit,"* 47; Emerson, *A Thanksgiving-Sermon Preach'd at Pepperell*; "Mr. Cooper's Sermon Occasioned by the Reduction of Quebec," Boston, 1759, Ms.q.3329, Boston Public Library; Guy S. Klett, *Minutes of the Presbyterian Church in America, 1706–1788* (Philadelphia, 1976), 424–426. For Isaac Watts, see John Hull, "Isaac Watts and the Origins of British Imperial Theology," *International Congregational Journal*, IV, no. 2 (February 2005), 59–79; J. F. Maclear, "Isaac Watts and the Idea of Public Religion," *Journal of the History of Ideas*, LIII (1992), 25–45; and McConville, *The King's Three Faces*, 261–262.

out of the discussions of the Declaratory Act, the Townshend Acts, and other similar measures. As long as they remained within the networks of transatlantic religion and committed to governments that were firmly inside the empire, the scaffolding of imperial protestantism constricted their capacity to use their connections and the institutions they led as a locus of political protest.

REAFFIRMING THE IMPERIAL ESTABLISHMENT

Just as religious leaders remained committed to British protestantism, so, too, did those in government. As the political controversies of the Stamp Act and subsequent pieces of legislation roiled the waters, political leaders repeatedly reaffirmed their commitment to the imperial establishment within its traditional boundaries through a series of religious controversies. These controversies originated in the ongoing frictions between Anglicans and dissenters, and they unfolded in multiple places, including London, New York, and finally in the more widespread "bishop controversy," which became a topic of public dispute on both sides of the Atlantic. Though the last of those three is by far the most discussed in the context of the American Revolution, its dynamics are more comprehensible when it is seen alongside other, similar conflicts within imperial protestantism. From many locations in the 1760s, Anglicans and dissenters agitated for the best position they could gain within the imperial establishment. In these episodes, however, the ultimate authority of governments over religious institutions remained uncontested, and those in power at the center—worried about the state of the empire—did not see the 1760s as a moment for change in Britain's long-standing religious settlement. (That those same leaders took a different approach in the ceded territories from the Seven Years' War is a topic taken up in Chapter 3.) Government commitment to the terms of the imperial establishment thus kept the scaffolding of imperial protestantism standing at the end of the decade, though not unscathed. The conflicts between Anglicans and dissenters, unlike the frictions over taxation that had been exposed by the Stamp Act crisis, were effectively contained.[17]

From the perspective of those in England, at the center of the empire's gov-

17. J. Patrick Mullins argues that the bishop controversy was a "prologue" to the Stamp Act; see Mullins, *Father of Liberty*, 154. Carl Bridenbaugh treats them as intimately interconnected. His influential work is still the primary work on the bishop controversy. See Bridenbaugh, *Mitre and Sceptre*, esp. 230–259. See also Clark, *Language of Liberty*, 277–278; Bell, *War of Religion*, 81–90; Kidd, *God of Liberty*, 59–63; and Kenneth R. Elliott, *Anglican Church Policy, Eighteenth Century Conflict, and the American Episcopate* (New York, 2011). For a historiographical overview of the bishop controversy, see Frederick V. Mills, Sr., "The Colonial Anglican Episcopate: A Historiographical Review," *Anglican and Episcopal History*, LXI (1992), 325–345. Other interpretations have turned to seeing the impact of the controversy on the Anglican and Episcopalian churches.

erning structure, the most significant contest between Anglicans and dissenters in the 1760s was probably that in London. That period marked the conclusion of the "Sheriff's Cause," a lengthy struggle to end what amounted to the legal extortion of wealthy dissenters by the City of London. As early as the 1730s, the City of London Corporation began to elect to public office individuals who, because of their religious scruples against conformity and the limitations of the 1661 Corporation Act (which required participation in the Anglican sacrament of Holy Communion for certain offices), could not serve the offices to which they were elected. When they failed to serve, they were fined substantial sums. As this source of revenue grew, the city turned these funds toward the large project of building Mansion House. The Protestant Dissenting Deputies, a group dedicated to protecting the rights of dissenters, decided to sue the city over a practice they considered both unethical and illegal, arguing that the city was disingenuous in electing those who could not serve, effectively fining its residents for their status as dissenters. In 1754, one Mr. Evans, along with two other men, "applied to this Committee to desire them to undertake his Defence for refusing to serve the said Office of the Sheriff in case the City should think fit to prosecute him for his said refusal." The deputies, of which Evans had previously been a member, took on his case and worked through legal channels for more than a decade before the case finally reached conclusion.[18]

Although the facts of the city's persecution of dissenters were self-evidently obnoxious, the case had to be taken through the courts because the terms of the imperial establishment—even in England—were at times vague. The will-

See Mills, *Bishops by Ballot: An Eighteenth-Century Ecclesiastical Revolution* (New York, 1978); Nancy L. Rhoden, *Revolutionary Anglicanism: The Colonial Church of England Clergy during the American Revolution* (New York, 1999), 37–63; Peter M. Doll, *Revolution, Religion, and National Identity: Imperial Anglicanism in British North America, 1745–1795* (Madison, N.J., 2000); Rowan Strong, *Anglicanism and the British Empire, c. 1700–1850* (Oxford, 2007), 111–117; and Peter W. Walker, "The Church Militant: The American Loyalist Clergy and the Making of the British Counterrevolution, 1701–92" (Ph.D. diss., Columbia University, 2016). For a related interpretation with regard to the bishop controversy, see Ned Landsman, "The Episcopate, the British Union, and the Failure of Religious Settlement in Colonial British America," in Chris Beneke and Christopher S. Grenda, eds., *The First Prejudice: Religious Tolerance and Intolerance in Early America* (Philadelphia, 2011), 75–97.

18. Protestant Dissenting Deputies, General and Committee Meeting Minutes (hereafter cited as PDD, Minutes), Aug. 7, 1754, CLC/181/MS03083/001, London Metropolitan Archives (LMA). The story of the Sheriff's Cause can be reconstructed in PDD, Minutes, especially CLC/181/MS03083/001, LMA. See also *A Sketch of the History and Proceedings of the Deputies Appointed to Protect the Civil Rights of the Protestant Dissenters to Which Is Annexed a Summary of the Laws Affecting Protestant Dissenters; with an Appendix of Statutes and Precedents of Legal Instruments* (London, 1813); Bernard Lord Manning, *The Protestant Dissenting Deputies*, ed. Ormerod Greenwood (Cambridge, 1952), 119–129. See also W. Pierce, "The Contributions of the Nonconformists to the Building of the Mansion House," *Transactions of the Congregational Historical Society*, IX (1924), 146–169. The case has received surprisingly little scholarly attention given its importance to dissenters in the 1760s.

ingness of all parties to submit to the authority of those courts reflected the close relationship between imperial protestantism and the governments that structured it. The case turned on whether dissenters were legitimate protestants who should be left unmolested, a fact that neither political nor Anglican leaders truly disputed in the 1760s despite the action of city leaders. If dissenters were appropriately "religious," even though they were not part of the Church of England, fining them served no civic purpose. There were more than enough lax Anglicans who could have been fined to raise funds for Mansion House if the goal had been to punish the irreligious. By selecting those dissenters who had scruples about conforming, the city depended on the religious character of its targets. The whole affair was vaguely embarrassing to the church hierarchy, which did not want to be associated with petty discrimination in a civil matter. The case was not a high priority for Archbishop Thomas Secker, and by its end the dissenters had the support of the government generally.[19]

When the case found its resolution in February 1767, it was a resounding success for the imperial establishment's mixed character and for its capacity to protect—and therefore define—legitimate protestantism. English authorities had no wish to alter it. William Murry, first earl of Mansfield, the great jurist, rendered the decision in favor of the dissenters, proclaiming, "It is now no crime for a man to say he is a Dissenter; nor is it any crime for him not to take the sacrament according to the rites of the church of England." Under the Act of Toleration, he argued, protestant "Dissenters' way of worship is permitted and allowed, . . . it is not only exempted from punishment, but rendered innocent and lawful." This was not, however, an attack on the imperial establishment more generally. To keep his statement of tolerance from becoming a slippery slope toward accepting all forms of religious expression, Mansfield stressed the importance of institutional protestant affiliation. Those who scrupled to participate in the Church of England but who did participate in other forms of institutional protestantism he deemed responsible citizens. These were the terms of loyal protestant dissent, the benefits of which accrued only to the individual who was "*bonâ fide* a Dissenter." That person "hath taken the oaths, and subscribed the declaration required by [the Act of Toleration.]" Moreover, that person's history would show his regular and longtime participation in the apparatus of a protestant church, one that was led by a member of the clergy, met regularly for worship, and fell generally within the wide spectrum of protestant theology. In this case, "there can be no doubt, therefore, that the defendant is a Dissenter, an honest conscientious Dissenter." "Atheists and Infidels," as well

19. Manning, *Protestant Dissenting Deputies*, ed. Greenwood, 125.

as Catholics, remained outside this protection because they were not included in the Act of Toleration. The ruling epitomized the imperial establishment; it limited legitimate protestantism to that which was defined by participation in a recognized denomination, embraced a strong establishment, and also refused to allow any one of those denominations to dominate another to the point of outright persecution.[20]

Mansfield's decision, despite its clear articulation of dissenters' right to exist without persecution, was reiteration, not an alteration, of Britain's mixed establishment. In the Sheriff's Cause, imperial authorities showed they had no desire to fundamentally alter the terms of the mixed protestant establishment, and neither did they wish to be bothered by those who abused it. That same description applied to officials' response to the next challenge to the system. Dissenters tried to capitalize on their success in the Sheriff's Cause by undertaking a series of initiatives between 1771 and 1774 to repeal requirements that dissenting clergy subscribe to the doctrinal components of the Thirty-Nine Articles. They made their case by appealing to the Act of Toleration, which, they argued, "as it now stands" was "inconsistent with itself," forcing compliance in some ways but not in others. They contended that the boundaries of toleration should reflect the act's goal in creating political loyalty and should thus be limited to matters that were required for the "Safety of the State." Differences in theology among protestants did not touch that "grand Line" of political danger. Liberal Anglicans, mostly unitarians who were increasingly uncomfortable with the theological strictures of the Thirty-Nine Articles, made a different sort of argument, based on liberty of conscience. Both efforts failed, and the terms of the imperial establishment held once again. As Prime Minister Frederick North, Lord North, phrased it when he opposed the Anglican "Feathers Tavern" petition: "The Union seems to me too fundamental a constitution to be lightly and wantonly altered." The mixed establishment—encapsulating both toleration and privilege for a single church—reached to the heart of British politics, and as such it could not be touched.[21]

A similar story emerged from across the Atlantic. There, too, church estab-

20. Ibid., 126; T. C. Hansard, *The Parliamentary History of England . . .*, XVI (London, 1813), 320, 323, 324; Peter N. Miller, *Defining the Common Good: Empire, Religion, and Philosophy in Eighteenth-Century Britain* (Cambridge, 1994), 305.

21. [Israel Mauduit], *The Case of the Protestant Dissenting Ministers and Schoolmasters, Humbly Submitted to Consideration* (London, 1773), 2–3 (quotations); "Report of the Committee for Conducting the Application to Parliament for the Relief of Protestant Dissenting Ministers," Apr. 17, 1772, in Minutes of the Body of Protestant Dissenting Ministers of the Three Denominations (hereafter cited as Minutes of the Three Denominations), 148–159, 38.106, Dr. Williams Library, London (DWL). For North, see William Cobbett et al., *The Parliamentary History of England, from the Earliest Period to the Year 1803 . . .*, XVII (London, 1813), 272. Not all dissenters

lishments were too foundational to the imperial structure to be altered. New York City's presbyterian church tried for many years, beginning in 1759 and more intensely after 1766, to gain a charter so that it could embark on a new building project. They based their case on the argument that they were a part of the established church of North Britain (Scotland), and they therefore were entitled to all the privileges of establishment in Britain's colonies. They petitioned the king in their case, as the center of the empire's mixed establishment. They also petitioned the General Assembly of the Church of Scotland, their fellow presbyterians, for support. The Scots formed a committee to advance their coreligionists' petition and then forwarded it to Lord Dartmouth, the awakened Anglican who was then first lord of trade. The London government bounced the issue back to New York, looking for the governor's advice. The petition met significant resistance from New York's Anglicans, both religious leaders and those in government. The New York Council was in a bind, unable to answer whether denying a charter to presbyterians—certainly legitimate protestants—crossed the frustratingly vague terms of the imperial establishment. They reported that the only charters in the colony that had been granted

agreed with this effort. Trinitarian conservatives resisted it, which they rightly saw as linked to the growth of unitarianism. The minutes of the Protestant Dissenting Ministers chronicle these efforts, including internal disagreements about strategy and the validity of the proposal. For lobbying, see also John Thornton to William Legge, Jan. 4, 1773, Dartmouth Papers, D(W) 1778/II/521; Richard B. Barlow, "Anti-Subscription and the Clerical Petition Movement in the Church of England, 1766–1772," *Historical Magazine of the Protestant Episcopal Church,* XXX (1961), 35–49; John Stephens, "The London Ministers and Subscription, 1772–1779," *Enlightenment and Dissent,* I (1982), 43–72; G. M. Ditchfield, "The Subscription Issue in British Parliamentary Politics, 1772–79," *Parliamentary History,* VII, pt. 1 (1988), 45–80; and Ditchfield, "'How Narrow Will the Limits of This Toleration Appear?' Dissenting Petitions to Parliament, 1772–1773," ibid., XXIV (2005), 91–106. Speeches in Parliament about the Feathers Tavern petition, including from Lord North and Edmund Burke, provided particularly strong articulations of the connection between religion, the civil state, and stability as well as the importance of the Act of Union. See Barlow, "Anti-Subscription," *Historical Magazine of the Protestant Episcopal Church,* XXX (1961), 45–46. English dissenting leaders spent a great deal of political energy on the repeal efforts. A committee, including presbyterian Richard Price, independent Philip Furneaux, and baptist Samuel Stennet, coordinated the projects. As the group itself reported, with the humility of a hard-pressed committee, "Almost their whole Time has been devoted" to the cause. "They have not had a day, scarce an hour, they could call their own; or in which, some or all of them have not been engaged in the prosecution of this business." They worked through the members of Parliament from whom they could count on for support, and the dissenting bill was brought before the Commons. In a move that showed the commitment of parliamentary leaders to some form of protestant establishment, the committee "were told" that "without a Declaration of their Christianity their Bill would not be admitted into the House of Commons." They agreed on a statement that was "an asserting of our great common principle, the Sufficiency of Scripture and the Right of private Judgment." The bill began moving through the Commons on April 3, 1772, and then successfully moved to the House of Lords. Dissenting lobbyists worked hard on the issue, but it foundered in the upper house in the face of significant episcopal opposition. A revival of the effort the following year also failed. See "Report of the Committee," Apr. 17, 1772, in Minutes of the Three Denominations, 148–150, 38.106, DWL.

to non-Anglican congregations had gone to the Dutch by virtue of their treaty rights. More importantly, the presbyterian petition had insisted that "the old English Statutes of Uniformity do not extend to America." In attacking the privileges of the Church of England in New York, in other words, the presbyterians also raised the specter of parliamentary authority in America. Here the council yielded jurisdiction: "Whether these statutes or [those from Queen Anne's reign establishing the Church of England in England] which is made an essential part of the Act of Union, do or do not extend to the Plantations, is a Question, of which the Committee do not conceive themselves competent Judges." New York's government did not, in the aftermath of the Stamp Act crisis and the Declaratory Act, want to weigh into territory that implicated both the extension of parliamentary rule to the colonies and the equality of the two components of Britain's mixed religious settlement. In London, the Privy Council authorities maintained the status quo once again, which meant denying the presbyterians' petition.[22]

In all these cases, those in government upheld the terms of Britain's imperial establishment. One could argue that the compromises necessary within this system could not have been sustained for much longer, or at the very least that pressure was building. Exactly that trajectory was suggested when the New York presbyterians were joined in their petitions by several other local churches that were certainly within the realm of legitimate protestantism, including the local Huguenot church, Dutch Protestant church, and Lutheran church. Either the presbyterian petition had to be granted on the terms that it was part of Britain's mixed establishment—an argument that essentially admitted that parliamentary law did not apply to the colonies because it discarded the Act of Uniformity there—or all of the petitions had to be granted on the terms that they were all

22. "Report of the Committee of the Council of New York re Presbyterian Incorporation," Mar. 24, 1767, Fulham Papers, XLI, fol. 308, Lambeth Palace Library, London (LPL). For the affair more broadly, see First Presbyterian Church in the City of New York, Minutes, April 1765, Record Group 413, Series 1, box 1, Presbyterian Historical Society, Philadelphia; Register of the Actings and Proceedings of the General Assembly of the Church of Scotland, 1766, Records of the General Assembly of the Church of Scotland, Ch1/1/58, National Records of Scotland, Edinburgh; Acts of the Privy Council, Mar. 18, 1766, in James Munro and Almeric Fitzroy, eds., *Acts of the Privy Council of England,* Colonial Series, VI, *The Unbound Papers* (London, 1912), 425–426; Legge to Dennys De Berdt, July 22, 1766, Dartmouth Papers, D(W) 1778/II/225; Richard Terrick to Lords of Trade, Feb. 9, 1767, Jared Sparks Collection, MS Sparks 43, IV, 44, Houghton Library, Harvard University, Cambridge, Mass. See also Samuel Auchmuty to Terrick, Feb. 21, 1767, Fulham Papers, XLI, fol. 306; and Myles Cooper to Terrick, Aug. 22, 1767, ibid., fol. 312. Archbishop Thomas Secker also framed the case in terms of the empire's core relationships when he opposed the petition. See Secker's abstract, Fulham Papers, XLI, fols. 296–298; Secker to Terrick, Feb. 15, 1767, ibid., fol. 304; and "Humble Address of the Ministers, Elders, and Deacons of the United Presbyterian Churches of the City of New York" to the General Assembly of the Church of Scotland, Oct. 20, 1773, Dartmouth Papers, D(W) 1778/II/728.

serving the same positive end of promoting religion, a tactic that led down a clear slippery slope. The most direct route out was to deny all of the petitions and maintain the status quo.[23]

The bishop controversy unfolded against this backdrop, another tempest in the teapot of transatlantic protestantism. Another fight between Anglicans and dissenters, it was precisely the kind of challenge that the structures of imperial protestantism contained most easily. It was not even a new issue. Attempts to install an Anglican bishop in America reached back decades. The idea had first been floated by Archbishop William Laud in 1638, and movements to bring it to fruition recurred several times in the eighteenth century. In the aftermath of the Seven Years' War, as imperial authorities embraced numerous efforts at reform, Anglicans on both sides of the Atlantic saw a new chance to solve an old problem. They diagnosed the American colonies as suffering on two grounds. First, American Anglicans had an incomplete church, lacking in discipline and the capacity to ordain clergy without a difficult ocean crossing. At the same time, Anglican leaders also believed that the unruly nature of the colonies stemmed from dissenters having too much influence; regularizing the structure of the Church of England, even if only in those colonies with an Anglican establishment, would, they believed, contain the disruptions. By installing a bishop in the colonies, they hoped both to ease the challenges faced by American Anglicans and also to inculcate a more disciplined empire. The scale of what they sought was enormous, however—no less than a reopening of the terms of the imperial establishment and the creation of an imperial church. Moreover, for the Church of England to install a bishop in the colonies would require an act of Parliament. Leaving aside that some colonists did not think Parliament *could* legislate for the colonies (that sentiment certainly did not hold Parliament back), the terms of the imperial establishment had been largely unchanged for decades, and there was little reason to think that they would be opened now.[24]

A key characteristic of the bishop controversy distinguished it from the other

23. For other congregations that also petitioned, see "Report of the Committee of the Council of New York re Presbyterian Incorporation," Fulham Papers, XLI, fol. 308.

24. For the history of efforts to place a bishop in the colonies, see Leslie W. Barnard, *Thomas Secker: An Eighteenth Century Primate* (Sussex, U.K., 1998), 123–139; Rhoden, *Revolutionary Anglicanism,* 39; Bell, *War of Religion,* 61–66; Elliott, *Anglican Church Policy,* 83–120. Anglicans drew up extensive documents imagining their newly expanded empire in the final years of the war and its aftermath. See, for example, "Thoughts upon the Present State of the Church of England in America," William Smith Papers, I, item 12, and "Queries Humbly Offered to the Consideration of the Friends of Protestant Episcopacy in North America," I, item 43, Hawks Collection, Archives of the Episcopal Church, Austin, Tex.; and "Thoughts on the Ecclesiastical Establishments in Canada," William White Papers, I, item 9, ibid. See also Mills, *Bishops by Ballot,* 139. The conquest of French territory, and therefore the presence of a significant number of Catholic subjects, also figured in this conversation. This topic will be discussed in Chapter 3, below.

fights over religious establishment in the decade: it never moved beyond the level of rhetoric and backroom discussions. Parliament never debated a bill proposing the creation of an American bishop. The consequently abstract nature of the fight is important. On the one hand, it shortened the duration of the whole affair. Because all sides understood that only a decision by Parliament could alter the terms of the imperial establishment, and because religious leaders on both sides accepted Parliament's authority over the system, neither Anglican nor dissenting leaders ever acted in political ways that went outside their normal channels of influence. As the Americans were moving into a Revolutionary moment, that forbearance from those in protestant institutions is significant. Religious leaders, at least, were not using the bishop controversy to transform the ways their institutions engaged imperial authorities.

At the same time, the fact that the bishop affair remained at the level of debate also meant that it was more subject to rumor and conspiracy theory than it otherwise might have been, and in that sense it was more consequential outside the confines of religious institutions. A great deal of the influence that has been ascribed to it has been just that: its symbolic capacity to activate fears that stretched far beyond the colonial hierarchy of the Church of England. Here the vantage point of imperial protestantism is particularly useful because it highlights the distinction between the effects of the bishop controversy for the scaffolding of protestantism (which were quite limited) and its potential consequences for the course of political radicalization in America, which are far harder to discern.

The bishop affair started in a dispute over the work of the Anglican missionary society, the Society for the Propagation of the Gospel in Foreign Parts (SPG). The society's missionary in Cambridge, Massachusetts, East Apthorp, picked a fight with congregationalist Jonathan Mayhew, who took the bait. Like scraping off a half-healed scab, asking questions about the SPG's work unleashed the specter of a bishop for the colonies. That latter terrain was far more charged because it was inherently linked to the structures of establishment, rather than merely being concerned with competition among missionaries. At the same time, its surfacing was unsurprising, as Anglican authorities in London were quite eager to reform their church in the postwar environment. Over the next couple of years, both Anglican and dissenting transatlantic networks became engaged in the argument over the justness and desirability of an American bishop. The printed debates occurred in both England and America. Even Thomas Secker, the archbishop of Canterbury, weighed in, and the topic animated the annual SPG sermon—always a widely circulated piece—preached by John Ewer, the bishop of Llandaff, in February 1767. Ewer infuriated colonists with his scolding assertion that the their irreligion was to blame for the SPG's poor showing since its founding. In short, Anglicans and dissenters alike were outraged and aggrieved: dissenters at a high-handed Anglican power grab, and Anglicans at dissenting hypocrisy in denying American Anglicans the liberties that dissenters demanded in England.[25]

All the complaints and barbs hurled by religious leaders went nowhere because the terms of the imperial establishment were not within their grasp. Parliament had no intention of altering that establishment, and that was the essential and irreducible truth shaping the bishop controversy. It was too much political trouble to touch. Archbishop Secker recorded in his autobiography that in the spring of 1767 he and Robert Hay, the archbishop of York, had appealed to William Petty, Lord Shelburne, the secretary of state, "to recommend to him the Ecclesiastical Affairs of Canada, and the Appointment of Bps in America." Secker, in his presentation, "dwelt chiefly on" the question of bishops "but could make no Impression at all upon" the secretary. The matter was deeply frustrating to Secker, who wrote to Richard Terrick, the bishop of London, in 1767, asking why he could not use his episcopal authority to consecrate a new bishop? He could "ordain priests for other Churches," he noted, so "why not Bishops?" Furthermore, why was this a political matter? The archbishop's train of thought is instructive. He wondered where the limits on government

25. [Thomas Secker], *An Answer to Dr. Mayhew's Observations on the Charter and Conduct of the Society for the Propagation of the Gospel* . . . (London, 1764), 18, 60; John Ewer, *A Sermon Preached before the Incorporated Society for the Propagation of the Gospel* . . . (London, 1767), 10, 19–20, 22. The sermon was soon reprinted in New York, and both Charles Chauncy in Boston and William Livingston, a presbyterian layman in New York, issued printed responses decrying the bishop's statements. The primary tracts in this first phase of the bishop controversy, in addition to Secker and Ewer, are East Apthorp, *Considerations on the Institution and Conduct of the Society for the Propagation of the Gospel* . . . (Boston, 1763), reprinted in London that same year; Jonathan Mayhew, *Observations on the Charter and Conduct of the Society for the Propagation of the Gospel in Foreign Parts* . . . (Boston, 1763), also reprinted in London the same year; and [Caleb Fleming], *The Claims of the Church of England Seriously Examined* . . . (London, 1764). Mayhew and Apthorp also printed further responses: Mayhew, *A Defence of the Observations on the Charter and Conduct of the Society for the Propagation of the Gospel* . . . (Boston, 1764), reprinted in London the same year; Apthorp, *A Review of Dr. Mayhew's Remarks on the Answer to His Observations on the Charter and Conduct of the Society for the Propagation of the Gospel in Foreign Parts* (London, 1765). Charles Inglis, a young Anglican minister in New York, wrote a rebuttal to Chauncy. See Charles Chauncy, *A Letter to a Friend, Containing Remarks on Certain Passages in a Sermon Preached by the Right Reverend Father in God, John Lord Bishop of Landaff* (Boston, 1767); William Livingston, *A Letter to the Right Reverend Father in God, John, Lord Bishop of Landaff* . . . (New York, 1768), and his "American Whig" columns published in the *New-York Gazette* in 1768; and [Charles Inglis], *A Vindication of the Bishop of Landaff's Sermon* . . . (New York, 1768). The spelling of Llandaff / Landaff appears to have been (and to be) remarkably fluid. The New Hampshire town of Landaff, named after Ewer, differs from Llandaff in Wales where the bishopric was seated. This was not Apthorp's first effort at controversy. See also *Boston Gazette*, Jan. 12, 1761, [3]; and East Apthorp, *The Constitution of a Christian Church* . . . (Boston, 1761). For Apthorp's role, see Bridenbaugh, *Mitre and Sceptre*, 212–213.

authority over the church really were. "If the Scheme, in Queen Anne's time, for establishing the English Episcopacy and Liturgy in Prussia, had taken Effect," he wrote, "would an Act of Parliament have been needed, to enable the then Bishops of this Nation to ordain Bishops for Prussia? Or, if they had done it without one, to what Penalties would they have been liable"? If Parliament had no role in affairs between European state churches (he wondered), why could it determine such matters within the empire? "And if without offence to the Law, or further Assistance from it, we may ordain Bishops for foreigners: why not for the Episcopalians of Scotland and America?" This question brought him to his main point, his own impotence: "The Moravians ordain as many Bishops as they please, for their own people, both in America, and even in England, and nobody calls them to account for it. Why may not we send Bishops to America as well as they?" Yet Secker knew they could not. The episcopacy of the Church of England was bound to the territory of England and Wales because its leaders submitted to Parliament's authority. Without fundamental imperial change, his authority as archbishop of Canterbury was only notional in North America.[26]

The archbishop knew that he and his peers on the bench could not create a bishop for the colonies without upsetting matters that were better left alone. It was a good thing, too, since many, probably the majority, of American Anglicans did not want one, despite the rhetoric emanating from the north. Many Anglican leaders in Virginia and Maryland, two substantial Anglican colonies, were wary of a bishop, as were lay members of the Church of England. In each of those colonies, local political arrangements meant that politicians (in Maryland the proprietary governor and in Virginia local vestries) exercised authority over the clergy. In neither colony did those groups wish to cede their responsibilities to an ecclesiastical outsider. Moreover, in each colony, disputes over ministerial salaries had marked the 1760s, so the duty to oversee clergy was more politically charged than it was farther to the north. In Maryland, reforms to the church in 1768 pushed some clergy to support the bishop plan in 1770, but petitions drafted to that effect were sent only to the governor's council, not to either the assembly or to England. The council responded to the petition by rebuking its writers for not following more proper channels of authority and asserting

26. John S. Macauley and R. W. Greaves, *The Autobiography of Thomas Secker, Archbishop of Canterbury* (Lawrence, Kans., 1988), 58–59 (quotation on 58); Secker to Terrick, Sept. 23, 1767, Thomas Secker, archbishop of Canterbury, Secker 7, fol. 227, LPL. For Parliament's unwillingness to create a colonial bishop because church matters were too disruptive politically, see Stephen Taylor, "Whigs, Bishops, and America: The Politics of Church Reform in Mid-Eighteenth-Century England," *Historical Journal*, XXXVI (1993), 331–356. Historians have offered a variety of explanations for the balance of factions that led to the impasse, though all agree that the impasse was both real and political. See also Rhoden, *Revolutionary Anglicanism*, 45–57; Bell, *War of Religion*, 90; Elliott, *Anglican Church Policy*, 180–193.

that "No degree of Support or Assistance is needed from episcopal Authority." Southern Anglicans were not particularly interested in tighter ties to Lambeth.[27]

The lack of political will in England or in the southern colonies to create a bishop did not stop Anglican leaders in the northern American colonies from doing everything they could within the bounds of imperial protestantism to promote one. The more ardent among them held conventions, in 1766 and 1767, to discuss the problems in their church. Thomas Bradbury Chandler, a clergyman from Elizabeth, New Jersey, published a pamphlet, *An Appeal to the Public, in Behalf of the Church of England in America,* in which he tried to convince the American public that a bishop was needed. It followed the conventions of imperial protestantism, quoting the Anglican hero of the Glorious Revolution, Bishop Gilbert Burnet, and sporting a dedication to Archbishop Secker. It rehashed the argument that Anglicans, too, deserved religious liberty. Indeed, Chandler believed that dissenters should not only support the idea of an American bishop but also should match the Anglicans' fervor for it because in doing so they furthered the broader cause of protestantism. "For certainly nothing can more degrade our national Religion, in the Eyes of Dissenters and others, both Protestants and Papists, at Home and abroad," he proclaimed, "than to see that it is in so small Estimation, and its Interest so little regarded, by those who profess it." Phrased in such terms, how could any true protestant object? This was the logic for a bishop articulated through imperial protestantism. Unfortunately for Chandler's *Appeal,* those in control of religious policy were not listening, while most of those who were listening—dissenters in America's northern cities—had no sympathy for Anglican appeals.[28]

Americans who were already wary of parliamentary authority saw calls for an Anglican bishop as something quite different from a harmless protection of religious liberty, or even a more extensive alteration of church establishments that might be contained to the realm of religious institutions. The political leaders who opposed a bishop believed it to represent the leading edge of parliamentary

27. Maryland Petition, September 1770, in William Hand Browne, ed., *Archives of Maryland: Proceedings of the Council of Maryland, April 15, 1761–September 24, 1770 . . .,* XXXII (Baltimore, 1912), 379–388 (quotation on 385); Bridenbaugh, *Mitre and Sceptre,* 208, 315–316, 322–323; Isaac, *Transformation of Virginia,* 181–189; Mills, *Bishops by Ballot,* 85–94; Rhoden, *Revolutionary Anglicanism,* 41–44, 56; Elliott, *Anglican Church Policy,* 184–187; Joan R. Gundersen, *The Anglican Ministry in Virginia, 1723–1766: A Study of a Social Class* (New York, 1989), 219–224; Carol van Voorst, *The Anglican Clergy in Maryland, 1692–1776* (New York, 1989), 79–87.

28. Thomas Bradbury Chandler, *An Appeal to the Public in Behalf of the Church of England in America* (New York, 1767), 83 (quotation); Walker, "The Church Militant," 83, 113–126. Chandler also appealed to other roles associated with imperial protestantism, arguing that a bishop was the best way to spread Christianity to Indigenous Americans, something that was the "indispensible Duty of every private Christian" and "still more strongly incumbent upon every Christian Nation" (61).

tyranny, quite beyond matters of church establishment. John Adams's "Dissertation on the Canon and Feudal Law," which he published in a Boston newspaper serially in 1765 during the height of the Stamp Act controversy, argued that before the Reformation, the intertwining of religious and political authority had debased both. Since the advent of protestantism, however, and particularly among the freedom-loving puritans and their New England descendants, there was a revulsion against such a system. Adams viewed the love of liberty as fundamentally political, however. The puritans had a "love of *universal Liberty,*" "not religion *alone,*" and that led to the settlement of America. They had also abolished episcopacy and "derid[ed], as all reasonable and impartial men must do, the ridiculous fancies of sanctified effluvia from episcopal fingers." Adams then explained that the actions of the British since the Seven Years' War, and specifically the projects of the SPG, inappropriately mingled church and state. They were a sign that the patterns of the corrupted, old Romish world, with its "domineering spirit," remained in England. For Adams, the danger lay not so much in the Church of England as in Parliament itself. As he wrote a half century later, this was a moment when Americans, regardless of denomination, "began to think of the secret latent principle, upon which all encroachments upon us, must be founded, the power of parliament." Political tyranny was the pressing issue, quite beyond matters of church establishment.[29]

In 1767, arguments about the political danger of an American episcopacy took on a new character, and they moved into a wider realm—coordinated newspaper polemics. These were the sorts of tools that those working within the mechanisms of imperial protestantism had eschewed. They were designed to stir up unrest, not to guide and lead with moral authority, as religious leaders generally sought to do. New York's William Livingstone, a presbyterian lawyer, and his fellows (some of whom were clergy) organized the effort. The team wrote a series of more than fifty articles to be printed in the *New York Gazette* that decried the potential imposition of a bishop. Livingston's goal was explicitly that of political speech. He planned to "shew them on the other side of the water that even the apprehension of a Bishop's being sent, has raised a Flame here." His intent was that dissenters in American be *"alarmed,"* while those in

29. John Adams, "III. 'A Dissertation on the Canon and the Feudal Law,' No. 1," "IV. 'A Dissertation on the Canon and the Feudal Law,' No. 4," in C. James Taylor, ed., *Adams Papers Digital Edition* (Boston, 2015), I, http://www.masshist.org/publications/adams-papers/index.php/volume/ADMS-06-01; John Adams to Jedidiah Morse, Dec. 2, 1815, *Founders Online,* National Archives, https://founders.archives.gov. See also Hatch, *Sacred Cause of Liberty,* 72–73. Michael Warner argues for Adams's deployment of puritan history here as a sign of a transformation in the public sphere in *The Letters of the Republic: Publication and the Public Sphere in Eighteenth-Century America* (Cambridge, Mass., 1990), 1–3.

the imperial government would be *"intimidated."* The pieces were reprinted in Boston and Philadelphia as well, spreading the reach of the public panic. A parallel project unfolded in Philadelphia. The point of the coordinated publications was to galvanize American sentiment to prevent Parliament from acting with regard to the colonies. Anglican polemicists, most of them also religious leaders, fought back, and for months the two sides warred in the press.[30]

In England, Thomas Hollis, a radical agitator who moved in dissenting circles, knew well that the controversy was now more about political gain than about an actual bishop. He wrote to Andrew Eliot in Boston that, because of "the time, unhappily, becoming critical both at home and in [North America,] the civil Ministers here will not adopt the Scheme" for an American bishop. His well-placed informant had reported that Wills Hill, the earl of Hillsborough, the first lord of trade, "knew of no Such Scheme" for a bishop. Hollis repeated the message in a subsequent letter, this time urging Eliot to use the fear of a bishop as a wedge despite its status as a dead proposal. "There is a great reason to believe, that the Scheme for *Bishoping* America has been dropped. . . . But that should, *by no means,* prevent the Non Episcopalians with You, from *urging on the Controversy concerning it in the public prints to the uttermost.*" Hollis emphasized this last by underlining it three times. The imperial establishment was not in danger from a new bishop for the colonies, but fear of it might be used to promote American protests.[31]

As the bishop controversy became something new, something political, it rapidly flamed out, even as it fed the larger conflagration of conflict between colonies and metropole. There was simply no way for a question of imperial establishment to become a sustained source of conflict between Parliament and colonists when Parliament refused to budge—the quarrel between the colonies and London, of course, was essentially about parliamentary overreach, not its opposite. The political version of the bishop controversy was therefore both limited and ineffective because neither side had the capacity to prevail over the other to bring about change in the terms of the imperial establishment. The

30. William Livingston, quoted in Bridenbaugh, *Mitre and Sceptre,* 297. Bridenbaugh delineates this period as the height of the "Great Fear of Episcopacy" (288–289). Bell also sees a transition to political voices at this time (*War of Religion,* 91). For the fullest description of the episode, see Bridenbaugh, *Mitre and Sceptre,* 296–307; see also Bell, *War of Religion,* 108–110. Many of the principal pieces were reprinted in *A Collection of Tracts from the Late News Papers, etc. Containing Particularly the American Whig, a Whip for the American Whig, with Some Other Pieces, on the Subject of the Residence of Protestant Bishops in the American Colonies, and in Answer to the Writers Who Opposed It, etc.* (New York, 1768). For Philadelphia and other efforts at harnessing newspapers in the cause, see Bridenbaugh, *Mitre and Sceptre,* 298–299.

31. William H. Bond, "Letters from Thomas Hollis of Lincoln's Inn to Andrew Eliot," Massachusetts Historical Society, *Proceedings,* XCIX (1987), 136–137, 140.

frustrations aired in northern colonial newspapers might well have nurtured American prejudices against both sides, but the imperial establishment was not a good means through which to organize revolution. Over time, because rumors about a bishop did not manifest themselves in legislative moves, tensions subsided. The paranoia some dissenters exhibited about a possible bishop, and the commitment of American Anglicans to British authority persisted, but neither side "won" the bishop controversy. The scaffolding of imperial protestantism once again held together because those who controlled it had no wish to alter the terms of the empire's mixed establishment.

The politicization of the bishop controversy in the American press had little impact on the terms of religious establishment, but the fight frayed the networks through which protestants communicated nonetheless. Perhaps surprisingly, the greatest damage was not between Anglicans and dissenters; it was within those separate networks. American Anglicans who desired a bishop had to work against their own superiors. Chandler's effort to reinvigorate the issue had been in no small part inspired by a frustration with what he perceived as inaction from Lambeth Palace. At the same time, some North American Anglicans took an opposite approach, seeking to diffuse the intensity of the calls coming from their fellows. Richard Peters and William Smith, both leaders in Philadelphia's Anglican community, believed their New Jersey and New York counterparts were too hotheaded when it came to a potential bishop, and they were gratified that Richard Terrick, the bishop of London, shared their views. Peters attended the 1766 convention led by Chandler and reported to Terrick shortly afterward that the men there were overeager on the subject of bishops. The clergy at the convention were "diligent in their cares and have religion at heart," he wrote, "but for all this they cannot observe any temper in the affair of bishops." A year and a half later, the gatherings were still a source of friction. William Smith wrote to the bishop of London in May 1768 that he had "much reason to fear the extraordinary warmth of the Jersey conventions might do hurt," and indeed they had "raised a great flame" when one viewed the newspaper reactions. Nonetheless, he felt the need to wade into the discussions. As he put it, the "Church here is now very rudely treated by a malevolent set of Writers and tho' I could have wished our side had not given any cause," he still felt compelled to defend his coreligionists. As long as the issue remained a viable source of political controversy in America, American Anglicans could not ignore it. It grew increasingly tiresome for those in London.[32]

32. Mills, *Bishops by Ballot,* 70 ("diligent"); William Stevens Perry, ed., *Historical Collections Relating to the American Colonial Church: Pennsylvania,* II (Hartford, Conn., 1871), 409–410, 427–429 ("malevolent" on 429). For frustrations with the church hierarchy, see Auchmuty to

A similar story unfolded within the dissenting network, where American conspiracy theories about an Anglican bishop were met with frustration from English dissenters who knew full well that no bishop would be forthcoming. The record from the eastern side of the Atlantic suggests that English dissenters, no matter how much they claimed allegiance to American coreligionists, had only limited political attention for their fellows' cause. They had long accustomed themselves to living with an establishment that included bishops and even saw them as protectors against the petty insults of local clergy. Ezra Stiles's incoming mail provided a steady stream of reminders that the American bishop controversy had no purchase in England. In 1768, Nathaniel Lardner wrote to Stiles: "You are much alarmed by the prospect of having Bps put among you." He was less worried, however, because "we are told, that the Arch Bp says, if Bishops were sent to America, they would have no courts," nor would they "have any power which could be injurious or oppressive to any, they would only perform the offices of the episcopal function: meaning, as I suppose, confirmation, ordination, and the like." From Thomas Wright, in Bristol, Stiles learned that "the Dissenters in England etc. enjoy greater liberty [than] is secured to them by the Act of Toleration," and he then recounted the dissenters' recent victory with the Sheriff's Cause. One particularly wearisome letter came to Stiles in 1772 from Phillip Furneaux, another leading English dissenter, again trying to reassure Stiles that he misunderstood the situation. "I do not apprehend that the Ministry here have yet shown any disposition to the scheme of sending Bishops to America," Furneaux stated, "and I am firmly convinced have never attempted to prevail upon any of our brethren to adopt that design in any shape." Certainly, he agreed, bishops were worth resisting, but he "believe[d] the ministry at present do not wish to be troubled with any such business." American panic met English quiescence.[33]

The disparity between English interest and American worries in the bishop issue was even more marked from the perspective of the Protestant Dissenting Deputies in London, a body that had a history of advocating for Americans in just such matters. In 1764, a group of Massachusetts ministers wrote to request aid in the event of the imposition of a bishop, and though notice of the letter was entered into the minutes of the London society twice, no record was taken

---

Richard Peters, Dec. 23, 1768, Richard Peters Papers, VI, part 2, 68, Historical Society of Pennsylvania, Philadelphia (HSP); and Bishop of London to Chandler, July 10, 1766, Fulham Papers, VI, 162–163. See also Walker, "Church Militant," 125–126.

33. Nathaniel Lardner to Ezra Stiles, June 30, 1767, Stiles Papers; Thomas Wright to Stiles, Mar. 24, 1768, ibid.; Phillip Furneaux to Stiles, Mar. 2, 1772, ibid. See also William Gordon to Joseph Bellamy, Aug. 21, 1764, Joseph Bellamy Papers, box 188, folder 2934, item 81311, Hartford Seminary Library, Conn.

of any action. The Massachusetts group wrote again in 1768, renewing their pleas for support in protesting the imposition of a bishop. They laid out the case against bishops at length, then concluded by saying that the "kind and generous Assistance you have afforded us upon all occasions, encourages us to apply to you in the present critical Season." As they had done in the past, the Bostonians "trust[ed]" that the plea would "encline You to appear with Zeal and Vigour now the Attempt is renewed." The deputies found that the former committee of correspondence had lapsed out of existence, and its members were no longer with them, with the exception of Jasper Mauduit, the chair. A new committee had to be constituted to look into the matter; two months later, the letter was referred to that committee so that they could "enquire of such Persons as they may think proper, in order to get the best information they can whether the design of introducing Bishops into America be dropt or not." One month after that, the unsurprising report came that there was no viable plan for a bishop in motion. Although subsequent requests from Americans continued to flow to the deputies, the appeals met with no significant response. One 1773 request waited more than a year for an answer. Tired of American pleas for help about a matter of dead policy, British dissenters tuned them out.[34]

What impact did the bishop controversy have on imperial protestantism? In the short term, as long as the scaffolding held, little new came of it. The friction between Anglicans and dissenters was an intrinsic part of the way British protestantism functioned; it was precisely the tension that the imperial establishment most effectively contained. Government officials refused to act to create a bishop, standing by the status quo, as they had with the Sheriff's Cause, the New York presbyterian church, and the various initiatives to change the requirements for subscription to the Thirty-Nine Articles in England. As a result, the bishop controversy died away as a focus of significant political agitation by 1770. Americans who were less concerned with religious institutions could find evidence of parliamentary tyranny in the Townshend duties or in the occupation of Boston, and so fears of the episcopacy ceased to captivate public attention, even as the political crisis festered. With the benefit of hindsight, it is possible to see the bishop issue as a harbinger of revolution. Tensions between American and British leaders, dissenters and Anglicans alike, could suggest growing national distinctions, and the politicization of religion could suggest an environment that would be sharply attuned to questions of church and state in the years of conflict that followed. Such extrapolations would have

34. PDD, Minutes, CLC/181/MS03083/001–002, esp. Apr. 18–Oct. 10, 1764, Mar. 9, 1768, Apr. 1–12, 1768, Jan. 15, Feb. 12, Mar. 1, 1772, Jan. 27, 1773, Oct. 19, 1774, LMA.

made little sense in 1770, however, in a protestant world where dissenters and Anglicans functioned as transatlantic networks and both sides embraced the importance of institutional religion to the stability of the state. At that moment, those in Parliament—and religious leaders around the empire—had every reason to assume that frayed relationships would be rebuilt and that Anglicans and dissenters would continue to push against each other within the imperial establishment, on both sides of the Atlantic, for years to come.

AWAKENED ENERGY

The fights between Anglicans and dissenters in the 1760s can too easily obscure the vitality of transatlantic protestantism during the decade. One of the reasons that tensions over a bishop did not overwhelm and fracture the empire's protestant scaffolding is that awakened protestants continued to launch new projects that bound together the system as a whole. Energy emanating from that quarter enabled leaders from many different denominational and geographic locations to connect with one another, even while dissenters and Anglicans battled over establishments and bishops. Notably, those in the awakening movement were persistently uninterested in the schisms between dissenters and Anglicans over questions of ecclesiastical organization. They worked from within all of the empire's dominant denominations, from within establishments and from places of dissent, and they communicated across all its regions. Even as they chafed at some of its strictures, awakened protestants greased the scaffolding of protestant empire.

Awakened protestants put great energy into building educational institutions as their movement matured into an increasingly solid form. For Americans, this process often meant leaning on their connections across the ocean. Some schools, like Pennsylvania's Log College, dated back to the early days of the revivals, but a significant number were founded in the 1760s, and many of those in America depended on transatlantic funding networks. A new baptist college in Rhode Island, later Brown University, was founded in 1764. Its early leaders depended on their connections in England to raise funds and to secure books. John Ryland, a leading baptist in Northampton, England, even sent that college's first president a list of men he thought worthy of honorary degrees from the new school, "to the End that we may attach as great a Number of active and learned Men to your Seminary as we can." (One was marked as an "old rich learned man that can leave 100£ to the College.") The College of New Jersey, originally founded in 1746, faced a leadership crisis after the rapid deaths of four illustrious presidents—Aaron Burr, Jonathan Edwards, Samuel Davies, and Samuel Finley—in only nine years. The school had benefited from English philanthropy in earlier years, and in 1767 its board was convinced that the best candidates for a new president were to be found among the awakened within the Church of Scotland. After a long recruiting campaign, they successfully secured John Witherspoon to lead the school in 1768. Transatlantic connections were strong within the awakened network, even as Americans and Britons squabbled over the terms of their political relationship.[35]

Significantly, that network also connected Anglicans and dissenters to one another, not through any intentional scheme to do so, but because the awakening movement bridged many communities. George Whitefield's vision to turn his Bethesda orphanage and school for Africans into a full-fledged college is a good example. He imagined the school as one that would rival any in America and would offer all the marks of prestige available at any university. It would provide for "the education of persons of superior rank; who thereby might be qualified to serve their king, their country, or their God, either in Church or State." His outline for the college noted that he intended it to make use of the money that had already been put into his hands "by many well-disposed persons of different denominations in various parts of Great Britain and the American Colonies," a sign that he was aware he pooled support from disparate sources. He also designed a leadership structure that drew from multiple denominations, excluding only Catholics from his potential college wardens. He planned an extensive panel of "corresponding" members in Britain and the "northward colonies" in America. It was a catalog of leading awakened protestants from around the empire. He included clergymen John Erskine and John Gillies in Scotland, philanthropists John Thornton, Robert Keen, and the earl of Dartmouth in England, as well as merchants Daniel Roberdeau in Philadelphia and Jonathan Mason in Boston. His reliance on wealthy donors reflected his fundraising experience and his anticipation of future needs. That most of these men were part of the dominant churches in their diverse communities provides evidence that awakened protestantism was thoroughly woven through, and provided connections between, the Anglican and dissenting networks.[36]

35. John Ryland, Sr., to James Manning, Apr. 9, 1772, James Manning Papers, MS-1C-1, box 1, folder 52, John Hay Library, Providence, R.I.; Manning to Samuel Stennett, June 7, 1770, ibid., box 1, folder 4; Isaac Backus to John Gill, n.d. 1765, Isaac Backus Papers, RG 280, Yale University Divinity School Library, New Haven, Conn.; Trustees to John Witherspoon, Nov. 19, 1766, John Witherspoon Papers, MG 58, folder 2, New Jersey Historical Society, Newark. See also the correspondence between Witherspoon and Benjamin Rush, John Witherspoon Collection, box 1, C0274, Special Collections, Princeton University Library.

36. L. Tyerman, *The Life of the Rev. George Whitefield,* II (New York, 1877), 479–480 (quotation on 479); George Whitefield, "A Plan of an Intended Act of Assembly," A3/1/10, Cheshunt College Archives, Westminster College, U.K.; Frank Lambert, *"Pedlar in Divinity": George Whitefield and*

The connections built through awakened projects were not merely hypothetical. The most successful transatlantic religious fundraising scheme of the eighteenth century might well have been the trip made between 1766 and 1768 by Mohegan presbyterian minister Samson Occom and Connecticut congregationalist Nathanael Whitaker to Britain and Ireland to raise money for Eleazar Wheelock's Connecticut Indian School. As they traveled, they mapped the web of connections that linked awakened protestants to Anglicans and dissenters across the empire. The trip fit within a long tradition of fundraising. Colonists assumed that deeper pockets resided in the metropole, and British protestants were accustomed to raising money for missions and for worthy religious projects in America. Wheelock's school seemed to be both of these. The New England minister had first become involved in Indian education in 1743, when Occom came to him to learn to read and write. By 1756, Occom was an ordained minister working with several Indigenous congregations, and Wheelock began seeking out more pupils for what became known as Moor's Indian School. Part of the school's mission was to "instruct" his students in the "Knowledge and Practice of the Protestant Christian Religion," and he trained missionaries from both European and Indigenous backgrounds. Like many North American missionaries, Wheelock relied on financial support from Britain, including from the Society in Scotland for Propagating Christian Knowledge (SSPCK) and the dissenting New England Company. Because his work possessed the legitimacy that derived from his place as an ordained minister and his ties to well-respected religious organizations, the congregationalist Wheelock did not hesitate to reach out to British officialdom for support when he needed it.[37]

After the end of the Seven Years' War, Wheelock also looked for a new home for the school, ideally within "Indian country." Money, of course, was Wheelock's primary obstacle. He turned to George Whitefield, with whom he had been acquainted since the early days of the revivalist's journeys to New England. Whitefield likely suggested that Occom undertake a tour to England to raise

the Transatlantic Revivals, 1737–1770 (Princeton, N.J., 2003), 210. See also William Smith to Terrick, June 25, 1765, in William Wilson Manross, *The Fulham Papers in the Lambeth Palace Library; American Colonial Section Calendar and Indexes* (Oxford, 1965), 114, telling him of Whitefield's plans; and Robert L. McCaul, "Whitefield's Bethesda College Project and Other Attempts to Found Colonial Colleges," *Georgia Historical Quarterly,* XLIV (1960), 263–277. For Whitefield and Roberdeau, see Kristen E. Beales, "Thy Will Be Done: Merchants and Religion in Early America, 1720–1815" (Ph.D. diss., College of William and Mary, 2019), 341–350.

37. Colin G. Calloway, *The Indian History of an American Institution: Native Americans and Dartmouth* (Hanover, N.H., 2010), 5–7, 9–10, 15–16; Margaret Connell Szasz, *Scottish Highlanders and Native Americans: Indigenous Education in the Eighteenth-Century Atlantic World* (Norman, Okla., 2007), 191. Edward E. Andrews outlines a similarly collaborative project, the education of two African missionaries, in *Native Apostles: Black and Indian Missionaries in the British Atlantic World* (Cambridge, Mass., 2013), 187–221.

funds. Whether out of cynicism or savvy, the image of an Indigenous minister in London seemed a promising plan. As one New Englander put it, "an Indian minister in England might get a Bushel of Money for the school." Wheelock procured endorsements for the project from many leading American figures before Whitaker and Occom left, including Superintendent of Indian Affairs William Johnson, and a tract printed and circulated in London spread that information widely. "The Friends of Religion in *America,*" it attested, backed what the writers called a "truly *catholic* and *charitable* Design." A long list of supporters' names attested to the project's legitimacy, including governors, lawyers, merchants, and ministers from the Anglican, presbyterian, Dutch Reformed, and various dissenting churches. In late 1765, after a short delay caused by the Stamp Act protests, Occom and minister Nathanael Whitaker set sail.[38]

The trip was a masterstroke of awakened fundraising, pulling together institutions and leaders from many corners of the British protestant world. Within days of their arrival, the travelers met with Lord Dartmouth; Dennys De Berdt, a Huguenot merchant who often advocated for dissenters; London awakened Anglicans Martin Madan and William Romaine; Quaker John Fothergill; and the German court preacher, Frederick Michael Ziegenhagen, with his colleague Friedrich Wilhelm Pasche, who reported on the events back to Halle. They moved in the circles of the awakened Anglican Selina Hastings, countess of Huntingdon, as well, and the countess supported Wheelock's project financially. She wrote that "Occum has been the instrument of great good to many of his tribe. . . . I hope yet to have it in my power, if the Lord should see fit to continue me in his service, to extend some aid to this interesting people." Awakened baptists were also well represented, including Andrew Gifford (who later sent books to Wheelock in Connecticut), John Ryland, and Samuel Stennett. Whitaker and Occom preached and traveled, and they met with hymnist and preacher John Newton at Olney in May 1766 and John Wesley in August 1767. This was the elite of English protestant society (see Figure 5).[39]

38. Leon Burr Richardson, ed., *An Indian Preacher in England . . .* (Hanover, N.H., 1933), 20; Eleazar Wheelock, *A Brief Narrative of the Indian Charity-School . . .* (London, 1767), 6, 10, 77–80. For Johnson, see "Testimonial about the Importance of the Indian School," Aug. 8, 1765, Dartmouth Papers, D(W) 1778/II/76. For Wheelock's plans and the subsequent trip, see Alden T. Vaughan, *Transatlantic Encounters: American Indians in Britain, 1500–1776* (New York, 2006). See also John Fea, "Wheelock's World: Letters and the Communication of Revival in Great Awakening New England," American Antiquarian Society, *Proceedings,* CIX (1999), 99–144.

39. [Aaron Seymour], *The Life and Times of Selina, Countess of Huntingdon . . .,* I (London, 1840), 412 (quotation); Albert C. Outler et al., eds., *Works of John Wesley* (Nashville, Tenn., 1984–), XXII, 97–98; Andrew Gifford to Eleazar Wheelock, Mar. 4, 1768, Gratz European Clergy Collection, case 12, box 25, HSP. Gifford was also a key figure in the Society for Promoting Religious Knowledge among the Poor; see Edwin Cannan and Roger Hayden, "Gifford, Andrew," September 2004, *Oxford Dictionary of National Biography,* https://www.oxfordnb.com.

FIGURE 5 "The Reverend Mr. Samson Occom, the first Indian minister that ever was in Europe. . . ." London, 1768. Print by Jonathan Spilsbury, after the engraving by Chamberlin I. Mason. 1902,1011.5130.

Occom and Whitaker, awakened dissenters, also moved in the highest levels of the Anglican world. Even George III, the symbolic embodiment of Britain's protestant empire, took part in the visit. The travelers had an audience with their sovereign in his robing room, and Occom commented in his journal that, "if an Earthly Crown is So grand—How great and glorious must the Crown of the glorious Redeemer be." Occom also met with Secker, archbishop of Canterbury, whom the American labeled "quite agreable and Friendly," and the archbishop of York, whom Occom thought "a greable Gentleman, and Friendly Dispos'd to our Cause." He even "Promis'd to do Something towards it." Such moments of pageantry were both important and symbolic. Although Wheelock had drawn much of his financial support from dissenting networks (and, like Occom and Whitaker, he had been ordained within the dissenting tradition), his representatives met with Dr. Daniel Burton, the secretary of the Anglican SPG. According to Occom, Burton suggested that he join the Anglican clergy. He "wou'd have feign perswaded me to Holier Orders," Occom wrote with a note of sarcasm. He declined the offer. "I modestly told him, I had no Such vew when I came from Home." He informed the Anglican that he "had been Ordained Six Years in a Dissenting Way." Yet Burton's brazen suggestion demonstrates the ready welcome the travelers had received from even the most conservative Anglican quarters. Their visit allowed leaders of Britain's governing classes to enact their commitment to promoting religion in all its legitimate forms. Although it did not unite religious leaders of the protestant system into a single whole—on the contrary, the pair received advice about how best to navigate its divisions—the journey nonetheless reinforced the idea that British protestantism was a single interwoven system at the very moment when Anglicans and dissenters were embroiled in the bishop controversy in America.[40]

As befitting a project of British imperial protestantism, Occom and Whitaker moved northward to Scotland in the spring of 1767. Their arrival in Edinburgh was eagerly noted by the *Caledonian Mercury,* with the information that Occom was a presbyterian and the *"first Indian preacher* that ever *set his foot* in *Britain."* In some ways, Scotland was home territory for Whitaker and Occom. The SSPCK had been one of Wheelock's primary supporters, and John Erskine, the energetic Scottish minister and proponent of the awakening movement, was one of its leaders. When the SSPCK and the visitors were disappointed

---

For meetings in London, see Friedrich Willhelm Pasche to Sebastian Andreas Fabricius, Apr. 29, 1766, afst m/1 D 10 60, Franckesche Stiftungen, Halle, Ger. For Occom's journal of his time in England, see Joanna Brooks, ed., *The Collected Writings of Samson Occom, Mohegan: Leadership and Literature in Eighteenth-Century Native America* (New York, 2006), 264–273.

40. Brooks, ed., *Collected Writings,* 268–270; Richardson, *An Indian Preacher,* 98–99.

in their effort to have the General Assembly of the Church of Scotland raise a subscription for the project, they used the tried-and-true methods of itinerant preaching coupled with widespread newspaper and pamphlet printing to raise funds. Occom and Whitaker preached frequently during their two months in Scotland, and they succeeded in raising relatively more money in Scotland than they had in England. Wheelock and Whitaker were granted the degree of Doctor of Divinity from the University of Edinburgh. London's William Gordon wrote of the honor to Joseph Bellamy in Connecticut that it did "not add at all to their work, tho' it may give them an air of importance." Nonetheless, he noted: "Great collections have been made for the school. May the application of them prove as successful as the more sanguine can wish." The fundraising trip represented the smooth promotion of religion around the empire, even as that empire had begun to show serious strains by the time the men returned to America in 1768.[41]

Occom and Whitaker's successful journey was one of several awakened projects during the decade that worked to integrate British protestants during a period most often associated with the growing frictions of coming revolution, particularly with the tensions between Anglicans and dissenters. That integration did not necessarily mean harmony—Wheelock, in particular, was a figure who attracted acrimony—but these collaborations nonetheless suggest that the kinds of quarrels over establishment that flared with the bishop controversy existed within a context where protestants from various places and denominations could work to a common purpose without much difficulty. They thus testify to the durability of the structures of imperial protestantism. The tensions between Parliament and the colonies and the fights over a bishop for the colonies had little impact on the transatlantic projects undertaken by awakened protestants because those who imagined new schools and new missions did not anticipate that the political struggles of the day would have any lasting impact on the relationships that had been built through decades of migration, revival, itinerancy, correspondence, and shared missionary work.[42]

At the same time, however, the awakened efforts of the 1760s were not without challenges. The cooperation they could generate through their enthusiastic labors could evaporate just as fast, leading to frustration and disappointment. Whitefield's college project in Georgia, for example, brought him into conflict

41. *Caledonian Mercury* (Edinburgh), May 16, 1767, quoted in Szasz, *Scottish Highlanders,* 204; John Erskine to Nathaniel Whitaker, June 12, 1767, in Richardson, *An Indian Preacher,* 263; Gordon to Bellamy, Oct. 14, 1767, Bellamy Papers, box 190, folder 2959, item 81623; Szasz, *Scottish Highlanders,* 162–196; Richardson, *An Indian Preacher,* 265.

42. For controversy around Wheelock, see Andrews, *Native Apostles,* 214–216.

with Archbishop of Canterbury Thomas Secker when the Anglican itinerant sought a royal charter for his college—a choice that itself reflected Whitefield's commitment to the kind of legitimacy that came only from the highest levels. Secker was not favorably disposed to the plan. According to the prelate's autobiography, he had been watching the affair develop over several years. Though he had heard from his friend, the dissenting minister Samuel Chandler, that the college was to have an Anglican head, he had later heard from William Smith, the Anglican provost of the College of Philadelphia, that "Mr Whitefields Design was to appoint a Number of Persons by Name for the Governors and Managers of his College, who sh[oul]d fill up Vacancies as they happened, and that thus it w[oul]d probably become a Methodist College." As he had with previous efforts to which he objected, Secker opposed the charter and effectively halted its progress.[43]

Whitefield—though an Anglican priest himself—responded with frustration and with resignation, first in conversation with Secker and then in print when he published their exchange. He insisted that "by far the greatest part of the Orphan-house collections and contributions came from dissenters, not only in New England, New York, Pennsylvania, South Carolina and Scotland, but in all probability here in England also." He had, "in most of the above-mentioned places, . . . solemnly declared from the pulpit, that it should be upon a *Broad Bottom, and no other*." The phrase "broad bottom," in British protestant circles, referred to conscious denominational inclusiveness in religious projects like the college Whitefield planned. He had felt confident when he made these claims "from the known long established mild and uncoercive genius of the English government—From your Grace's moderation towards protestant dissenters—From the unconquerable attachment of the Americans to toleration principles, as well as from the avowed habitual feelings and sentiments of my own heart." Despite such dramatic language, however, Whitefield knew he was trapped. He could not found his college as an exclusively Anglican institution and follow the awakened protestant model he had envisioned. Yet to build an institution with the kind of legitimacy he sought in Georgia, where Anglicanism was established, he needed a charter the archbishop would support. He acquiesced and assured Secker that he "intend[ed] troubling your Grace . . . no more about

43. Macauley and Greaves, *Autobiography of Thomas Secker*, 64–65; Robert Henley, Lord Northington to Secker, Aug. 27, 1767, Frederick Cornwallis to Northington, Aug. 28, 1767, both in SPG Papers, XI, 245, 255, LPL. See also McCaul, "Whitefield's Bethesda College," *Georgia Historical Quarterly*, XLIV (1960), 263–277; and Peter Y. Choi, *George Whitefield: Evangelist for God and Empire* (Grand Rapids, Mich., 2018), 219–225.

this so long depending concern." His loud protests and his submission to the archbishop's authority spoke at cross purposes, objecting to and reaffirming the position of awakened protestants within the Church of England's hierarchy.[44]

Wheelock's new Indian school also ran into difficulties when he resisted the usual structures of transatlantic protestantism, in this case the tradition of funds being administered from Britain. Before Occom and Whitaker even returned home, disagreements arose about how to structure and distribute funds raised in England and in Scotland. Wheelock wanted the money in his control, and he was unconvinced by a proposed English trust, even when its terms required representatives of "every denomination of Protestants of undeniable Characters." To make matters more complicated, Wheelock had also been busily trying to find a new home for the planned school. Various locations on the westward edge of British settlement had been considered, and landowners and government leaders in those places recruited the project. Wheelock sought advice from a variety of sources at once, including from Whitaker in London, and he petitioned Lord Dartmouth for assistance. For Wheelock, incorporation of his school—if he could pull it off, his college—would give his endeavor the legal solidity it needed to endure. Although Connecticut authorities supported the idea in principle, Connecticut, a corporate colony, could not itself issue a corporate charter. Wheelock considered the Ohio Valley and New York, but he eventually settled on New Hampshire, where he procured a charter for his college from its royal governor, John Wentworth. His planned institution had evolved also, shifting from an Indian school to a college that would train European-descended missionaries as well. He knew the changes in the college's purpose and location would anger the English trustees of his funds, who had donated on behalf of the more traditional goal of missionary work.[45]

Facing restrictions that echoed those Whitefield had struggled with but with his charter (from a colony rather than from the king) in hand, Wheelock outmaneuvered his English funders. His victory came at the cost of cooperation with Anglican leaders that Whitaker and Occom had carefully built. Wheelock's newly minted charter placed control of the college in the hands of its American leadership, though it also preserved a place on the board of trustees for the

44. George Whitefield, *A Letter to His Excellency Governor Wright, Giving an Account of the Steps Taken* . . . (London, 1768), 6–7, 16–18 (quotations on 17, 18); Choi, *George Whitefield*, 209–217. For "broad bottom," see also Whitefield to Secker, Oct. 16, 1767, SPG Papers, XI, 259; and Walter Herbert Stowe, ed., *The Life and Letters of Bishop William White* . . . (New York, 1937), 57.

45. Scots who had been involved in fundraising through the SSPCK were also skeptical of English control. See Richardson, *An Indian Preacher*, 93–95, 156–157, 162–164, 167–171 (quotation on 171), 263–267; and Jere R. Daniell II, "Eleazar Wheelock and the Dartmouth College Charter," *Historical New Hampshire*, XXIV, no. 4 (Winter 1969), 9.

bishop of London. Lord Dartmouth, after whom the college had also now been named, contacted the bishop, Richard Terrick, in the summer of 1771. Terrick was not pleased and responded that, though he would "always be willing to take a part in encouraging and protecting any scheme for the propagation of true Religion," it was nonetheless "impossible, that I could think of accepting a Trust for the erection and endowment of a College, the charter of which has never been communicated to me; nor has the least intimation been given to me, that a Provision is made in the charter, either that the Head of the College shall be of the Church of England, or that the Prayers made use of shall be those of our Liturgy." All the worse, Terrick blistered, he could "not help remarking, that in the List of Trustees . . . there are several Dissenting Ministers and not one of the Church of England." The interdenominational cooperation on which awakened protestants relied evaporated once good will toward the project at hand was in doubt. Wheelock's reorganization of his college put it beyond the limits of what Terrick would support.[46]

It is important to distinguish between the kinds of denominational rivalries evident in Wheelock's and Whitefield's colleges and the growing rift between colonies and Parliament. Those surrounding the projects of awakened protestants did not feed into the Americans' anger against Britain, as the bishop controversy had. Quite the contrary, when Whitefield invoked the colonial crisis in 1768 it was to the opposite purpose. That spring, six awakened Anglican students were expelled from Oxford. Whitefield published a pamphlet about the incident that blistered with righteous indignation on behalf of the awakening movement. He championed the biblical nature of extemporaneous prayer and small religious gatherings, the importance of singing hymns, and the superior character of students whose crimes stemmed from piety rather than those that arose from baser instincts. In the middle of this argument he pointed out that the university's actions had already harmed the "venerable Society," the SPG, because the expulsions would exacerbate the already significant problem of finding missionaries to go to America. Moreover, since Americans were already worried that the "Society for propagating the Gospel, hath been all the while rather a Society for propagating Episcopacy in foreign parts," it was all the worse to provide evidence that the religion of the Church of England was hollow. "How will the very thought of the introduction of Lords Bishops even make them shudder," he lamented, "if their Lordships should

46. Terrick to Lord Dartmouth, July 9, 1771, Dartmouth Papers, D(W) 1778/II/347, pt. 2; Daniell, "Eleazar Wheelock," *Historical New Hampshire,* XXIV, no. 4 (Winter 1969), 3–31. For Lord Dartmouth's participation and the trustees' view, see B. D. Bargar, *Lord Dartmouth and the American Revolution* (Columbia, S.C., 1965), 13–14.

think proper to countenance the expulsion of such worthy and truly religious Students, whilst those who have no religion at all perhaps, may not only meet with countenance, but approbation and applause?" Whitefield's real anger was directed at limitations on what he saw as vital religion; a bishop for America was a side issue in this case.[47]

The position of awakened protestants in the 1760s can only be described as complicated. Leaders in England, particularly George Whitefield and John and Charles Wesley, remained consistent in their commitment to the Church of England throughout the decade. They preferred to use their influence to transform Anglo-American protestantism from a position of insider authority. The same was true for Americans within that movement, men like Eleazar Wheelock and Joseph Bellamy, whose privilege as ministers of loyal, legally established denominations gave them direct entrée into the realm of legitimate religion, into the public pulpit, and into donors' pockets. Awakened leaders saw ample work to be done from within the empire's dominant protestant institutions. They stayed there, building collaborations across distances and denominations, connecting the various factions of British protestantism with one another. Placing the transatlantic projects of awakened protestantism alongside the contemporaneous fights over the imperial establishment between Anglicans and dissenters allows the durability of British protestantism during the period to come more fully into view. It was not without conflict and competitions, but it never had been. Yet searching for signs of revolution within the decade's religious conflicts gives a false weight to disputes that participants assumed would be overcome. The scaffolding of imperial protestantism, populated by three competing and yet overlapping networks, still stood when George Whitefield, the Grand Itinerant, died in 1770.

Little had altered within British protestantism as a result of the decade's disputes. Parliament had declined to make changes to the imperial establishment, and religious leaders had rejoiced when the ill-advised Stamp Act had been repealed. Meanwhile, work in the various missions and projects around

47. George Whitefield, *A Letter to the Reverend Dr. Durell, Vice-Chancellor of the University of Oxford; Occasioned by a Late Expulsion of Six Students from Edmund-Hall* (London, 1768), 25–26 (quotations on 20, 21). The tract was reprinted in Edinburgh and also in Boston, and answering tracts were also written. Awakened protestants discussed the expulsions widely. See John Thornton to Sebastian Fabricius, Mar. 18, 1768, Stab/F 30 5 4, microfilm roll 21, images 137–140, Franckesche Stiftungen; and Theophilus Lindsey to Selina Hastings, Apr. 29, 1768, in G. M. Ditchfield, ed., *The Letters of Theophilus Lindsey (1723–1808)*, I, *1747–1788* (Woodbridge, U.K., 2007), 106. See also Outler et al., eds., *Works of John Wesley*, XXII, 164; and Choi, *George Whitefield*, 225–227. Hastings founded her college at Trevecca in response to the Oxford expulsions. See Boyd Stanley Schlenther, *Queen of the Methodists: The Countess of Huntingdon and the Eighteenth-Century Crisis of Faith and Society* (Durham, N.C., 1997), 75–77.

the empire had continued with all the energy, partnership, and discord that had always characterized transatlantic protestantism. But stability within imperial protestantism did not mean all was well within Britain's empire as the decade came to a close. Religious observers watched as the relationship between Britain and the colonies deteriorated. London baptist Samuel Stennett commented to James Manning in Providence, Rhode Island, in the summer of 1770 that "the sovereignty of Parliament over all the British dominions seem to be the great object of governm.t," though he still "believe[d] they wou'd be glad to have peace and harmony restor'd." The devil would be in the details of any political improvement, however, and details of policy were rapidly becoming major shocks to the imperial system. When the new prime minister, Lord North, lowered some of the duties levied by the Townshend Acts, leaving in place the tax on tea, Scot John Erskine lamented to Connecticut's Joseph Bellamy that he was "heartily sorry so imperfect a relief has been given to North America as to the revenue laws." "People in Scotland in general," he continued, "seem infatuated and blind to our Danger." Equally pessimistic, New York Anglican Samuel Auchmuty wrote to Richard Peters in Philadelphia that "such is the infatuation of Americans, that they seem to be running fast, not to the prize of the high calling in Christ Jesus, but to their own destruction." The political fight, he believed, was likely to be a disaster. "They are endeavouring to shake off their Dependency from Great Britain," but if they "persisted in" this course, it "must terminate in their Ruin." Their worries were well placed. The disruptions of the years to come would be far more consequential for the structures and communities of imperial protestantism than those of the past decade had been.[48]

48. Gordon to Benjamin Rush, 1770, Yi 2 7260 F 7, Rush Family Papers, Library Company of Philadelphia at HSP; Stennett to Manning, Aug. 10, 1770, Manning Papers, MS-1C-1, folder 55; Erskine to Bellamy, Mar. 16, 1770, Bellamy Papers, box 188, folder 2936, item 81355; Auchmuty to Peters, May 6, 1770, Peters Papers, VI, pt. 2, 109.

3 Bending Apart, 1773–1774

In 1773 and 1774, the British Empire stumbled toward war. When the fissure finally arrived, it was—like most significant historical moments—the result of both long-term tensions and more immediate causes. Its origins had not been derived from imperial protestantism; the religious institutions and networks that spanned the distant parts of Britain's empire had not, over the course of the 1760s, become tools in the organization of protests the way that colonial assemblies and committees of correspondence had. Colonists angry about the military occupation of Boston, the limits on westward expansion caused by the Proclamation Line of 1763, or the potential threat to slavery posed by the Somerset decision in 1772 did not rely on their religious leaders to send complaints back to coreligionists in Britain. In addition, there were signs that the divisions of the previous decade might be fading. The Stamp Act had been repealed, as had most of the Townshend duties, with the exception of the tax on tea. The nonimportation and nonconsumption agreements that colonists had used to pressure Parliament had lapsed. Troops had been removed from Boston in the wake of the Boston Massacre. For all these reasons, the scaffolding of imperial protestantism was relatively intact at the crucial moment, in late 1773, when Bostonians disposed of tea in their harbor and triggered the ruptures that led to war.[1]

In that chain of events, religious leaders were primarily reactive. Rather than guiding public sentiment, as has often been assumed, they worked within the structural imperatives created by Britain's mixed establishment, and those structures guided—and sometimes restricted—their options. But as the empire fractured, the imperatives created by Britain's mixed establishment pushed

1. For a broad survey of the coming of the Revolution, see Alan Taylor, *American Revolutions: A Continental History, 1750–1804* (New York, 2016), 55–128. For more specific studies, see S. Max Edelson, *The New Map of Empire: How Britain Imagined America before Independence* (Cambridge, Mass., 2017), 289–316; Eliga H. Gould, *Among the Powers of the Earth: The American Revolution and the Making of a New World Empire* (Cambridge, Mass., 2012), 79–110; Christopher Leslie Brown, *Moral Capital: Foundations of British Abolitionism* (Williamsburg, Va., and Chapel Hill, N.C., 2006), 105–153; and Woody Holton, *Forced Founders: Indians, Debtors, Slaves, and the Making of the American Revolution in Virginia* (Williamsburg, Va., and Chapel Hill, N.C., 1999).

in opposing directions, with rebelling colonies going one way and Britain's imperial administration going in another. As a result, the political crisis had significant consequences for the scaffolding that had once wrapped around the empire. It is useful to consider the course of these pivotal years in terms of chronological stages, as events unfolded first on one side of the Atlantic, then on the other, because doing so brings new clarity to the relationship between protestant leaders and political events in the various parts of Britain's mixed establishment. The first period, before and directly after the Boston Tea Party, saw religious leaders articulate their commitment to a vision of protestant empire, and that perspective informed the immediate response of New England's religious leaders to the Tea Party. They urged caution at a moment that seemed precarious. But, whereas New Englanders were wary, British authorities, when they learned what had happened in early 1774, were outraged. Their deliberations on the best response to Boston's destructive protest, including religious leaders' role therein, provide a second moment of consideration.[2]

When news of Parliament's response—the Coercive Acts—reached America that summer, the third period began. Colonists, working through their governments when they could, reacted with fury. They asked for the support of colonial religious leaders and received it when the structures that shaped the public pulpit made it possible. In all three of these moments, throughout 1773 and 1774, the pressures of Britain's mixed establishment were evident because religious leaders made choices that hewed closely to the agendas set by the dominant government around them. As the crisis of empire deepened, the close ties that existed between protestant leaders and their local governments—a result of the empire's decentralized, rather than consolidated, establishment—guided the voices of most protestant leaders. But the mixed establishment, the pillars

2. This chronological approach is informed by Sarah Knott's interpretation of "hot chronology." See her "Narrating the Age of Revolution," *William and Mary Quarterly*, 3d Ser., LXXIII (2016), 3–36. The argument that religious leaders provided a theology of revolution is particularly strong within the Christian nationalist tradition, but it also resonates in academic work, particularly where ideology is seen to drive action. See, for example, Thomas S. Kidd, *God of Liberty: A Religious History of the American Revolution* (New York, 2010), esp. 75–95; and Harry S. Stout, *The New England Soul: Preaching and Religious Culture in Colonial New England* (New York, 1986), 283–287. The influential work of Ruth H. Bloch (*Visionary Republic: Millennial Themes in American Thought, 1756–1800* [Cambridge, 1985]) and Nathan O. Hatch (*The Sacred Cause of Liberty: Republican Thought and the Millennium in Revolutionary New England* [New Haven, Conn., 1977]) avoids such oversimplifications but nonetheless underestimates the institutional conservatism of religious leaders. The idea of Revolutionary theology driving the imperial crisis is particularly common in works with an emphasis on the literarily productive dissenting groups, which leave as an unexplored issue the sizable number of southern Anglican clergy who followed their congregants—though not the church hierarchy—into support for the American resistance.

of the scaffold, was only part of the whole system. Finally, in the last months before the outbreak of war, the protestant networks, the planks that bound the empire together, protested the course of events. Radical voices within both the dissenting and the Anglican networks spoke out, disparaging the spiral toward division. The fruitlessness of their outcries, and the anger with which they were voiced, should not obscure the fact that these strident outliers represent the primary religious efforts to slow the descent into war.

TEA PARTY

The benefit of hindsight makes it clear that the Boston Tea Party was a significant turning point in the history of Britain's eighteenth-century empire. The speed with which matters went awry after 1774 can too easily suggest that tensions must have started much earlier and grew in a neat line from the Stamp Act, through the Townsend Acts, and on to the Tea Act and the party that followed. But that narrative oversimplifies a complex story and, for present purposes, obscures the uncertainty and caution of the early 1770s. In the first years of the decade, many religious leaders were hopeful for their protestant empire's shared future, though concerns about the danger Parliament posed to colonial rights could also be heard from a few, particularly dissenting, quarters. A brief survey of these sentiments provides important context within which to interpret the responses from religious leaders to the Tea Party itself at the end of 1773 and the start of 1774. At that tense moment, they had every reason to assume their connections to empire would continue. Though the flash of colonial anger that had been evident in Boston had the potential to reignite tensions between Parliament and colonists, protestant leaders hoped cooler heads would prevail.

During the early 1770s, religious leaders reaffirmed the British Empire as a champion of protestantism, putting the difficulties of the past decade behind them. The most significant such statement came from Anglican Jonathan Shipley, the bishop of St. Asaph, who preached the 1773 annual sermon for the Society for the Propagation of the Gospel in Foreign Parts (SPG). It was an important venue, given the antagonism that had circled around the SPG's work in New England during the previous decade. Shipley was also an interesting choice of speaker. He was a latitudinarian in ecclesiastical politics, and he had been advanced to the episcopacy by the duke of Grafton, who was moderate in his perspective on colonial affairs. In the Revolutionary crisis, Shipley tended to side against Lord North. But, whereas Britons might well have read the sermon within that partisan context, Americans saw in it a welcoming picture of their future role in the empire.[3]

The bishop took as his text Luke 2:14: "Glory be to God in the highest, and on earth peace, good will towards men." The words spoken by the angel at Jesus's birth had heralded a new age, and perhaps the colonists hoped Shipley's would, as well. He stated simply that the "chief object" of the SPG, the body that had been at the center of so much controversy, was "instructing distant countries in religious truths to promote the peace and happiness of mankind." He refrained from scolding colonists for irreligion the way the bishop of Llandaff in 1767 had, instead employing the tropes of hereditary heathenism to explain Indigenous peoples' "untameable savage spirit" behind their rejection of the gospel. If labor among those communities was difficult, he suggested that the society turn to the opportunities created by the empire's expanding Euro-American population and to forming "new congregations." This point, too, was more conciliatory than what had come before, as it implied that SPG missionaries would avoid pulling congregants from the well-established churches of New England and the Middle Colonies, welcome news to colonial clergy. Building on this foundation, Shipley conjured a prosperous British Empire with a peaceful and glorious future. He asked his audience to "reflect that to whatever limits the population of our colonies may extend, whatever states and kingdoms they may form," the SPG would "continue to operate with an increasing influence" and "give it's *[sic]* character hereafter to the religion and morals of a powerful state." Rather than division, Shipley foresaw harmony that would "tend to revive that union and cordiality between the mother-country and it's *[sic]* colonies, which for the common utility ought never to have been interrupted." From this basis, Shipley went on to recommend a benevolent and liberal policy toward the colonies, in the spirit of brotherly love.[4]

The sermon met with positive reactions on both sides of the Atlantic. A review in the London-based *Gentleman's Magazine* noted that it "exhibits a lively picture of that benevolent spirit, and of those equitable principles and

3. See G. M. Ditchfield, "Shipley, Jonathan (1713–1788), Bishop of St Asaph," Jan. 3, 2008, *Oxford Dictionary of National Biography*, https://www.oxforddnb.com; Colin Bonwick, *English Radicals and the American Revolution* (Chapel Hill, N.C., 1977), 9. See also Peter Brown, *The Chathamites: A Study in the Relationship between Personalities and Ideas in the Second Half of the Eighteenth Century* (London, 1967), 325–338.

4. Jonathan [Shipley], *A Sermon Preached before the Incorporated Society for the Propagation of the Gospel in Foreign Parts; at Their Anniversary Meeting in the Parish Church of St. Mary-le-Bow, on Friday, February 19, 1773* (London, 1773), iii, v–vi, xiii–xiv. Rebecca Anne Goetz coined the term "hereditary heathenism"; see Goetz, *The Baptism of Early Virginia: How Christianity Created Race* (Baltimore, 2012), 6.

measures, by which alone [Great Britain and her colonies in America can return to] their old concord and mutual prosperity can be restored." American protestant leaders were also pleased with Shipley's effort, and their responses point to their sense that the colonies were part of a shared protestant empire, even as they were on their guard against new parliamentary encroachments. William Gordon, an awakened dissenter from London who had recently relocated to Massachusetts, wrote that the sermon was "read with avidity, is talked of in all companies, [and] is greatly approved by the high sons of liberty." He reported that Americans had even purchased enough copies to justify a second printing, "a rare thing for such a kind of publication in America." He was right. Shipley's sermon was reprinted in at least five different cities in the colonies, beyond the original printing in London. Samuel Magaw, an SPG minister in Delaware, reported to his superiors, "The last Sermon preached before the Society, pleases and delights the Americans; and My Lord the Bishop of St. Asaph is universally beloved and admired." Even the dissenter Ezra Stiles recorded in his literary diary that he had read the sermon, and "it is greatly in favor of America." An inclusive vision of empire from the SPG had the support of American religious leaders. They saw themselves as part of that empire, though they wanted respect within it.[5]

Hopeful views of Britain's protestant empire came from other quarters, as well. Philadelphia awakened Anglican Jacob Duché published a series of essays in that city's newspapers in 1772 and 1773, describing Pennsylvania's capital in glowing terms from the perspective of an English visitor. When completed, the essays were published together as a single volume. In the text, Duché's imagined traveler, a churchman (that is, an Anglican), noted sagely that if he were to move across the Atlantic permanently, he "should never say a word in favour of an established episcopate, till the powers of the intended Bishop were accurately defined, and a satisfactory security given by act of Parliament against any future encroachments." Such a move was warranted, because Philadelphia's dissenters were "all warmly attached to the British constitution, and whilst their civil and religious liberties are secured to them, will remain as affectionate and obedient

5. "[Review:] 32. A Sermon Preached before the Incorporated Society for the Propagation of the Gospel in Foreign Parts . . . ," *Gentleman's Magazine,* XLIII (1773), 393–396, esp. 393; William Gordon to William Legge, second earl of Dartmouth, June 16, 1773, in Papers of the Legge Family, Earls of Dartmouth (hereafter cited as Dartmouth Papers), D(W) 1778/II/637, Staffordshire Record Office, Stafford, U.K.; Samuel Magaw to SPG, Nov. 6, 1773, Records of the Society for the Propagation of the Gospel in Foreign Parts (SPG), Series B, XXI, item 156, British Online Archives, https://microform.digital/boa; Franklin Bowditch Dexter, ed., *The Literary Diary of Ezra Stiles, D.D., LLD., President of Yale College, I, January 1, 1769–March 13, 1776* (New York, 1901), 388. According to the English Short Title Catalogue, the sermon was printed in Philadelphia; Norwich, Connecticut; New York; Boston; and Newport, Rhode Island.

subjects, as any in his Majesty's dominions." American voices, too, championed a harmonious relationship between colonies and empire, perhaps willing it into being. Their aspirations were further supported by the appointment, in 1772, of awakened Anglican William Legge, the second earl of Dartmouth, as secretary of state for the colonies. Across the various circles of religious leaders, he was well known and, more important, widely trusted. There were any number of reasons to assume that affairs across the empire would improve.[6]

The prospect of a future in which Britain and her American colonies flourished together may sound a bit like whistling past the graveyard, and there were reasons for ongoing concern. On June 10, 1772, a mob in Providence, Rhode Island, burned the stranded customs ship *Gaspee* (after removing its crew and contents), and the investigations the following winter spurred the Virginia House of Burgesses to initiate a committee of correspondence with other colonies. Some religious leaders sounded an alarm about British actions' posing a threat to American liberty. Baptist minister John Allen, a recent arrival from England, published a fast-day sermon "on the essential rights of Americans." The printed edition was dedicated to Lord Dartmouth, whom he called to task for failing as a Christian to protect American liberties. Allen went further than most were willing to when he advocated vigorous resistance, but even he concluded his sermon with the hope that, when an American parliament would be equal to the English one, "the *British* nation may be come the most glorious that ever existed since time began." His views were shared by some others, including Swiss presbyterian John Joachim Zubly in Georgia. The balance between the optimism of men like Duché and the more alarmist positions of the likes of Allen and Zubly—at a point when most religious leaders said nothing about their expectations—suggests an uneasy calm. William Gordon gave unsolicited advice to the new secretary of state: "The only effectual method to set all right in the speediest manner, is, for government to bring things back as far as possible, to the same state they were in at his Majesty's ascension" in 1760. "Great Britain must either decline making obnoxious acts of parliament

6. [Jacob Duché], *Observations on a Variety of Subjects, Literary, Moral, and Religious: In a Series of Original Letters, Written by Tamoc Caspipina, a Gentleman of Foreign Extraction, Who Resided Some Time in Philadelphia* (Philadelphia, 1774), 62–64. Duché's *Caspipina* was printed as a single volume twice in Philadelphia and then again in Bath in 1771. It saw more reprintings in the 1790s. See also Kevin J. Dellape, *America's First Chaplain: The Life and Times of the Reverend Jacob Duché* (Bethlehem, Pa., 2013), 65–67. For Legge, see Gordon to Dartmouth, Oct. 4, 1772, Dartmouth Papers, D(W) 1778/II/442; James Alice to [Dartmouth], Nov. 5, 1772, ibid., D(W) 1778/II/453; B. D. Bargar, *Lord Dartmouth and the American Revolution* (Columbia, S.C., 1965), 57–58; and Gordon to Joseph Bellamy, Sept. 9, 1766, Joseph Bellamy Papers, box 190, folder 2959, item 81621, Hartford Seminary Library, Conn. See also Nick Bunker, *An Empire on the Edge: How Britain Came to Fight America* (New York, 2014), 194–195; and Benjamin Woods Labaree, *The Boston Tea Party* (1964; rpt. Boston, 1979), 83–84.

for America," he wrote, or the mother country would have to choose between "patiently [submitting] to see them neglected and despised" or "supporting them by military power." The reasonable assumptions of many religious leaders that an imperial relationship would endure did not eliminate concern over the immediate course of affairs.[7]

It was an inauspicious moment for Parliament to bail out the East India Company by giving it a monopoly on the American tea market. Bostonians were certainly not thinking about Dartmouth's devotion to Christianity when they decided to destroy the tea awaiting customs clearance in Boston Harbor in December 1773. It was an explicit and direct protest against parliamentary authority performed on behalf of an imagined America. Samuel Cooper, the pastor of the Brattle Street Church, wrote to Benjamin Franklin in London, "Two or three hundred Persons in Dress and appearance like Indians, pass'd by the old South Meeting House where the Assembly was held, gave a War Hoop, and hasten'd to the Wharf where all the Tea Ships lay, and demanding the Tea, which was given up to them without the least Resistance, they soon emptied all the Chests into the Harbor, to the Amount of about three hundred and forty." Cooper recounted that the men did so "with out Injury to any other Property, or to any Man's Person." Stressing what he saw as the upright nature of the proceedings, he called it "a remarkable Instance of Order and Justice, among Savages," who, when they had finished, "silently departed, and the Town has been remarkably quiet ever since." Cooper emphasized the decorum of these quintessentially unlawful acts. But, as much as the Boston patriots might have wished to legitimate their actions, it was difficult to disguise that the city was out of British control.[8]

7. [John Allen], *An Oration on the Beauties of Liberty; or, The Essential Rights of the Americans: Delivered at the Second Baptist-Church in Boston, upon the Last Annual Thanksgiving, Dec. 3d, 1772 . . .*, 4th ed. (Boston, 1773), 63–64. Allen had a shaky reputation. His willingness to transgress boundaries might have made him more willing to be more radical, earlier, than many other voices. For "Effectual method," see Gordon to Dartmouth, June 16, 1773, Dartmouth Papers, D(W)1778/II/637. See also John M. Bumsted and Charles E. Clark, "New England's Tom Paine: John Allen and the Spirit of Liberty," *WMQ*, 3d Ser., XXI (1964), 561–570; and James P. Byrd, *Sacred Scripture, Sacred War: The Bible and the American Revolution* (New York, 2013), 35–36. See also Ezra Stiles's thoughts at this period in Dexter, ed., *Literary Diary of Ezra Stiles*, I, 343–351. It is worth noting that Stiles also maintained an intense interest in the goings-on in England's dissenting community (see 302–322). Zubly wrote a series of pamphlets between 1769 and 1775 advocating against parliamentary authority in the colonies; see Randall M. Miller, ed., *"A Warm and Zealous Spirit": John J. Zubly and the American Revolution, a Selection of His Writings* (Macon, Ga., 1982); and Spencer W. McBride, *Pulpit and Nation: Clergymen and the Politics of Revolutionary America* (Charlottesville, Va., 2016), 89–93.

8. Samuel Cooper to [Benjamin] Franklin, Dec. 17, 1773, *Benjamin Franklin Papers Online*, http://franklinpapers.org. For more complete retellings of the legendary episode, see Benjamin L. Carp, *Defiance of the Patriots: The Boston Tea Party and the Making of America* (New Haven,

After the Boston Tea Party, the immediate reaction of religious leaders in New England was cautious. They had to balance their assumption that imperial authority would continue in America, their belief that civil disorder was undesirable, and their personal views on the events themselves. Duxbury, Massachusetts, minister Charles Turner preached a sermon only a few days after the destruction of the tea, at a ceremony commemorating the founding of Plymouth. Turner was no fan of parliamentary authority. His Massachusetts election-day sermon, a few months before, had urged resistance. But now he spoke in less strident terms. He vindicated the Pilgrims' devotion to religious liberty but also defended them against being "reproached" as *"schismatics."* Devotion to a dissenting view of religious liberty, in other words, did not mean embracing division. At the same time, he argued that Plymouth's beginnings had been "pregnant with empire," the first plantings of great things to come, and he reinforced his point with an explicit quotation from Shipley's recent SPG sermon: "Perhaps the annals of history have never afforded a more grateful spectacle to a benevolent and philosophic mind, than the growth and progress of the british Colonies of *North-America*." He added, "We chearfully hoped, that all the absurd popish doctrines and wicked devices of spiritual and civil oppression will fall into utter contempt" and that balance "between the power of rulers and privileges of the people, in matters civil and ecclesiastical, will be held with a steady, wise, and unerring hand." He applauded resistance to an Anglican bishop and rejoiced in the "future greatness and happiness of our country," but his spirits were "damped" when he thought of their "present political embarrassments, together with our sinfulness." Better, he argued, to "nourish that spirit of christianity, which implies the spirit of liberty and *union"* so that they might find "deliverance out of all tribulation" and "not be ruined thereby." Turner omitted specific comment on the destruction of the tea and avoided explicit rejection of parliamentary authority. In a moment where the best course of action was not clear, pious contemplation of basic principles was called for. If *"standing fast* in the cause of liberty and dissenting religion" was the "cause of God," then they should do so, but it was not a step to be taken lightly.[9]

Conn., 2010), 117–140. For the politics and circumstances of the Tea Act, see Labaree, *Boston Tea Party*, 66–73; and Jane T. Merritt, *The Trouble with Tea: The Politics of Consumption in the Eighteenth-Century Global Economy* (Baltimore, 2017), 89–100. It does not appear that Cooper leveraged his connections to leaders of clerical or denominational networks in Britain or that he tried to raise an outcry over the bill using religious language. See Charles W. Akers, *The Divine Politician: Samuel Cooper and the American Revolution in Boston* (Boston, 1982), 163–168; Akers emphasizes, instead, how much Cooper was in step with the sentiments of his congregants.

9. Charles Turner, *A Sermon Preached at Plymouth December 22d: 1773; Being the Anniversary Thanksgiving, in Commemoration of the Landing of the Fathers There, A.D. 1620* (Boston, 1774), 19, 28, 31, 33–34, 40–42, 45.

A worry that underlay responses to the Tea Party was that, if the Americans were sinful, then whatever punishment followed from the destruction of the tea was just. A few days after Turner preached his sermon, awakened baptist Israel Holly of Suffield, Connecticut, cast the conflict between the colonies and Britain in scriptural terms. His text was quite a propos: 1 Kings 12:15, part of a chapter that told of the wicked King Rehoboam's failure to listen to his people's protests when he burdened them with heavy taxes and the subsequent division of King David's realm into two competing kingdoms. In a theologically dense sermon, Holly mapped out an argument for God's providential direction of affairs for the purpose of chastising sinners. "So by way of punishment God is threatening of us now, and if he should suffer arbitrary and tyrannical edicts to issue from the highest seat of power in our nation, tending to abridge the colonies in America of their natural and constitutional liberties; and the people should refuse to subject thereto, let the risque be what it will," proclaimed Holly. In the present crisis, God's use of human action to punish sin portended "mutual ruin, the ruin of Britain as well as of the colonies." If the "king of Great-Britain will not hearken to the people in the colonies of America," as King Rehoboam had not, then this was evidence of God's using the "corruptions of those he means to punish, as the means to bring it about." The colonists had "reason to fear, that God is now about to chastise, and in great severity, to punish such a wicked land and nation as our's *[sic]*." Holly sounded the notes of a traditional jeremiad, decrying the sins of America and Britain alike.[10]

Holly's lament for the spiritual state of the world struck a markedly different tone than Turner's celebration of faithfulness, yet their prescriptions were quite similar. In response to the question "What must be done?" Holly advised the colonies to unite to "maintain their threatened rights and liberties," but at the same time, like Turner, he avoided weighing in on what he saw as political questions. "I leave it to others to plan," he remarked, "in those affairs which relate to state policy, and give my advice in another character." Like the Ninevites, if the colonists turned from sin, they might be spared. "And God in his providence now, as well as in his word, is setting life and death before us, and is bidding us choose: and therefore, O, America, O, New-England, be wise, and choose

10. Israel Holly, *God Brings about His Holy and Wise Purpose or Decree, concerning Many Particular Events, by Using and Improving the Wicked Dispositions of Mankind in Order Thereto; . . .* (Hartford, Conn., 1774), 15–16. Holly's sermon is discussed by Byrd in *Sacred Scripture, Sacred War*, 37–38. Byrd's overall survey of Revolutionary-era sermons finds that this chapter of 1 Kings, which tells of the division of David's kingdom, was one of the most frequently used in the era (appendix, 169–170). See also Eran Shalev, *American Zion: The Old Testament as a Political Text from the Revolution to the Civil War* (New Haven, Conn., 2013), 7.

life." Again echoing Turner, Holly also reminded the colonists of the dangers of tyranny, for the loss of civil liberty could lead to the loss of religious liberty, and ultimately to popery, the religious tyranny that lay at the end of this slippery slope. In this light, resistance was necessary, but, from Holly's perspective, the turn away from sin was crucial.[11]

From elsewhere in the empire, continued hope for unity and peace marked a third sermon preached in the aftermath of the Tea Party. Like the others, it was cautious, though it came from a very different location than the others. Edmund Law, bishop of Carlisle, gave the annual SPG sermon for 1774 on February 18, a few weeks after the news of the Boston Tea Party reached England. A bishop (and therefore also a member of the House of Lords) preaching from St. Mary-le-Bow in the heart of London, representing the "Venerable Society," Law wielded all of the official gravitas a British religious leader could. Despite these credentials, Law was a striking spokesman for the SPG and the Church of England at this moment. Like his predecessor the year before, Jonathan Shipley, Law was a latitudinarian, allied with England's dissenters on political issues and comfortable with a wide variety of opinions on key theological matters within the church. He had sympathized with the effort to exempt Anglican clergy from the requirement to subscribe to the Thirty-Nine Articles, and he was a close colleague of Archdeacon Francis Blackburne, who moved in dissenting circles. Indeed, given the historical connections dissenters shared across the Atlantic and the perception that dissenters were active in the American protests because of their role in the bishop controversy, Edmund Law was a decidedly conciliatory choice of speaker.[12]

Law's sermon at this tense moment in the relationship between Parliament and colonies was telling. Rather than excoriating the Bostonians—who were, of course, largely dissenters—for their lawlessness, he reiterated Shipley's positive vision of the British Empire. He imagined a peaceful and united Christian future and even offered "some few cautions that seem more especially needful in these trying times," lest anything distract from the "principal aim" of the

11. Holly, *God Brings*, 19–21. Holly's use of anti-Catholic rhetoric was more robust than Turner's. "No wonder then," he wrote, "that men of sense and honor, no wonder that men of piety and religion, no wonder that men of conscience and fidelity, are loth to submit to that, which they have reason to think is leading towards" the Church of Rome (22).

12. I have not yet found any discussion on the selection of these two speakers or comment on the choice, though it would be very interesting to know whether this circumstance was planned or accidental. For more general discussion of SPG annual sermons, see Edgar Legare Pennington, "The S.P.G. Annual Sermons, 1702–1783," *Historical Magazine of the Protestant Episcopal Church*, XX (1951), 10–43; and Laura M. Stevens, "Why Read Sermons? What Americanists Can Learn from the Society for the Propagation of the Gospel in Foreign Parts," *History Compass*, III (2005), 119.

society and thus from the "*common cause* of religion." The distressing matters of politics, he seemed to say, could be laid aside with the right kind of labor. For the SPG, a missionary society, this naturally meant missionary work. Like Shipley the year before, Law blamed past failures on the peoples whom the missionaries sought to convert. As to the failings of Christians in America, whether missionaries or colonists, Law dismissed the subject as "disagreeable talk." Instead, he urged the society to pay attention to core principles: the dissemination of the "plain primitive doctrines of our common faith" and the avoidance of theological controversy. Second, he urged missionaries to work alongside rather than compete with the colonists. They should not, he said, "set up *altar against altar;* neither openly interfering with, nor secretly opposing any labours of other men in their respective provinces." Use care in handling divisive issues, Law advised, "discreet and wary caution," and "under the divine protection we shall be secure from either open violence, or secret enmity and opposition." Someday, he hoped, they would be able to spread the gospel and "meet with suitable encouragement from all true friends of our common Christianity; from those especially, who are best acquainted with the state and circumstances of these countries." The differences of experiences between colonies and metropole could even be an asset and facilitate the promotion of protestantism.[13]

It was a careful way to promote imperial peace, with a gentle suggestion of how to avoid further crisis. By reiterating the themes that had been laid out by his predecessor a year before and using them to articulate ways of overcoming differences between colonists, Law acted as though colonial matters were unchanged. By staying the course and collaborating effectively and tolerantly with the colonists, the ship of state might steer through rocky shoals. Taken together, the voices of Law, Holly, and Turner were remarkably cautious. From their prominent positions, their words reminded hearers and readers that much was at stake in the imperial relationship and that the consequences for resis-

13. Edmund [Law], *A Sermon Preached before the Incorporated Society for the Propagation of the Gospel in Foreign Parts; at Their Anniversary Meeting in the Parish Church of St. Mary-Le-Bow, on Friday February 18, 1774* (London, 1774), xiv–xv, xvi, xviii (this section quotes 2 Corinthians 10:14, 16), xx. Travis Glasson discusses Law's sermon, and Shipley's, from the perspective of attitudes toward enslaved and Native peoples, seeing the sermons as part of a longer-term trend toward pessimism about the ability of those peoples to become Christian (Glasson, *Mastering Christianity: Missionary Anglicanism and Slavery in the Atlantic World* [New York, 2012], 70–71). Laura M. Stevens notes the same issue regarding Shipley's sermon (Stevens, *The Poor Indians: British Missionaries, Native Americans, and Colonial Sensibility* [Philadelphia, 2004], 195). In this context, the discourse of religion as a unifying force between colonists and the British reinforced emerging racial distinctions.

tance and division could be dear. Rather than representing a particularly unified political stance—or even polarization on the two sides of the Atlantic—the responses of religious leaders to the Tea Party reinforce the essential conservatism of those deeply embedded within institutions. In this case, as religious leaders, such men might also have felt moral responsibility for encouraging peace and unity and, at the very least, pressures not to encourage division or disobedience. It is intriguing to wonder whether they might have celebrated a repeal of the Tea Act with the same vigor that they had the Stamp Act, but events did not move in that direction. The moment when advocating for caution was the safest course passed quickly.

It passed because those who controlled the levers of power in Britain were less concerned with not angering the colonists than they were with asserting Parliament's authority. Even Lord Dartmouth, who was more apt than most to listen to clergymen, had no interest in biblical visions of unity as a solution to the problem of disobedient colonists. He expressed his sentiments to John Thornton, the awakened Anglican philanthropist who served as Dartmouth's go-between with the prolific William Gordon. "Whenever you write to that Gentleman," he requested, "I wish you would represent to him, in the strongest terms, the impression which the late outrageous madness of the people of Boston has made upon the minds of men in general here." He warned Gordon, and any "leading people" of Massachusetts he might be able to reach, "how fatally and effectually they have now shut the door against all possibility of present relief from any of the things they complain of, and how utterly vain it must be to expect that Parliament will ever give it them, till there appears to be a change in their temper and conduct." Dartmouth confided to Thornton that he hoped for a peaceful route out of the mess, but he did not sound confident. "If it is meant (which I am very unwilling to suppose, but can hardly persuade myself not to suspect) to drive this Country to Extremities, there is an end of all schemes and plans of Reconciliation, and both sides must be content to take what follows." The events of the Boston Tea Party changed matters, as far as those in Britain were concerned. Though some had hoped to cool tempers in its wake, the North government saw the demonstration as an offense that demanded a swift and powerful response. The second stage of the process through which the scaffolding of protestantism bent apart was thus in Britain, as imperial leaders decided what course of action to pursue.[14]

14. Dartmouth to John Thornton, Feb. 12, 1774, Dartmouth Papers, D(W) 1778/II/827; Bunker, *Empire on the Edge*, 250–252.

PROTESTANT EMPIRE?

The political crisis of 1774 flowed from the problem of how to hold the colonists accountable for the massive destruction of property in Boston, as well as how to reestablish British rule in the colonies firmly and permanently. In March, the frustrated prime minister, Lord North, summed up the issues over which the colonies and Parliament had struggled for nearly a decade and brought it to a head. "We are not entering into a dispute between internal and external taxes," he argued, "not between taxes laid for the purpose of revenues and taxes laid for the regulation of trade, not between representation and taxation, or legislation and taxation; but we are now to dispute the question whether we have, or have not any authority in that country." In the spring of 1774, within weeks of learning about the Tea Party, North proposed a series of bills that were known as the Coercive Acts. The most immediately dramatic, the Boston Port Act, closed the Boston harbor as of June 1, 1774. It was quickly followed by the Massachusetts Regulatory Act, which significantly increased royal authority in that colony, and the Impartial Administration of Justice Act, which allowed a royal official accused of capital crimes to be tried in England by an English jury. Although these latter two measures generated significant debate in Parliament, they became law on May 20, 1774, followed by a new Quartering Act, a further attempt to solve a long-term problem of colonial aversion to housing British troops.[15]

These legislative moves were controversial in England, but, from the perspective of imperial protestantism, the most important issue came from a different quarter. In June 1774, just after the coercive measures, the Quebec Act passed. This last piece of legislation organized the government for the Quebec territory, which the British had taken in the 1763 Treaty of Paris that ended the Seven Years' War. Though it was grouped with the coercive measures in the popular imagination, it was more properly the final step in a lengthy process designed to incorporate large swaths of ceded territory from the decade-past war that were home to predominantly Catholic populations. In addition to most of what had been New France on the North American mainland, the British Empire now included the Caribbean islands of Grenada, Dominica, Saint Vincent, and Tobago, as well as Florida. When Quebec had surrendered in 1759, the British guaranteed the "free exercise of the Catholic, Apostolic, and Roman

15. Henry Cavendish's shorthand notes, Egerton MSS, 254, fols. 109–110, British Museum, London, cited in Bernard Donoughue, *British Politics and the American Revolution: The Path to War, 1773–75* (London, 1964), 73–104, esp. 77; Andrew Jackson O'Shaughnessy, *The Men Who Lost America: British Leadership, the American Revolution, and the Fate of the Empire* (New Haven, Conn., 2013), 51–54.

religion," and Grenada received the same privileges. In the years that followed, imperial administrators experimented with a variety of pragmatic solutions for managing their Catholic subjects, including extending civil rights to Catholic Grenadans as well as permitting Catholics to serve in the island's assembly and as judges. The extensions of civic rights were not without controversy, including in Britain, but the government had moved pragmatically nonetheless, eschewing philosophical or ideological arguments. The desire to limit political conflict and ensure the empire's integrity—the same motives that had led to the creation of the mixed establishment—proved dominant.[16]

When they finally got to organizing Quebec in 1774, imperial administrators acted similarly. The vast majority of the territory's European-descended inhabitants were French Catholics. The Quebec Act, though it stopped short of formally establishing the Roman Catholic Church in Canada, permitted Catholics to pay tithes to the church, and it also permitted a Catholic bishop to reside there. In addition, the act organized the government of Quebec, which now extended into the Ohio Valley, without a legislature. Colonists in the coastal provinces that claimed the Ohio Valley saw the Quebec Act as an enormous land grab. Many Britons throughout the empire read the act as a sign that the government was hostile to popular rule more generally. The official toleration of Catholicism (to some, any official acceptance of Catholicism seemed to be a Roman Catholic establishment) on the edges of and even within the scaffolding of imperial protestantism aroused anger and fear from dissenters, who viewed the government with distrust to begin with, but they were not the only ones who objected. To the outrage of many across the empire, the British government, it seemed, might no longer be committed to the protestantism that defined it.[17]

16. "Articles of Capitulation, Quebec, Sept. 18, 1759," and "Articles of Capitulation, Montreal, Sept. 8, 1760," in Adam Shortt and Arthur G. Doughty, eds., *Documents Relating to the Constitutional History of Canada, 1759–1791*, I, pt. 1 (Ottawa, Ont., 1918), quoted in Jessica L. Harland-Jacobs, "Incorporating the King's New Subjects: Accommodation and Anti-Catholicism in the British Empire, 1763–1815," *Journal of Religious History*, XXXIX (2015), 203–223, esp. 209. See also Harland-Jacobs, "Multi-Confessional Governance: Incorporating Catholics in the British Empire, 1713–1783," in Robert A. Olwell and James M. Vaughn, eds., *Envisioning Empire: The New British World from 1763 to 1773* (London, 2020), 83–108; and Aaron Willis, "The Standing of New Subjects: Grenada and the Protestant Constitution after the Treaty of Paris (1763)," *Journal of Imperial and Commonwealth History*, XLII (2014), 1–21.

17. Grenada was a key testing ground for these political issues. See Willis, "Standing of New Subjects," *Journal of Imperial and Commonwealth History*, XLII (2014), 1–21; and Harland-Jacobs, "Incorporating the King's New Subjects," *Journal of Religious History*, XXXIX (2015), 203–223. For the Quebec Act, see Edelson, *New Map of Empire*, 309–316; David Milobar, "Quebec Reform, the British Constitution, and the Atlantic Empire: 1774–1775," *Parliamentary History*, XIV (1995), 65–88; and Donoughue, *British Politics*, 105–126, esp. 125. See also Charles H. Metzger, *The Quebec Act: A Primary Cause of the American Revolution* (New York, 1936). For responses to the Quebec Act, see *Nova Scotia Gazette*, Sept. 13, 20, 1774. See also James E. Bradley, *Religion, Revolution, and English Radicalism: Nonconformity in Eighteenth-Century Politics and Society* (Cambridge,

The anger in Britain stirred up by the Quebec Act had implications for protestant leaders because of widespread assumptions that legitimate religious institutions within the empire defended and promoted their faith in partnership with government. In practice, antipopery was a complicated beast that intermingled theological and political prejudices emanating both from powerful institutions—churches and governments—and from more popular, cultural sources beyond the control of those institutions. On the popular level, it was a rhetorical knot that looped together fear of political conspiracy at the highest levels with fear of ecclesiastical tyranny (the opposite of religious liberty), worry about the presence of Roman Catholic people within the polity, and the vision of Britain as an empire that furthered the interests of protestantism. At the elite level, it functioned as a source of unity and, therefore, stability. The empire's mixed establishment of dominant protestant denominations had been justified as a bulwark against Catholicism, and religious leaders had long promoted anti-Catholicism as part of their support of the empire's goals. That the British government could be seen as guilty of promoting popery—for the political act of establishing a large government without a legislature and for extending toleration to the Catholic population of Quebec—meant the North ministry and George III were suspect leaders, at home and in the colonies. For those who opposed North's policy, antipopery now conjured up a worst-case scenario of the British government's true nature: that it might be corrupted by forces hostile to all kinds of liberty. Caught in this morass were religious leaders, particularly those in the Church of England. By habit, they supported government, and the Quebec Act was designed, in part, to make the colonies easier to administer. But the appearance that they were not sufficiently zealous in their protection of protestantism was damning.[18]

The issue came up in parliamentary debate, where opponents of the Quebec Act cast themselves as champions of protestantism and demanded that the king's government uphold its duties as head of the protestant cause. William

1990), 150; and Troy Bickham, *Making Headlines: The American Revolution as Seen through the British Press* (DeKalb, Ill., 2009), 57–62.

18. For discussions of antipopery, anti-Catholicism, and protestant political identity more generally in Britain, see Colin Haydon, *Anti-Catholicism in Eighteenth-Century England, c. 1714–80: A Political and Social Study* (Manchester, N.Y., 1993); Raymond D. Tumbleson, *Catholicism in the English Protestant Imagination: Nationalism, Religion, and Literature, 1660–1745* (Cambridge, 1998); Hannah Smith, "The Idea of a Protestant Monarchy in Britain, 1714–1760," *Past and Present*, no. 185 (November 2004), 91–118; Kathleen Wilson, *The Sense of the People: Politics, Culture, and Imperialism in England, 1715–1785* (Cambridge, 1995); Linda Colley, *Britons: Forging the Nation, 1707–1837* (New Haven, Conn., 1992); and Robert Kent Donovan, *No Popery and Radicalism: Opposition to Roman Catholic Relief in Scotland, 1778–1782* (New York, 1987). For dissenting anti-Catholicism in this moment, see Bradley, *Religion, Revolution, and English Radicalism*. Popular

Pitt, Lord Chatham, spoke against the measure. He asserted that "by the Bill the Catholic religion was made the established religion of that vast continent," and "it was impossible" that those who guarded the true faith "could be silent on the occasion." It violated the essentials of the British law, which "constitute[d] a clear compact that all establishments by law are to be Protestant." Those who argued for the bill took an opposite approach, insisting that the persecution of Catholics was inconsistent with the liberty cherished by a protestant government. The bill's advocates in Parliament included the pious Lord Dartmouth, who spoke in its favor, as did another lord, who averred that "no true Protestant" could promote intolerance. The king supported the bill, along with the majority of both Houses of Parliament and the bishops' bench, sending it on its way to a speedy enactment.[19]

But popular opinion nonetheless rejected the religious protections the Quebec Act offered to French Canadians. John Wilkes, the famous radical who had become lord mayor of London, organized a "Petition and Address" to demand that George III protect the protestant empire. It argued that the Quebec bill opened the door to persecution of "our Protestant fellow subjects of the Church of England" in America. Moreover, the Hanoverian claim to the throne rested on "the express stipulation that they should profess the Protestant Religion." George, at his coronation, they reminded him, "solemnly swore that you would, to the utmost of your power, maintain the Laws of God, the true profession of the Gospel, and the Protestant Reformed Religion established by Law." On those grounds, the petitioners pleaded with the king not to support the bill. Some 150 people went to St. James's to present the address on the day that George planned to give his assent. They failed. George carefully avoided them, approved the Quebec Act, and prorogued Parliament as he had intended. The moment set popular and institutional understandings of protestantism in stark contrast with each other. Which of the two was more authentically religious is not a question that can be answered. The more important point is that those

---

anti-Catholicism became a major issue during the war, with movements for Catholic emancipation in England and Scotland and anti-Catholic riots (including the Gordon Riots) in both places. These subjects will be central to subsequent chapters. Antipopery in America has also received significant attention. See, for example, Brendan McConville, *The King's Three Faces: The Rise and Fall of Royal America, 1688–1776* (Williamsburg, Va., and Chapel Hill, N.C., 2006); and Owen Stanwood, *The Empire Reformed: English America in the Age of the Glorious Revolution* (Philadelphia, 2011).

19. William Cobbett, *The Parliamentary History from the Earliest Period to the Year 1803 . . .*, XVII, *A.D. 1771–1774* (London, 1813), 1403–1404; John Fortescue, ed., *The Correspondence of King George* (London, 1928), III, 109–113; Donoughue, *British Politics*, 125. In general, the bishops supported the position of government in this era, though not universally. See William C. Lowe, "Bishops and Scottish Representative Peers in the House of Lords, 1760–1775," *Journal of British Studies*, XVIII (1978), 86–106.

who governed the empire believed their policies toward Quebec would be effective and would not harm anything essential about British protestantism. The leaders of religious institutions largely acquiesced in this vision, at least to the extent that there were few protests from that quarter (as distinguished from Wilkes's petitioners) against either the Quebec Act or the measures designed to bring New England to heel.[20]

Throughout the debates of the Quebec Act and the coercive measures, the goal of those in power—Lord North, George III, and even Lord Dartmouth—was to achieve the greatest level of stability and smooth governance. This task was not particularly religious, in the sense that it did not touch on protestant religious institutions. These men believed that the best course of action in solving the colonial problems was, first, to regularize the government of Quebec while protecting the rights of conquered French Catholics and, second, to force those in Massachusetts to fall into line. Though far from all Britons believed this to be good policy—dissenters, in particular, objected—the institutional bodies that represented protestantism in England mostly stayed out of the fray. Of course, the path of least resistance for leaders of established denominations was always to support the government's actions, and the bishops of the Church of England overwhelmingly supported the administration in its harsh response to the Tea Party. The most notable exception to this trend came from Jonathan Shipley, the whig bishop of St. Asaph, who had promoted a unifying vision of imperial religious community for the SPG just a few short months before. In the House of Lords, he opposed the coercive measures aimed at the Americans and even published an anonymous tract presenting his case for reconciliation. The pamphlet went to many editions, and Benjamin Franklin, who was a close associate of Shipley's, wrote to him that he "had the great Pleasure of hearing in all Companies the Speech extoll'd as a Master-piece of Eloquence and Wisdom. Great Numbers of them have been printed and dispers'd over the Nation: And I think one may see already its beginning Effect." Shipley's voice was quite isolated among his Anglican coreligionists. Neither the king nor the archbishop of Canterbury pushed for a formal recognition of the Boston Tea Party or colonial disobedience in religious terms. No special day of fasting or thanksgiving was declared in Britain between 1763 and 1776 for any occasion other than the (astonishingly regular) births of princes and princesses to King George and Queen Charlotte. As the empire plunged into disarray and war, the most powerful tool of public protestantism lay untouched.[21]

20. *Jackson's Oxford Journal,* June 25, 1774, 1–2.

21. [Jonathan Shipley], *A Speech Intended to Have Been Spoken on the Bill for Altering the Charters of the Colony of Massachusett's Bay* (London, [1774]); Franklin to Jonathan Shipley, Sept. 28,

Dissenting institutions' general silence on the coercive measures, including the Quebec Act, deserves particular consideration. The Protestant Dissenting Deputies, based in London, made no mention of Boston's sufferings in its minutes, or of the potential dangers presented to religious liberty by the Quebec Act. On October 19, 1774, the deputies met after a summer's hiatus. One of the letters entered in their minutes was from Scottish émigré and New Jersey presbyterian John Witherspoon, who acted on behalf of a nascent collaboration between American presbyterians and congregationalists. In a move that was probably covering up a moment of sloppiness, the deputies entered the Scot's letter as having been written only a few weeks previously, on September 1, 1774, when it was, in fact, dated a year earlier, September 1, 1773. The letter addressed, as many previous ones had, the threat of a bishop for the colonies, and it complained about the continued failure of the English body to respond to American correspondence. Witherspoon's letter, of course, said nothing about the tumultuous events that had unfolded during the period between the two Septembers, and the English dissenters did not bring them up. The minutes mention only that the secretary was directed to answer the letter and to "give the reason why the last was not answered, and that the Committee will be glad to have the Accounts they mention." The presbyterian General Assembly of the Church of Scotland also made no mention of the brewing crisis. The established church of North Britain, like the Church of England, reflexively supported government and largely stayed out of colonial policy. This quiescence from religious institutions is an essential counterpoint to the well-known partisan lean of dissenters in favor of the Americans. The alignment of political sentiments and the actions of religious institutions were not synonymous. Where they diverged, the pressure of the imperial establishment comes into view.[22]

1774, *Franklin Papers Online*. For days of special prayer, see Natalie Mears et al., eds., *National Prayers: Special Worship since the Reformation*, 3 vols. (Woodbridge, U.K., 2013–), 557–562.

22. For English dissenters, see Protestant Dissenting Deputies, General and Committee Meeting Minutes, Oct. 19, 1774, CLC/181/MS03083/002, London Metropolitan Archives. See also *Minutes of the Convention of Delegates from the Synod of New York and Philadelphia and from the Associations of Connecticut: Held Annually from 1766 to 1775, Inclusive* (Hartford, Conn., 1843), 39–43. For the Church of Scotland, see *The Principal Acts of the General Assembly of the Church of Scotland Convened at Edinburgh, the 19th Day of May, 1774 . . .* (Edinburgh, 1774). The Church of Scotland generally worked through British official structures when issues with the colonies arose. For example, when the Presbyterian Church of New York appealed to the Church of Scotland for support in its quest for incorporation, the Church of Scotland forwarded the issue to Lord Dartmouth for his action. See United Presbyterian Churches of New York to Dartmouth, New York, Oct. 20, 1773, Dartmouth Papers, D(W) 1778/II/728. For the partisanship of dissenters in the American crisis, see Bradley, *Religion, Revolution, and English Radicalism;* and Bonwick, *English Radicals and the American Revolution*.

Religious leaders' failure to speak out effectively in terms that advocated for the empire's protestant character did not go unnoticed. Those who came in for direct attacks were the Anglican bishops, who, as members of the House of Lords, had mostly supported the Quebec Act. For political commentator Horace Walpole, the overarching message was one of hypocrisy. He excoriated the bishops, calling them "hardened to shame and infamy" in part because they had "boldly voted in the recent instance of sending an army to cut the throats of the Bostonians." Those who abstained from voting (it was said that some bishops walked out of the chamber when Lord Chatham castigated them directly) were "too good courtiers and too bad Christians" to render an opinion on the bill. In Walpole's opinion, the response to the threat of popery presented by the Quebec bill had been inadequate. Popery was now established, he charged, in Britain's protestant empire, and the blame lay on "the Clergy of the Established Church, whose duty it was to oppose it." They were, in his view, "not only too apt to connive at Popery when countenanced by the Crown," but, for self-interested reasons, they went along with the court. Noting the irony that the church's hierarchy supported rights for Catholics in the empire and limited them to protestant dissenters at home, he bitterly added, "For the present Bench of Bishops, they had neither piety enough to care about their religion, sense enough to see the danger of the constitution, nor virtue enough, if they saw the danger of both, to care about either." Further evidence from American policy sealed his case: the bishops wanted an Anglican bishop in the colonies, a step that would doubtless be easier with a Catholic bishop in Quebec. Public cynicism about the failure of the Church of England to protect protestantism appeared in satiric form, as well. The *London Magazine* printed a cartoon entitled the *Mitred Minuet* in July 1774, often reprinted on both sides of the Atlantic, which shows Lord North and Lord Bute pointing at a cabal of Catholic bishops dancing ritualistically around the Quebec bill (see Figure 6). Members of the Church of England sit idly by. Another print, entitled *Fame's Rewards,* depicts a corrupted churchman reaching for his bishop's mitre and his "living" (his salary) while he stepped on the Bible and a paper labeled "protestant religion" (see Figure 7). Though imperial leaders—including the bishops' bench—believed that they were promoting Britain's best interest, the public expectation that religious leaders would defend the boundaries of protestantism was strong.[23]

23. A. Francis Steuart, ed., *Last Journals of Horace Walpole during the Reign of George III from 1771–1783*, I (London, 1910), 354–357. For more on Walpole and religion, see G. M. Ditchfield, "'That Most Useful Part of All History, a Picture of Human Minds': Horace Walpole's *Memoirs of the Reign of George III," Parliamentary History,* XXI, part 2 (2002), 255–268. Walpole also tied the recently failed effort to repeal the subscription requirements to the Quebec Act. *The Mitred Minuet* appeared in the *London Magazine* in July 1774, XLIII, facing page 312. The accompanying

FIGURE 6 *The Mitred Minuet.* 1868,0808.10061. © The Trustees of the British Museum.

The public anger directed at the bishops' bench about the Quebec Act suggested that many people imagined bishops to have a level of influence over imperial policy that they simply did not possess. Britain's mixed establishment, foundational for the empire's "Constitution in Church and State," created the impression that protestant institutions partnered with government leaders in steering the empire when it came to religious matters. In practice, however, the political issues with which they concerned themselves, such as competitions between Anglicans and dissenters, largely stayed within the confines of the mixed establishment. They appeared, in other words, locked inside the scaffold that they had helped build. Their position was at once protected and precarious. They benefited from the privileges accorded them through their connections with government, and they drew the ire of those who believed they ought to be held to a higher moral standard. In the summer of 1774, both the privilege and the critique were in full view.

---

essay ("The Mitred Minuet: A Vision") described a dream scene in which the dreamer awoke after being "Struck to the very soul at the apostacy *[sic]* of the church" (312). See Mary Dorothy George, ed., *Catalogue of Political and Personal Satires Preserved in the Department of Prints and Drawings in the British Museum,* V ([London], 1935); and Edward W. Pitcher, "Edward Thompson (1738?–86): The Contributions of a Satirist to the 'London Magazine' and the 'Westminster Magazine,'" *Papers of the Bibliographical Society of America,* XCII (1998), 135. Paul Revere reprinted the engraving in the colonies in October 1774, and it is sometimes misattributed to him. For a description of *Fame's Rewards,* which also depicts Sir John Fielding, see *Whimsical Repository,* I (1774), 49–50.

FIGURE 7 *Fame's Rewards.*

After the passage of the coercive measures and the Quebec Act, the main stage of action passed back to the colonies, but before it did so there was one more scene in Britain. During the fall of 1774, Lord North called for, and won, a general election. His political victory in some measure vindicated the support religious leaders had given him. Though, during those elections, some within the dissenting network advocated strongly for a change in course on American affairs, as will be discussed below, North's victory gave him political security as he pursued more aggressive measures against America. Most Britons concurred with the coercive posture toward America and the regularization of administration represented by the Quebec Act. Religious leaders presented few objections to that course of action, and protestant institutions offered none. The criticisms of the administration for its failure to support protestantism in Quebec were portentous, but that was far from evident to imperial leaders in 1774. More clear was the fact that religious leaders in Britain would not alter the direction of the fight rapidly taking shape between Parliament and the colonies.[24]

RELIGION AND AMERICAN PROTESTS

In 1774, British government leaders charted a course, and religious leaders largely fell in line. Leaders of the American rebellion, facing a far different task, hoped they could count on protestant leaders, on religion, to do the same for them. When rumors of the Coercive Acts and the Quebec Act reached America, those Americans who opposed both the legislation and Parliament seized on public religion, especially the public pulpit, as a means to legitimate their case. They had the support of an outraged public, as well. From Newport, Ezra Stiles recorded on June 15, 1774, that events had "spread an amazing Alarm thro' the Colonies" and added, "Boston is in great Distress!" Colonial governments—some long-standing, others emerging in response to royal governors' dissolving assemblies—quickly began selecting delegates to send to a meeting for the early fall, even as Parliament still debated the exact terms of the Quebec Act. The final version of that bill, which was viewed by many in both Britain and North America as part of the Coercive Acts, reached the colonies by late summer. Like their counterparts in Britain, many colonists interpreted the Quebec Act as providing damning evidence of Parliament's abandonment of protestantism. As colonial anger grew, however, American protestant leaders did not remain quiet the way that many British religious leaders had done. Instead, the forces

24. For the 1774 election, see Bunker, *Empire on the Edge*, 318–325; Donoughue, *British Politics*, 177–200. For a close examination of dissenting and radical Anglican participation in the election (and in 1780), see Bradley, *Religion, Revolution, and English Radicalism*, 195–311.

of resistance in America leveraged the support of protestant leaders to their cause. When they did so, American leaders—both those at the head of religious institutions and those in the political resistance movement—twisted a key part of British protestantism to a Revolutionary purpose, first by holding colonial-level fast days and then by employing public religion to validate the new General Congress in Philadelphia.[25]

Britain's eroding control over the colonies can be traced in the colonists' ability to deploy the fast day to their advantage, a tool used only with difficulty during the Stamp Act crisis. The first fast day declared in response to the Coercive Acts occurred, not in New England, but in Virginia, where the House of Burgesses declared a day of "fasting, humiliation, and prayer" for June 1, 1774, the day Boston's port was to be "stopped by an armed force." The proclamation's wording was significant. The members "set apart" the day "devoutly to implore the Divine Interposition for averting the heavy Calamity which threatens the destruction of our civil Rights, and the Evils of civil War." Clearly, the Virginians viewed the threats to Massachusetts as threats to themselves, as well. Both the danger to rights and the specter of civil war were cause to seek God's help. To prevent these awful fates, the Virginians prayed for God to "give us one Heart, and one Mind, firmly to oppose, by all just and proper Means, every injury to American rights." The Virginians asserted the righteousness of their political cause, but they stopped short of claiming the British threatened their "civil and religious liberties," the phrase so often used by dissenters. Instead, they prayed for unity of heart and purpose, a goal within the realm of imperial protestantism. The language of Christianity here did not so much sacralize the coming conflict as it positively unified the people who would fight.[26]

Any care the Virginia legislators had taken to solemnize and validate their cause through religion was lost on the colony's royal governor, John Murray, Lord Dunmore, who viewed the fast day as an act of open defiance. He reported to Lord Dartmouth, his superior in London, that the goal of the day was to "prepare the minds of the people" to follow the House of Burgesses, whose intent, he assumed, was to "inflame the whole Country, and instigate the people to Acts that might rouse the indignation of the Mother Country against them." Dunmore dissolved the legislature to prevent such a turn of events. Richard Gwatkin, the William and Mary professor who had been tapped to deliver the address on June 1, gracefully demurred and reported to Dunmore and to Dartmouth that he had not been asked beforehand if he would perform the duties

25. Dexter, ed., *Literary Diary of Ezra Stiles*, I, 443.

26. Fast-day proclamation printed in the *Virginia Gazette* (Williamsburg), May 26, 1774, [2]; McBride, *Pulpit and Nation*, 15–16.

in question. Gwatkin might have been a logical choice for the House—he had been an outspoken opponent of an Anglican bishop of the colonies—but his liberalism apparently did not extend as far as they wished. He remained loyal to the crown and his church in the ensuing controversies, and he fled back to England with Lord Dunmore.[27]

Meanwhile, in New England, colonists observed fast days in response to the Coercive Acts and used the venerable tradition to validate the decisions they made (on both sides) through the voices of their clergy. Rhode Island observed the occasion on June 30, 1774, and its diverse body of clergy expressed both support for and opposition to the colonists' resistance to British legislation. Stiles's congregants had the choice of attending two services that day, and those in his church were two among many available in a town where nearly all churches were "hearty in the Cause of Liberty." In the morning, awakened protestant Levi Hart preached for Stiles, and in the afternoon Stiles himself preached from the book of Esther: "And in every province, whithersoever the king's commandment and his decree came, there was great mourning among the Jews, and fasting, and weeping, and wailing; and many lay in sackcloth and ashes." The story, about a king's mistaken ruling against a faithful people, likely appealed to what Stiles called "a very crouded Assembly of all Denominations." Hart used the same text from Esther to preach in Samuel Hopkins's church in the afternoon, evidence of its aptness to the moment. Newport's Anglican minister, however, took a different tack, drawing on Matthew 6:16, a verse that condemned hypocritical shows of devotion. In Stiles's words, the Anglican "preached a high Tory Sermon inveig[h]ing (by Allusions) against Boston and N. England as a turbulent ungoverned people." The form of the fast-day sermon provided space for clergymen to support whatever view they wished, but the vast majority of New England's religious leaders supported the colonists' anger toward the British government and used their pulpits to justify resistance.[28]

In Massachusetts, the fast day marking the Coercive Acts was itself a revolutionary act. In the preceding few years, formulaic fast-day proclamations from the governor had been met with annoyance from ministers who had interpreted them as chiding. The day of thanksgiving declared by Lieutenant Governor

27. Dunmore to Dartmouth, May 29, 1774, CO 5/1352, fols. 81–82, June 6, 1774, CO 5/1352, fols. 108–110, both in The National Archives, Kew, U.K. (TNA). See also *Virginia Gazette*, June 2, 1774, [2]; Rhys Isaac, *The Transformation of Virginia, 1740–1790* (Williamsburg, Va., and Chapel Hill, N.C., 1982), 184–205, 243–245; and Carl Bridenbaugh, *Mitre and Sceptre: Transatlantic Faiths, Ideas, Personalities, and Politics, 1689–1775* (New York, 1962), 318–319.

28. Dexter, ed., *Literary Diary of Ezra Stiles*, I, 447–448; Esther 4:3 AV ("in every province"). The text of Matthew 6:16 is: "Moreover when ye fast, be not, as the hypocrites, of a sad countenance: for they disfigure their faces, that they may appear unto men to fast. Verily I say unto you, They have their reward" (AV).

Thomas Hutchinson in 1771 had been either rejected or modified by clergy, who found the proclamation inappropriate. In the spring of 1774, it was hardly surprising that the newly appointed governor, General Thomas Gage, would not declare a fast day in response to the coercive measures. He reported to Dartmouth in London that such an event would "give an opportunity for Sedition to flow from the Pulpits." Boston's clergy thus acted independently. The Associated Pastors of Boston noted that the "late house of assembly of this Province, taking into consideration the gloomy state of our public affairs, recommended a day of fasting and prayer, that the people through the province might in a solemn manner humble themselves before God, and implore his mercy." As colonists took control of the declarations from the royal governors in the months after the Coercive Acts, the public pulpit was an important means for expressing colonial sentiments with the imprimatur of legitimate religion.[29]

The Massachusetts sermons preached by members of the dissenting network on that colony's most prominent fast day, July 14, 1774, focused on issues of justice in government and righteous resistance against oppression. The traditional gravitas of the fast day thus authorized increasingly revolutionary pronouncements. Peter Whitney, the minister at the Church of Christ in Northboro, Massachusetts, told his listeners that civil government had been established by God and that the "British constitution, in its primitive purity, is the most perfect form of civil government, because it derives and secures the greatest *good* to the whole nation," a goal Whitney considered the purpose of "all civil government." Invoking the coalition of good government and religion, he went so far as to state that "Reason will direct, and interest lead, all chearfully to submit to the laws and government" of "good 'princes,'" and he went on to quote both Paul and Peter to prove that "religion most strongly enforces the same duty." But when leaders overstepped their bounds, "the people must be judge of the good or ill conduct of their rulers." Using one of the most frequently cited biblical passages of the Revolutionary era, Galatians 5:1, Whitney quoted Paul to urge his hearers to "stand fast in the liberty wherewith Christ hath made us free, and be not entangled again with the yoke of bondage." Nathan Fiske, preaching on the same day in Brookfield, Massachusetts, addressed

29. Thomas Gage to Dartmouth, May 30, 1774, in Clarence Edwin Carter, ed., *The Correspondence of General Thomas Gage . . .* (New Haven, Conn., 1931), I, 356; Boston Association of Ministers, Minutes, June 20, 1774, BMS 71/1, Andover-Harvard Theological Library, Cambridge, Mass. The fast days in Massachusetts were not uniform. See *Essex Gazette* (Salem, Mass.), June 14–21, July 19–26, 1774, and the note in the Boston Association of Ministers minutes that the Old Brick Church observed its fast day on May 19. See also W[illiam] DeLoss Love, Jr., *The Fast and Thanksgiving Days of New England* (Boston, 1895), 332–335; Akers, *Divine Politician,* 175; James S. Leamon, *The Reverend Jacob Bailey, Maine Loyalist: For God, King, Country, and for Self* (Amherst, Mass., 2012), 105–107.

the same theme, this time working from the text (Isaiah 5:7): "And he looked for judgment, but behold oppression; for righteousness, but beheld a cry." Fiske detailed the abuses of the Parliament specifically. "Our harbour is blocked up by ships of war; armed soldiers, in hostile appearance, are planted in our metropolis; the trade of that once flourishing Town is destroyed; its inhabitants greatly distressed and impoverished; and multitudes in danger of being starved, were it not for the charity of others," he lamented. Like Whitney, Fiske used Paul, with a little improvement, to inspire his listeners: "We have no design to oppose any authority that is constitutionally founded and exercised; but only to *stand fast in the liberty wherewith God,* and our charter, *hath made us free.*" Rebellion against constituted government was not easily justified through the tools of imperial protestantism, but if need be Fiske would legitimate it from his public pulpit.[30]

Liberty was not usually the starting point of the July 14 Massachusetts sermons but, rather, the conclusion. It was a cautious perspective. Preachers remained first and foremost concerned with identifying oppression and finding relief from it in the best and most pious way. "We should seek to God for deliverance from the oppression of man," wrote Timothy Hilliard, because he "is ever disposed to pity and relieve those that are oppressed." Such interposition required the suffering people to repent, of course, even when the people were justified in resistance. "Now can we consider these things and not be convinced that we are under the oppression of man?" Hilliard queried. "Can we help trembling for fear that our precious rights and privileges will at length be all extorted from us, and that we shall be reduced to a state of abject slavery? Can we help trembling for the ark of God, the interest of religion, at such a season as this is?" The colonists' cause was righteous because their oppressors were unjust, not because they, themselves, were necessarily fighting for right. This concern with justifying resistance, a position that stopped well short of any unrestrained championing of liberty, served the moment and the venue well. Colonists who were wary about what was to come could hear, from their religious leaders, comforting words that they had not gone too far. In keeping with the cautious tone of the moment, Massachusetts's preachers largely steered clear of the conspiracy-laden discourse of antipopery. In July, the full details of the Quebec Act were not yet known. Antipopery would come to play a more

30. Peter Whitney, *Mr. Whitney's Discourses on the Public Fast* (Boston, 1774), 10, 15, 17, 19; Nathan Fiske, *The Importance of Righteousness to the Happiness, and the Tendency of Oppression to the Misery of a People* (Boston, 1774), 36, 37. Timothy Hilliard also took oppression as his theme, reminding his hearers that, while they asked for deliverance, they also had to remember to follow, with added strength, the dictates God laid out (Hilliard, *The Duty of a People under the Oppression of Man . . .* [Boston, 1774]). See also Samuel Webster, *The Misery and Duty of an Oppress'd and Enslav'd People . . .* (Boston, 1774); and Byrd, *Sacred Scripture,* 129–136, 170.

significant role on Connecticut's fast day just over a month later, on August 31, 1774. By that time, conjecture about the government's Quebec policy became knowledge of the law, which was signed by the king in London on June 22, and the meeting of the Continental Congress was imminent.[31]

When Connecticut's fast day arrived, Samuel Sherwood, pastor of Christ Church in Fairfield, Connecticut, published one of the most complete versions of why Americans should feel confident that their resistance to Parliament was righteous. Like his dissenting fellows, he outlined a contractual view of government, the rightness of opposing tyranny, and the connection between civil and religious liberties. The Connecticut minister also added a stronger note of alarm to his text than his predecessors, broadening the scope of his critiques. Sherwood, like many of his fellows, worked from a text that dealt with the limits of good government: 2 Samuel 23:3 ("He that ruleth over men must be just, ruling in the fear of God"). Governments had their basis in "voluntary compact," argued Sherwood, and they were bound by the principles of good government. "Public good is the end of government," he argued, and when governments failed to work for that end, they "govern in an arbitrary, tyrannical manner." Tyranny could hardly be justified by religion.[32]

Sherwood's text used the history of British protestantism to argue for revolution against Britain. It was an important step to take as he repurposed ideas that had long served the empire. The British people had been justified when they removed the tyrannical James II, and likewise the Americans were justified in sending their representatives to "meet in general congress." Sherwood recounted the abuses the British had heaped on the Americans, but his next step was even more significant. British tyranny could be headed in only one direction: "We are awfully threatened with being deprived of the liberty of our consciences, the liberty of professing the important truths of the gospel; and

31. Hilliard, *Duty of a People,* 12, 25. While still unaware of the Quebec Act's full details, Whitney, for example, noted that governments must be judged by their people, saying, "It is the highest popery to affirm otherwise"; in his sermon's final pages, he speculated that the cause of the present troubles might be papist influence at court. But these speculations remained separate from his core biblical argument. See Whitney, *Mr. Whitney's Discourses,* 17, 61–64; and Donoughue, *British Politics,* 125.

32. Samuel Sherwood, *A Sermon, Containing Scriptural Instructions to Civil Rulers, and all Free-Born Subjects . . .* (New Haven, Conn., 1774), [11], 12, 19, 21–22. The same pamphlet contains an appendix by Ebenezer Baldwin, "An Appendix, Stating the Heavy Grievances the Colonies Labour under from the Several Late Acts of the British Parliament . . . " (43–81). Baldwin's appendix is continuously numbered within the same pamphlet. Much has been written about the connections between protestantism, Calvinism, and philosophies of government. For the definitive work, see Mark A. Noll, *America's God: From Jonathan Edwards to Abraham Lincoln* (New York, 2002). For the British side, see Bradley, *Religion, Revolution, and English Radicalism,* 142–147. J. C. D. Clark, *The Language of Liberty, 1660–1832: Political Discourse and Social Dynamics in the Anglo-American World* (Cambridge, 1994), takes a transatlantic approach.

attending those sacred ordinances which God has instituted with a view to advance the glory of the Redeemer, and promote the salvation of his people." The specific invocation of religious matters was unmistakable and powerful. The Coercive Acts threatened, not a vague political protestantism that eschewed fine points of theology, but specifically that which was required for salvation. Finally, he rallied his audience with a vision that resonated with the unity that British protestantism had formerly promoted, but he put it to an immediate, anti-imperial political end: "Considering our present critical situation, it would, no doubt, be our wisdom and prudence to make up, unite, and gather into one common interest, all the good *protestants* in this land; notwithstanding lesser differences among them; that we may stand or fall together." He evoked a new protestant unity, this one centered in America only.[33]

Sherwood's use of the phrase "good *protestants* in this land" here is noteworthy. It took religious leaders to differentiate between the good and the bad, and it was the duty of those in government who declared the fast day at which he spoke, and those in the public who would act as part of the body politic, to encourage "good" protestants. His second word, "protestants," calls on a key element of the British political-religious culture that would have been very familiar to the colonists. They had fought on the side of the protestant interest in the Seven Years' War and for the British constitutional system, perfected in the Glorious Revolution. In a striking choice, however, when he laid out the history of that event in his sermon, Sherwood did not discuss James II's Catholicism or William and Mary's protestantism directly. James was merely a "tyrannical oppressive prince," Sherwood explained, who "tended to deprive the subjects of their dear liberties, and their best rights and properties." If it was wrong to resist arbitrary authority (as the colonists were doing), then "we must throw up the present constitution of England and the *Hanover* family" and "return back in our allegiance to the *Stuart* family; and to their popish plan of government." Such was the "doctrine of *passive obedience and non-resistance.*" Sherwood's entire context here invoked the struggle between protestantism and Catholicism that had marked the century before the Revolutionary crisis. It could not be missed. But he reserved the use of the word "protestant" for his discussion of "good *protestants* in this land." Those final words, "in this land," point to protestantism's capacity to unify. Sherwood's invocation of the phrase

33. Taking a page from the subscription issue in England, Sherwood noted, "It must be a pleasure to all lovers of liberty and virtue" that ever more people "wish that no penal laws might be enacted in matters merely religious" and "that no person might be liable to any penalty, or lie under any incapacity, on account of any opinion or practice in religion, which does not at all affect the peace and happiness of human society" (Sherwood, *A Sermon Containing Scriptural Instructions,* 19, 21–22, 28–31, 37, 41).

thus transposed the political unity provided by protestantism from the House of Hanover—and the empire it led—onto the colonists.[34]

Sherwood's sermon was followed in the printed edition by an appendix (of nearly equal length to the sermon), in which fellow minister Ebenezer Baldwin detailed the political context at hand, including a dramatic and extended warning of the dangers of popery introduced by the Quebec Act. Regarding the measure, he asked: "Have we not just grounds to fear that all this will not be the completion of their oppressive plan?" invoking the encroaching tyrannical spirit that characterized popery. He enumerated a series of governmental sins in the Quebec Act. The central problems were the lack of trial by jury and the appointed council (as opposed to an elected legislature) in the new government, yet these were "gilded over with a full establishment of that religion, of which [the Quebecois] are such bigoted professors." The danger to New England came from the fact that "by the same right" the Parliament could treat the older colonies similarly, and the Coercive Acts made it look as if the government intended to do just that. In light of this terrible prospect, Baldwin expressed the central logic of antipopery: "And when our civil rights and privileges shall have thus fallen a sacrifice to tyranny and oppression, our religious liberties cannot long survive: for where hath it ever been known that civil and ecclesiastical tyranny and despotism have not yet gone hand in hand together[?]" At this most essential level, where protestant and papist laws and government collided, true religion needed the care and shepherding of protestant ministers and governments. Baldwin, like Sherwood, made the case for why the colonists had to resist the British, who were now portrayed as papists. This was a time of crisis—a house burning around a soundly sleeping family, in his analogy—and, as a clergyman, Baldwin felt compelled to speak.[35]

The timing and nature of Sherwood's and Baldwin's texts mattered. Fast days, like the one on which Sherwood preached, were essential public rituals connecting government and religious authority. Colonial assemblies certainly knew this, and by giving religious leaders the pulpit in the late summer of 1774, they asserted that their resistance to Parliament was moral and just. New England's clergy, those who most frequently were given such an opportunity, generally responded by supporting American anger at Parliament. Their voices matched the stances of the growing Revolutionary political leadership and also the opinions of a notable portion of the population. From that position, they coherently articulated an increasingly pro-resistance political theology and depicted British rule as akin to tyranny—even, at times, popery. The sermons were an important

34. Ibid., 28–29.
35. Ibid., 71–72.

blend of thoroughly predictable and utterly revolutionary. Clergy, as voices of stability, generally supported the powers that be, and in places where colonists resisting the British had control of the public pulpit, clergy responded with their validation. They worked, in other words, within a traditional structure. Yet it was equally true that, in presenting and publishing these sermons, American clergy—following the lead of the public around them—used a key mechanism of imperial protestantism for an end that did not support imperial unity. In their hands, the public pulpit became a wedge that splintered the empire along the developing political boundary.[36]

The powerful voices of New Englanders like Sherwood and Baldwin seem to be definitive of "American" sentiments in retrospect, but a broader survey of the colonies suggests that the situation was more complex in the summer of 1774. As the resistance to imperial authority grew, religious leaders faced varied challenges. Once again, the nature of the collaboration between religious institutions and local governments proved significant in determining the extent to which religion became a part of the discussions of resistance. In the Middle Colonies, governments did not call fast days, making that tool far less significant than it was in New England. In its absence, religious groups did not coordinate their responses to the public controversy, or the means of expressing them. An effort by Philadelphia's Committee of Correspondence to create a collective religious observance about the Coercive Acts for June 1, 1774, caused controversy, and the city's influential Quakers explicitly stood apart from the observance. The presbyterian Synod of New York and Philadelphia called for a fast day for the third Thursday in June, but without the partnership with government, the day was far less noticeable than parallel events in New England. The synod considered the "dark and threatening aspect of our public affairs both civil and religious as loudly calling for deep humiliation before God," and its leadership, acting as a religious body on its own authority, declared a "solemn day of fasting and prayer" for its members. The synod hoped the day of prayer would "avert those calamities which on account of our manifold provocations we have great reason to fear." Newspaper reports of the fast's observance made the actions of that denomination visible to the public, but however the day was

36. Loyalist historian Peter Oliver famously blamed New England's clergy for inciting rebellion, naming Charles Chauncy, Samuel Cooper, and Jonathan Mayhew (who had died in 1766) (Douglas Adair and John A. Schutz, eds., *Peter Oliver's Origin and Progress of the American Revolution: A Tory View* [San Marino, Calif., 1967], 41–45). John Leacock's faux-biblical *First Book of the American Chronicles,* which began circulating in Boston in 1774, pointed to the role of that city's clergy in the events, though, as literary scholar Carla Mulford has argued, focusing on the role of the clergy also emphasized the interpretation of events that cast the colonists as righteous and the British as persecutors (Mulford, ed., *John Leacock's the First Book of the American Chronicles of the Times, 1774–1775* [Newark, Del., 1987]).

marked, it did not yield waves of printed sermons such as the kind evident in New England. That absence is intriguing. Perhaps mid-Atlantic clergy believed the local audience less receptive to their arguments; perhaps, without the imprimatur of the state-sponsored date, their views were less authoritative; perhaps the mid-Atlantic population was less unified in its support for the resistance. Whatever the mix of reasons, mid-Atlantic clergymen's words from the pulpit did not achieve the same reach as the printed views of their peers to the north.[37]

In the southern colonies, matters were more complicated still. Where Anglicanism was established, clergy were in a particularly difficult position. As their congregants joined the resistance to Parliament, the church's hierarchy in London remained steadfastly opposed. Anglican clergy in the South had to move cautiously, and there is no reason to assume they agreed on what course of action would be best. Yet, though they did not publish many sermons about the importance of resistance in 1774, as New Englanders had done, quite a few southern clergy defied parliamentary authority in more local and personal ways while also keeping their voices out of the transatlantic political fight. This was the first stage in what historian Nancy Rhoden has called a "depoliticization" of the Anglican clergy over the coming years. Across the rebelling colonies, the frequency with which religious leaders took public positions or interpreted the Coercive Acts and American resistance to Parliament in religious terms was as much a function of institutional influences as it was a reflection of their personal political sentiments. The powerful forces resulting from the long-standing partnerships between denominations and governments, from Britain's mixed establishment, continued to matter a great deal for determining how and when clergy spoke out, even as those disparate establishments no longer aligned consistently around the empire.[38]

The political situation worsened in the fall. On September 1, 1774, Massachusetts governor General Gage secretly transferred a significant part of the colony's gunpowder and cannon to Castle William, a fort in Boston's harbor. News spread quickly. Rumor and panic outpaced solid information in what became known as the Powder Alarm. New England's colonists responded with a combination of mass mobilization and crowd action that drove some leading loyalists into permanent exile. The region was on a hair trigger. Ezra Stiles

37. Guy S. Klett, ed., *Minutes of the Presbyterian Church in America, 1706–1788* (Philadelphia, 1976), 536; *Pennsylvania Gazette* (Philadelphia), June 22, 1774; *Connecticut Gazette; and the Universal Intelligencer* (New London), June 24, 1774, [1]; *New York Journal; or, The General Advertiser,* June 30, 1774, [3]; *Essex Gazette* (Salem, Mass.), June 21–28, 1774, 187; Sally Schwartz, *"A Mixed Multitude": The Struggle for Toleration in Colonial Pennsylvania* (New York, 1987), 272–273.

38. Nancy L. Rhoden, *Revolutionary Anglicanism: The Colonial Church of England Clergy during the American Revolution* (New York, 1999), 88–89, 92; McBride, *Pulpit and Nation,* 80–85.

reported from Newport that "the Body of the people in the Towns for 30 Miles round Boston instantly took Arms and crouded into Cambridge." The First Continental, or General, Congress convened in Philadelphia on September 5, 1774, just days after the Powder Alarm. It sat until October 26 of that year. The assembly included many of the Revolutionary movement's leading figures, including George Washington and Patrick Henry of Virginia, cousins John and Samuel Adams from Massachusetts, Roger Sherman of Connecticut, John Jay of New York, and John Dickinson from Pennsylvania. The Congress took several measures, all of which increased its standing as "a full and free representation of these colonies." Unity was both the purpose and the challenge of the Congress, since the colonists were divided regionally, politically, and also by denomination. As leaders of the Continental Congress came together, they, like the Revolutionaries in the various colonies who had declared fast days, used public religion to validate their cause.[39]

Formal prayer functioned for the Congress as fast days had for the colonies in the preceding months, solemnizing events and creating the impression that political leaders were concerned with God's truth when they acted. But the Congress, as an American body, now faced the same challenge that British authorities had faced nearly a century earlier when they wanted to create unity through religion. The colonists were divided into separate establishments with different—often competing or even hostile—denominations. If they shared a faith, it was what they shared as subjects of Britain's protestant empire, a politically constructed protestantism that conjured unity out of division. John Adams described to his wife how the delegates negotiated these divisions. As he told it, Thomas Cushing, Adams's fellow delegate from Massachusetts, called for a prayer at the convening of the body. John Jay and another delegate objected on the grounds that the Congress was "so divided in religious Sentiments." This was always the danger with matters of faith: they were a source of conflict if handled in the wrong way. Samuel Adams, however, deftly avoided this pitfall and invoked, implicitly, protestantism's capacity to unify across denominations. He "arose and said he was no Bigot, and could hear a Prayer from a Gentleman of Piety and Virtue, who was at the same Time a Friend to his Country." In an ecumenism highlighted by the divisions that had just been alluded to, Samuel

39. Dexter, ed., *Literary Diary of Ezra Stiles*, I, 457; "Declaration and Resolves of the First Continental Congress," Oct. 14, 1774, House Document no. 398, in Charles C. Tansill, ed., *Documents Illustrative of the Formation of the Union of the American States* (Washington, D.C., 1927), https://avalon.law.yale.edu/18th_century/resolves.asp. For the Powder Alarm, see David Hackett Fisher, *Paul Revere's Ride* (New York, 1994), 44–48. For the Continental Congress as a body, see Benjamin H. Irvin, *Clothed in Robes of Sovereignty: The Continental Congress and the People out of Doors* (New York, 2011).

suggested a moderate, local Anglican minister sympathetic to the awakening movement: Jacob Duché. The Congress assented.[40]

Duché rose to the challenge, and he enacted a ceremony of public religion that became iconic for those in subsequent generations who have seen the American Revolution as an event in providential history. He arrived at the congressional session "in his Pontificallibus," his Anglican clerical robes, and he first "read several Prayers, in the established Form; and then read the Collect for the seventh day of September, which was the Thirty fifth Psalm" (see Figure 8). This liturgical ritual was likely comforting for those who craved the stability of tradition in the midst of an act of revolution, all the more so because it was led by an Anglican. His presence highlighted the care and precision the Congress was taking and preserved it from the charge that its members were merely destructive. The episode would be striking enough if he had stopped there, but, instead (again in John Adams's retelling), Duché

> unexpected to every Body struck out into an extemporary Prayer, which filled the Bosom of every Man present. I must confess I never heard a better Prayer or one, so well pronounced. Episcopalian as [Duché] is, Dr. [Samuel] Cooper himself never prayed with such fervour, such Ardor, such Earnestness and Pathos, and in Language so elegant and sublime—for America, for the Congress, for The Province of Massachusetts Bay, and especially the Town of Boston.

Adams concluded his reverie on Duché's prayer with an entreaty that Abigail read both Psalm 35 and his own letter to one and all, and he cast the event in providential terms. Duché's impression on Congress was such that he was appointed that body's first chaplain.[41]

Duché's theatrical prayer gave Congress moral authority, but, put into the wider context of religious voices in the 1774 resistance movement, what it rep-

40. John Adams to Abigail Adams, Sept. 16, 1774, in Paul H. Smith, ed., *Letters of Delegates to Congress, 1774–1789,* 26 vols. (Washington, D.C., 1976–2000), I, 74–75. There is some dispute about who made the first motion to have a chaplain. For the present purposes, Samuel Adams's role is more significant. See also Derek H. Davis, *Religion and the Continental Congress, 1774–1789: Contributions to Original Intent* (New York, 2000), 73–75. For more on this episode, see Kevin J. Dellape, *America's First Chaplain: The Life and Times of the Reverend Jacob Duché* (Bethlehem, Pa., 2013), 71–93. Christopher C. Lund places Duché's prayer in a longer-term legal context and emphasizes persistent American anti-Catholicism (Lund, "The Congressional Chaplaincies," *William and Mary Bill of Rights Journal,* XVII [2009], 1171–1214).

41. John Adams to Abigail Adams, Sept. 16, 1774, in Smith, ed., *Letters of Delegates,* I, 74–75. Psalm 35 is a series of pleas for justice and assistance against unjust treatment. In addition to the letter, see Sept. 7, 1774, entry in John Adams diary 22, 4 September–9 November 1774 (electronic edition), *Adams Family Papers: An Electronic Archive,* Massachusetts Historical Society, http://www.masshist.org/digitaladams/archive.

FIGURE 8 *The First Prayer in Congress.* By T. H. Matteson. Engraved on steel by H. S. Sadd. Matteson immortalized Jacob Duché's sermon in the 1840s. It depicts a foundational moment in an American tradition but also a revolutionary moment from the perspective of British protestantism. Courtesy of the Library of Congress Prints and Photographs Division, Washington, D.C.

resented—and what it did not—is also important. In choosing a local, moderate Anglican to lead them in prayer, Congress summoned protestantism's capacity to unify diverse denominations and, indeed, the role of religion generally in uniting a people. But Duché's voice did not represent a unified population, or even the unity of clergy behind Congress, in any meaningful way. American Anglican clergy, in particular, were divided about the Congress's legal and moral standing. Congress's choice to ask for Duché's services and then to name him a chaplain reflected its sense that its authority would be enhanced by continuing the partnership between protestant institutions and government that had characterized British and colonial life. Duché's prayer was part of Congress's effort to establish legitimacy through protestant institutional tradition.

Congress drew on the traditions of British protestantism in other ways, as well, but the almost random way in which it did so suggests that the body was far more concerned with its survival and success than it was with any coherent religious ideology. Consider the documents it produced. The first, the "Declaration of Colonial Rights and Grievances," detailed the steps by which Parliament had undermined the rights of the colonists and justified Congress's meeting so that "their religion, laws, and liberties may not be subverted." The phrase "religion, laws, and liberties" here was neither an accident nor a spontaneous declaration of faith. It came directly from the documents produced by both William of Orange and Parliament in the Glorious Revolution. Its repetition by the Congress reiterated that body's place in a British, protestant lineage and suggested the Congress's commitment to stability and reason that the term brought with it. At the same time, the phrase's generality avoided any specific concerns about religion that might divide the delegates—there was no American protestant system that they could easily define, and they were not ready to take on such difficult questions anyway. Was religion something that bound them to Britain or something that could be used to build a new national cause? They could not decide. A letter from Congress to the "Inhabitants of the Province of Quebec" acknowledged "difference of religion" between the Congress and those in Quebec, but it used the example of Switzerland as reason to hope that protestants and Catholics might work together, suggesting a future polity that embraced more than protestants. At the same time, when writing to the people of Britain, the delegates once again drew on fear of Roman Catholics in Canada and the importance of the "Protestant cause," pleading for help from the colonists' fellow protestants. Representatives of a politically fragile and probably treasonous movement, the delegates invoked religion in whatever way they could to garner support from wherever they could.[42]

Across the summer and fall of 1774, those who led the emerging American resistance called on protestant leaders for support in prayers and at fast days. Where institutional logic and public support made it possible, they found it. The General Congress, seeking to speak for the colonies as a whole, called on

42. "Declaration and Resolves," House Document no. 398, in Tansill, ed., *Documents*, Avalon Project: Documents in Law, History, and Diplomacy, https://avalon.law.yale.edu/18th_century/resolves.asp; "To the Inhabitants of the Province of Quebec," Oct. 26, 1774, in *Journals of the Continental Congress, 1774–1789 . . .*, 34 vols. (Washington, D.C., 1904–1937), I, 105–113 (quotation on 112). See also Pauline Maier, *American Scripture: Making of the Declaration of Independence* (New York, 1997), 51–54; "Prince of Orange's Declaration," Dec. 19, 1688, in *Journal of the House of Commons, X, 1688–1693* (London, 1802), 1–6, *British History Online*, https://www.british-history.ac.uk/commons-jrnl/vol10/pp1-6; "Declaration of Colonial Rights and Grievances," Oct. 1, 1774, in Merrill Jensen, ed., *English Historical Documents*, IX (Oxford, 1955), 805–808; Davis, *Religion and the Continental Congress*, 151–154, 239–246; and "A Letter from the General Congress to the People of Great-Britain," Philadelphia, Sept. 5, 1774, printed in the *London Magazine*, XLIII (1774), appendix, 628–633.

aspects of public religion and the colonies' protestant heritage to justify its actions. The irony, of course, is that those institutional possibilities had been created by the structures of Britain's mixed establishment, which had built imperial unity out of regional diversity. Because many of the ties between protestant institutions and the empire had run through local governments, when those local governments turned firmly against Parliament, as they did in New England, religious leaders followed suit. Where matters were more complicated, the voices of religious leaders become harder to find. But events in New England were indicative of much that was to come. The pillars of the scaffold were being wrenched away from the empire. The tools that rebelling colonists employed with such facility—the public pulpit and public prayer—had long been key ways to connect colony to empire in crucial matters of national import, particularly war. Now, as war approached again, they promoted revolution.

For the Americans, it was a moment of remarkable consistency but also of radical change. Viewed as a moment in distinct and separate British or American histories, the choices of the vast majority of religious leaders matched what they had done before and what they would do after—generally, support the direction set by the leaders in government. But that is only part of the story; in 1774, they were not yet inhabiting separate histories. It was a dramatic departure from the traditions of imperial protestantism for American religious leaders to lend their voices to an intercolonial cause represented by an extralegal body. American Revolutionaries' successful deployment of the tools of public religion bent a key structure of imperial protestantism to a revolutionary end.

NETWORKS PROTESTING

The flexibility and diversity that flourished within Britain's protestant empire had the effect of dividing colonists and Parliament in 1774, when religious leaders in England, Scotland, and the rebelling colonies all generally supported their own governments through their distinctive traditions of establishment. For this reason, there were remarkably few religious protests as the empire descended into war. But what of the planks that bound the scaffolding together, the networks through which protestant leaders had built connections to one another and incorporated the goals and distant reaches of that empire into their sense of religious work? As colonial affairs worsened, in the last stage of the process set off by the Boston Tea Party, voices from within those networks tried to stop the downward spiral. Outspoken dissenters protested British policy, and radical Anglicans in the colonies challenged the legitimacy of the General Congress. Historians have viewed these protests as further polarization of the struggle between Anglicans and dissenters. They were that, but they were also more. They grew out of the connections, based in a sense of shared imperial protestant community, that had once bound the empire together.[43]

Though these protests failed to shift policy in either location, they were, nonetheless, important last gasps of the imperial protestantism that had been nurtured through transatlantic networks. The disparate voices—directly opposed to one another and often lacking the support of many of their dissenting and Anglican fellows—reflected a deep commitment to the ideal of the British Empire as a promoter of protestant liberty, even as they disagreed about the threats facing that ideal. As the crisis increased, so, too, did these protests and their instigators' efforts to reach out across the Atlantic to coreligionists within their separate networks.

English dissenters who saw the loss of colonial rights as a crucial issue corresponded with their fellows in North America and spoke out publicly, even as the London-based institutions of dissent remained quiet. The ensuing discussions were remarkably political. Presbyterian minister Richard Price, for example, was a proponent of relief for the Americans, and he corresponded with Boston divine Charles Chauncy on the subject. The New Englander wrote to Price multiple times, expressing his firm conviction, in providential terms, that the Coercive Acts would be counterproductive because they would sway American public opinion. "The British edict, which, without all doubt, was an intended blow at the liberties of all the American Colonies," he wrote, "will, I believe, under the blessing of providence, be the very thing which will bring salvation to us." No longer would they trust greedy merchants, Chauncy vowed. They would instead count on their own self-sufficiency. "Our dependence, under God," he wrote, "is upon the *landed interest,* upon our Freeholders and Yeomanry." Though he sprinkled his letters with language of the righteousness of his cause, Chauncy articulated a version of the crisis that had earthly origins (he blamed the "British edict"), and he called on earthly political remediation in the form of the shared action of the American people, not the intervention of protestant loyalties or institutions. Another Bostonian, Josiah Quincy, expressed a similar sentiment at a dinner with Theophilus Lindsey, Benjamin Franklin, Joseph Priestley, and Price. "We began and ended with the Americans," Lindsey

43. For English dissenters, see Bonwick, *English Radicals and the American Revolution;* James E. Bradley, *Popular Politics and the American Revolution in England: Petitions, the Crown, and Public Opinion* (Macon, Ga., 1986); and Bradley, *Religion, Revolution, and English Radicalism.* For American Anglicans in opposition to the process of revolution, see Peter W. Walker, "The Church Militant: The American Loyalist Clergy and the Making of the British Counterrevolution, 1701–92" (Ph.D. diss., Columbia University, 2016); Rhoden, *Revolutionary Anglicanism;* and James B. Bell, *A War of Religion: Dissenters, Anglicans, and the American Revolution* (Basingstoke, U.K., 2008).

reported to a friend. Quincy shared the latest news, and the group pored over the latest letters from New England, "all of which concurred to assure us that our brethren on the other side of the Atlantic *will be free*." For British dissenters who sympathized with the Americans, this was a time to speak out. In the fall of 1774, during the snap elections called by Lord North, they published pamphlets and worked hard to alter the course of policy, for their own sakes and for their American counterparts.[44]

English dissenters who championed American rights as part of a vision of the British Empire in 1774 and 1775 represented only a portion of that community, a fact that helps explain the silence of dissenting organizations on the subject. But those who fought passionately against the North administration's policies included well-known writers like Priestley, and they argued for American rights within a British Empire that, when rightly ordered, protected religious and civil liberty. Whereas William III and the first two Georges had been "friendly" to liberty, Priestley maintained in his 1774 *Address to Protestant Dissenters of All Denominations,* Britons now found themselves in a moment of peril. "Be assured," he wrote, that the "peculiar privileges" dissenters enjoyed in Britain's mixed establishment were dependent on civil liberties that had to be defended. Priestley viewed the assault on "our brethren in America" as a harbinger of future attacks on liberties at home. He also believed that the most promising future lay in keeping the empire together, though with a diminished role for Parliament. The strength of the empire "depend[ed] on UNION and on LIBERTY." It is worth noting that these calls for beneficence toward the Americans were not based merely in altruism born of shared protestantism. Priestley hoped to use the ties between English dissenters and their coreligionists to get the former to act in an English political context, to protect all their liberties. But, setting aside the question of whether English dissenters would have been moved if they felt their own liberties to be secure, they believed the relationship of Britons to Americans, and that of the British Empire to the promotion of liberty, were all worth saving. Yet all that shared sentiment had little impact on the course of the Revolution. Though dissenting radicals arguably shifted the margins of the 1774 parliamentary elections, their influence was not sufficient to change the direction of North's American policy.[45]

44. Charles Chauncy to Richard Price, May 30, 1774, in D. O. Thomas and Bernard Peach, eds., *The Correspondence of Richard Price,* I (Durham, N.C., 1983), 169–171, esp. 170. Quincy's visit is described in Price's correspondence, and also by Theophilus Lindsey to W. Turner, Jan. 17, 1775, in H. McLachlan, ed., *Letters of Theophilus Lindsey,* I (Manchester, U.K., 1920), 78–79. See also Bradley, *Religion, Revolution, and English Radicalism,* 190–191.

45. [Joseph Priestley], *An Address to Protestant Dissenters of All Denominations on the Approaching Election of Members of Parliament . . .* (London, 1774), 4, 14–15. Bonwick outlines

Across the Atlantic, a small but vocal group of American Anglicans faced similar challenges to their English dissenting counterparts, and, like their dissenting fellows, they reached out across their network for support. Anglicans corresponded about how to buttress their transatlantic church, often through enhancing its legal position. In New York, Anglicans continued to seek the appointment of a bishop to the colonies. The hierarchy in London was surprisingly responsive, given the political situation. Lord Dartmouth wrote to the New Yorkers in July 1774, just as colonial protests were swelling, to "assure you of my very hearty concurrence with you in your sentiments and wishes on the great and important subject of an American Episcopate." In August, New York's Anglican clergy sought a royal charter for King's College. The endorsing letter from Lieutenant Governor Cadwallader Colden praised the plan "not only on account of Religion, but of good Policy, to prevent the growth of republican Principles, which already too much prevail in the Colonies," reinforcing the common notion that Anglicanism supported the kind of government that royal authorities needed.[46]

As dissenters did in Britain, American Anglicans also entered the political fray and tried to sway their compatriots that their vision of protestant empire would stem the tide of revolution. Also like their dissenting counterparts, the American Anglicans who spoke out represented a radical, minority position, as many Anglicans, particularly in the southern colonies where they dominated, supported the colonists' resistance. But vocal Anglicans fought back against that resistance, conjuring an American populace that was immature, divided, and easily led astray. It needed the guidance of the imperial government. Jonathan Boucher, in his *Letter from a Virginian to a Member of Congress,* described the colonists as "undebauched and innocent, compared with those of the Inhabitants of older Countries," but this just made them more vulnerable. "You will surely beware how you inflame the Minds of such honest deluded Citizens," he warned Congress, or "you will wish, when it will be too late, to calm the Storm you have raised." Thomas Bradbury Chandler, in his voice as the *American Querist,* asked "whether the *American* colonies do not consider themselves as

---

these arguments in a close chronological fashion (*English Radicals and the American Revolution,* 67–80). See also Bradley, *Religion, Revolution, and English Radicalism,* 58–59, 123–124, 148–149, 195–196, 311; and Bonwick, "English Dissenters and the American Revolution," in H. C. Allen and Roger Thompson, eds., *Contrast and Connection: Bicentennial Essays in Anglo-American History* (Athens, Ohio, 1976), 89–91, 95.

46. Bishop of London to Dartmouth, July 14, 1774, Dartmouth Papers, D(W) 1778/II/929; [Dartmouth] to the episcopal clergy of New York and New Jersey, July 14, 1774, ibid., D(W) 1778/II/930; Cadwallader Colden to William Tryon, CO 5/1106, fols. 123–126, TNA; meeting approving draft charter for King's College, CO 5/1106, fols. 59–62, TNA. See also John Vardill to Dartmouth, Sept. 1, 1774, Dartmouth Papers, D(W) 1778/II/955.

composing one distinct political body; and whether this body does not appear at this time to be deeply disordered?" Samuel Seabury's "Westchester Farmer" was more direct: "The American Colonies are unhappily involved in a scene of confusion and discord. The bands of civil society are broken; the authority of government weakened, and in some instances taken away." As these clergymen depicted the crisis, it was not one between the colonies and Britain but within the colonies themselves. The problem was not with tyranny but with unrest and disorder.[47]

The British Empire, in the hands of these Anglican polemicists, had religion on its side. Chandler's *Friendly Address to All Reasonable Americans* was an angry declaration of the rebelling colonists' moral failures. He asserted that British rule had been essentially good, and "the subjects of Great-Britain are the happiest people on earth." But now the colonies were in peril. "The darkness of a rising tempest is beginning to overspread our land," he warned. "It is high time therefore to awaken the thoughtless to a sense of their danger, and to think of providing for our common safety." The fault for this situation lay squarely with the colonists. The "crime of the Bostonians was a compound of the grossest injury and insult," and now some New Englanders had "openly bid defiance to the united authority of the King, Lords and Commons assembled in Parliament" and had "set up in *direct opposition* to their authority, a government of their own." Such actions violated the colonists' responsibilities as Christians. Citing Romans 13, he chided: "For rulers are not a terror to good works, but to the evil. Wilt thou then not be afraid of the power? Do that which is good, and thou shalt have the praise of the same." Imperial rebellion signaled a failure of protestant loyalty by the American laity.[48]

47. [Jonathan Boucher], *A Letter from a Virginian to the Members of the Congress to Be Held at Philadelphia, on the First of September, 1774* ([New York?], 1774), 15–16; [Thomas Bradbury Chandler], *The American Querist; or, Some Questions Proposed Relative to the Present Disputes between Great Britain, and Her American Colonies; by a North-American* ([New York], 1774), 3; [Samuel Seabury and Isaac Wilkins], *Free Thoughts, on the Proceedings of the Continental Congress Held at Philadelphia Sept. 5, 1774: Wherein Their Errors Are Exhibited, Their Reasonings Confuted, and the Fatal Tendency of Their Non-Importation, Non-Exportation, and Non-Consumption Measures, Are Laid Open to the Plainest Understandings . . .* (New York, 1774), 3.

48. [Thomas Bradbury Chandler], *A Friendly Address to All Reasonable Americans, on the Subject of Our Political Confusions: In Which the Necessary Consequences of Violently Opposing the King's Troops, and of a General Non-Importation Are Fairly Stated* ([New York], 1774), 3–4, 15, 23, 29. Chandler set the stage for the *Friendly Address* with the final section of the *Querist,* which quotes directly from 1 Peter 2:13–14 and Romans 13:1–2: *"Submit to every ordinance of man for the Lord's sake;* and require us on pain of *damnation,* to be duly *subject to the higher powers,* and *not to resist* their lawful authority" (*Querist,* 30). In his selection of these two verses, Chandler had a great deal of company. James Byrd finds that they are the first and fifth most cited passages during the Revolutionary era because of their central concern with obedience to civil authority. See Byrd, *Sacred Scripture, Sacred War,* 116–142.

The problem, Chandler argued, was the troublesome dissenting spirit that animated New Englanders. Chandler's anti-dissenting rhetoric functioned much as the language of antipopery did. He railed that the people who had brought on the crisis were "obstinate, hot-headed Zealots, who are at the bottom of all our confusions." Like papists, these irrational souls were unfit to govern and would deprive good citizens of their religious liberties. If the Americans should win against Britain, he suggested that they consider "the character of our future masters." In that dystopia, all would be ruled by the "republican zealots and bigots of New-England; whose tender mercies, when they had power in their hands, have been ever cruel, towards all that presumed to differ from them in matters either of religion or government." Their future targets, according to Chandler, were "the members of the Church of England, the Friends or people called Quakers, the Baptists, those that belong to the German and Dutch Churches, and the moderate and candid part of the Presbyterians themselves." Against this religious tyranny, Chandler juxtaposed the just treatment of the Catholics in Quebec. Although they had been accused of promoting popery, Parliament had, in the Quebec Act, been liberal and benevolent by furthering religious harmony. Chandler's sense that dissenters had caused the present crisis mirrored the belief among dissenters that Anglicans—or papists—were at the heart of the loss of religious and civil liberties.[49]

Radicals on both sides of the Atlantic, working within the visions of empire that had been nurtured by their separate networks, argued the crisis between Parliament and colonists imperiled an empire that had protected and promoted religious liberty. The outrage within both networks resulted from years of shared communications and a deep investment, by both dissenters and Anglicans, in the idea that the British constitution, rightly constructed with protestant institutions at its heart, was the best safeguard for the future. But by the fall of 1774, in the midst of British elections and the American General Congress, their voices were relatively isolated, both geographically and in their own networks. Radical Anglicans in the northern colonies were doubly isolated, from their more cautious and divided southern counterparts and from their northern, largely dissenting, neighbors. Radical dissenters in England faced similar challenges. Though their English dissenting compatriots were sympathetic to the Americans, the institutions of dissent—including the Church of Scotland—did not speak out against the North administration in 1774. American dissenters, meanwhile, found more productive ways to fight for their liberties by allying with the apparatus of a newly forming American state.

49. [Chandler], *Friendly Address,* 20–21, 47, 49.

It is tempting to imagine what might have happened if the radical voices within the Anglican and dissenting networks, each working to halt the political rupture, had found a common strategy or a common language based in shared protestantism that could have smoothed over the political crisis. But such a course of events was never feasible. Submission to a shared central government had created Britain's imperial protestantism, and that submission was exactly what the rebelling colonists refused to give. In that fight, political differences were not defined by denomination, and therefore religious differences received little attention from rival governments. In December 1774, just after the seating of the new Parliament, Lord Dartmouth reached out through intermediaries to Benjamin Franklin, seeking terms for reconciliation. None of the issues Franklin raised touched on religion. It had not been the basis for the political rupture, and it could not bring Parliament and colonies back together. Ultimately, the failure of the networks' most radical voices exposed the precariousness of connections built through imperial protestantism when the political bonds of empire could no longer be assumed.[50]

Over two years, 1773 and 1774, the political crisis that had begun to split the British Empire had twisted and bent the scaffolding of imperial protestantism. Most religious leaders had responded to the course of events in ways that reflected their positions within its pillars, its mixed establishment. As a result of that tendency, Americans from all three networks—dissenters, Anglicans, and awakened protestants—and from a variety of denominations could unify behind an emerging American national religion, whereas most religious institutions in Britain acquiesced to the North administration's harsh policies. Noting that alignment, and its relationship to local religious establishments, is not a matter of cynicism. It is, rather, a recognition of the strength of the ties to local governments that had been built through the preceding decades. Equally important, however, are the transformations brought by those continued loyalties. In Britain, the willingness of the church hierarchy to support the Quebec Act raised the question of whether the empire's leaders were insufficiently protestant. In the rebelling colonies, the same structures that had supported empire were now put to a revolutionary cause. Despite the calls of a few radicals to resist the empire's widening rift, the capacity of the British Empire to unify protestant leaders across great distances was ebbing quickly as imperial authorities lost control.

50. See also O'Shaughnessy, *Men Who Lost America,* 54–55; Barger, *Lord Dartmouth and the American Revolution,* 133–136; and Albert Henry Smyth, ed., *The Writings of Benjamin Franklin,* 10 vols. (New York, 1905–1907), VI, 327–330. A parallel outreach by Lord Howe to Franklin at this time followed similar lines and produced similar results. See "Franklin's Proposals to Lord Howe for Resolving the Crisis," Dec. 28–31, 1774, *Franklin Papers Online.*

The result of these changes was that the scaffolding of imperial protestantism no longer encircled the empire in a meaningful way by early 1775—even though most of its structures and habits still stood, and most of those who guided its institutions continued to behave as they always had. The changes were subtle but important. The collective submission to imperial authorities that had linked together disparate places into a single, mixed establishment could no longer be relied upon. Neither could the commitment to protestantism on the part of either the imperial government or the emerging American government be assumed, as both sides recruited (for very different reasons) the support of Canadian Catholics. Finally, without the centripetal force of the empire, what place would there be for the relationships, the networks, built under its care? The failures of radical dissenters and Anglicans raised precisely this question. The scaffolding of imperial protestantism had not been torn down, but its component parts were bent, repurposed, and ragged—no longer welded together.

In the tense days before fighting broke out in Lexington and Concord, Ezra Stiles wrote several of his dissenting counterparts in Britain, confessing that he had cast his lot in with the Americans. One letter, to dissenting pamphleteer Samuel Wilton, included the declaration: "As to religious Liberty, you yourself have described my sentiments most exactly. I am a Lover of all good men of all Denominations, but will be brot under the Power of none; I inherit from my Ancestors who came out of England among the first Accessions of the last Century, an ardent inextinguishable Love of *Liberty civil and Religious*." He added, "An ultimate [annihilation] of *religious* Liberty on the English Territories in America is the evident Tendency, if not primary Design of the Quebec Bill. Who could have thot that a [Protestant Parliament] would have armed Papists [against] Protestants?" With others, Stiles used even stronger language. To Philip Furneaux, he wrote that he felt he had been forced to turn his back on his English friends: "If deserted by our ~~Friends~~ Brethren in G. Britain, and abandoned by the World, we confidently trust in our God that he will deliver us." Stiles expressed a new religious geography: "Our fathers fled hither for Religion and Liberty—if extracted from hence, there is no new World to flee to. God has located us here, and by this Location has commanded us to make a stand, and see the Salvation of the Ld. The Event is with the Lord of Hosts." If his participation in transatlantic protestantism was to continue, it had to be on different terms. The events of the following months, the outbreak of military conflict in New England, would ensure that would come to pass.[51]

51. Stiles to Samuel Wilton, Apr. 13, 1775, Stiles to Philip Furneaux, Apr. 12, 1775, both in Ezra Stiles Papers, Beinecke Rare Book and Manuscript Library, Yale University, New Haven, Conn.

4 National Wars

Public Religion in the First Years of the Revolution

The crisis of 1774 had damaged the scaffolding of imperial protestantism, yet the strains caused by disagreements over taxes, or even the Quebec Act, did not immediately create two separate religious nations ready to wage war against each another. That process took time, and it took the efforts of government leaders in both nations who understood the value of public religion, and the public pulpit in particular, for shaping a national cause. That both sides used the same tools to define the war's purpose was a reminder of the decades during which Britain and the United States had been part of a shared protestant system. At the same time, the very different ways that British and American leaders employed public religion point to the starkly divergent challenges they faced in the war's first months.

In 1775, there was no scaffolding of American national religion because there was no nation. When American leaders employed public religion, they conjured a collaboration between themselves and protestant leaders in an effort to legitimate the Revolution and the nation it founded. They were successful. Willing American clergy—who sometimes supported public religion for its own sake and sometimes supported the American resistance out of conviction—participated in fast days, government prayers, and militia musters. They stayed within the boundaries of the political moment, holding out room for reconciliation in 1775 and then finally embracing independence in 1776. But, to borrow historian John Murrin's famous phrase, this new national religion was "a roof without walls." It rhetorically united a nation without any of the legal and institutional structures that had characterized British imperial protestantism, a fact that became clear when members of Congress crafted the new nation's first government, the Articles of Confederation, in 1776.[1]

1. John M. Murrin, "A Roof without Walls: The Dilemma of American National Identity," in Richard R. Beeman, Stephen Botein, and Edward C. Carter II, eds., *Beyond Confederation: Origins of the Constitution and American National Identity* (Williamsburg, Va., and Chapel Hill,

Tracing the use of public religion on the British side of the Atlantic tells a very different story. There, where the structures and habits of imperial protestantism were largely intact, if increasingly disconnected from their former American partners, the question was not whether the government could command public religion but, rather, when. In the war's first months, the government took no religious notice of the war, creating a vacuum in which religious leaders struggled to cast the conflict in the context of British protestantism. Their debates played out in the press. Though historians have long noted the partisan character of these discussions, more important for tracing the shifts in imperial protestantism are the difficulties British religious leaders had in framing the war's relationship to a protestant heritage they shared with colonists. But British protestant leaders still very much worked within a system that linked

N.C., 1987), 333–348. The point at which a new American religious nation came into being has often been subsumed into other discussions. Those who argue for the importance of religion in causing the American Revolution, for example, frequently place it long before 1775. Carl Bridenbaugh identified in the dissenting tradition "the essential ingredient of the nascent American sense of nationality" (Bridenbaugh, *Mitre and Sceptre: Transatlantic Faiths, Ideas, Personalities, and Politics, 1689–1775* [New York, 1962], xiv). The literature on American religious nationalism during the Revolution is still heavily influenced by the work of Nathan O. Hatch, *The Sacred Cause of Liberty: Republican Thought and the Millennium in Revolutionary New England* (New Haven, Conn., 1977); and Ruth H. Bloch, *Visionary Republic: Millennial Themes in American Thought, 1756–1800* (Cambridge, 1985). By treating the second half of the eighteenth century in an American intellectual context, each of these works links traditions of British imperial protestantism to the Revolutionary cause and eventually to American religion but does not emphasize, as the present project does, the chronological shifts within the period of the war. Bloch argues, more generally, that millennialism "can illuminate how many Americans understood the ultimate meaning of the revolutionary crisis and the birth of the American nation" (xiii). Also influential is Harry S. Stout, *The New England Soul: Preaching and Religious Culture in Colonial New England* (New York, 1986), esp. 282–311, which treats New England preaching as nationally normative and argues for May 1775 as the pivotal moment—an argument that works for New England but not nationally. James P. Byrd's careful study of the Bible in Revolutionary-era sermons notes the importance of mid-1776 as an inflection point in biblical references (Byrd, *Sacred Scripture, Sacred War: The Bible and the American Revolution* [New York, 2013], 46–47). Benjamin H. Irvin, *Clothed in Robes of Sovereignty: The Continental Congress and the People out of Doors* (New York, 2011), weaves religious concerns into the concerns of Congress about self-definition. Nicholas Guyatt, *Providence and the Invention of the United States, 1607–1876* (Cambridge, 2007), argues that British and American traditions of providentialism had diverged in the period before the war, and he notes the importance of fast days to articulating the new American vision, an interpretation with which the present project largely concurs. Spencer W. McBride, *Pulpit and Nation: Clergymen and the Politics of Revolutionary America* (Charlottesville, Va., 2016), 11–37, also frames discussion of the first war year around fast days. Works that look at American religious nationalism as it formed in the early Republic include Benjamin E. Park, *American Nationalisms: Imagining Union in the Age of Revolutions, 1783–1833* (Cambridge, 2018); and Sam Haselby, *The Origins of American Religious Nationalism* (New York, 2015). Though they posit different dynamics, both share the present study's stance that a national American religious identity, encompassing both clergy and a substantial number of Americans, did not exist in any meaningful way until after the Revolutionary era. The literature on American nationalism more broadly is enormous. David Waldstreicher, *In the Midst of Perpetual Fetes: The Making of American Nationalism, 1776–1820* (Williamsburg, Va., and Chapel Hill, N.C., 1997), is a good place to start.

them to the empire, and when the king declared the first national fast for the war in December 1776, it became quite clear that imperial leaders still commanded public religion within the realm.[2]

This structural analysis of public religion pays as much attention to when those in government deployed the public pulpit as it pays to what was said from it. It also purposefully avoids the question of how religious rhetoric inspired those who consumed it, choosing not to assume that eighteenth-century Americans and Britons acted primarily based on what they heard from religious leaders, as compared with the myriad other influences on their actions. And, indeed, knowing whether they did is not necessary for tracing the connections between religious and governmental institutions. From the perspective of imperial protestantism's transformation, the importance of public religion lies, not in its persuasiveness, but in its capacity to connect the leaders of culturally dominant protestant institutions to the state—a crucial task at a time of war, revolution, and state building.[3]

2. The religious historiography of the American Revolution in Britain is naturally not framed around national origins but, rather, situates controversies over the American crisis within the context of national political leanings. Henry P. Ippel has argued for the importance of the public pulpit in debates on the subject. See Ippel, "Blow the Trumpet, Sanctify the Fast," *Huntington Library Quarterly,* XLIV (1980), 43–60; and Ippel, "British Sermons and the American Revolution," *Journal of Religious History,* XII (1982), 191–205. Robert Hole, *Pulpits, Politics, and Public Order in England, 1760–1832* (Cambridge, 1989), 44–50, treats the war as one of a series of religio-political controversies. Stephen Conway, *The British Isles and the War of American Independence* (Oxford, 2000), 139–144, summarizes the divisions within British public opinion based on religion, most of which happened in the first part of the war. The work of James E. Bradley has been particularly important. See his *Popular Politics and the American Revolution in England: Petitions, the Crown, and Public Opinion* (Macon, Ga., 1986); Bradley, *Religion, Revolution, and English Radicalism: Nonconformity in Eighteenth-Century Politics and Society* (Cambridge, 1990); and Bradley, "The Anglican Pulpit, the Social Order, and the Resurgence of Toryism during the American Revolution," *Albion,* XXI (1989), 361–388. See also Nigel Aston, "Archbishop Markham and Political Preaching in Wartime England, 1776–77," in Robert D. Cornwall and William Gibson, eds., *Religion, Politics, and Dissent, 1660–1832: Essays in Honour of James E. Bradley* (Farnham, U.K., 2010), 185–217.

3. Eighteenth-century public preaching has been studied in a variety of contexts. Pasi Ihalainen, *Protestant Nations Redefined: Changing Perceptions of National Identity in the Rhetoric of the English, Dutch, and Swedish Public Churches, 1685–1772* (Leiden, 2005), studies the evolution of "state sermons" as a "ceremony" that expresses "concepts of the nation" and "connects the identity of an individual to the collective identity of the nation" (25). Hole, *Pulpits, Politics, and Public Order in England,* uses the religious discourse, including the public pulpit, as a way to access broad political thought. For public preaching within the wider subject of preaching generally, see Jennifer Farooq, *Preaching in Eighteenth-Century London* (Woodbridge, U.K., 2013), esp. 255–256, 259–260. Public sermons form an important basis for Stout, *New England Soul,* in his analysis of New England's path through the Revolution, and he argues, generally, that religious leaders were particularly important (see esp. 281–311). Gordon S. Wood expressed a not-infrequent assumption in 1997 when he wrote, "Despite the growth of Enlightenment among elites in the eighteenth-century America, Protestantism in one form or another still remained the principal means by which most common people ordered and explained the world and made it meaningful." Such assumptions allow the privileging of the voices of institutional protestant leaders without contextualizing what their actual influence might have been. It is the present author's contention

LEGITIMATING REBELLION

Protestants around the British Empire had long been accustomed to public religion as an aspect of war. Military sermons, fast days proclaimed to unify and focus the attention of the public, days of thanksgiving to celebrate divine assistance in victories—these were traditions of imperial protestantism that colonists knew well. Why would the Revolutionary War be any different? On the one hand, it was not. Colonists preserved those traditions of public religion inherited from imperial protestantism as they went to war against the British, a process made easier by the fact that, at the provincial level, Revolutionary governments usually supplanted royal ones without immediately rejecting the voices of religious leaders within their borders. But that conservatism should not mask the essential function of public religion for those new governments. Reenacting the traditions of imperial protestantism's public religion created moments when Revolutionary governments invited the leaders of protestant institutions to bless their revolution, lending the authority of institutional protestantism to governments that British imperial leaders most definitely did not approve of. Protestant tradition thus sanctified revolution. And yet, we should also remember that political leaders drove this process. The spokesmen of American public religion followed, rather than led, the charge toward an independent nation.[4]

Massachusetts's religious leaders found it easy to transpose the traditions of imperial protestantism to the American cause after fighting broke out in the towns of Lexington and Concord on April 19, 1775. In that province, where most colonists were united in resistance to Parliament and where the colony's religious establishment—always a local matter under the terms of the imperial establishment—was untouched by the formation of the Revolutionary government, it made little practical difference that the established congregationalist clergy advocated for a Massachusetts that resisted Britain rather than a Massachusetts that was subsumed in the British Empire. That transition had already started before the April battles. William Emerson, a congregationalist minister in Concord, supported the Boston resistance in the early 1770s, and in January 1775, four months before the war's opening salvos, he was already preaching

---

that we must measure the influence of such preaching in comparison to other influences on action. See Wood, "Religion and the American Revolution," in Harry S. Stout and D. G. Hart, eds., *New Directions in American Religious History* (New York, 1997), 173–205, esp. 175. For a more recent iteration of this argument, see T. H. Breen, *American Insurgents, American Patriots: The Revolution of the People* (New York, 2010), esp. 241–261.

4. For martial preaching, see Byrd, *Sacred Scripture, Sacred War,* 20–27. For other aspects of public religion, see Chapter 1. For public preaching more generally, see note 3, above.

before militia gatherings called for by the Provincial Congress, the body seeking to control that colony after the regular colonial assembly had been dissolved by Governor Thomas Gage in October 1774. In March 1775, at a militia review in Concord, Emerson reminded listeners, without any innovation in colonial traditions, that God fought with the righteous and therefore they need not fear daunting odds and that those who had "acted up to their Character as Christians" would have "Courage and Resolution in the Day of Battle." The "conscientious Soldier" would also make sure he had an upright and moral character, avoiding those "Blots and Blemishes" that might tarnish a "Man who sincerely aims at serving God and his Country in the military Character." A moral soldier would be a credit to his cause, and God would fight on his side. The assembled men certainly knew they prepared to oppose militarily an empire they had been a part of, but the message they heard and the voice from which they heard it were comfortingly familiar parts of imperial protestantism.[5]

Yet the remnants of imperial frameworks could get New Englanders only so far in a war against Britain, the polity at the heart of imperial protestantism. This conflict demanded new terms to describe who fought whom. As Emerson detailed the ways that Massachusetts hoped its fighting men would acquit themselves, his focus on individual behavior neatly sidestepped the complicated fact that the country they now fought against was the same they had fought for in decades of imperial warfare. Using the authority of the pulpit and the power of scriptural argument, Emerson rhetorically constituted a "Country" that would be useful to the fight at hand. Following in the long-standing puritan tradition, he argued that New England was his country, and he insisted that his country's founders, the "Fathers" and "provident Parents" of his assembled listeners, had "carefully guarded against any implied Acknowledgement of the Power of the British Parliament." Ever virtuous, the New Englanders were "cruelly charged with Rebellion and Sedition; when perhaps there never was any Part of the British Dominions since Civil Government was invented, that ever less deserved so reproachful a Character." Emerson employed the word "our" to describe the people under attack. There was "a Standing Army" in "our Country Towns," but he was "satisfied" with "our Military Preparation here for our own Defense."

5. Amelia Forbes Emerson, ed., *Diaries and Letters of William Emerson, 1743–1776, Minister of the Church in Concord, Chaplain in the Revolutionary Army* (n.p., 1972), 53, 57, 59–60, 62, 63; Robert Middlekauff, *The Glorious Cause: The American Revolution, 1763–1789* (New York, 1982), 252–253; Alan Taylor, *American Revolutions: A Continental History, 1750–1804* (New York, 2016), 121–123; Byrd, *Sacred Scripture, Sacred War,* 20–27; Stout, *New England Soul,* 289–291; David Hackett Fischer, *Paul Revere's Ride* (New York, 1994), 151–155, 158. For the role of chaplains in the Revolutionary War, see McBride, *Pulpit and Nation,* 38–67; and Byrd, *Sacred Scripture, Sacred War,* 41–44.

He asserted an emotional and familial tie to New England that would easily resonate with his audience. But it also created a problem. New England was not alone in rebelling against Britain. It needed partners from other colonies, many of which had no positive emotional connection to a puritan heritage.[6]

The vagueness apparent in Emerson's use of "Country" reflected the political reality that new governments were being created under the cover of traditional rituals of public religion. This was true at both the provincial and national levels. Provincial governments had the easier task, of course, because they inherited religious establishments and traditions. Congregationalist clergy, members of Massachusetts's established church, had prayed for its government in the past and continued to do so. The new Massachusetts Provincial Congress drew on that habit when it named chaplains for itself and held regular prayers, a move that gave added legitimacy to a government that was certainly, in 1775, extralegal. The Massachusetts body had already asked Nathaniel Appleton and William Emerson to become its chaplains in late 1774, when it met in Cambridge and Concord, respectively. Emerson reprised the role in March 1775. William Gordon also took a turn in the Congress's pulpit, and Samuel Cooper received an invitation that he turned down. That the Provincial Congress preferred rotating through preachers in proximity to its meeting places is noteworthy, as it suggests that such official duties were the proper role of every clergyman rather than a post assigned according to the representatives' partisan positions. The new government, and its New England neighbors, supplemented the use of chaplains by keeping other traditional rituals of public religion, including election-day sermons and regular fast and thanksgiving days. As protestant ministers participated in these events, they gave their institutional credibility to the Revolutionary governments.[7]

Protestant leaders did not always support these governments out of sheer enthusiasm for the Revolutionary cause. Sometimes commitment to the importance of public religion for its own sake pushed religious leaders to participate in the rituals created by Revolutionary governments. This was evident in

6. Emerson, ed., *Diaries,* 64–66. See also Christopher Grasso, *A Speaking Aristocracy: Transforming Public Discourse in Eighteenth-Century Connecticut* (Williamsburg, Va., and Chapel Hill, N.C., 1999), 72.

7. Emerson, ed., *Diaries,* 58; *The Journals of Each Provincial Congress of Massachusetts in 1774 and 1775, and of the Committee of Safety . . .* (Boston, 1838), Oct. 11, 12, 17, 1774, Mar. 22, 23, May 3, 4, 1775, 16–17, 22, 109, 184–189. For Massachusetts's election-day sermon in 1775, see Stout, *New England Soul,* 293–294. For this process in Virginia, see John A. Ragosta, *Wellspring of Liberty: How Virginia's Religious Dissenters Helped Win the American Revolution and Secured Religious Liberty* (New York, 2010), 89–106. For a list of New England days of fasting and thanksgiving during the period, see W[illiam] DeLoss Love, Jr., *The Fast and Thanksgiving Days of New England* (Boston, 1895), 502–503.

New York, where the new government also deployed public religion to unite its factions and legitimate its efforts. The province possessed a vocal Anglican community as well as a diverse range of other denominations. Patriot leaders in its newly formed Provincial Congress (which operated parallel to the not-yet-defunct royal government) sought the imprimatur of public religion to prove its inclusiveness. One of its first actions was "to apply to all the ministers in this city, who can pray in English, and to request them to make such an arrangement among themselves as will enable them alternately to open the Congress every morning with prayer." The move was not uncontroversial, though it passed. Nearly twenty of Congress's delegates objected to the plan. That all English-speaking ministers were included suggested the kind of pan-protestant approach to the boundaries of religious community that imperial authorities had embraced. This idea is further reinforced by the participation of outspoken loyalist Samuel Auchmuty, whose communication with British troops had been the subject of public controversy, so that few could have missed his pro-British sympathies. On May 25, 1775, Auchmuty and the presbyterian John Rodgers "delivered to the President an arrangement of the clergy" to take up the duty of leading prayers in the body. They included, in addition to themselves, the awakened baptist John Gano, a range of Anglican clergy, and the presbyterian Joseph Treat. The group also included Archibald Laidlie, the first English-speaking minister of New York's Dutch Reformed Church. The list replicated the boundaries around legitimate protestantism that had been enforced by Britain's imperial establishment. Auchmuty led the prayer before the Provincial Congress on May 26, the first day on which the regular ritual was performed. The scene, noted only in passing in the Congress's *Journal,* highlights the symbolic and political nature of the public pulpit. The loyalist Auchmuty did not pass up the opportunity provided by New York's Revolutionary congress, though he certainly did not embrace its aims. Perhaps he felt he could sway the rebels from his authoritative vantage point; perhaps he felt fulfilling his public duties as a member of the clergy was too important to turn down, even though he legitimized the Congress in the process.[8]

8. *Journals of the Provincial Congress, Provincial Convention, Committee of Safety and Council of Safety of the State of New-York, 1775–1776–1777,* I (Albany, N.Y., 1842), May 23, 25, 26, 1775, 9–11, 13; Randall Balmer, *A Perfect Babel of Confusion: Dutch Religion and English Culture in the Middle Colonies* (New York, 1989), 143; Michael Kammen, *Colonial New York: A History* (New York, 1975), 366–367. For the Auchmuty controversy, see "Extract of a Letter from Philadelphia, Dated May 25, 1775," *New-York Journal; or, the General Advertiser,* June 1, 1775, [3]; "Dr. Auchmuty's Letter to Capt. Montresor, Chief Engineer at Boston. New-York, April 19, 1775," *New-England Chronicle: or, the Essex Gazette* (Cambridge, Mass.), May 12–18, 1775, [3]; "The Following Remarks Were Intended to Have Been Inserted Directly after Mr. Auchmuty's Vile Letter . . . ," ibid., May 18–25, 1775, [2]; "Dr. Auchmuty's Letter to Capt. Montresor, Chief Engineer, at Boston. New-York,

South Carolina's new provincial government also leaned on religious leaders as a way to shore up its legitimacy. Dominated by lowcountry planters, it badly needed the support of those in the backcountry, many of whom were either presbyterians or baptists. The Provincial Congress sent three emissaries to the region, including William Henry Drayton, a leader of the Revolutionary movement in the colony, and two clergymen, awakened presbyterian William Tennent and baptist Oliver Hart. Tennent had been active and vocal in the Revolutionary movement, and he was also a delegate to the Provincial Congress, so he was a logical choice. He and Drayton set out together, and he recorded meetings in which he preached a sermon and then "harangued" his hearers about the Continental cause, a direct blending of religious and political authority. In one place, "after . . . making an apology for the necessity of treating on the subject of my mission on the Lord's day, [he] harangued at large." Tennent was not universally successful—he recorded one group refusing to sign a pledge to the American side on the advice of "two gainsaying Baptist preachers"—but the strategy on the part of South Carolina's Revolutionary organization to depend on protestant leaders highlighted that such men could bestow a certain type of legitimacy on the cause of rebellion that those in government could not assert for themselves.[9]

Unlike the states, the new national government, the Continental Congress, had no long-standing relationship to religious leaders or habits of American national public religion to draw on. There were no legal or institutional connections between the Congress and any ecclesiastical body. Even more worrisome, there were reasons to believe that religion would be more divisive than uniting. Without the guiding force of the imperial establishment creating rough parity among the dominant protestant denominations, it was not clear which protestant voices ought to speak for the new nation. The competitions between Anglicans and dissenters, kept in check by imperial protestantism, might become a source of division. The balance between establishment and

---

April 19, 1775," *Norwich Packet and the Connecticut, Massachusetts, New-Hampshire & Rhode-Island Weekly Advertiser*, May 11–18, 1775, [2]; "Dr. Auchmuty's Letter to Capt. Montresor, Chief Engineer, at Boston. New-York, April 19, 1775," *Newport Mercury* (R.I.), May 22, 1775, [2–3]; *Pennsylvania Journal and Weekly Advertiser* (Philadelphia), May 31, 1775; *Dr. Auchmuty's Letter to Capt. Montresor, Chief Engineer, at Boston* ([Boston], 1775); and C. J., *A Letter to the Rev. Dr. Auchmuty* ([New York?], 1775).

9. "A Fragment of a Journal Kept by Rev. William Tennent . . . ," Aug. 13, 20, 1775, in R[obert] W. Gibbes, ed., *Documentary History of the American Revolution: Consisting of Letters and Papers Relating to the Contest for Liberty, Chiefly in South Carolina, from Originals in the Possession of the Editor, and Other Sources*, I, *1764–1776* (New York, 1855), 225–239, esp. 228, 229; McBride, *Pulpit and Nation*, 37–38; Newton B. Jones, ed., "Writings of the Reverend William Tennent, 1740–1777," *South Carolina Historical Magazine*, LXI (1960), 129–145.

toleration was also a potential problem, one the first General Congress in 1774 had avoided addressing. In that year, Massachusetts's baptists had attempted to petition the Congress for redress of what they viewed as unfair tax policies within the colony. The petition was shunted into the shadows and never heard before the whole Congress, partly to protect the reputation of the Massachusetts contingent—which insisted anyway that its establishment was "a very slender one"—and also to avoid a potential quagmire. Afterward, there had been rumors that the baptists were insufficiently committed to the American cause, even though their deference to the nascent American government might have been interpreted as an act of patriotism. With such events a recent memory, and with the challenges of war barreling down on them, the Continental Congress needed public religion to legitimate it and unify people behind it. Delegates to this new legislative body knew they had to move carefully.[10]

Despite the dangers it posed to national unity, the power of public religion was too great for the Continental Congress to ignore. Convening just weeks after the battles at Lexington and Concord, Congress quickly attended to its own schedule for prayer and moved for a resolution for a national fast day. The year before, the first General Congress had selected Philadelphia Anglican Jacob Duché to preach because he was a moderate voice, and the Second Congress also requested his services. He opened the second day of sessions, on May 11, 1775, with prayer. A few weeks later, on June 7, Congress resolved that July 20 would "be observed throughout the twelve United Colonies, as a day of humiliation, fasting and prayer." (Georgia had not yet joined.) The date was not an accident; it was selected to coincide with the date Parliament had chosen for enforcing prohibitions on some aspects of American trade. Congress thus not only sought to communicate its own piety and conjure unity in the new nation but also to demonstrate its specific distaste for Parliament's perceived cruelty. From its first days, the Congress would create connections to institutional protestantism as a means of asserting its moral legitimacy.[11]

This first fast day presented special challenges because the political goals of the Congress were not clear. Though Congress was rapidly organizing the resistance at a level that would eventually become national, its delegates were not ready to declare independence, and reconciliation to Britain was very much

10. Derek H. Davis, *Religion and the Continental Congress, 1774–1789: Contributions to Original Intent* (New York, 2000), 126–127; William G. McLoughlin, *New England Dissent, 1630–1833: The Baptists and the Separation of Church and State*, I (Cambridge, Mass., 1971), 556–568.

11. *Journals of the Continental Congress, 1774–1789 . . .*, 34 vols. (Washington, D.C., 1904–1937), II, 12–13, 81. Congress paid close attention to many symbolic issues as it worked to legitimate itself. See Irvin, *Clothed in Robes of Sovereignty*, 109–117. For issues of religion more directly, see McBride, *Pulpit and Nation*, 53–63; and Davis, *Religion and the Continental Congress*, 57–72.

on the table. Did Congress ask clergy to preach on behalf of a new nation? A temporary agent of resistance? The national fast day required a text laying out its logic, and the delegates struck a cautious tone, balancing between outrage and deference. The proclamation was written by New Englanders John Adams and Robert Treat Paine as well as North Carolinian William Hooper. (It was therefore regionally diverse, though all three men had attended congregationalist Harvard.) The text they wrote professed the Congress's "indispensible duty devoutly to acknowledge [the] superintending providence" of "the great Governor of the World," who "by his supreme and universal Providence . . . frequently influences the minds of men to serve the wise and gracious purposes of his providential government." The Congress "earnestly recommend[ed] . . . a day of public humiliation, fasting and prayer" when colonists might confess their sins, "bless our rightful sovereign, King George," and "inspire him with wisdom to discern and pursue the true interest of all his subjects, that a speedy end may be put to the civil discord between Great Britain and the American colonies, without farther effusion of blood." When this happened, they prayed, peace and prosperity would return, and "virtue and true religion may revive and flourish throughout our land." The proclamation, which was printed as a broadside and also appeared in newspapers, asserted the Congress's capacity to deploy national-level rhetoric of public religion but stopped short of saying that Congress led an independent nation.[12]

The careful tone set by the fast-day proclamation received a boost even before the day itself arrived, when Anglican William Smith delivered a sermon to a militia body in Philadelphia. It was the most influential sermon of the summer, distributed widely in America, Britain, and even in Europe. In it, Smith sought to strengthen the rebels' resolve, but he also held out hope for reconciliation. Long a public figure, Smith was the provost of the College of Philadelphia, and he preached "on the Present Situation of American Affairs" before the city's third battalion. His text was from Joshua 22:22: *"If it be in Rebellion, or in Transgression against the Lord*—Save us not this Day." He argued the familiar position that the colonists, "his fellow-citizens," had not forsaken their rights or their loyalties when they moved across the ocean and that they were not setting themselves up against the British. He lamented that "no Embassy of great or good men has been raised" in Britain to handle the American situation, find the Americans true, and negotiate a peace. Since that diplomacy had not taken place, Smith proclaimed that "CONTINUED submission to violence is no tenet of our church." They were "now engaged in one of the grandest struggles, to

12. *Journals of the Continental Congress,* II, 87–88. See also McBride, *Pulpit and Nation,* 20–24.

which freemen can be called . . . contending for what you conceive to be your constitutional rights, and for a final settlement of the terms upon which this country may be perpetually united to the Parent State." Smith's simultaneous call to arms and hope for peace within the empire reflected the Congress's tenuous position in the summer of 1775.[13]

The deeply rooted belief that protestantism united British lands in liberty helped Smith to walk this line and made it easier for him not to overstep the political moment. Protestantism was the glue that bound the empire together. It was a matter of providence, he preached, that "the most important part of this continent fell to the sons of a protestant and free nation" who were "enthusiasts to that scared plan of civil and religious happiness, for the preservation of which they have sacrificed from age to age." Those in Britain need only "Behold your own religious and civil institutions, and then examine the frames of government" and laws in America to see that they were "sprung from the same stock." Yet at the same time protestantism unified the British Empire it could also justify rebellion because of the failures of British policy. Contrasting the successful embassy of Phineas in the Joshua story with the situation the colonists faced, Smith found that "*Jewish* tenderness has put *Christian* benevolence to shame." Because "religion and liberty must flourish or fall together in America," the Americans had to fight. The careful sermon attempted to hold out the hope of reconciliation and also justify war. To do this, Smith needed British protestantism to both unify Britons and permit rebellion—and, above all, he needed it to stand outside the awfulness of war.[14]

The national fast day, held on July 20, 1775, was a triumph of public religion, widely observed by congregations across the new nation in a clear demonstration that protestant leaders (and Americans more generally) were paying attention to Congress. It continued the same, cautious tone set by Smith. Congress had sent the Olive Branch Petition, a final plea for reconciliation that the king ultimately ignored, and many in America still held out hope that it would be successful. On the day of the fast, delegates to the Continental Congress heard one sermon from the Anglican Duché and one from presbyterian leader Francis Alison. Silas Deane recorded: "Such a Fast was never before observed in this City. Sunday was never so strictly kept." In Newport, Ezra Stiles noted that the

13. William Smith, *A Sermon on the Present Situation of American Affairs: Preached in Christ-Church, June 23, 1775 . . .* (Philadelphia, 1775), i, 1, 17, 20, 23; Irvin, *Clothed in Robes of Sovereignty*, 105–106. Guyatt similarly pairs William Smith and Jacob Duché in *Providence and the Invention of the United States*, 108–109. See also William Pencak, "Out of Many, One: Pennsylvania's Anglican Loyalist Clergy in the American Revolution," in Pencak, ed., *Pennsylvania's Revolution* (University Park, Pa., 2010), 99–100.

14. Smith, *A Sermon on the Present Situation*, 13, 15, 18, 20.

day saw "the most crouded Assembly that I ever preached to in my Meeting-house. It has been a serious and solemn and I hope sincere Fast!" He also noted that the local Anglican Church held prayers, "but without preachg or afternoon service." Even the Jews and Moravians marked the day, according to Stiles. Awakened Anglican William Piercy, then preaching in New York, reported that he "never remembered to have seen a Day that was observed with so much seriousness and solemnity as in this City. Every Thing and every Person wore the Appearance of Mourning and Lamentation." The scope of these events is noteworthy. The ritual of public prayer offered a means for Americans to mark collectively and solemnly the importance of what was unfolding around them, even—as the example of Newport Anglicans suggests—when they did not agree about the causes or best course of action in those events. Public religion solemnized and unified an American public without erasing internal divisions, just as it was supposed to do. Daniel Batwell, an Anglican preacher in Pennsylvania who would later remove to England, asked whether his hearers "ever expect to see the day, when all the various communions of this wide-extended continent should be bowed as the heart of one man to deprecate the wrath, and to entreat the protection of heaven, in one and the same hour, in one and the same cause?" The reach of the public ritual was remarkable.[15]

Despite the success of the fast-day ritual in marking support for the Revolutionary movement, the published sermons on the occasion were circumspect, fitting for a moment when the nascent nation's political leaders had not yet committed to outright rebellion. Whether this was a cause or a product of the disproportionate number of Anglican contributions to the corpus is difficult to say. Anglicans, who had taken oaths to support both church and state, faced particular challenges. Batwell lamented in his sermon that the Americans were *"at variance with those whom hitherto we have revered as fathers, honoured as teachers, loved as brethren, and dealt with as friends."* He prayed that God would *"suffer not those to remain long divided, whom the same language, the same descent, the same manners, the same constitution, the same religion, have so intimately united."* Yet he gingerly blamed the crisis on the British, referencing "those fatal misconceptions that have gone forth on the other side of the atlantick," and though he pleaded that it was not his place to judge, he nevertheless thought moderate aims were

15. Silas Deane to Elizabeth Deane, July 20, 1775, in Paul H. Smith, ed., *Letters of Delegates to Congress, 1774–1789*, 26 vols. (Washington, D.C., 1976–2000), I, 640; Franklin Bowditch Dexter, ed., *The Literary Diary of Ezra Stiles, D.D., LL.D., President of Yale College*, I, *January 1, 1769–March 13, 1776* (New York, 1901), July 20, 1775, 590–591; William Piercy to Selina Hastings, July 28, 1775, A4/2/18A, Cheshunt College Archives, Westminster College, Cambridge; Daniel Batwell, *A Sermon, Preached at York-Town, before Captain Morgan's and Captain Price's Companies of Rifle-Men . . .* (Philadelphia, 1775), 10–11; McBride, *Pulpit and Nation*, 57–59. For the Olive Branch Petition, see Irvin, *Clothed in Robes of Sovereignty*, 72–73.

legitimate. "If to preserve our rights and privileges be the sole aim of the Continental Congress, and of those who assemble at their biddings," he wrote, and "if no sparks of disloyalty, no desire of change, no intentions of removing the ancient land marks, lie concealed beneath the fair outside of public good; . . . then we have a good cause." This was a tactfully articulated stance; defense of American liberties was appropriate, even when disloyalty was not. Jacob Duché's fast-day sermon, *The American Vine,* followed this same vein of both stressing union with Britain and justifying American complaints. Like that of his fellow Philadelphia Anglican, William Smith, it circulated widely. Following a common theme, it pointed to both the value of past ties to Britain and the virtues of standing up for American liberties. Duché condemned the "UNNATURAL WAR" that had "burst forth in the very bowels of our native land" and stressed "the blessings of Providence" and "the nurturing care and protection of the mother country" that America had hitherto enjoyed. Nonetheless, the fault was Britain's. "AND happy, my dear brethren, should we still remain, if the parent would be satisfied with such returns from the children, . . . and not exact such an illegal and unrighteous tribute." Preaching before the Continental Congress, Duché went one step further. He legitimated the Congress that Batwell had only tacitly approved. "Go on, ye chosen band of Christian Patriots!" Duché announced. His words validated Congress's invitation to him to be its chaplain, and he used his religious authority to endorse their actions. Of course, not every voice from the pulpit on July 20, 1775, struck a moderate tone—baptist David Jones's fervently pro-American sermon, *Defensive War in a Just Cause Sinless,* was an important exception—but uniformity of opinion was less significant than the Congress's capacity to command the ritual, and the general tone of the day fell easily in line with Congress's goals.[16]

16. Batwell, *A Sermon, Preached at York-Town,* 2, 4, 12, 16–17; Jacob Duché, *The American Vine: A Sermon, Preached in Christ Church, Philadelphia, before the Honourable Continental Congress, July 20th, 1775* (Philadelphia, 1775), 16, 19–20, 24, 27–29. See also Thomas Coombe, *A Sermon, Preached before the Congregations of Christ Church and St. Peter's . . .* (Philadelphia, 1775); Smith, *A Sermon on the Present Situation,* esp. iv, 12; and David Jones, *Defensive War in a Just Cause Sinless: A Sermon, Preached on the Day of the Continental Fast, at Tredyffrin, in Chester County* (Philadelphia, 1775), 19. Jones, in particular, stressed the Declaratory Act as a cause, then pointed out, "Even our religion is not excepted" (19). See also John J. Zubly, "The Law of Liberty: A Sermon on American Affairs, Preached at the Opening of the Provincial Congress of Georgia; Addressed to the Right Honourable the Earl of Dartmouth," in Randall M. Miller, ed., *"A Warm and Zealous Spirit": John J. Zubly and the American Revolution; a Selection of His Writings* (Macon, Ga., 1982), 123–161 (blame for the war's origins is variously presented on 126 and 145); and Joseph Montgomery, *A Sermon, Preached at Christiana Bridge and Newcastle, the 20th of July 1775 . . .* (Philadelphia, 1775), for a similar call to defensive war. For a significant Anglican outlier, see Samuel Andrews, *A Discourse Shewing the Necessity of Joining Internal Repentance, with the External Profession of It: Delivered upon the General Fast, July 20th. 1775* (New Haven, Conn., 1775). For Anglican clergy at this time, see Nancy L. Rhoden, *Revolutionary Anglicanism: The Colonial Church of England Clergy during the American Revolution* (Basingstoke, U.K., 1999), 93.

The 1775 fast day firmly established the Continental Congress as a power commanding a national public religion, both similar to and yet in direct opposition to the public religion that had so long linked British protestants to their empire. It was a remarkable achievement for an upstart government representing a polity that had no prior existence. Conjuring a united public religion was an important and—in political terms—revolutionary mark of moral legitimacy for both Congress and for the Revolutionary provincial governments. The accomplishment of wresting control of public religion from the structures of the British Empire was significant, precisely because of their deep roots in imperial protestantism. With the assistance of American protestant leaders, the new governments had taken up and repurposed tools that had long justified British imperial actions.

OUTSIDE AND INSIDE THE PUBLIC PULPIT IN BRITAIN

The period of American caution in 1775 had a counterpart in Britain, both politically and in the rhetoric of imperial protestantism. During the first year of the war, King George proclaimed no day of fasting or other special public religious notice of the war. To do so would have been out of the ordinary for a localized colonial fracas, and in 1775 leaders in Britain hoped that was all the conflict in the colonies would turn out to be. The Church of England's hierarchy, the king, and Lord North all had reasons to avoid casting the rebellion as a dramatic threat. They would not invoke the tools of public religion in response to the conflict until late in 1776, more than a year after the fighting had started. (The delay did not stem from a lapse in the use of such tools entirely, as a day of public thanksgiving had been declared for the birth of Princess Mary in April 1776.) In the months while such tools lay untouched, religious discussions about the American crisis in Britain occurred outside the public pulpit, and they ranged across the political spectrum. Those early debates illustrate how difficult it was for religious leaders to frame the war in the terms of imperial protestantism, the language they had used for decades to describe the empire's wars. Those debates did not last long, however. Once the rituals of public religion were brought to bear on the conflict, a far more unified voice emerged, condemning the colonists and justifying the fight.[17]

17. Philip Williamson et al., eds., *National Prayers: Special Worship since the Reformation*, II, *General Fasts, Thanksgivings, and Special Prayers in the British Isles, 1689–1870* (Woodbridge, U.K., 2017), 262. For public opinion in the early months of the conflict, see Conway, *The British Isles and the War of American Independence*, 129–131; Bradley, *Popular Politics and the American Revolution in England;* and Colin Bonwick, *English Radicals and the American Revolution* (Chapel Hill, N.C., 1977), 85–86. For the challenges Anglican religious leaders faced at this moment, see

Though the British government did not take official religious notice of the war, protestant religious leaders in Britain worried about what the fighting meant for the empire and what it might bring. Awakened Anglican John Newton wrote to his friend and patron John Thornton: "The alarming news lately receivd from Boston, gives me a mournful prospect of the issue of our unhappy disputes." Lamenting events was insufficient, however. Upon learning that war had broken out, he took the astonishing step of calling "a Prayer meeting extraordinary on a National account on Tuesday mornings at 5 o'clock." Despite the early hour, he was "much pleasd and encouraged to find my proposal so well seconded, for at that early hour we had between 150 and 200 people." He even penned a hymn for the day, entitled "The Gathering Clouds, with Aspect Dark," subsequently published in 1779 (see Figure 9). Thornton responded, "Our American Affairs look sad, indeed." Others also saw the start of war in religious terms. An anonymous pamphleteer published a woeful lament that "there is no sensible, reflecting Christian heart, in all his Majesty's dominions, that does not bleed at the dreadful prospect opened to us by the unnatural civil war" in which the empire found itself. The propensity to see the war as a potential religious crisis extended beyond the clergy. Charles Wesley received a letter asking, "Does it not Dear Sir evidently appear that God has a Controversy with the land? Pray what do you think of the present state of this Nation; what is like to be the end of this quarrel between the Crown and the Colonies?"[18]

This was a war within the protestant fold, something awakened Anglican leader John Wesley fretted about to both his friends and to powerful allies in government. His socially conservative Anglicanism did not permit protests of legitimate government, and he saw no reason to think of Britain's government as illegitimate. Even so, he still worried about the course of events in the colonies, and he was personally sympathetic to colonists' outcries that their liberties were being unfairly restricted. To his brother Charles, he wrote: "Just what I thought at first, I think still of American affairs. If a blow is struck, I give *America* for lost, and perhaps *England* too. Our part is to continue instant in prayer." After learning of the fighting across the Atlantic, he wrote to Thomas Rankin, an

Aston, "Archbishop Markham and Political Preaching in Wartime England," in Cornwall and Gibson, eds., *Religion, Politics, and Dissent*, 186.

18. John Newton to John Thornton, June 13, 1775, John Newton: Correspondence with John Thornton, Add. MSS, 7826/1/A, Cambridge University Library (CUL); "On the Commencement of Hostilities in America," in *Olney Hymns: In Three Parts* (London, 1855), 211; Thornton to Newton, July 29, 1775, Thornton Family Papers, Add. MSS, 7674/1/X/35, CUL; Christianus, *The Voice of God: Being Serious Thoughts on the Present Alarming Crisis . . .* (London, 1775), 5; William Smith to Charles Wesley, Sept. 13, 1775, Early Preachers Collection, DDPr 1/74, John Rylands Library, University of Manchester, U.K.

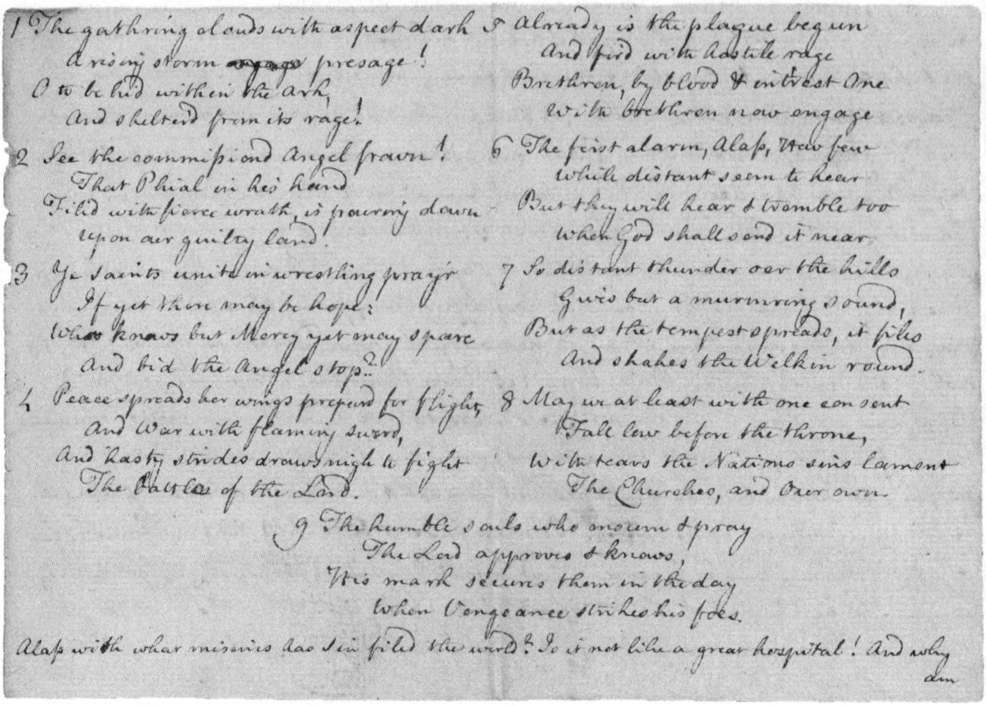
1 The gathring clouds with aspect dark
A rising storm presage!
O to be hid within the ark,
And sheltred from its rage!

2 See the commission'd Angel frown!
That Phial in his hand
Fill'd with fierce wrath, is pouring down
Upon our guilty land!

3 Ye saints unite in wrestling pray'r
If yet there may be hope:
Who knows but Mercy yet may spare
And bid the Angel stop?

4 Peace spreads her wings prepar'd for flight,
And War with flaming sword,
And hasty strides draws nigh to fight
The battles of the Lord.

5 Already is the plague begun
And fir'd with hostile rage
Brethren, by blood & int'rest One
With brethren now engage

6 The first alarm, Alas, tho' few
While distant seem to hear
But they will hear & tremble too
When God shall send it near

7 So distant thunder oer the hills
Gives but a murmuring sound,
But as the tempest spreads, it fills
And shakes the Welkin round.

8 May we at least with one consent
Fall low before the throne,
With tears the Nations sins lament
The Churches, and our own.

9 The humble souls who mourn & pray
The Lord approves & knows,
His mark secures them in the day
When Vengeance strikes his foes.

Alas with what miseries has sin fill'd the world! Is it not like a great hospital! And why
don

FIGURE 9 John Newton's Hymn. Anglican John Newton wrote a hymn expressing his worry that the American Revolution represented divine punishment for Britain. Ms.Add.7826/1a. Reproduced by kind permission of the Syndics of Cambridge University Library

awakened itinerant then in the colonies, "What will the end of these things be either in Europe or America? It seems, huge confusion and distress, such as neither we nor our fathers had known!" Wesley also wrote urgent letters to those in power he hoped to sway, including two in June 1775 to the pious Lord Dartmouth and his stepbrother, Lord North. Though assuring the men (in separate letters that were virtually identical) that "all my prejudices are against the Americans," he nonetheless stated, "An oppressed people asked for nothing more than their legal rights." Moreover, he was pessimistic about British chances against a people made up of "calm, deliberate enthusiasts," and he feared that, within England, folk were "ripe for open rebellion" because of the poor economic conditions. Wesley's concerns, his capacity to empathize with all sides, and his uneasiness that a war that started in America might spread to Britain were all reflections of the bonds Wesley believed connected the various parts of the protestant empire.[19]

Wesley led the way among British protestant leaders in public discussions about the justice of the British military actions in America. In October 1775, he published one of the most widely circulated tracts in support of the North ministry, *A Calm Address to Our American Colonies*. It was not original work. After reading Samuel Johnson's *Taxation No Tyranny*, Wesley abridged that text and represented it as his own in his *Calm Address*. The pamphlet sold cheaply and by the thousands. It made the famous clergyman an effective communicator for the North administration—despite his position as a leader of the awakening movement and an irritant to the Church of England's hierarchy. He argued forcefully that Parliament had a right to tax the colonies as part of its sovereign power. Wesley's pamphlet (along with Johnson's, to which it was clearly linked) formed an important part of public discussions about the rightness of the North ministry's coercive actions. That debate galvanized the attention of the British political nation and appeared in newspapers, pamphlets, magazines, and a broad petition drive both for and against military measures in America. Wesley's

19. John Wesley to Charles Wesley, June 2, 1775, in John Telford, ed., *The Letters of the Rev. John Wesley, A.M.: Sometime Fellow of Lincoln College, Oxford*, VI, *December 11, 1772, to March 12, 1780* (London, 1931), 152; John Wesley to Thomas Rankin, June 13, 1775, ibid., 154; John Wesley to William Legge, second earl of Dartmouth, June 14, 1775, ibid., 156, 159; John Wesley to Frederick North, second earl of Guilford, June 15, 1775, ibid., 161, 163. For John Wesley's social and political attitudes, see David Hempton, *Methodism and Politics in British Society, 1750–1850* (Stanford, Calif., 1984), 20–54. Wesley's conservative tendencies were noted by E. P. Thompson, *The Making of the English Working Class* (New York, 1966), 41. There is some dispute among historians about Wesley's positions toward the Americans in the years before the outbreak of the crisis. See Allan Raymond, "'I Fear God and Honour the King': John Wesley and the American Revolution," *Church History*, XLV (1976), 316–328. For Wesley's early contacts with North America, see Dee E. Andrews, *The Methodists and Revolutionary America, 1760–1800: The Shaping of an Evangelical Culture* (Princeton, N.J., 2000).

pamphlet provided a point of entrée for other religious voices. Bristol dissenter Caleb Evans took on Wesley most directly, and the pamphlet fight that ensued between Evans, Wesley, Wesley's colleague John Fletcher, and dissenter Richard Price was widely publicized. In the discussions, dissenters tended to side with the parliamentary opposition and Wesley's friends with the ministry.[20]

Although historians have attended closely to the debate's partisan character, more important for present purposes are religious leaders' challenges in formulating the conflict's relationship to British protestantism. Wesley's tactic was avoidance: he mostly focused on taxes and representation. He stressed what he saw as the natural logic of parliamentary authority over the colonies. "Nothing can be more plain," he wrote, "than that the supreme power in England has a legal right of laying any tax upon [the colonies] for any end beneficial to the whole empire." His tone was anything but conciliatory, and he suggested that, if the Americans "can yet give yourselves time to think, you will see, the plain case" was for submission. When religion appeared in his text, it was mostly in the form of "religious liberty," which he treated as an extension of a more general notion of the concept. "After all the vehement cry for liberty, what more liberty can you have? What more religious liberty can you desire, than that which you enjoy already?" Wesley's general avoidance of religion, coupled

20. John Wesley, *A Calm Address to Our American Colonies* (London, 1775); Samuel Johnson, *Taxation No Tyranny: An Answer to the Resolutions and Address of the American Congress* (London, 1775); Caleb Evans, *A Letter to the Rev. Mr. John Wesley, Occasioned by His Calm Address to the American Colonies* (London, 1775), 24. For discussions of the *Calm Address,* see Jeffrey Williams, *Religion and Violence in Early American Methodism: Taking the Kingdom by Force* (Bloomington, Ind., 2010), 50–53; Glen O'Brien, "John Wesley's Rebuke to the Rebels of British America: Revisiting the Calm Address," *Methodist Review,* IV (2012), 31–55; Frank Baker, "The Shaping of Wesley's 'Calm Address,'" *Methodist History,* XIV (1975), 3–12; Raymond, "'I Fear God and Honour the King,'" *Church History,* XLV (1976); David T. Morgan, "'The Dupes of Designing Men': John Wesley and the American Revolution," *Historical Magazine of the Protestant Episcopal Church,* XLIV (1975), 121–131; and Hempton, *Methodism and Politics in British Society,* 45–46. Historians have discussed the influence of Wesley's politics and pamphlet in a variety of contexts. See Andrew Jackson O'Shaughnessy, *The Men Who Lost America: British Leadership, the American Revolution, and the Fate of the Empire* (New Haven, Conn., 2013), 58–59, 75; Ragosta, *Wellspring of Liberty,* 83–86; Andrews, *Methodists and Revolutionary America,* 49–50; Kathleen Wilson, *The Sense of the People: Politics, Culture, and Imperialism in England, 1715–1785* (Cambridge, 1995), 359; and Bradley, *Popular Politics and the American Revolution in England,* 93–95. Wesley might have been encouraged to write by North. Lord Dartmouth read and approved John Fletcher's *Vindication* of Wesley. See Fletcher to Charles Wesley, Oct. 10, 1775, in Peter S. Forsaith, ed., *"Unexampled Labours": Letters of the Revd John Fletcher to Leaders in the Evangelical Revival* (Peterborough, U.K., 2008), 332–333. The North government was involved in the publication of two pamphlets by Scots John Home and Adam Ferguson during this period, as well. See Richard B. Sher, *Church and University in the Scottish Enlightenment: The Moderate Literati of Edinburgh* (Princeton, N.J., 1985), 263–268. Wesley's reactions to Evans and subsequent acknowledgment of his plagiarism are discussed in Donald H. Kirkham, "John Wesley's 'Calm Address': The Response of the Critics," *Methodist History,* XIV (1975), 13–23; Albert M. Lyles, "The Hostile Reaction to the American Views of Johnson and Wesley," *Journal of the Rutgers University Library,* XXIV (1960), 1–13; and Bradley, *Religion, Revolution, and English Radicalism,*

with his personal reservations about what might result from the conflict, are striking. They suggest that, even though he believed his government was in the right, he was not able—or, perhaps, not willing—to articulate those opinions in the language of protestantism that normally formed such a dominant part of politico-religious discussions.[21]

Others in the debate engaged religious issues, but they invoked protestantism for varied purposes. The idea that a protestant tradition should guide policy, for example, did not mean the same thing to all, so it could be employed to different ends. Dissenters who attacked the North ministry's military policy worked from the assumption that imperial protestantism and religious liberty were on the American side of the argument—presuming, of course, that the Americans would return to the British fold when that policy was corrected. In a sermon preached on Guy Fawkes Day, November 5, 1775, Caleb Evans asserted the perfection of the British constitution in protecting both civil and religious liberty, recounting the nation's historic struggles from the Spanish Armada to the Glorious Revolution. He told his British congregants to stand for the best of protestant governing values: "*Ye* are not called to give your voices for the destruction of your brethren, though they should have erred! YE are not called to appear as the patrons of POPERY and ABSOLUTE POWER, in any part of the

128. For discussions of these debates about American policy, see Troy Bickham, *Making Headlines: The American Revolution as Seen through the British Press* (DeKalb, Ill., 2009), 71–87; Eliga H. Gould, *The Persistence of Empire: British Political Culture in the Age of the American Revolution* (Williamsburg, Va., and Chapel Hill, N.C., 2000), 150–155; Hole, *Pulpits, Politics, and Public Order in England*, 44–47; Bonwick, *English Radicals*, 81–90; Bradley, *Popular Politics and the American Revolution in England*, 207–216; and Linda Colley, *Britons: Forging the Nation, 1707–1837* (New Haven, Conn., 1992), 138–141. Historians, particularly James E. Bradley and Colin Bonwick, have emphasized the role of dissenters in public debates about the British response to the American crisis—though, to use Bonwick's framing, more as political "radicals" than as leaders of religious institutions per se. Bradley's *Religion, Revolution, and English Radicalism* is the most thorough treatment of the subject. Stephen Conway argues, "Opinions on the American war were influenced in many cases by religious affiliation, though care should be taken not to adopt a simplistic religious determinism" (Conway, *British Isles and the War of American Independence*, 139–140). The particular importance of Richard Price's pamphlets is discussed in Bernard Peach's introduction to Peach, ed., *Richard Price and the Ethical Foundations of the American Revolution* (Durham, N.C., 1979), 13–40. Sheldon S. Cohen, *British Supporters of the American Revolution, 1775–1783: The Role of the "Middling Level" Activists* (Woodbridge, U.K., 2004), places dissenting support within a wider political context; see esp. 6–21.

21. Wesley, *Calm Address*, 4, 11, 15. Wesley also referenced the biblical figure of Ahithophel, comparing those in England who sought to undermine the legitimate government and made "dupes" of the Americans to him (17). He also attacked William Smith's *Sermon on the Present Situation of American Affairs*, placing himself in conversation with other religious leaders even as he did not explicitly address religious themes in depth (19–23). Conway, *British Isles and the War of American Independence*, 139–144, summarizes the divisions within British public opinion based on religion, most of which happened in the first part of the war. See also Bradley, *Popular Politics and the American Revolution in England*; Bradley, *Religion, Revolution, and English Radicalism*; Bradley, "Anglican Pulpit," *Albion*, XXI (1989); and Bonwick, *English Radicals*.

world!"[22] Awakened Anglican John Fletcher similarly invoked British protestantism, though he took an opposite political stance from Evans. He assured his readers "that the American controversy is closely connected with Christianity in general, and with Protestantism in particular; and that, of consequence, is of a *religious,* as well as of a civil nature." He did this by arguing what he viewed as the central principles of protestant government. Citing Romans 13:1—*"Let every soul be subject to the higher powers"*—Fletcher demonstrated the scriptural basis for taxation and divine origins of government in general. Like Evans, he also walked his reader through a careful explication of protestant history, but he did it to argue that a tendency to disorder and lawlessness had been with the tradition since the beginning. It thus necessitated American submission. Fletcher asked that Evans moderate his perspective. "Be intreated, Sir, to rectify your false notions of liberty. The liberty of Christians, and Britons, does not consist in bearing no yoke; but in bearing a yoke made easy by a gracious Saviour and a gracious sovereign." Both Evans and Fletcher presumed that British protestantism was a basis for peace, but they imagined very different routes to achieve it.[23]

Scot John Erskine, an awakened minister with deep ties to North America, also deployed imperial protestantism in the hope of halting military measures. In 1776, he republished in Edinburgh a tract he had originally written anonymously in 1769, *Shall I Go to War with My American Brethren?* in which he argued there were far greater problems before the empire than that of American rebellion. His new appendix made a painful plea: "Can we hate men who have taken up arms, not from hatred of us, but from a too jealous love for fair liberty? Can we triumph in the slaughter of our fellow men, our fellow-Christians, our fellow Protestants; and in the burning of cities and churches, where fervent prayer used to be put up for Britain and Britain's king? Is it not time to listen to the whispers of compassion?" He struck a similar note in a second, anonymous tract he published in 1776, in which he suggested that justice and prudence ought to prevail ahead of hasty war. Citing Joshua, the same biblical story about

22. Caleb Evans, *British Constitutional Liberty: A Sermon, Preached in Broad-Mead, Bristol, November 5, 1775* (Bristol, U.K., [1775]), 4, 29. Galatians 5:1, rather than 5:13, was a favorite of American ministers during this period. See Byrd, *Sacred Scripture, Sacred War,* 129–136. New England baptist Isaac Backus used Galatians 5:13 in 1773. See Mark A. Noll, *In the Beginning Was the Word: The Bible in American Public Life, 1492–1783* (New York, 2016), 235–236, 262. When the sermon was reprinted in Belfast a few months later, it included a notice from the *Monthly Review,* saying, "This discourse, in favour of our civil and religious liberties, seems to have been particularly seasonable, at a time when Mr. Wesley's Toryism is making so rapid a progress through the country" ("Monthly Catalogue: Sermons," *Monthly Review,* LIII [1775], 528).

23. John Fletcher, *A Vindication of the Rev. Mr. Wesley's "Calm Address to Our American Colonies": In Some Letters to Mr. Caleb Evans* (London, [1775]), iii, 12, 45, 50–51.

which William Smith had preached in Philadelphia, he wrote that, when "the children of Israel" had readied themselves for war, they had "not reckon[ed] it a debasing their dignity, to send an honourable embassy, and to expostulate with them on their offensive conduct." In such a way, war was avoided. He advised that the government change course and avoid the coming disaster, and he directed his sentiments at "men, whom unfeigned piety, sincere attachment to Protestant principles, and undissembled regard to our present happy establishment in church and state, render incapable of such malevolence" lest "God come, and smite the British empire with a curse!" If imperial leaders sufficiently attended to their "Protestant principles," in other words, war would be averted.[24]

Not all religious leaders believed that shared protestantism could prevent war. Two prominent voices, again on opposite sides of the political spectrum, argued for a version of future Anglo-American relations that would abandon protestant unity, with the connection between government and protestant institutions it implied. On one end was Richard Price, a prominent dissenter and philosopher who opposed the military response in America. He roundly dismissed British protestantism's purpose (and that of religion in general) of unifying a polity in his *Observations on the Nature of Civil Liberty, the Principles of Government, and the Justice and Policy of the War with America*, published in February 1776. He rejected the notion that the war was necessary to preserve unity in the empire. "Pleas of this sort have, in all ages, been used to justify tyranny. They have in religion given rise to numberless oppressive claims and slavish hierarchies." Most obviously, "the Pope claims the title and powers of the supreme head on earth of the Christian church, in order to preserve its unity." Driving his point home, he wrote, "With respect to the British Empire nothing can be more preposterous than to endeavor to maintain its unity by setting up such a claim." Where others hoped to use the bonds of protestant history to inspire empathy, Price saw a dangerous tendency to compel conformity. If the bonds created by "one supreme executive head, an exchange of kind offices, ties of interest and affection," and the like, were not sufficient, "let it, in the name of God, want unity" rather than have one part enslaved to another. Price rejected the concept that religion should justify a person's coerced membership in a polity—even as, in his conclusion, he condemned Britons for being less pious than their American foes. He pointedly remarked that the colonists (unlike

24. John Erskine, *Shall I Go to War with My American Brethren? A Discourse Addressed to All Concerned in Determining That Important Question* (Edinburgh, 1776), 29–30; [Erskine], *The Equity and Wisdom of Administration, in Measures That Have Unhappily Occasioned the American Revolt, Tried by Sacred Oracles* (Edinburgh, 1776), 6, 19.

Britons) had already participated in the important rituals of public prayer and fast. He also asked whether his British fellows could legitimately say "that we are not the aggressors in this war." Whatever the future relationship between the colonies and Great Britain—and in 1775, Price did not advocate for American independence—he did not believe it should include a perpetuation of the kind of imperial protestantism that had existed before.[25]

There were intriguing parallels between the perspective taken by Price and that taken by Anglican economist Josiah Tucker, who was also the dean of Gloucester. Tucker objected to Britain's role as a colonial power and opposed the North ministry's policies aimed at keeping the colonies, even though he also rejected the version of imperial protestantism promoted by dissenters like Caleb Evans. He supported a radical freedom of religion, and with regard to religion in the colonies he argued that, if Americans had "taken it into their Heads to believe" that the Church of England, "under the Masque of Religion," was just another form of obligation "to the Mother-Country," then Britain should simply "resign up all Claim of Authority over them, as well Ecclesiastical as Civil; let her declare *North-America* to be independent." Outliers though they were, Price and Tucker stretched the range of debate about the nature of the bonds shared protestantism ought to create.[26]

Although some religious leaders entered the political debate in 1775 and early 1776, denominational bodies did not, with the important exception of the Church of Scotland. Its debates over the war in May 1776 distinguished it from the Church of England, the Protestant Dissenting Ministers of the Three Denominations, and the Protestant Dissenting Deputies, none of which took special notice of the outbreak of war. The silence of those English institutions likely reflected the absence of rituals of public prayer, which could only be commanded by the government, and the comparative distance of Britons from the violence of the war. Scotland's main presbyterian organization was in a different position. Like the rest of their British compatriots, Scots were very interested in American affairs, and there was healthy debate in the Scottish press and among

25. Richard Price, "Observations on the Nature of Civil Liberty, the Principles of Government, and the Justice and Policy of the War with America," in Peach, ed., *Richard Price and the Ethical Foundations of the American Revolution*, 83, 116; Bonwick, *English Radicals*, 91–98. Guyatt discusses Price's passing reference to providence here; see Guyatt, *Providence and the Invention of the United States*, 115–116. For Price's evolving opinions on American ties to Britain in this period, see Emma Macleod, "A Proper Manner of Carrying on Controversies: Richard Price and the American Revolution," *Huntington Library Quarterly*, LXXXII (2019), 285.

26. Josiah Tucker, *Four Tracts on Political and Commercial Subjects*, 3d ed. (Gloucester, U.K., 1776), 222–223. See also Conway, *British Isles and the War of Independence*, 324–326. Tucker also became enmeshed in the Wesley-Fletcher-Evans debates. See Caleb Evans, *A Reply to the Rev. Mr. Fletcher's Vindication of Mr. Wesley's Calm Address to Our American Colonies* (Bristol, U.K., [1776]).

Scottish clergy about both government actions and the Americans' rebellion. But Scotland did not have its own parliament, and the General Assembly of the Church of Scotland provided a significant venue through which Scots could speak collectively. It met in Edinburgh each spring, and one of its first acts was always to send an address to the king. The important ritual gave a distinctly independent platform to the Church of Scotland that not even the Church of England, more closely entwined with both royal and parliamentary authority, could employ to such direct effect.[27]

In 1776, the General Assembly was dominated by moderate and elite voices who were closely allied to London, but the "Popular party," a large but loose coalition of clergy who supported a more democratic ecclesiastic structure and tended toward the awakening movement, formed a powerful faction. Both groups, however, largely supported the British constitution as the best means for preserving both social welfare and liberty. In advance of the May 1776 assembly, controversy broke out between those who, in the words of the *Scots Magazine,* "were for addressing the King, to recall the troops from America, and to put an end to so unnatural a war" and those who wanted to maintain the church's expected and traditional stance of loyalty. If Scots decided to mount a protest of imperial policy through the General Assembly, it would represent a significant breach in the protocols of imperial protestantism, which were uniformly loyal.[28]

Such a protest was too much for moderate Scots, and particularly their leader, William Robertson, to permit. In the event, the meeting of the assembly itself was anticlimactic (though a larger-than-usual number of church leaders assembled and the galleries were quite full) because Robertson thwarted the protests before they could come to a head. The king's commissioner, Lord Cathcart, began the day by expressing his and the king's gratitude for the assembly's past loyalty. He then raised the matter of "the present alarming situation of public affairs in America," but, deflecting the issue, he asked the body for its forgiveness and declined to go into detail about the conflict. He said "it was not now time for discussions of that sort; the affair of the moment was the business of the moment: That it was sufficient to observe, that many of the provinces had already revolted from the parent-state, and were now in actual rebellion against the mother-country." Since the colonists "were now no longer

27. D. B. Swinfen, "The American Revolution in the Scottish Press," in Owen Dudley Edwards and George Shepperson, eds., *Scotland, Europe, and the American Revolution* (New York, 1976), 68. See also Colley, *Britons,* 140–141.

28. "Historical Affairs," *Scots Magazine,* XXXVIII (1776), 271; John R. McIntosh, *Church and Theology in Enlightenment Scotland: The Popular Party, 1740–1800* (East Linton, U.K., 1998), 20, 82–83, 155.

acting on the defensive" and aimed at independence, military measures were justified, though the king also assured his Scottish subjects that he was in the midst of offering an "olive-branch." Cathcart concluded by saying it was his "duty" to bring these matters to the attention of those who might be unaware, and he "concluded with recommending to them, to draw up a loyal and dutiful address to his Majesty on the present situation of affairs." The committee, including William Robertson, assembled to write the requested document. When it was read the following day, Robertson apparently commented "that it breathed a spirit of mildness becoming the church of Scotland." Mildness, in this moment, meant reenacting the General Assembly's traditional submission to imperial policy.[29]

The text of the final address the General Assembly sent to King George demonstrated that the established protestant body of Scotland would support the aims of the empire, as defined by the king's ministers. It laid the blame for the American situation on the "progress of that spirit, which hath prompted our fellow-subjects in North America to take arms, in opposition to your Majesty's authority, and the supremacy of the British legislature." It even reiterated the special role that religious leaders played in supporting the government, noting that its signers "consider ourselves as called upon in the present situation of public affairs to exert our utmost diligence in discharging the important functions of our sacred office." Those functions, as befitting the acts of religious leaders, would "confirm the people committed to our charge in their reverence for the laws of their country, in their attachment to the system of legal government established by the glorious revolution, and in their loyalty towards your Majesty." They also sent their "fervent prayers" with British forces that were abroad to "put a speedy period, without effusion of blood, to the present dangerous and unnatural rebellion." As clergy, the ministers of the Church of Scotland had a duty to uphold the authority of the British state, and though the conflict the empire faced was "unnatural," they also had a responsibility to support the measures taken by its leaders to end it. Though not a few ministers disagreed with this stance, having been outmaneuvered at the General Assembly, they lacked an official means to take that stand. The voices with the loudest—bully—pulpit were those that were closest to the government that supported them.[30]

29. "Historical Affairs," *Scots Magazine,* XXXVIII (1776), 271–272. For secondary accounts of these events, see Dalphy I. Fagerstrom, "Scottish Opinion and the American Revolution," *William and Mary Quarterly,* 3d Ser., XI (1954), 275; Sher, *Church and University in the Scottish Enlightenment,* 269–270; and Robert Kent Donovan, "The Popular Party of the Church of Scotland and the American Revolution," in Sher and Jeffrey R. Smitten, eds., *Scotland and America in the Age of the Enlightenment* (Princeton, N.J., 1990), 86–87.

30. "Historical Affairs," *Scots Magazine,* XXXVIII (1776), 272–273.

The affair in the General Assembly demonstrated that, when the links between protestant institutions and government were invoked, they could be very effective from the perspective of the government. Calls increased for a national day of fasting to mark the war. A few months after news of the Declaration of Independence arrived at the end of August 1776, King George proclaimed Britain's first fast day for the conflict, setting the date of December 13. The observance would allow king and people to "send up our prayers and supplications to the Divine Majesty for . . . imploring [God's] intervention and blessing speedily to deliver our loyal subjects within our colonies . . . from the violence, injustice, and tyranny, of those daring rebels," as well as "open the eyes of those who have been deluded, by specious falsehoods, into acts of treason and rebellion." The accompanying forms of prayer largely followed those used during the Seven Years' War, a foreign war, but Archbishop Frederick Cornwallis substituted some passages from the Jacobite rebellion in 1745, as they were more appropriate to the context. The fast day elevated the American war to a national event and provided the occasion to reenact a central ritual of public religion. Anglican leaders now took powerful and public stands in favor of the government's war, a contrast to their comparative quiet during the previous year despite widespread public backing for the government's policies. The connections between the goals of empire—in this case, pacifying the Americans—and the rhetoric of its protestant spokesmen largely, if not entirely, fell into place.[31]

The sermons preached on the December 13 fast day firmly established that the British military effort fitted within the traditions of British protestantism. The dominant argument made in the sermons was—in the words of "A Country Curate"—that "Obedience is the Subject's Duty." The Americans had

31. "By the King: A Proclamation of a General Fast," *Gentleman's Magazine,* XLVI (1776), 505. Williamson et al., eds., *National Prayers,* II, 562–569, esp. 563, describes the sources of the proclamation and forms of prayer; see also Guyatt, *Providence and the Invention of the United States,* 115–116. For calls for the fast, see Christianus, *Voice of God,* 20. Additionally, Price called for a fast day in his *Observations.* See also Bickham, *Making Headlines,* 86–87. The fast day was not met with universal approval; Edmund Burke condemned it in the House of Commons because it asked Britons "to go to the altar of the Almighty, with war and vengeance in our hearts, instead of the peace of our blessed Savior." For Burke, see "Debates in the House of Commons," *Gentleman's Magazine,* XLVII (1777), 7. For the British fast days during the war in general, see Ippel, "British Sermons and the American Revolution," *Journal of Religious History,* XII (1982), 191–205; and Ippel, "Blow the Trumpet, Sanctify the Fast," *Huntington Library Quarterly,* XLIV (1980), 43–60. For Burke, and also for Anglican attitudes before and after the first fast day, see Paul Langford, "The English Clergy and the American Revolution," in Eckhart Helmuth, ed., *The Transformation of Political Culture: England and Germany in the Late Eighteenth Century* (New York, 1990), 275–290; and Bradley, *Religion, Revolution, and English Radicalism,* 126–133. The *Scots Magazine* carried reviews of many of the published sermons; see "New Books," *Scots Magazine,* XXXIX (1777), 32–36, 39–40. For the overall conformity of Anglicans with the position of government, see W. M. Jacob, *The Clerical Profession in the Long Eighteenth Century, 1680–1840* (New York, 2007), 80–82; and Bradley, "Anglican Pulpit," *Albion,* XXI (1989), 361–388.

clearly failed in that duty. The Scottish presbyterian George Campbell took the sentiment one step further, stating that it was "undeniable" "that our religion strongly inculcates the duty of subjects to the magistrate." Myles Cooper, an Anglican who had fled New York in the early days of the war, asked that his audience "humble ourselves before our ALMIGHTY CREATOR" and prayed that he "put a speedy End to that *enormous* wickedness,—to that wanton and barbarous REBELLION" troubling the empire. East Apthorp, another Anglican who had played a part in the early days of the bishop controversy but had been serving a church in Croydon since 1764, wrote that "religion" did not "ever authorize the taking up arms on the part of the subject, except only in a case that cannot happen under a Protestant and free government." Those sermons that explicitly addressed the rebellion condemned it almost uniformly. Nearly as notable, however, two tracts widely distributed by the Society for Promoting Christian Knowledge (SPCK)—a sermon preached by Robert Pool Finch on the fast day and an earlier pamphlet entitled *Seasonable Reflections, Adapted to the Approaching Fast*—left out all discussion of the war and focused instead on the providence through which God punished the unwise, "thus asserting his rightful government, and thus vindicating the honour of his laws." Most of those who heard or read sermons related to the day received the strong message that the duty to submit to the state had the imprimatur of religious authority, a belief that served as both a judgment on the Americans' actions and a demand for future compliance from Britons.[32]

For many Britons, the war was very much a civil war, the goal of which was reunion through the submission of the colonists. It was, therefore, a cause for contrition even as it was necessary. Richard Hurd, the bishop of Litchfield and a favorite of the king's, preaching before the House of Lords, reminded his august audience that "a civil war is the most dreadful of those instruments, by which the moral government of God is administered in this world" and that, under such circumstances, "we shall do well to *learn righteousness*." Such a war was a special moral judgment from God, "the sword of civil fury." George Campbell

32. "A Country Curate," *American Resistance Indefensible: A Sermon, Preached on Friday, December 13, 1776, Being the Day Appointed for a General Fast* (London, [1776]), 22; George Campbell, *The Nature, Extent, and Importance of the Duty of Allegiance* . . . (Aberdeen, U.K., 1777), 33; Myles Cooper, *National Humiliation and Repentance Recommended, and the Causes of the Present Rebellion in America Assigned* . . . (Oxford, 1777), 2; East Apthorp, *A Sermon on the General Fast* . . . (London, 1776), 20; Robert Pool Finch, *The Denunciation of Christ against Jerusalem, Considered and Applied* . . . (London, 1777), 6; Society for Promoting Christian Knowledge (SPCK), Minutes, Nov. 26, Dec. 3, 1776, Jan. 14, 1777, XXVIII, CUL. Campbell's sermon was well received by the Church of England. The dean of Gloucester sent one hundred copies of it to the SPCK, presumably for distribution through its networks (SPCK, Minutes, Mar. 31, 1778, XXVIII). The importance of preaching on obedience was not limited to the Revolutionary context. See Bradley, "Anglican Pulpit," *Albion*, XXI (1989), 364.

framed his remarks with the comment that "the miseries of a civil war, whether incurred by immoderate stretches of power on the one side, or by a wanton abuse of liberty on the other," required correcting national sins. Myles Cooper concurred that "CIVIL WAR is one of the severest scourges of Heaven: it is the Sword of Divine Vengeance, which is two-edged, and wherever it strikes brings double ruin and accumulated destruction." There were limits to British contrition in this new mood, however. As the "Country Curate" protested, "But how the *Americans* could be said to be our Fellow-Subjects, whilst they refused Submission to the supreme Authority of the State, does not seem obvious to a plain Understanding." The civil war might be chastening, but it was also the fault of the Americans.[33]

Several of those who preached on the fast day took pains to point out that the war was just, or, at the very least, a necessary fight. Myles Cooper, who felt himself personally wronged, argued, "If it be right in a Sovereign State, to attempt the forcible suppression of a wicked and unprovoked Rebellion, . . . then this War is just." Even George Campbell, a more moderate voice, believed that the colonists' actions had "now laid [the government] under a necessity of seeking by arms to bring back to their duty those insolent and rebellious subjects." His fellow Scot, Alexander Carlyle, took it as one of his sermon's central charges "to shew the justice and necessity of this war." John Butler, a rising clerical voice who would end up as bishop of Hereford, was handpicked to preach before the House of Commons. He stated that the colonists had "provoked the application of a naval and military force, so valuable for their defence as well as ours, to the purpose of restoring them to a sense of their Interest and Duty." The message from the pulpit clarified any lingering doubts about who was to blame for the war among coreligionists, and it aimed at creating unity within the population behind the war effort.[34]

When the king and his subordinates took up the tools of public religion, they shifted the balance of religious debate about the American war from the justice of British military actions to justifications for a war that was well under way and, ultimately, the responsibility of the colonists. The unity of religious leaders after

33. Richard [Hurd], *A Sermon Preached before the Right Honourable the House of Lords . . .* (London, 1777), 6, 9; Campbell, *Nature, Extent, and Importance,* 1; Cooper, *National Humiliation,* 10; Country Curate, *American Resistance Indefensible,* 13. See also Gould, *Persistence of Empire,* 154; Bonwick, *English Radicals,* 101; and David Armitage, *Civil Wars: A History in Ideas* (New York, 2017), 128–147.

34. Cooper, *National Humiliation,* 18; Campbell, *Nature, Extent, and Importance,* 35; Alexander Carlyle, *The Justice and Necessity of the War with Our American Colonies Examined . . .* (Edinburgh, 1777), 4; John Butler, *A Sermon Preached before the Honourable House of Commons . . .* (London, 1777), 6–7. For Butler's selection, see Langford, "The English Clergy," in Helmuth, ed., *Transformation of Political Culture,* 279.

the 1776 fast day should not be overstated, of course. Dissenters continued to assert support for the American positions, but they did not boycott the ritual of the public fast. Nevertheless, after the 1776 fast day it was easier to find validation for government policy in the form of a sermon than to find its opposite. The moment of uncertainty had passed, and public religion helped to reinforce what had been a potential weakness in the connection between the religious institutions of the empire and the government that backed them.[35]

The ease with which such structures functioned highlights the profoundly divergent tasks the two warring countries faced in explaining their fight. Whereas the Continental Congress turned immediately to public religion to justify itself, even in advance of clear war aims, the British government faced no such pressing need. But there were consequences for the British choice to employ the tools of public religion against the Americans. It created the very real possibility that, if the Americans should wind up outside the British political fold, they would also be outside the reach of British protestantism. Just what that might mean for transatlantic protestant community was yet to be seen.

RHETORIC AND REALITY OF AMERICAN RELIGION

Whereas British imperial authorities could count on deep habits of obedience and connection between themselves and protestant leaders within their remaining empire, Americans faced a far different situation as the war deepened. In the summer of 1776, Americans found themselves simultaneously at the zenith and the nadir of American national religion, expressing some of its loftiest nationalizing rhetoric and grappling with the sheer impossibility of creating a unified American religious scaffolding. The summer's central event was the Declaration of Independence, dated July 4, 1776. It was a turning point from which Congress never retreated. After that moment, American success meant becoming an independent nation, with all that entailed.[36]

35. In addition to the published sermons by men like William Turner and Newcome Cappe, which challenged the moral basis for the war, Price's powerful arguments about liberty continued to reverberate on the fast day in the works of those who opposed it. See Country Curate, *American Resistance Indefensible;* and, from Scotland, Carlyle, *Justice and Necessity of the War,* esp. 39. John Erskine and the "Popular" party in Scotland continued to protest the war, as had Church of England minister Richard Watson, though his most widely known piece on the subject was not preached on the fast day; see Watson, *The Principles of the Revolution Vindicated in a Sermon Preached before the University of Cambridge, on Wednesday, May 29, 1776* (Cambridge, 1776). See also Gould, *Persistence of Empire,* 152–153.

36. *Journals of the Continental Congress, 1774–1789 . . . ,* 34 vols. (Washington, D.C., 1904–1937), V, 428–433. There is no shortage of work on the Declaration of Independence. Two recent transatlantic perspectives can be found in Steve Pincus, *The Heart of the Declaration: The Founders' Case for an Activist Government* (New Haven, Conn., 2017); and David Armitage, *The Declaration*

Though the Declaration of Independence—a remarkably secular document, despite its references to "Nature's God" and "divine Providence"—has rightly received the bulk of historical attention for the period, two other documents are more important for assessing matters of religion in 1776 because they reveal the complex transitions under way as Americans formally founded a new nation and had to peel away from the scaffolding of British protestantism. The nation's second fast day occurred on May 17, 1776. John Witherspoon's widely circulated fast-day sermon, *The Dominion of Providence over the Passions of Men,* outlined a distinct religious purpose for that new nation, free of the shackles of its British protestant heritage. He triumphed in his effort to depict the Americans as united and their cause as righteous. Then, sometime over the subsequent weeks, Pennsylvania lawyer John Dickinson penned the outline of the plan that would become the United States' first government. But his hope to promote religious liberty in the new nation foundered on the unfeasibility of simply replacing the imperial establishment with an American national equivalent. Setting these two documents side by side points to the potential, and to the limits, of the Americans' ability to create their own version of British imperial protestantism in the midst of war. Rhetorical religious unity worked; protestant establishment was elusive, even impossible.[37]

Witherspoon's fast-day sermon launched a fresh vision for American religion, free of any need to delve into the origins of the conflict with Britain. Instead, it offered a providential view of the war; an optimistic, even prophetic, future; and a weak attachment to historical British protestantism. This position represented a rearrangement, rather than complete innovation, on traditional themes within public religion. The sermon stressed the capacity of providence to work through political events that were not themselves godly, and it universalized the struggles of the Americans, disconnecting the war from the specific historical circumstances that had brought it about. The trials of human life, derived from the sinful

---

of Independence: A Global History (Cambridge, Mass., 2007). On the American side, see Robert G. Parkinson, *The Common Cause: Creating Race and Nation in the American Revolution* (Williamsburg, Va., and Chapel Hill, N.C., 2016), 251–263; and Pauline Maier, *American Scripture: Making the Declaration of Independence* (New York, 1997). McBride discusses the use of public religion to support the Declaration in *Pulpit and Nation,* 25–26. John Fea approaches the document from the perspective of its subsequent interpretation by American Christians (Fea, *Was America Founded as a Christian Nation? A Historical Introduction* [Louisville, Ky., 2011], 122–135).

37. John Witherspoon, *The Dominion of Providence over the Passions of Men . . .* (Philadelphia, 1776). Witherspoon's sermon has been widely analyzed in a variety of contexts. See Noll, *In the Beginning Was the Word,* 298–301; Gideon Mailer, *John Witherspoon's American Revolution* (Williamsburg, Va., and Chapel Hill, N.C., 2017), 259–268; Byrd, *Sacred Scripture, Sacred War,* 102; Guyatt, *Providence and the Invention of the United States,* 96–100; Mailer, "Anglo-Scottish Union and John Witherspoon's American Revolution," *WMQ,* 3d Ser., LXVII (2010), 709–746; and Richard B. Sher, "Witherspoon's *Dominion of Providence* and the Scottish Jeremiad Tradition," in Sher and Smitten, eds., *Scotland and America in the Age of the Enlightenment,* 46–64.

nature of man, would ultimately fulfill God's will whether men understood it or not. Sin was bad enough, "but war and violence," he wrote, were "a spectacle, still more awful." Witherspoon did not lay fault for the war exclusively at the feet of the British, instead pondering "that the lust of domination should be so violent and universal." War was war—the main point was that God would providentially use it to his ends. This reframing of the war from a result of the specific grievances perpetrated by the British into a vehicle for God's larger plan took some of the burden off the moral problem of the rupture within Britain's protestant community. "THERE is no part of divine providence in which a greater beauty and majesty appears," he argued, "than when the Almighty Ruler turns the councils of wicked men into confusion," as he had with bungling British military policy in the preceding months. God's intervention in history mattered far more than the details of why Americans had quarreled with Parliament.[38]

Witherspoon also asserted a direct American relationship to God, one that did not need the framing contexts of British protestantism. "It would be a criminal inattention not to observe the singular interposition of providence hitherto, in behalf of the American colonies," he wrote. Placing providence so firmly on the side of the Americans was hardly unprecedented. The trope of Christianity and civilization moving westward was centuries old. In the seventeenth century, English poet George Herbert had penned the couplet "Religion stands on tip-toe in our land, / Readie to passe to the *American* strand" in "The Church Militant." Yet Witherspoon's assertion of God's favor for the Americans and against the British was powerful despite the long history it drew on. As an independent nation freed from its ties to a protestant empire, the image of God's chosen land took on added force. When so much hung in the balance, those who supported the American rebellion needed to believe that God was on their side. "Some have observed," Witherspoon wrote, "that true religion, and in her train dominion, riches, literature, and arts, have taken their course in a slow and gradual manner, from east to west since the earth was settled after the flood, and from thence forbode the future glory of America." This repurposed rhetoric smoothed the transition from imperial protestantism to American national religion. The new American nation was—and had always been meant to be—the place where God's plan would thrive. Similar notes could be heard from the young awakened minister Timothy Dwight, who proclaimed before Yale's community, just after the Declaration of Independence, that God had made America particularly bountiful. In a fit of profound understatement, Dwight added that, although America faced obvious challenges "which arise

38. Witherspoon, *Dominion of Providence*, 9, 21.

from events altogether political and accidental," it nonetheless had a glorious and even prophetic future. "This is emphatically that uttermost part of the earth, whose songs and happiness so often inspired Isaiah with raptures," and it was also the "wilderness, which shall rejoice, and blossom as a rose." In the most dramatic terms, America was the place where "shall a King reign in righteousness, whose kingdom shall be an everlasting kingdom, and whose dominion shall not be destroyed." This glorious image of an American future, created through the trial of a war that lacked historical specificity, allowed religion to lift up the American cause without the burden of civil war or rupture.[39]

The new American vision did not abandon its roots in British protestantism, but it softened them and left them to the distant past. Witherspoon noted, in the context of examples from both scripture and the Reformation, that providence had favored the protestant cause in the loss of the Spanish Armada and in the fortuitous careers of "Mr. Hampden and Oliver Cromwell." But he did not, as was common in British sermons of an earlier era, stress the importance of the Glorious Revolution or the British commitment to fighting popery throughout the century. Rather, he noted the hand of providence in the flight of puritans to New England. Dwight—notably not within the genre of a sermon—wrote, "Even the boasted *British-constitution* is but an uncouth *Gothic* pile, covered and adorned by the elegance of modern architecture." As Witherspoon put it, civilization and religion thus moved westward, freed of their roots in the British protestant cause, and took on a new purpose: "the cause of justice, of liberty, and of human nature." He was "satisfied that the confederacy of the colonies, has not been the effect of pride, resentment, or sedition, but of a deep and general conviction, that our civil and religious liberties, and consequently in a great measure the temporal and eternal happiness of us and our posterity depended on the issue." Independence was the only course of action, and God undoubtedly approved. If spiritual reunion were to happen in the future, it would not be because of reconstituted political ties.[40]

39. Ibid., 34, 39; George Herbert, "From 'The Church Militant'" (1633), in Myra Jehlen and Michael Warner, eds., *The English Literatures of America, 1500–1800* (New York, 1997), 535; [Timothy Dwight], *A Valedictory Address to the Young Gentlemen, Who Commenced Bachelors of Arts, at Yale-College, July 25th, 1776* (New Haven, Conn., 1776), 7–8, 14–15. Dwight refers here to Isaiah 35:1–2 and 32:1, and Daniel 7:14. See also Levi Hart, manuscript sermon preached on May 17, 1776, Levi Hart Papers, Connecticut Historical Society, Hartford. John Adams also heard a sermon that made him contemplate independence as the "Design of Providence" on the fast day. See Byrd, *Sacred Scripture, Sacred War,* 46–47; and Guyatt, *Providence and the Invention of the United States,* 95–100. Dwight's vision of America is discussed in Grasso, *A Speaking Aristocracy,* 330–334.

40. Witherspoon, *Dominion of Providence,* 27–28, 40; Dwight, *Valedictory Address,* 12; Mailer, *John Witherspoon's American Revolution,* 267–268. On reinterpretations of Oliver Cromwell in the Revolutionary period, see Brendan McConville, *The King's Three Faces: The Rise and Fall of Royal America, 1688–1776* (Williamsburg, Va., and Chapel Hill, N.C., 2006), 270–272.

This independent nation was united in religion, Witherspoon asserted. There had never been "in history" a war "from which religious differences have been so entirely excluded." On the contrary, "true and undefiled religion" should animate their cause. That spirit would manifest in overcoming religious distinctions, as "there are few surer marks of the reality of religion, than when a man feels himself more joined in spirit to a truly holy person of a different denomination, than to an irregular liver of his own." For the awakened presbyterian Witherspoon, this public spirit of religious unity grew out of an inward form of vital religion—or, as he defined it, "an inward temper and outward conduct suited to your state and circumstances in providence at any time." That religion was the basis for "the uncorrupted patriot, the useful citizen, and the invincible soldier," in his eyes. As he concluded his text, he added: "God grant that in America true religion and civil liberty may be inseparable, and that the unjust attempts to destroy the one, may in the issue tend to the support and establishment of both." It was powerful rhetoric, but it was also powerfully vague. It seemed to suggest the strength of establishment in both civil liberty and religion in the new United States. Nothing could have been further from the truth in that moment.[41]

The religious unity and purpose Witherspoon conjured from the public pulpit was aspirational and inspirational. Those in Congress knew that governing a diverse people was far harder than striking a rhetorical posture, however. The model they had, the British Empire, allowed local protestant diversity but also built imperial unity explicitly through protestantism, from the Glorious Revolution through the Hanoverian succession and beyond. Even George III had invoked the importance of such unity at his coronation in 1761, when he swore to "inviolably maintain and preserve the foresaid settlement of the true Protestant religion." He reiterated it in his first speech to Parliament, when he promised to "adhere to and strengthen this excellent Constitution in Church and State, and to maintain Toleration inviolable." Protestantism, an institutional compromise between dominant denominations, was inextricable from British political unity. It was the foundation around which imperial protestantism had been constructed.[42]

When Americans set about founding their first government, they did not build it on protestantism. No one seriously proposed it—a noteworthy fact,

41. Witherspoon, *Dominion of Providence*, 46, 51–52, 60.

42. For George III's approach to religion, see G. M. Ditchfield, "The Religion of George III," in Ditchfield, *George III: An Essay in Monarchy* (Basingstoke, U.K., 2002), 77–108. For the oath, which relates to Scotland, see "Act for Securing of the Protestant Religion and Presbyterian Church Government," in K. M. Brown et al., eds., *The Records of the Parliaments of Scotland to 1707* (St Andrews, U.K., 2007–2020), http://www.rps.ac.uk/trans/1706/10/251. For George III's inaugural speech before Parliament, see William Cobbett, *The Parliamentary History from the Earliest Period to the Year 1803 . . . , XV, A.D. 1753–1765* (London, 1813), 982.

given that all must have been aware of its utility in a British context. Early sketches of the new government omitted it. Benjamin Franklin had proposed a plan in July 1775, but it said nothing about religion. A proposal from Silas Deane, also from 1775, similarly made no such mention. Each of these plans included a reference to mutual defense—the essence of union in the context of war—but they asserted the colonies' willingness to protect one another's "Liberties," without specification to type, neglecting the language of "civil and religious liberty" that was ubiquitous in British discourse. The absence of discussions of religion in those early plans probably reflected a general sense that religion would not be an effective means to create national unity. Because religious sentiments could be difficult to manage and because each state had its own religious laws, the specifics details of policy regarding religion were best left to the state level. This was a significant omission, however, from the perspective of the imperial protestant system the Americans were exiting. Though the Congress regularly called on the public pulpit to unify and justify its actions, particularly through days of fast and thanksgiving, those same congressmen made no effort to reconstruct the institutional aspects of imperial protestantism.[43]

The challenges the Americans faced in constructing their religious nation appear more clearly when viewed from a different angle: not through any effort to create a religious establishment, but rather through an attempt to ensure religious liberty. John Dickinson made just such an effort when he wrote a first draft for the Articles of Confederation, the United States' first government. In his initial draft, he included a lengthy, convoluted article about religious freedom, just after an article that preserved the freedom of the individual colonies (see Figure 10). A close examination of its complexities points to the difficulties Americans would have faced if they had tried to create their own parallel to the British imperial establishment.[44]

Dickinson started with a statement of religious liberty, insisting that a person "living peaceably under the Civil Government" could not "be molested or prejudiced in his or her person or Estate for his or her religious persuasion, Profession or practice, nor be compelled to frequent or maintain or contribute

43. For Franklin's plan, see *Journals of the Continental Congress,* II, 195–199; for Deane's, see "Silas Deane's Proposal to Congress," in Smith, ed., *Letters of Delegates to Congress,* II, 418–419. For discussion of the various plans and drafts, see Jack N. Rakove, *The Beginnings of National Politics: An Interpretive History of the Continental Congress* (New York, 1979), 136–149.

44. Dickinson's draft article appears in "Josiah Bartlett's and John Dickinson's Draft Articles of Confederation," in Smith, ed., *Letters of Delegates,* IV, 233–235. For the handwritten version, see "Draft of the Articles of Confederation by John Dickinson, 1776," R. R. Logan collection of John Dickinson papers [collection 0383], Historical Society of Pennsylvania, Philadelphia. For discussion of the article, see Rakove, *Beginnings,* 152–153; Jane E. Calvert, *Quaker Constitutionalism and the Political Thought of John Dickinson* (Cambridge, 2009), 251–252; and Davis, *Religion and the Continental Congress,* 157–163.

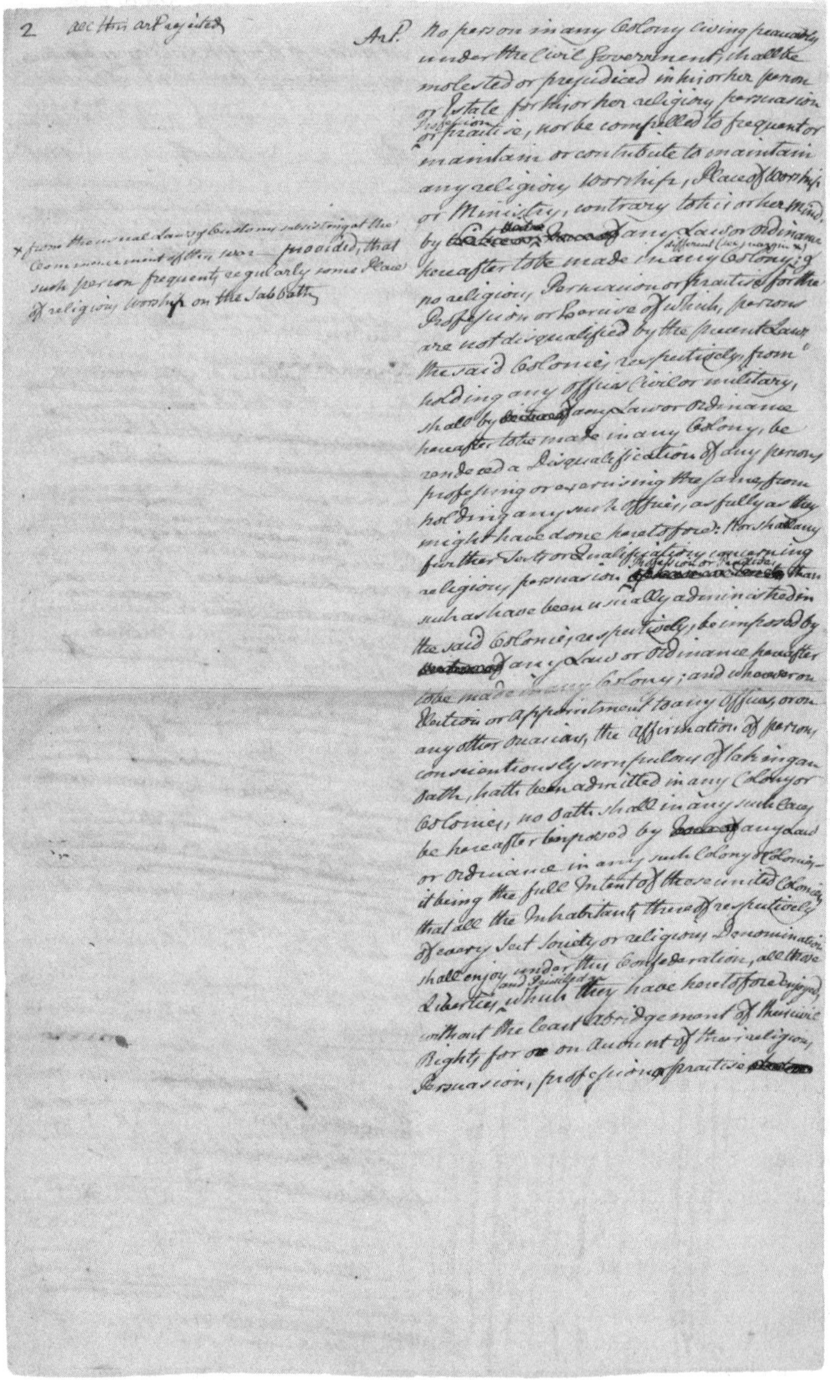

2 Section art rejected

Art. No person in any Colony living peaceably under the Civil Government, shall be molested or prejudiced in his or her person or Estate for his or her religious persuasion Profession or practise, nor be compelled to frequent or maintain or contribute to maintain any religious Worship, Place of Worship, or Ministry, contrary to his or her Mind, by any Law or Ordinance hereafter to be made in any Colony different (see margin x); no religious Persuasion or practise for the Profession or Exercise of which, persons are not disqualified by the present Laws of the said Colonies respectively from holding any offices Civil or military, shall by any Law or Ordinance hereafter to be made in any Colony, be rendered a Disqualification of any persons professing or exercising the same from holding any such offices, as fully as they might have done heretofore: Nor shall any further Tests or Qualifications concerning religious persuasion Profession or practise than such as have been usually administered in the said Colonies respectively, be imposed by any Law or Ordinance hereafter to be made in any Colony; and whereas on Election or Appointment to any Offices, or on any other occasion, the Affirmation of persons conscientiously scrupulous of taking an Oath, hath been admitted in any Colony or Colonies, no Oath shall in any such Case be hereafter imposed by any Law or Ordinance in any such Colony or Colonies, it being the full Intent of these united Colonies that all the Inhabitants thereof respectively of every Sect Society or religious Denomination shall enjoy under this Confederation, all these Liberties and Privileges which they have heretofore enjoyed, without the least Abridgement of their civil Rights for or on Account of their religious Persuasion, profession or practise.

x from the usual Laws & Customs subsisting at the Commencement of this war — provided, that such person frequent regularly some Place of religious Worship on the Sabbath

FIGURE 10 "Second Page of Draft of the Articles of Confederation by John Dickinson, 1776." R. R. Logan collection of John Dickinson papers [collection 0383], Historical Society of Pennsylvania. The draft includes a provision for religious liberty. Reproduced with permission from the Historical Society of Pennsylvania

to maintain any religious Worship, Place of Worship, or Ministry" against their conscience. It was a bold, and remarkably gender-neutral, assertion of religious rights. But Dickinson then limited those rights by adding language that echoed the imperial establishment in its structuring of legitimate protestant religion. First, the rights guaranteed by the article applied only to "any Law or ordinance hereafter to be made in any Colony different from the usual Laws and Customs subsisting at the Commencement of this War." The complex heritage of colonial laws about religion, therefore, would be preserved. This move was only practical; a frame of government that immediately dismantled a huge body of law and cultural practice in all the states would be doomed from the start. At the same time, because the new nation lacked the imperial arbiter that had imposed boundaries on those establishments and the new national government declined to step into its place, the continuance of colonial establishments would now potentially become chaos. The second limitation on the religious liberty he proposed was even more interesting. The protection from molestation only applied to a "person [who] frequents regularly some Place of religious Worship on the Sabbath." The formulation assumed irreligion or nonreligion would remain unacceptable and, in keeping with long-standing British practice, restricted legitimate religion to those practices that involved "Place[s] of Worship" and keeping the Sabbath. Although this was not an explicitly protestant version of religion, it gestured toward institutional religion in a way that, for most, would have conjured protestantism as well as Catholicism; it left open a question of how much further the proposed toleration would stretch. The two limitations, each of which preserved some incomplete version of imperial protestantism, reduced the proposed religious liberty into an oddly frozen version of policies developed under Britain's mixed establishment.[45]

Even then, Dickinson's tortured sentence was not yet over. He went on to stipulate that no new laws could disqualify persons from "any offices Civil or military," though former religious tests continued to apply, and no "further Tests or Qualifications concerning religious persuasion, Profession or Practise, than such as have been usually administered in the said Colonies respectively, be imposed by any Law or Ordinance hereafter to be made in any Colony." Finally, he asserted the continuing validity of Oaths of Affirmation where they had been permitted before. Only after this extensive discussion, which perpetuated religious establishments, did the article state that it was "the full Intent of these united Colonies that all the Inhabitants thereof respectively of every

45. "Josiah Bartlett's and John Dickinson's Draft Articles of Confederation," in Smith, ed., *Letters of Delegates*, IV, 234.

Sect, Society or religious Denomination shall enjoy under this Confederation, all the Liberties and Priviledges which they have heretofore enjoyed without the least abridgement of their civil Rights for or on Account of their religious Persuasion, profession or practise." But what rights would such a pronouncement ensure? Dickinson's declaration of principle had left untouched the mix of establishment and toleration from the colonial period, a reflection of the political realities that worked against any kind of uniform, centralized religious arrangement. The article was hardly a ringing statement of clarity. It was, rather, a remarkable foray into the impossible task the United States would face if it ever tried to build a national religion with institutional coherence.[46]

Dickinson's article was struck in its entirety by the committee, as were many other parts of his plan. On the subject of religion, members of Congress likely had no desire to poke at a hornet's nest. They knew that the diversity of establishments in the different colonies had to be respected, but they no longer had any clear way to define who deserved toleration or the privileges of establishment at the national level. For the state to be just, as the British constitution once presumably had been, it had to preserve religious liberty, but for whom? There were many protestant denominations, not to mention Catholics and Jews, and religious liberty meant not privileging any one. Yet, without any national mechanism to decide which protestant groups were worthy of toleration—or, more important still, to adjudicate between conflicting state establishments—the question was better left alone. Moreover, it was difficult for even Dickinson to imagine that toleration might be extended to those who did not attend any service. The final draft of the articles, presented to Congress on July 12, 1776, made only one reference to religion: that the colonies would defend one another from attacks "on Account of Religion," a statement that vaguely conjured the days of protestant-Catholic warfare and the idea that religion was worth fighting for. This limited mention encapsulated the issue. Presumably the colonies, at least, had some shared religion and would defend it, but how that might be defined was a matter lacking either institutional or legal clarity.[47]

The silences about religion in the nation's first government reflected political realities in the United States. It would not be a protestant nation, at least, not in any way that would have been familiar to the empire's religious leaders a generation before. Protestantism—viewed either as a contrast to popery or a

46. Ibid., 234–235.

47. Calvert, *Quaker Constitutionalism,* 252–253. For a related argument, see Evan Haefeli, "Toleration and Empire: The Origins of American Religious Pluralism," in Stephen Foster, ed., *British North America in the Seventeenth and Eighteenth Centuries* (Oxford, 2013), 103–135. For the draft presented to Congress on July 12, 1776, see *Journals of the Continental Congress,* V, 546–547 (quotation on 547). Dickinson's handwritten draft clearly has "Religion" capitalized. His rendering

grouping of denominations that were officially recognized or tolerated—was not particularly helpful during the war. Most obviously, Congress wanted to coax the Quebecois into its cause, and it desperately needed assistance from the French. Even more important, however, the dynamics of establishment and toleration within the British Empire had been built on the two poles of the Church of England and the Church of Scotland, each of which, in its home nation, exerted enormous influence. Those churches had created a binary protestant center of gravity in the empire that could not be simply replicated in the colonies. Had New England congregationalists, Middle Colony presbyterians, and southern Anglicans imagined that the United States ought to have a tripartite establishment, such a "protestantism" might have been constructed, but the farcical nature of such a counterfactual highlights the realities that militated against such a vision. New England congregationalists were themselves a divided group; many Middle Colony presbyterians had acculturated to a system of local disestablishment; and southern Anglicans had resisted the idea of an American bishop and were unlikely to support any national establishment, much less one they had to share. Although the religious arrangements in all three regions were organic products of British protestantism, no mechanism or political will existed to create a national American protestant establishment—in 1776 or, as Americans would find, at any time since. Whatever it was becoming through the process of war, the United States would not be a protestant nation in the way that its predecessor state had been. There would be no scaffolding of American protestantism that organized local variations into a common system. The ideal of national American religion that was advocated from the public pulpit stood apart from the structures of institutional protestantism, and its aspirational pronouncements lacked any clearly defined connection to the new national government.

Public religion was a powerful tool that occupied a long history within imperial protestantism. Both American and British government leaders recognized its utility. Where Americans seized on its potential to legitimate their fight, Britons moved more slowly. At the same time, where Americans confronted real limits on their political capacity to unite their new nation through religion, the imperial government faced no parallel difficulty. Despite the Americans'

---

of "account" is less clear; see "Draft of the Articles of Confederation by John Dickinson [1776]." The document printed by Congress in 1777, when it was finally submitted to the states, did not capitalize either word. The printed version is at *Articles of Confederation and Perpetual Union between the States of New Hampshire, Massachusetts Bay, Rhode Island, and Providence Plantations, Connecticut, New York, New Jersey, Pennsylvania, Delaware, Maryland, Virginia, North Carolina, South Carolina, and Georgia* (Williamsburg, Va., [1777]), esp. [2], https://www.loc.gov/item/rbpe.17802600.

defection, the structures and habits of imperial protestantism within Britain were strong enough to rally behind the war. By the end of 1776, two separate religious nations were emerging, if (on the American side) only in rhetoric. But that rhetoric was significant. It developed because the same scaffolding that had once supported the British Empire had been bent apart enough for the Continental Congress to marshal the support of men like Smith, Duché, and Witherspoon. They used their credibility as protestant leaders to buttress the new nation and articulate a future for it, even as its survival was very much in doubt. Imperial protestantism simultaneously permitted British leaders to fall in line behind a national war, despite their political differences about its execution.

But public religion was only one component of imperial protestantism, and it was one that had been built mainly out of the scaffold's pillars—its mixed and, therefore, decentralized establishment. The religious communities and institutions that had bridged the empire before the war—its planks—were not immediately reshaped by the Declaration of Independence or by George III's proclamation that the colonies were in rebellion. The process of personal and communal disentanglement within the networks of transatlantic protestantism was far more complicated than the lofty words of John Witherspoon or the condemnatory rhetoric of British fast-day sermons implied. That separation unfolded, rather, through the gritty realities of war.

5 The War's Consequences for Protestant Communities

The Revolutionary War transformed the connections that had bound distant protestants across the empire to one another, and it did so in ways that were often sharp and painful. The war's violence destroyed many of the shared projects that had been nurtured in the colonial era, and it forced religious leaders to choose between pressing political realities and long-standing loyalties. Those traumas and the decisions made in response wrenched apart the planks of imperial protestantism's scaffolding. The consequences reached far beyond the rapid collapse of the Church of England in America. The war had implications for the nature of community across the wider fabric of the empire's protestantism.[1]

As the war raged on, religious leaders on both sides of the Atlantic turned away from former partners. They came to see erstwhile fellows as unreliable or inconstant, even as enemies. The crisis had particularly strong consequences for the ties that sustained the Anglican and dissenting networks of the colonial period. Both of those networks broke down, and their now-separate remnants retreated into separate nations. The fighting also destroyed, in quite physical ways, the projects that had been built by transatlantic partnerships, further weakening the presence of British imperial protestantism on what was now United States soil. British religious leaders, meanwhile, betrayed by the Americans, put their energies toward supporting protestants in colonies that were more faithful. It was a difficult and unsettling time for protestant communities and for their leaders. The losses of the past era were visible, but the tools for rebuilding could not yet be found.

1. Previous scholarship has treated awakened protestants, Anglicans, and dissenters separately. The assumption that the Anglo-American conflict was relatively inconsequential for transatlantic protestantism is largely based on missionary connections, usually from the awakened protestant community, which were rapidly rebuilt in the 1790s—a subject that will be taken up in Chapter 7. See, for example, Emily Conroy-Krutz, *Christian Imperialism: Converting the World in the Early American Republic* (Ithaca, N.Y., 2015), 7–8; Kariann Akemi Yokota, *Unbecoming British: How Revolutionary America Became a Postcolonial Nation* (New York, 2011), 159–161; and Gordon S. Wood, *Empire of Liberty: A History of the Early Republic, 1789–1815* (New York, 2009), 490–491. The awakened movement's history is usefully examined by Mark A. Noll, who describes this

AMERICAN RELIGIOUS LEADERS CHOOSE

The relationship between religion and wartime loyalties has often been depicted as a matter of ideological affinities, but such a perspective obscures the ways that the war actually transformed the boundaries of colonial-era religious communities. The creation of a separate American nation—of political bonds that united colonists and separated them from the British Empire—triggered the reorientation of the networks that connected American religious leaders to distant protestants. Though the full implications of the war's disruptions would not become clear until it was concluded, the process began as Americans incorporated the new political boundary into their allegiances. They did so at a moment of great conflict. The empire did not divide through a series of bureaucratic niceties; intense antagonism and war caused its fracture. For American religious leaders, bringing the United States into their religious communities sometimes meant pushing out—rejecting—the networks and connections of the colonial era. Understanding how the war changed the networks of the colonial era thus means asking when and how New Englanders and mid-Atlantic presbyterians (for example) stopped being "dissenters." But charting this transition also means watching American Anglicans come to terms with the Church of England's demand of loyalty to the British government as a condition of church membership. Not all American religious leaders had the choice to remain in connection with their British fellows.[2]

---

period as one of "diversification" (Noll, *The Rise of Evangelicalism: The Age of Edwards, Whitefield, and the Wesleys, A History of Evangelicalism: People, Movements, and Ideas in the English-Speaking World,* I [Downers Grove, Ill., 2003], 194–232). The disruption of the dissenting network in North America has been overlooked by historians who have largely confined their work on that group to the colonial period, most influentially in Carl Bridenbaugh, *Mitre and Sceptre: Transatlantic Faiths, Ideas, Personalities, and Politics, 1689–1775* (New York, 1962). Catherine A. Brekus, "Dissent in the American Colonies before the First Amendment," in Andrew C. Thompson, ed., *The Oxford History of Protestant Dissenting Traditions,* II, *The Long Eighteenth Century, c. 1689–c. 1828* (Oxford, 2018), 183–199, treats the subject of transatlantic dissent from the perspective of church-state relations rather than as an affective community. The absence of the category of "dissenters" from scholarship on religion in the early American Republic is not generally remarked. Work on Anglicanism in the Revolutionary period does emphasize the war's disruptions, though not in the broader context of transatlantic community. See, for example, Peter W. Walker, "The Church Militant: The American Loyalist Clergy and the Making of the British Counterrevolution, 1701–92" (Ph.D. diss., Columbia University, 2016); Nancy L. Rhoden, *Revolutionary Anglicanism: The Colonial Church of England Clergy during the American Revolution* (New York, 1999); and Frederick V. Mills, Sr., *Bishops by Ballot: An Eighteenth-Century Ecclesiastical Revolution* (New York, 1978). For Methodists and the impact of the Revolution, see Christopher Cannon Jones, "Methodism, Slavery, and Freedom in the Revolutionary Atlantic, 1770–1820" (Ph.D. diss., College of William and Mary, 2016); and Anna M. Lawrence, *One Family under God: Love, Belonging, and Authority in Early Transatlantic Methodism* (Philadelphia, 2011).

2. Anglicans and dissenters had blamed each other for political tensions for years, a situation that did not stop with the coming of the war. For scholarly works that investigate connections

American dissenters began the war as part of a transatlantic community that had existed for more than a century. In the war's first months, there was a short-lived flurry of activity between dissenters on the two sides of the Atlantic, even though that network had lagged and struggled after the frustrating years of the bishop controversy. Key New England divines responded to the war's outbreak by sending urgent letters across the Atlantic to London dissenter Richard Price, an outspoken proponent of the Americans' cause. John Winthrop, Jr., wrote to Price, "The blow has been struck—the sword is drawn—and I suppose the scabbard thrown away." Charles Chauncy assured Price that the Americans would stand united together, despite the "hope of [Lord North's] ministry" that the resistance might fracture or collapse. "Our Spirits continually rise in warmth," he wrote, and "our union is daily growing in strength and vigor." Price also received lengthy accounts of military affairs and of goings-on in Congress. New Englanders tried desperately to convey their position on the American cause across the Atlantic, and they hoped Price would communicate with his influential friends in the capital. But these attempts were fleeting. As the war continued, such correspondence became less frequent, and American references to being dissenters became far more scarce.[3]

As the war separated Britons and Americans, the dissenting network faced an existential problem: imperial policy and Britain's mixed establishment had defined its creation and boundaries. The very term "protestant dissenters" derived from English legal constructions of toleration. Over time, the network had developed into more. It had simultaneously advocated for stability within the

between denomination and political loyalty, see, for example, Spencer W. McBride, *Pulpit and Nation: Clergymen and the Politics of Revolutionary America* (Charlottesville, Va., 2016), 69; James B. Bell, *A War of Religion: Dissenters, Anglicans, and the American Revolution* (Basingstoke, U.K., 2008); Joseph S. Tiedemann, "Presbyterianism and the American Revolution in the Middle Colonies," *Church History,* LXXIV (2005), 306–344; and Bradley J. Longfield, *Presbyterians and American Culture: A History* (Louisville, Ky., 2013), 41–44. For the Quaker experience, see Sarah Crabtree, *Holy Nation: The Transatlantic Quaker Ministry in an Age of Revolution* (Chicago, 2015), 73–81; and Jack D. Marietta, *The Reformation of American Quakerism, 1748–1783* (Philadelphia, 1984), 222–248. For Germans, see John B. Frantz, "Religion, the American Revolution, and the Pennsylvania Germans," in William Pencak, ed., *Pennsylvania's Revolution* (University Park, Pa., 2010), 76–96. For Moravians, see Katherine Carté Engel, *Religion and Profit: Moravians in Early America* (Philadelphia, 2009), 216–225; and Kenneth Gardiner Hamilton, *John Ettwein and the Moravian Church during the Revolutionary Period* (Bethlehem, Pa., 1940), rpt. in Moravian Historical Society, *Transactions,* XII (1940), 85, 87–99, 101–213, 215–429.

3. John Winthrop to Richard Price, June 6, 1775, in D. O. Thomas and Bernard Peach, eds., *The Correspondence of Richard Price,* 3 vols. (Durham, N.C., 1983–1994), I, 208–212; Charles Chauncy to Price, July 18, 1775, ibid., 215–221; William Gordon to Price, Sept. 12, 1775, ibid., 225–229. See also Theophilus Lindsey to William Turner, June 28, 1775, in G. M. Ditchfield, ed., *The Letters of Theophilus Lindsey (1723–1808), I, 1747–1788,* Church of England Record Society, XV (Woodbridge, U.K., 2007), 213–214; John Jebb to Lindsey, May 7, 1775, Simon Gratz European Clergy Collection, case 12, box 25, Historical Society of Pennsylvania, Philadelphia (HSP).

imperial establishment—that is, against a colonial bishop—and raised money for missions, to support colleges, and to promote the dissenting faith more generally. American religious leaders within the network conceived of themselves as "dissenters," even when they enjoyed the privileges of establishment. During the war years, most of the transatlantic relationships that sustained those partnerships had to be—at best—put on hold, and their resurrection would depend on the outcome of the war. In the meantime, internal American religious connections grew in strength.

Dissenters did sustain a few connections during the war, when possible, but even those demonstrated precious little in the sense of shared religious community. In 1779, for example, Chauncy was able to send a letter via Holland to Price. It attested to the Americans' political and military strength: Chauncy insisted to his friend that the Americans were "*richer* now in *reality* . . . than they ever were in any former period of time, and they are much better able to carry on the war than when they began it." In promoting American might, Chauncy did not seek to protect or reinforce ties to his British fellows, and that omission—though certainly logical in the context—is worth noting. Chauncy still considered Price a friend, and he clearly wanted to maintain the personal tie. But nothing in his letters, or indeed any surviving evidence, suggests that either American or British dissenters put effort into retaining their shared ties as a protestant community. It is difficult to put an exact date on when those ties frayed—the relationship had been worn thin in some areas by disagreements over how to manage the threat of an American bishop—but the war terminated Americans' attempts to reach out on those grounds.[4]

A part of that dissolution, for some Americans, was likely military service. The Continental Congress set out the structures and pay for the chaplaincy at the same time as it structured the rest of the army, and local militias called on chaplains, as well. From the government's perspective, the chaplaincy was an important position in both symbolic and practical ways. It brought legitimacy to the Congress, as all displays of public religion did, and military leaders also believed it helped keep discipline. According to one estimate, more than two hundred chaplains served on the American side during the Revolutionary War, with about two-thirds of them coming from dissenting (congregationalist, pres-

4. Chauncy to Price, May 20, 1779, in Thomas and Peach, eds., *Correspondence of Richard Price*, II, 39–41, esp. 40. Although the gaps in surviving correspondence make it impossible to say positively that letters were not sent or received, the level of correspondence between American and British dissenters seems to have dropped precipitously, as measured by the surviving correspondence of Richard Price and Ezra Stiles as well as a general survey of the collections used for this study, including those in Dr. Williams's Library (London). For Price, see Thomas and Peach, eds., *Correspondence of Richard Price*, I, II; for Stiles, see Harold E. Selesky, ed., *A Guide to the Microfilm Edition of the Ezra Stiles Papers at Yale University* (New Haven, Conn., 1978).

byterian, or baptist) backgrounds. Service could be of long duration or very short, and its duties varied tremendously. But whatever their exact responsibilities, chaplains built loyalties to the United States at the expense of colonial-era imperial connections. In his diary, during the battle for New York in September 1776, chaplain Phillip Vickers Fithian laid blame for the carnage at the feet of George III, lamenting "so many Mothers robbed of their beloved Children—So many Lovers forever divided." A few days later, he prayed for divine interposition on the American side. "We are a Sinful Nation, O Lord," he wrote, "but is it written in thy Book concerning us that we must always fly before our Enemies?" Chaplains necessarily interwove the goals of the Revolution with their pastoral responsibilities to soldiers and to nation. Supporting the fight against the British while also believing oneself to be part of a transatlantic religious community—even just with dissenters—must have been very difficult.[5]

Perhaps the most definitive evidence that American presbyterians, congregationalists, and baptists had ceased to think of themselves as dissenters during the war comes from the end of an organization that had been created to advance the dissenting interest. The last collective meeting of the Consociated Churches of Connecticut and the Synod of New York and Philadelphia was held in September 1775. The partnership, which had begun in the 1760s, had been enabled by an explicit consciousness of the wider imperial system that incorporated American protestants. Its purpose had been to advocate for dissenters in the empire against the threat posed by Anglicans. When the war started, the need for that advocacy ended abruptly. Without the political bonds of empire, there was no longer any reason for collaboration defined by dissenting status—because Anglicans were no longer a threat backed by Parliament. American presbyterians and congregationalists repositioned themselves within an emerging United States government in which dissent was no longer a major organizing category of religious community.[6]

5. Robert Greenhalgh Albion and Leonidas Dodson, ed., *Philip Vickers Fithian Journal, 1775–1776: Written on the Virginia-Pennsylvania Frontier and in the Army around New York* (Princeton, N.J., 1934), Sept. 15, 1776, 234, cited in John Fea, *The Way of Improvement Leads Home: Philip Vickers Fithian and the Rural Enlightenment in Early America* (Philadelphia, 2008), 204, 206. Fithian's chaplaincy is detailed on 189–208. McBride, *Pulpit and Nation,* 41–53, provides the best overall treatment of the Continental army's chaplaincy. For estimates by denomination, see Parker C. Thompson, *The United States Army Chaplaincy,* I (Washington, D.C., 1978), xix. Jack Darrell Crowder, *Chaplains of the Revolutionary War: Black Robed American Warriors* (Jefferson, N.C., 2017) does not take an academic perspective, but it identifies and lists chaplains with sources.

6. [David Dudley Field, ed.], *Minutes of the Convention of Delegates from the Synod of New York and Philadelphia and from the Associations of Connecticut: Held Annually from 1766 to 1775, Inclusive* (Hartford, Conn., 1843), 46. For a fuller history of this collaboration, see Benjamin Gilbert Wright, "Gospel of Liberty: Antislavery and American Salvation" (Ph.D. diss., Rice University, 2014), 113–117; and Edmund S. Morgan, *The Gentle Puritan: A Life of Ezra Stiles, 1727–1795* (Williamsburg, Va., and Chapel Hill, N.C., 1962), 239–250.

As they left the imperial network of dissenters behind, American protestant institutions affiliated themselves to the new national government in a transfer of allegiance from one centralizing government to another. This included Connecticut's General Association as well as some of its more local consociations, which made fervent statements in support of resistance to Parliament by the Americans. It also included the presbyterian Synod of New York and Philadelphia, a particularly interesting group because it had strong connections to the dissenting world, evident in its just-ending cooperation with Connecticut coreligionists, but it also had ties to the Church of Scotland. At its May 1775 meeting, it supported the American resistance. Its delegates took up the "alarming state of public Affairs" and found it their "duty to call all the Congregations under their care to solemn fasting humiliation and prayer." Though the delegates set a date for this observance, they also deferred to the Continental Congress, "who may probably appoint a Fast for the same purpose." The move echoed the kind of protestant cooperation for the United States that had been a hallmark of imperial protestantism. The synod allowed Congress to lead in this matter for the sake of "greater harmony with all other deno[mi]nations, and for the greater public order." The tone used by the synod was remarkably establishmentarian, conjuring authority for the Continental Congress though it had no formal relationship to that body. Its choice to transfer its allegiance from the British Empire—and from the Church of Scotland—to the American entity offered the Revolutionary cause an important vote of support at a precarious moment. But it also signaled a rupture between American presbyterians and their British counterparts. The network of dissent had been a significant part of imperial protestantism's scaffold binding the colonies to Britain, but when the empire dissolved into war, Americans left it behind.[7]

7. *The Records of the General Association of the Colony of Connecticut, Begun June 20th, 1738, Ending June 19th, 1799* (Hartford, Conn., 1888), 86; "A Book of Records for the Revd. the East-Association in the County of Fairfield Humbly Presented Samuel Cooke Junr., New Haven, Novbr. 24th 1735," minute book, Fairfield East Association, General Association of Connecticut Collection, 1734–1813, 98, Congregational Library and Archives, http://www.congregationallibrary.org/nehh/series3/CTGA5311; Guy S. Klett, ed., *Minutes of the Presbyterian Church in America, 1706–1788* (Philadelphia, 1976), 541. John Witherspoon also drew up a lengthy pastoral letter at this juncture. See ibid., 543; and *A Pastoral Letter from the Synod of New-York and Philadelphia to the Congregations under Their Care* . . . (New York, 1775), 3–4. Distributed by the synod, it exhorted presbyterians to "maintain the union which at present subsists through all the colonies" and advised "that a spirit of candour, charity and mutual esteem be preserved, and promoted toward those of different religious denominations" (ibid., 6). Religious unity and "the experience of our happy concord hitherto in a state of liberty should engage all to unite in support of the common interest" (ibid.). The solemn and authoritative tone of the presbyterian pronouncements is significant. For Witherspoon, see Gideon Mailer, "Anglo-Scottish Union and John Witherspoon's American Revolution," *William and Mary Quarterly*, 3d Ser., LXVII (2010), 709–746.

Without shared imperial ties reinforcing their membership in the dissenting community, Americans became, separately, congregationalists, presbyterians, and baptists, some of whom enjoyed the benefits of establishment in New England and some of whom did not. Moreover, those three groups did not all agree on their support for the American cause. Newport congregationalist Ezra Stiles accused James Manning, the baptist president of Rhode Island's baptist college (later Brown University), of being "particul[arl]y . . . against his Country in heart," and Stiles scorned "biggoted Baptist Politicians" in general. Some baptists faced mob violence from congregationalists who considered them tories. Of course, anti-baptist antagonism was nothing new in New England, but appeals to English dissenting bodies or to British imperial authorities could no longer offer baptists any hope of a check on American congregationalists' domineering tendencies. Like the mixed imperial establishment from which it derived, the idea of dissenters, as such, was no longer a useful construct for organizing American denominations and their rivalries. New, American conceptions of religious community would have to develop in the space "dissent" had once occupied.[8]

American Anglicans, like their dissenting fellows, also left the connections of the colonial period behind, but the process was much messier, and the personal stakes for religious leaders were often quite a bit higher. The church's hierarchy in London was unified in its opposition to colonial resistance and its sense that the boundaries of Anglican authority lay within the empire. As a result, the fate of the Anglican network in the rebelling colonies was dependent on the outcome of the war: if the British prevailed, the church would continue to consider American Anglicans within the fold; if the Americans won, those protestants would no longer be Anglicans. The stance reflected the belief among Anglicans that their church was territorial in nature—universal, but only within the bounds of a particular polity. But what was fairly cut-and-dried in London was far more complicated on the ground in the colonies during the war. American Anglican leaders faced wrenching choices balancing the pulls of local community, political opinions, church allegiance, and even personal safety. In the end, a substantial number of them simply fled. More than 20 percent of the Anglican clergy present in the colonies in 1775 were gone by 1783. The rate of flight was higher north of the Chesapeake, where more than 40 percent fled. Behind these numbers were complex personal choices.[9]

8. Franklin Bowditch Dexter, ed., *The Literary Diary of Ezra Stiles, D.D., LL.D., President of Yale College, II, March 14, 1776–December 31, 1781* (New York, 1901), 23; William G. McLoughlin, *Soul Liberty: The Baptists' Struggle in New England, 1630–1833* (Hanover, N.H., 1991), 196–201.

9. Bell, *War of Religion*, 222–240. There are a number of scholarly treatments of Anglicans during the war years. Many emphasize the experience of loyalist Anglicans as part of a larger political

In the early days of the war, some American Anglican leaders sought compromises. They tried to serve rebelling American congregations and remain true to their Anglican faith. The actions of the largely moderate Anglican clergy in Philadelphia, including William Smith and Jacob Duché—men who preached prominent moderate sermons in the same period—are suggestive of the challenges Anglican leaders faced. They were accustomed to supporting government and religion from the public pulpit, but doing so had become increasingly difficult as the Revolutionary Congress had grown in strength. On June 30, 1775, they penned a collective letter to the bishop of London "under deep affliction of mind." Though they had prayed that "the unhappy controversy between the Parent Country and these Colonies might be terminated upon Principles honourable and advantageous to both, without proceeding to the extremities of civil war and the horrors of Bloodshed," their wishes had not been granted. They assured the bishop that they had done what they could, but "as to public advice we have hitherto thought it our Duty to keep our Pulpits wholly clear from every thing bordering on this contest." They had, instead, pursued "Reason and Moderation" and "avoid[ed] whatever might irritate the Tempers of the people, or create a suspicion that we were opposed to the Interest of the Country in which we live." Yet the time had passed when they felt they could remain silent, particularly since the Continental Congress had declared a public fast. Members of their congregations were "determined never to submit to the Parliamentary claim of taxing them at pleasure," and, for Philadelphians, the outbreak of violence was a turning point. "The Blood already spilt," they wrote, "is unhappily alienating the affections of many from the Parent Country, and cementing them closer in the most fixed purpose of a Resistance, dreadful even in Contemplation." In such a context, they felt compelled to act in accordance with their pastoral responsibilities. When asked to preach before militia companies and at other public occasions, the Anglicans "thought it adviseable to take our Turn with the Ministers of other Denominations" and noted that they had heard their fellows in New York had done the same. It was a difficult spot to be in, not wanting to abandon their duties to the public pulpit but also not fully backing the patriot cause.[10]

---

narrative. For an important exception, see Rhoden, *Revolutionary Anglicanism,* 88–115. Bell, *War of Religion,* argues for a tight connection between loyalism and Anglicanism and provides essential numerical data about the choices of Anglican clergy by colony. See also Mills, *Bishops by Ballot,* 150–154. For an important treatment that emphasizes the consequences loyalist Anglicans faced for postwar British Anglicanism, see Walker, "Church Militant."

10. "Letter to the Lord Bishop of London," in William Stevens Perry, ed., *Papers Relating to the History of the Church in Pennsylvania, A.D. 1680–1778* (Philadelphia, 1871), 470–472.

The pressures of war eliminated the possibility that many Anglicans would be able to thread the needle between loyalties the way Philadelphia's Anglicans had attempted. In the northern colonies, public prejudice forced Anglican clergy to take sides, either violating the will of their ecclesiastical superiors or facing personal, often physical, penalties. During the war's first months, some ran afoul of test oaths and even faced imprisonment. Jacob Bailey, a missionary with the Society for the Propagation of the Gospel in Foreign Parts (SPG) in Pownalborough, Maine (then still part of Massachusetts), had suffered through repeated conflicts with local congregationalist leaders in the years before the war started, and that antagonism only accelerated as waves of patriot vigilantism forced Anglican missionaries to flee. In May 1776, amid rumors that independence might be declared soon, Pownalborough's Committee of Correspondence—its effective government at that time—resolved that Bailey had "been guilty of a criminal neglect in not reading Proclamations issued by the continental and provincial Congresses for days of publick fasting and prayer," by which acts he had "denied [the Congresses'] Authority." Bailey, in his report of his subsequent appearance before the body, described his behavior as exhibiting an admirable sangfroid. His antagonist—a local grandee who was simultaneously a part of the committee, the local sheriff, and a representative to the Provincial Congress—cut a different figure. In Bailey's retelling, the man "fell immediately into a violent passion, abused me with the most illiberal and virulent language, and having worked himself into a perfect frenzy, he stamped on the floor, smote on the table and exclaimed, *now for it Gentlemen,* as if he meant to excite the people to tear me into pieces." But no matter his calm, Bailey did not have the upper hand in Maine. In October, he was called in again, for "neglecting and refusing to read the declaration of the Right Hon.ble, the continental Congress for Independency, for preaching a seditious Sermon Lords day" and for other crimes "against the States of America." He insisted that his oaths as an Anglican "ought to be observed as sacred" and, moreover, that "a church or place of religious worship ought to be sacred to truth, and no minister ought to publish anything but what he realy believes agreable to the truth." His defense was not heeded. Bailey managed to dodge his opponents and stay in New England for several more years, but ultimately the die was cast against him, and he settled in Nova Scotia before the end of the war. Like other Anglicans who fled, Bailey could continue to be an Anglican—as long as he remained within the loyal British Empire.[11]

11. Jacob Bailey, "A Copy of the Proceedings of the Committee against the Rev. Jacob Bailey of Pownalboro," Richard Peters Papers, I, item 26, HSP; James S. Leamon, *The Reverend Jacob Bailey, Maine Loyalist: For God, King, Country, and for Self* (Amherst, Mass., 2012), 115–147. See also Walker, "Church Militant," 144–146.

During the course of the war, New York became a center of outspoken Anglican loyalists. Though Myles Cooper, the head of King's College in that city, and New Jersey's Thomas Bradbury Chandler left for England in May 1775, Charles Inglis and Samuel Seabury stayed in the region through the years of British occupation. Their robust communication with their coreligionists in England and with the church's hierarchy kept the Anglican network alive for a time. Inglis, from his post at New York's Trinity Church, published a pamphlet intended to refute Thomas Paine's *Common Sense,* answering a call from a loyalist publisher in the city, but his effort was almost destroyed in a frenzy of mob violence. As he later wrote in his memoir, the crowd seized the text mid-printing, then "carried one copy to a Beer House, where [they] read and unanimously condemned it." The next night, the mob returned to the printer and "burnt the whole impression." But Inglis and Seabury knew that the Anglicanism they sought to maintain was dependent on military success. As that became less likely, their spirits deteriorated. Seabury wrote as much to Cooper in 1778: "I wish I had something clever to tell you, but every thing on this side of the water is most confoundedly out of spirit." But he "expect[ed]" nonetheless that his compatriots would "support their own Honor and Dignity, and will finally crush this infernal Rebellion." That, of course, would not happen. Both Seabury and Inglis would eventually become bishops, but the former outside the Church of England and the latter outside the boundaries of the United States. There was no path forward that would allow them to be Anglican Americans.[12]

Southern Anglicans faced a very different set of choices from their northern colleagues, as they were caught between local congregations and vestries that often supported the rebellion and a church that emphatically did not. The difficulty was particularly evident for Maryland's Jonathan Boucher, a clergyman in Prince George's County. His congregation was broadly sympathetic to the rebellion, though Boucher was not. Additionally, he had, in the years before

12. For the correspondence between Cooper, Chandler, Seabury, and Inglis, see, especially, the Fettercairn Papers in the National Library of Scotland, Edinburgh, and the Samuel Seabury Papers at the General Theological Seminary, New York. See also Ross N. Hebb, *Samuel Seabury and Charles Inglis: Two Bishops, Two Churches* (Madison, N.J., 2010), 33. Inglis's controversial tract was *The Deceiver Unmasked; or, Loyalty and Interest United: In Answer to a Pamphlet Entitled Common Sense; by a Loyal American [Ten Lines of Quotations]* (New York, 1776). At least three copies of it survived. See "Memoires of Bishop Inglis, Nova Scotia," MG 1, CCCCLXXIX, Charles and John Inglis Fonds, Nova Scotia Archives, Halifax. See also Bell, *War of Religion,* 151–152; Samuel Seabury to Miles Cooper, Jan. 26, 1778, Fettercairn Papers, MSS, acc. 4796/75; and Robert G. Parkinson, *The Common Cause: Creating Race and Nation in the American Revolution* (Williamsburg, Va., and Chapel Hill, N.C., 2016), 205–206. Inglis also published Charles Inglis, *The True Interest of America Impartially Stated, in Certain Stictures* [sic] *on a Pamphlet Intitled Common Sense: By an American* (Philadelphia, 1776). See also Charles Inglis to Cooper, July 24, 1777, Fettercairn Papers, MSS, acc. 4796/75.

the fighting started, alienated many of the colony's elite through his advocacy of higher clerical salaries and a bishop in the early 1770s, despite Marylanders' preference for a locally dominated Anglican polity. He published a tract highly critical of the Continental Congress in 1774, and in early 1775 he was forcibly brought before the leaders of Maryland's revolution because of his political sentiments. As he wrote to William Smith in Philadelphia on May 4, 1775, he believed the Anglican Church in Maryland had "received its Death's Blow," and no establishment at all would exist in a few more years. He wanted Anglicans to take up the charge against the rebels, and he asked Smith to pen "some acc't of the sad Convulsions which are about to rend in Pieces this once happy Country." The Marylander reported that those in neighboring Virginia were even more agitated than New Englanders, and he could not "help suspecting, that they hope to carry their Point by blustering and looking big." Despite these sentiments, he was not outspoken in his support of British actions, either. "It is not easy to say to which side a real Friend to Liberty, Order and good Government would incline. For my Part I equally dread a Victory on either Side." Boucher's distress at the situation was palpable, as was his frustration that his own voice—already aligned with the British, in the eyes of his neighbors—could not be seen as a neutral, moral authority.[13]

Matters came to a head rapidly for Boucher, and it was clear to him that he could not minister a flock that promoted revolution. When it came to Maryland's fast day, on May 11, 1775, he declined to preach, thinking it the better part of valor not to have to define the occasion in a way that was empty or duplicitous. His reputation for controversy drew attention anyway. The day had been set aside for "fasting and humiliation" because of the "distressed and perplexed situation of British America, the weakness of all human counsels," and because "the hearts of all men are in the disposal of the Supreme Being." Maryland's de facto government called on this traditional ritual to validate and legitimate itself as it transformed the lines of authority in the colony. As Boucher recounted later, Maryland's pro-rebellion voices became increasingly hostile to his preaching, and he eventually began to carry weapons with him into the church. The situation was not tenable in the long term. Maryland's new government demanded that Boucher sign articles of association that he considered in violation of his oaths to church and state. He left for England in August.[14]

13. Anne Y. Zimmer, *Jonathan Boucher: Loyalist in Exile* (Detroit, 1978), 119–130, 164–168; Jonathan Boucher to William Smith, May 4, 1775, William Smith Papers, II, letter 7, ser. C, Hawks Collection, Archives of the Episcopal Church, Austin, Tex.; also published as "Letters of Rev. Jonathan Boucher," *Maryland Historical Magazine,* VIII (1913), 237–240.

14. *Proceedings of the Conventions of the Province of Maryland, Held at the City of Annapolis, in 1774, 1775, and 1776* (Baltimore, 1836), 13; Zimmer, *Jonathan Boucher,* 172–174, 183–191.

The accounts of Anglicans-turned-Revolutionaries could be as vivid as those of their loyalist counterparts, but they were not typical. The most famous story in the first category relates to Peter Gabriel Muhlenberg, a Halle-trained Anglican serving a congregation in Virginia. He resigned his position as a minister to join the army, earning himself—through the labors of his descendant-cum-biographer—a place in the lore of American Christian nationalism with the (apocryphal) story that he dramatically removed his clerical robes while in the pulpit to reveal his Virginia military uniform (see Figure 11). Several other Anglicans also became military chaplains on the American side, including Virginians David Griffith and John Hurt. Far more common, however, were the quieter choices by Anglican clergy to support the Americans. Some served on local Committees of Safety or supported the new governments in other ways. But these were hard choices, in light of their professional responsibilities. Although the Anglican Church was established in Virginia and Maryland, and powerful members of the laity (including, of course, George Washington) in both those colonies supported the rebellion, the decisions made by southern Anglican clergy were not eased by any denominational body. There was, in other words, no Anglican parallel to the Synod of New York and Philadelphia, with its strong statements of support for Congress. Overall, according to the work of historian James Bell, more than 40 percent of Anglican clergy present in 1775 joined the American side, whereas close to another 20 percent kept their political leanings from this historical record. Whatever their choices, none of those American Anglican leaders who chose to support the United States would be Anglicans in 1783 for the simple reason that the Church of England no longer recognized any relation to them.[15]

Because the Church of England's hierarchy remained steadfast in its com-

15. Muhlenberg's story grew to mythic proportions over the centuries. For an academic treatment, see Bell, *War of Religion,* 171–173. For discussion of it in Christian nationalist circles, see Kate Carté Engel, "The Founding Fathers in Modern America," in Matthew Avery Sutton and Darren Dochuk, eds., *Faith in the New Millennium: The Future of Religion and American Politics* (New York, 2016), 19. Thomas Buchanan Read's poem "The Rising" was published in Read, *The Wagoner of the Alleghanies: A Poem of the Days of Seventy-Six* (Philadelphia, 1862), 82–92; see esp. 89–91, for the lines quoted with Figure 11. For Griffith and Hurt, see Bell, *War of Religion,* 174–176. Historians have evaluated the choices of Anglican clergy, noting both the prevalence of loyalism among northern Anglican clergy and the general tendency toward support for the Revolution in the southern colonies, where Anglicanism was established and Revolutionary governments took hold. See Bell, *War of Religion,* esp. 170–186, app. 1. Rhoden gives a careful and thorough analysis in *Revolutionary Anglicanism,* 88–115. See also G. MacLaren Brydon, "The Clergy of the Established Church in Virginia and the Revolution," *Virginia Magazine of History and Biography,* XLI (1933), 11–23. For fast days, see Derek H. Davis, *Religion and the Continental Congress, 1774–1789: Contributions to Original Intent* (New York, 2000), 84; and Charles Wilbanks, ed., *The American Revolution and Righteous Community: Selected Sermons of Bishop Robert Smith* (Columbia, S.C., 2007), xviii–xix, 20–22.

mitment to upholding imperial policy, only those people and places who took the same view remained within the transatlantic Anglican network. Although American Anglicans who backed the Revolutionary cause might remain within local churches if they had the support of their congregations and local authorities, they lost their connections to their counterparts in other areas of the empire. They also lost their access to bishops, a deep wound for an episcopal church that would not be mended until several years after the war concluded. For a time, American Anglicans who aligned with London were able to maintain robust communications and count on continued assistance, moral and sometimes financial, from their Anglican counterparts, but their options, too, declined in the war's later years. They would have to leave the United States or find a new ecclesiastical home. The transatlantic Anglican network that had characterized imperial protestantism continued to exist, but without its American branch. American Anglicans faced a new United States in which their church, which had benefited directly from its privileged place in the empire, was now little more than a series of state-based remnants.[16]

What of the awakened network? Because its structures were often personal and informal, bridging all of the major denominations and establishment structures of imperial protestantism, it was most successful weathering the war's disruptions. More than either of the other two networks, its members had space to lament the war's divisions. In December 1775, Thomas Rankin, an awakened Anglican connected to John Wesley's growing movement, wrote to Lord Dartmouth from Philadelphia. In a neat summation of imperial protestantism's ethos, he explained to his high-placed patron that he wrote out of a sense of duty "to God, My Prince, and my fellow Subjects, in Great Britain, Ireland, and America." He decried the terrible state of colonial affairs, but rather than rehash how matters had devolved, he wrote that it was "the future that engages my attention, and the attention of Millions; and Millions yet unborn, [that] may be interested in the important Scene." At the present moment, matters were bleak: *"Britannia weeps,"* he wrote with emphasis, *"while wicked men and Devils triumph!"* He saw no easy solution. Quoting Jeremiah, he added: *"Is there no balm in Gilead? Is there no Phisician there?"* Rankin tried to remain impartial (though he must have known his correspondent was not) and claimed he could not "help from thinking, that Great Britain and her Colonies, might be restored to their late harmony, without the sheding of any more human Blood. Surely they may, unless God has a determined controversy with these lands." Regardless,

16. The richest collections of transatlantic Anglican correspondence during the war years revolve around the loyalists who remained in occupied New York. See, for example, the Fettercairn Papers and the Seabury Papers.

FIGURE 11 *"General Pete" Muhlenberg.* Photograph of watercolor by Helen Richards Horn. 1942. Used by permission of Trexler Library, Muhlenberg College.

The idea of religious leaders' guiding their congregants into battle has a powerful history in U.S. national mythology. Those myths simplified the complicated path American religious leaders took from participation in imperial protestantism to spokesmen for a new, independent United States. A statue of Peter Gabriel Muhlenberg is one of Pennsylvania's two contributions to the U.S. Capitol's Hall of Statuary. It was produced in 1889 by Blanche Nevin. At that time, the story of Muhlenberg's choice to join the Virginia army was replicated in verse in the popular McGuffey Readers series as part of a poem that included the verses of Thomas Buchanan Read's 1862 poem "The Rising":

> The pastor rose: the prayer was strong;
> The psalm was warrior David's song;
> The text, a few short words of might,—
> "The Lord of hosts shall arm the right!"
> He spoke of wrongs too long endured,
> Of sacred rights to be secured;
> Then from his patriot tongue of flame
> The startling words for Freedom came.
> The stirring sentences he spake
> Compelled the heart to glow or quake,
> And, rising on his theme's broad wing,
> And grasping in his nervous hand
> The imaginary battle-brand,
> In face of death he dared to fling
> Defiance to a tyrant king.
>
> Even as he spoke, his frame, renewed
> In eloquence of attitude,
> Rose, as it seemed, a shoulder higher;
> Then swept his kindling glance of fire
> From startled pew to breathless choir;
> When suddenly his mantle wide
> His hands impatient flung aside,
> And, lo! he met their wondering eyes
> Complete in all a warrior's guise.
>
> A moment there was awful pause,—
> When Berkley cried, "Cease, traitor! cease!
> God's temple is the house of peace!"
> The other shouted, "Nay, not so,
> When God is with our righteous cause:
> His holiest places then are ours,
> His temples are our forts and towers
> That frown upon the tyrant foe:
> In this the dawn of Freedom's day
> There is a time to fight and pray!"

he continued, "present disturbances, are not at all favourable to the spreading of the gospel." He and his awakened fellows certainly hoped the opportunity for religious work would soon return, but, for the moment, it had to wait.[17]

Rankin's letter reflected an important characteristic of the awakened network that differentiated it from both its dissenting and Anglican peers. Whereas those networks were, at least in part, built from denominational or institutional structures, the awakened network in the colonial period was essentially personal. It connected like-minded religious leaders across all the dominant denominations and establishment arrangements. Because of that distinctive structure, many connections, such as those between Scotland's John Erskine and New England's awakened leaders, or even between South Carolina's William Tennent and Selina Hastings, the countess of Huntingdon, could essentially be paused. Participants could merely wait for an opportune moment to communicate again. Sometimes they were successful and sometimes not; Erskine reconnected with Joseph Bellamy in 1784, but Tennent did not survive the war. For many awakened protestants, transatlantic ties escaped the taint of politics that plagued their dissenting and Anglican colleagues.[18]

One important exception to that generalization warrants discussion, however. John Wesley's outspoken stance in favor of the North ministry's coercive measures in 1775 was widely discussed on both sides of the Atlantic. His followers in North America (mostly awakened Anglicans, as the formation of the American Methodist Episcopal Church in 1786 was a consequence of the war) suffered persecution because of their connections to him. Moreover, the Wesleyans' commitment to remain within the Church of England forced them to deal with some of the same difficulties as loyalist Anglicans. George Shadford, who worked with Rankin in Virginia, petitioned that state's government in October 1776 in favor of maintaining its Anglican establishment on the grounds that the "methodists" were no "Dessenters, but a Religious Society in Communion with the Church of England." They "pray that as the Church of England ever hath been, so it may continue to be Established." It was an inauspicious moment to be making such a petition. The association between Wesley and the British side in the cause did his followers in America no favors. As a result of antagonism from Americans who supported the rebellion, most of his missionaries fled the growing jurisdiction of the United States during the war.

17. Thomas Rankin to William Legge, second earl of Dartmouth, Dec. 20, 1775, in Papers of the Legge Family, Earls of Dartmouth (hereafter cited as Dartmouth Papers), D(W) 1778/II/1616, Staffordshire Record Office, Stafford, U.K. The biblical citation is Jeremiah 8:22 (AV).

18. John Erskine to Joseph Bellamy, Sept. 21, 1784, Joseph Bellamy Papers, box 188, folder 2938, item 81393, Hartford Seminary Library, Conn.

Afterward, only one, the indefatigable Francis Asbury, remained. The personal nature of the awakened network was a blessing and a curse when it came to managing the politics and disruptions of the war. For Wesley's followers, it hurt, but for the larger awakened community, the network's personal nature would become a source of resilience.[19]

The dislocations and violence of war forced American religious leaders to test connections to their British counterparts, religious and political. The networks that had structured so much transatlantic community within imperial protestantism bore the greatest strain. American dissenters, though they largely concurred on the politics of the war with their British fellows, turned away from an imperial conception of the dissenting interest to lend their support to American religious institutions. The Anglican network contracted, leaving behind American coreligionists who chose to stay in the new United States. Even awakened protestants paused in their labors, unsure of their future. The primary channels of connection that structured the transatlantic protestant community during the colonial era—the planks of the scaffolding—no longer connected American protestants to coreligionists in Britain.

WAR'S DESTRUCTION

The Revolutionary War was long and brutal. The fighting ranged from Nova Scotia to Georgia and also raged at sea. It battered the churches, colleges, and missions painstakingly built before the war, many of them funded and supported through the organizations of imperial protestantism. The material ruin brought by the war played a significant role in dislodging the United States from the connections that had bound it to Britain. It erased from the landscape the physical reminders of past collaborations, replacing them with scars more easily understood—by Americans—as signs of unchristian British behavior. The war did more than reorient the attentions of American religious leaders toward a new polity and new protestant communities. It damaged and destroyed much of what the cooperation of the previous era had produced.[20]

The war on the North American landscape can be outlined in the damage

19. "Methodist Petition, Oct. 28, 1776," in "Virginia Legislative Papers (Continued)," *VMHB*, XVIII (1910), 140–150, esp. 143–144; Jones, "Methodism, Slavery, and Freedom in the Revolutionary Atlantic," 20–23; Anna M. Lawrence, *One Family under God: Love, Belonging, and Authority in Early Transatlantic Methodism* (Philadelphia, 2011), 196–199; Dee E. Andrews, *The Methodists and Revolutionary America, 1760–1800: The Shaping of an Evangelical Culture* (Princeton, N.J., 2000), 49–55.

20. For the war's violence and destruction, see Holger Hoock, *Scars of Independence: America's Violent Birth* (New York, 2017), esp. 40.

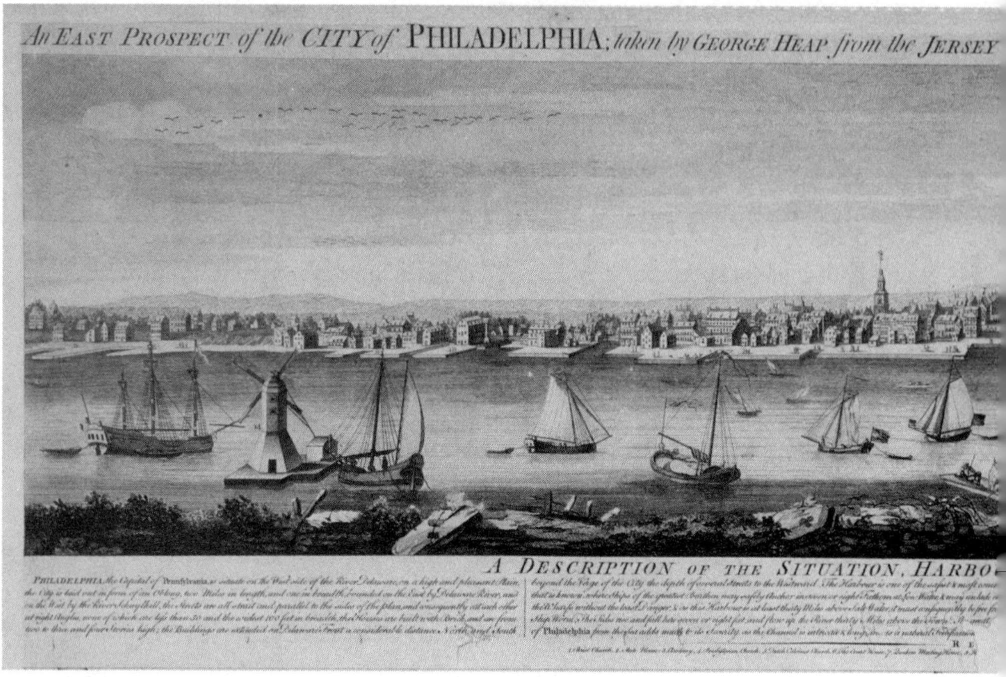

FIGURE 12 *An East Prospect of the City of Philadelphia; Taken by George Heap from the Jersey Shore, under the Direction of Nicholas Skull Surveyor General of the Province of Pennsylvania.* Engraved by T. Jefferys. This 1768 view of Philadelphia suggests the prominence of churches in the city's landscape. Four of the seven numbered buildings in the plan were churches. Courtesy of the Library of Congress Prints and Photographs Division, Washington, D.C.

done to its religious architecture. The physical infrastructure associated with institutional protestantism accounted for some of the most dramatic and spacious buildings in North America. Colonial cityscapes showed rows of church spires (see Figure 12). Congregations put substantial funds into building churches and meetinghouses, and the colleges funded and organized by religious leaders—Harvard, Yale, the College of New Jersey, the baptist college in Providence, King's College—all possessed substantial buildings. The story of the war was thus, at least in part, a history of violence against sites associated with religion. One of the earliest examples was among the most infamous. During the occupation of Boston, Old South Church was "taken possession of" by a regiment of British dragoons. The "Pulpit, pews and seats, [were] all cut to pieces and carried off in the most savage manner as can be expressed," according to one diarist. A "beautiful carved pew with the silk furniture" was turned into a "hog stye." These acts were blamed on General John Burgoyne. Those same insults were recounted years later by William Gordon, who, at the time of the war, had

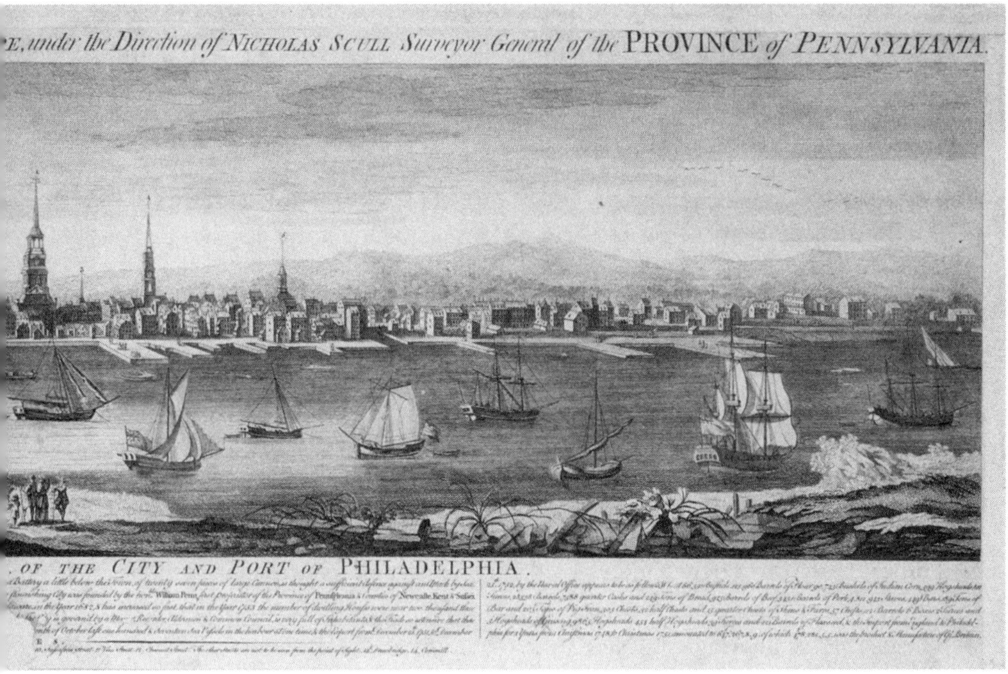

been a minister in Roxbury, Massachusetts. After telling the story in his history of the Revolution, he assured his reader that such damage would not have been done to an Anglican church, effectively blaming the British for a crime of prejudice as well as an act of war. "Had the meeting house and its contents been honored with episcopal consecration," he wrote, "these proceedings would be deemed by multitudes profane and sacrilegious." In many ways, the story, and its gloss by Gordon, set the paradigm for how patriot religious leaders experienced the war. They were angry at what they viewed as desecration, and the stories of assaults on these embodiments of institutional protestantism became—and remained for generations—particular marks of British cruelty.[21]

21. Timothy Newell, "A Journal Kept during the Time Y[e]t Bolton Was Shut up in 1775–6," in Massachusetts Historical Society, *Collections*, 4th Ser., I (Boston, 1852), 269; William Gordon, *The History of the Rise, Progress, and the Establishment of the Independence of the United States of America . . .*, II (London, 1788), 140; J. Franklin Jameson, *The American Revolution Considered as a Social Movement* (1926; rpt. Princeton, N.J., 1967), 92. Sermons after the war recounted the damage. See Samuel Miller, ed., *Memoirs of the Rev. John Rodgers, D.D., Late Pastor of the Wall-Street*

The list of churches that were damaged, destroyed, and repurposed was long and often repeated. Andrew Eliot, one of Boston's ministers who stayed during the siege, wrote to a fellow New Englander who was then in London about the "contempt thrown upon our places of worship." Listing churches by their ministers, Eliot reported that, in Boston, "Dr. Cooper's, Mr. Steward's, and Dr. Byles's turned into barracks without any appearance of necessity. Mr. Moorhead's filled with hay, Mr. Stillman's made an hospital. Such conduct w.d disgrace barbarians." When British troops occupied Newport, Rhode Island, in December 1776, Ezra Stiles, who had already evacuated the town, recorded that "Officers were taking up houses for Barracks, and among others have taken my House and Meetinghouse—which last it is said they intend to make an Assembly Room for Balls etc after taking down the Pews." After the occupation ended, Stiles reported that soldiers "had run up a Chimney in the middle of the Meetinghouse, and demolished all the Pews and Seats below and in the Galleries." In a stroke of luck, "they left the Pulpit Stand[in]g, tho' they destroyed the pulpit in the other Presb. Meetingh. and in two Baptist Meetings." Newspapers, too, paid particular attention to assaults on churches. The *Norwich Packet,* recounting a British attack on Kingston, New York, that took place October 16, 1777, noted that the "whole town except one house was reduced to ashes, the church itself not escaping." Another newspaper reported of a British raid on Bristol, Rhode Island, in 1778 that the soldiers had moved into the town "burning, plundering, and destroying whatever their haste would permit, not sparing the episcopal church, a large edifice near the centre of the town." Explaining the war's destruction by emphasizing its damage to churches brought the conflict into the core of colonial life.[22]

Applying blame for the destruction was complicated. For some, the damage and chaos were merely facts of war—armies were apt to behave in ways that religious leaders did not like. When Andrew Eliot described the destruction of Boston's churches, he followed it up with the statement that he was "quite sick

---

and Brick Churches in the City of New-York (New York, 1813), 334–337. Jedidiah Morse listed Connecticut losses in his *Annals of the American Revolution,* 324n. See also David Ramsay, *The History of the Independent Congregational Church in Charleston, South Carolina* (Philadelphia, 1815), 35–36.

22. Andrew Eliot to Isaac Smith, Jr., Apr. 9, 1776, Smith-Carter Family Papers, 1669–1880, microfilm, P 147, reel 2, Massachusetts Historical Society, Boston; Dexter, ed., *Literary Diary of Ezra Stiles,* I, 426, II, 96; *Norwich Packet* (Conn.), Dec. 15, 1777, [1]; *Pennsylvania Evening Post* (Philadelphia), July 4, 1778, 220; Andrews Hill Hamilton, *The History of the Old South Church (Third Church) Boston, 1699–1884* (Boston, 1889), 176–177. Jameson suggested, but did not document, the destruction of "more than fifty places of worship in various parts of the country" (*American Revolution Considered as a Social Movement,* 92). For German churches in Pennsylvania, see John B. Frantz, "Religion, the American Revolution, and the Pennsylvania Germans," in Pencak, ed., *Pennsylvania's Revolution,* 83–85. See also Thomas S. Kidd, *God of Liberty: A Religious History of the American Revolution* (New York, 2010), 194; and Crabtree, *Holy Nation,* 45.

of armies, and am determined, if possible, never to live in the same place, with any considerable body of forces." Though Eliot was a supporter of the American cause and saw no prospect of reunion with Great Britain, he did not blame the British for specific crimes against churches when he reported them to his friend. Similarly, Charles Inglis recounted to his former colleague, Myles Cooper, who had fled to Britain, that the "College Library and Apparatus" of King's (where Cooper had been the president before the war) were "plundered and dispersed by the [British] Soldiery." He added that the matter "has chagrined me as much as any thing during the whole Rebellion." He saw the negative consequences of the army's behavior clearly. "The Ravages committed every where on Friends and Foes indiscriminately by our Army, [are] really shameful; and if not checked, will be productive of the most fatal Consequences. The Army will be ruined, and the Colonists totally disaffected." The consequences of war—the actions of marauding armies—became a force unto themselves, separate from the prejudices that led to the conflict.[23]

The damage was vast. The British destroyed Boston's churches in 1775; fire took down New York's in 1776. As Inglis reported, before that city's great conflagration on September 20, 1776, the Anglicans had "three Churches, of which Trinity Church was the oldest and largest." It, along with many auxiliary facilities, burned. "St. Paul's Church and King's College [would have] shared the same Fate," Inglis wrote, as they were "directly in the Line of Fire, had I not been providentially on the Spot, and sent a Number of People with Water on the Roof of each." The occupying British did not rebuild Trinity but instead transformed it into an area for entertainment, earning the anger of local Anglicans. Nor were the British the only offenders. SPG minister Daniel Batwell reported to his superiors that "Churches of York and Carlisle [Pennsylvania], have been converted into Magazines by the Rebels." The war took a very direct toll on the structures that colonists and their religious leaders used and considered sacred.[24]

That both armies damaged the religious landscape did not stop such actions from becoming politicized, including in religious terms. The new American government actively connected the damage to American religious symbols with

23. Eliot to Smith, Apr. 9, 1776, Smith-Carter Papers, P 147, reel 2; Inglis to Cooper, Feb. 8, 1777, Fettercairn Papers, MSS, acc. 4796/75.

24. Inglis to Richard Hind, secretary of the SPG, Oct. 31, 1776, in John Wolfe Lydekker, *The Life and Letters of Charles Inglis: His Ministry in America and Consecration as First Colonial Bishop, from 1759 to 1787* (London, 1936), 168; Journal of the Society for the Propagation of the Gospel in Foreign Parts (SPG), June 19, 1778, XXI, 317, Colonial Missionaries' Papers from America and the West Indies, 1701–1870, British Online Archives, https://microform.digital/boa; Judith L. Van Buskirk, *Generous Enemies: Patriots and Loyalists in Revolutionary New York* (Philadelphia, 2002), 33–34.

British perfidy. In the aftermath of the New Jersey campaigns in 1776 and early 1777, Congress appointed a committee of seven members, including Princeton president John Witherspoon, to investigate the "conduct of the British and Hessian generals and officers." Witherspoon believed that the behavior of the British was "dreadful." As he told his son, "At Trenton they killed Mr. Roxburgh, Presbyterian minister." The story carried with it a particular viciousness. "Though he fell down on his knees and begged his life," Witherspoon continued, "yet they pierced him through and through with their bayonets, and mangled him in a most shocking manner." Witherspoon had also heard a rumor that the offenders had mistaken Roxburgh for himself, a point on which Witherspoon was not sure; regardless, he believed "the fact of his death and the manner of it is beyond all doubt." The committee's report found that the "conduct of the enemy" included a long litany of abuses, but "above all, places of worship, ministers and religious persons of some particular protestant denominations, seem to have been treated with the most rancorous hatred, and, at the same time, with the highest contempt." The suggestion that the largely Anglican British had targeted New Jersey's presbyterians was unmistakable, but it also served a more general argument that the British destroyed and attacked that which was holy.[25]

Important symbols of imperial protestant cooperation over the preceding decades also suffered. This included most of the colonial colleges. The College of New Jersey—long a recipient of transatlantic fundraising efforts—was caught between the two warring armies. It passed back and forth between them, incurring damage from each side. British forces turned the college's main building, Nassau Hall, and the nearby presbyterian church into barracks. A British soldier later reported that his fellows "spoiled and plundered" the library, a particularly galling loss since religious leaders so assiduously contributed to colonial college libraries. On January 3, 1777, the Battle of Princeton resulted in an American victory, but it came with costs—among them, further damage to Nassau Hall (see Figure 13). The college that London merchant Dennys De Berdt had once championed to Lord Dartmouth as "the only Colledge where Vital Religion is Regarded" could not easily be rebuilt. No one could rely on the transatlantic

25. *Journals of the Continental Congress, 1774–1789 . . .*, 34 vols. (Washington, D.C., 1904–1937), VII, 42–43, 276, 277; John Witherspoon to David Witherspoon, Feb. 2, 1777, in Paul H. Smith, ed., *Letters of Delegates to Congress, 1774–1789*, 26 vols. (Washington, D.C., 1976–2000), VI, 269–270. The Synod of New York and Philadelphia recorded that "the Revd. Mr John Rosbrugh was barbarously murdered by the Enemy at Trenton on January 2d [1777]." See Klett, ed., *Minutes of the Presbyterian Church in America*, 555; see also David Hackett Fischer, *Washington's Crossing* (New York, 2004), 300. William Gordon, who was himself a dissenting minister, reprinted this report in his history, verbatim. See Gordon, *History of the Rise, Progress, and the Establishment*, II, 458.

FIGURE 13 *Death of General Mercer*. By Jonathan Trumbull. This work depicting the Battle of Princeton resembled a painting by Trumbull's mentor, Benjamin West, which portrayed the death of General Wolff at Quebec in 1759 as a Christ-like martyr for the British cause. Trumbull's painting transposed that religious iconography to the American cause. This early pen-and-ink sketch dates from 1786, ten years after the battle. John Trumbull, Battle of Princeton Prints Collection (GC155), Graphic Arts Division, Department of Special Collections, Princeton University Library

ties that had financed its development and even supplied Witherspoon as its illustrious president. Severed from the empire, it now had a far more circumscribed range of potential patrons.[26]

The same difficulties troubled Anglican institutions, which were also cut off from British support by the war. Anglican leaders in occupied New York continued to appeal to London for help. They hoped that a British victory would allow the Church of England to be put on a stronger footing, including a better role for King's College. Their case vacillated between desperation at the college's current state and almost delusionary hopes for future expansion.

26. "Petition to the Council of Assembly for the State of New Jersey," John Witherspoon Collection, C0274, box 1, folder 3, Princeton University Library; Dennys De Berdt to [Dartmouth], Aug. 22, 1766, Dartmouth Papers, D(W) 1778/II/229; *History of the College of New Jersey, from Its Commencement, A.D. 1746, to 1783, by a Graduate* (Princeton, N.J., 1844), 47; Mailer, *John Witherspoon's American Revolution*, 289–901; Fischer, *Washington's Crossing*, 131–132, 338; Alfred Hoyt Bill, *The Campaign of Princeton, 1776–1777* (Princeton, N.J., 1948), 33–34; Jeffrey H. Morrison, *John Witherspoon and the Founding of the American Republic* (Notre Dame, Ind., 2005), 14–15. See also "Correspondence of Ezra Stiles, President of Yale College, and James Madison, President of William and Mary College, 1780," *WMQ*, 3d Ser., VII (1927), 292–296.

Inglis admonished the college's absent president, Myles Cooper, not to think of coming back to New York, as Cooper could better serve the college by procuring a new royal charter for it in London. In the meantime, Inglis told his friend, "Remember, the College is an Hospital—the small Partitions are all knocked down, and the large and small Rooms thrown into one, for the Benefit of the Patients." Moreover, without either books or equipment, "It will require at least a thousand Pounds to put the College in proper Repair." The loyalist Anglican cohort had no realistic hope of American support, and help from Britain could only come if the British won the war. Either way, King's College, like Princeton, was in shambles.[27]

The withdrawal of the SPG from the rebelling regions was the most dramatic and widespread collapse of a colonial-era project during the war, one that intertwined with the contraction of the Anglican network. The sprawling missionary society had been the basis of the vast majority of communications between British Anglican leaders and their American counterparts. Though it did not formally end activities in the United States until after the war's conclusion, roughly a third of all SPG missionaries in North America fled their posts. Daniel Batwell, who had been stationed in York, Pennsylvania, wrote to the SPG in 1778, after a two-year lapse, to say that "thro' the violence of the times he has lost his labor; his money, and his health, but, by the blessing of God, has saved his family, and not made shipwreck of his conscience." Nonetheless, he had an extreme tale of woe. As these missionaries fled, the vision of the imperial missionary church retreated with them. There were ninety-two missionaries, catechists, and schoolmasters on the SPG's payroll in 1775 working in colonies that rebelled. After the war, any who remained in the United States had to find new employers. As the SPG disappeared from the United States, one of the most significant planks of the imperial protestant scaffold came crashing down.[28]

27. Inglis to Cooper, Feb. 8, 1777, July 15, 1777, Fettercairn Papers, MSS, acc. 4796/75.

28. Journal of the SPG, June 19, 1778, XXI, 312. Batwell had been ignominiously dragged from his sickbed and thrown into prison by Americans who thought him loyal to the king. He also wrote to both John Hancock and Henry Laurens to protest his plight. See Daniel Batwell to Hancock, Oct. 1, 1777, and Batwell to Laurens, Nov. 7, 1777, Simon Gratz American Clergy Collection, case 8, box 21. See also James P. Myers, Jr., "Homeland Security in the Pennsylvania Backcountry, 1777–1778: The Example of the Reverend Mr. Daniel Batwell, SPG," *Pennsylvania History,* LXXVIII (2011), 247–271; and [Barrington] Shute, *A Sermon Preached before the Incorporated Society for the Propagation of the Gospel in Foreign Parts . . .* (London, 1775), 7–15. Cross-referencing the catalog that appears at the back of Shute's printed sermon in the society's annual report with Bell's appendix to *War of Religion,* 222–240, permits one to glean more about the choices of individual ministers. From the perspective of the SPG, however, work did not continue within the bounds of the United States. For discussions of the plight of SPG ministers, see Travis Glasson, *Mastering Christianity: Missionary Anglicanism and Slavery in the Atlantic World* (New York, 2012), 207–208; Bell, *War of Religion,* 197–198; and Rhoden, *Revolutionary Anglicanism,* 127–128.

The damage done to George Whitefield's plantation and orphan house (turned college) in Bethesda, Georgia, also revealed the war as a turning point for imperial protestantism. The Grand Itinerant had spent decades raising money for the project, and when he sought a charter for it to become a college, he had explicitly imagined it as a body that bridged the empire's regional and denominational divisions. The estate had passed to the countess of Huntingdon when Whitefield died in 1770. She had sent a group of missionaries to Georgia, only to have much of Whitefield's establishment burn to the ground in 1773. When the war broke out, Huntingdon's staff struggled to maintain control of a project that made little sense in the middle of a revolution. A group of the countess's enslaved Africans, uninterested in laboring to support missionaries, ran away to a British ship. One of her representatives, Richard Piercy, appealed to the captain of the *Raven* for their return on the grounds that they were part of a religious project, telling him that the Africans "[belonged] to a publick Charity, a Charity not confined to America, but equally beneficial to England as Georgia." When the captain rejected this argument, Piercy tried a different tactic—"I insisted upon it that they were British Property and mentioned your Ladyship as the sole Proprietor"—but that had no better result. Neither Bethesda's religious purpose nor its ties to its English patron could protect it. Worse was yet to come, though the countess was not to know it until years later, when a report arrived from a servant, Margaret Floyd. As she recounted, when British forces took Savannah at the end of 1778, they "took all the best of the things at the Orphanhouse." Shortly after, "the Hessians came out first and plundered the house of all the poultry and meat and likewise Sugar Tea coffee candles and every thing of that kind." On yet a third visit from the invading army, Floyd reported that she "show'd your Name and mark on the Sheets and Table linen and other Things of which there was a great plenty but they did not mind it." Between the fire and the war, there was little left to show for decades of transatlantic philanthropic labor.[29]

29. Piercy later reported the ship had made its way to Saint Augustine, and if he was right, perhaps the Bethesda group eventually made its way to freedom in Nova Scotia or Sierra Leone. In an interesting twist, the captain of the *Raven* claimed to be a relative of the countess. See Richard Piercy to Selina Hastings, June 10, 1777, A4/2/19, William Piercy to Hastings, Oct. 3, 1777, A4/2/20, Margaret Floyd to Hastings, 1785, A3/1/38–39, all in Cheshunt College Archives, Westminster College, Cambridge (CCA); and Harvey H. Jackson, "The Battle of the Riceboats: Georgia Joins the Revolution," *Georgia Historical Quarterly*, LVIII (1974), 229–243. For Whitefield's relationship to Bethesda and the bounds of empire, see Peter Y. Choi, *George Whitefield: Evangelist for God and Empire* (Grand Rapids, Mich., 2018), 219–225. For the countess of Huntingdon's connections there, see Boyd Stanley Schlenther, "'To Convert the Poor People in America': The Bethesda Orphanage and the Thwarted Zeal of the Countess of Huntingdon," *Georgia Historical Quarterly*, LXXVIII (1994), 225–256. For the fire, see James Habersham to Hastings, June 3, 1773, A3/3/3, CCA.

New opportunities developed within an American rather than a transatlantic context. At the start of the war, Samuel Kirkland, a presbyterian missionary and former associate of Eleazar Wheelock, received funds from the New England Company (NEC) and from the Society in Scotland for Propagating Christian Knowledge (SSPCK). Both British societies ceased sending payments during the war. But Kirkland offered his expertise in Indigenous matters to the new Congress, and he was reimbursed for expenses he had already incurred in its cause. Moreover, "for the propagation of the Gospel amongst the Indians, and conciliating their affections to the United Colonies, and thereby preserving their friendship and neutrality," Congress continued his employment. For the struggling government, this intertwining of missionary and political work was natural. It fitted with the body's willingness to harness protestant institutions and their leaders to support its cause. Eleazar Wheelock also received money from Congress for his Indian School, now in New Hampshire. Although the new partnerships signal Kirkland's and Wheelock's political proclivities in the war, they also mark the reorientation of protestant work toward new funding sources and authorities. As connections to distant fellows failed, religious leaders needed new partners. The shifting of political masters was not pleasing to those in Britain. Ambrose Serle, an aide to General William Howe who moved in awakened protestant circles, wrote to Lord Dartmouth in London complaining that religious leaders were a cause of the war. He was "sorry to hear, that Mr. Wheelock [supported the American cause], as well as Mr. [William] Gordon, both of whom I believe are known to your Lordship. One Kirtland also does immense Harm in the back Country about Lake Champlain." Serle's discomfort pointed to a new reality. Religious leaders who had promoted the ends of empire during the colonial period could now put those same skills to serve the United States. A national boundary now cut through the old imperial protestant system, and those on either side had to make choices accordingly.[30]

The physical and financial destruction brought by the war reinforced the weakening of imperial protestantism's transatlantic networks that had begun in the war's first years. Numerous congregations faced the practical work of rebuild-

30. *Journals of the Continental Congress*, III, 351; Ambrose Serle to Dartmouth, Nov. 8, 1776, in *B. F. Stevens's Facsimiles of Manuscripts in European Archives Relating to America, 1773–1783 . . .*, XXIV (London, 1895), doc. 2045, also available in Dartmouth Papers, D(W) 1778/II/1710; General Court and Committee Minutes, New England Company, Nov. 10, 1775, CLC/540/MS07920/001, London Metropolitan Archives; Alan Taylor, *The Divided Ground: Indians, Settlers, and the Northern Borderlands of the American Revolution* (New York, 2006), 81–82; Christine Sternberg Patrick, "The Life and Times of Samuel Kirkland, 1741–1808: Missionary to the Oneida Indians, American Patriot and the Founder of Hamilton College" (Ph.D. diss., State University of New York at Buffalo, 1993), 225–228, 289–290; Colin G. Calloway, *The Indian History of an American Institution: Native Americans and Dartmouth* (Hanover, N.H., 2010), 42.

ing churches, and after the war they would do that as part of a new, American religious community, not as extensions of Britain's imperial protestantism. At the same time, the work that had been produced by transatlantic partnerships during the colonial period—colleges, missions, even the Sphinxlike Bethesda—had been damaged and disconnected from its British patrons. American protestant leaders, when they had the time and space to construct their protestant work again, would have to think very carefully about whom they could ask for support.

BRITAIN'S WAR

The planks that spanned the scaffolding of imperial protestantism had two ends. The war's destruction of those planks occurred on both sides of the Atlantic, though naturally not in the same way. Whereas those in the United States lost their connections to imperial protestantism and underwent the reorientation of their religious communities, what happened in Britain and its remaining empire could, more rightly, be framed as amputation. In the metropole, the scaffolding of imperial protestantism still joined Britain to a truncated version of its empire. The societies and connections nurtured by that scaffold, particularly in its Anglican incarnation, functioned during the war to serve the empire's new goal—cutting off the Americans, both in sentiment and in practice, from what remained of the empire.

Britons followed the war closely, and religious leaders worried about their fellows who were caught up in it. Their sympathies flowed most easily to those still within the empire who were endangered by the Americans' rebellion. As early as the summer of 1775, an Anglican clergyman in Bermuda wrote home to the bishop of London that "the Times, to us in this little remote Island, look dismally bad." The island did not raise enough food to support itself, and it depended on the North American mainland. "We have had report upon report that the ports will be shut and none of our Vessels permitted to Trade," and shortly, "if it should not please Almighty God to send us assistance from some Quarter," they would "inevitably perish or quit the Island." He prayed that the Americans would relent, so "that the Royal favour may be extended to them, that peace may be restored, and all united in Love and Friendship. esteeming ourselves to be possess'd of one common Interest." A 1781 letter from awakened Anglican Mary Gilbert in Antigua reached awakened Anglican philanthropist John Thornton in Clapham detailing the terrifying scale of death that island faced through starvation and disease. Antiguans were "in such a critical situation, with respect to our national Enemies that all opportunities of conveyance may soon be obstructed as we have every reason to fear the being deprived of our liberties as subjects of great Britain." She concluded with an invocation of scripture: "Surely this is the time of which our Lord speaks, when there should be distress of Nations, with perplexity." Such reports built sympathy for the victims of a war prosecuted by the Americans and pushed British religious leaders to see their own community as composed of only those who were loyal.[31]

Concern for those who suffered because of the American war was mirrored by distrust for former fellows who were now on the far side of the political boundary. Robert Keen detailed his frustrations to the countess of Huntingdon. He could not find any reliable information about William Piercy, the leader of the Bethesda group, but he heard damning rumors. His correspondent told him, "The Indians are harassing the frontiers of Carolina and Georgia and have killed many—Georgia is in a most deplorable situation, they have a *Low life Dutchman, a Quandam Cattle Driver* for their President—Mr. Piercy is amongst them and is appointed *Rebel Rector* of the Church of Savannah, I wish I could say somewhat in favor of him, but cannot—His Brother is a Major amongst them." On the other hand, Keen did not trust this informant either, as "in all his letters [he] appears so deeply prejudiced against the Americans and all their proceedings, that one does not know whether to credit what he says or not." The choices of moderate Anglican William Smith came in for scrutiny in England, as well. His 1775 *Sermon on the Present Situation of American Affairs* prompted much discussion. A rumor crossed the Atlantic that the printed version was "very different from the one delivered." When Smith had preached it, the reports said, it was "most audaciously seditious and unworthy of the Clerical Character, and the Obligations and Oaths he had taken." Smith did not see his own behavior as out of line, a case he tried to make to his superiors in subsequent months. Nonetheless, in 1778, the SPG "unanimously Resolved that Dr. Smith should no longer supply the Church at Oxford in Pennsylvania," cutting off his salary. Smith appealed, saying that the "Sermon w.ch seems to have been the cause of offence, was not delivered in his character, as connected with [the] Oxford Mission, but was only of a political nature," and "he should have hoped that it would not have come under the cognizance of the Soc[iety] with whom he was connected only in a religious vein." The SPG recorded, one suspects with a caustic tone, that he said he might "without offence continue his services"

31. Thomas Lyttelton to Richard Terrick, June 25, 1775, Fulham Papers, microfilm, reel 9, XVII, 39–40, Lambeth Palace Library, London (LPL); Mary Gilbert to Sir, Nov. 29, 1781, Thornton Family Papers, Add. MSS, 7674/1/C/9, Cambridge University Library, U.K. (CUL); Andrew Jackson O'Shaughnessy, *An Empire Divided: The American Revolution and the British Caribbean* (Philadelphia, 2000), 161–162. The biblical reference is to Luke 21:25 (AV). See also Samuel Farley to Charles Wesley, Apr. 5, 1778, Early Preachers Collection, DDPr 1/127, John Rylands Library, University of Manchester, U.K.

to his congregation, as the society could not soon send a replacement. "Tho' he has been unkindly treated," the record stated, "he shall indeavor, if he stays in the country, to support what may be left of the Church in it." Political tests eroded both trust and material support.[32]

Victims of American aggression generated sympathy from Britons, and Anglican leaders employed the same philanthropic structures that had promoted protestantism in the colonies to rescue the victims of colonial rebellion. The Church of England's most direct response to the war was to raise funds to support the cause of the distressed and suffering American clergy, an important project that actually brought the traditions of imperial protestantism to bear against the Americans. The archbishop of Canterbury, Frederick Cornwallis, supported a formal subscription that began in early 1776, and fundraising continued throughout the war. Over the years, thousands of pounds were collected and disbursed to refugee clergy. A wide swath of interested Anglicans donated, including bishops and clergy and some of the same men who were active in other societies, such as the Society for Promoting Christian Knowledge (SPCK). In 1779, those who raised the subscription printed notices across a range of London newspapers because "it is thought proper to lay before the public" the amounts raised and paid out, a total that came to £6,684. At that point, according to the printed report, seventy-three American clergymen had received payments. That same year, the SPG gained support from King George to raise a special collection for its efforts, including help for persecuted clergy. The royal letter of support indicated that, "notwithstanding the present separation of a considerable part of *North America* from their allegiance to our Crown," those "Clergy, who refused to renounce their allegiance, though for a time deprived of their churches," were "still intitled to a support from the Society." The fundraising efforts reinforced the connection between loyalty to the church and loyalty to the empire, and it created opportunities for Anglicans worried about the war to be active in their support for protestant institutions.[33]

The sufferings of the SPG clergy in North America also redefined rebelling

32. Robert Keen to Hastings, Jan. 10, 1778, A1/14/14, CCA. Halle's pietist group also struggled to get news of their cadre of ministers. See, for example, Friedrich Willhelm Pasche to Sebastian Andreas Fabricius, AFST/M 1 D 14 12, Franckesche Stiftungen, Halle, Ger. For rumors of Smith, see John Milner to Cooper, Aug. 10, 1775, Fettercairn Papers, MSS, acc. 4796/75. For Smith's discussions with the SPG, see Journal of the SPG, Mar. 21, Sept. 18, 1778, XXI, 179, 335–336. The society disagreed with Smith and considered him in its debt financially. See ibid., 357.

33. "Record of the American Subscription," SPG Collection, SPG VI, fol. 378, LPL. See also "Subscriptions for the Missionarys in America," Frederick Cornwallis, Archbishop of Canterbury, Cornwallis 4, LPL; "Subscription book for American Clergy," SPG VI, fol. 379, LPL; *Morning Chronicle and London Advertiser,* May 14, 1779, [1]; John [Thomas], *A Sermon Preached before the Incorporated Society for the Propagation of the Gospel in Foreign Parts . . .* (London, 1780), 59;

Americans as threats to the work of British protestants. The society's printed reports became a vehicle to share these stories. In 1776, readers learned that "numerous indeed and truly pitiable are the accounts received by the Society" from persecuted missionaries because of the "present unhappy state of America." Those sufferers were counting on the SPG, and "cases of such distress must needs affect the Society with deep concern, under their present inability to do more." In 1777, annexed to its annual sermon, the SPG gave what amounted to a history of the war from the perspective of the suffering clergy. It began with the assertion that "little or no Correspondence hath subsisted between the society and it's *[sic]* missionaries" because of the "deplorable State of our Plantations." As a result, "their churches are shut up, the pastors imprisoned, or driven from their flocks to places of greater security." Echoing a theme with which those in North America were quite familiar—that religion itself had been targeted by the war—SPG readers learned of many events that were "indeed a disgrace to humanity and religion." The report exposed the "baleful nature of persecution," and readers were invited to agree that "the sufferings of the American clergy . . . would be no bad supplement to *Walker's Sufferings of the clergy,"* a reference to an early-eighteenth-century work that catalogued Anglican leaders persecuted by puritans during the seventeenth-century civil war. The printed reports of the SPG reached many more readers than the letters of individual religious leaders could, and they served to direct attention from those concerned with religious matters onto the Americans' treachery and cruelty.[34]

Other Anglican societies also turned their attentions to efforts that supported the war and excluded the rebelling colonists from Britain's ongoing religious projects. The SPCK directed its energies toward supporting the Christian morale of British soldiers and sailors. Beginning in the spring of 1776, it provided devotional materials "for the use of the Fleet and Army in America." They printed volumes like the *Soldier's Monitor* and the *Seaman's Monitor* by the thousands and distributed them with the assistance of Secretary of State

---

and Francis Rufford, *Compassion to Men's Souls the Greatest Charity; and the Necessity of a Subscription for the Support and Relief of Missionaries . . .* (Worcester, U.K., 1779). See also Walker, "Church Militant," 189–191.

34. John [Hinchliffe], *A Sermon Preached before the Incorporated Society for the Propagation of the Gospel in Foreign Parts . . .* (London, 1776), 38; William [Markham], *A Sermon Preached before the Incorporated Society for the Propagation of the Gospel in Foreign Parts . . .* (London, 1777), 43, 58. See also Nigel Aston, "Archbishop Markham and Political Preaching in Wartime England, 1776–77," in Robert D. Cornwall and William Gibson, eds., *Religion, Politics, and Dissent, 1660–1832: Essays in Honour of James E. Bradley* (Farnham, U.K., 2010), 185–217. See also Laura M. Stevens, *The Poor Indians: British Missionaries, Native Americans, and Colonial Sensibility* (Philadelphia, 2004), 25, 29–30; and Edgar Legare Pennington, "The S.P.G. Annual Sermons, 1702–1783," *Historical Magazine of the Protestant Episcopal Church,* XX (1951), 10–43.

Lord George Germaine's office. The project of building pious soldiers and sailors expanded over the next few years, and an accounting at the end of 1781 detailed more than forty-seven thousand distributed texts. Indeed, building a moral military was so valuable a task that a separate group formed in 1779 for the purpose of "purchasing Bibles to be distributed among the British Soldiers and Seamen of the Navy." In addition to its work among the troops, the SPCK also maintained its decades-long support of work in India through the East India Company and the collaboration of the Halle pietists, and the group continued to send books to support work in Britain's Caribbean possessions. The war, and the remaining empire, provided plenty of work for enterprising Anglicans.[35]

The transition away from North America as a field of work was not always easy, to be sure, although most groups found their footing fairly quickly. An exception was the Associates of Doctor Bray, which struggled. Its leaders decided that further work in North America was impossible and turned their attention to the Scilly Isles, where the overlapping SPCK also worked. The associates also did work in Bermuda in 1779 and Antigua in 1781. But, during those years, its leadership barely met, and the group struggled for a clear purpose, cut off from its primary work in North America. Its experience was, in many ways, the exception that proved the rule. The remarkable ease with which Anglicans transitioned from promoting protestant causes in North America to supporting a war against the American colonies reflected the capacity of British leaders to turn the protestant scaffolding they dominated to a new imperial-driven end.[36]

Britain's imperial protestant scaffolding fractured to cut off its American portions with deceptive ease. The same organizations and tools that had once joined Britons and their erstwhile American partners regrouped, through the demands of war, to unite against the Americans. The quickness of the transition should not obscure the significance of what was happening, however. As

35. Society for Promoting Christian Knowledge (SPCK), Minutes, May 14, 1776, XXVII, CUL; Josiah Woodward, *The Seaman's Monitor; or, Advice to Sea-Faring Men, with Reference to Their Behaviour before, in, and after Their Voyage: With Prayers for Their Use* (London, 1776); Woodward, *The Soldier's Monitor: Being Serious Advice to Soldiers, to Behave Themselves with a Just Regard to Religion and True Manhood*, 7th ed. (London, 1776). Woodward's tracts were originally printed in 1701. Beginning in 1780, the SPCK printed Thomas Broughton, *The Christian Soldier; or, The Duties of a Religious Life Recommended to the Army, from the Example of Cornelius: In a Sermon* (1738; rpt. London, 1780), in quantity. See SPCK, Minutes, Mar. 7, 14, Oct. 3, 1780, May 8, 1781, XXVIII, CUL. For "purchasing," see F. W. B. Bullock, *Voluntary Religious Societies, 1520–1799* (St. Leonards-on-Sea, U.K., 1963), 236. For Halle, see SPCK, Minutes, Dec. 2, 1777, Mar. 16, Aug. 3, 1779, XXVIII, CUL. For the Caribbean, see ibid., Sept. 5, 1780, Jan. 23, Feb. 6, Dec. 11, 1781.

36. Minutes of the Associates of Dr. Bray, Nov. 13, 1777, June 23, 1779, Feb. 8, 1781, British Online Archives, https://microform.digital/boa. The associates' secretary "reported having accidentally heard that there are many poor Children in the Parish of St. Mary's in the Scilly Islands." The SPCK, including overlapping members, had begun considering the Scilly Isles in 1773.

Britons raised money to support refugees and blamed the war on treacherous former partners, they reimagined their empire and reshaped their protestant scaffold to exclude much of a continent that had been central to its very functioning since its inception.

MOURNING TRANSATLANTIC CONNECTIONS

When does a relationship—always attenuated by great distance—end? Much of the reckoning for the war's damage to transatlantic community had to wait until the dust settled. But even in the midst of the war, a few American religious leaders paused to comment on what was happening. They provide important soundings of how deeply the reconfiguration of imperial protestantism registered, and they offer a counterpoint to the religious nationalism that is so often evident in times of war. The American Revolution reconfigured transatlantic protestant communities that had framed the work and lives of those who invested in them. For a few who paused to note the transition, this was a moment of sadness.

Dissenter Ezra Stiles experienced the decline of his membership in the transatlantic community of dissent as a personal loss. In the colonial period, he had been more invested than most American religious leaders in both the community's opportunities and the frictions with Anglicans it structured. He had spent the two decades preceding the war in Newport, Rhode Island. From that city, he had corresponded with dissenting leaders around the protestant world, and there he had penned his widely circulated sermon on *Christian Union,* a text that simultaneously celebrated the potential for cooperation among protestants and excoriated Anglican threats to dissenters. At the outbreak of the war, Stiles was strongly partisan in favor of the Americans. He stayed in Newport when the city's residents first started to evacuate in the fall of 1775, but in March 1776, now a widower, he and his children left their home and moved inland to Dighton, Massachusetts, where he had received an invitation from a small congregation. In 1778, he accepted an offer to become the president of Yale College, a position he was "desirous of looking upon . . . not in a *secular* but a *religious Light.*" The unusual level of reflection Stiles recorded about the role of religion and political matters in his own life provides a fleeting window into the uneven process by which imperial protestantism splintered and religio-national loyalties changed.[37]

37. Ezra Stiles, *A Discourse on Christian Union: The Substance of Which Was Delivered before the Reverend Convention of the Congregational Clergy in the Colony of Rhode-Island; Assembled at Bristol April 23, 1760* (Boston, 1761); Morgan, *Gentle Puritan,* 280–281; Dexter, ed., *Literary Diary of Ezra Stiles,* II, 268.

Stiles's writings over the war years suggest a person who embraced new religious communities yet lamented the loss of the old. In September 1776, he reached out to John Rodgers, a leading presbyterian in New York, when that place was under British attack. "Let us be beheld by God," Stiles wrote, "as a people using indeed but not trusting in Arms, in the numerous Hosts now assembled for Battle." He hoped for victory and prayed that "we be delivered with such a Salvation as shall cause all Nations to acknowledge that God is with us of a Truth." The protestant universalism of previous decades had been altered by war. As he told Rodgers, "By the Declaration of Independence, the Congress have tied a Knot, which G. Britain can neither untie or cut. The American Republic is formed." Stiles's lofty vision of a Christian unity, evident both in his *Discourse on Christian Union* and his plans for an international dissenting organization (the origins of the more limited collaboration between Connecticut and Middle Colony presbyterians that had just folded), had been replaced by membership in a new nation.[38]

Even as he embraced an American religious community, Stiles also found himself depressed at the divisions and divisiveness among different religious groups. The old competitions between Anglicans and dissenters had been replaced by chaos. As 1777 began, he "took a Review of all the Religions of Every Age and Nation in the World, and examined my Heart as to its preference of the Christian Religion." His first observation was the "Indignation" he felt when noting "so little Charity among Xtian Sects, and such an Engagedness and Zeal to build up Sects rather than to make Xtians." He felt that in his own life he had started "with an extensive Charity to all Protestants," and at that time he had assumed "their Differences [were] founded in conscientious Judgment." Unfortunately, he now believed that nearly everyone—Anglicans, baptists, Quakers, Moravians, even Sandemanians—failed to embrace his standards for charity. Only the "Congregationalists and Presb. of America" passed muster as "the most truly Charitable and Catholic of any part of Xtendom." Separated from transatlantic religious community that he had long embraced, Stiles lost his characteristic optimism for protestant collaboration. Though he did not articulate it, the loss of the imperial establishment, with its ground rules for cooperation among dominant denominations, left a void in which fractiousness overwhelmed coordination.[39]

38. Dexter, ed., *Literary Diary of Ezra Stiles,* II, 45–47, 49. On Stiles's vision for the dissenting society, see Stiles to John Devotion, June 27, 1766, Ezra Stiles Papers, microfilm, reel 2, Beinecke Rare Book and Manuscript Library, Yale University, New Haven, Conn.

39. Dexter, ed., *Literary Diary of Ezra Stiles,* II, 113–114.

Stiles continued to hope for Christian fellowship, but in a moment of profound political transition, he also despaired that it was realizable. He wrote that he had given up on chances to build "Coalescences," a vague term for connections of any kind. He was, he felt, "perhaps, more than any man of extensive Acquaintance and Correspondence—ALONE—and unconnected in the World." One cannot help but hear the war refugee and grieving widower in these statements, but the loss of his religious community—a community that had been intrinsically transatlantic—was also very real to Stiles and left him isolated. He took solace in spiritual fellowship with the invisible church of God, but he feared he could not find any real fellowship on earth. "But to love a whole Character, or a whole [Church], or any whole Fraternity whether literary, religious or politic," he wrote, "I do not find within me." He "never shall cordially and externally unite with Mankind in any of their Affairs, Enterprizes and Revolutions." These lonely laments were the close companions of the nascent religious nationalism Stiles articulated. The national and earthly allegiances that he saw created—and destroyed—around him paled in comparison to the loftier Christian cause. The war brought a loss of shared protestant community alongside the creation of the new nation. He did not explicitly name the loss of his membership in the "dissenting interest," but because it had been so central to his intellectual life in the decades before the war, it is hard to imagine he did not miss it.[40]

Stiles might well have seen Anglican Jacob Duché as a kindred spirit in the midst of the war, mourning the end of a former religio-political regime, though Duché's response was far more dramatic than Stiles's lonely pen scratchings. Duché also cherished a sense of transatlantic religious fellowship. That faith led him into one of the war's greatest blunders. Like Stiles's, Duché's career had been wrapped around the scaffolding of imperial protestantism. He was a third-generation Philadelphian whose grandfather, a Huguenot, had arrived in William Penn's colony during its earliest days. The family had conformed to the Church of England before Jacob's birth, and he grew up as a member of the city's Anglican elite. Duché had studied under presbyterian Francis Allison and Anglican William Smith at the College of Philadelphia before he went to Cambridge, in England, to complete his education. In 1759, after his ordination, he became the assistant minister at the new Christ Church in his hometown. He also became allied with the awakened protestant faction within Philadelphia's Anglican community, and he continued to praise protestant cooperation. About Philadelphia, he wrote: "There is less religious bigotry here, than in any place

40. Ibid., 115. This passage is also excerpted and analyzed in Morgan, *Gentle Puritan*, 286–288.

I have yet visited." In light of his amiable spirit, Duché had been a likely choice when the first General Congress looked for a minister to overcome their divisions and sanctify their proceedings in 1774.[41]

Duché had embodied a flexible and unifying vision of Anglican clerical leadership, and he had willingly lent that authority to the Congress in the war's early days. But after the Declaration of Independence, he was increasingly uncomfortable with that position. Like many other Anglicans, he found himself forced to take a personal stand. His own church was divided between those who supported and those who opposed independence. On July 4, 1776, the church's vestry approved the omission of the king and royal family from the liturgy. The language of the resolution placed the onus for the choice on the laity, providing Duché some cover if he disagreed with the move, but it nonetheless "requested [Duché and the assistant ministers] in the Name of the Vestry and their Constituents" to omit the prayers. Still keeping his reservations about the course of the war private, Duché became chaplain to the Congress once again in October 1776, but he quickly resigned the role. The British army entered Philadelphia on September 26, 1777, a year later. Because he had been a visible figure in support of the Congress, he had much to fear. He was arrested and detained overnight by British authorities. Traumatized, he decided to appeal directly to George Washington to end a war that he found increasingly unsupportable.[42]

His letter, penned October 8, 1777, held out quixotic hope that Washington would, by an act of conscience, stop the war. The letter was foolhardy, suicidal, even. Duché pleaded with Washington to abandon the cause of the Revolution because it simply could not be won. "How fruitless the expense of Blood!" he wrote, as he urged the general to reconsider everything he had fought for. Rather than place the argument in the abstract, Duché recounted his own history as a reluctant patriot. He claimed that even his most famous sermon had "disclaim[ed] the idea of independency" and he had "persisted until the very last moment in using prayers for my sovereign." He had believed, as his friends did, that Washington "shuddered at the thought of a separation

41. [Jacob Duché], *Observations on a Variety of Subjects, Literary, Moral, and Religious: In a Series of Original Letters* (Philadelphia, 1774), 9, 25–26, 62. Duché also quoted George Herbert's "Church Militant" poem to argue for the true faith moving to America (ibid., 110–112). See also Kevin J. Dellape, *America's First Chaplain: The Life and Times of the Reverend Jacob Duché* (Bethlehem, Pa., 2013), 3–4, 20, 25–27, 44–49.

42. Dellape, *America's First Chaplain,* 103–107 (quotation on 104); *Journals of the Continental Congress,* V, 530, VI, 886; "Ein guter Freund" to Heinrich Melchior Mühlenberg, Sept. 30, 1777, in Kurt Aland and Hermann Wellenreuther, eds., *Die Korrespondenz Heinrich Melchior Mühlenbergs: Aus der Angangzeit des Deutschen Lutertums in Nordamerika,* V, 1777–1787 (Berlin, 2002), 59–60; Nelson Waite Rightmyer, "Churches under Enemy Occupation, Philadelphia 1777–8," *Church History,* XIV (1945), 33–60.

from the mother country." From Duché's perspective, independence was the wrong move. The costs it brought were simply too high. If Washington took steps to reunite the empire, "thousands, who are now ardently wishing and praying for such a measure, will step forth and declare themselves the zealous advocates of constitutional Liberty." Britain's constitution would reunite what had been wrenched apart. Concluding, he reiterated that this was a private letter and that he wrote it out of "the Love of Truth, the Love of Peace, and the Love of my God." The letter was a desperate plea from Duché's conscience to Washington's and a direct outgrowth of the former's belief that the bonds of empire, supported by protestantism, were too strong to break.[43]

Duché's idealism ran straight into Washington's pragmatism. The general knew the Anglican's letter smacked of treason, so he got it out of his hands almost as soon as it fell into them. Washington turned the letter over to Congress; it was promptly published in the newspapers. Pennsylvania's government named Duché a traitor, and the Anglican was exiled from Pennsylvania. He left for London on December 12, 1777, reaching England in June 1778 after a difficult voyage and delay in the West Indies. Amazingly, he inspired more pity than anything else, perhaps because those around him believed he had spoken from the heart. Washington confessed to Duché's brother-in-law, Francis Hopkinson, that he was "not more surprised than concerned, at receiving so extraordinary a letter from Mr. Duché, of whom I had entertained the most favorable opinion." Hopkinson, for his part, scolded Duché almost like a child. Even the frequently abrasive Charles Inglis found sympathy for Duché. "He has made all the atonement in his power for any Error of Judgment or Conduct he may have unhappily fallen into," Inglis wrote. "His Head, I am confident, has erred much more than his Heart; and considering how many persist, unreclaimable, in open, avowed Rebellion, I think he should be considered in an favourable Light, all Things considered." The case was both pathetic and tragic, but that should not obscure the sentiments from which it grew. Duché believed he had a moral responsibility, derived from his role as a religious leader and his personal faith, to try to keep the Americans within an empire he viewed in religious terms. He therefore went further than merely condemning the American rebels, as many American

43. Jacob Duché to George Washington, Oct. 8, 1777, in Worthington Chauncey Ford, ed., *The Washington-Duché Letters* (Brooklyn, N.Y., 1890), 9–25, esp. 10, 13, 15–20, 22, 24. For versions of Duché's story, see Dellape, *America's First Chaplain*, 124–167; William Pencak, "Out of Many, One: Pennsylvania's Anglican Loyalist Clergy in the American Revolution," in Pencak, ed., *Pennsylvania's Revolution*, 104–105; McBride, *Pulpit and Nation*, 63–67; and Nicholas Guyatt, *Providence and the Invention of the United States, 1607–1876* (New York, 2007), 110–111. Duché's letter was reprinted widely, including in the *Scots Magazine*, XXXIX (1777), 692–695.

loyalists and their counterparts in Britain did. The risk he took reflects how greatly he valued what was being lost through the war.[44]

A final lament for the damage done to imperial protestantism by the war bears mentioning. Its disgust at the war's destruction is an important complement to Stiles's sadness and Duché's desperation. Writing in 1776, Mohegan minister Samson Occom tried to prod a fellow religious leader—philanthropist and awakened Anglican John Thornton—into serious reflection about the consequences of the war for the work of religion that British protestant leaders had promoted so vigorously within the old empire. Occom wrote that he was "very sorry to see the white people on both sides use their influence with the poor Indians to get them on their side, I wish they would let the Indians alone." He saw the war as an Anglo-American problem, but also a pointless one. "This contention amongst you Amazes and astonishes the ignorant Heathen in the Wilderness," he continued. "There never was the like, or such instance amongst all the Tribes of Indians, they are ready to say. What? Brethren and Christians kill one another?" The war was frankly destructive to the religious work in which they all had been engaged: "This Quarrel is a very great stumbling block before the Heathen." The critique must have lingered with Thornton because he included it in a letter he wrote to a friend two years later. He prefaced the excerpt by saying Occom was "one of the few American Ministers that are in a right Spirit." But Thornton left the passage unremarked, and he turned immediately to matters closer at hand: "We are expecting an invasion here or in Ireland." Thornton's quick change of subject away from the deeper implications of the conflict is frustrating but apt. The exigencies of war, with its demands for loyalty and its ever-changing threats, did not really leave room for reflection.[45]

The passage of time makes clear what the demands of the present obscure. The Revolutionary War transformed the connections that had linked American and British protestants, the planks that surrounded the scaffolding of imperial protestantism. It did so by damaging the American religious landscape and by reconfiguring the networks and societies that had bound distant coreligionists to one another. For Americans, the dissenting community had less and less relevancy, as congregationalists, presbyterians, and baptists moved outside the

44. Dellape, *America's First Chaplain,* 137–138; Washington to Francis Hopkinson, Nov. 21, 1777, in Ford, ed., *Washington-Duché Letters,* 28; Hopkinson to Duché, Nov. 14, 1777, ibid., 30–34; Inglis to Cooper, Dec. 5, 1777, Dec. 23, 1778, Fettercairn Papers, MSS, acc. 4796/75.

45. John Thornton to William Richardson, June 5, 1778, Thornton Family Papers, Add. MSS, 7674/1/C/8. Occom's original letter, along with another expressing similar sentiments and lamenting the difficulty of getting funds for missionary work in the context of the war's disruptions, dated Jan. 1, 1777, appear in Joanna Brooks, ed., *The Collected Writings of Samson Occom, Mohegan: Leadership and Literature in Eighteenth-Century Native America* (New York, 2006), 113–115.

imperial establishment and away from inevitable competition with Anglicans. Denominational bodies, clear supporters of the new American regime, now connected American congregationalists and presbyterians to their government. The Anglican network, for its part, retreated away from America, in a painful process that involved exiles, persecutions, and sometimes wrenching personal decisions. As Anglicans left the rebelling colonies behind, they abandoned American Anglicans who supported the Revolution with few reliable connections to their former fellows. Even awakened protestants, though partially insulated by their distinctive network, suffered as the projects that had been built through their work languished.

The violence and damage of the war had powerful consequences for the transatlantic religious community, as well. Decades of work—collaborations, politicking, and fundraising that had gone into supplying missions for North America, building its universities, filling its libraries, and caring for its souls—were laid waste by armies, by fleeing missionaries, by changing loyalties. This destruction gave the lie to the cheerful words of the English-born Massachusetts minister William Gordon, who told the Massachusetts General Court on the first anniversary of the Declaration of Independence, "No damage can ensue to the continent, on the score of religion," from the "separation" of the colonies from Great Britain. If, by "religion," he referred to the institutions and connections of the imperial protestantism, then he was utterly wrong.[46]

That same violence looked very different from the other side of the Atlantic. British sensibilities smarted at evidence of American treachery, and British leaders turned their labors toward protecting those who remained loyal. The connections of imperial protestantism thus fell away from both ends at once. A comparison of 1773 and 1783 provides a stark contrast. In the former year, the scaffolding of imperial protestantism was bound together by a dense web of personal and organizational relationships and the extensive projects of groups like the SSPCK, SPG, NEC, and SPCK. Awakened leaders John Wesley and the countess of Huntingdon supported itinerant ministers in the colonies. Leaders from all the branches of the wider religious community appealed, ultimately, to the same set of political leaders and constitutional principles to structure protestant life. By 1783, Britons had contracted their vision of their protestant empire so that it now excluded a region that had been a site of religious promise since the sixteenth century. Many details remained to be handled in the postwar era, but the damage had been done.

46. William Gordon, *The Separation of the Jewish Tribes, after the Death of Solomon, Accounted for, and Applied to the Present Day: In a Sermon Preached before the General Court, on Friday, July the 4th, 1777; Being the Anniversary of the Declaration of Independency* (Boston, 1777), 31.

Destruction of the connections that bound Anglo-American protestants to one another did not exhaust the consequences of the war for religion and religious institutions in the two warring nations, however. In both countries, the war also forced a reckoning with two of the most foundational characteristics of the early modern Euro-American world: that states were either protestant or Catholic and that governments and protestant institutions were joined in their labors to defend Britain's protestant empire.

6 Antipopery and the End of the Protestant State

In its first years, the Revolutionary War pushed religious leaders on both sides of the Atlantic to fall in line behind their now-opposing governments and the armies they fielded. It reshaped the transatlantic connections that had been nurtured by the scaffolding of imperial protestantism. As the war dragged on, it also forced religious leaders—and many of their followers—to accept that their governments were no longer really protestant in character. The American Revolution was, in that sense, the final punctuation on the confessional era, the centuries during which European imperial politics were framed by the competitions between protestants and Catholics. Britain's imperial protestantism had developed at the turn of the eighteenth century as a direct result of confessionally defined political imperatives. The meaning of *protestant* sustained by that system was capacious enough to link the episcopal Church of England, the presbyterian Church of Scotland, congregationalist dissenters, and baptists into one loyal polity. It expanded to embrace first a Dutch Reformed then a German Lutheran king. That flexibility existed in large measure because protestants did not have to compromise on their shared enemy: Catholicism and popery. Protestants could be trusted as subjects; Catholics—papists—could not. These prejudices were built through decades of war against Spain and France and fears of Jacobite rebellion. Through it all, religious leaders supported the connection between protestantism and national goals. They reinforced it through countless sermons that championed the protestant cause and decried the evils of popery. Both those in government and religious leaders deployed protestantism to common ends in their mutual partnership.

The American Revolution revealed fault lines between government commitments to protestantism and those maintained by religious leaders. The fractures began to emerge during the imperial crisis. The commitment of British imperial leaders to the protestant interest on the global stage began to fade after 1763, at the end of the Seven Years' War. Although anti-Catholicism had been an effective political tool during the war, its outcome gave British leaders reason to be utilitarian when it came to Catholics. The territories ceded by France to Britain in the Peace of Paris included many Catholics, as of course Ireland long had. Thus, the idea of a purely protestant empire became harder and harder to sustain on a governing level, while the potential contributions of Catholic subjects became more appealing. In the same period, some religious leaders also relaxed their objections to Catholics, and elites increasingly embraced abstract ideas of religious toleration. When the imperial crisis came to a head, the place of protestantism in the conflict was ambiguous, to say the least. The heated rhetoric around the Quebec Act had demonstrated that anti-Catholicism remained a powerful political force in the popular imagination on both sides of the Atlantic. In Britain, Parliament and Anglican bishops had borne the brunt of antipopery attacks for permitting Catholicism to remain in place in Quebec in 1774, and the Continental Congress had proved no great friend to protestantism either. That American body's gymnastic willingness to appeal for support from both the Quebecois and British suggested no particular allegiance to protestantism per se. Governance, for imperial authorities and for the rebelling Americans, was not particularly a protestant affair.[1]

In the war's later years, the relationship between protestantism, antipopery, and the state reemerged as an important theme on both sides of the Atlantic. Religious leaders faced the reality that their partners in government pursued policies that were no longer distinctly protestant. Historians have neglected the importance of the French alliance and the 1778–1780 anti-Catholic violence in Britain for the religious history of the American Revolution; the former is often seen as too focused on military or diplomatic issues to be significant within religious history, and American historians have generally seen the latter as too distant geographically to be relevant. As a result, the war's destabilizing

1. Works on protestantism as a major factor in British politics and foreign relations emphasize the first half of the eighteenth century. See, for example, Tony Claydon, *Europe and the Making of England, 1660–1760* (Cambridge, 2007); and Linda Colley, *Britons: Forging the Nation, 1707–1837* (New Haven, Conn., 1992). See also Jeremy Black, "Confessional State or Elect Nation? Religion and Identity in Eighteenth-Century England," in Tony Claydon and Ian McBride, eds., *Protestantism and National Identity: Britain and Ireland, c. 1650–c. 1850* (Cambridge, 1998), 53–74. For North America, see Owen Stanwood, *The Empire Reformed: English America in the Age of the Glorious Revolution* (Philadelphia, 2011); and Thomas S. Kidd, *The Protestant Interest: New England after Puritanism* (New Haven, Conn., 2004). In scholarship on the coming of the Revolution, anti-Catholicism plays a major role in the Quebec Act, discussed in Chapter 3. For an assessment of the "confessional era" (primarily used in European historiography), see Ute Lotz-Heumann, "The Concept of 'Confessionalization': A Historiographical Paradigm in Dispute," *Memoria y Civilización*, IV (2001), 93–114. Scholarship on the Age of Revolutions, rooted in the work of R. R. Palmer, tends to trace the rise of Enlightenment thinking at the expense of a more "religious" early modern era. See, for example, Palmer, *The Age of the Democratic Revolution: A Political History of Europe and America, 1760–1800: The Challenge* (Princeton, N.J., 1959); or, in a more philosophical form, Charles Taylor, *A Secular Age* (Cambridge, Mass., 2007).

effect on long-standing conventions about protestant nations in both places at nearly the same moment has also been largely overlooked. Yet these events, taken together, point to the American Revolution as the final coda to the early modern confessional era.[2]

Reintegrating these pieces of the story is important for understanding the shifting relationship between protestant institutions and governments on both sides of the Atlantic. In the United States, where the boundaries around any national religious unity were vague at best, the French alliance meant partnership with a long-hated papist foe. Religious leaders, valuing military success and national survival over traditions of antipopery, largely embraced the alliance and the widening vision of legitimate religion it brought to the new nation. In Britain, the course of events was more complicated because popular anti-Catholicism forced religious leaders to decide between their commitment to public order or their commitment to protestantism. As the stakes became higher, their response became clearer: the partnership between governing authorities and protestant institutions outlasted any increasingly abstract commitment to the protestantism of a former age.

PROTESTANTISM AND THE FRENCH ALLIANCE

The idea that one of Europe's Catholic powers, particularly France, might assist American colonists in a war against Britain circulated even before the fighting started. It was a natural alliance; the French had decades of antipathy for the British and had recently lost most of their American empire. Some religious

2. The French alliance and its implications is absent or barely touched on in most studies of religion and the American Revolution. See, for example, Spencer W. McBride, *Pulpit and Nation: Clergymen and the Politics of Revolutionary America* (Charlottesville, Va., 2016), 26–27; James P. Byrd, *Sacred Scripture, Sacred War: The Bible and the American Revolution* (Oxford, 2013); Thomas S. Kidd, *God of Liberty: A Religious History of the American Revolution* (New York, 2010); Nicholas Guyatt, *Providence and the Invention of the United States, 1607–1876* (Cambridge, 2007), 101; and Nathan O. Hatch, *The Sacred Cause of Liberty: Republican Thought and the Millennium in Revolutionary New England* (New Haven, Conn., 1977), 73–76, 89–91. The most thorough treatment of the subject is Francis D. Cogliano, *No King, No Popery: Anti-Catholicism in Revolutionary New England* (Westport, Conn., 1995). See also Charles P. Hanson, *Necessary Virtue: The Pragmatic Origins of Religious Liberty in New England* (Charlottesville, Va., 1998), 85–118; and William C. Stinchcombe, *The American Revolution and the French Alliance* (Syracuse, N.Y., 1969), 91–103. There is a substantial historiography on the Gordon Riots and their Scottish counterparts, though that literature is largely disconnected from American historiography on antipopery or on the American Revolution. For a historiographical treatment of the Gordon Riots, see Ian Haywood and John Seed, "Introduction," in Haywood and Seed, eds., *The Gordon Riots: Politics, Culture, and Insurrection in Late Eighteenth-Century Britain* (Cambridge, 2012), 7–12. See also Stephen Conway, *The British Isles and the War of American Independence* (Oxford, 2000), 246–259. For the Scottish events, see, especially, Robert Kent Donovan, *No Popery and Radicalism: Opposition to Roman Catholic Relief in Scotland, 1778–1782* (New York, 1987). For work

leaders predictably protested that such an alliance was unnatural. Edinburgh's John Erskine wrote in 1776 that the Americans' "political and religious principles are incompatible with submitting to the government, or asking the protection of France or Spain." But Erskine's views were not shared by the shepherds of the American war effort, and those in America knew it. In November 1776, New York loyalist Anglican Charles Inglis wrote to a colleague in London that the Americans seemed determined to "protract the War till some European Power steps in to their Assistance." Benjamin Franklin, he noted, had left Philadelphia. "It is said that he is gone to France, to try if he can rouse that Nation in Behalf of America." He assumed the French would not "be so infatuated as to support our Rebels against their Sovereign, as the Example and Consequences might be very dangerous to themselves." Of course, both Erskine, the pro-American Scot, and Inglis, the pro-British American, were completely wrong. Assumptions based on religious and political ideology fell before political pragmatism. American leaders welcomed military assistance from the French. In doing so, they placed the new nation's religious leaders in an interesting spot. Long reliable purveyors of theological anti-Catholicism, those who supported the Revolution now had to welcome Catholics into the fold. Furthermore, they had to put rhetorical distance between their nation and the familiar constructs of British protestantism. They did so, and the results sharply limited any potential for an explicitly protestant American state.[3]

For those caught up in the intensity of the war effort, news of the American victory at Saratoga—with its hope for French assistance—brought joy. Bos-

---

that looks at those events in a transatlantic context, see Brad A. Jones, "'In Favour of Popery': Patriotism, Protestantism, and the Gordon Riots in the Revolutionary British Atlantic," *Journal of British Studies*, LII (2013), 79–102.

The Age of Revolutions is most commonly framed as a fracturing of early modern empires caused by shifting political ideologies. See, for example, Janet Polasky, *Revolutions without Borders: The Call to Liberty in the Atlantic World* (New Haven, Conn., 2015), 5; and J. H. Elliott, *Empires of the Atlantic World: Britain and Spain in America, 1492–1830* (New Haven, Conn., 2006), 325–326. Sarah Knott, "Narrating the Age of Revolution," *William and Mary Quarterly*, 3d Ser., LXXIII (2015), 3–36, helpfully chronicles the shifting efforts to define and narrate the period, a story in which confessionalism has played only a small role. The broader historical conception of the era remains dependent on the work of Palmer, *Age of Democratic Revolution*. The role of political protestantism, or the timing of its decline, has not been a primary topic of investigation for the American Revolution. See, for example, Robert G. Parkinson, *The Common Cause: Creating Race and Nation in the American Revolution* (Williamsburg, Va., and Chapel Hill, N.C., 2016), 3–4. Parkinson notes the protestant roots of the phrase "common cause" but, in a study that begins in 1775, is not concerned with when protestantism as such ceased to be a major part of that cause. Brendan McConville argues for the ongoing influence of political protestantism in the Revolutionary era; see McConville, *The King's Three Faces: The Rise and Fall of Royal America, 1688–1776* (Williamsburg, Va., and Chapel Hill, N.C., 2006).

3. A Freeholder [John Erskine], *Reflections on the Rise, Progress, and Probable Consequences, of the Present Contentions with the Colonies* (Edinburgh, 1776), 2; Charles Inglis to Myles Cooper, Nov. 5, 1776, Fettercairn Papers, MSS, acc. 4796/75, National Library of Scotland, Edinburgh

ton's Samuel Cooper wrote to Franklin, then negotiating for the Americans in Paris, "to congratulate you upon the most important and glorious success of the Arms of the American States." He rejoiced that, "thro the Course of the War; at the same Time, divine Providence has supported and sav'd us in Ways we little thought of." Just as important, Cooper asked the diplomat, "What Effect" will the battle "have upon the European Powers? Will they think us respectable enough to have an acknowledg'd Place among the Nations?" To celebrate, Cooper also dusted off the sermon he had preached after the repeal of the Stamp Act more than a decade before. The text was from 1 Samuel 12:24, "Only fear the Lord, and serve him in truth with all your heart: for consider how great thing he hath done for you." Cooper's hopes were rewarded. Shortly after learning of the outcome of Saratoga, on February 6, 1778, "His Most Christian Majesty," Louis XVI, entered into a treaty with the Americans.[4]

American religious leaders who supported the war effort celebrated, and they brought the French alliance into their understanding that God was on the American side. Franklin wrote to Cooper in Boston with the news. The letter arrived right as the minister "was stepping into the Pulpit," and he immediately "gave public Thanks, and implor'd the Blessing of Heaven on the King of France and his Dominions." The irony of the moment was not lost on him. "It was a new Thing in more Senses than one," he wrote, "and struck the whole Congregation with an agreable Surprize, who most cordially joyn'd in that Act of Devotion." The next day he added a further note, describing "what Joy the Treaties with France have diffus'd among all true Americans" and "the chagrine they have given to the few interested and slavish Partizans of Britain among us." His choice of the word "slavish" is interesting. Slavishness was an attribute often connected with papists, who, because they were not taught the

---

(NLS). See also A Friend to the King, "For the London Magazine" ("Extract from a Book of Chronicles"), *London Magazine: Or, Gentleman's Monthly Intelligencer,* April 1774, 185–187. For the diplomatic history of the Revolution, see Paul W. Mapp, "The Revolutionary War and Europe's Great Powers," in Edward G. Gray and Jane Kamensky, eds., *The Oxford Handbook of the American Revolution* (Oxford, 2013), 311–326; Leonard J. Sadosky, *Revolutionary Negotiations: Indians, Empires, and Diplomats in the Founding of America* (Charlottesville, Va., 2009); and Stinchcombe, *American Revolution.*

4. Samuel Cooper to Benjamin Franklin, Oct. 25, 1777, Samuel Cooper Papers, Huntington Library, San Marino, Calif. (this letter also appears in *The Papers of Benjamin Franklin,* Digital Edition, XXV, *October 1, 1777, through February 28, 1778,* https://franklinpapers.org/framedVolumes.jsp?vol=25&page=104); Samuel Cooper, Manuscript Sermon, Ms.q.3329, Boston Public Library; Andrew Jackson O'Shaughnessy, *The Men Who Lost America: British Leadership, the American Revolution, and the Fate of the Empire* (New Haven, Conn., 2013), 155–158. For a brief summary of the diplomatic timing, see Parkinson, *Common Cause,* 362–363; and Robert Middlekauff, *The Glorious Cause: The American Revolution, 1763–1789* (New York, 1982), 380–384. For works on the French alliance more generally, see Stinchcombe, *American Revolution.*

habits of protestant liberty, could not be trusted as members of the body politic. In this new world, slavishness now applied to loyalists, and the assistance the French gave to the Americans was a blessing. Congregationalist William Gordon wrote to missionary Samuel Kirkland, calling the French alliance a sign of "the over-rulings of Providence in our favour." He believed that "God indeed hath been working marvellously for us all along, and his hand is so exceeding evident, even his stretched out arm, that we should be highly criminal not to acknowledge it." Elbridge Gerry, one of Massachusetts's representatives in Congress, commented that there had been "a marvellous Change in the System of the political Worlds." As he saw it, "England advocates for Despotism," and "France Advocates for Liberty, espousing the Cause of Lutherans and Calvinists." Even more on point, he saw "the King of Britain establishing Popery, the King of France endeavouring to free his people from this ecclesiastical Tyranny." This was revolutionary indeed. After centuries in which—according to imperial protestant tradition—the British promoted protestant liberty and the French fought for popish tyranny, American protestants fought British tyranny with providential help provided by France.[5]

While pro-American religious leaders embraced the French, loyalists had the easier job, only needing to take up the well-tested rhetorical tool of antipopery. The Americans, they claimed, furthered popery by taking aid from the French. Samuel Adams told a friend that "Popery is particularly held up" by the loyalists. The royalist *Pennsylvania Ledger* printed news of the treaty with the warning that the French would make the Americans regret their choice to forego reunion with Britain and the chance "of securing our civil and religious freedom." In these dire times, the Americans seemed to "wish for a final separation from Britain, the ancient and chief support of the protestant religion in the world," for the sake of a corrupt Congress that had made "a treaty with that ambitious and treacherous power, whose religious and political maxims have so often disturbed the peace and invaded the rights of mankind!" The writer justly reminded his readers of the outrage over Britain's "bare *toleration*" of Catholicism in Quebec, which was then described as "'a sanguinary faith, which had for ages filled the world with blood and slaughter!'" Now, Congress had made the Americans into "instruments of weakening the best friends, and of

5. Cooper to Franklin, May 13, 14, 1778, *Franklin Papers,* Digital Edition, XXVI, *March 1, 1778, through June 30, 1778,* https://franklinpapers.org/framedVolumes.jsp?vol=26&page=453a; William Gordon to Samuel Kirkland, May 30, 1780, Hamilton College Library Digital Collections, Samuel Kirkland Collection, https://sparc.hamilton.edu/islandora/object/hamLibSparc%3A12351661#page/1/mode/1up; Elbridge Gerry to James Warren, May 26, 1778, in Paul H. Smith, ed., *Letters of Delegates to Congress, 1774–1789,* 26 vols. (Washington, D.C., 1982), IX, 751. For immediate reaction to the French alliance, see Parkinson, *Common Cause,* 387.

strengthening the most powerful and ambitious enemies of the reformation, to such a degree as must do more than all the world besides could do, towards the universal re-establishment of Popery through all Christendom." Antipopery could now be deployed as a tool of war against the Americans.[6]

American leaders simply ignored such loyalist aspersions, declining to frame their conflict in confessional terms. Already in 1775, when the target alliance was the Quebecois rather than the French, George Washington had called a halt to Pope's Day celebrations in the army, with their mocking effigies of Catholic authority, because "we are soliciting and have really obtained the friendship and alliance of the people of Canada." Congress ceremonially accepted the Catholic French into the American fold, expanding their usage of acceptable public religion to include Catholics for diplomatic purposes, at least. The French ambassador, Conrad-Alexandre Gérard, arrived in Philadelphia in July 1778. Congress, only recently back in control of that city, greeted him as the representative of "his most Christian Majesty," the traditional title used by the French monarchy. Congress granted Louis XVI a new title as well. According to its president, Henry Laurens, France's king "throughout Christendom, will be stiled 'protector of the Rights of Mankind.'" The new moniker, according to Laurens, was "better founded than" the title used by the British monarchy, "'Defender of the Faith.'" His comment was perhaps a reference to the ongoing royal usage of a term that had been bestowed on Henry VIII by the pope *before* the former's break with Rome, or perhaps Laurens meant to signify that George III no longer adequately defended protestantism. In either case, the new title the Americans offered to Louis, Laurens continued, was "an excellent adjunct to 'Most Christian,'" and the best part was that it would gall his royal British rival.[7]

Members of Congress validated the faith of their new allies in other ways as well. On July 4, 1779, they attended three religious services, one of them Catholic. The sermon, given by Gérard's chaplain, was printed in the *Pennsyl-*

6. Samuel Adams to James Warren, June 1, 1778, in Smith, ed., *Letters of Delegates to Congress,* X, [3]; "From the York-Town Rebel Paper of May 4," *Pennsylvania Ledger; or the Philadelphia Market-Day Advertiser,* May 13, 1778. See also Inglis to Cooper, Nov. 10, 1777, Fettercairn Papers, MSS, acc. 4796/75; and Helvetius [John Zubly], "Number 2" (Aug. 3, 1780) and "Number 3" (Aug. 31, 1780), in Randall M. Miller, ed., *"A Warm and Zealous Spirit": John J. Zubly and the American Revolution, a Selection of His Writings* (Macon, Ga., 1982), 179–180, 185. Huguenot-descended John Jay came in for particular criticism from loyalists. See Papinian [Charles Inglis], "Letter III. To John Jay, Esq." and "Letter IV. To John Jay, Esq.," in Inglis, *The Letters of Papinian; in Which the Conduct, Present State, and Prospects of the American Colonies Are Examined* (New York, 1779), 42–43. See also Hanson, *Necessary Virtue,* 95–98.

7. Washington's Pope's Day order, quoted in Cogliano, *No King, No Popery,* 67; Benjamin H. Irvin, *Clothed in Robes of Sovereignty: The Continental Congress and the People Out of Doors* (Oxford, 2011), 175 ("his Most Christian Majesty"), 184–186; Henry Laurens to the Chevalier de Mauduit Du Plessis, May 11, 1778, in Smith, ed., *Letters of Delegates to Congress,* IX, 640.

vania Packet in both English and French. Like countless public sermons before it, it proclaimed the unity of those who heard it. France, the chaplain told his American audience, had "blended her interests with your interests, and her sentiments with yours." She "unites her voice to yours at the foot of the altars of the Eternal God, to celebrate that glorious revolution, which has placed the sons of America among the Free and Independent nations of the earth." At this highly symbolic moment, the new nation's governors embraced a version of "religious" leadership that extended beyond what could have been contained within the category of protestant.[8]

American religious leaders were a bit more subdued in their enthusiasm for French Catholicism than their counterparts in the Revolutionary government were, but they stood behind the alliance nonetheless, giving the legitimacy of institutional protestantism to a nation that accepted help from Catholics. They did not promote the vision of protestant-Catholic unity espoused by Gérard's chaplain, but neither did they raise the specter of anti-Catholic fear—or connect it to the French—in a way that would have been natural only a few years before. Some in New England preached sermons that used providence to justify the alliance. Phillips Payson, in Massachusetts, preached that his hearers "must be infidels," if they did not see that it was God who had "dispose[d] his most Christian Majesty, the King of France, to enter into the most open, and generous alliance, with these independent states." It was "an event in providence, which like the beams of the morning, cheer and enliven this great continent." Connecticut's James Dana used an election day sermon on May 13, 1779, to preach that "the interference of foreign powers" in the conflict was divine. He asserted, too, that "the common interest European nations will have in protecting" the states would help ensure the new country's future. "Popery" he attached, not to France, but to a "late establishment . . . by a British parliament" in Quebec, where "the protestant religion, founded in principles of liberty, is barely tolerated." He added, without any sense of irony, that he hoped to see "our allies have their eyes opened on the blessings" of a protestant government so they might "at once renounce their superstition." David S. Rowland, preaching in Providence, found in the French alliance proof "that God, whose kingdom is over all, and in whose hand are the hearts of the kings of the earth, which he can turn as the rivers of water, hath disposed one of the most powerful monarchs in Europe to own and espouse the cause of his injured people in this country." Dismissing generations of confessional conflict, he glibly noted that there were ample precedents for

8. Irvin, *Clothed in Robes of Sovereignty*, 194–195; "Philadelphia," *Pennsylvania Packet or the General Advertiser* (Philadelphia), July 10, 1779, [1].

alliances across boundaries of faith. "Differences in religion have no operation in the political system," even though, he added, "advantage may arise by such an alliance, in a moral or religious view." This pragmatic vision of international affairs smoothly abandoned the logic of a protestant empire advancing God's plan and replaced it with a utilitarian support for the American cause.[9]

Some religious leaders went further still. Samuel Cooper, in Boston, was one of the most active promoters of Franco-American relations. He preached in support of the alliance, he learned French, he helped manage difficult days when the French army was present in Boston, and he ultimately took a pension from France for his support of the two nations' ties. Perhaps most striking, he helped to facilitate the Catholic burial of a French nobleman who was killed in a brawl. The site chosen was Boston's King's Chapel, a shocking mingling of sacred space. Yale College, where Ezra Stiles was presiding, granted the French representative, Gérard, an honorary degree in 1779, potentially the first degree given by the college to a Roman Catholic. The degree chosen, Doctor of Laws, gestured toward public affairs. At the same time, Stiles—and the Yale Corporation—balked at a French professor for the school. The corporation cautioned "that great Delicacy is requisite" when pondering any change that "the People at large" could construe "to bring them under a foreign Influence" or "to affect their internal state as to Policy or Religion." Many remained wary of just what it would mean to build close ties to Catholics.[10]

9. Phillips Payson, *A Sermon Preached before the Honorable Council, and the Honorable House of Representatives, of the State of Massachusetts-Bay . . .* (Boston, 1778), 30–31; James Dana, *A Sermon, Preached before the General Assembly of the State of Connecticut, at Hartford, on the Day of the Anniversary Election, May 13, 1779* (Hartford, Conn., 1779), 10, 12, 15 (Dana also made a plea for public support of the institutions of religion, including ministers, schools, and public worship); David S. Rowland, *Historical Remarks, with Moral Reflections: A Sermon, Preached at Providence, June 6, 1779 . . .* (Providence, R.I., [1779]), 30–32; Cogliano, *No King, No Popery,* 75–78. It is remarkably difficult to prove a negative. The comparative lack of emphasis on anti-Catholicism is noted explicitly by Melvin Endy, Jr., "Just War, Holy War, and Millennialism in Revolutionary America," *WMQ,* 3d Ser., XLII (1985), 3–25, esp. 21. Of course, cultural anti-Catholicism remained a persistent cultural thread in North America, despite its political ebb. In that sense, Alan Heimert's assertion that the "evangelical mind had grown indifferent to and weary with the archaic battle lines of the Reformation" takes matters a bit too far, though in the 1760s and 1770s most anti-Catholic discussion was of a cultural-political rather than theological nature (Heimert, *Religion and the American Mind: From the Great Awakening to the Revolution* [Cambridge, Mass., 1966], 85). For views that trace persistent popular anti-Catholicism in colonial America, see Maura Jane Farrelly, *Anti-Catholicism in America, 1620–1860* (Cambridge, 2018); Jason K. Duncan, *Citizens or Papists? The Politics of Anti-Catholicism in New York, 1685–1821* (New York, 2005); Thomas S. Kidd, "Recovering *The French Convert*: Views of the French and the Uses of Anti-Catholicism in Early America," *Book History,* VII (2004), 97–111; and Brendan McConville, "Pope's Day Revisited, 'Popular' Culture Reconsidered," *Explorations in Early American Culture,* IV (2000), 258–280.

10. Edmund S. Morgan, *The Gentle Puritan: A Life of Ezra Stiles, 1727–1795* (Williamsburg, Va., and Chapel Hill, N.C.,1962), 338–339 (quotation on 339); Franklin Bowditch Dexter, ed., *The Literary Diary of Ezra Stiles, D.D., LL.D., President of Yale College, II, March 14, 1776–December 31, 1781*

As American religious leaders lent their support to Congress's choice of allies, anti-Catholicism ebbed in the new country, although that decline had little impact on the anti-Indigenous sentiment to which popery had been attached during the era of imperial warfare. For the moment, European Catholics benefited from the shift. Although there were (relative to protestants) few Catholics in the United States and they practiced their faith under significant legal penalties, Catholics participated in the Revolutionary movement in numbers greater than their presence in the population. In Maryland, Charles Carroll was one of several Catholics who served in the state's Revolutionary government, though he and his coreligionists had lacked full political rights in the colonial regime. More than half of Catholic men in Saint Mary's County, Maryland, actively sided with the Americans, whereas closer to 40 percent of protestant men in the area did so. Catholics would, as new Revolutionary governments formed, leverage this Revolutionary loyalty into new civic rights. The decline in American anti-Catholicism had a less welcoming corollary. Although Euro-American protestants accepted Euro-American Catholics into the body politic, they found new ways to exclude Indigenous peoples who had previously been smeared with the language of antipopery. Although that subject is too vast to be investigated here, that the United States could not, as a result of the French alliance, be configured as a military power fighting for protestantism might well have helped create the circumstances for an increasingly racialized language of the American war. When those supporting rebellion from Britain defined the enemy against which they fought, they depicted savagery, and they linked it to Indians and slave revolt, with the British playing ringleaders. Euro-American Catholics thus benefited from the French alliance, whereas France's former Indigenous allies suffered all the more.[11]

(New York, 1901), 332; Charles W. Akers, *The Divine Politician: Samuel Cooper and the American Revolution in Boston* (Boston, 1982), 264–267, 278–281; Cogliano, *No King, No Popery*, 95–97, 103–106.

11. Farrelly, *Anti-Catholicism in America*, 78, 96–98; Maura Jane Farrelly, *Papist Patriots: The Making of an American Catholic Identity* (Oxford, 2012), 241–246; Cogliano, *No King, No Popery*, 62–67. Chris Beneke has noted that the Revolutionary era overall experienced a marked lack of religious violence; see Beneke, "'Not by Force or Violence': Religious Violence, Anti-Catholicism, and Rights of Conscience in the Early National United States," *Journal of Church and State*, LIV (2012), 5–32. Parkinson's *Common Cause* touches very little on subjects related to religion; nonetheless, religion's absence within his study suggests its relative weakness in newspaper sources. His exploration of Jane McCrea's death provides a clear example of a highly publicized episode used for political purposes, but without the invocation of religion (340–350). See also Samuel Fisher, "Fit Instruments in a Howling Wilderness: Colonists, Indians, and the Origins of the American Revolution," *WMQ*, 3d Ser., LXXIII (2016), 647–680, for an argument that places the development of "savagery" in a British protestant context; and Peter Silver, *Our Savage Neighbors: How Indian War Transformed Early America* (New York, 2008), 232, for the timing of the transfer from an American perspective.

The Revolutionary War thus signaled the end of the early modern political language of protestant-Catholic rivalry in America, a paradigm that had animated imperial competition since the sixteenth century. The unlikely character of Benedict Arnold provided proof of the shift. The one-time American military hero betrayed his country after being named the commander of the essential post at West Point, on the Hudson River. He planned to deliver that key strategic spot to the British in exchange for funds, and he tried to sweeten the deal by seizing on a chance to hand over George Washington as well. In a moment of high drama on September 25, 1780, the plot was interrupted; his British confederate, Major John André, was captured; and Arnold made a hasty escape. Arnold's defection came at a difficult time for those who supported the American cause. The war was dragging into its sixth year. American losses in the South, including Savannah, Georgia, and Charleston, South Carolina, did not bode well for the future. In light of these difficulties, Arnold's treachery outraged an already weary American public. Samuel Adams reported that Arnold "has been gibbeted in the Streets by the Populace, anathematizd by the Clergy in the Pulpit, and his Name has with Indignation been struck out of the List of Officers by Order of Congress." Americans were eager to demonize, literally, their former hero.[12]

The outcry around Arnold's actions—framed by his treachery having been discovered in time to prevent its intended damage—allowed Americans the opportunity to articulate divine favor for their cause. On September 30, the *Pennsylvania Packet* carried the news of "the providential detection of the perfidy and treachery of a late distinguished general officer." A broadside published for the event proclaimed that he had "been discovered by the goodness of the Omniscient Creator," a moment now celebrated "with joyful acclamation, another instance of the interposition of bounteous Providence." Philadelphians paraded and burned him in effigy (see Figure 14). The dummy showed a two-faced Arnold with the Devil at his back, "a mark in his left hand, and a letter in his right from Belzebub, telling him that he had done all the mischief he could do, and now he must hang himself." A large paper lantern in front of the Arnold figure showed "General Arnold on his knees before the Devil, who is pulling him into the flames—a label from the General's mouth with these words, 'My

12. Samuel Adams to Betsy Adams, Oct. 10, 1780, in Harry Alonzo Cushing, ed., *The Writings of Samuel Adams*, IV, *1778–1802* (New York, 1908), 209–210. For Arnold's story, see Barry K. Wilson, *Benedict Arnold: A Traitor in Our Midst* (Montreal, 2001), 145–159; and Charles Royster, "'The Nature of Treason': Revolutionary Virtue and American Reactions to Benedict Arnold," *WMQ*, 3d Ser., XXXVI (1979), 171–179. John André also captured a great deal of attention. See Sarah Knott, *Sensibility and the American Revolution* (Williamsburg, Va., and Chapel Hill, N.C., 2009), 153–193; the reaction in Philadelphia is described on 155–156, 170.

FIGURE 14 *A Representation of the Figures Exhibited and Paraded through the Streets of Philadelphia, on Saturday, the 30th of September, 1780*. Courtesy of the Library of Congress Prints and Photographs Division, Washington, D.C.

dear Sir, I have served you faithfully;' to which the Devil replies, 'And I'll reward you.'" The effigy was burned at the end of the procession. Arnold, in the American mind, had sold his soul to the Devil for money (and money had most certainly been a part of his transaction with the British). His virtue was compromised, and as a poet wrote in the *Pennsylvania Packet,* those who behaved like him would "follow Arnold and the Devil to Hell." The enemy of a nation God favored was easily named.[13]

Whereas Americans interpreted Arnold's betrayal as a devilish assault on a favored nation, the man himself used a very different—and, in late 1780, outdated—construct of imperial protestantism to justify his behavior. He wrote an address that first appeared in New York's *Royal Gazette* on October 11. It was a rehearsal of loyalist claims, and it embraced the logic of protestant connection. He pleaded with "the Inhabitants of America" that he had always been

13. *Pennsylvania Packet or the General Advertiser* (Philadelphia), Sept. 30, 1780, [2]; *A Representation of the Figures Exhibited and Paraded through the Streets of Philadelphia, on Saturday, the 30th of September, 1780* ([Philadelphia, 1780]); *Pennsylvania Packet,* Oct. 7, 1780, [2]. See also ibid., Oct. 3, 10, 31, 1780; Parkinson, *Common Cause,* 477–478, 501–502; and Catherine L. Albanese, *Sons of the Fathers: The Civil Religion of the American Revolution* (Philadelphia, 1976), 94–95. Abuse appeared in newspapers for weeks. See, for example, *Pennsylvania Packet,* Oct. 24, 1780.

faithful in his loyalties, although circumstances had changed around him. He claimed, as Jacob Duché had done before him, that he had found the Declaration of Independence too hasty, "precipitate" in his words. Now, the participation of the French in the war made the issue clear to him. Britain's "enemies [were] in her own bosom," and he could not support the American cause any longer. The original fight against the British, undertaken with limited goals, he argued, had been righteous, but now the proper course was to fight against—not with—the French. The Americans and their protestant British fellows had suffered through the period when they had "raised our arms against a brother," and now he asked that "God incline the guilty protractors of these unnatural dissentions, to reign their ambition, and cease from their delusions, in compassion to kindred blood." Rehearsing the history of the French alliance, Arnold did not find it binding. He now thought "it infinitely wiser and safer, to cast my confidence upon [Britain's] justice and generosity, than to trust a monarchy too feeble to establish your independency, so perilous to her distant dominions; the enemy of the Protestant Faith, and fraudulently avowing an affection for the liberties of mankind, while she holds her native sons in vassalage and chains." He sought "the re-union of the British empire, as the best and only means to dry up the streams of misery that have deluged this country." He called on Americans to remember the strong ties between protestantism, liberty, and the British Empire that had long protected them and to turn their backs on their new—false—friends.[14]

Arnold's formulation of his loyalties in terms of protestantism and its French foe fell flat for an American population that would rather see his actions as part of an alliance with the Devil. An article printed in both Philadelphia and Boston in December 1780 listed one of Arnold's crimes as *"Hypocrisy*. The Traitor ARNOLD had the face to speak of *religion* in his address," it lambasted. "He had so totally sold himself to the English, and was so entirely lost to every moral sentiment, as not to perceive that Providence itself had patronized the cause of our independence, by discovering his plots in a manner next to miraculous." Juxtaposing the two paradigms—Arnold's positioning of his actions within a protestant-Catholic rivalry and Americans' associating him with a Christian symbol for depravity and evil—highlights Americans' rapid movement away from the confessional era. Their fears of Catholic France, and the dangers that popery might pose to their earthly or spiritual freedoms, were far less powerful

14. B. Arnold, "To the Inhabitants of America," *Pennsylvania Packet,* Oct. 17, 1780, [2]. For discussion of Arnold's address, see Willard M. Wallace, *Traitorous Hero: The Life and Fortunes of Benedict Arnold* (New York, 1954), 263–265 ("Inhabitants" on 263). I would like to thank Adam Sanchez, Southern Methodist University (class of 2018), for his help with this research.

than their anger at Arnold's betrayal of their trust through an alliance with the British. It was a symbolic moment that spoke to a very real shift for the role religious boundaries played in organizing geopolitics.[15]

Americans, already outside the imperial protestant scaffold on a practical level, also turned their backs on the idea that their new nation would be defined by protestantism. The French alliance made it impossible for Americans to place their war in the history of a grand conflict between protestant and Catholic empires. Embrace of Catholic allies did not require American religious leaders to fight for Catholicism, of course, and deep reserves of popular and theological anti-Catholicism persisted. But the willingness of American religious leaders to support the French alliance brought their voices, and the institutions they led, in line with a state in which protestant and Catholic souls collaborated for collective political ends. Protestant institutions now served a state that was not necessarily protestant. That embrace did not immediately ensure that Catholics would receive full civil rights in the new governments that formed out of the Revolution; that process would be fought out at the state level in the coming years. But, although it is important not to overstate the gains for Catholics from the French alliance, one should not underestimate the significance of the alliance for Americans' exit from the protestant scaffolding that had bound the colonies' religious institutions to London and its mixed establishment. It closed the door on the language of the confessional era, the territory on which Britain's mixed establishment had been formed. It would not be replicated in the new country.

PROTESTANTISM MOBILIZED

The British experience of anti-Catholicism during the American Revolution was the inverse of the American experience, though they both led to much the same result—the weakening of protestantism as a viable form of political rhetoric. Whereas Americans largely followed their governmental and religious leaders to embrace collaboration with a Catholic army in order to win the war, rank-and-file Britons rejected similar moves, violently so. Anti-Catholic riots broke out in Glasgow and Edinburgh in the winter of 1778–1779, and then even more dramatically in London's Gordon Riots in the summer of 1780. A second contrast, and the most telling from the perspective of imperial protestantism, emerges most strongly from the first phase of the British story. In

15. *Pennsylvania Journal* (Philadelphia), Dec. 27, 1780, [1] reprinted from *Independent Chronicle and the Universal Advertiser* (Boston), Dec. 8, 1780, [1].

Scotland, some religious leaders energetically supported the rising tide of anti-Catholicism and political protest because they viewed the boundaries between protestants and Catholics as essential to preserving the British constitution. As their protests increased and became more political, their voices came into conflict with those, both fellow religious leaders and those in government, who believed that the role of protestant institutions was to support the government and the stability it provided. It was a contest between those who believed protestantism must be protected, even from the British government, and those who believed protestantism could not support disorder. In Scotland, the outcome was to preserve the boundaries around protestantism, but it came at a cost.

The events began in the exigencies of a war that was lasting too long already and was now made worse because it had become a European conflict as well. War with France was an inauspicious development, to say the least, from the British perspective. Samuel Farley, a colleague of awakened Anglican Charles Wesley, was peeved that "after waiting near three years in the pleasing expectation of Peace, the Trumpet of war is sounding afresh." He was clear about whom he wanted to blame. "America *unnaturally* allied with France against England," he explained, "must produce such a Change in the Political System of Europe, that the ablest statesmen will be puzzled to settle for a century to come. Where or how the Contest *will end* the God of Armies only knows." He found hope, however, in the idea that it was "not improbable but this will bring about *a reconciliation on better* terms than any red heel'd Commissioners [a reference to the unsuccessful Carlisle Commission] could ever obtain from those rough unpolish'd Demagogues in greasy night Caps and old woolen Jackets." In this inauspicious military environment, Parliament began discussing limited Catholic relief in 1778, proposing to lift prohibitions on saying masses and on Catholic education and some restrictions on passing down property. The immediate impetus came from the need for more soldiers; the North administration viewed Catholics as potential military recruits. Though Catholic military service was formally outlawed, it had been discretely occurring for years, and the hope was that easing some of the penal restrictions on Catholic practice would encourage Catholic elites to, in turn, support more enlistments in their communities.[16]

There were a variety of reasons for the North administration, the primary

16. Samuel Farley to Charles Wesley, Mar. 28, 1778, Early Preachers Collection, DDPr 1/28, John Rylands Library, Manchester, U.K. See O'Shaughnessy, *The Men Who Lost America,* 61–65; Conway, *The British Isles and the War of American Independence,* 246–252; and Robert Kent Donovan, "The Military Origins of the Roman Catholic Relief Programme of 1778," *Historical Journal,* XXVIII (1985), 79–102. The Carlisle Commission was an ill-fated British attempt to negotiate a peace treaty in 1778. Congress, now with France in its corner, rejected the proposals because they did not include independence.

supporters of the bill, to think Catholic relief might be successful from the perspective of government. It seemed a logical extension of measures already taken. The incorporation of Quebec and Grenada into the empire after the Seven Years' War, and the 1774 Quebec Act, tended to acknowledge that Catholics ought to be treated as loyal and valuable subjects, though certainly not without controversy in either case. Moreover, the decline of the Jacobites since 1745 made Catholics less of a threat to the monarchy. Catholics in England and in Scotland recognized the potential of the moment and mobilized their support. They argued their loyalty in contrast to American rebellion, and they pointed to the untapped resource of Catholic subjects. Baron Robert Petre, a prominent Catholic from Norfolk, for example, supported the "laudable purpose of adopting some plan to assist his majesty in suppressing his Rebellious Colonies," clearly drawing the link between renewed Catholic political activity and the war. The disloyalty of Americans created an opportunity for British Catholics to prove their worthiness as part of the body politic, and the North administration seized the moment.[17]

Catholic relief's passage through Parliament was surprisingly quick, reflecting its pragmatic origins. It was framed as supporting, rather than undermining, British protestantism. A bill was introduced on May 14, 1778, by George Savile, a member of the parliamentary opposition, putting the measure at arm's length from the North administration. Savile appeared a friend to both toleration and protestantism. He had supported the 1772 Feathers Tavern petition to grant relief to Anglican clergy who did not want to subscribe to the Thirty-Nine Articles, but he had also sought to repeal the Quebec Act because of its leniency toward Catholics. Saville argued that the restrictions repealed by the new Catholic relief bill were consistent with British protestantism. It was thus necessary "to vindicate the honour, and to assert the principles of the Protestant religion, to which all persecution was, or ought to be, wholly adverse." In the

17. Robert Petre to [unknown], Jan. 23, 1778, 366 (quotation), Petre to William Jerningham, Apr. 15, 1778, 335, both in Jerningham Collection, Norfolk Record Office, Norwich, U.K.; Donovan, "Military Origins," *Historical Journal,* XXVIII (1985), 90–92; Jessica L. Harland-Jacobs, "Incorporating the King's New Subjects: Accommodation and Anti-Catholicism in the British Empire, 1763–1815," *Journal of Religious History,* XXXIX (2015), 203–223; Aaron Willis, "The Standing of New Subjects: Grenada and the Protestant Constitution after the Treaty of Paris (1763)," *Journal of Imperial and Commonwealth History,* XLII (2014), 1–21; David Milobar, "Quebec Reform, the British Constitution, and the Atlantic Empire, 1774–1775," *Parliamentary History,* XIV (1995), 65–88; Colin Haydon, *Anti-Catholicism in Eighteenth-Century England, c. 1714–80: A Political and Social Study* (Manchester, U.K., 1993), 171–175, 200–201. See also Haydon, "'I Love My King and My Country, but a Roman Catholic I Hate': Anti-Catholicism, Xenophobia, and National Identity in Eighteenth-Century England," in McBride and Claydon, eds., *Protestantism and National Identity,* 33–52; and John Wolffe, "A Comparative Historical Categorisation of Anti-Catholicism," *Journal of Religious History,* XXXIX (2015), 182–202.

ensuing—brief—discussion, members of Parliament supported the limited relief under discussion, and it was noted that a bill in the British Parliament might set an example for Ireland. Henry Dundas, the lord advocate of Scotland, pointed out that, because "the acts intended to be repealed were made before the union of England and Scotland," repealing them would also require an act for Scotland, and he would bring a motion to that effect. A few days later, the bill passed the Commons and moved into the House of Lords.[18]

In the upper chamber, the primary objections to Catholic relief came from John Hinchliffe, the bishop of Peterborough, who protested that the matter had been carried out too speedily. In addition, he noted the essential conundrum of expanding the notion of religious toleration—which traditionally applied only to those groups that largely worked within the systems of British protestantism—to Catholics, whose faith was antithetical to protestant liberty. Hinchcliffe claimed to "disapprove of all laws which are calculated to oppress men for their religious persuasion," but he pointed out that he was "not so ignorant of the genius of popery, as not to know it is a very difficult matter to consider its religious principles altogether distinct from that political superstructure which has been raised upon them." No matter what rights to religious principles Catholics might have, he "[could not] but fear, that should occasion offer," those principles "might still be made too subservient." A Catholic could not, reliably, be free from outside pressures. The concept of "religious toleration" necessarily extended only to those who could be trusted to be loyal to the British state, not because they shared particular beliefs (even the Trinity was under debate among protestants by 1778), but because they existed within the system of British protestantism. Hinchcliiff's objections were noted in passing, however. Facing threats from rebellion in America, a failing war effort, and worries of invasion from France, the House of Lords thought British Catholics worthy of a bit more trust, and the bill passed easily.[19]

England's religious leaders greeted Catholic relief cautiously. Dissenters, who were often outspoken in their anti-Catholicism as part of demonstrating

18. *The Parliamentary History of England, from the Earliest Period to the Year 1803 . . .*, XIX, *Comprising the Period from the Twenty-Ninth of January 1777, to the Fourth of December 1778* (London, 1806), 1137 ("vindicate"), 1142 ("acts intended"); Milobar, "Quebec Reform," *Parliamentary History*, XIV (1995), 80–81; Donovan, "Military Origins," *Historical Journal*, XXVIII (1985), 87. An Irish relief measure worked its way through the Irish Parliament in the summer of 1778. See Robert E. Burns, "The Catholic Relief Act in Ireland, 1778," *Church History*, XXXII (1963), 181–206; and Conway, *The British Isles and the War of American Independence*, 246–252.

19. *Parliamentary History of England*, XIX, 1143 (quotations); Samuel Wilde to Lord Hardwicke, May 25, 1778, Add. MS 35614, fol. 239, British Library, London; Eugene Charlton Black, *The Association: British Extraparliamentary Political Organization, 1769–1793* (Cambridge, Mass., 1963), 133–134.

their loyal protestantism, for the most part did not make common cause with Catholics in arguments for greater religious freedom. The organizations that coordinated the dissenting community, the Protestant Dissenting Ministers of the Three Denominations and the Protestant Dissenting Deputies, made no mention of Catholic relief at their meetings. Theophilus Lindsey, the unitarian-Anglican who had led the push for the Feathers Tavern petition, attended the debates in the House of Commons on May 14. He clearly approved of the bill, writing to a friend that he [the friend] "would have been delighted with the feeling and humanity and justice that Sr George [Saville] spoke with." But, he continued, "the body of Dissenters . . . wisely resolved not to meddle at present, for many reasons." Having suffered a series of disappointments in earlier efforts to repeal subscription and still living with the restrictions imposed by the Test and Corporation Acts, they did not want to link their cause to Catholic relief. In general, English religious leaders seem to have reacted to the measure in the way members of Parliament had. Limited relief for Catholics from outdated punitive measures was not overly troubling, even if protestant leaders were not eager for Catholic toleration in principle.[20]

The most consequential part of Parliament's discussion, it turned out, was not the debate over its merits; rather, it was the comment from the lord advocate for Scotland that a bill for that country would be forthcoming. Scots, like many in England, worried that the Catholic population was on the rise, though in reality that Scottish Catholic population was small and impoverished, even in the Highlands. But the symbolic role of protestantism for Scots was even more important. The connections built through shared protestantism were crucial to how many Scots understood their role in Britain and its empire. The most important moment in the creation of British imperial protestantism was certainly the Act of Union in 1707, which formed a protestant state with a mixed establishment. Scotland's status within the Kingdom of Great Britain was linked

20. Theophilus Lindsey to William Turner, May 14, 1778, in G. M. Ditchfield, ed., *The Letters of Theophilus Lindsey (1723–1808)*, I, *1747–1788*, 257–259 (quotations on 258); Minutes of the Body of Protestant Dissenting Ministers of the Three Denominations, II, Apr. 7, 14, 1778, Mar. 18, 1779, 189–192, Dr. Williams Library, London; Protestant Dissenting Deputies, General and Committee Meeting Minutes (hereafter cited as PDD, Minutes), Mar. 27, Apr. 24, May 29, 1778, CLC/181/MS03083/002, London Metropolitan Archives (LMA). One explanation for the silence of the Dissenting Deputies may be that its members were, at that time, preoccupied with a small 1776 riot that had targeted awakened Anglicans in Lingfield. As they struggled to decide whether such Anglicans counted as dissenters and worked to counter the anger turned against them by English crowds, they might not have wanted to poke the hornet's nest of antipopery. The Lingfield matter, which the deputies explicitly decided would not set a precedent, stretched from Aug. 13, 1776, to Oct. 9, 1778; see PDD, Minutes, CLC/181/MS03083/002, LMA; Bernard Lord Manning, *The Protestant Dissenting Deputies*, ed. Ormerod Greenwood (Cambridge, 1952), 117–119; and Anthony Lincoln, *Some Political and Social Ideas of English Dissent, 1763–1800* (Cambridge, 1938), 236–238.

to protestantism, and any alteration in that principle was destabilizing. Moreover, the primary collective entity Scots possessed was the General Assembly of the Church of Scotland, a body that naturally considered religious matters as central to its purpose in a way that Parliament did not. The idea of Catholic relief therefore resonated differently in Scotland than it had in England, and, furthermore, it would be discussed in a very different venue. News of the potential bill for Scotland reached Edinburgh just as the General Assembly was gathering for its 1778 meeting. The American war was a significant presence, as it had been in 1776. Discussions about Catholic relief in the press wound their way through mentions "of the unnatural and unjust revolt of his Majesty's subjects in North America," a circumstance that created a "season of public danger and alarm." Fears that Catholics might be brought into the body politic merged with worries about the war in a tense General Assembly, where some felt the presbyterian institution ought to act to protect protestantism from Parliament and others felt a duty to continue their tradition of loyal support for London's government.[21]

The Edinburgh debates in the General Assembly were the first stage in the Scottish drama. They vacillated between arguments for extending relief based on the harm that was done to Catholics by persecuting them, and, on the other side, a new, darker discussion about how popery injured protestantism. Anti-relief clergy, often associated with the same "Popular party" that had supported the Americans two years before, worried about the "tendency to hurt the interest of the Protestant religion," which might be unleashed by a bill for Scotland. Glasgow's John Gillies, a leader in the popular faction, wanted the assembly to watch carefully so that it could "stand forth in opposition to whatever might tend to hurt the Protestant religion, which he insisted the bill in question would most unquestionably do." On the other hand, the assembly's moderates saw

21. "Scotland," *Scots Magazine,* May 1778, 267 (quotations); Donovan, *No Popery and Radicaslism,* 8–11, 168–170; Mark Goldie, "The Scottish Catholic Enlightenment," *Journal of British Studies,* XXX (1991), 24; Margaret Connell Szasz, *Scottish Highlanders and Native Americans: Indigenous Education in the Eighteenth-Century Atlantic World* (Norman, Okla., 2007), 90; Richard B. Sher, *Church and University in the Scottish Enlightenment: The Moderate Literati of Edinburgh* (Princeton, N.J., 1985), 279–280; "Representation and Petition of the Presbytery of Strathbogie," May 6, 1778, Assembly Papers of the Church of Scotland, Ch1/2/120/2, 209–210, National Records of Scotland, Edinburgh (NRS). Religion as a part of Scottish political identity is discussed in Richard J. Finlay, "Keeping the Covenant: Scottish National Identity," in T. M. Devine and J. R. Young, eds., *Eighteenth Century Scotland: New Perspectives* (East Linton, U.K., 1999), 121–133; and Colley, *Britons.* Colin Kidd traces Scottish investment in protestantism both as part of British identity and separate from it; see Kidd, *Subverting Scotland's Past: Scottish Whig Historians and the Creation of an Anglo-British Identity, 1689–c. 1830* (Cambridge, 1993). See also Craig Gallagher, "Covenants and Commerce: Scottish Networks and the Making of the British Atlantic World" (Ph.D. diss., Boston College, 2017).

the potential measure as righting a wrong in the form of persecution. Moderator William Robertson described the existing penal statues against Catholics as "sanguinary" and "cruel." Moreover, if the assembly reacted too strongly, it would create a problem where one might not be. Once again, as he had in 1776, Robertson outmaneuvered his colleagues from the Popular party in the assembly so that no formal resolution to act was taken by the body, leaving the matter to Parliament. Those who feared a growing Catholic threat could not let the issue drop, however, and they continued to speak out actively in what they viewed as an increasing crisis.[22]

Having failed to make the General Assembly a venue for formal protest that could be sent back to London, anti-relief voices next supported a rising tide of antipopery in lower-level presbyterian bodies, the synods and kirk sessions of the Church of Scotland. These organizations were closer to and more representative of popular sentiment than the General Assembly. Their politicization was important, as protestant institutions usually demonstrated and reiterated their loyalty to government, not its opposite. Several synods passed resolutions against Catholic relief. At Glenelg, those gathered took "into their most serious consideration, the alarming progress of Popery" and the potential for a bill relieving Catholics. They "resolved to give this public testimony of their disapprobation of said bill," which might embolden "the indefatigable assiduities and artifices of trafficking priests," a reference to an imagined population of infiltrators who labored to deliver Scotland to the pope. In October 1778, the Synod of Glasgow and Ayr met, and it drew up an address to the king "to express . . . the anxious fears which we and our people are under, from the present apparent growth of Popery among us, and of the fatal consequences which must necessarily ensue to the eternal concerns of the People committed to our care, and to the interests of this Church as by law established, if by any means that unhallowed superstition, equally unfriendly to your Majesty's Family and Government, and to the Religion and Morals of your loyal subjects, should gain further ground among us." The address did not mention the English repeal law or the idea that such a law might be proposed for Scotland, but by asserting the "apparent growth" of popery, it continued to push the discussion toward the dangers of popery and away from any value to toleration. The synod employed the public pulpit as well. It appointed a fast day for December 2, 1778, "on account of the various evils which at present much abound, but particularly on

22. "Scotland," *Scots Magazine,* May 1778, 266–271 (quotations on 267, 270); Donovan, *No Popery and Radicalism,* 10–12; Sher, *Church and University,* 280–282; John R. McIntosh, *Church and Theology in Enlightenment Scotland: The Popular Party, 1740–1800* (East Linton, U.K., 1998), 160–161.

the rapid progress of infidelity, and the encouragement given to Popery." Other presbyterian bodies throughout Scotland likewise made anti-Catholic resolutions. Only a few voices spoke out against the rising antipopery; the Synod of Lothian (which included Edinburgh) resolved that there was little to fear from Catholic relief, for example. But the opposition to Catholic relief was both visible and organized. Regional church governments resisted the position taken by the pro-London General Assembly, which had seemed to endorse the pro-relief Parliament in London.[23]

For Scotland's anti-relief presbyterians, guarding protestantism entailed maintaining a boundary around civic participation. They made the case that Catholics were religiously incapable of being a part of Britain's body politic. Glasgow preacher William Porteous argued on the city's fast day "that in Britain, Popery has always been in league with despotism,—not only so, but in all Europe, we can find no popish state of any consequence, that can be managed without tyranny in the civil government." A large part of Porteous's case, and a large part of the debate as a whole, centered on the belief among protestants that, for Catholics, *"no faith is to be kept with heretics in matters where the interest of Popery is concerned."* If that were the case, then no oath of loyalty made by a Catholic could be trusted, and a central logic of the imperial protestant system—that those within it were loyal to the state—was undermined. In this argument Porteous drew from another that had been made earlier by William Abernethy Drummond, a leader in the Scottish Episcopal Church, and then debated by Scotland's Catholic bishop, George Hay, in a widely circulated exchange. The accusation recurred in a variety of forms, including a long satirical poem entitled *The Repeal,* published in 1779:

> They'll promise and subscribe by dispensations,
> And swallow oaths with mental reservations.

Rhyming couplets reinforced a serious argument. The boundary around protestantism must be defended. Britain's protestant empire depended on a body of protestant subjects.[24]

23. "Provincial Synod of Glenelg," July 3, 1778, and "Synod of Glasgow and Ayr," Oct. 13, 1778, in *Scotland's Opposition to the Popish Bill: A Collection of All the Declarations and Resolutions, Published by the Different Counties, Cities, Towns, Parishes, Incorporations, and Societies, throughout Scotland . . .* (Edinburgh, 1780), 4; "Ministers and Elders of the Provincial Synod of Glasgow and Ayr: Petition on the Growth of Popery," Oct. 16, 1778, SP 54/47, fol. 203, The National Archives, Kew, U.K. (TNA). See also "Scotland," *Scots Magazine,* October 1778, 565–566; *Protestant Interest: Or the Unanimous Resolution of about Forty Thousand Inhabitants in and about Glasgow, to Oppose the Popery Bill . . .* (Glasgow, 1779), SP 54/47, fol. 210, TNA.

24. William Porteous, *The Doctrine of Toleration, Applied to the Present Times . . .* (Glasgow, 1778), 15–16, 18; W[illiam] A[bernethy] D[rummond], *The Lawfulness of Breaking Faith with*

Affairs turned violent on October 18, 1778, in Glasgow, when a mob attacked the house of a Catholic combmaker and stoned some Catholics who had heard Mass. While some synods continued to make anti-Catholic resolutions, other nonreligious civil organizations also began to form to support the cause. The trend of the protests thus moved away from protestant institutions. The model of the American committees of correspondence served the Scots well, as they formed what were essentially paralegal structures of protest. A group calling itself the "Protestant Interest" formed in Edinburgh, and new organizations in other places issued statements as well. In Selkirk, the "Magistrates, town-council, and deacons of several incorporations within this burgh" met. Their collective statement attested to their "unanimous" "resolve," and they proposed "to use every legal method to oppose such bill, and to request their representative in parliament to oppose the same." One group put its institutional focus into its lengthy name: The Eighty-Five Private Societies, in and about Glasgow, United in a General Correspondence, to Take What Legal Steps Might Appear Conducive, Oppose a Repeal of the Penal Statutes against Papists in Scotland. They began meeting on January 8, 1779, and they elected officers and set agendas. They noted when clergy attended, but they focused their attention on the formal structures of government that might address popery legally, including a letter to Henry Howard, Lord Suffolk, the secretary of state. They also, in a move that appears ironic in hindsight, "offered their service to the Lord Provost, to check any mobs, or riots in the town." By the spring of 1779, the protest movement had, in large measure, moved beyond the Church of Scotland to encompass an increasingly organized and self-conscious manifestation of Scottish civil

---

Heretics Proved to Be an Established Doctrine of the Church of Rome; in a Letter to Mr G. H. (Edinburgh, 1778); G[eorge] H[ay], *An Answer to Mr W. A. D's Letter to G. H. . . .* (Edinburgh, 1778); *The Repeal: An Occasional Poem, Calculated for the Times; in Two Parts* (Edinburgh, 1779), 15. The two lines that followed were: "All this was done in our last Scottish reign; / And what has been before may be again." A footnote to the couplet cited here included the following reinforcement: "In 1580, Lord D'Aubigny, a young nobleman born and bred in France, and cousin-german to the King, came over to Scotland. He was most kindly received, and soon turning a mighty favourite, was created Earl of Lennox. His being of the Roman profession, and in high favour with the King, raised the hopes of the Roman-Catholics. Priests and Jesuits swarmed into the country, and such as were Popishly affected at home, began openly to avow that religion.—On the other hand, the Protestant clergy were as much offended, and began in their sermons to regret the countenance that was given to Papists at court. The King, in order to quiet them, was at great pains to make a convert of his cousin; and accordingly, by one mean or other, got him openly, in St Giles's church, to renounce the errors in which he had been educated.—'Yet this (says he) did not remove the jealousies of the people; which were increased by the intercepting of certain dispensations from Rome, whereby the Catholics were permitted to promise, swear, subscribe, and do what else should be required of them, so as in mind they continued firm, and did use their diligence to advance in secret the Roman faith.' *Spottis. Hist. p.* 308. &c.—How applicable this may be to the present case, needs no commentary" (ibid., 21–22 n. 9).

society. At a public level, popular protest thus began to eclipse the resistance to Catholic relief that had been led by religious leaders.[25]

Religious leaders were not just left behind in these protests; the imperially linked institutions they worked within functioned to thwart and silence them. In the case of the Society in Scotland for Propagating Christian Knowledge (SSPCK), moderate voices together with the society's noble patrons urged church bodies to be cautious. The SSPCK was a natural vehicle to employ in the fight against popery. Like many such organizations, its very foundation had been made in the midst of fear of a Catholic threat. As a 1714 "Account" of the group stated, its "Design" began among those concerned about "Ignorance, Atheism, Popery and Impiety, that did so much abound in the Highlands and Isles of *Scotland*." When the SSPCK met on December 9, 1778, however, the members found that they could not agree on the subject of the "popery bill," and thus, in the tradition of bureaucracies everywhere, they created a subcommittee to handle the issue. That subcommittee included John Erskine, a leader of the Popular party that had promoted resistance to the popery bill in the General Assembly. The subcommittee drew up two resolutions, one explicitly objecting to the English bill and any potential future bill in Scotland and a second making a more general, but strong, statement against "Popish Idolatry and Superstition" and professing "their detestation of the Popish principle and practise of persecuting Men for worshiping God according to their consciences." In another careful move, the general committee then decided to consult with the body's patrons, the earls of Kinnoull and Leven, before going forward. The earls urged caution, even as they were sympathetic to the cause, and Kinnoull "endeavoured to convince [Erskine] that it w[oul]d be improper for the Committee of the Society to take up the Business of the intended Repeal of the Popish Acts." In the end, the SSPCK simply "resolve[d] to oppose, by every constitutional method in their power, the passing of any law that may obstruct the success of their endeavours to answer the ends of their institution," and it printed as much in the Edinburgh papers.[26]

25. "Provincial Synod of Galloway," Oct. 28, 1778, "The Synod of Lothian and Tweedale," Nov. 11, 1778, "Provincial Synod of Ross," Nov. 25, 1778, "Protestant Interest in Edinburgh," Dec. 1, 1778, and "Magistrates, Two-Council, etc. of Selkirk," Dec. 8, 1778, in *Scotland's Opposition*, 8–11; *Transactions of the Eight-Five Private Societies, in and about Glasgow; United in a General Correspondence, to Take What Legal Steps Might Appear Most Conducive, to Oppose a Repeal of the Penal Statutes against Papists in Scotland* (Glasgow, 1779), 6; Donovan, *No Popery and Radicalism*, 14, 51–62; Black, *The Association*, 136–140.

26. *An Account of the Rise, Constitution, and Management, of the Society in Scotland, for Propagating Christian Knowledge* (London, 1714), 6; Society in Scotland for Propagating Christian Knowledge (SSPCK), Minutes, Dec. 9, 18, 1778, GD95/2/9, 284–287, NRS; Kinnoull to Levin, Dec. 22, 1778, GD26/13/253/1 ("endeavoured to convince"), Minute of the Committee of Directors, Dec. 18, 1778, GD26/13/253/9, Kinnoull to Leven, Jan. 15, 1779, GD26/13/253/16, Robert

The caution that permeated the SSPCK's discussions reflected deep connections between the institutional protestant bodies in Britain and the state's governing social and political structures. Clergy in the SSPCK were part of an established state church. The society's noble patrons and leaders, from the earl of Leven to the king himself, saw the goals of the society and the British state as intertwined and mutually supportive, leaving little room for the society to disagree with matters of government policy. Thus, although men like Erskine—a deeply anti-Catholic thinker who believed papists were incapable of being trustworthy citizens—actively promoted antipopery with vigor, it was difficult for him to turn Scotland's protestant institutions to the purpose of political protest. The men of the SSPCK did not know how they might lobby government precisely because religious institutions, including the General Assembly, were deeply interconnected with government, local and imperial. Without a way to promote their concerns through religious institutions, the protests first raised by protestant leaders and through their institutions were quickly absorbed into newly organized groups, such as the Eighty-Five Private Societies in Glasgow and the Protestant Interest in Edinburgh, that could seize a wider platform and were not as intertwined in promoting stability and loyalty. Popular groups clearly drew moral authority from clerical participation—as had American rebels who sought to legitimize their cause—but the new civil institutions they created were not part of the scaffolding of British protestantism. That distinction, even as they spoke on behalf of protestantism, gave them more freedom.[27]

As the mechanics of organization shifted, so, too, did the arguments. Anti-Catholic civic organizations presented constitutional arguments against relief and depicted protestantism as the bulwark of Britain, hardly a coincidence when Britain was in the midst of a war of dismemberment. A declaration from the County of Kinross attested to its writers' duty "as Protestants and loyal subjects" to prevent "a measure so opposite to the interests of religion, and so subversive of all their valuable rights and privileges," which they had enjoyed "since the happy Revolution, and the accession of the present illustrious family of Hanover to the British throne." One 1778 tract, *A Short View of the Statutes etc. against Popery,* made the case that the repeal of limitations on Catholics violated the Act of Union. In the author's reasoning, "the security of church and state

Walker to Leven, Jan. 9, 1779, GD26/13/253/14, all in "Letters by or to David, Earl of Leven, as President of the SSPCK . . . Mainly with Regard to Measures to Be Taken to Halt the Repeal of the Penal Laws against Catholics in Scotland," NRS; "Society for Propagating Christian Knowledge," Jan. 7, 1779, in *Scotland's Opposition,* 22–23 ("resolve[d] to oppose"); Donovan, *No Popery and Radicalism,* 66–67.

27. Sher, *Church and University,* 285–286.

seem to be *inseparably* connected with the abolition of Popery." It showed the centrality of the fight against popery to both the settlement of the Glorious Revolution in Scotland and to the Act of Union, and the case was ultimately confirmed with the words of King George's oath to *"inviolably maintain* and preserve the settlement of the *true Protestant religion,* with the government, worship and discipline, *rights* and privileges of the church of Scotland, as established." This reassertion of Britain's history, alongside frequent retellings of purported Catholic abuses, made a positive argument for British protestantism as a core part of the nation's political fabric, but unlike the argument about keeping faith with heretics, it was an argument made *about* religion, rather than one made primarily through its leaders and institutions.[28]

As the anti-relief movement became more political, religious leaders who traded in antipopery found themselves on the defensive in the face of critiques from those in government. In late 1778, Erskine told readers of his tract *Considerations on the Spirit of Popery, and the Intended Bill for the Relief of Papists in Scotland* that he was "well assured, from ministers in that neighbourhood, that the disturbance given to a Popish meeting in Glasgow, about which some have raised so hideous an outcry, was occasioned by the insolent behaviour of a Papist to a few idle boys who had followed him from curiosity." William Porteous wrote, also after the Glasgow riot, that, "if any violent methods are employed, we will injure the best of causes, and do service to the worst." Yet, from the perspective of the state, clergy were a part of the problem. Adolphus Oughton, military commander-in-chief in Scotland, wrote to William Robertson urging him to speak out for quiet. "As religious heats are of all others the most dangerous," he wanted Robertson to use "the great Weight you so justly possess" to quiet matters in a way only the church could. Oughton had misdirected his request because Robertson had no influence with the mob. In December, the prominent Edinburgh minister had even received anonymous threats. "A Lover of Truth" told him that "provock'd revengence from Heaven will make an Example of you unless you recal your former conduct in as public a manner" as he had supported the "Popish Bill." On January 21, 1779, Oughton reported to his superiors in London that "the Pulpits, Presbyteries, Synods, Burgess meetings, and Associations all speak the same language, expressive of their Fears," intended to oppose relief measures. "The most moderate Clergy of the established Church are obliged," he continued, "for their own sakes, to

28. "County of Kinross," Jan. 11, 1779, "Town-Council of Kinghorn," Jan. 11, 1779, "Society of Journeymen Hammermen in Glasgow," Jan. 12, 1779, and "Parish of Kinglassie," Jan. 13, 1779, in *Scotland's Opposition,* 35 (quotations), 36, 46, 51; *A Short View of the Statutes at Present in Force in Scotland against Popery . . .* (Edinburgh, 1778), 16, 19–20.

join in the Cry; the enthusiastick Preachers, Nonjurors, and Republicans of all Denominations labour asiduously to spread the alarm." All religion seemed to him to be in the hands of the mob.[29]

Violence broke out again, this time in Edinburgh between January 30 and February 2, 1779. Anonymous leaflets urged residents "to pull down that pillar of Popery lately erected" in Leith Wynd, a reference to a house recently built by Bishop George Hay. That house was attacked first on January 30, and then during the next three days more anti-Catholic violence ensued. As Oughton reported, "Last Night a considerable Mob rose, and set Fire to an House which the Papists employed as a Chapple, and attacked that where Mr Hay (titular Bishop of Edinburgh) resided." The disorder required calling in troops. Oughton wrote: "The Magistrates, supported by 250 of the Military, prevented any further Excesses for that time, and took four of them Prisoners. But the Tumult has by no means subsided. This Morning the Magistrates inform me that the Mob threaten the Houses of Principal [Robertson], the Lord Advocate, and Counsellor Crosbie, supposing them Friends to the Popery Bill, and of Lord Linton as a Roman Catholick." Order was only restored after several days, and in the ensuing weeks all sides would plead they had not been responsible for the problems, but clearly the stability and loyalty that protestantism was supposed to promote had broken down.[30]

Tempers cooled quickly in Scotland because of the shock of the Edinburgh riots and because those in government made clear that Catholic relief in Scotland would go no further. On February 3, in the immediate aftermath of the riots, the lord provost of Edinburgh issued a formal proclamation, printed on a broadside, that there would be no relief for Catholics in Scotland (see Figure 15). Those who had organized to protest Catholic relief quickly distanced themselves from the rioting. The lord justice clerk reported on February 4, 1779, "The Leaders of the Opposition to the Repeal Act profess great indignation at the conduct of the Mob, and I hope they are sincere." Of course, from the view of Britain's authorities, those same leaders "would have done better, if they had

29. John Erskine, *Considerations on the Spirit of Popery, and the Intended Bill for the Relief of Papists in Scotland* (Edinburgh, 1778), 23–24; Porteous, *Doctrine of Toleration,* 38; Adolphus Oughton to William Robertson, Oct. 27, 1778, MS 3943–80, "A Lover of Truth" to Robertson, Dec. 29, 1778, MS 3943–85, both in Robertson-MacDonald Collection, NLS; Oughton to [Suffolk?], Jan. 21, 1779, SP 54/47 206, TNA. See also Thomas Miller to Suffolk, Jan. 25, 1779, SP 54/47 208, TNA.

30. [George Hay], *A Memorial to the Public, in Behalf of the Roman Catholics of Edinburgh and Glasgow* . . . (London, 1779), 15 ("pull down"), 18–28; Adolphus Oughton to Suffolk, Feb. 3, 1779, SP 54/47/212, TNA; *A Narrative of the Late Riots at Edinburgh; and a Vindication of Its Magistracy, against the Charges Advanced in the Memorial for the Papists of Scotland* (Edinburgh, 1779); Anonymous to Robertson, [Feb. 3, 1779], Robertson-MacDonald Collection, MS 3943–86, 89; Sher, *Church and University,* 287–290.

conducted their opposition from the beginning with more Moderation, and not have sounded the Alarm so loud to the People, who when once inflamed, will follow the direction of their own rage, without regard to the Dictates of their Leaders." Even some of the organizations that had formed specifically to fight the bill began to soften their rhetoric. The Parish of Cockpen reported that, just as its leaders rejected popish tyranny, so, too, do they "express [their] warmest indignation at those outrages that have of late taken place in the metropolis of this country." The Committee of Correspondence in Glasgow reported itself "deeply grieved with the unworthy behavior of those seditious rioters" in their city who had burned the house of a Catholic family. Now that those who opposed Catholic relief had achieved their end, riots would not be tolerated by either civic bodies or by religious institutions.[31]

Scotland's midwar wave of antipopery represented a challenge to the habits of imperial protestantism, all the more so because it was carried on in the name of protecting exactly that system and, in its early phases, was encouraged by many of the institutions and leaders that constituted imperial protestantism. The war against America had pushed British leaders in London to envision a state that included Catholics in some limited ways. But Scots considered protestantism to be an essential part of their connection to the government of Great Britain, and they resisted Parliament's attempt to push it in a direction that included those they considered politically suspect. The protests made clear to the imperial leaders—both those in government and those, like William Robertson, who supported them—the strength of the entrenched prejudices that supported political protestantism and the willingness of at least some among the ranks of religious leaders to support it. As far as Scotland was concerned, Parliament relented. But, at the same time, a counter-lesson was also being learned by religious leaders. Allying themselves with popular political protests had led to destruction and violence that could not easily be defended by those who represented the stability of institutional protestantism. It was a lesson to which their southern neighbors attended with particular care.

"THE PRETENCE OF RELIGION"

The violence that shook London in June 1780 in the name of protestantism overshadowed that in Scotland by a significant order of magnitude. At the same

31. "Proclamation Stating That the Bill to Repeal . . . ," Feb. 3, 1779, SP 54/47/216, TNA; Miller to ?, Feb. 4, 1779, SP 54/47/217, TNA; "Sub-Committee of Farmers," Feb. 6, 1779, "Parish of Cockpen," Feb. 9, 1779, "Committee of Correspondence in Glasgow," Feb. 10, 1779, and "Eighty-Three Societies," Feb. 10, 1779, in *Scotland's Opposition,* 243, 250 ("indignation"), 252 ("grieved").

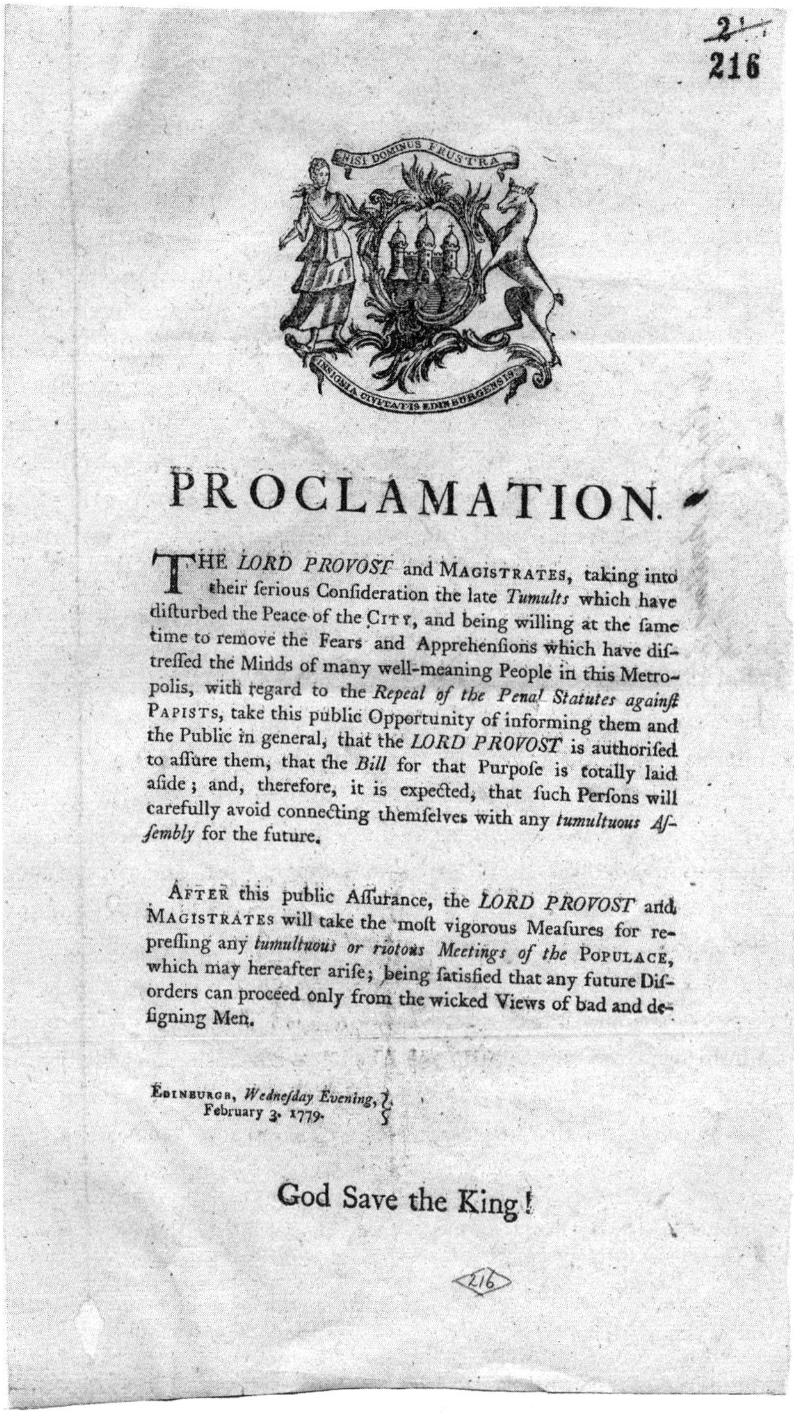

2
216

NISI DOMINUS FRUSTRA

INSIGNIA CIVITATIS EDINBURGENSIS

PROCLAMATION.

THE *LORD PROVOST* and MAGISTRATES, taking into their ſerious Conſideration the late *Tumults* which have diſturbed the Peace of the CITY, and being willing at the ſame time to remove the Fears and Apprehenſions which have diſtreſſed the Minds of many well-meaning People in this Metropolis, with regard to the *Repeal of the Penal Statutes againſt* PAPISTS, take this public Opportunity of informing them and the Public in general, that the *LORD PROVOST* is authoriſed to aſſure them, that the *Bill* for that Purpoſe is totally laid aſide; and, therefore, it is expected, that ſuch Perſons will carefully avoid connecting themſelves with any *tumultuous Aſſembly* for the future.

AFTER this public Aſſurance, the *LORD PROVOST* and MAGISTRATES will take the moſt vigorous Meaſures for repreſſing any *tumultuous or riotous Meetings of the* POPULACE, which may hereafter ariſe; being ſatiſfied that any future Diſorders can proceed only from the wicked Views of bad and deſigning Men.

EDINBURGH, *Wedneſday Evening*, February 3. 1779.

God Save the King!

216

FIGURE 15 “Proclamation Stating That the Bill to Repeal . . . ,” Feb. 3, 1779, SP 54/47/216, The National Archives, Kew. Authorities in Scotland declared Catholic relief a dead letter after the Edinburgh riots. Courtesy of The National Archives, Kew, U.K.

time, the issues involved, from the perspective of imperial protestantism, were much less complicated. Religious leaders in England were far less involved in the organized anti-Catholic movement than their counterparts in Scotland had been; faced with the choice between defending protestantism in the street or supporting the policies of the imperial government, they overwhelmingly chose the latter. When the activities of London's Protestant Association, the movement's organizers, spun out of control under the guidance of the unpredictable Scottish demagogue Lord George Gordon, religious and governmental leaders alike created the narrative that what had happened had little to do with religion because the protestant institutions they led could never engage in such riotous behavior. Separating a movement on behalf of protestantism from the idea of religion seems counterintuitive, but it was successful. Blame for the riots was not laid at the feet of protestant institutions, and these institutions continued to collaborate with a government that was no longer so closely allied with protestantism. Government and religious leaders in Britain, like those in the United States, distanced themselves from the political rhetoric of the confessional era.[32]

The links between Scotland's anti-Catholic moment and England's were quite direct, even though the riots were separated by more than a year. The Protestant Interest in Edinburgh and the Eighty-Five Private Societies in Glasgow, unsatisfied with merely stopping Catholic relief in Scotland, reached out to Lord George Gordon in the months after the Edinburgh riots. Gordon was a younger son of a Scottish noble family, and after a short career in the navy that included service in America he had entered Parliament representing a rotten borough in 1774. He made no contributions to Parliament's discussions about Catholic relief in 1778, but when he was recruited to the cause by Scots in early 1779, he was an enthusiastic leader. He framed his first discussion of the anti-Catholic uproar in terms of the American war, suggesting that the British might be as unsympathetic to the Scots as they had been to the Americans. One London paper reported that he "treated the whole in a humorous and a very

32. Conway, *The British Isles and the War of American Independence,* 252–253. The literature on the Gordon Riots emphasizes their history as a popular uprising, following the scholarship of George Rudé, who deemphasized religion as a motivation in the riots and argues that "behind the slogan of 'No Popery,' and the other outward forms of religious fanaticism there lay a deeper social purpose: a groping desire to settle accounts with the rich, if only for a day, and to achieve some rough kind of social justice" (Rudé, *Paris and London in the Eighteenth Century: Studies in Popular Protest* [New York, 1971], 289). See also E. P. Thompson, *The Making of the English Working Class* (New York, 1966), 70–72. For a thorough reassessment of the event's parameters and consequences, see Haywood and Seed, eds., *The Gordon Riots.* For the Protestant Association in Newcastle, see Kathleen Wilson, *The Sense of the People: Politics, Culture, and Imperialism in England, 1715–1785* (Cambridge, 1995), 365–370, and, more generally, 265–267. As an event in English anti-Catholicism, see Haydon, *Anti-Catholicism,* 204–244. For a transatlantic perspective on the events, see Jones, "'In Favour of Popery,'" *Journal of British Studies,* LII (2013), 79–102.

jocular manner, mixing at the same time a deal of satire with his facetiousness, and concluding very seriously" that Catholic relief in Scotland "would produce a civil war," though that policy had already been abandoned. Gordon also voiced his opposition to Lord North's administration in terms that combined the American conflict and Catholic relief. North, he claimed, had brought on a war with the colonies and with Europe, and now his government had "at last shewn their intention to sap the very foundation of our liberties at home, by attempting the repeal of our ancient and independent laws, in favour of the Protestant Religion." Gordon quickly became the figurehead of the protestant movement, and he was feted on a trip through Scotland in the late summer of 1779, a few months after the Edinburgh riots.[33]

The leaders of the English anti-Catholic movement were outside institutional protestantism from the outset. In November 1779, Gordon joined his efforts with a new English group calling itself the Protestant Association, after he received an invitation from its leader, James Fisher. The group, which met at Coachmakers Hall (notably not a church), described itself in the press as "deeply affected at the alarming appearance of POPERY . . . and generally attached to the PROTESTANT FAITH, and our happy Constitution." It also "disclaim[ed] every idea of a party, or of supporting any particular sect of Christians," and declared that "Protestants of every denomination" were welcomed into "this cause against the common enemy of the Protestant religion." Though they leveraged the label of "Protestant," the group had few connections to organized protestantism. An awakened Anglican clergyman from Eastcheap, Erasmus Middleton, was an early leader in the association, and it included some other awakened clerical members, but their numbers paled in comparison to the masses who supported the cause, and no prominent protestant institution endorsed it.[34]

33. "House of Commons. Thursday," *General Advertiser, and Morning Intelligencer* (London), Mar. 19, 1779, [3]. David Grant, a minister in the Edinburgh body, initiated correspondence with Gordon in March 1779 and connected him with another leader of the Protestant Association, Ralph Bowie. From Glasgow, John Paterson of the Eighty-Five Societies reached out to Gordon. See *Transactions of the Eighty-Five Private Societies*, 11, 12 ("at last shewn"); "Rex v Lord George Gordon for High Treason in Regarding to the 'No Popery Riots' of 1780; . . .", TS 11/388/1212, TNA; *Parliamentary History of England*, XIX, 1093–1094; Black, *The Association*, 147–149; and Robert Watson, *The Life of Lord George Gordon: With a Philosophical Review of His Political Conduct*, 2d ed. (London, 1795), 9–10. Black asserts that Gordon had already corresponded with the General Assembly of the Church of Scotland, but he provides no citation. See also Colin Haydon, "Gordon, Lord George (1751–1793)," September 2004, *Oxford Dictionary of National Biography Online*, https://www.oxforddnb.com; Donovan, *No Popery and Radicalism*, 31, 36–37, 241–243; and O'Shaughnessy, *The Men Who Lost America*, 151. Gordon also invoked the story of Jane McCrea to implicate the English in anti-presbyterian savagery.

34. "Protestant Association," *General Advertiser, and Morning Intelligencer*, May 25, 1779, [4]; Watson, *Life of George Gordon*, 12; John Seed, "'The Fall of Romish Babylon Anticipated': Plebian Dissenters and Anti-Popery in the Gordon Riots," in Haywood and Seed, eds., *The Gordon*

The leaders of the Protestant Association wanted the legitimacy that connections to protestant institutions might provide nonetheless. They attempted to bring the Church of England, by far the largest protestant body in England, into their effort; their failure points to the disreputable state of the cause of political protestantism in 1779, after the Scottish riots. The group printed an invitation stating that "it was determined, in forming the PROTESTANT ASSOCIATION, that the CLERGY *of the Established Church* should be requested to take the Lead in the important Business thereof." Its members forwarded the document, along with some anti-Catholic materials, to archbishops and bishops, saying they were "anxiously solicitous to have the approbation and concurrence" of those men "in the steps they take to stem the progress of Popery." There is no evidence that the church's hierarchy embraced the effort, though a few Anglican clergy were among the petitioners in 1780. Later, Beilby Porteus, the bishop of Chester, remarked that "the Bishops and the English Clergy did not see that Act in the same light and had no reason to believe either that Popery was increasing or the Protestant Religion in any Danger," and thus "they did not accept the Invitation." There was some support from among dissenting circles as well, though neither of the organizations of dissent in London made any mention of the cause in their records. Of course, the bishops' bench had already acquiesced to the relief measure more than a year before and continued to support the government.[35]

Awakened Anglican John Wesley provided the most significant public support for the group from a well-known religious leader. In 1779, he published a tract, *Popery Calmly Considered,* that was printed in England, Scotland, and Ireland before the year was out. He also published two letters, one in the *Public Advertiser* and one in the *Arminian Magazine,* praising the Protestant Association and laying out in a few paragraphs the core argument that, although one

---

Riots, 70, 74. The same notice also appeared in "Protestant Association," *St. James's Chronicle; Or, British Evening-Post* (London), May 25–27, 1779, [1]. For a broader exploration of the episode and the American war that stretches beyond religion, see Nicholas Rogers, "The Gordon Riots and the Politics of War," in Haywood and Seed, eds., *The Gordon Riots,* 21–45. The Protestant Association also extended beyond London. See Black, *The Association,* 152–153; and Wilson, *Sense of the People,* 364–370.

35. James Fisher to archbishops and bishops, n.d., Fulham Papers: Papers of the Bishops of London, Papers of Beilby Porteus 16 (hereafter cited as FP Porteus 16), fol. 21, Lambeth Palace Library, London (LPL); and printed broadside from the Protestant Association, n.d., FP Porteus 16, fol. 16. These two documents are undated, but the printed statement refers to the next meeting of the group on Friday, June 4. June 4, 1779, was a Friday, and June 4, 1780, was a Sunday and fell in the middle of the riots. See also Beilby Porteus, "Occasional Memorandums and Reflexions on Several Subjects Principally Religious, Moral, Ecclesiastical and Literary Begun in the Year 1771," I, Diary, MS 2098, 133 ("Danger"), LPL; and Seed, "The Fall of Romish Babylon," in Haywood and Seed, eds., *The Gordon Riots,* 77–78.

should "persecute no man for his religious principles," in this case an exception must be made, as Catholics could not take oaths that would be trusted. Wesley's support for the Protestant Association is intriguing to ponder, as is the presence of a few other awakened protestants among the signatories to the group's subsequent petition to Parliament. An outspoken figure with his own following, Wesley might well have felt less bound by the institutions in which he was enmeshed than other leaders, who for the most part kept their distance from the growing fracas. In a similar way, awakened leaders might have been less concerned with embracing the stability provided by institutions than their Anglican and dissenting counterparts. The small number of awakened clergy among the petitioners, and the fact that no collective awakened body—no awakened institution—promoted the cause, renders absolute conclusions elusive, and perhaps that is finally the point. Where the conservative pressure of protestant institutions was more palpably felt, religious leaders eschewed the Protestant Association. Where those pressures were weaker, as they were with Wesley, more antipopery sentiment could be found.[36]

The Protestant Association also sought the assistance of George III. As Britain's sovereign, he was at the center of the empire's protestant system, and he had personally sworn to uphold protestantism. Gordon used his position as a member of the peerage to meet with the king on several occasions, and, in Gordon's retelling, he insisted that the king protect the "Protestant Interest" that was the basis of the British constitution and threatened George with the specter of the late Stuart dynasty. But, according to Gordon, when the king was pressed on the issue, just a few weeks before the riots, he responded: *"I am myself a Protestant; but must confess I am a Friend to Toleration."* Though the king did not see these two as contradictory, Gordon and his fellows did. Lacking widespread support from religious leaders or from those in government, they turned to more direct political action.[37]

36. John Wesley, "To the Printer of the *Public Advertiser,*" Jan. 12, 1780, in John Telford, ed., *The Letters of the Rev. John Wesley, A.M.: Sometime Fellow of Lincoln College, Oxford,* VI (London, 1931), 370–371 (quotation on 371); Reginald Ward and Richard P. Heitzenrater, eds., *The Works of John Wesley,* XXIII, *Journal and Diaries, VI (1776–86)* (Nashville, Tenn., 1995), 159; David Butler, *Methodists and Papists: John Wesley and the Catholic Church in the Eighteenth Century* (London, 1995), 56–57; Haydon, *Anti-Catholicism,* 210–211; Seed, "The Fall of Romish Babylon," in Haywood and Seed, eds., *The Gordon Riots,* 74–76. For awakened protestant worries about Catholics, see also John Newton to John Thornton, July 4, 1778, Thornton Family Papers, Add. MS 7674/1/B/24, Special Collections, Cambridge University Library; and John Erskine to John Ryland, Sr., Nov. 1, 1779, John Erskine Papers, E99.14, Edinburgh University Library. Seed points out that Erasmus Middleton was one of the awakened Anglicans who had been expelled from Oxford in 1768, suggesting his position on the fringes of respectable Anglicanism was already well established.

37. George Gordon, *Innocence Vindicated, and the Intrigues of Popery and Its Abettors Displayed, in an Authentic Narrative of Some Transactions, Hitherto Unknown, Relating to a Late Act of the*

With Gordon's leadership, the Protestant Association decided to submit a petition to Parliament requesting repeal of the Catholic Relief Act of 1778. In November 1779, the group issued *An Appeal from the Protestant Association to the People of Great Britain,* in which it laid out, once again, the arguments against bringing Catholics into the public body. Papists could not be trusted as loyal citizens, and though persecution was antithetical to protestantism, the *Appeal* argued that it was absolutely necessary for British protestants to protect themselves from the popish menace. They recounted the hasty passage of the bill and the successful movement to stop relief in Scotland. Finally, they declared it was an *"absolute necessity"* that *"an application to Parliament for redress"* be made. The urgency, as with much of the events in the antipopery episode, came from the American war. Britons "lately had striking proofs" of how untrustworthy papists were. In the first years of the colonial conflict, the French had "publicly protested against the conduct of our American colonies," upholding the principle of imperial, monarchical rule. That nation had even—in what now appeared to be a *"plan of duplicity"*—demanded "*American privateers to leave her ports.*" But now, "at the very time when Papists were receiving favours from this government," the French forgot "their public disavowals of the American cause, and their solemn protestations to the British ministry; their *most Christian and Catholic majesties,* without the least provocation, contrary to the faith of treaties, and to the law of nations, united for our destruction." Bitter anger and sarcasm drove the point home: loyal British protestants needed to act.[38]

The Gordon Riots, as they unfolded between June 2 and June 9, 1780, were the most violent and destructive mob action in eighteenth-century Britain. They began when the Protestant Association, under the leadership of Lord Gordon, gathered by the thousands to deliver its massive petition—forty-four thousand signatures—to Parliament. Petitioners marched to Westminster, where the mood turned from orderly to restive. Members of Parliament, including bishops, were harassed and threatened, and the situation deteriorated from there. Over the next six days, the mob destroyed both Catholic chapels and prominent symbols of government authority. The home of the chief justice, Lord Mansfield, was ransacked; Newgate Prison and other jails were dismantled and their inmates released. On the night of June 6, fires raged through the city.

British Legislature in Favour of English Papists, and the Petition Presented to Parliament for Its Repeal; Part II, 2d ed. (London, 1783), 15–16.

38. *An Appeal from the Protestant Association to the People of Great Britain concerning the Probable Tendency of the Late Act of Parliament in Favour of the Papists* (London, 1779), 56–58; Haydon, *Anti-Catholicism,* 210. The *Monthly Review* quipped in response to the Protestant Association's tract, "Shall we act like Papists in supporting Protestantism?" (*Monthly Review,* LXII [January 1780], 67).

The following night was even worse, with the burning of a distillery and an attack on the Bank of England. Scottish politician John Anstruther reported back home to William Robertson's son what he saw: "When we sett out the whole sky was covered w.t Black Clouds of Smoke with Gleams of fire from every side you turned to." "From every quarter," he wrote, "you heard the shrieks of those who were saving themselves mixed with the yells and huzzas of the Mob the [unclear] of falling houses and now and then a Platoon which for a term hushed the storm." At the distillery, "Not five Minutes after we arrived," he continued, "30000 Gallons of Sherets of different sorts blew up at once and formed a column of Flame as high as your eyes could reach casting a light brighter than the brightest sun." London seemed to burn.[39]

Order was restored when the military, on the orders of the king, intervened. The results were bloody. Before it was over, hundreds were reported dead. London's Catholic community suffered particularly, but the mob terrified many others as well. Politicians, jails, and the Bank—symbols of power and authority—were principal targets. Yet some protestant figures also had reason to worry. Awakened Anglican leader Charles Wesley, unitarian Theophilus Lindsey, and London's Moravian community all reported threats or worse. The Protestant Association, presumably without the leadership of Lord Gordon, who by then was already imprisoned, distributed a statement saying that their petition had not been considered because of "the unhappy distractions occasioned by an unruly and tumultuous mob, who, under pretence of opposing Popery, have been guilty of many most heinous offences." The subsequent actions by "the military power which has been called in" had thus been aimed, not at "the Protestants of London," but at its criminal elements. Rumors of French involvement continued. "Many letters from abroad confirm[ed] the prophecy of the French Ambassador at the Hague, concerning the burning of London," according to the *London Chronicle*. There were other tidbits that seemed to validate those suspicions, including "a man habited shabbily," but who wore silks "under his coarse stockings . . . , and in his bosom a picture set 'round with diamonds." Peace returned, but the enormity of the damage and destruction required an explanation.[40]

39. John Anstruther to William Robertson, Jr., June 9, 1780, Robertson-MacDonald Collection, MS 3943–124. For brief summations of the events, see Rudé, *Paris and London*, 270–275; and Haywood and Seed, "Introduction," in Haywood and Seed, eds., *The Gordon Riots*, 1–7. For contemporary accounts, see *The Annual Register; or, A View of the History, Politics, and Literature, for the Year 1780* (London, 1780), 254–287; and William Vincent [Thomas Holcroft], *A Plain and Succinct Narrative of the Late Riots and Disturbances in the Cities of London and Westminster, and Borough of Southwark* . . . (London, 1780).

40. "London," *London Chronicle*, June 13–15, 1780, 570; Thomas Jackson, *The Life of the Rev. Charles Wesley* . . . , II (London, 1841), 321; Lindsey to William Tayleur, June 10, 1780, in Ditchfield,

FIGURE 16 *No Popery or Newgate Reformer*. The anti-Catholic Gordon Riots were followed by a major effort to blame the conflict on rabble and to protect the motivations of the "protestants" who instigated it. 1868,0808.4694.

In the aftermath, Britons quickly rallied to the idea that the riots were lawless and chaotic, rather than a righteous defense of a core part of British public life (see Figure 16). Similar to the Americans' dismissal of Benedict Arnold's insistence on an outdated protestant-Catholic rivalry, Britons in 1780 could not believe that defending protestantism could justify such disorder. Preserving peace and order was more important than maintaining the strict boundary between protestants and Catholics. In his first public proclamation of the riots, King George declared that the attacks on foreign chapels were done "to the great Scandal and Offence of all truly pious and good protestants," and he described the riots as a "Reproach of so frantick and Atrocious an Outrage against the precepts of Religion." A letter writer to the *Morning-Post* directly addressed the Protestant Association's statement disavowing responsibility. The writer

ed., *Letters of Theophilus Lindsey*, I, 317; Charles Wesley to Sally Wesley, June 12, 1780, Charles Wesley Papers, DDCW 7/42, John Rylands Library, University of Manchester, U.K. See also James Fisher, "Protestant Association," *Public Advertiser* (London), June 12, 1780, [1]; "By the King, a Proclamation," and "Morning Post London," *Morning Post, and Daily Advertiser* (London), June 12, 1780, [2–3].

asked if the associators condemned the attacks on innocent Catholics, and he guessed not. "But popery, you tell us, is a blood thirsty and destructive religion." In the present moment, that charge, he argued, could be laid elsewhere. "Which religion am I to prefer? That, which silently submits, from a love of peace and order, to insults and the wild attacks of enthusiasm, or that, which *persecutes,* which destroys property, and which exposes to cruel danger even the lives of our fellow creatures," he asked. "The *real* protestant religion is by no means of the latter description, it breaths peace and good will to *all men.*" The riots had brought shame to "the established religion of this kingdom," and he urged the association "to assume some other appellation better adapted to the character of *your* religion." The *Monthly Review,* which had favored the relief bill, responded to a tract by Scottish minister John Erskine supporting the actions in Scotland that must have been published before the riots in England. The *Review* provided a blanket condemnation of the tumult. "We totally disapproved of the opposition which was made in Scotland to the Bill in favour of the Roman Catholics," the piece stated. "It was begun in malice, and ended in outrage." More recent events framed the force of their comments: "What a disgrace will the remembrances of some late events in Scotland and England stamp on the annals of Protestantism! The pretence of religion only aggravated the guilt of sedition." Another writer concluded, "The Protestant religion had nothing to do with the late disturbances." Religion—the stable institutions of the nation's dominant protestantism—had to be separated from the ignominy of riot.[41]

The effort to separate loyal religion from the causes of riot also permeated the legal case against Gordon. Prosecutors seized Gordon's papers. They prepared a catalog of the documents, arguing that Gordon had acted alone and had worked against the advice of reputable religious leaders. David Grant, the Scottish minister who had corresponded with Gordon, provided the one example of religious respectability, and, in the prosecutors' telling, even he admitted that "None of the Reverend Fathers" in Scotland, "however great their aversion to Popery, will imitate the example of the *first Pope* in *drawing the sword* in Defence of their Master, and his Religion: We have few Peters among us; and as few *Lord G. Gordon's.*" Prosecutors used the dossier to trace how Grant and

41. Privy Council Minutes, June 5, 1780, PC 2/125, fols. 131–33, TNA; "For the Morning Post. To Mr. Fisher, Secretary of the Protestant Association," *Morning Post, and Daily Advertiser,* June 20, 1780, [4]; "Monthly Catalogue: Religious," *Monthly Review,* LXII (June 1780), 502; [Thomas O'Beirne], *Considerations on the Late Disturbances, by a Consistent Whig* (London, 1780), 6, 14–15, 29. The English Short Title Catalogue attributes this anonymous pamphlet to O'Beirne. Bishop Beilby Porteus attributed it to Edmund Burke in his diary; see Porteus, "Occasional Memorandums and Reflexions on Several Subjects," I, Diary, MS 2098, 149, LPL. See also Vincent [Holcroft], *Plain and Succinct Narrative of the Late Riots and Disturbances,* 2d ed. (London, 1780), 46, note M (appendix).

Gordon found themselves at odds with the General Assembly after its 1779 meeting. Grant was *"astonished"* and "incredulous" to learn "that the sober part of the Nation and of the Clergy was *satisfied"* by reassurances that there would be no bill for Scotland. Through the summer of 1779, Gordon and his Scottish colleagues, principally Ralph Bowie and Grant, continued to agitate, gradually despairing of adequate support from the now tranquil Scots. In a May 1780 letter to Gordon, Grant shared "his Concern that the People [in Scotland] did not Act more heartily with his Lordship." Grant insisted to those with whom he corresponded that Gordon could be trusted as a *"Patron of Protestantism,"* even if others could not. The dossier's preparers then noted: "What [Grant] means 'by Protestantism' he explains, 'I am sorry that the Publications in England have rather viewed it in a *Religious,* than a *Political* Light.'" The meanings twisted back on themselves. Apparently Grant, the Scottish cleric, lamented that English writers viewed protestantism as a religious rather than a political category, thus asserting—presumably to the relief of those preparing for Gordon's trial—that the movement was actually political and could not be blamed on religion. The importance of these categories to those who spoke for the government in the months after the rioting is striking; just as urgent as holding perpetrators accountable was ensuring that their motives could not undermine the role of religion, and the institutions that structured it, as a stabilizing force in society.[42]

Protestant leaders, too, jumped into the fray in the aftermath of the riots to protect the reputation of their work and to lay blame for the events. Bishop Beilby Porteus addressed those he held responsible. He drafted a letter to the "late Protestant Association" insisting that, "however pure and peaceable your Intentions may have been," they had led to "fatal consequences." He called on them to make amends "by doing their utmost to quiet the minds and calm the fears of those" whom they had "alarmed and terrified" of the "late Act." He also wrote to John Wesley, taking him to task for his role in the events. He blamed the popular preacher for stirring up anti-Catholicism in the newspapers and for spreading the idea that Catholics could not be trusted to make oaths. Although he believed himself a "sincere Protestant" and saw "popery as a most corrupt system of superstition and bigotry," he still considered the "rage against papists, and those vain [fears?] about the danger [to] Protestantism" as the cause of "all the late mobs, outrages, and commissions." Wesley, Porteus blasted, had "a great

42. "Rex v Lord George Gordon," TS 11/388/1212, TNA. For the 1779 General Assembly of the Church of Scotland, see [John Erskine], *A Narrative of the Debate in the General Assembly of the Church of Scotland, May 25, 1779; Occasioned by Apprehensions of an Intended Repeal of the Penal Statutes against Papists* (Edinburgh, 1779). See also Donovan, *No Popery and Radicalism,* 104–106; McIntosh, *Church and Theology,* 161–166; and Sher, *Church and University,* 290–294.

FIGURE 17 *Fanat[i]cism Revived.* The print places Wesley in the center of the Gordon Riots, arms stretched out. The caption reads, "Religious strife is rais[e]d to Life, / by canting whining John; / No Popery he loud doth cry, / To the deluded throng." 868,0808.4738.

deal to answer for to God and to your country, and unless you make the best amends you can to both—by confessing your mistake and setting those deluded people right whom you have unhappily mislead, all men will justly entertain a much more unfavourable opinion of you than they have hitherto done." The enthusiasm that was frequently associated with Wesley's followers, coupled with his virulent anti-Catholicism, had for Porteus overstepped the bounds of responsible leadership. Dissenter and pro-American cleric Joseph Priestley published a brief pamphlet in which he urged toleration as the best method to support protestantism, essentially promoting the same stance as Bishop Porteus. John Wesley himself was not in London when the riots occurred, but his brother Charles composed and published a series of poems on the occasion, expressing his distress at the insurrection. With seeming uniformity, religious leaders condemned what had been done in the name of protestantism (see Figure 17).[43]

43. Beilby Porteus to the Protestant Association, n.d., FP Porteus 16, fols. 29–31, LPL; Porteus to John Wesley, draft, n.d., FP Porteus 16, fols. 29–31, LPL. I am grateful to the assistance of Randy Maddox in transcribing this challenging draft. The draft appears to say "danger of Protestantism" rather than "danger to," which makes little sense, unless Porteus was moving in one sentence from antipopery fears to fears generated *by* the riots, which does not fit in context. See also A Lover of

The general consensus, from the courts, from religious leaders, and eventually from historians, was that the riots grew from popular outrage, from a mob led astray. In his memoirs, Bishop Porteus opined that the "dreadfull Tumult and Insurrection," which was "supposed to take its rise from Religious Zeal," had as an "Original cause" "the extravagant and enthusiastic Zeal of the Protestant Association," but those sentiments had mainly planted "the first seeds of discontent amongst the Populace, inflamed their Passions, excited their Rage, alarmed their Fears, and prepared them for any violences." The "dreadfull Consequences that followed" were the fault of "a Band of Ruffians, who had no Religion at all, by Felons and Murderers let out of Goals, and as some also supposed by the French and American Agents who thought this a most favourable opportunity of exciting insurrection." By distancing "Religion" from the riots, and dismissing the possibility that the responsible institutions they led could be behind such dramatic popular protest, those who defended religion from riot threw their lot in, once again, with government authorities and stability—even when faced with popular resistance that advocated for protestantism. The idea of a state that extended limited rights to Catholics was simply less threatening than mass protest. Their position was hardly surprising given that England's religious leaders had raised few objections two years before when Catholic relief was passed. The scaffolding of imperial protestantism was hard-pressed to protest imperial policy under any circumstances. But the Gordon Riots were highly symbolic nonetheless. Institutional champions of protestantism were more invested in the stability of the British state than they were in any existential threat posed by Catholicism.[44]

Of course, the real challenge faced by the British in 1780 came from the American war. The protests of the Gordon rioters were a frustrating distraction. Faced with a rapidly expanding conflict against the largely protestant United States and its widening number of European allies, both antipopery and unity based on protestantism were beside the point. The appeal of Ireland's Catholics as a resource for the military remained strong, and Catholic relief continued there. As the dust settled in England, Parliament and leaders from the Church of

---

Peace and Truth [Joseph Priestley], *A Free Address to Those Who Have Petitioned for the Repeal of the Late Act of Parliament, in Favor of the Roman Catholics* (London, 1780); [Charles Wesley], *Hymns Written in the Time of the Tumults, June 1780* (Bristol, U.K., 1780); [Wesley], "Hymns Written in the Time of the Tumults, June 1780," in G. Osborn, ed., *The Poetical Works of John and Charles Wesley: Reprinted from the Originals, with the Last Corrections of the Authors; Together with the Poems of Charles Wesley Not Before Published* (London, 1870), VIII, 263–280; and Seed, "The Fall of Romish Babylon," in Haywood and Seed, eds., *The Gordon Riots,* 70–71, 87–88.

44. Porteus, "Occasional Memorandums and Reflexions on Several Subjects," I, Diary, MS 2098, 147–149, LPL.

England reaffirmed their faith in the principle of toleration and also investigated the notion that perhaps there had been an increase in the number of Catholics since the 1778 repeal. George Savile, the same member of Parliament who had introduced Catholic relief in 1778, introduced a Bill to Secure the Protestant Religion in Great Britain from Any Encroachments of Popery to Parliament, and although it passed the Commons, it was defeated in the House of Lords. These were bureaucratic responses to the riots, and they marked a return to the religio-political order in which government determined the ways that religious institutions functioned. Thus, much of the scaffolding of British protestantism—understood as the institutional ties between protestant institutions and government structures—survived the violent disorder that had been, theoretically, perpetrated in its name. The old antagonism between protestants and Catholics, the backbone of the confessional era, was far less relevant in this new, revolutionary, age.[45]

Between 1778 and 1781, the last years of the Revolutionary War, government leaders in both the United States and in the British Empire revaluated their relationship to protestantism, not as a theology or a series of institutions, but as a foundation for political unity. Though historians have often seen the decline of confessional politics and the rise of religious toleration as part of the same conversation, the events of these years illustrate the need for a more-nuanced reading. The political investment in protestantism as a unifying concept did not end merely because Britons and Americans became more tolerant of religious outsiders (though intellectual elites were certainly moving in that direction) or because policymakers became less pious; it ended because the demands of the American Revolution made the framework for politics that it represented—and had represented for a century—politically unsustainable. The war's exigencies pushed the governments of the United States and Great Britain to embrace Catholic partners, relaxing the connection between the boundaries around protestantism and those around civic participation.[46]

The shifts made by governments had implications for their partners in protestant institutions. In the United States, matters were fairly straightforward. The new nation had already distanced itself from the scaffolding of imperial protestantism, and protestant leaders had already thrown their lot in with a

45. Ibid., 150; "A Bill [with the Amendments] to Secure the Protestant Religion in Great Britain from Any Encroachments of Popery," FP Porteus 16, fols. 14–15, LPL; Conway, *The British Isles and the War of American Independence*, 250–252.

46. Historians have analyzed the Gordon Riots with an eye toward evaluating the progress of religious toleration. See, for example, Haydon, *Anti-Catholicism*, 243–244, which argues that residual conservativism in English society linked the anti-Catholic population to its seventeenth-century forebearers. See also Conway, *The British Isles and the War of American Independence*, 263–266.

Revolutionary government. They had already described—and even sanctified—a nation that had no clear relationship to religious institutions or establishments. There, religious leaders quite easily became champions of the French alliance, embracing the providential possibilities for both military triumph and the spread of protestant Christianity that it brought.

In Britain, leaving the politics of protestantism behind was more complicated. The spasms of anti-Catholicism that erupted in 1779 and 1780 pointed to the foundational role that protestantism continued to play in Britons' understanding of their nation, particularly in Scotland, even as some of their more elite leaders, men like William Robertson in Scotland and Beilby Porteus in England, were ready to imagine subjecthood in ways that were less contingent on confession. Yet, when British religious leaders and their political partners rescued religion from the Gordon Riots, they also distanced the institutions they led from the popular notion of protestantism the rioters championed. On both sides of the Atlantic, the essential protestant character of the scaffolding that connected religious institutions to the state had been tested and found wanting. The politics of the new era would look different.

7 The New Protestant Order

The scaffolding linking religious institutions to goverments across the British Empire had, for nearly a century, kept protestantism's schismatic tendencies largely in check. As Americans and Britons divided through war, they were freed from the connections and pressures that scaffolding had produced. They began to remake the Anglo-American denominational order of the preceding era. In the colonial period, Anglicans, presbyterians, and congregationalists, with a smaller number of baptists among them, had dominated the protestant landscape in nearly every part of the empire, both demographically and in terms of government privilege. The vibrant awakening movement had, for the most part, stayed within those boundaries, and one single church—the Church of England—predominated in vast regions on both sides of the Atlantic.[1]

After the war, in the absence of the imperial protestant scaffold, the balance within that denominational order shifted toward fracture and the creation of new denominations. There were two overlapping causes for the shift, both rooted in the war. In areas where the war had broken down habits and structures of religious leadership, new religious leaders from a fresh wave of awakenings—people who in some cases bore little resemblance to the kind of men who had been recognized as legitimate protestant leaders in the colonial period—started movements and founded denominations. At the same time, the Church of England dismembered itself. Its American branches were cut off, and the Protestant Episcopal Church in the United States was formed. In a further, overlapping development, many awakened Anglicans, those who followed John Wesley, moved outside Anglicanism on both sides of the Atlantic. In the United States, the consequences of this divide were staggering. The new Methodist Episcopal Church in America, the body that gathered most of Wesley's American followers, grew to include a remarkable 34 percent of the nation's religious adherents in 1850. Meanwhile, the percentage of Americans who belonged to congregationalist, episcopal, and presbyterian bodies declined. Those groups

1. For a critical investigation of denominationalism, in both its eighteenth-century British and more recent U.S. contexts, see Russell E. Richey, *Denominationalism: Illustrated and Explained* (Eugene, Ore., 2013).

collectively accounted for slightly more than 55 percent of religious adherents in 1776 but less than 20 percent in 1850.[2]

The end of one denominational system and the creation of a new one had its counterpart in the realm of transatlantic partnerships intended to do the religious work of spreading Christianity. The war had eroded most of the connections—the planks—of the imperial protestant scaffold. The postwar period saw the sweeping away of the residue of those older partnerships, but it also witnessed the formation of new relationships, on different terms, for a new world. By the early 1790s, a new transatlantic protestant order began to emerge. It sponsored an energetic missionary movement that was independent of the trappings of imperial protestantism and the confessional age that had shaped its eighteenth-century predecessor.

THE NEW AMERICAN RELIGIOUS LANDSCAPE

A primary consequence of the American Revolution was the declining influence of a few dominant denominations and the rapid increase of awakened protestant sects. This story has often been told through the growth of awakened protestantism among Americans. The movement's appeal is generally ascribed to its easy alliance with the political realities and ideals of the new nation—and also to the eagerness with which awakened groups reached out to, and were

2. For statistics, see Roger Finke and Rodney Stark, "How the Upstart Sects Won America, 1776–1850," *Journal for the Scientific Study of Religion,* XXVIII (1989), 31. If anything, these numbers underestimate the scale of the decline because by counting adherents—people who affiliated with churches—they obscure the influence of established churches on the religious options of the unchurched. It is also important to note that Finke and Stark include Catholics in their calculations, with that church making up 1.8 percent of religious adherents in 1776 and 13.9 percent in 1850. That fact reinforces the overall loss of cultural dominance by the colonial denominations. The percentage of baptists remained deceptively stable, going from 16.9 percent to 20.5 percent, but that stability needs to be balanced against the stark decline of the other colonial denominations. Their survival was success. For Methodist statistics, see Katherine Carté Engel, "Dissent in the Atlantic World, 1787–1830," in Andrew C. Thompson, ed., *The Oxford History of Protestant Dissenting Traditions,* II, *The Long Eighteenth Century, c. 1689–c.1828* (Oxford, 2018), 200–222. The rise of awakened denominations in the United States, the foundation of the American Episcopal Church, and the separation of the Wesleyan denominations from the Church of England are generally told as separate stories. The present project argues that they are part of a single whole. For discussions of the growth of awakened denominations, see note 3 below. For the foundation of the American Episcopal Church and its Canadian counterpart, see Peter M. Doll, *Revolution, Religion, and National Identity: Imperial Anglicanism in British North America, 1745–1795* (Madison, N.J., 2000); Nancy L. Rhoden, *Revolutionary Anglicanism: The Colonial Church of England Clergy during the American Revolution* (New York, 1999); and Frederick V. Mills, Sr., *Bishops by Ballot: An Eighteenth Century Ecclesiastical Revolution* (New York, 1978). For the Wesleyan separation from the Church of England, see Frank Baker, *John Wesley and the Church of England* (1970; rpt. London, 2000). A more typical way to discuss early Methodism, as a movement rather than as an institution, can be found in David Hempton, *Methodism: Empire of the Spirit* (New Haven, Conn., 2005).

embraced by, African Americans. That narrative is important, but by focusing on how Americans chose awakened protestant institutions because of their theological or experiential characteristics, the story sidesteps important questions of institutional formation in the longer history of the awakening movement. In short, it obscures the significance of the American Revolution, with its attendant destruction of imperial protestantism, to the formation of those new churches and denominations. Before new groups could begin to garner followers, they first had to be free of the constraints of the British protestant order. The growth of awakened institutions, in this sense, was not the first act of the United States' religious history; it was the final dissolution of imperial protestantism.[3]

As had long been the case for awakened protestantism, revivals continued to play a key role in the growth of the movement. After the war, however, they often unfolded beyond the geographic limits of imperial protestant institutions or in places where the war had swept such institutions away. They also brought dramatic institutional change in ways that their predecessors had not. Baptist

3. The dominant historiographical story of American religious history in the early Republic is the growth of "evangelicalism," a term this work has eschewed for its historical slipperiness. The most influential works in the field are Nathan O. Hatch, *The Democratization of American Christianity* (New Haven, Conn., 1989); Mark A. Noll, *America's God: From Jonathan Edwards to Abraham Lincoln* (New York, 2002); and Noll, *The Rise of Evangelicalism: The Age of Edwards, Whitefield, and the Wesleys* (Downers Grove, Ill., 2003). For a neat summary of the story, see David Hempton, *The Church in the Long Eighteenth Century* (London, 2011), 191. In some cases, the emphasis on the early Republic in the scholarship on evangelicalism has the effect of minimizing connections to the Revolutionary and colonial eras, though the collapse of Anglican establishments is often noted as an important precursor. See, for example, Christine Leigh Heyrman, *Southern Cross: The Beginnings of the Bible Belt* (New York, 1997), 22–27, who argues that awakened protestants had comparatively little success in the South before the Revolution. Monica Najar, *Evangelizing the South: A Social History of Church and State in Early America* (New York, 2008), esp. 117–130, treats the Revolution as part of a larger argument about the influence of baptist innovations on American religious and civil life. Philip N. Mulder, *A Controversial Spirit: Evangelical Awakenings in the South* (New York, 2002), 89–109, depicts the Revolution as a stage in the conflict between evangelical denomination. For Methodists, see Cynthia Lynn Lyerly, *Methodism and the Southern Mind, 1770–1810* (New York, 1998); and Dee E. Andrews, *The Methodists and Revolutionary America, 1760–1800: The Shaping of an Evangelical Culture* (Princeton, N.J., 2000). For African Americans, see Charles F. Irons, *The Origins of Proslavery Christianity: White and Black Evangelicals in Colonial and Antebellum Virginia* (Chapel Hill, N.C., 2008). Amanda Porterfield challenged the logic of the appeal of evangelicalism in Porterfield, *Conceived in Doubt: Religion and Politics in the New American Nation* (Chicago, 2012). These scholars certainly acknowledge the role of the Revolution (especially disestablishment), particularly in the South, to the growth of the evangelical movement, but the current project seeks to complement that narrative with a greater emphasis on the war as a serious rupture and necessary precursor to the growth of awakened denominations. Other scholars who have advanced similar arguments in an American context include Stephen A. Marini, *Radical Sects of Revolutionary New England* (Cambridge, Mass., 1982); and Shelby M. Balik, *Rally the Scattered Believers: Northern New England's Religious Geography* (Bloomington, Ind., 2014). For a summary of the state of the field, see Christopher Grasso, *Skepticism and American Faith: From the Revolution to the Civil War* (New York, 2018), 5–6, 514 n. 4.

groups became particularly important. Members of that tradition had been within the dissenting and awakened movements before the war, but always in a contingent way because, alone among the major Anglo-American denominations (that is, unlike congregationalists, presbyterians, and Anglicans), they did not directly enjoy the benefits of establishment. Thus, although they were seen as legitimate protestants, they were at a greater remove from government authorities than their peers. Though other awakened communities (of all denominations) also swelled during the postwar period, a major part of the energy of these new movements gathered in baptist groups both because of the appeal of the doctrine of believers (or adult) baptism and because the baptist polity, which was congregationally based, allowed for more flexibility, including in the process of ordination. But this choice also meant that much of the energy of the new revivals spun away from, rather than toward, the centers of governmental power—such as they were—in the new United States.[4]

The choice to found, join, or lead baptist congregations thus carried with it a comparative freedom from older institutional habits and connections. The awakened leaders of the preceding era, men like Samuel Davies, Jonathan Edwards, John Erskine, Joseph Bellamy—even baptists like James Manning and Isaac Backus—had understood American awakenings as part of a transatlantic movement that unfolded largely though the structures of imperial protestantism and the systems of establishment in their regions. In contrast, many of the postwar generation's most important figures did not see their own efforts in the same way. They worked in regions that were characterized by migration, religious competition, and the absence of stable protestant institutions. They inherited the theological and spiritual legacies of the colonial revivals, but they could not rely on the transatlantic networks their predecessors had built, and often they did not seek them. As a result of all these factors, this new

4. The literature on early American and Canadian baptists is vast and regionally segregated. For Canada and New England, see Balik, *Rally the Scattered Believers;* Daniel C. Goodwin, *Into Deep Waters: Evangelical Spirituality and Maritime Calvinistic Baptist Ministers, 1790–1855* (Montreal, 2010); and William G. McLoughlin, *New England Dissent, 1630–1833; the Baptists and the Separation of Church and State,* 2 vols. (Cambridge, Mass., 1971). For baptists in the context of New England's revivals, see Douglas L. Winiarski, *Darkness Falls on the Land of Light: Experiencing Religious Awakenings in Eighteenth-Century New England* (Williamsburg, Va., and Chapel Hill, N.C., 2017). For mid-Atlantic and southern baptists, see Janet Moore Lindman, *Bodies of Belief: Baptist Community in Early America* (Philadelphia, 2008); Najar, *Evangelizing the South;* Jewel L. Spangler, *Virginians Reborn: Anglican Monopoly, Evangelical Dissent, and the Rise of the Baptists in the Late Eighteenth Century* (Charlottesville, Va., 2008); and Mulder, *A Controversial Spirit.* For transatlantic connections, see Hywel M. Davies, *Transatlantic Brethren: Rev. Samuel Jones (1735–1814) and His Friends: Baptists in Wales, Pennsylvania, and Beyond* (Bethlehem, Pa., 1995). For a survey of British baptists in this period, see Karen E. Smith, "Baptists," in Thompson, ed., *Oxford History of Protestant Dissenting Traditions,* II, 54–76.

generation of religious leaders was different from its forebearers. Its members were less white and less likely to be formally educated than those of the colonial period. Their movements—and consequently the new denominational order—were both geographically and organizationally independent of imperial protestantism.

Two regions dominated the American revivals of the 1780s, each just beyond areas into which, in the 1750s, imperial protestant organizations had poured resources in order to spread and secure protestant Britain. The area where northern New England abutted Maritime Canada marked the first such region. Over the war years, it saw dramatic population growth and dislocation. Wartime refugees were joined by postwar migrants, as thousands moved into backcountry regions in search of new land. The population of Maine, particularly in its interior settlements, tripled between 1775 and 1790. Similarly, Nova Scotia became home to a flood of people seeking to flee the war to their southwest. At the same time, government support for religious establishments was quickly ebbing. Massachusetts struggled to realize its traditional congregationalist system in its Maine territory; both town organization and ministerial placement lagged. In Nova Scotia, the war's migrations swelled dissenting populations. Many newcomers arrived from regions in New England where their churches had received state support, but their new province provided no local government mechanism to finance congregational (that is, dissenting) churches. The area's Anglicans fared little better. Dislocation and rapid growth made it difficult for older protestant structures to serve these new regions.[5]

A similar story unfolded many miles to the south. Before the war, Virginia, the Carolinas, and Georgia all supported Anglican establishments. That system collapsed rapidly when the Revolution started, as did the willingness of the social elites who maintained those establishments to police preaching by non-Anglican ministers. Between 1776 and 1778, all four jurisdictions ended mandatory tax support for the Church of England. That, along with the continued growth of dissenting congregations and the loss of many Anglican ministers who fled the war, threw the region's institutional protestant life into chaos, in-

5. Maya Jasanoff, *Liberty's Exiles: American Loyalists in the Revolutionary World* (New York, 2011), 157–175; Alan Taylor, *Liberty Men and Great Proprietors: The Revolutionary Settlement on the Maine Frontier, 1760–1820* (Williamsburg, Va., and Chapel Hill, N.C., 1990), 15; James S. Leamon, *Revolution Downeast: The War for American Independence in Maine* (Amherst, Mass., 1993), 209–212; Elizabeth Mancke, *The Fault Lines of Empire: Political Differentiation in Massachusetts and Nova Scotia, ca. 1760–1830* (New York, 2005), 36, 112–114, 121–123; Balik, *Rally the Scattered Believers*, 77–78, 81, 92, 225 n. 13; Marini, *Radical Sects*, 25–39; Winiarski, *Darkness Falls on the Land of Light*, 386–387; Maurice W. Armstrong, *The Great Awakening in Nova Scotia, 1776–1809* (Hartford, Conn., 1948), 55–60.

cluding the idea that any one institutional church ought to serve all of an area's residents. A diverse range of protestant groups staked out new claims, none of them seeking or expecting to become the basis of a new establishment. The region's population, both Black and white, also grew. Georgia's numbers more than doubled between 1770 and 1780; the lower South as a whole increased by nearly 50 percent in the same period. Virginia and Maryland saw smaller but notable increases, and the growth continued in the following decade. When the war concluded, a flood of migrants pushed into western North Carolina and Kentucky. As in northern New England, these areas lacked a settled religious infrastructure, and no new state (besides Vermont) seriously contemplated creating a church establishment that might serve them. The new nation's populations rapidly moved, geographically and in terms of sheer numbers, beyond the reach of colonial protestant institutions. At a time when the infrastructure of imperial protestantism had been swept away by war, there was no way for older colonial institutions to keep up with the pace of new need.[6]

These were the sorts of areas where, before the war, voluntary societies and transatlantic networks had promoted institutional protestantism. They had focused the attention of protestants in London or in Boston on frontier places, recruited missionaries, and fielded appeals from congregations seeking clergy. Such help was sharply curtailed by the war. In 1774, the Society for the Propagation of the Gospel in Foreign Parts (SPG) listed thirteen missionaries and teachers in Nova Scotia; in 1783, that number had fallen to eleven, despite rapid gains in population. A missionary posted in Halifax reported that, "by a large influx of people from New England, and other American provinces," the number of people under his care had increased considerably. Connecticut's congregationalist General Association initiated a plan to send missionaries to the frontier in 1774, but in the following year it acknowledged the near impossibility of putting the plan into effect during the war. Meanwhile, Anglican clergy fled or were driven out of areas under rebellion. It was a distressing spiral from the perspective of settled clergy, who considered the presence of

6. For legal shifts and denominational responses, see Rhoden, *Revolutionary Anglicanism,* 117; John A. Ragosta, *Wellspring of Liberty: How Virginia's Religious Dissenters Helped Win the American Revolution and Secured Religious Liberty* (New York, 2010), 43–70, 109–133; Spangler, *Virginians Reborn,* 195–199; Thomas J. Curry, *The First Freedoms: Church and State in America to the Passage of the First Amendment* (New York, 1986), 134–158; Mulder, *A Controversial Spirit,* 89–109; Heyrman, *Southern Cross,* 22–23; and Rhys Isaac, *The Transformation of Virginia, 1740–1790* (Williamsburg, Va., and Chapel Hill, N.C., 1982), 278–295. For population figures, see John J. McCusker and Russell R. Menard, *The Economy of British America, 1607–1789* (Williamsburg, Va., and Chapel Hill, N.C., 1991), 136, 172. For the growth of awakened groups in the South, see Najar, *Evangelizing the South,* 96–98; for northern New England, see Balik, *Rally the Scattered Believers,* 75–80.

institutional churches and regular public worship to be the hallmark of a stable, pious society.[7]

A group of energetic religious leaders emerged in the midst of these wartime dislocations, individuals who often lacked the imprimatur of formal education and who were only tangentially connected to the institutional protestantism of the prewar period. In Nova Scotia, the young preacher Henry Alline documented his story in a journal that was published after his death. Its general outlines matched those of other wartime and postwar revivalists. In 1775, Alline was living in Falmouth, Nova Scotia, a small town on the Bay of Fundy side of the peninsula. His parents, like most of his neighbors, were originally from New England. They had moved north in 1760, when Alline was twelve, and though they lived in a region dominated by congregationalists, there was no church in the town. Alline's spiritual journey started in the early years of the war. He had a profound religious experience, and he came to believe that "the Lord discovered to me my labour in the ministry and call to preach the gospel." He was confident in his vocation as a preacher, but he knew that for many the path to ordination lay through "going to the seats of learning to be prepared for the ministry, and then authorized by men." Though he would soon leave that belief behind, in 1775 he "still . . . retained a strong persuasion, that I could not preach until I had acquired learning, and therefore must proceed to New-England." According to his journal, his parents endorsed the move, not only because they had relatives in Boston but also because they feared he otherwise might be drafted into the military if he stayed home. (Alline's narrative does not address that Boston was then under siege.) When his ship from Cornwallis, Nova Scotia, to New England was seized (a further impact of the war), he lingered where he was and then decided to preach without the benefit of a degree. Such a career was plausible in the dislocation of the postwar Maritimes in a way it would not have been within the strictures of the congregational establishment Alline had been born into.[8]

7. Edmund [Law], *A Sermon Preached before the Incorporated Society for the Propagation of the Gospel in Foreign Parts; at Their Anniversary Meeting in the Parish Church of St. Mary-le-Bow, on Friday February 18, 1774* (London, 1774), 8–10; Beilby [Porteus], *A Sermon Preached before the Incorporated Society for the Propagation of the Gospel in Foreign Parts; at Their Anniversary Meeting in the Parish Church of St. Mary-le-Bow, on Friday February 21, 1783* (London, 1783), 41–42; Marini, *Radical Sects*, 36; *The Records of the General Association of the Colony of Connecticut, Begun June 20th, 1738; Ending June 19th, 1799* (Hartford, Conn., 1888), 76, 85–86; James B. Bell, *A War of Religion: Dissenters, Anglicans, and the American Revolution* (Houndmills, U.K., 2008), 224–225.

8. *The Life and Journal of the Rev. Mr. Henry Alline* (Boston, 1806), 36, 42–44. The journal also appears in George A. Rawlyk, ed., *Henry Alline: Selected Writings* (New York, 1987), 55–99. Rawlyk's introduction is also helpful. For Alline's biography and the Allinite revivals, see Rawlyk, *The Canada Fire: Radical Evangelicalism in British North America, 1775–1812* (Kingston, Ontario, 1994); Rawlyk, *Ravished by the Spirit: Religious Revivals, Baptists, and Henry Alline* (Kingston,

Many in Alline's neighborhood accepted his leadership as preacher, even though the war had prevented his gaining a formal education. Whether they were hungry for his distinctive message or for any kind of religious community, they helped him become the nexus around which both revivals and churches formed. He first "came out and spoke by way of exhortation" on April 18, 1776, a "day set apart for fasting and prayer." He met with almost immediate success. Word of his preaching "spread abroad over the whole place," and crowds continued to grow. As the young revivalist recounted it, "Some came to hear what the babler had to say; some came with gladness of heart that God had raised up one to speak in his name; and some c[a]me to make a scoff, but it did not seem to trouble me much; for I trust God was with me." In September 1776, Alline and his followers formed their own church in a nearby town, a step that angered both the baptist and the congregationalist churches that were already in that area. Alline dismissed their critiques because "we did not think the churches in those parts were churches of Christ, but had only a dry form without religion." The young preacher continued to itinerate around Nova Scotia and New Brunswick, spreading revival, and controversy, wherever he went. He declined a request to stay permanently in a town with the comment: "I had no call from God to settle any where." Over the next several years, he traveled in Nova Scotia, and a series of churches organized around his teachings. Three of those congregations, from around the Minas Bay area, gathered on April 6, 1779, and Alline "received the imposition of hands by nine delegates, three chosen out of each church." The delegates then "gave [him his] credentials," and he then began itinerating in a wider region, including both Saint John's, in New Brunswick, and eventually New England. He died in New Hampshire in 1784, at age thirty-five.[9]

Alline had fellow travelers in this homegrown awakening movement. Together, their activities soon spawned new denominations that were both theologically and logistically independent of the old structures of imperial protestantism. In New Hampshire, Benjamin Randel became, like Alline, a leading religious figure who moved outside the traditional structures of institutional protestant authority. Randel, born in 1749, attended one of George Whitefield's last sermons in 1770. He was moved by hearing the Grand Itinerant, especially after Whitefield died only a week later. The young man became a licentiate of a

---

Ontario, 1984); J. M. Bumsted, *Henry Alline, 1748–1784* (Toronto, 1971); and Armstrong, *The Great Awakening in Nova Scotia*.

9. Armstrong, *The Great Awakening in Nova Scotia*, 65–66; *Life and Journal of Henry Alline*, 46, 47, 48, 54, 70.

nearby Calvinist baptist church, but he moved away from Calvinism and from his church as his theology developed further.[10]

As it had done for Alline, the war disrupted Randel's path to the ministry, even more so because he was closer to the fighting. He enlisted in the army as a commissary in October 1775 and served at least two three-month terms around the time he was to become a preacher. In 1780, Randel was ordained by several of his followers, and by the end of the year the group organized into what amounted to a new sect of baptists, known for their Freewill teachings. Its members rejected the Calvinism that dominated among New England's baptists and embraced Randel's views of universal atonement. Randel drew from a range of influences, including the models set by Whitefield and Alline, but having those men as inspirations did not bring him inside the dominant baptist circles in the region—or into any remaining circles of transatlantic protestantism. His focus remained local, and he steered his energies into organizing in the new American environment. In 1783, Randel and his colleagues at New Durham, New Hampshire, created a more formal structure to coordinate their work, providing the origins of the Freewill Baptists in New England. The new movements led by Alline and Randel flourished outside colonial-era protestant institutions. The war had made it difficult for their leaders to join up with their clerical colleagues, and its destruction kept the older systems of protestant expansion—funds from government and the sending of missionaries from more settled areas—from functioning.[11]

Alongside the more radical homegrown awakenings led by Alline and Randel, wartime and postwar revivals moved through older baptist groups as well. As the structures of religious establishment weakened in the postwar years, particularly in places like northern New England, the pressures keeping those inclined toward revival within the privileged congregationalist community weakened dramatically. In the wake of New England's Whitefieldian revivals at midcentury, more than a few congregations that had separated from town churches had moved into the baptist fold. They settled on the baptist polity as the most appropriate way to organize both because it expressed their desire

10. Marini, *Radical Sects*, 64–67, 103–104; Balik, *Rally the Scattered Believers*, 50–52; Scott Bryant, *The Awakening of the Freewill Baptists: Benjamin Randall and the Founding of an American Religious Tradition* (Macon, Ga., 2011), 62–89. The main source for Randel is John Buzzell, *The Life of Elder Benjamin Randal, Principally Taken from Documents Written by Himself* (Lumerick, Maine, 1827).

11. Buzzell, *The Life of Elder Benjamin Randal*, 32, 43; Rawlyk, *Ravished by the Spirit*, 54–58. Randel's surviving correspondence shows a local focus, rather than one concerned with reaching out to wider revivals. See Benjamin Randel Letter Book, Ephraim Stinchfield Collection, no. 44, Brown Research Library, Maine Historical Society, Portland.

to have churches that reflected as closely as possible the invisible church—by accepting for baptism only those adults who were deemed worthy of it—and also because its radical decentralization allowed for maximum local control over such issues as selecting and dismissing ministers. That movement accelerated during the war years, with the "New Light Stir," a revival within Calvinist baptist circles. In late 1779, the Warren Association in Massachusetts reported that "in those troublesome times the Lord hath been pleased to revive his work, as appears by the very agreeable accounts we have received from a number of our churches, more especially to the Westward and Northern frontier settlements of our country." Over the next few years, large numbers of new members joined the Warren Association's churches, and the total number of congregations within the association came close to doubling. Particularly in areas where the war prevented the effective extension of colonial establishments, baptists flourished.[12]

So, too, in the South. In that region, one of the most important features of the period was the emergence on the institutional religious scene of a significant cadre of African American protestant leaders. Such preachers had existed largely outside the realm of the imperial protestant system during the colonial period. Even (or especially) work by free Black preachers was controversial, as David Margrett—a missionary in the employ of the countess of Huntingdon who was forced to flee Georgia in 1775 in the face of white fury at his message of spiritual and earthly freedom—found out. As a result, the historical record yields only a few tantalizing hints of those Black preachers who worked within the Black community before the Revolution. On the eve of Margrett's forced departure from the lowcountry, for example, one of the Bethesda group's white associates reported that "Faithful Thomas, a Black who was called by my Ministry about 12 months ago," had sent a message to Margrett warning him that he was in danger. Little is now known of who such leaders might have been and how they viewed their relationship to the organized protestantism that dominated public religious life in pre-Revolutionary British North America. Even simple dates are sometimes difficult to uncover and are contested. Extant evidence mostly suggests that Black leaders were able to move into the white-controlled structures of institutional protestantism only after the dislocations of war began. A preacher known as Moses, for example, organized a Black baptist congregation

12. *Minutes of the Warren Association, in Their Meeting at Attleborough, September 7th and 8th, 1779* ([Boston?] 1779), 6; Winiarski, *Darkness Falls on the Land of Light*, 387–391, 394–402, 427; William G. McLoughlin, *Soul Liberty: The Baptists' Struggle in New England, 1630–1833* (Hanover, N.H., 1991), 6–7; David W. Bebbington, *Baptists through the Centuries: A History of a Global People* (Waco, Tex., 2010), 78–81; Marini, *Radical Sects*, 45–46; Thomas S. Kidd, *The Great Awakening: The Roots of Evangelical Christianity in Colonial America* (New Haven, Conn., 2007), 313–314.

in Williamsburg, Virginia, in 1776, but he was "arrested and whipped" for his efforts. Moses's wartime claims to institutional religious authority are significant nonetheless for the evidence they provide of Black leaders' seizing the moment. As the interlocking structures of religious and governmental institutions strained under the forces of the Revolution, opportunities appeared to break down the old rules of legitimacy for protestant leadership.[13]

As in the North, the southern revivals that began before the war accelerated significantly afterward and developed new institutional structures that challenged old models. George Liele, a key figure in this process, was enslaved from his birth in Virginia around 1740. While still enslaved in the early 1770s, Liele had a conversion experience in a church led by his master's brother-in-law, a baptist minister named Matthew Moore, on a plantation on the South Carolina side of the Savannah River. After Liele's gifts as a preacher came to

13. John Edwards to William Piercy, Jan. 11, 1775, A3/6/9, Cheshunt College Archives, Westminster College, Cambridge (CCA) ("Faithful"); *The Negro in Virginia* (New York, 1940), 100 ("arrested and whipped"). The connection between Margrett and Liele is also discussed in Sylvia R. Frey and Betty Wood, *Come Shouting to Zion: African American Protestantism in the American South and British Caribbean to 1830* (Chapel Hill, N.C., 1998), 112–113, 116. Margrett / Margate's history is discussed in J. William Harris, *The Hanging of Thomas Jeremiah: A Free Black Man's Encounter with Liberty* (New Haven, Conn., 2009), 73–79; and Robert G. Parkinson, *The Common Cause: Creating Race and Nation in the American Revolution* (Williamsburg, Va., and Chapel Hill, N.C., 2016), 86–87. For Moses and Williamsburg, see Frey and Wood, *Come Shouting to Zion,* 114–115; Frey, *Water from the Rock: Black Resistance in a Revolutionary Age* (Princeton, N.J., 1991), 37–40; Robert B. Semple, *A History of the Rise and Progress of the Baptists in Virginia,* revised and extended by G. W. Beale (Richmond, Va., 1894), 148; and Albert J. Raboteau, *Slave Religion: The "Invisible Institution" in the Antebellum South* (Oxford, 1978), 138–139. During the colonial period, local elites committed to the maintenance of racial slavery had pushed hard against Black leaders who sought to preach to free and enslaved African Americans, and they were often unwilling to have Christianity preached at all among slaves. Leading white awakened protestants, not least George Whitefield but also the likes of Samuel Davies and those employed by Selina Hastings, countess of Huntingdon, had preached among slaves, but as they worked within the dominant denominations they quickly learned to tailor their message to the expectations of local elites, and they did not ordain Black clergy. For accommodations between missionaries and planters, see Sylvester A. Johnson, *African American Religions, 1500–2000: Colonialism, Democracy, Freedom* (New York, 2015), 138–142; Rebecca Anne Goetz, *The Baptism of Early Virginia: How Christianity Created Race* (Baltimore, 2012); Travis Glasson, *Mastering Christianity: Missionary Anglicanism and Slavery in the Atlantic World* (New York, 2012); Frey and Wood, *Come Shouting to Zion,* 63–79, 93–101; Frey, *Water from the Rock,* 21–26; and Raboteau, *Slave Religion*. The Moravians, outside the system of imperial protestantism, did encourage limited African leadership. They led large communities of Afro-protestants in the Caribbean, and they included smaller numbers of free and enslaved Africans within their North Carolina and Pennsylvania communities. Black leaders known as Helpers, an important—though nonordained—role within Moravian life, worked in places like Saint Thomas where there were few white missionaries and large congregations. See Katharine Gerbner, *Christian Slavery: Conversion and Race in the Protestant Atlantic World* (Philadelphia, 2018), 138–163; Edward E. Andrews, *Native Apostles: Black and Indian Missionaries in the British Atlantic World* (Cambridge, Mass., 2013), 88–105; Jon F. Sensbach, *Rebecca's Revival: Creating Black Christianity in the Atlantic World* (Cambridge, Mass., 2005), 94–100; Sensbach, *A Separate Canaan: The Making of an Afro-Moravian World in North Carolina, 1763–1840* (Williamsburg, Va., and Chapel Hill, N.C., 1998); Frey and Wood, *Come Shouting to Zion,* 83–88; and John W. Catron, *Embracing Protestantism: Black Identities in the Atlantic World* (Gainesville, Fla., 2016), 50–51.

Moore's attention, he ordained Liele, who has generally been recorded as the first Black baptist minister licensed in North America. He preached widely and with the permission of his master, who eventually freed the dynamic minister. Liele's influence grew almost exponentially from there. He and another baptist itinerant known as Brother Palmer preached at the Silver Bluff, Georgia, plantation of George Galphin, a devout planter who moved in the same circles as the missionaries of Selina Hastings, the countess of Huntingdon, at Bethesda. At Silver Bluff, Liele preached movingly, and his words shaped the career of another future minister, David George. As George wrote decades later when he heard Liele preach, "His whole discourse seemed for me." There was a personal tie too; George noted that he had known Liele "ever since he was a boy." Soon George felt a calling to "pray with the people myself." His old friend helped him overcome his reservations. At that point, Palmer "formed us into a church, and gave us the Lord's Supper at Silver Bluff." Soon thereafter, George was "appointed to the office of an Elder" by Palmer. These organizing efforts were stopped by the war, but both Liele and George found ways to leverage the subsequent dislocations to become recognized religious leaders within the Black community.[14]

These new leaders flourished within the large streams of African American migrants set in motion by the war. When the British invaded Savannah in 1778, they drew heavily on support among enslaved African Americans, who, in turn, pushed the British to make good on promises to free those who fought against American rebels. British commander-in-chief Henry Clinton issued a proclamation in 1779 offering "full security" to African Americans who would support the king's cause, and thousands took him up on his offer. George's Silver Bluff congregation was disrupted when its patriot owner, Galphin, fled. The baptist preacher and his family first traveled to Ebenezer, Georgia, where he was briefly

14. John Rippon, *The Baptist Annual Register, for 1790, 1791, 1792, and Part of 1793; Including Sketches of the State of Religion among Different Denominations of Good Men at Home and Abroad* [London, 1793?], 475–476 (hereafter cited as *BAR*). George's story also appears in Vincent Carretta, ed., *Unchained Voices: An Anthology of Black Authors in the English-Speaking World of the Eighteenth Century* (Lexington, Ky., 1996), 325–332. For discussion of Liele's career, see Thomas J. Little, "George Liele and the Rise of Independent Black Baptist Churches in the Lower South and Jamaica," *Slavery and Abolition*, XVI (1995), 188–204; Catron, *Embracing Protestantism*, 200–202; Noel Leo Erskine, *Plantation Church: How African American Religion Was Born in Caribbean Slavery* (New York, 2014), 84–88; and Frey and Wood, *Come Shouting to Zion*, 114–117. For the timing of the revivals, see also Johnson, *African American Religions*, 142–145; and Sylvia R. Frey, "'The Year of Jubilee Is Come': Black Christianity in the Plantation South in Post-Revolutionary America," in Ronald Hoffman and Peter J. Albert, eds., *Religion in a Revolutionary Age* (Charlottesville, Va., 1994), 92–102. Some churches, particularly those within the awakening movement, were open to interracial congregations during the colonial period, though such arrangements required complicated negotiations. See Irons, *The Origins of Proslavery Christianity*, 47; Lindman, *Bodies of Belief*, 130–132.

imprisoned, and then to Savannah, where he met up with Liele again, and the two preached together for a time. George spent the remainder of the war in British-occupied Savannah, before fleeing to Charleston and evacuating with his family to Nova Scotia—a place already in the midst of its own domestic revival.[15]

As many as fifteen thousand now-free Blacks left Charleston. The Georges, joined by about five hundred others, traveled to Nova Scotia, becoming part of a new community consisting of more than four thousand free and enslaved Blacks. George continued his ministry there, though he "found the White people were against" him. He quickly developed a following nonetheless, and he was "so overjoyed with having an opportunity once more of preaching the word of God, that after I had given out the hymn, I could not speak for tears." Over the next few years, he pursued an extensive ministry among both Blacks and whites, building on the groundwork already laid by Henry Alline in the region, and in spite of ongoing opposition from some quarters. George became one of the leading political as well as religious leaders in his community, and he was among those who persuaded large numbers of Black loyalists in Nova Scotia to emigrate to Sierra Leone in 1792. He accompanied them, taking his message of protestant awakening to another continent. In those efforts, he became part of the new era of transatlantic protestantism.[16]

George Liele also left the new United States, but his journey took him on a different path. In Jamaica, he built protestant congregations that would receive government recognition in a colony that remained within Britain's protestant umbrella. He had evacuated Savannah in 1782 with loyalists bound for the British sugar island; many of the white refugees took with them those they enslaved. Jamaica's planter elite had remained loyal to the crown, and slavery continued to dominate both culture and society there. Liele began his career on the island as a free Black man who was indentured to a British officer. Once he obtained his full freedom, he resumed preaching. What started as a small but a "good smart congregation" grew, in less than a decade, to 350 souls. Liele proudly reported that his efforts received the imprimatur of the Jamaican government.

15. James W. St. G. Walker, *The Black Loyalists: The Search for a Promised Land in Nova Scotia and Sierra Leone, 1783–1870* (New York, 1976), 2–4 (quotation on 2). For African Americans and the military events of the period, see Edward Countryman, *Enjoy the Same Liberty: Black Americans and the Revolutionary Era* (Lanham, Md., 2012), 48; Alan Gilbert, *Black Patriots and Loyalists: Fighting for Emancipation in the War for Independence* (Chicago, 2012), 124–126; Andrew Jackson O'Shaughnessy, *The Men Who Lost America: British Leadership, the American Revolution, and the Fate of the Empire* (New Haven, Conn., 2013), 223–227; Catron, *Embracing Protestantism*, 197–199; Irons, *The Origins of Proslavery Christianity*, 44–47; and *BAR*, 476–477.

16. *BAR*, 478–482 (quotation on 478); Jasanoff, *Liberty's Exiles*, 76, 160, 279–284, 291–295; Walker, *Black Loyalists*, 74–77; Catron, *Embracing Protestantism*, 203–205, 216.

This group had "applied to the HONORABLE HOUSE OF ASSEMBLY, with a petition of our distresses, being poor people, desiring to worship Almighty God according to the tenets of the Bible," he wrote, and "they have granted us liberty, and given us their sanction." He reiterated his point further, stressing its importance: "Thanks be to God we have liberty to worship him as we please in Kingston." They soon coupled that official recognition with more physical symbols of institutional solidity. The congregation bought land and began building a church in 1789. Liele's efforts—alongside those of Wesleyan ministers who joined him, part of a new era of awakened missionary outreach from Britain—initiated a rapidly growing awakening movement on the island.[17]

African American religious leaders took their place at the fore of the awakening movement outside the United States, but reciprocal developments occurred within that nation as well, as African American protestantism further diversified the American denominational landscape. Andrew Bryan, another erstwhile companion of Liele's, founded the First African Baptist church of Savannah. That congregation faced significant struggles; a 1790 letter printed in London's *Baptist Annual Register* reported that, although the congregation had permission from a landowner to "erect a rough building," they were later "artfully dispossessed" of it. They also faced more violent opposition. Worshippers were "imprisoned and whipped," including Bryan and his brother. The former was *"cut, and bled abundantly"* as he was whipped, but he reportedly "held up his hands, and told his persecutors that he rejoiced not only to be whipped, but *would freely suffer death for the cause of Jesus Christ.*" Bryan's movement grew despite their hardships, as Liele's and George's had, as did the baptist movement more generally among African Americans in the later 1780s and in subsequent decades. Gowan Pamphlet, Moses's successor in Williamsburg, led his congregation into the baptist Dover Association in 1791. The difficulties of navigating either independent congregations or participation in white-led congregations did not diminish in the slave territories of the South after the war, but the institutions of protestant leadership were not wholly closed to African Americans either.[18]

Just as the revivals led by Alline and Randel on the northern coast had been paralleled by revivals within older baptist communities, a similar process un-

17. Jasanoff, *Liberty's Exiles*, 247–251; Carretta, *Unchained Voices*, 327 (quotations); Little, "George Liele," *Slavery and Abolition*, XVI (1995), 194. See also Christopher Cannon Jones, "Methodism, Slavery, and Freedom in the Revolutionary Atlantic, 1770–1820" (Ph.D. diss., College of William and Mary, 2016), 142–145.

18. *BAR*, 340; Lindman, *Bodies of Belief*, 151–155; Catron, *Embracing Protestantism*, 172: Irons, *Origins of Proslavery Christianity*, 48; Frey and Wood, *Come Shouting to Zion*, 115; Sarah Barringer Gordon, "The African Supplement: Religion, Race, and Corporate Law in Early National America," *William and Mary Quarterly*, 3d Ser., LXXII (2015), 385–422.

folded in the South. In Virginia, between 1785 and 1792, the number of baptists tripled, in part through the leadership of John Leland, an itinerant originally from Massachusetts who worked in Virginia for fifteen years. Leland described what he saw as the "glorious work of God," which "broke out, on the banks of James river," in 1785. Over the following years, he reported dramatic revivals in which it was "nothing strange to see a great part of the congregation fall p[r]ostrate upon the floor or ground." These demonstrations could last for hours. He proudly reported that there were "some ministers now living in Virginia, who have baptised more than 2000 persons." The results were that in 1790 there were "about 150 ordained preachers of the Baptist denomination, and a number besides who exercise a public gift." As Leland's reports suggest, awakened protestants also reaped rewards in terms of new congregations, new adherents, and new clergy in more traditional ways—among Euro-Americans who turned to the clergy of traditional denominational structures. The connections between these successes and the Revolution were strong, even if they were sometimes indirect. The failure of the Anglican establishment in the southern regions of the United States created a religious organizational vacuum, and baptists were among the first to fill it. As adherents flocked to them, the newly forming congregations eschewed the benefits of establishment that had accrued to their predecessors of a prior era.[19]

The rapid growth of awakened protestantism in the war's wake transformed the options that were available within the spectrum of American protestant institutions, its denominational order. The contrast to the colonial period was stark. Before the war, almost all officially sanctioned religious institutional life in British North America existed within the scaffolding of imperial protestantism. The dominant denominations, beneficiaries of Britain's mixed establishment, had followed roughly uniform habits when it came to who qualified as a religious leader, while the scaffolding of connections that had linked distant regions pulled them into a common organizational system. Awakened protestants, even the baptists, had usually chosen to remain within that system, seeing its benefits as outweighing its limitations.

After the war, much changed. While in some places new revivals invigorated older baptist groups, they also led to the organization of new protestant bodies that were outside the boundaries of the old imperial protestant scaffold and the benefits of establishment, both geographically and in the diversity of its reli-

19. John Leland, *The Virginia Chronicle: With Judicious and Critical Remarks under XXIV Heads* (Norfolk, Va., 1790), 33, 35. See also Irons, *The Origins of Proslavery Christianity*, 52–53; Wesley M. Gewehr, *The Great Awakening in Virginia, 1740–1790* (Durham, N.C., 1930), 173–177. For the broader context of Baptist history in Virginia, see Spangler, *Virginians Reborn*.

gious leadership. After a period in which some of Alline's New Lights explored more radical forms of spiritual expression (compared at the time to the Shakers who were also then flourishing), a traditional Calvinist baptist community took hold in Nova Scotia led by several of Alline's former followers. Randel's followers in northern New England founded Freewill Baptist organizations, and they elaborated their structures over the rest of the eighteenth century. The baptist congregations led by George Liele, David George, and Andrew Bryan could trace connections back to the growth of the awakening movement in the South in the 1760s and 1770s—a movement that continued to grow dramatically, as leaders like Isaac Backus and John Leland happily noted—but the efforts by Liele, George, and Bryan were independent of older structures as well. They took on their own energy and did not lightly submit to the authority of baptist associations. Overall, the multiplying groups of awakened protestants on American frontiers, led by both Black and white clergy, showed little interest in the religious monopolies of the previous era, from which they would have garnered few benefits in any case. In the later 1780s, as the ripples of the war's dislocations and disestablishments spread, a new generation of religious leaders charted their own paths. Postwar American protestants faced a widening group of protestant options and a far broader definition of "legitimate" protestantism.[20]

DISMANTLING THE CHURCH OF ENGLAND

The development of new awakened congregations in the United States was often a local phenomenon led by individuals far from the centers of power, but the prewar denominational order also collapsed from its very center, in a process managed—and mismanaged—by some of the most influential religious leaders in the Anglo-American world. The largest protestant institution in the imperial system had been the Church of England. The Revolution fractured Anglicans along the new political border between Britain and the United States, but it also opened the way for a further rupture between its awakened and non-awakened wings. The two fractures reinforced each other, and they must be considered together in order to see the full implications of the Revolution for the structures of imperial protestantism. As American episcopalians and

20. Goodwin, *Into Deep Waters;* Rawlyk, *Ravished by the Spirit,* 83–90; Rawlyk, *The Canada Fire,* 61–71; Balik, *Rally the Scattered Believers,* 51–53. Although this study focuses on innovations within dominant protestant circles, the creativity of the Revolutionary moment extended beyond such limits, as Susan Juster argued in *Doomsayers: Anglo-American Prophecy in the Age of Revolution* (Philadelphia, 2003).

British Anglicans dithered and made false starts on the road to settling their ecclesiastical affairs, they opened the space for John Wesley's followers to exit the Anglican fold, not just in the United States but in Britain as well, creating independent Methodist churches. When the dust settled, where there had been one denomination there were now at least four. Where imperial protestantism gave way, many different institutions—including an increasing number of awakened denominations—sprang up to rebuild.[21]

The first people to take up the problem of what to do about American episcopalians did so in a theoretical way, before the war even ended. They knew that no national religious establishment would be forthcoming, and they knew that the war had separated them from the bishops who had long consecrated their clergy. Philadelphia's William White, an Anglican clergyman, offered the first solution in 1782, when he published a vision for a new ecclesiastical body that would unite all Americans who had been Anglicans. White was politically moderate and the rector of the united congregations of Christ Church and Saint Peter's Church in Philadelphia. There he was the successor to the idealistic Jacob Duché, who had fled to London after his ill-fated attempt to get George Washington to end the war. White believed that organizing the new nation's episcopalians was essential to creating a unified American church and also to the "piety and morals of its members." This proposed church would join all episcopalian residents of the United States, even though it would have no connection to the national government. It was a notable leap in national thinking because Britain's mixed establishment had been determined by colony, and the American colonies had shared few connections to one another. But White's very title referenced "the United States," and in his tract he discussed the war with Great Britain—the process that had unified the various colonies into a nation. Indeed, in a move that would ultimately be set aside, he proposed that the vast American territory be broken down into "small districts" that would aggregate into "three different bodies," with no mention of the states. The proposed new American episcopal church would unite distant territories, just as the Church of England had aspired to do in the imperial era.[22]

21. These stories have generally been told separately, with the founding of American Methodism as part of the growth of awakened protestantism in the early Republic and the organization of the American Episcopal Church as a coda to colonial Anglicanism. See, for example, Mills, *Bishops by Ballot;* and Andrews, *The Methodists and Revolutionary America.* The story of Methodist separation in England was far more complicated. See Baker, *John Wesley and the Church of England,* 283–303.

22. [William White], *The Case of the Episcopal Churches in the United States Considered* (Philadelphia, 1782), iv ("piety and morals"), 5, 8, 12 ("small districts"). For discussion of White's plan, see Mills, *Bishops by Ballot,* 183–188. For investigations of White's biography and intellectual positions in this transitional moment, see Gregory K. Hotchkiss, "The Revolutionary William

More controversially, White envisioned a democratic episcopal church within that national project that lacked any benefits of legal establishment. Although it would have bishops (and thus in that sense be "episcopal"), White's proposed structure vested power in the clergy and the laity of the new nation. He "presumed, that, in general, the members of the episcopal churches are friendly to the principles, on which the present governments were formed." He also assumed that the new church must be independent of the "temporal authority of a foreign state," so it could no longer depend on the bishop of London for the ordination of clergy. In other words, since American episcopalians lacked either a bishop or any other means to ordain clergy, they would have to create their own bishops. He proposed that clergy and laity representing the three geographic districts of the extensive new nation gather to elect "a superior order of ministers," his euphemism for the elected bishops. In addition, each individual church—seen as an original sovereign body, not a subdivision of an episcopal diocese—would "retain . . . every power that need not be delegated for the good of the whole." The bishops chosen by the clergy would thus administer and perpetuate the church, but they would not rule it outright.[23]

Bishops selected under White's radical proposal would receive no government support, nor would they be able to claim any part in the history of Christian episcopal succession. Traditionally, bishops, both protestant and Catholic, received consecration from three existing bishops through the laying on of hands, theoretically ensuring their place in a continuous historical chain that stretched back to Saint Peter and Jesus. For the time being, White believed the issue of the historic episcopate would have to be set aside for pragmatic reasons, so that church leaders could prioritize the institutional health and unity of the episcopal communion in America. "From the parent church," he wrote, "most unquestionably" such a sanction could not be obtained. "The peculiar circumstances of the war in which our country is engaged," he continued, "preclude us from procuring the succession in those quarters, to which alone application could consistently be made; the danger of offending the British government constraining (perhaps) a refusal of what, it would of course be indelicate in us to

White and Democratic Catholicity," *Anglican and Episcopal History,* LXX (2001), 40–74; and John F. Woolverton, "Philadelphia's William White: Episcopalian Distinctiveness and Accommodation in the Post-Revolutionary Period," *Historical Magazine of the Protestant Episcopal Church,* XLIII (1974), 279–296. He was too young to have been deeply embedded in the prewar bishop controversy, and the 1782 pamphlet, laying out his agenda for a new "episcopal" church, was his first notable publication. For an earlier, abortive attempt to organize Anglicans in Virginia, see Thomas E. Buckley, *Church and State in Revolutionary Virginia, 1776–1787* (Charlottesville, Va., 1977), 43–44.

23. [White], *Case of the Episcopal Churches,* 6–7, 10–12 (quotations on 6, 10, 11).

ask." The right course of action, from White's perspective, was thus democratic, national, and immediate.[24]

While White imagined a democratic episcopal church independent of the nation's new government, an influential English Anglican spun out a different scheme. In Oxford, George Berkeley, Jr., the son of the bishop of Cloyne, who, decades before, had attempted to plant an Anglican college in Bermuda, saw the political division created by the war as an opportunity. He maintained an elevated opinion of the traditions and authority of bishops, but, unlike many of his Anglican peers, he could easily imagine an American episcopacy that received little state support. At the same time, he also believed that three traditionally consecrated bishops should be found to bring the new American bishops into the historical episcopate. The vehicle he envisioned for building the new American church was the tiny episcopal church in Scotland. In 1782, he wrote to John Skinner, a leader in that church, making the case. "A *consecration* from a persecuted depressed Church which is barely tolerated would not alarm the prejudices of Opponents," Berkeley argued. The Scots already understood from experience what had to be true in the United States also, "that an Episcopal Church may exist without any *Legal* encouragement or establishment—and without the definition of country into *regular* and *bounded* Dioceses." The war had made the moment urgent: "In a *short time,* we must expect all Protestant Episcopalian Principles to be totally lost in America." A few months later he wrote again to Skinner, this time saying that the persecuted Scots might be the *"plant in a dry ground"* from which "a most important good may e're long be derived to the suffering and nearly neglected sons of *Protestant Episcopacy* on the other side of the Atlantic." It was the inverse of the plan so long promoted by the Church of England. Rather than extending episcopacy to the colonies to support the empire through religion, the Scots would take advantage of the dismembered empire to extend episcopacy without political connection.[25]

24. Ibid., 16–17. I have chosen to use the phrases "episcopal succession" and "historic episcopate" here rather than apostolic succession because the discussions through the 1780s were largely practical rather than theological, concerning connection to the Anglican or Scottish episcopal churches, not the nature of apostolic succession. Though the latter term appears in some primary sources, it can conjure for a modern reader discussions that were largely left out at the time.

25. George Berkeley, Jr., to John Skinner, Mar. 21, 1782, CH12/12/1988, Episcopal Chest, CH12/12/1989, National Records of Scotland, Edinburgh (NRS); Berkeley to Skinner, Oct. 9, 1782, CH12/12/1989, ibid. "Plant in a dry ground" is probably a reference to Isaiah 53:2. For Bishop Berkeley, see Scott Breuninger, *Recovering Bishop Berkeley: Virtue and Society in the Anglo-Irish Context* (New York, 2010), esp. 95–115. Berkeley was part of High Church Anglican circles that included loyalist Anglicans. See Peter W. Walker, "The Church Militant: The American Loyalist Clergy and the Making of the British Counterrevolution, 1701–92" (Ph.D. diss., Columbia University, 2016), 124, 238–239; and Peter Benedict Nockles, *The Oxford Movement in Context: Anglican High Churchmanship, 1760–1857* (Cambridge, 1994), 13–14, 46–47.

Connecticut's episcopal clergy was the first group to move from the theoretical to the practical in this conversation. In an intriguing mix of pragmatism, subterfuge, and theological commitment, they attempted to salvage both the historic episcopate and ties to the Church of England. They also abandoned White's national project and worked instead as a state body. Gathering in Woodbury on March 23, 1783, they kept their actions, and even the complete list of their names, secret because they worried about political backlash. Their goal, in keeping with Berkeley's, was to ensure that their church had a proper foundation through episcopal succession, but they wished "to retain the religious Polity—the primitive and evangelical Doctrine, and Discipline, which at the Reformation were restored and established in the Church of England." These ties to the mother church were exactly what they felt White's democratic plan endangered. They wrote as much to the archbishops of Canterbury and York. They outlined White's "extraordinary" scheme "lately formed and published in Philadelphia," and they asserted that they found "it our Duty to reject such a spurious Substitute for Episcopacy, and as far as may be in our Power, to prevent its taking Effect." To create "a valid and regular Episcopate in America," they continued, "we earnestly intreat your Grace, that in your archiepiscopal Character, you will espouse the Cause of our sinking Church, and at this important Crisis, afford her that Relief, on which her very Existence depends, by consecrating a Bishop for Connecticut." They sent loyalist minister Samuel Seabury to England for consecration, with a backup plan that he might also journey on to Scotland, following Berkeley's proposal, if necessary.[26]

While competing groups of episcopalians vied to organize those in North America who had been part of the Church of England, John Wesley also turned his attention to his American followers, quite irrespective of their relationship to the Church of England or any successor body in the United States. Despite the challenges American Wesleyans faced by being connected with the outspoken American critic during the war years, their small movement was growing rapidly, and their numbers nearly doubled between 1778 (6,095) and 1782 (11,785), with the majority in Maryland, Virginia, and Delaware. A significant number of those who joined Wesleyan (known as methodist) societies—as much as 10 percent by 1786—were African American. In addition, many more

26. Clergy of Connecticut to archbishop of York, Apr. 21, 1783, CH12/12/1995, NRS; Petition to Scotland from the Convention of the Episcopal Clergy of Connecticut, Apr. 21, 1783, CH12/12/1994, NRS; Mills, *Bishops by Ballot*, 210–213; E. Edwards Beardsley, *Life and Correspondence of the Right Reverend Samuel Seabury, D.D. First Bishop of Connecticut, and of the Episcopal Church in the United States of America*, 2d ed. (Boston, 1881), 76–96.

than those captured in the statistics kept by ministers were hearers or adherents of the vibrant movement.[27]

At the same time, because most American Wesleyans were still formally a part of whatever it was the episcopal church was becoming after the war, they faced the same practical problem that their formerly Anglican fellows did: clergy eligible to administer the sacraments had to be ordained by the Church of England, now politically cut off from the United States. They had the further difficulty, too, of their marginal status within the Church of England, as many bishops in England declined to ordain clergy who were part of the Wesleyan awakening movement. The power to resolve the problem lay with Wesley. While he remained committed to the church, his followers would as well—even though it had become a matter that required repeating rather than one that could be assumed. Should he change his mind and move outside the Anglican fold, they would follow him. Anglican organizations on both sides of the Atlantic were thus profoundly vulnerable to shifts in Wesley's commitment to the church that ordained him.[28]

While Connecticut's Seabury worked through his options in London, Wesley decided to act alone. According to Thomas Coke, one of the principal figures in the development of the American Methodist Episcopal Church, Wesley informed Coke "of his design of drawing up a plan of Church-government, and of establishing an ordination for his *American* societies," directly in response to missionary Francis Asbury's stated need for sacramental ministers in the United States. To meet this perceived need, Wesley took for himself the authority to ordain ministers—authority that was, in the Church of England, reserved for bishops. He felt empowered to assume these duties for the new country, even though he did not take such liberties at home, because he believed the Revolution had placed Americans outside the Church of England. When he facilitated ordinations for America, therefore, Wesley acted, not (only) as a priest of the

27. Numbers of adherents found in [Methodist Episcopal Church], *Minutes of the Methodist Conferences, Annually Held in America, from 1773 to 1794, Inclusive* (Philadelphia, 1795), 25, 53. See also Andrews, *Methodists and Revolutionary America,* 61–62, 259–261.

28. For the problem of the sacraments, see Elmer T. Clark, J. Manning Potts, and Jacob S. Payton, eds., *The Journals and Letters of Francis Asbury,* III (London, 1958), 24–25, 29–32; and Andrews, *Methodists and Revolutionary America,* 63–64. Wesley reiterated his expectation that American Wesleyans would defer to him, as well to Asbury, in 1783 ([Methodist Episcopal Church], *Minutes of the Methodist Conferences,* 72–73). Wesley's exchange with Asbury in the summer and fall of 1783 is described in Baker, *John Wesley and the Church of England,* 240–241; and Andrews, *Methodists and Revolutionary America,* 65. See also Jesse Lee, *A Short History of the Methodists, in the United States of America; Beginning in 1766, and Continued till 1809; to Which Is Prefixed, a Brief Account of Their Rise in England, in the Year 1729, etc.* (Baltimore, 1810), 85–86; and John Telford, ed., *The Letters of the Rev. John Wesley, A.M.: Sometime Fellow of Lincoln College, Oxford,* VII (London, 1931), 191.

Church of England, but rather as a religious leader working beyond its limits. Through these actions, Wesley also came to understand the role of the bishop differently than he had before. He began to argue that presbyters, a biblical term for religious elders, had the right to ordain "superintending" presbyters in situations where there was no alternative. He claimed to be just such a presbyter, and with the assistance of other presbyters, he believed his followers, an emerging church, might ordain their own clergy in places where there was no functioning church structure in place. At the moment, that meant the United States. As Coke, whom Wesley "set apart as a Superintendent," framed it, *"The power of ordaining others should be received by me from you* [Wesley], by the imposition of your hands, and that you should lay hands" on two others headed to America as well. With three such church administrators, American Wesleyans could ordain new clergy in the United States. They would not be recognized by the Church of England. Nonetheless, Coke and Wesley believed, this was the "primitive" Christian mechanism of transmitting clerical authority. Although it might not be permissible in England, it could be in the new United States. Wesley ordained Coke and two others as elders for America in early September 1784.[29]

It was a dramatic step. The act allowed his followers in North America to construct an institutional body that would soon become one of the United States' largest denominations. It would also be separate from whatever episcopal institution would ultimately develop there, virtually ensuring there would be no continuation of the colonial cohabitation between Wesley's awakened followers and Anglicans. Wesley interpreted his own actions in pragmatic political terms, obscuring the rupture within the residual body of the colonial Anglican Church. Because those in North America were "totally disjoined from their Mother-Country, and erected into Independent States," they had been left without any spiritual oversight. He implicitly acknowledged that what he had done would have been disruptive in England, where there were "Bishops who have legal jurisdiction." America, though, was "[widely] different." Continuing to rely on the Anglican Church there was impossible, not to mention impractical, so he had done only what was necessary. "If any one will point out a more rational and scriptural way," he wrote, "of feeding and guiding those poor sheep in the wilderness," he would "gladly embrace it." For the moment, however, he

29. [Thomas] Coke and [Henry] Moore, *The Life of the Rev. John Wesley, A.M.: Including an Account of the Great Revival of Religion, in Europe and America, of Which He Was the First and Chief Instrument* (London, 1792), 458 (quotation); Baker, *John Wesley and the Church of England,* 240–241, 260–270 (quotation on 265, 270). Coke began contemplating his own journey to America in October 1783. See John A. Vickers, ed., *The Letters of Dr. Thomas Coke* (Nashville, Tenn., 2013), 45, 56–59. See also John Wesley to Barnabas Thomas, Mar. 25, 1785, MA 1977/502/1/31, John Rylands Library, University of Manchester, U.K (JRL).

"[could] not see any better method than I have taken." The political reality of the empire's dismemberment justified an urgent, schismatic, ecclesiastical act.[30]

It is hard to overstate the importance of Wesley's ordinations for the postwar denominational order. It hastened the process by which protestant institutions came into alignment with the new national borders, solidifying the fracture that ran through the heart of imperial protestantism, and it eroded the habits that had kept awakened protestants within the fold. Counterfactuals are always challenging, but it is plausible that Wesley could have used his influence to press for a solution to the entire problem of episcopal and sacramental authority for former Anglicans in the United States, rather than attending only to his own flock. Indeed, during the war years, he had written to the bishop of London about that more general problem, folding his followers in with the larger church of which they were a part. After the war, however, he accepted the complete end of connections between Wesleyans and episcopalians in the new country as a correlate part of the end of British political authority there. In the United States, he wrote, "no one either exercises or claims any Ecclesiastical Authority at all," and yet "thousands of the Inhabitants of these States desire my advice." He believed that ordinations of his ministers to go to the United States would not be forthcoming from Anglican officials, and "as our *American* Brethren are now totally disentangled both from the State and from the *English* Hierarchy, we dare not entangle them again, either with the one or the other." He was, of course, right. American Wesleyans felt themselves part of a distinctive community, only partially connected to the Church of England and dubiously tied to American episcopalians. Yet even though Wesley's move largely formalized what was already a fait accompli, it was nonetheless a mighty blow to the remaining connections of the older protestant system. When Wesley ordained clergy for the colonies, he actively supported the creation of a new mainstream denomination, something that had not happened on such a scale since before the Act of Toleration. The forces that kept Wesley within the protestant scaffold had lost their strength with the imperial rupture.[31]

Wesley acted on his own authority in creating his American church, but, unfortunately for Connecticut's Anglicans, Samuel Seabury could not do the same. For British authorities, the creation of a bishop (among other, more theological, matters) was an issue of government action, and taking the step

30. "To Dr. Coke, Mr. Asbury, and Our Brethren in North-America," Sept. 10, 1784, printed document, MA 1977/502/3/7, JRL. A handwritten copy is also in the SPG Collection, SPG X, fols. 197–197a, Lambeth Palace Library, London (LPL). The text reads "widley," which seems likely to be a typo, and, indeed, the handwritten copy at Lambeth renders it as "widely."

31. "To Dr. Coke, Mr. Asbury," Sept. 10, 1784, printed document, MA 1977/502/3/7, JRL; Baker, *John Wesley and the Church of England*, 253, 260.

first required assurances that consecrating bishops for the United States would not cause diplomatic problems. When Seabury reached out to the English archbishops, he learned that the prelates worried that the government of Connecticut would reject a bishop and that "there would be no adequate support for him." This last issue reflected deep-seated British assumptions that a true bishop was not merely a clerical functionary but rather a figure of dignity and respect, centrally tied to the authority of the state in the way that the structures of imperial protestantism had long assumed. Seabury wrote home to request that "the State of Connecticut should be applied to for their consent" to his appointment as a bishop for the state. He received the stumbling reply that his friends had "consulted with several persons whose Judgement we can depend upon, concerning the Application, you propose to be made to the Assembly; who give it, as their Opinion, *That a formal Application to the Assembly would be improper, if not highly imprudent.*" Connecticut could not guarantee what the bishops needed to hear: that there would be no political objections to an episcopacy. A similarly awkward situation arose when several Americans in London, including Mason Locke Weems, George Washington's future biographer, ran into difficulties obtaining ordination in 1783. The request was hardly innovative; American clergy had always had their ordinations in England, but after the war exemption from the normal loyalty oaths to the crown required an act of Parliament. Weems turned to American diplomat John Adams for help, who replied that, "however dangerous it maybe for an American Minister of State, to intermeddle, in a matter of Religion especially without Orders from his Superiors," he would offer his help "as a private Citizen, in a matter of so serious Concern." Fortunately for Weems and his fellows, Parliament resolved the short-term problem of their ordinations with a one-off act, but the larger issue of episcopal consecration lingered.[32]

In August 1784, Seabury made a tally of the "objections" he faced. High on

32. Beardsley, *Life and Correspondence,* 109–110; Jeremiah Leaming to Samuel Seabury, January 1784, Samuel Seabury Papers, 1/60, General Theological Seminary, New York; Mason Locke Weems to John Adams, circa Feb. 27, 1784, Adams to Weems, Mar. 3, 1784, both in *Founders Online*, National Archives, https://founders.archives.gov. See also Richard G. Salomon, "British Legislation and American Episcopacy," *Historical Magazine of the Protestant Episcopal Church,* XX (1951), 278–293, esp. 279–282. Weems's efforts to find ordination provoked the comment: "An hundred Years hence, when People are more enlightend, it will be wonder'd at, that Men in America, qualified by their Learning and Piety to pray for and instruct their Neighbours, should not be permitted to do it till they had made a Voyage of 6000 Miles going out and home, to ask leave of a cross old Gentleman at Canterbury: Who seems, by your Account, to have as little Regard for the Souls of the People of Maryland, as King Williams' Attorney General Seymour had for those of Virginia" (Benjamin Franklin to Mason Weems and Edward Gant, July 18, 1784 [unpublished], *The Papers of Benjamin Franklin,* Digital Edition, https://franklinpapers.org). See also Frederick V. Mills, *Bishops by Ballot,* 203.

that list was that Congress had not "requested" nor even "acquiesced in the measure." If Connecticut appeared to, it was only a state, and its "consent [was] not explicitly declared." Seabury gave up trying to procure consecration from the Church of England and turned to Scotland's episcopalians. The first consecration of a bishop in the Anglican tradition designed to serve in North America was thus performed in Aberdeen on November 14, 1784 (see Figure 18).[33]

While Seabury was in Scotland, news spread about Wesley's ordinations for America among his English followers. Wesley's actions raised issues of the greatest magnitude about the nature of ecclesiastical fellowship and Christian community. Many were not pleased by this breach with a church they cherished, and not least among the protesting voices was John's younger brother and lifelong collaborator, Charles. John had anticipated his brother's objections, and he had kept Charles in the dark for a while after his September ordination of Coke and his fellows. Charles thus learned about them only through a third party, and the younger sibling described himself as *"thunderstruck"* by John's choice. He turned his skilled poet's pen against his older brother:

So easily are Bishops made
By man's, or woman's whim?
Wesley his hands on Coke hath laid,
But who laid hands on him?

The core problem for Charles Wesley, and many of his peers, was that in his view John's actions went against the imperatives of ecclesiastical unity. Although the ordained men were destined for the United States, Charles believed that John's assumption of the power of ordination represented a breach in Christian community far greater than that created by the division of governments

33. Samuel Seabury, "Objections Made to the Connecticut Episcopacy," August 1784, Samuel Seabury Papers, box 1, folder 65-Removed. See also Beardsley, *Life and Correspondence,* 110–136. Beilby Porteus recounted a succinct version of this story that he heard from Seabury after the latter's return to England in 1785. See Beilby Porteus, "Occasional Memorandums and Reflexions on Several Subjects; Chiefly Religious, Moral Ecclesiastical and Literary," III, Diary, 1781–1786, MS 4983, 87, LPL. Seabury reached out to Scotland via Myles Cooper, who was in Edinburgh, shortly after drawing up this list. See Samuel Seabury to Myles Cooper, Aug. 31, 1784, Ch12/12/2007, NRS; and Beardsley, *Life and Correspondence,* 136–139. Records of the lengthy final negotiations are in Ch12/12/2008–2016, and also Ch12/24/486 and 537, NRS. William Smith, the longtime Philadelphia Anglican minister who was then in Maryland, attempted to stop Seabury's consecration through gossip (Beardsley, *Life and Correspondence,* 142–146; Mills, *Bishops by Ballot,* 219–224). The key issue for the Scottish bishops was the Concordat signed with Connecticut episcopalians, a document that gave the tiny and persecuted Scottish Church a partner in the world of transatlantic protestantism. A copy can be found at "Original Concordat," Ch12/12/2015A, NRS. Seabury maintained a correspondence with the Scottish church in furtherance of this spirit of cooperation. See also Salomon, "British Legislation," *Historical Magazine of the Protestant Episcopal Church,* XX (1951), 278–293.

FIGURE 18 *The Right Reverend Samuel Seabury, D.D. Bishop of Connecticut.* Engraving by William Sharp. When Samuel Seabury, newly consecrated, passed through London on his way back to Connecticut, he stopped to visit the exiled Jacob Duché. The latter's son Thomas was studying to be a portraitist and painted a dramatic image of Seabury as an America bishop, on which this engraving was based. © National Portrait Gallery, London

accomplished through the war. Charles's worries were embodied in the phrase "Ordination is separation," a pithy formulation from his school friend, William Murray, Lord Mansfield, whose opinion Charles had solicited in the matter. When John, "Did boldly on himself confer / The Apostolic Character!" to quote another piece written by Charles, the elder Wesley had both transformed his followers into presbyterians (by creating a church order that did not require bishops to be consecrated through the historic episcopate) and ruptured the body of the national church.

By laying on his hasty hands;
The mighty Babel to erect,
And found a new Dissenting Sect,
His Mother-Church to rend, disclaim,
And brand the Party with his Name.

These lines, penned in 1785, suggest the enormity of the problems involved with the formation of new ecclesiastical bodies in America from the perspective of the unity that the territorial church was supposed to provide, particularly because for Wesley's followers it might also mean the same would happen in England.[34]

Charles Wesley's objections found a ready audience among American episcopalians, who similarly worried about the loss of episcopal succession among Wesleyans and the possibility that these former Anglicans would leave their churches, resulting in both schism and a diminishment of their own numbers. The younger Wesley had in his papers an extract of a letter from New York, probably written by clergyman Benjamin Moore, that outlined these fears in strong language. "Wesley has just sent over three Preachers, one of them a Man in Orders," the report read. They had been canny in their actions: "In order to take Advantage of the present Moment of Uncertainty and Distraction in our Church Affairs, they hurried away from England, and brought their Prayer Books with them unbound.... What is become of all their Professions of steadfast Attachment to the Church?" The writer went on, expressing the same sense of panic that Charles Wesley put in his verse: "We shall oppose their Pretensions, and the Consequence will be Division and Animosity." If the Americans

34. Frank Baker, *Charles Wesley: As Revealed by His Letters* (London, 1948), 134 (*"thunderstruck"*); John R. Tyson, ed., *Charles Wesley: A Reader* (New York, 1989), 140 ("Ordination"), 429 ("So easily"), 431 ("By laying"), 432 ("Did boldly"). See also Henry Durbin to Charles Wesley, Oct. 10, 1784, Early Preachers Collection, DDPr 1/123, JRL; William Pine to Charles Wesley, Nov. 25, 1784, Charles Wesley Papers, DDCW 6/83A, JRL; Sarah Wesley to Charles Wesley, Aug. 18, 1785, ibid., DDCW 6/42; Gareth Lloyd, *Charles Wesley and the Struggle for Methodist Identity* (Oxford, 2007), 198–212; and Baker, *John Wesley and the Church of England*, 273.

were "Blessed with the Presence of a Bishop," he mused, "our Difficulties would vanish in an Instant; all Pretensions for Innovation would be obviated, and we would hold the Church in this Country on an equal Footing with any other religious Denomination." Blame was easy to assign. "Are the great Men in England mad? Or are they besotted? . . . This is an Independent Country—true—but the Cause of Religion ought to be the Cause of every good Man." The divisions, first between branches of the Anglican Church and now between Wesleyans and Anglicans, went counter to the core of the church's ideals.[35]

There was no stopping the postwar denominational fracture that was well under way, but Charles Wesley tried anyway. Hearing of Seabury's consecration, he wrote a long letter to Thomas Bradbury Chandler, a loyalist Anglican minister who had recently returned to New Jersey from London, seeking to use Seabury's new position to halt the disintegration. The letter, which Charles intended to be shared, outlined the long relationship between the two Wesley brothers. "For 50 years we kept the sheep in the fold," but now he could "scarcely yet believe it that in his 82d year, my Brother, my old intimate Friend and Companion should have *assumed the Episcopal Character*[,] ordained Elders, Consecrated a Bishop and sent him to ordain the Lay-preachers in America!" He then, in a postscript, connected the American episcopal and Wesleyan issues. "What will become of those poor sheep in the wilderness, the American Methodists? How have they been *betrayed* into a Separation from the Church of England!—which their Preachers and They no more intended than the Methodists here[.]" Seabury's consecration created a sliver of hope. "Had they had patience a little longer, they would have seen a *REAL Primitive Bishop* in America *duly* Consecrated by Three Scotch Bishops, who had *their* Consecration from the English Bishops, and are acknowledged by them as the same with Themselves. There is therefore not the least difference betwixt the Members of Bishop Seabury's Church, and the Members of the Church of England." The man in question, Seabury, did take up the charge of maintaining Wesley's followers within his episcopal church, even ordaining two nonseparating Wesleyan preachers. These

35. "Extract of a Letter from a Clergyman from New York to Dr. Inglis, Dated New York, November 29, 1784," MA 1977/502/3/9, JRL. The letter writer refers to himself as one of the men selected to be an officer of the "Corporation for the Support of Clergymen's Widows." At the Oct. 5, 1784, meeting in New York of that society, Moore was elected secretary. See John William Wallace, *A Century of Beneficence, 1769–1869: Historical Sketch of the Corporation for the Relief of the Widows and Children of the Clergymen in the Communion of the Protestant Church, in the Commonwealth of Pennsylvania . . .* (Philadelphia, 1870), 40; and Mills, *Bishops by Ballot*, 229. Inglis was then in London, and it seems plausible that Moore would have corresponded with him. See Ross N. Hebb, *Samuel Seabury and Charles Inglis: Two Bishops, Two Churches* (Madison, N.J., 2010), 41, 84. The letter had been forwarded to Charles Wesley by Charles Inglis, then in London as a refugee. Inglis, of course, had been a strong supporter of Seabury.

efforts were too little, too late, however. Connecticut's bishop did not have the influence to stop the schismatic energy of Wesley's American followers, led by Thomas Coke and Francis Asbury.[36]

In Baltimore, in 1784, Coke and Asbury organized the Methodist Episcopal Church in America, at what became known as the Christmas Conference. The proceedings laid the groundwork for a church that was independent of connections to any ecclesiastical body beyond itself. The preachers gathered there, some dozens, elected Asbury and Coke to be superintendents of the new church. That democratic process mattered because it added a second component to their leadership beyond that provided by Wesley's selection and ceremonial elevation to authority. In addition to matching with the mode of governance that prevailed in the new United States, it distanced the new Methodist Episcopal Church from Wesley's direct authority and also from whatever American episcopal church would be reconstructed in the coming years. Coke preached a sermon at the occasion of Asbury's elevation to superintendent, justifying their actions in words that cast aside both Wesley's opposition to the American cause in the war and his followers' long-standing position within the Church of England. Instead, he appealed directly to an American audience. "Blessed be GOD, and praised by his HOLY NAME," he wrote, "that the memorable Revolution has struck off these intolerable fetters, and broken the antichristian union which before subsisted between Church and State." He continued to excoriate American episcopalians as "hirelings *who ate the fat and cloathed themselves with the wool,*" quoting Ezekiel 34:3. With this rejection accomplished, he proceeded to lay out Wesley's justification for ordination, and even to push further by saying that he was "cheerfully ready to answer at the Bar of GOD" for *"this schism"* from an ecclesiastical institution that was in error on fundamental teachings. Here was a positive embrace of separation. Lingering ties remained to Wesley and the British religious community he led, but Asbury's church rapidly became an independent actor in the postwar denominational order.[37]

36. Charles Wesley to Thomas Bradbury Chandler, Apr. 28, 1785, Wesley Family Letters, DDWes 1/38, JRL. There are many copies of this letter. Samuel Seabury had an extract in his papers (Samuel Seabury Papers, box 1, folder 86). It also appeared in William Jones Seabury, *Memoir of Bishop Seabury* (New York, 1908), 377–380. The transcription here follows the outgoing copy. For Chandler's making use of it, see Thomas Bradbury Chandler to Charles Wesley, Jan. 31, 1786, Wesley Family Letters, DDWes 2/93. For discussion of the Wesleyan-Anglican split in the United States, see Seabury to Charles Wesley, Jan. 23, 1787, MA 1977/502/3/12, JRL. For Seabury's ordinations, see Chandler to Charles Wesley, Jan. 31, 1786, Wesley Family Letters, DDWes 2/93; and Baker, *John Wesley and the Church of England,* 275.

37. Thomas Coke, *Substance of a Sermon, Preached at Baltimore, in the State of Maryland, before the General Conference of the Methodist Episcopal Church, on the 7th of December, 1785, at the*

Wesleyans in Britain did not abandon the ideals of ecclesiastical unity as quickly as their American counterparts, but the process of denominational multiplication continued there as well. Though John Wesley did not formally separate from the church in his lifetime (he died in 1791), he laid the groundwork for the transformation. The essential first step, ordaining ministers for America, happened alongside a legal move transferring Wesleyan chapels to a self-sustaining body of leaders (and thus not back to the control of the church hierarchy). He also ordained ministers for Scotland, a land at the heart of British protestantism. Wesley eventually ordained clergy for England in 1787. At the same time, these actions were hardly triumphant. Wesley expressed some regrets; some measures were kept secret or at least private. In addition, both English Wesleyans and their American counterparts initiated moves to join with other denominations, seeking to stem the tide of protestant fracture. Thomas Coke, like Wesley another principal actor in the process of division, was one of the leaders who also sought reunion. In 1786, in England, he took part, along with Charles Wesley and Moravian Benjamin Latrobe, in discussions about joining their respective groups. The Moravians had been fellow travelers, if also sometimes combatants, with the Wesleys since the 1730s, and their concept of an ecclesiastical "Tropus," in which religious communities were loosely joined and yet remained separate, appealed. A few years later, in North America, Coke was involved in a further effort, trying to reconnect the American Protestant Episcopal and Methodist Episcopal Churches. Both projects failed, but that they were conceived of at all suggests that protestant leaders felt unsteady about the schisms within the Church of England. They continued to strive for the largest possible church communities, often unsure of precisely which issues would define new boundaries.[38]

Ordination of the Rev. Francis Asbury, to the Office of a Superintendent (Baltimore, 1785), 6–7, 10–11. The title page of the printed sermon mistakenly has the date as 1785. A footnote in the published version exempted some Anglicans from his condemnations. See also John Wigger, *American Saint: Francis Asbury and the Methodists* (Oxford, 2009), 139–148, 159–165; and Andrews, *The Methodists and Revolutionary America,* 62–72; Anna M. Lawrence, *One Family under God: Love, Belonging, and Authority in Early Transatlantic Methodism* (Philadelphia, 2011), 202–206. For ongoing ties to Wesley among American Methodists, see *Minutes of Several Conversations between the Rev. Thomas Coke LL.D. the Rev. Francis Asbury, and Others . . .* (Philadelphia, 1785) 3–4.

38. Baker, *John Wesley and the Church of England,* 218–233, 278–282. For Wesley's personal view on separation, see Richard P. Heitzenrater, "Methodists," in Thompson, ed., *Oxford History of Protestant Dissenting Traditions,* II, 99–115. For the Moravian-Methodist initiative, see Baker, *John Wesley and the Church of England,* 305–306; and Vickers, ed., *Letters of Dr. Thomas Coke,* 74–80. In 1791, Coke reached out to William White and to Samuel Seabury in a failed effort to reunite the American Methodist and American episcopal churches. See ibid., 133–137, 141–146. Coke was touchy on the point of separation. See also Thomas Coke to William Wilberforce, Aug. 24, 1790, Papers of Thomas Coke, PLP 28/7/5, JRL; and Vickers, ed., *Letters of Dr. Thomas Coke,* 123.

American episcopalians, led by William White, finally found their path forward in 1785. They were assisted by Seabury, if only because his appearance in London as a bishop claiming ordination from Scotland prodded English Anglicans to action. Two things happened to bring the Americans back to the front of Anglican attentions. The first was Seabury's appeal to the SPG for support, which pushed the issue of the status of American missionaries within that society. Its leaders followed the course so many other transatlantic religious organizations had charted in previous years, and the SPG formally retreated so that its missionary efforts followed the new political boundary. The second effect of Seabury's consecration, which was more indirect, was to push the bishops' bench into overcoming the political obstacles to an Anglican ordination of an American episcopal bishop. New political energy in the effort came from Granville Sharp, an awakened Anglican who dedicated his life to ending slavery. Sharp had for some time been supporting, through letters and in print, the idea that the Americans ought to have a "primitive," elected episcopacy, whose bishops would nonetheless be consecrated by Anglicans into the traditions of episcopal succession. He began politicking for the Anglican hierarchy to support such a move even before Seabury was consecrated, and he accelerated those efforts afterward. In addition to believing that an elected episcopacy—legitimately consecrated according to tradition—was both legal and scriptural, he also explicitly opposed the idea of a succession derived through Scotland. It was "very doubtful how *a succession* of [the non-jurors] Authority could be continued," Sharp argued, "amongst persons, who have *no real Congregation or* Episcopal Charge, but only a nominal or mere *titular appointment* over an *invisible Church;* and that granted by *the pretender,* a foreign Prince, who has no authority whatsoever in these Kingdoms! This must be the case, I fear, with the *present Scotch Bishops.*" The undesirability of American bishops implicitly elevating the status of the Scots, rather than being descended from the Anglican Church, made action more likely.[39]

39. Granville Sharp to James Manning, Feb. 22, 1785, copies in Samuel Seabury Papers, box 1, folder 81; and in Papers of John Moore, archbishop of Canterbury (hereafter cited as Moore Papers), Moore 6, fols. 111–114, LPL. The copies vary slightly, and the transcription here follows the copy in the Lambeth Palace Library. See also Benjamin Rush to Sharp, Apr. 27, 1784, in L. H. Butterfield, ed., *Letters of Benjamin Rush,* I (Princeton, N.J., 1951), 330–331. For discussions of Seabury and his movements, see Jacob Duché to William White, Dec. 1, 1784, William White Papers, I, item 50, Hawks Collection, Archives of the Episcopal Church, Austin, Tex.; and Michael Lort to Samuel Henley, Jan. 10, 1785 (item misdated from 1784), Samuel Henley Papers, Ch.H.2.25, Boston Public Library. See also "Dr. Seaberry," *Public Advertiser* (London), Feb. 11, 1785, [3]. Granville Sharp referenced this publication in Sharp to Manning, Feb. 22, 1785, Samuel Seabury Papers, box 1, folder 81. For the SPG, see Journal of the Society for the Propagation of the Gospel in Foreign Parts, Apr. 15, 1785, XXIV, 83, Colonial Missionaries' Papers from America and the West Indies, 1701–1870, British Online Archives, https://microform.digital/boa; Seabury

When the Anglican hierarchy received a petition from the Americans in 1785, it was ready to act. The event was the culmination of the efforts that had been started by White with his pamphlet three years before. The new Protestant Episcopal Church in the United States used the democratic forms to which Americans were now accustomed. They largely followed White's 1782 plan, but they relied on states as internal units to the newly constituted national church, rather than White's three districts. It gave a place of honor to bishops, not surprisingly, but it also retained leadership for the laity that differed markedly from the parent Church of England. In addition, while the new body prepared an address to send to the archbishops in England, requesting consecration for the new American bishops, it also set in motion a process for state conventions to "elect persons for this purpose," thus limiting its own centralized authority over the selection of bishops. It "recommended" to the states, however, "that the persons who shall be sent . . . for consecration are desired in the character of Bishops, as well by the Laity as by the Clergy of this Church," to prevent the embarrassing possibility of a candidate for the dignified office being a source of dispute and controversy. The careful actions of the General Convention embraced the voice of the laity, allowed for regional differences, and took very little authority to the national organization itself. Seabury, now at home in Connecticut, made his objections to the process well known, and he did not participate. Members of the convention did not embrace him as an ecclesiastical authority.[40]

---

to SPG, Samuel Seabury Papers, Autograph material no. 82; and Statement of the SPG respecting Missionaries in the Independent States, Apr. 15, 1785, ibid., box 1, folder 87. American missionaries also watched closely what was going on. See Richard Mansfield to Samuel Peters, May 26, 1785, ibid., box 1, folder 89. Bishop Beilby Porteus mused on the events in his diary; see Porteus, "Occasional Memorandums and Reflexions on Several Subjects," III, Diary, MS 4983, 87–90, 94, LPL. For the British political context, see Doll, *Revolution, Religion, and National Identity,* 221. For a detailed discussion of Sharp's activities, see Frederick V. Mills, Sr., "Granville Sharp and the Creation of an American Episcopate: Ordo Episcoporum Est Robur Ecclesiae," *Anglican and Episcopal History,* LXXIX (2010), 34–58; and Doll, *Revolution, Religion, and National Identity,* 228. Sharp also wrote a biting letter to Robert Findlay in Glasgow, which he also forwarded to Archbishop Moore, dated Mar. 8, 1785 (Moore Papers, Moore 6, fols. 115–116, LPL). Sharp also communicated with Beilby Porteus on the subject of the American episcopacy; see Porteus, "Occasional Memorandums and Reflexions on Several Subjects," III, Diary, MS 4983, 94–101, LPL.

40. Francis L. Hawks and William Stevens Perry, eds., *Journals of the General Conventions of the Protestant Episcopal Church in the United State of America from A.D. 1785 to A.D. 1853, Inclusive* (Philadelphia, 1861), 10, 17–18, 21–25 (quotations on 25). The New York meetings "resolves" were also reported by Seabury to John Skinner in Aberdeen, as all parties continued to watch the various settlements play out. See Seabury to Skinner, Dec. 27, 1784, Ch12/12/2017, NRS. For the Episcopal Church's organizational process in the United States, see Mills, *Bishops by Ballot,* 237–242. White's correspondence with Seabury was not uncivil, and he was addressed with the title "Right Reverend." See William White et al. to Seabury, July 22, 1785, Samuel Seabury Papers, box 1, folder 91.

The convention's petition of the archbishops of Canterbury and York for consecrations was a straightforward act with far-reaching consequences. It ably handled political issues created by American independence. The petitioners wrote that their "Forefathers, when they left the land of their nativity," had not left the "bosom of that Church, over which your Lordships now preside." Because it had then "pleased the supreme Ruler of the Universe, that this part of the British Empire should be free, sovereign, and independent," the Anglican bishops had now to provide for the "continuance" of the American church. The petitioners frankly admitted that they did not know if their "request will meet with insurmountable impediments, from the political regulations of the Kingdom in which your Lordships fill such distinguished stations," and they added that "in these States there is a separation between the concerns of policy and those of religion," so "our civil rulers cannot officially join in the present application." It was a simple statement of the profound transformation brought about within protestant circles by the Revolution. It was also a practical hurdle. To address the lack of government support for their petition, they also sent letters of endorsement from influential episcopalian politicians Richard Henry Lee and John Jay. These last were actually addressed to the American diplomat John Adams, based in London, who once again found himself required (in Lee's words) to "remove mistaken scruples from the mind of [the British] administration, by representing how perfectly consonant it is with our Revolution principles professed thro-out all the States, that every denomination of Christians has a right to pursue its own religious modes, interfering not with others." The petition was dispatched, and Adams presented it to the archbishops early in 1786. One is forced to wonder whether anyone paused to consider the transformation that placed that job in the hands of a man who had, twenty-one years earlier, during the Stamp Act crisis, celebrated how his puritan forebearers had "demolished the whole system of Diocesan episcopacy" and "derid[ed], as all reasonable and impartial men must do, the ridiculous fancies of sanctified effluvia from episcopal fingers."[41]

This time, the Anglican hierarchy was sympathetic to the Americans' pleas, and events went smoothly, though the bishops poured over with care the

41. "Petition to the Archbishops," Oct. 5, 1785, SPG X, 200–209, LPL; Hawks and Perry, eds., *Journals of the General Conventions*, 26–27; Samuel Provoost to White, Nov. 7, 1785, William White Papers, I, item 78, Hawks Collection; Richard Henry Lee to John Adams, Oct. 24, 1785, John Jay to Adams, Nov. 1, 1785, both in *Founders Online*. Lee also wrote to Beilby Porteus, the bishop of Chester; see Porteus Notebooks, MS 2099, 135, LPL. For "all reasonable and impartial," see John Adams, "Dissertation on the Canon and the Feudal Law," No. 2, Aug. 19, 1765, in C. James Taylor, ed., *Adams Papers Digital Edition* (Boston, 2015), I, http://www.masshist.org/publications/adams-papers/index.php/view/ADMS-06-01-02-0052-0005 (originally printed in the *Boston Gazette*, Aug. 19, 1765, [2]).

specific changes to the liturgy and structure of the church proposed by the Americans. A letter sent to the American convention and signed by most of the bishops stated that "nothing is nearer to our hearts than the wish to promote your Spiritual Welfare, to be instrumental in procuring for you the complete Exercise of our holy Religion, and the enjoyment of that Ecclesiastical Constitution, which We believe to be truly Apostolical, and for which you express so unreserved a Veneration." They went to on say that, since the Americans were not likely to face difficulties "from the Civil Powers under which you live," the bishops would "on our Parts . . . use our best Endeavours, [inserted: which we have good reason to hope will be successful] to acquire a Legal Capacity of complying with the Prayer of your Address." A few small issues remained to be hashed out, but the bishops submitted a bill to the House of Lords in June 1786. It received royal assent early the next month. During the same period, the second American episcopal convention met and completed its side of the process. Three bishops had already been elected by state meetings: William White for Pennsylvania, Samuel Provoost for New York, and David Griffith for Virginia. Griffith fell ill, but White and Provoost traveled to England and were consecrated early in 1787. The internal divisions within the American church over Seabury's role lingered, but with three men (including Seabury) now duly consecrated, the issues were no longer related to the nature of transnational episcopacy, and they were confined instead to domestic harmony. Seabury eventually came within the American Episcopalian fold, and a fourth bishop, Virginia's James Madison, cousin to the future president of the same name, was consecrated in England in 1790.[42]

An intriguing footnote to the whole era, a proposed meeting in London between John Wesley and William White, failed to come to fruition, leaving one to speculate about what might have been said had it come to pass. The two men, both architects of enduring ecclesiastical institutions in the new denominational order, had started the Revolutionary era within the same church, but by 1787 they were in opposite corners of a disintegrated protestant system. The process by which the colonial-era Church of England devolved into American

42. Beilby Porteus, Notebooks, MS 2099, 136–141, LPL; "Draft of Reply from Archbishops and Bishops . . . ," Feb. 27, 1786, SPG X, fols. 210–210a, LPL; Salomon, "British Legislation," *Historical Magazine of the Protestant Episcopal Church,* XX (1951), 284–288. Charles Inglis, then in London, helped facilitate the process. See Inglis to White, June 6, 1786, in John Wolfe Lydekker, *The Life and Letters of Charles Inglis: His Ministry in America and Consecration as First Colonial Bishop, from 1759–1787* (London, 1936), 241–245; Doll, *Revolution, Religion, and National Identity,* 226–229; and Mills, *Bishops by Ballot,* 252–256. Provoost to White, Dec. 28, 1785, William White Papers, I, item 87, Hawks Collection, discusses ongoing problems with Seabury. The political maneuvering between the Seabury and White organizations is discussed in Mills, *Bishops by Ballot,* 264–288.

and British segments, and through which Wesley's followers began to leave the fold, was a direct result of the American Revolution. Without the scaffold of imperial protestantism organizing the relationship between denominations and keeping the structures of establishment in place, the number of protestant denominations within the Anglo-American world multiplied. As they did, the idea—embraced by the Church of England—that one ecclesiastical body joined colonies to metropole collapsed. In the United States, the Methodist Episcopal Church grew and expanded quickly, independent of the limitations Wesley's followers had faced as a movement inside the Church of England. Within a few years, it was also independent of most limitations that came from dependence on Wesley. The national boundary had also become a religious boundary.[43]

QUARRELS OVER MONEY AND THE FINAL SEPARATION OF COLONIAL PROJECTS

In the post-Revolutionary era, energy and dynamism belonged to awakened protestants who pioneered new denominations and left the limitations of old systems behind. The very vibrancy of those movements can easily distract from a separate, more dismal process that was also under way. Though the networks that had encircled Britain's imperial protestant scaffold had largely ceased to function during the war years, there were lingering attachments and expectations once peace returned. After the war, protestants on both sides of the Atlantic moved to sweep them away, and not without rancor. This was the final housekeeping necessary to disentangle American and British protestants. Its inclusion here, a sour note amid the more hopeful postwar reorganization of the denominational order, points to the full incorporation of the new national boundaries into the communities of protestantism.

Many of the lingering issues had to do with relationships written into trusts and charters. What to do with British organizations founded on the premise that missions to America furthered British protestantism? The New England Company (NEC) provides a good example of the way that old ties were tested, then eliminated. In 1775, payments to areas under rebellion had been suspended, a policy reaffirmed in 1779 "during the Continuance of the present Rebellion and until the Restoration of Peace Order and Good Governance." After the conclusion of the fighting, neither the British nor the Americans involved in the NEC seemed clear about the nature of the ties that connected them in this new world, but the mood in London favored disentanglement from the rebellious

43. Mills, *Bishops by Ballot*, 256.

Americans. Those in Massachusetts sent numerous letters across the Atlantic in 1782, including several from Gideon Hawley, a missionary in Mashpee, as well as the former treasurer of the NEC's Boston Commissioners, Isaac Smith. The Londoners were torn about how to act. They reviewed their past minutes and resolutions, and they ultimately honored some, but not all, of the Americans' requests in May 1783. The following year it appeared that New England and England might be growing closer again. The group's London leaders moved to remit to Harvard College the remainder of a large bequest held for it in trust, and the NEC's members asked for more information about positions left vacant by the war. They even entertained a visitor, Nathaniel Gorham, who was seeking funds for a new missionary school in Massachusetts. In 1785 and 1786, however, the group changed course again. It consulted lawyers and decided it must confine its activities to areas that remained subject to the British crown. It therefore began to set up operations in New Brunswick. The brief window for potential collaboration was closed; national boundaries would henceforth shape the work of the NEC.[44]

Underneath the NEC's legalistic process lay anger at the Americans over the war. Israel Mauduit, a dissenting lawyer and pro-government pamphleteer who would be prominent in the efforts to repeal the Test and Corporation Acts, published a speech he gave before the NEC in 1785, just as the group pivoted toward New Brunswick. Mauduit was not typical among dissenting leaders. He had stood out during the war years in his support of government, and he was a lay figure rather than a clergyman, but he had a persuasive voice in the dissenting community. His speech (and pamphlet) detailed the parameters of the NEC's charter and emphasized how much the organization was dedicated to the furtherance of English goals. Now that the Americans were independent, however, the former colonies had "become alien or foreign states." In this new position, the New Englanders were "as distinct as *Spain* and *Portugal* are; more truly a different nation than *France* is: for the Crown of *England* has never renounced its title to *France,*" but it had concluded a treaty with the Americans. It is noteworthy that Mauduit did not frame his list of examples in any way to emphasize protestant nations, though his recitation of the charter had stressed the NEC's goals to convert and educate protestant Indigenous people. The ties

44. General Court and Committee Minutes, New England Company, Nov. 10, 1775, May 19, 1779, May 2, 1783, July 14, 1784, CLC/540/MS0790/001, London Metropolitan Archives. The Corporation for the Support of [Anglican] Clergymen's Widows was similarly unsure. See "Extract of a Letter from a Clergyman from New York to Dr. Inglis, Dated New York, November 29, 1784," MA 1977/502/3/9, JRL. New Brunswick received attention from several groups looking for a new American site for projects. See Ann Gorman Condon, *The Loyalist Dream for New Brunswick: The Envy of the American States* (Fredericton, N.B., 1984), 184–190.

that linked protestants together ceased to bind, and they faded from view. Now the work of religion was explicitly bound by nation.[45]

The NEC's case was not isolated. It was a part of the larger disassociation between Britain and the United States that left behind the imperial protestant system and its many connections between Britain and America. A trust established through the will of Robert Boyle, who died in 1691, directed funds to be used "for and towards the Advancement and Propagation of the Christian Religion amongst Infidells." Harvard and the New England missionaries through the NEC, as well as a school for Indigenous students at William and Mary, all benefited from the trust. These last funds were administered through the bishop of London. When the bishop sought to stop further payments after the war, the College of William and Mary went through the courts to get them reinstated. The Court of Chancery ultimately found in 1790 that the trust could be redirected on the grounds that there were no more Indigenous people in the vicinity of the college to educate and that William and Mary was now subject to a foreign power. The case set an important precedent about charities and the treaty of 1783, but, more importantly for the present purposes, the lengthy dispute showed the unwillingness of the Anglican hierarchy in England to work with Americans, even American Episcopalians, on the terms they had before the war, within the imperial protestant system. It had made sense for the liberal Boyle, nearly a century before, to create a benefaction that served Indian education in multiple colonies (even though these schools were variously staffed by dissenters and Anglicans), but after the war both the dissenting NEC and the bishop of London viewed their ties to religious fellows now in the United States as fundamentally changed by the political alteration. They unwound the philanthropic ties that bound them to their former compatriots.[46]

45. Israel Mauduit, *The Substance of a Speech Made before a General Court of the Company for the Propagation of the Gospel in New England and the Parts Adjacent, in America* (London, 1785), 6. Mauduit argued particularly that the stance of the Stockbridge Indians against the British justified the termination of relations with their American counterparts. For more on Mauduit generally, see Robert Taylor, "Israel Mauduit," *New England Quarterly*, XXIV (1951), 208–230.

46. "Brafferton Manor and the Indian School at the College of William and Mary, Virginia," Nov. 26, 2015, borthwickinstitute.blogspot.com/2015/11/brafferton-manor-and-indian-school-at.html; Mauduit, *Substance of a Speech*, 17; "Letter from the President and Professor of William and Mary College to the Bishop of London," Aug. 15, 1786, CFS F/3, fol. 132, LPL. Records of William and Mary's suit can be found at CFS F/3, fols. 134–135, LPL. The ultimate judgment from the Chancery Court is Attorney-General v. City of London, (1790) Ves. Jc 243 3 Bro. CC 171. The case is discussed in Herbert Lawrence Ganter, "Some Notes on 'The Charity of the Honourable Robert Boyle, Esq., of the City of London, Deceased,'" *William and Mary Quarterly*, 2d Ser., XV (1935), 1–39, 207–228, 346–384. This era also marked the rise of a new kind of nonreligious philanthropy. See Amanda B. Moniz, *From Empire to Humanity: The American Revolution and the Origins of Humanitarianism* (New York, 2016).

Americans came to understand only gradually, and sometimes with embarrassment, that Britons no longer wished to finance what had formerly been joint projects. The College of New Jersey, in Princeton, the site of much transatlantic attention before the war—including the fundraising journey by Samuel Davies and William Tennent in the early 1750s and the effort to hire John Witherspoon in the 1760s—had been severely damaged in the fighting, and its trustees turned to Britons to help rebuild it. So great was their faith in the willingness of former benefactors to assist that they sent the infirm Witherspoon, along with General Joseph Reed, to London. The trip was a disaster. Witherspoon wrote to John Jay, then in Paris, that "there is little or no Prospect of success here." Jay replied from France that he was not surprised. "While our Country remained part of the british Empire," he explained, "there was no Impropriety in solliciting the aid of our distant Brethren and fellow Subjects, for any liberal and public purpose." Matters had altered since the war, however. Now that the United States was independent, its stature "implies ability to provide for all the ordinary Objects of their Governments; and as the Diffusion of Knowledge among a republican People is and ought to be one of the constant and most important of those Objects," that, too, should be financed on its own. It was not just independence but also the war through which it was achieved that caused problems. As John Wesley commented to an associate, Witherspoon should not be "surprised if most Englishmen are strongly prejudiced on the other side: when they consider him as the grand instrument of tearing away children from their parents to which they were united by the most sacred ties, so that I know not with what face I can mention him, or with what probability of success." When Witherspoon returned to New Jersey, he and the college trustees made a new round of applications, this time directed at American "friends of religion and learning . . . who wish success to an institution of such importance to our civil and religious interests." They also asked the Scot's fellow presbyterians for help and sought to "impress them with a warm sense of the absolute necessity of a general exertion throughout all our churches for the support of the college under its present state of depression." Funding American colleges was now an American responsibility. It surely did not escape Witherspoon's notice that his own presence in New Jersey had been the product of an intensive transatlantic effort, in many ways the epitome of the connections that bound the religious community of the empire together. Twenty-five years later, no such common effort could be reconstructed.[47]

47. John Witherspoon to John Jay, March 1784, *John Jay Papers*, https://dlc.library.columbia.edu/jay/ldpd:48214; Jay to Witherspoon, Apr. 6, 1784, C0274 1/21C, and Witherspoon to the Presbytery of New Brunswick, Sept. 30, 1784, C0274 1/12A, John Witherspoon Collection, Princeton

A similar story unfolded with respect to Dartmouth College. Once the recipient of a tremendous outpouring of support from religious leaders across the empire, it now found itself cut off from further British support after the war. John Wheelock, president of the college after his father Eleazar's death, traveled to Europe and Britain in search of funds. In London, he met with John Thornton, long a benefactor of transatlantic religious projects, and also with the school's namesake, the earl of Dartmouth. Thornton informed Wheelock that the "spirit of the nation for the present would not admit" of a new solicitation, but he was "civil and kind," as was Dartmouth. Wheelock was less successful when he reached out to John Erskine, in an attempt to gain access to the funds that had been raised in Scotland before the war. Members of the Society in Scotland for Propagating Christian Knowledge (SSPCK), which held the funds, were still angry about the move by Wheelock père of the college to New Hampshire, and they protested that "nothing could be done till public affairs were settled." The case lingered for years; Wheelock did not see any money for some time. The SSPCK was not completely against supporting Americans, however. Daniel Simon, a Narragansett missionary who had graduated from Dartmouth in 1777, applied to the organization at about the same time Wheelock did. Its members decided they could not simply appoint a new missionary, since the disruption of communication meant that they did not even know "whether the four Missionaries who were in their service at the commencement of the War be alive," but they provided Simon with some funds to defray his costs in Britain and referred him on to their New Jersey board. Wheelock received far less sympathy, and he returned home nearly empty-handed.[48]

The desire to confine religious projects within political borders did not come only from the British side. Americans, too, became jealous of protecting their own projects and territory. Selina Hastings, the countess of Huntingdon, still mired in a messy set of ties to Bethesda in Georgia, began an initiative in 1783 designed to spread the gospel among American Indigenous people. In keeping

University Library; John Wesley to Brian Bury Collins, Mar. 11, 1784, in Telford, ed., *Letters of John Wesley*, VII, 214. For fundraising, see also Richard Price to Benjamin Rush, Jan. 1, 1783, in D. O. Thomas, ed., *The Correspondence of Richard Price*, II (Durham, N.C., 1991), 162–164. Reed had been married to Esther De Berdt, the daughter of a prominent Huguenot family, which might have made him a good choice for the trip. For details on the trip from Witherspoon's perspective, see David Walker Woods, Jr., *John Witherspoon* (New York, 1906), 124–129.

48. Leon B. Richardson, ed., "John Wheelock's European Journey," *Dartmouth Alumni Magazine*, XXV, no. 3 (December 1932), 6–10, XXV, no. 4 (January 1933), 11–14 (quotations on 11–12); Society in Scotland for Propagating Christian Knowledge (SSPCK), Minutes, Apr. 15, 1783, GD95/2/9, NRS; Linford D. Fisher, *The Indian Great Awakening: Religion and the Shaping of Native Cultures in Early America* (New York, 2012), 250 n. 129; Colin G. Calloway, *The Indian History of an American Institution: Native Americans and Dartmouth* (Hanover, N.H., 2010), 49.

with traditions of partnership between religious projects and governments, she reached out to those in prominent places who could advance her plan: George Washington (to whom she believed herself related) and the governors of several states. With the help of Sir James Jay, John Jay's brother, she composed a letter to "the Friends of Religion and Humanity, in America," laying out her plan to purchase a large tract of land, "in one or more of the united States," "among the Indians, or very near to them, and so situated, in regard to the bulk of the more distant Indian Nations," where she would settle "Protestants of all denominations" as well as clergy so that the place could be both a site of missionary work and one where Indigneous people would gradually learn from the dutiful and religious protestants, who would "be constant Examples to them." She wrote to the governors of North Carolina, Virginia, Pennsylvania, and New York in hopes of receiving a tract of land. She played on their patriotism, saying that she "rejoice[d] in thinking that the late Revolution opens a way to this great work": the "Conversion and Civilization" of Indigenous people in order to make "them good Christians and useful Citizens." For her part, she wanted to return to the partnerships of the colonial era, and although she acknowledged the political shift, she still contemplated a scheme that could have been started at nearly any point in the eighteenth century.[49]

Initially, American leaders were receptive, but not for long. Washington attempted to further the plan with Richard Henry Lee in Congress, to whom Patrick Henry, as governor of Virginia, had also forwarded word. Lee explained to Washington, however, that the project was impossible. He referred to "those religious people whom her Ladyship had in prospect to transplant and fix on our frontier" as "remarkable in the late war for an unanimous and bitter enmity to the American cause." Lee did not spell out exactly what he meant by "those religious people," but probably he meant Wesleyans, who had a reputation for loyalism that followed from their leader's outspoken support for Britain's position. Lee worried that such people "might form a dangerous settlement at so great a distance, contiguous to the Indians, and easily accessible to Canada." It might be a threat to the United States, he suggested, "especially in the present very unfriendly temper of mind that we now suppose the British nation possesses with respect to us." The countess, with her talk of "Protestants of all denominations," had attempted to resurrect, in a new national context, the projects of a

49. "V: Lady Huntingdon's Plan for Settlement, 8 April 1784," "VI: Lady Huntingdon's Circular Letter to the Governors of North Carolina, Virginia, Pennsylvania, and New York, c. 8 April 1784," both in *Founders Online*. See also Boyd Stanley Schlenther, "'To Convert the Poor People in America': The Bethesda Orphanage and the Thwarted Zeal of the Countess of Huntingdon," *Georgia Historical Quarterly*, LXXVIII (1994), 245–246.

previous generation. But Americans were wary of a return to older connections, and they declined to participate. Eventually, Hastings turned her efforts, as the NEC had done, to the Canadian Maritime province of New Brunswick. The countess's Georgia project also fell on hard times. The state passed a special law to allow her to continue to maintain her trust, but it was deemed for her life only, and it was confiscated when she died in 1791.[50]

The disentanglement of transatlantic charity efforts, coupled with the thwarting of any new ones, ensured that Americans and Britons, going forward, would imagine religious work within the boundaries of their particular nations. These limitations certainly did not preclude cooperation. Indeed, when new missionary efforts—particularly those spearheaded by awakened denominations—started, their proponents reached out across the Atlantic to find partners. But these were now international cooperations, consciously connecting separate nations. The far more complicated and intimate ties of the imperial era were gone.

A NEW MISSIONARY ERA

When new transatlantic protestant connections developed in the postwar era, they reflected, first and foremost, the vibrancy of the awakened movement in the new denominational order. Americans, overwhelmed with the tasks of starting new movements and building domestic institutions, were not the first movers, however. The new missionary movement, spearheaded first by baptists, started in England. An explicitly denominational project free of the old imperial protestant scaffold, the effort built on a profoundly different understanding of empire than its predecessors a century earlier had used. The alphabet soup of societies that had promoted imperial protestantism had worked within the premise that Catholic empires were the greatest threat to the survival of protestantism, that "protestant" rather than a particular denomination was the best way of understanding true Christianity, and that missions were most usefully sent to the Indigenous and enslaved peoples that had been brought within Britain's protestant empire. The new era of British missionary societies, in contrast, was confident of its global reach and unfettered by the pressures of competition with Catholic empires.

50. Richard Henry Lee to George Washington, Feb. 27, 1785, and "V: Huntingdon's Plan for Settlement," both in *Founders Online*. Patrick Henry supported the effort, but without effect. See Thomas Kidd, *Patrick Henry: First among Patriots* (New York, 2011), 173–174. For the outcome of the Bethesda project, see Edwin Welch, *Spiritual Pilgrim: A Reassessment of the Life of the Countess of Huntingdon* (Cardiff, U.K., 1995), 168–175. See also Kidd, "Jefferson, Madison, Henry, and the Context for Religious Liberty in Revolutionary America," in Allen D. Hertzke, ed., *Religious Freedom in America: Constitutional Roots and Contemporary Challenges* (Norman, Okla., 2015), 42–43.

The baptist missionary movement of the 1790s was built out of a new wave of revivals that began within British baptist circles. Like those unfolding at the same time in America, the postwar revivals had roots in the prewar awakening movement. Central to this history was the network nurtured by the awakened Scottish leader, John Erskine. He had maintained a correspondence with several Americans, and he had been instrumental in helping Jonathan Edwards, Jr., publish and distribute his father's works in Britain. In 1784, Erskine sent a copy of the senior Edwards's *Humble Attempt to Promote Explicit Agreement and Visible Union of God's People* to John Ryland, Jr., a baptist minister in Northampton, England. That 1747 work, which had called for a transatlantic and interdenominational Concert of Prayer, led Ryland to begin organizing for prayer and renewal in the baptist Northamptonshire Association. The desire to build a more activist faith—one in which humans actively engaged in evangelizing even those who might not ultimately be saved—also came from other quarters at the same time. In 1781, baptist Robert Hall promoted such a vision in his sermon, *Help to Zion's Travellers,* and in 1785 Andrew Fuller, yet another baptist minister influenced by Jonathan Edwards, published a work entitled *The Gospel of Christ Worthy of All Acceptation,* making a similar case. These revivals built in energy across the 1780s, matching, though quite organizationally separate from, the rise of new baptist movements in the United States at the same time.[51]

Though the baptist revivals began within well-established protestant institutions, with the founding of the Particular Baptist Society for the Propagation of the Gospel amongst the Heathen (known as the Baptist Missionary Society, or BMS, for short) its leaders turned their energies to an innovative project that differed significantly from the missionary efforts of the past. A prime mover in the society, William Carey, was a young baptist minister whose interest in the wider world had been piqued by reading the travels of Captain James Cook. In 1792, Carey published *An Enquiry into the Obligations of Christians to Use Means*

51. Brian Stanley, *The History of the Baptist Missionary Society, 1792–1992* (Edinburgh, 1992), 4–6; John Erskine to John Ryland, July 15, 1783, John Erskine Papers, Edinburgh University Library. For Hall's and Fuller's contributions, see Robert Hall, *Help to Zion's Travellers: Being an Attempt to Remove Various Stumbling Blocks out of the Way, Relating to Doctrinal, Experimental, and Practical Religion* (Bristol, U.K., [1781]); and Andrew Fuller, *The Gospel of Christ Worthy of All Acceptation; or, The Obligations of Men Fully to Credit, and Cordially to Approve, Whatever God Makes Known; Wherein Is Considered the Nature of Faith in Christ, and the Duty of Those Where the Gospel Comes in That Matter* (Northampton, U.K., [1785?]). For a wider perspective on these revivals within the communities of dissent, see Richard Carwardine, *Transatlantic Revivalism: Popular Evangelicalism in Britain and America, 1790–1865* (Westport, Conn., 1978), 60–62. See also Noll, *The Rise of Evangelicalism,* 207; A. C. Underwood, *A History of the English Baptists* (London, 1947), 160–161. For historical context on debates among baptists, see Geoffrey F. Nuttall, "Northamptonshire and *The Modern Question:* A Turning Point in Eighteenth-Century Dissent," *Journal of Theological Studies,* n.s. XVI (1965), 101–123.

for the Conversion of the Heathens. The text laid out the case for embarking on missionary work, arguing that such work had languished miserably and most of the world was in dire need of conversion. His portrait of protestant mission history differed significantly from what would have been envisioned by his colonial-era dissenting predecessors—an identity he did not claim explicitly, in any case. The modern heroes of his tale were the previously ostracized Moravians, whom Carey believed had taken up the mantle of missionary work once held by men such as John Eliot and David Brainerd. Just as striking as his willingness to praise the once-controversial Moravians was the near complete absence of imperial political context in Carey's call to arms. The word *protestant* did not appear anywhere in the main text, suggesting he did not imagine that the mere fact of Catholics in the world was a strong motivation for missionary work, quite a shift from the prewar years. In addition, no particular distinction was made in Carey's global religious demography between those areas where British imperial reach was strong and those areas where it was nonexistent. Though Catholics, whom Carey called papists, clearly did not possess the faith Carey wished to inspire, the confessional competition between empires did not drive the narrative, as it had for groups like the SPG and the Society for Promoting Christian Knowledge decades before.[52]

Having shed some of the explicit imperial context for structuring missionary work, Carey also shed the language of protestant denominational cooperation that had characterized earlier mission groups. Although he did not intend, he wrote, "in any wise to confine [his call to missionary action] to one denomination of Christians," he proposed that the new society come from the Particular Baptists alone. Should other bodies of protestants wish to labor alongside them, "there is room enough for us all, without interfering with each other." They could all engage in "the great cause of true religion," while knowing that "if all were intermingled, it is likely their private discords might throw a damp upon their spirits, and much retard their public usefulness." Carey's vision paralleled that of his eighteenth-century predecessors in that it sought the spread of protestant Christianity, but the geopolitical context that shaped his goals was new. Though British imperial power clearly influenced the parameters of nineteenth-century missionary work, the tight connection between the imperial expansion, confessional competition, and work of protestant missionaries

52. Stanley, *History of the Baptist Missionary Society*, 6–12; William Carey, *An Enquiry into the Obligations of Christians to Use Means for the Conversion of the Heathens . . .* (Leicester, U.K., 1792); Andrew Porter, "Church History, History of Christianity, Religious History: Some Reflections on British Missionary Enterprise Since the Late Eighteenth Century," *Church History*, LXXI (2002), 555–584, esp. 563.

shifted considerably. Gone was the intense focus on North America and the concern for the threat of papist empire. Notably, this new wave of missionaries had—as Carey outlined—a global vision that included regions, like Tahiti, that were not always directly under British control. Carey's work offered a fairly explicit indictment of Britain's past protestant establishment and its failure to adequately spread the gospel. Within a few years, Carey's Baptist Missionary Society would be joined by a series of others led by British Congregationalists, Methodists, and Anglicans. American groups would eventually join the movement, but they acted through their own separate organizations, institutionally distinct from the British groups.[53]

British missionary work embraced a new imperial era, and awakened denominations built new transatlantic ties that largely supplanted the personal connections that had existed among awakened protestants during the colonial era. The energy, particularly among baptists, stood in stark contrast to the lapsed dissenting network and the increasing divisions between American Episcopalians and British Anglicans in the postwar period. Among the baptists, the *Baptist Annual Register,* a publication that began appearing in 1793 from London's John Rippon, played a significant role in building transatlantic ties. It published reports and vital statistics from baptist churches around the globe, and, like Carey had done, it envisioned a global baptist community. The first issue included a brief verse on its cover, written by hymnist Thomas Gibbons:

From East to West, from North to South,
Now be his Name ador'd!
EUROPE, with all thy millions, shout
Hosannahs to thy Lord!
ASIA and AFRICA, resound
From shore to shore his Fame;
And thou, AMERICA, in songs,
Redeeming love proclaim!

53. Carey, *An Enquiry,* 84; Andrew Porter, *Religion versus Empire? British Protestant Missionaries and Overseas Expansion, 1700–1914* (Manchester, U.K., 2004), 45–46. For a similar argument in favor of denominational particularity and against the traditions of protestant cooperation of an earlier era, see Benjamin Rush to Jonathan Armstrong, Mar. 19, 1783, in Butterfield, ed., *Letters of Benjamin Rush,* I, 294–297. There is a significant literature on the development of the American mission movement that began in the 1790s. See, for example, Emily Conroy-Krutz, *Christian Imperialism: Converting the World in the Early American Republic* (Ithaca, N.Y., 2015); Christine Leigh Heyrman, *American Apostles: When Evangelicals Entered the World of Islam* (New York, 2015); Porter, *Religion versus Empire?* 39–63; and Elizabeth Elbourne, *Blood Ground: Colonialism, Missions, and the Contest for Christianity in the Cape Colony and Britain, 1799–1853* (Montreal, 2002). For transatlantic Methodism in the postwar period, see Jones, "Methodism, Slavery, and Freedom in the Revolutionary Atlantic"; Hempton, *Methodism,* 151–177.

Global visions here replaced the protestant perspective of the imperial era. Baptists were ready to convert the world.[54]

A slightly more practicable estimation of the *Baptist Annual Register*'s reach came at the bottom of the title page, which listed the ways a reader might procure the volume, including booksellers in London, Edinburgh, and through a list of eight baptist ministers in North America, stretching from Boston to Savannah. The volume was dedicated to "all the baptized ministers and people in America England Ireland Scotland, Wales, the United Netherlands France Switzerland Poland Russia Prussia and Elsewhere." It was a project designed to unite, as Rippon put it, "good men"—that is, awakened, Calvinist, and generally Particular Baptist men—across the protestant world.[55]

Rippon explicitly sought to create a transnational *baptist* community, largely leaving behind both the "protestant" and "dissenting" communities that had characterized similar efforts of the previous era. He left open the possibility that fellow travelers beyond the denomination—presumably those who embraced the same message of awakening that the Particular Baptists did—might be included, but unity across denominations was no longer a primary purpose. Instead, through the publication, he emphased denomination and hoped to address the failure of baptists to tell their own stories and to develop the kind of organizations that groups like the Moravians and "the followers of the late Mr. Wesley" had. In Rippon's view, the baptists within England were insufficiently connected and organized, and they were "less, much less acquainted with the condition of our Brethren abroad." Though "formerly, several of our senior Ministers in *England* were in the habit of correspondence with the *American* churches," some of those men had died, "and the unhappy war with the Colonies, shut up almost every friendly intercourse between us." Rippon was happy to report, however, that since "peace was restored, it was thought by several persons an object of considerable importance, to open a new correspondence with the western world." Happily, they had met with an eager response from the United States, and the resulting information about the state of the baptist denomination was thus published.[56]

54. *BAR*, title page. Rippon had first advertised for the *Register* in 1790, and there is an extant, twelve-page section for a 1790 register. See John Rippon, *The Baptist Annual Register for 1790, Part the First; Including Sketches of the State of Religion among Different Denominations of Good Men at Home and Abroad* (London, 1791). This earlier *Register* also includes the opening epigraph.

55. *BAR*, dedication, [i] (Preface).

56. Ibid., iii, iv. Rippon's list of important publications (118–127), including works by both John Erskine and Jonathan Edwards, his effusive praise for the recently deceased awakened Anglican leader John Thornton (130), and an obituary for Joseph Bellamy (143–150), also highlighted the awakened context for the baptist resurgence. See also Ken R. Manley, *"Redeeming Love Proclaim": John Rippon and the Baptists* (Carlisle, U.K., 2004), 139–195.

The most strikingly new aspect of the *Baptist Annual Register* was its inclusion of African American voices and its embrace of antislavery politics. It was a departure from the era when protestant ministers focused primarily on inoffensively preaching to the enslaved without irritating those who maintained the slave system. Rippon included in the *Register* a lengthy report about the work of George Liele, a man "so highly favoured of God, as to plant the first Baptist Church in Savannah, and another in Jamaica." The description of Liele reached Rippon by way of Joseph Cook, a minister in South Carolina who had originally traveled to America with the countess of Huntingdon's Georgia group. Both Cook and Rippon treated Liele as a full member of the clergy, and in the *Register* Liele's own words were designated with quotations. A few pages later, the *Register* printed an account of the new Particular Baptist Society, but it amended the short history that Carey had used in his *Enquiry* to include the "Labours of brother *George Liele,* the Baptist negro in *Jamaica.*" Similarly, the *Register* printed "An Account of the Life of Mr. David George, from Sierra Leone in Africa," a text that attested to the barbarity of slavery but also highlighted the clerical labors of its author. Subsequent issues of the *Register* referred to George as the "Negro Minister." The baptist movement crystalized by Rippon possessed a notably biracial community of both congregants and clergy, a shift that paralleled the wider move to new forms of religious leadership in other sectors.[57]

The movement that began among English baptists spread widely, and within the next decade a new series of similar societies and projects also launched. Awakened protestants across a variety of other denominations founded their own organizations, often in conversation with the baptists who had begun the work first. These included the London Missionary Society in 1795, which was largely congregationalist, and the Anglican-based Church Missionary Society in 1799. These groups focused their energies on Britain's expanding presence in places like India and Africa; America was no longer a target of their missionary fervor. New energy also flowed into other forms of benevolent work, including tract societies. London's Religious Tract Society, founded in 1799, and the British and Foreign Bible Society, founded in 1804, provided new channels for religious labor. Although their American counterparts, such as the Philadel-

57. For Liele, see *BAR*, 332–344 ("highly favoured" on 332), 373 ("Labours"). See also Carretta, *Unchained Voices*, 325–332. For George, see *BAR*, 473–484 ("Account" on 473); and John Rippon, *The Baptist Annual Register, for 1784, 1795, 1796-1797, Including Sketches of the State of Religion among Different Denominations of Good Men at Home and Abroad* [London, 1797?], 94. George's writings are printed in Carretta, *Unchained Voices*, 333–350 ("Negro Minister" on 342). See also accounts of Black churches in *BAR*, 540–545, 561. For Cook, see, for example, Joseph Cook to Selina Hastings, Feb. 28, 1778, A3/1/25, 26, CCA; and Cook to Hastings, Mar. 24, 1785, ibid., A3/12/17. A biography of Cook appeared in *BAR*, 501–509.

phia Bible Society (founded in 1808) looked to British models, they remained institutionally distinct.

Whereas the differences between the old and the new missionary societies were largely in focus and organization, a final effort undertaken in these years points to an even greater scale of change. British religious and political actors from many quarters—from the Anglican Granville Sharp, to a range of awakened Anglicans, to bishop Beilby Porteus, and even to unexpected new Quaker partners—joined forces in a movement to abolish the international slave trade. In that movement they followed the leadership of African-descended abolitionists, such as Phillis Wheatley, Ukawsaw Gronniosaw, and Olaudah Equiano, who used their protestantism and their pens to decry the hypocrisy of slavery. The abolitionist movement, as it grew, created new kinds of links among British protestant groups in service of its political goals. In 1789, for example, Sharp wrote to the Western Baptist Association on behalf of the Society for the Abolition of the Slave Trade, thanking them for a subscription and for their "approbation of the endeavours of this committee, and their so hearty concurrence with us in the purposes of our institution." The letter was printed in Rippon's *Baptist Annual Register* a few years later. A movement aimed directly at bringing about political change through the lobbying of Parliament, abolitionism could never have been undertaken by religious leaders within the old imperial protestant scaffold.[58]

The missionary projects and transatlantic connections that emanated from English baptist circles, and those that joined them, bore little resemblance to those undertaken by the missionaries who worked within the imperial protestant scaffold. Through these new organizations, and through their Wesleyan counterparts, awakened protestants now controlled their own denominations and institutions. They built their own transatlantic connections and envisioned their own global missionary projects. They built upon and worked with the changing British Empire, to be sure, but as the new generation of religious

58. *Society Instituted in 1787, for the Purpose of Effecting the Abolition of the Slave Trade* [London, 1787]; *BAR*, 60 ("our institution"); John Fea, *The Bible Cause: A History of the American Bible Society* (New York, 2016), 10–12; Hilary M. Carey, *God's Empire: Religion and Colonialism in the British World, c. 1801–1908* (Cambridge, 2011), 75–38; Porter, *Religion versus Empire?* 39–63; Noll, *The Rise of Evangelicalism*, 231–232. For the catalytic activities of Africans in the abolition movement, see James Albert Ukawsaw Gronniosaw, "A Narrative of the Most Remarkable Particulars in the Life of James Albert Ukawsaw Gronniosaw, an African Prince . . . ," in Carretta, ed., *Unchained Voices*, 39, 45–47; Vincent Carretta, *Equiano the African: Biography of a Self-made Man* (Athens, Ga., 2005), 169–200; David Waldstreicher, "The Wheatleyan Moment," *Early American Studies*, IX (2011), 522–551; and Srividhya Swaminathan, *Debating the Slave Trade: Rhetoric of British National Identity, 1759–1815* (Farnham, U.K., 2009), 114–117. For the abolition movement, more generally, see Christopher Leslie Brown, *Moral Capital: Foundations of British Abolitionism* (Williamsburg, Va., and Chapel Hill, N.C., 2006). See also Moniz, *From Empire to Humanity*.

leaders looked toward the nineteenth century, they were no longer preoccupied with the concerns of the confessional age and the close partnership between imperial aims and protestant institutions that it had produced. Their principal tasks were no longer converting the empire's American souls and fending off the Catholic imperial threat. Their ability to look forward to a new age was made possible by the ruptures and transformations bought about by the American Revolution.

The new denominational order that developed after the American Revolution was far more varied than its predecessor. Rather than a few dominant denominations prevailing in the empire's distant reaches, the territories formerly under British control supported an ever-multiplying number of protestant institutions, all vying for legitimacy, often outside the boundaries of older systems of establishment. Within that order, the energy of the awakened groups—which had been channeled back into the dominant denominations in the colonial period—moved in its own institutional and organizational directions.

The growth of awakened protestant denominations, and the missionary work they and their successors undertook in the nineteenth and twentieth centuries, transformed protestantism globally. But the scale of expansion within awakened protestant circles in the 1780s and 1790s should not overshadow the pivotal importance of the American Revolution to the timing of these transformations. In the wake of the war, protestants cleared away the detritus of imperial protestantism's scaffold. They dismembered the Church of England as the Anglo-American world's largest protestant institution. They cut longstanding philanthropic ties, and they broke with tradition to move outside long-dominant denominations. They ignored a previous generation's assumptions that tensions between protestant and Catholic empires ordered sacred history and thus demanded the extension of protestant institutions within the context of Britain's protestant empire. Leaving the old order behind was more complicated than a simple act of will, however. At the same time that protestants transformed the denominational order, their partners in governments also altered the connections between protestant institutions and the state. It is to that story, the last piece of the imperial history of religion and the American Revolution, that we now turn.

8
Transforming Religious Establishments

In 1798, then president John Adams wrote, "Our Constitution was made only for a moral and religious People. It is wholly inadequate to the government of any other." His comments conjure for many the belief that the country's framers presumed a strong protestant culture would undergird the nation they built. His successor, Thomas Jefferson, wrote to the baptists in Danbury, Connecticut, in 1802 that he "contemplate[d] with sovereign reverence that act of the whole American people which declared that their legislature should 'make no law respecting an establishment of religion, or prohibiting the free exercise thereof,' thus building a wall of separation between Church and State."[1] For centuries, Americans have debated statements like these, politicizing the realignment between church and state after the American Revolution to suit particular aims. Historians have also offered competing narratives. For some, the withdrawal of state support for particular churches in the United States, known as *disestablishment,* had profound consequences for American religion because it created a marketplace of denominations, an environment in which all religious groups competed equally. Others dispute that any truly consequential disestablishment happened in the early Republic, arguing that the new nation's influential protestant majority dominated both church and state for decades, even centuries, to come. Still others depict a rising acceptance of religious diversity as part of an increasingly secular public sphere, minimizing the mechanics of disestablishment in favor of longue durée trends. The contemporary political stakes of these discussions are high as Americans continue to struggle over issues of church and state, and the temptation to reduce a complicated history into a simple verdict has always been strong.[2]

1. Quotations from John Adams to Massachusetts Militia, Oct. 11, 1798, *Founders Online,* National Archives, https://founders.archives.gov. Thomas Jefferson's letter to the Danbury baptists can be found at https://www.loc.gov/loc/lcib/9806/danpre.html. For discussion of the letter, see John Fea, *Was America Founded as a Christian Nation? A Historical Introduction* (Louisville, Ky., 2011), 163–167; Johann N. Neem, "Beyond the Wall: Reinterpreting Jefferson's Danbury Address," *Journal of the Early Republic,* XXVII (2007), 139–154; and James H. Hutson, Thomas E. Buckley, and Robert M. O'Neil, "Forum: Thomas Jefferson's Letter to the Danbury Baptists: A Controversy Rejoined," *William and Mary Quarterly,* 3d Ser., LVI (1999), 775–800.

2. The end of state support for institutional protestantism, particularly in the South and in the

The political investments in discussions about American disestablishment are so significant that they can easily overshadow the historical events, disconnecting them from the transatlantic revolutionary context in which they happened. Such discussions neglect, above all, the historically specific nature of what was being "disestablished." Configured as the end point to the American Revolution rather than the start of a new era, this period of disruption in the relationship between governments and protestant institutions comes into view as a wider, Anglo-American process made up of three distinct components. Each was a separate aftereffect of the war that Britons and Americans had fought against one another. Each resulted from the loss of the protestant scaffold that had joined the empire before the war. First, at the state level in the United States, Americans had to adjust to being outside Britain's mixed establishment. For the

---

newer western states, has been seen as the turning point in the development of an "American" religion, particularly exemplified by awakened protestantism. See, for example, Christine Leigh Heyrman, *Southern Cross: The Beginnings of the Bible Belt* (New York, 1997), 22; and Nathan O. Hatch, *The Democratization of American Christianity* (New Haven, Conn., 1989), 59–60. For a parallel story in northern New England, see Shelby M. Balik, *Rally the Scattered Believers: Northern New England's Spiritual Geography* (Bloomington, Ind., 2014); and Mark A. Noll, *America's God: From Jonathan Edwards to Abraham Lincoln* (New York, 2002), 174–175. Works emphasizing older regions of New England, where state establishments persisted well into the early Republic, trace a longer period of continuities. See Jonathan D. Sassi, *A Republic of Righteousness: The Public Christianity of the Post-Revolutionary New England Clergy* (New York, 2001), 11. More recently, scholars have seen the moment as one of anxiety. See Christopher Grasso, *Skepticism and American Faith: From the Revolution to the Civil War* (New York, 2018), 31–32; and Amanda Porterfield, *Conceived in Doubt: Religion and Politics in the New American Nation* (Chicago, 2012), 7–10. For an informal, or moral, establishment of protestantism in the United States that was enduringly powerful, see David Sehat, *The Myth of American Religious Freedom* (New York, 2011); and Daniel Walker Howe, *What Hath God Wrought: The Transformation of America, 1815–1848* (New York, 2007), esp. 164–166. This protestant establishment, according to scholars of religious studies, configured itself as a "secular" state. See Tisa Wenger, *Religious Freedom: The Contested History of an American Ideal* (Chapel Hill, N.C., 2017); Tracy Fessenden, *Culture and Redemption: Religion, the Secular, and American Literature* (Princeton, N.J., 2007), esp. 60–64; Kathleen Flake, *The Politics of American Religious Identity: The Seating of Senator Reed Smoot, Mormon Apostle* (Chapel Hill, N.C., 2004). For works that emphasize a long-term trend toward freedom of religion (or decreasing religious influence), see, for example, Nicholas P. Miller, *The Religious Roots of the First Amendment: Dissenting Protestants and the Separation of Church and State* (New York, 2012); Christopher S. Grenda, "Faith, Reason, and Enlightenment: The Cultural Sources of Toleration in Early America," in Chris Beneke and Grenda, eds., *The First Prejudice: Religious Tolerance and Intolerance in Early America* (Philadelphia, 2011), 23–52; and Christopher Grasso, *A Speaking Aristocracy: Transforming Public Discourse in Eighteenth-Century Connecticut* (Williamsburg, Va., and Chapel Hill, N.C., 1999). Disestablishment is indirectly implicated by Charles Taylor in *A Secular Age* (Cambridge, Mass., 2007), 196–198, as part of creating a sovereign people. See also Michael Warner, *The Letters of the Republic: Publication and the Public Sphere in Eighteenth-Century America* (Cambridge, Mass., 1990). The narrative that American religious pluralism, exacerbated by the Great Awakening, led to disestablishment is also important in this context, though scholars working in this vein have contributed much to the discussion of disestablishment's historical context. See, for example, Chris Beneke, *Beyond Toleration: The Religious Origins of American Pluralism* (New York, 2006); and Frank Lambert, *The Founding Fathers and the Place of Religion in America* (Princeton, N.J., 2003).

most part, they chose to leave its remnants behind, separating protestant institutions from government support and jurisdiction. Second, across the Atlantic, Britons watched events in America. They were shaken by the loss of the colonies, and their religio-political dynamics entered a period of transition, without the counterbalance long provided by the colonies. By the 1790s, however, Britons—concerned over the turn of events in France—responded by retrenching. They affirmed their commitment to a renewed imperial protestantism, even, finally, placing a bishop in the remaining American colonies. But the greatest changes of all came at the national, American level. The framers and leaders of the new United States government refused to codify or formalize any national public religion of the sort that had been employed by both their British and Revolutionary predecessors. Their decisions turned American national religion into a field of contest between those who championed an informal national religion, on the one hand, and a legal apparatus that worked to the opposite effect, on the other. As Anglo-Americans worked through the war's final reverberations for transatlantic protestantism, they solidified the changes wrought by the conflict. Their choices determined that it was not merely a bump in the road; it was a transformative event for both nations' religious communities.

SEPARATING STATE GOVERNMENTS AND RELIGION

The first governments to rework the connections between themselves and protestant institutions were the rebelling American states. Within Britain's mixed establishment, each colony had maintained a distinctive set of arrangements regarding the relationship between government and institutional protestantism. For this reason, the shifts that occurred at this level in the wake of the imperial rupture are particularly interesting, not because they were a precursor to later events on the national scene, but because they most directly reflected Americans' efforts to grapple with the remnants of the now-defunct imperial system. Because these states began to adjust their relationships to protestant institutions well before the war ended, tracing that process requires a brief excursus back to the war's early years. Immediately after the imperial rupture, several states tried to instantiate some version of a collective religious polity to maintain governmental control over the scope of legitimate protestant institutions. As the war came to a close, however, these efforts increasingly faltered. In most places, they eroded and disappeared. In states where they remained, the trend was toward more local control. Religious leaders entered these new waters cautiously, unsure whether they should support more religious freedom or seek to retain the connections to government that had validated and elevated their work during the colonial period. By the end of the 1780s, a different version of "religion" began to appear in law, freer of state control and less tied to protestant institutions and behavior. Religion, in this form, was no longer a potential threat to state stability and could be made the basis of far wider "religious freedom." This new freedom—enshrined in the 1786 Virginia Statute for Religious Freedom—marked a new phase in American religious history.[3]

The easiest step for states to take when the war broke out was to cease paying for colonial-era establishments, particularly where those establishments had been Anglican. In those areas, the movement against establishment came swiftly in the first months after the war started, and it was seen as part of rejecting Britain's authority. The Church of England's financial support evaporated even in advance of constitutional changes. Virginia suspended its religious establishment in 1776 by ceasing to pay for it. Maryland, North Carolina, and South Carolina also ended public funding for their former Anglican establishments. Georgia, too, undermined its former establishment by eliminating compulsory payments to the Church of England. In New York, where the nature of the local establishment was a matter of significant contention, the Revolutionary government wrote a constitution that "abrogated and rejected" any laws then on the books that "may be construed to establish or maintain any particular denomination of Christians or their ministers." Whatever connections would survive between protestant institutions and the states, it would be difficult for the empire's largest church to regain its former status.[4]

As Anglican establishments fell away, new questions arose. Under Britain's imperial protestant regime, colonies had been implicitly protestant because of their ties to the empire. Now some considered making those ties explicit.

3. For the process of disestablishment and the varied experiences of the states, see Carl H. Esbeck and Jonathan J. Den Hartog, eds., *Disestablishment and Religious Dissent: Church-State Relations in the New American States, 1776–1833* (Columbia, Mo., 2019); and Thomas J. Curry, *The First Freedoms: Church and State in America to the Passage of the First Amendment* (New York, 1986). See also Sarah Barringer Gordon, "The Landscape of Faith: Religious Property and Confiscation in the Early Republic," in Daniel J. Hulsebosch and R. B. Bernstein, eds., *Making Legal History: Essays in Honor of William E. Nelson* (New York, 2013), 13–48; and Gordon, "The First Disestablishment: Limits on Church Power and Property before the Civil War," *University of Pennsylvania Law Review,* CLXII (2014), 307–372. Esbeck and Den Hartog contest the idea that any one state was more influential than any other (*Disestablishment and Religious Dissent,* 10).

4. "Constitution of New York—1777," in Francis Newton Thorpe, ed., *The Federal and State Constitutions, Colonial Charters, and Other Organic Laws of the States, Territories, and Colonies Now or Heretofore Forming the United States of America,* 7 vols. (Washington, D.C., 1909), V, 2636 (quotations); Edwin S. Gaustad, "Colonial Religion and Liberty of Conscience," in Merrill D. Peterson and Robert C. Vaughan, eds., *The Virginia Statute for Religious Freedom: Its Evolution and Consequences in American History* (Cambridge, 1988), 23–42; Thomas E. Buckley, *Church and State in Revolutionary Virginia, 1776–1787* (Charlottesville, Va., 1977), 36; Nancy L. Rhoden, *Revolutionary Anglicanism: The Colonial Church of England Clergy during the American Revolution* (New York, 1999), 117–118.

State leaders took up the issue of their governmental religious arrangements with care when they rewrote their constitutions. Several states altered their religious arrangements and yet preserved some measure of protestant—or Christian—identification for the polity as a whole, however vague. Maryland's 1776 Constitution created provisions through which taxes might be raised "for the support of the Christian religion" and required an oath stating the "belief in the Christian religion" for officeholders. In South Carolina, legislators declared that the "Christian Protestant religion shall be deemed, and is hereby constituted and declared to be, the established religion of this State." A list of five specific theological points, reminiscent of England's Thirty-Nine Articles, defined legitimate protestantism more precisely. Moreover, any religious body meeting South Carolina's criteria could incorporate, one of the crucial rights non-established denominations coveted from state authorities. In 1779, Virginia's legislators, who struggled for years to define a new religious settlement, entertained, then rejected, a bill for an establishment of the "Christian Religion" that followed South Carolina's religious articles closely. A 1779 petition from Lunenburg, Virginia, said that "the Christian religion, free from the errors of popery, and a general contribution to the support thereof, ought to be established from the principle of public utility" and requested that "the reformed Protestant religion, including the different denominations thereof," receive such privilege. Massachusetts's Constitution of 1778, which was rejected by the state's towns in part because of disagreements over religious establishment, provided for "free exercise and enjoyment of Religious profession and worship" but limited it to "every denomination of protestants." These complicated efforts point to the difficult reality state lawmakers faced. Without Britain's mixed establishment defining the boundaries of legitimate religion, they had to enact such limits locally. General agreement that protestantism mattered in some way—the kind of sentiment behind South Carolina's assertion that the "Christian Protestant religion" was "established" there—did little to define precisely which institutions should get privilege. Few of these early attempts survived the Revolutionary era.[5]

5. For Maryland, see "Constitution of Maryland—1776," in Thorpe, eds., *Federal and State Constitutions,* III, 1689, 1690. For South Carolina's Revolutionary revisions, see "Constitution of South Carolina—1778," ibid., VI, 3255; and James Lowell Underwood, "The Dawn of Religious Freedom in South Carolina: The Journey from Limited Toleration to Constitutional Right," in Underwood and W. Lewis Burke, eds., *The Dawn of Religious Freedom in South Carolina* (Columbia, S.C., 2006), 1–57. For Virginia, see Charles F. James, *Documentary History of the Struggle for Religious Liberty in Virginia* (Lynchburg, Va., 1900), 94; Thomas E. Buckley, *Establishing Religious Freedom: Jefferson's Statute in Virginia* (Charlottesville, Va., 2013), 57–58; John Ragosta, *Religious Freedom: Jefferson's Legacy, America's Creed* (Charlottesville, Va., 2013), 58–73; and Buckley, *Church and State in Revolutionary Virginia,* 56–59, 185–187. For Massachusetts, see "The Constitution of 1778,"

Massachusetts was more successful in its second attempt to create a religious establishment that could work outside the protestant scaffold. After its failed 1778 effort, it adopted a new constitution in 1780 that affirmed a strong connection between the state and its protestant institutions. Its second article declared that it was the "right as well as the duty of all men in society, publicly, and at stated seasons, to worship the SUPREME BEING" but that no one should be "molested" for doing so in their own way, provided they did not "disturb the public peace." Its third article then made a much stronger statement directly justifying public support of religious institutions: "The happiness of a people, and the good order and preservation of civil government essentially depend upon piety, religion and morality; and as these cannot be generally diffused through a community, but by the institution of the public worship of GOD, and of the public instructions in piety, religion, and morality. . . ." On this basis, the Massachusetts government justified public funding for clergy, essentially perpetuating, with slight alterations, its colonial system until 1833. The 1780 Massachusetts Constitution did not pass without controversy; baptists, in particular, led by Isaac Backus, objected to the requirement that everyone be assessed for ministers. But the constitution became law, and in the early Republic Massachusetts (along with neighboring Connecticut) retained strong connections between government and protestant institutions. Already in 1780, these states stood out for their ability to roughly reconstruct a form of protestant establishment in the United States.[6]

In most states, however, the shifts in religious arrangements that occurred as the war progressed happened in an intellectual environment that progressively embraced religious freedom on a broader scale and rejected state involvement in protestant institutions. By 1777, the mid-Atlantic states as well as Maryland, North Carolina, and Georgia had all adopted constitutions that contained clauses formally disestablishing religion or asserting that the state could not give any single denomination preferential treatment. Historians have offered a variety of explanations for the attitudinal shifts that made these transitions pos-

---

in Robert J. Taylor, ed., *Massachusetts, Colony to Commonwealth: Documents on the Formation of Its Constitution, 1775–1780* (Williamsburg, Va., and Chapel Hill, N.C., 1961), 58. Documents outlining the 1778 constitution's rejection appear on 59–89. See also John Witte, Jr., "'A Most Mild and Equitable Establishment of Religion': John Adams and the Massachusetts Experiment," *Journal of Church and State*, XLI (1999), 213–252, esp. 220–221; and Charles H. Lippy, "The 1780 Massachusetts Constitution: Religious Establishment or Civil Religion?" ibid., XX (1978), 535–536.

6. "The Constitution of 1780," in Taylor, ed., *Massachusetts*, 128 (quotations). For Massachusetts's 1780 Constitution and religious issues, see John Witte, Jr., and Justin Latterell, "The Last American Establishment: Massachusetts, 1780–1833," in Esbeck and Den Hartog, eds., *Disestablishment and Religious Dissent*, 403–414; and William G. McLoughlin, *New England Dissent, 1630–1833; the Baptists and the Separation of Church and State* (Cambridge, Mass., 1971), I, 591–635.

sible and changed the world that protestant institutions inhabited, explanations that are collectively persuasive. This Revolutionary generation of Americans conceived of their new polities in ways that were not defined by their position in a divine order; they associated religious establishments (particularly Anglican ones) with British tyranny; they were more tolerant of religious diversity within their political communities; and they yielded to a combination of persuasive arguments made by religious dissenters and Enlightenment leaders. Wartime constitutional revisions made it possible to enact new systems that reflected new beliefs. Moreover, they happened at the same time as the national American government embraced the Catholic French, bringing to a close the confessional politics of the prior era. All of these changes influenced the crafting of new constitutions. They made the sorts of connections between protestant institutions and states that had been widespread in the colonial period seem less essential to grounding the new states.[7]

The elimination of privilege for established denominations began to morph into the creation of a new kind of religious freedom. As Americans became less interested in having their governments privilege or establish particular churches, states struggled with how to define precisely who should be eligible to inhabit the realm of legitimate religion. South Carolina's detailed article concerning religion in its 1778 Constitution is again instructive. It outlined with remarkable specificity the terms through which the state would identify a legitimate protestant group, eligible for participation in its protestant establishment. It stipulated that any fifteen men, over the age of twenty-one, who "profess[ed], the Christian Protestant religion" and "agree[d] to unite themselves in a society for the purposes of religious worship" could be considered part of its establishment. Even creating new names was attended to, as "every society of Christians so formed shall give themselves a name or denomination by which they shall be called and known in law, and all that associate with them for the purposes of worship shall be esteemed as belonging to the society so called." Though religious societies could elect their own clergy, "the State may have sufficient

7. For a summary of the various state constitutional measures, see David Sehat, "The American Moral Establishment: Religion and Liberalism in the Nineteenth Century" (Ph.D. diss., University of North Carolina at Chapel Hill, 2007), appendix, 266–286; as well as Esbeck and Den Hartog, eds., *Disestablishment and Religious Dissent*. For new definitions of an American political community that were not rooted in religion and were a part of the rise of the public sphere, see Grasso, *A Speaking Aristocracy;* Warner, *Letters of the Republic;* and Benedict Anderson, *Imagined Communities: Reflections on the Origin and Spread of Nationalism,* rev. ed. (London, 1991). For increasing religious toleration, see Beneke, *Beyond Toleration*. For competition among denominations, leavened with Enlightenment principles, see Buckley, *Church and State in Revolutionary Virginia;* and John Ragosta, *Wellspring of Liberty: How Virginia's Religious Dissenters Helped Win the American Revolution and Secured Religious Liberty* (New York, 2010).

security for the due discharge of the pastoral office, by those who shall be admitted to be clergymen." A required oath elaborated the terms. Furthermore, the document also noted that "no person whatsoever shall speak anything in their religious assembly irreverently or seditiously of the government of this State." South Carolinians were ready to imagine a religious establishment separate from the Church of England, even without any single privileged church. They were unwilling as yet, however, to give up oversight of religion completely, or to imagine religion in noninstitutional forms.[8]

South Carolina's 1778 document was particularly elaborate in its effort to regulate the religious marketplace for the security of the state. Other states relied more simply on the idea that religious freedom was limited to those who were peaceful. Loyalty to government had been the defining characteristic of legitimate protestantism within the British Empire, and the new states saw no reason to alter that expectation. Those worthy of religious recognition—and through it, legal protection—had to "demean" themselves "peaceably." It was an oft-repeated phrase. John Dickinson, in his 1776 draft of an article ensuring religious liberty at the national level had proposed extending it only to those "living peaceably under the Civil Government," but the language long predated the Revolutionary era. Charles II had used the phrase in his speech opening Parliament in February 1662/3, and it had appeared in contexts related to religious toleration across the eighteenth century. When the newly independent American state legislatures contemplated states without either a religious establishment or the guiding frame of Britain's mixed establishment, the idea that a religious body could be legitimate only when it was peaceful became more important. New Jersey's 1776 Constitution guaranteed religious freedom to all and permitted any protestant "who shall demean themselves peaceably under the government" the right to hold office. Maryland's 1776 Constitution varied the language but strengthened the terms, explicitly excluding from protection those who "under colour of religion . . . disturb the good order, peace or safety of the State" or "infringe the laws of morality, or injure others, in their natural, civil, or religious rights." The same language also appeared in South Carolina's 1778 Constitution and in Virginia's proposed 1779 "Bill concerning Religion." Most influentially, the phrase recurred in the Massachusetts Constitution of 1780, which, after laying out the terms of tax support for "public worship of GOD" and for "the support and maintenance of public protestant teachers of

8. "Contstitution of South Carolina—1778," in Thorpe, ed., *Federal and State Constitutions,* 3256–3257. See also Underwood, "The Dawn of Religious Freedom in South Carolina," in Underwood and Burke, eds., *The Dawn of Religious Freedom,* 26–35; and John Wesley Brinsfield, *Religion and Politics in Colonial South Carolina* (Easley, S.C., 1983), 105–128.

piety, religion and morality," guaranteed equal protection to "every denomination of christians demeaning themselves peaceably." In the colonial period, the coexistence of protestant groups in a mixed establishment, coupled with toleration of loyal protestants, had been designed to stabilize the support of contending denominations for the state. Now, as state leaders came to extend religious liberty, they presumed such freedoms were viable only insofar as they were confined within a framework that ensured the state's right to protect itself from unruly religion.[9]

Despite such statements asserting the state's right to regulate legitimate religion for its own benefit, the overall trend was for the new state governments to remove themselves from religious questions. Even the New England states, which had retained establishments, placed those establishments in local hands. New Hampshire's 1784 Constitution perpetuated its colonial tradition of allowing towns to provide for the "support and maintenance of public protestant teachers of piety, religion and morality," and it guaranteed no one would have to support a minister of a different denomination. The state thus set the terms for competition but ensured that it would be managed at the local level, rendering it unnecessary for the state to provide more concrete direction. The "right to worship" was protected for all, provided that it "doth not disturb the public peace, or disturb others, in their religious worship." Locally, congregationalists continued to exert control over most ministerial posts in New Hampshire, but by virtue of their majority, not because of a dictate from above. Baptists, and others, had to fight to have their rights not to pay ministerial taxes honored. Vermont similarly allowed for local variation, thus acknowledging in principle that the state viewed institutional religion as a public good and at the same time declining to decide what shape that would take. Because no one involved in these discussions could assume that a single denomination would ever include all protestants, the decision not to regulate the religious marketplace effectively

9. John Dickinson's draft article appears in Paul H. Smith et al., eds., *Letters of the Delegates to Congress, 1774–1789*, IV, *May 16–August 15, 1776* (Washington, D.C., 1979), 234–235 (quotation on 234). For Charles II, see *Journal of the House of Lords: Volume 11, 1660–1666* (London, 1767–1830), 478–479, *British History Online*, https://www.british-history.ac.uk/lords-jrnl/vol11/pp478-479. The phrase recurs with respect to British Jews both in the Restoration period and in the 1751 naturalization act. The phrase was in no way limited to religious contexts, but its recurrence in statutes related to religious liberty is nonetheless notable. For Virginia, see Buckley, *Church and State in Revolutionary Virginia*, 56, and, for the text of the proposed bill, 185–187. For New Jersey, see "Constitution of New Jersey—1776," in Thorpe, ed., *Federal and State Constitutions*, V, 2597. For Maryland, see "Constitution of Maryland—1776," ibid., III, 1689. For Massachusetts, see "The Constitution of 1780," in Taylor, ed., *Massachusetts*, 128–129. For the debates around religion in the 1780 Massachusetts Constitution, see Curry, *First Freedoms*, 163–167; Beneke, *Beyond Toleration*, 137–145; and Lippy, "The 1780 Massachusetts Constitution," *Journal of Church and State*, XX (1978), 533–549.

meant endorsing the idea that many different forms of religion could claim equal status. Even more important, it meant accepting the likelihood that some localities would choose to have no public support for religion. At the state level, lawmakers in New Hampshire and Vermont did just that. Even Connecticut, in the nation's erstwhile puritan core, dropped the early-eighteenth-century Saybrook Platform from its books in 1784. This devolution of religious organization to a more local level, even in most places that maintained an establishmentarian ethos, marked the disintegration—rather than the rejection—of a core component of imperial protestantism, the state regulation of who qualified as legitimate protestants, upon whom the state could depend to promote stability. In 1790, even South Carolina abandoned its protestant establishment, replacing it with a statement that "free exercise and enjoyment of religious profession and worship, without discrimination or preference, shall forever hereafter be allowed within this state." Though some states retained symbolic measures, such as religious tests for office, most states (with the notable exception of Massachusetts) largely withdrew from the business of religion.[10]

In some places, religious leaders entered the political fray caused by these changes. They argued both for and against establishments in ways that only highlighted the kinds of contradictions that had been easily managed by Britain's mixed establishment. Even as early as 1776, some among Pennsylvania's religious leaders sought to place tests on officeholders in that state in order to strengthen the sense that the state was in some way linked to a religious identity. A conflicted approach to future establishments on the part of religious leaders appeared in the South as well. In 1783, Maryland's governor, William Paca, proposed that the House of Delegates "[make] such a provision" for supporting religion "as the constitution in this case authorises and approves." He urged this action because the "sufferings of the ministers of the Gospel of all denominations, during the war, have been very considerable," and those who had stayed at their posts through such hardships "claim our acknowledgements and thanks."

10. "Constitution of New Hampshire—1784," in Thorpe, ed., *Federal and State Constitutions,* IV, 2454; Balik, *Rally the Scattered Believers,* 80–85; Curry, *First Freedoms,* 180–181, 185–187. For Vermont, see Article XXXVIII, "Constitution of Vermont—1786," in Thorpe, ed., *Federal and State Constitutions,* VI, 3760. For Connecticut, see Robert J. Imhold, "Connecticut: A Land of Steady Habits," in Esbeck and Den Hartog, eds., *Disestablishment and Religious Dissent,* 333–334. South Carolina's 1790 Constitution did, however, also include the obligatory remark that such freedom "shall not be so construed as to excuse acts of licentiousness, or justify practices inconsistent with the peace or safety of this State." See "Constitution of South Carolina—1790," in Thorpe, ed., *Federal and State Constitutions,* VI, 3264. See also James Lowell Underwood, "'Without Discrimination or Preference': Equality for Catholics and Jews under the South Carolina Constitution of 1790," in Underwood and Burke, eds., *The Dawn of Religious Freedom,* 64. For Massachusetts's continued establishment, see Witte and Latterell, "The Last American Establishment," in Esbeck and Den Hartog, eds., *Disestablishment and Religious Dissent,* 403–414.

He was "thoroughly convinced," he argued, "of the powerful influence of religion, when diffused by its respectable teachers." Local presbyterians, who did not want the former influence of the Anglican Church reconstituted through the Episcopalians, opposed the bill. Episcopalian William Smith observed, "There is considerable Opposition to the Religious Bill, from some Men who call themselves Christians." He found them disingenuous, however, telling his friend William White that such Christians "seem never to be pleased with any Thing however *Christian,* or however *Catholic* [that is, universal]; where their Numbers will not enable them to be the *sole* or *chief* Directors." After months of legislative and political jockeying, the bill failed in late 1785. Maryland's religious establishment continued in an ambiguous state for some years, but no further public moneys were used for its explicit support. These were messy political situations in which it was hard for religious leaders to argue for the continued privilege of some protestants without opening up such freedoms to all comers.[11]

The chain of events that unfolded in Virginia after the war's conclusion combined many of the elements that had been evident in other states, but its conclusion was more extreme—a clear separation of protestant institutions from the state. The process began in late 1783, when those who believed that religious institutions should receive support from taxes renewed their efforts

11. William Paca, quoted in *Votes and Proceedings of the House of Delegates of the State of Maryland, April Session, 1783; Being the Second Session of This Assembly* (Annapolis, Md., 1783), 6; William Smith to William White, Jan. 26, 1785, William White Papers, I, item 56, Hawks Collection, Archives of the Episcopal Church, Austin, Tex. The text of the bill appears in Maryland, General Assembly, House of Delegates, *An Act to Lay a General Tax for the Support of Ministers of the Gospel of All Societies of Christians within This State* (Baltimore, 1785). Patrick Allison laid out his position in [Allison] Vindex, *Candid Animadversions, respecting a Petition to the Late General Assembly of Maryland in Behalf of the Episcopal Ministers in the Same* (Baltimore, 1783). For discussions of the events in Maryland, see also Curry, *First Freedoms,* 155–157; and John Corbin Rainbolt, "The Struggle to Define 'Religious Liberty' in Maryland, 1776–85," *Journal of Church and State,* XVII (1975), 443–458. The bill's proponents leveraged the words of English legal theorist William Blackstone (who had objected to both civil liberties for dissenters and to the American Revolution), who said that "the preservation of Christianity, as a national religion, is, abstracted from its own intrinsic truth, of the upmost consequence to the civil state." See William Blackstone, quoted in J. C. D. Clark, *The Language of Liberty, 1660–1832: Political Discourse and Social Dynamics in the Anglo-American World* (Cambridge, 1994), 176–179 (quotation on 177); and Wilfred Prest, *William Blackstone: Law and Letters in the Eighteenth Century* (Oxford, 2008), 292. For Pennsylvania, see Sehat, *Myth of American Religious Freedom,* 17–20; William Pencak, *Jews and Gentiles in Early America, 1654–1800* (Ann Arbor, Mich., 2005), 210–217; and Curry, *First Freedoms,* 160–161. For a summary of Pennsylvania's colonial arrangements, see Sally Schwartz, *"A Mixed Multitude": The Struggle for Toleration in Colonial Pennsylvania* (New York, 1987 [1988]), 30–33. The connection between religion and education was particularly visible in Article III of Massachusetts's 1780 Constitution, which referred to ministers as "public teachers" ("The Constitution of 1780," in Taylor, ed., *Massachusetts,* 128–129). Virginia's 1784 assessment similarly provided for "teachers of the Christian Religion." The bill is reprinted in Buckley, *Church and State in Revolutionary Virginia,* 188–189.

for a general assessment of funds to support religion in the state, alongside measures that would allow the Virginia episcopal church to incorporate and to give clergy from all denominations the ability to perform marriages. Petitions in the matter largely favored the episcopal establishment, reflecting the organizational efforts of the episcopal community. In the fall 1784 session of the General Assembly, the subject of an assessment came to a head. Assembly members, acting as a Committee of the Whole and led by Patrick Henry, agreed to an assessment in principle, and in their preliminary vote they embraced, forty-seven to thirty-two, "the support of the Christian religion, or of some Christian church, denomination, or communion of Christians, or of some form of Christian worship." The lengthy list of nouns they used in their statement attests to the difficulties they faced in defining just what they were supporting. Other than a clear preference for the word "Christian" over the potentially competing terms "protestant" or, more simply, "religion," the assembly had no clear sense of what sort of institution they described. Without the boundaries around legitimate protestantism provided from the imperial center, or from some other body, there was no easy resolution to the vocabulary problem.[12]

Those from denominations that had supported imperial protestantism, but had only been tolerated in colonial Virginia, now faced a dilemma. Did they wish to be included in a more extended establishment, or would it be better for all if there was no public funding of religious institutions? Conditioned by the traditions of the imperial protestant system, there were good arguments to be made for equalizing access to establishment, and thus protecting a privileged space for those who could claim to be "some Christian church, denomination, or communion of Christians." Those limits would provide a basis for excluding outsiders and troublemakers while still allowing the old dissenters—especially baptists and presbyterians, who had been considered legitimate protestants in an imperial sense even though they had to contend for that privilege in Virginia—more solidly into the realm of privilege. Virginia's baptists, encouraged by their successes during the war years, formed the General Committee of Baptist Associations in October 1784. They petitioned the General Assembly with regard to the marriage issue but did not take a position on an assessment,

12. Virginia, General Assembly, House of Delegates, *Journal of the House of Delegates* (Richmond, Va., 1785), 17, quoted in Ragosta, *Wellspring of Liberty: How Virginia's Religious Dissenters Helped Win the American Revolution and Secured Religious Liberty* (New York, 2010), 119. There is an extensive literature on the Virginia bill. See Ragosta, *Religion Freedom,* 74–100; Buckley, *Establishing Religious Freedom;* Ragosta, *Wellspring of Liberty,* 117–136; Rhys Isaac, "'The Rage of Malice of the Old Serpent Devil': The Dissenters and the Making and Remaking of the Virginia Statute for Religious Freedom," in Peterson and Vaughan, eds., *The Virginia Statute for Religious Freedom,* 139–169; and William Henry Foote, *Sketches of Virginia: Historical and Biographical* (Philadelphia, 1850), 333–347.

suggesting some among their ranks might have supported it. That possibility is striking, since baptists had never benefited directly from establishment as their dissenting fellows had done in Scotland and New England, and, indeed, the General Committee's minutes opposed assessment. In their petition, however, they did not take the traditional baptist stance of opposition to any form of government connection to religious institutions. Less surprising is the position taken by the Hanover Presbytery, the leading body of that denomination in Virginia. Although it strenuously opposed an incorporation measure permitting episcopalians to take hold of all property that had been acquired by the Church of England through general taxation during the colonial period, its October 1784 petition supported the idea of a general assessment. The authors of the petition argued that the "support of religion and its solemn institutions" was "absolutely necessary to the existence and welfare" of any state. Because of that principle, they accepted the right of the government "to interfere in religion," but "this interference ought only to extend to the preserving of the public worship of the Deity, and the supporting of institutions for inculcating the great fundamental principles of all religion, without which society could not easily exist." These were articulations that fit well within the tradition of imperial protestantism. Institutional religion formed the basis of a stable society for those who led protestant institutions, and they advocated for that position as they could.[13]

The petitions for establishment from dissenters and—far more frequently—from episcopalians failed, despite significant support from many influential politicians, including Patrick Henry and Richard Henry Lee. Working against a general assessment for religion, James Madison, then in the General Assembly, skillfully maneuvered the conversation before the final vote on assessment in 1785, and in doing so he articulated a version of religion that was remarkably deinstitutionalized and also could not be construed as a threat to the state. He offered a useful stance for states that did not wish to solve the problem of which religious institutions could be trusted to demean themselves peaceably or which kinds of nouns described legitimate religious institutions. Madison's *Memorial and Remonstrance against Religious Assessments,* a fifteen-point argument,

13. "Memorial: The Presbytery of Hanover, to the Assembly, in October, 1784," in Foote, *Sketches of Virginia,* 337; Charles F. Irons, "The Spiritual Fruits of Revolution: Disestablishment and the Rise of the Virginia Baptists," *Virginia Magazine of History and Biography,* CIX (2001), 171; Ragosta, *Wellspring of Liberty,* 119; James H. Smylie, "Jefferson's Statute for Religious Freedom: The Hanover Presbytery Memorials, 1776–1786," *American Presbyterians,* LXIII (1985), 355–373; Fred J. Hood, "Revolution and Religious Liberty: The Conservation of the Theocratic Concept in Virginia," *Church History,* XL (1971), 170–181; Buckley, *Establishing Religious Freedom,* 69–70; Philip N. Mulder, *A Controversial Spirit: Evangelical Awakenings in the South* (New York, 2002), 94–96.

cast the debate in terms that made protestant institutions largely irrelevant. It argued that religion did not need the support of the state and that, when religious establishments existed, they tended to harm both civil harmony and the goals of religion.[14]

The words he used are worth considering closely. His discussion undercut the traditions of imperial protestantism in two ways. First, he separated "religion" from the dominant denominations and their reasonable claims to parity. This move served to transcend the internal fights that had characterized the preceding decades. He referred to Christianity, and compared it to "all other Religions" and "all other Sects," insisting the reader imagine, not the traditional diversity among the dominant denominations—with the attendant tensions between dissenters and Anglicans—but rather the variety that extended beyond it. Furthermore, he specifically referenced "Quakers and Menonists" as groups that did not require establishments. These pacifist groups, of course, had been outside Britain's protestant scaffold, and yet, as incidental beneficiaries of its toleration, they were not deemed political threats, as Catholics were. Madison's choice of references chipped away at the connection between religion and the dominant protestant categories, and it simultaneously asked its readers to envision religion as nonthreatening, even when not associated with Britain's stolid protestantism.[15]

Second, Madison reinforced the idea that "religion" meant transcendent, protestant Christianity, *independent from any institution*. He drew on traditions that described religion as individual conscience, but he did not frame that conscience within other terms that conjured institutions, such as "denomination" or "society." Instead, he described a faith that was beyond political intervention or support, albeit in recognizably protestant terms. He quoted the Virginia Declaration of Rights, which described "religion" as "the duty which we owe to our Creator and the manner of discharging it." Later, he argued that if religion was used as "an engine of Civil policy," it was essentially "an unhallowed perversion of the means of salvation." Finally, he discussed how the "Christian Religion" required no human laws and that it was at its best in its "primitive State." Indeed, any establishment would be "adverse to the diffusion of the light of Christianity." Christians' "first wish . . . ought to be that it may be imparted to the whole race of mankind," which the assessment bill would not further. The true missionary impulse was tainted, rather than enhanced, by connection to the state. Madison's *Memorial* perfectly articulated the religion of a new age:

14. Ragosta, *Wellspring of Liberty*, 123–132.

15. James Madison, *Memorial and Remonstrance against Religious Assessments*, June 20, 1785, https://press-pubs.uchicago.edu/founders/documents/amendI_religions43.html.

normatively Christian and protestant and yet disassociated from any particular institutional or political form. After the tide turned on assessment, the Virginia Assembly passed Thomas Jefferson's Statute for Religious Freedom. Originally introduced years before, its moment had finally come. The act declared that "no man shall be compelled to frequent or support any religious worship, place, or ministry whatsoever" and that "all men shall be free to profess, and by argument to maintain, their opinion in matters of religion." This was not institutional religious freedom; it was a personal freedom. Virginians thus codified what most states were stumbling toward: the elimination of connections between protestant institutions and government.[16]

A further point about the Virginia story. Neither Madison's *Memorial* nor the Virginia Bill contained a clause reserving religious freedom to those who demeaned themselves peaceably, a common limit on toleration within imperial protestantism and in the early state constitutions. Such provisions, commonsensical to those who drafted them, ensured that religion would not be used to disrupt the public peace, whether by fanaticism or by any practice too far from dominant protestantism. They faded from use in favor of bolder statements of religious freedom in the early Republic. In Madison's articulation, we see the disappearance of the explicit statement that government had the capacity to confine religion—protestantism in Britain's case—into an institutional form that supported the stability of the state and demanded loyalty, while excluding whatever might be called religion that did not meet those qualifications. One can argue that Madison presented his religion as essentially harmless, too important to restrict and yet too personal and intellectual to be a threat to the state. The 1786 Virginia act depicted religion—rendered in noninstitutional form as "opinion"—as offering no *cause* for civil adjudication because it could not inflict public harm. If government officials were to "intrude . . . into the field of opinion and to restrain the profession or propagation of principles on supposition of their ill tendency," they would only substitute their own opinions. And there could be no need anyway, the act continued. "It is time enough for the rightful purposes of civil government for its officers to interfere when principles break out into overt acts against peace and good order." Religious conflict—here the competition among opinions—could even be positive: "Truth is great and will prevail if left to herself." "Truth," the act continued, "has nothing to fear from

16. Ibid. The *Memorial and Remonstrance* has received extensive historical treatment. For discussions within the current context, see Gideon Mailer, *John Witherspoon's American Revolution* (Williamsburg, Va., and Chapel Hill, N.C., 2017), 347–355; and Ragosta, *Wellspring of Liberty*, 130–131. For the act, see Foote, *Sketches of Virginia*, 347; and Buckley, *Church and State in Revolutionary Virginia*, 190–191.

the conflict unless by human interposition disarmed of her natural weapons, free argument and debate; error ceasing to be dangerous when it is permitted freely to contradict them." This construction of religion as primarily intellectual, detached from any institution or interest in society that could cause harm, did not require its advocates to demean themselves peaceably. It moved outside the realm of government oversight and adjudication where it had been for almost a century.[17]

Virginia's 1786 measure is often, if somewhat misleadingly, cast as a precursor to the First Amendment to the Federal Constitution of 1787. In the present context, seen as the culmination of the dismantling of Britain's protestantism establishment in America, it has a different meaning. It was a dramatic step away from traditions of imperial protestantism that were, across former British colonies, already withering. In the decade after the imperial rupture, states reconfigured their religious arrangements, progressively removing government control from religion. Whereas nearly every state had possessed a protestant establishment in one form or another before the war, by 1790 they were nearly all gone. In most places where establishments of some kind remained (Massachusetts's stronger system being the notable example), they were increasingly managed at the local level so that the states—the units of establishment from the colonial period—lost most ties to institutional religion. The process in no way eliminated religious strife, but it shifted the context of the discussions: if religion was largely a personal or a local matter, was the state—let alone the nation—still bound by a shared religion? The answer, increasingly, was no. Outside the imperial protestant scaffold, states limited their connections to institutional protestantism.[18]

THE WAR'S REVERBERATIONS INSIDE THE BRITISH FOLD

In the years after the American Revolution, as American states revised their church establishments, Britons, too, rethought the nature of their church-state connections. For British leaders, the sense that the wheels of history were turning quickly, that a new era had begun, created both optimism for change and its

17. Buckley, *Church and State in Revolutionary Virginia,* 190–191. Both Richard Price and Ezra Stiles presented similar arguments, in which protestant truth would have a competitive advantage on a level playing field. For related points to those presented here, see J. G. A. Pocock, "Religious Freedom and the Desacralization of Politics: From the English Civil Wars to the Virginia Statute," 43–73, and Isaac, "'The Rage of Malice of the Old Serpent Devil,'" 139–169, both in Peterson and Vaughan, eds., *The Virginia Statute for Religious Freedom.*

18. Esbeck and Den Hartog, eds., *Disestablishment and Religious Dissent,* 12; Steven K. Green, *The Second Disestablishment: Church and State in Nineteenth-Century America* (New York, 2010).

opposite, a strong desire to retrench and to strengthen a system that had proven itself too weak. Moreover, without the colonies that had formed the United States, the religious dynamics in Britain and in its remaining empire changed substantially. The old balance between Anglicans and dissenters was disrupted. The result was both renewed struggle in Parliament and dramatic change in religious policy for the remaining empire, as Anglicans finally achieved their long-standing goal of a bishop in the colonies.[19]

In the unsettled postwar years, even before the French Revolution upset European politics, British dissenters were frustrated that they continued to suffer under legal disadvantages while English Catholics now enjoyed greater toleration than they had before the Catholic Relief Act. As religious establishments were crumbling in the United States, the time seemed right for change in late 1786. Parliament had agreed to the church hierarchy's role in consecrating bishops for an American episcopal church, and the text of Jefferson's Virginia Statute for Religious Freedom was circulating widely in the English press. Both were markers that the war, and old imperial ties, were being set aside. Members of the Protestant Dissenting Deputies formed an extraordinary committee for the purpose of repealing the Test and Corporation Acts. The movement blossomed quickly. The group enlarged its committee to include sympathetic political voices, made its case to the public in print, and lobbied Prime Minister William Pitt for his support. Three times between 1787 and 1790 dissenters sought to remove limitations on their civic participation that resulted from the Test and Corporation Acts. Their efforts reveal much about the way the

19. For the relationship between the American Revolution and reform in Britain, see Peter W. Walker, "The Church Militant: The American Loyalist Clergy and the Making of the British Counterrevolution, 1701–92" (Ph.D. diss., Columbia University, 2016); Maya Jasanoff, *Liberty's Exiles: American Loyalists in the Revolutionary World* (New York, 2011); Christopher Leslie Brown, *Moral Capital: Foundations of British Abolitionism* (Williamsburg, Va., and Chapel Hill, N.C., 2006); Eliga H. Gould, *The Persistence of Empire: British Political Culture in the Age of the American Revolution* (Williamsburg, Va., and Chapel Hill, N.C, 2000); Stephen Conway, *The British Isles and the War of American Independence* (Oxford, 2000); Kathleen Wilson, *The Sense of the People: Politics, Culture, and Imperialism in England, 1715–1785* (Cambridge, 1995); and Linda Colley, *Britons: Forging the Nation, 1707–1837* (New Haven, Conn., 1992). The idea of a contagion of liberty, or a democratic age, figures influentially in R. R. Palmer, *The Age of Democratic Revolution: A Political History of Europe and America, 1760–1800* (Princeton, N.J., 1959). For the spread of revolutionary ideas, see Janet Polasky, *Revolutions without Borders: The Call to Liberty in the Atlantic World* (New Haven, Conn., 2015). For a summary of Anglican history that uses the end of the American Revolution as a framing event, see Mark Smith, "The Anglican Churches, 1783–1829," in Jeremy Gregory, ed., *The Oxford History of Anglicanism*, II, *Establishment and Empire, 1662–1829* (Oxford, 2017), 68–87. Joanna Innes notes a shift in the connotations of "reform" around this time to be more political and institutional, though she does not connect it explicitly to the American Revolution; see Innes, "'Reform' in English Public Life: The Fortunes of a Word," in Innes and Arthur Burns, ed., *Rethinking the Age of Reform: Britain, 1780–1850* (Cambridge, 2003), 84–86. Arthur Burns dates the origins of ecclesiastical reforms within the Church of England to this period as well; see Burns, "English 'Church Reform' Revisited, 1780–1840," ibid., 149–150.

American Revolution reverberated within British protestantism and opened the way for more polarizing fights over ecclesiastical policy.[20]

As they prepared their arguments for repeal of the Test and Corporation Acts, dissenters emphasized that times had changed, that Britain was in a new era. They stressed the anachronistic nature of punitive religious restrictions. According to the pamphlet they published in anticipation of the parliamentary effort, principles "now universally acknowledged" demanded the end to a regime put in place in a long-past moment. When the acts had been passed in the seventeenth century, "Papists were indulged in their Religion." They had worked in prominent positions in government. Moreover, "the King himself was suspected of Popery, and the Duke of *York,* his presumptive heir, had openly declared himself of that Religion." The measures, they claimed, had been designed to target Catholics, not loyal protestants. Nonconformists had even, "in their zeal to rescue the nation from the dangers which were at that time apprehended from Popish Recusants, . . . contributed to the passing of the Bill; willingly subjecting themselves to the disabilities created by it rather than obstruct what was deemed so necessary to the common welfare." More than a century later, that crisis—which had led to the Glorious Revolution and the establishment of Britain's mixed protestant constitution—was distant history. It was time to rectify old injustices.[21]

20. *At a General Meeting of the Deputies of the Three Denominations of Dissenters, Held at Dr. Williams's Library, Red Cross Street, London, on Friday the 5th of January, 1787, to Consider of an Application to Parliament, for the Repeal of the Corporation and Test Acts* (London, 1787); *The Case of the Protestant Dissenters with Reference to the Test and Corporation Acts* ([London?], 1787), 1; "Committee Appointed to Conduct the Application to Parliament for the Repeal of the Test and Corporation Acts: Minutes, 1786–90," in Thomas W. Davis, ed., *Committees for Repeal of the Test and Corporation Acts: Minutes 1786–90 and 1827–8* (London, 1978), 1–22, *British History Online,* http://www.british-history.ac.uk/london-record-soc/vo114/pp1–22; *A Sketch of the History of the Proceedings of the Deputies Appointed to Protect the Civil Rights of the Protestant Dissenters . . .* (London, 1813), 46–48. For the parliamentary side of the story, see G. M. Ditchfield, "The Parliamentary Struggle over the Repeal of the Test and Corporation Acts, 1787–1790," *English Historical Review,* LXXXIX (1974), 551–577. See also Colin Bonwick, *English Radicals and the American Revolution* (Chapel Hill, N.C., 1977), 204–209. For a survey of the politics of rational dissent in this period, see John Seed, "'A Set of Men Powerful Enough in Many Things': Rational Dissent and Political Opposition in England, 1770–1790," in Knud Haakonnssen, ed., *Enlightenment and Religion: Rational Dissent in Eighteenth-Century Britain* (Cambridge, 1996), 140–168. For the impact of the American Revolution on the British religious settlement, see Innes and Burns, eds., *Rethinking the Age of Reform,* 8–9. For the preceding attempt to repeal the Test and Corporation Acts, see Andrew C. Thompson, "Toleration, Dissent, and the State in Britain," in Thompson, ed., *The Oxford History of Protestant Dissenting Traditions,* II, *The Long Eighteenth Century, c. 1689–c.1828* (Oxford, 2018), 277–279. For the 1787–1790 effort, see Ditchfield, "The Parliamentary Struggle," *English Historical Review,* LXXXIX (1974), 551–577; and Richard Burgess Barlow, *Citizenship and Conscience: A Study in the Theory and Practice of Religious Toleration in England during the Eighteenth Century* (Philadelphia, 1962), 223–271.

21. *The Case of the Protestant Dissenters,* 1, 2.

Similarly stressing the turning of the age, dissenting lawyer Samuel Heywood published a volume arguing for the "right of protestant dissenters to a compleat toleration." He began by "rejoic[ing] to behold the spirit of every government in Europe becoming daily more mild and indulgent to those, who cannot conscientiously conform to the established religion of their country." Old "prejudices, formerly entertained against Nonconformists," were "worn out." The residual laws against dissenters, therefore, should be repealed, particularly since "the punishment of *their religious* opinions was not in contemplation of the Legislature when either of these acts was passed." If once it had made sense to limit civic participation on the basis of one's ties to the established church, it was no longer so. The proposed changes were far more limited than those occurring in the United States in the same period, but they had the same thrust: religious opinions ought not to limit civil participation.[22]

British dissenters couched this argument for change within a conservative framing that harkened back to a prior era. They continued to affirm their nation's tradition and the logic of loyal protestantism. Heywood cited liberal Anglican William Paley's 1785 work, *The Principles of Moral and Political Philosophy,* in which that divine outlined his utilitarian establishment. Paley (and then through quotation Heywood) argued that, among the "sects of Christianity which actually prevail in the world, we must confess, that with the single exception of refusing to bear arms, we find no tenet in any of them, which incapacitates men for the service of the state." The test laws were thus unnecessary because Britain's protestant "sects" would be loyal. It was possible to eliminate the old restrictions on dissenters because Britain's system of mixed establishment ensured that dominant denominations exerted enormous gravity on religious life. (Paley noted that the same system might not work in a place like North America.) In other words, establishments per se were not the problem, provided that they were sufficiently liberal. Rather, they enabled religious freedom. Nonetheless, the civil restrictions that divided those within the dominant denominations needed reforming. In addition to England's dissenting population, Heywood also treated "the injustice of a test which excludes the natives of Scotland" from government office in England, so that "a member of the church of England has full and free access to all the offices of Scotland, while a member of the kirk of Scotland is incapacitated from holding one in England" without conformity to the Anglican Church. This was an argument

22. [Samuel Heywood], *The Right of Protestant Dissenters to a Compleat Toleration, Asserted . . .* (London, 1787), 1–3.

for perfecting Britain's mixed establishment of loyal protestants, not one for its dissolution.[23]

The dissenters' rhetorical embrace of Britain's protestant system, even as they challenged its suitability for the postwar era, could not eliminate the discomfort Anglican leaders felt about altering the terms of religious establishment when the war had so recently offered proof that it needed to be strengthened. In February 1787, William Pitt—after meeting with the dissenters but before the matter came to the floor in Parliament—solicited the advice of the bishops' bench. John Moore, archbishop of Canterbury, assembled those bishops then resident in London to discuss the matter, and they voted, fourteen to two, against the repeal. Moore also provided a brief critique of the arguments raised by the dissenters. "Their *Writers* certainly breath *[sic]* not the Language of Peace," he wrote. They would, he continued, "rather be tolerated than persecuted." But to Moore and his peers, the dissenters' moderate tone contrasted with the ample proof (provided over the preceding decade) that dissenters fomented objectionable political views. "I know not what farther Pretensions they have to the name of good Subjects," he continued. "Their almost avowed Republican Principles, their constant and active Endeavours to depress the power of the Crown; Their Conduct in fomenting the Revolt of America"—these political proclivities made full civil participation for dissenters unwise. The dissenters might have hoped to ride an American wave of increased religious liberty, but the lesson learned from the war in the halls of power in London was that such liberties led nowhere good.[24]

Perhaps wary of such sentiments, English dissenters stuck with their moderate case for repeal when it finally came up for debate in Parliament in 1787, blending arguments for their increased rights with recognition of both Britain's protestant heritage and the turning of the times after the Revolution. Their advocate, Henry Beaufoy, "humbly solicit[ed] a restoration of [dissenters'] Civil Rights, not an enlargement of their Ecclesiastical Privileges." Indeed, Beaufoy stated explicitly that dissenters did not seek to "diminish the provision which the Legislature has made for the established church." Moreover, his case was

23. Ibid., 109–111, 121; William Paley, *The Principles of Moral and Political Philosophy* (London, 1785), 554–586 (quotation on 582). Heywood also took care to argue that repealing the Test Act would not harm the Act of Union, pointing to the ongoing centrality of religious structures to the constitution (192–199). In an appendix, he also discussed the positive example in America. See Bonwick, *English Radicals,* 208; and Barlow, *Citizenship and Conscience,* 229–230.

24. "Meetings to Discuss Dissenters Relief," Feb. 12, 1787, Papers of John Moore, archbishop of Canterbury, Moore 8, fol. 36, and "Answer to the Case of the Protestant Dissenters," Moore 8, fol. 40, fols. 14–15, Lambeth Palace Library, London. Moore was not confident that his side would prevail, despite its influence with Pitt. See Ditchfield, "The Parliamentary Struggle," *English Historical Review,* LXXXIX (1974), 552.

not for universal civic participation regardless of religion. He argued only that protestant dissenters be included fully in the body politic, keeping in place a line that was rapidly dissolving in the United States. Beaufoy carefully delineated how, upon repeal of the Test and Corporation Acts, Parliament could still trust that Roman Catholics, "Mahometan[s]," Jews, or "a worshipper of fire" would still be excluded, either by oaths or merely through social and political pressure. At the same time, however, notes of a more universalistic hope for political liberty, for a new age free from the constraints of the old, crept into Beaufoy's rhetoric. As he reached his crescendo, moderation gave way to more dramatic visions for the future. Beaufoy argued that even Catholics should have greater rights, if they could prove they were truly loyal and independent of Rome. More to the point, he believed that if Parliament would remove religious tests from civic life, as had been done in "most of the enlightened nations of Europe," it would be only just. "Shall then England alone adhere to an exploded system which all the other enlightened nations of Europe, upon a full conviction of its weakness, have already abandoned, or are now preparing to abandon?" Dissenters were politically prudent actors within a long-established protestant system, but they also believed that history was on their side.[25]

Unfortunately for dissenters, the vote against repeal that followed this round of debate made clear that the majority in the government considered the establishment of the Church of England and the limits placed on dissenters as foundational to the British constitution. They did not plan to alter that arrangement. But, rather than demonstrating impermeability to change, the conservative stance of Parliament at this moment instead reflected the shifting nature of Britain's religious settlement in the new era. Without the political challenges of keeping the dissenting New England colonies in the empire, proponents of a strong Anglican Church had fewer reasons to humor the mixed establishment's lesser members. Lord North called the Test Act "the great bulwark of the constitution," something "to which we [owe] those inestimable blessings of freedom which we now happily [enjoy]." He recalled the turmoil dissent-

25. *The Parliamentary Register; or, History of the Proceedings and Debates of the House of Commons . . .*, XXI (London 1787), 529, 530, 544, 548, 549. See also Barlow, *Citizenship and Conscience*, 231–238. For a broader discussion of legislation around religion during these years, see Joanna Innes, "Parliament and Church Reform: Off and on the Agenda," in Gordon Pentland and Michael T. Davis, eds., *Liberty, Property, and Popular Politics: England and Scotland, 1688–1815: Essays in Honour of H. T. Dickinson* (Edinburgh, 2016), 39–57; G. M. Ditchfield, "Ecclesiastical Legislation during the Ministry of the Younger Pitt, 1783–1801," *Parliamentary History*, XIX (2000), 64–80; and Ditchfield, "The Parliamentary Struggle," *English Historical Review*, LXXXIX (1974), 551–577. For a firsthand account of the discussions, see Theophilus Lindsey to William Tayleur, Apr. 5, 1787, in Ditchfield, ed., *The Letters of Theophilus Lindsey (1723–1808)*, I, *1747–1788* (Woodbridge, U.K., 2007), 505–507.

ers had caused before the Glorious Revolution and pointed out that the Test Act had been instrumental in James II's fall. Pitt, too, spoke against the repeal. "The church and state are united upon principles of expediency," he posited, "and it concerns those, to whom the well-being of the state is intrusted, to take care that the church should not be rashly demolished." He also reminded the chamber that not all dissenters were as "moderate" as those who asked carefully for repeal. Others were enemies to establishment altogether. These arguments held sway in a chamber that looked warily at radical change to the nature of church establishment.[26]

After 1787, the debate over the Test and Corporation Acts became increasingly radicalized—also a reflection of the era's shifting politics—before it ultimately subsided in 1791, in the midst of the conservative fears opened by the French Revolution's early days. As the discussions wore on, prominent dissenting writers Joseph Priestley and Richard Price, well known for their pro-American sentiments during and after the war, published tracts in response to the debates, convincing many Britons that the dissenting agenda was in reality no less than the dismantling of the church entire. Conservative forces within the Church of England rallied to protect the church as "one branch of our excellent constitution, established for the religious benefit of the subjects of this realm," in the words of a document prepared by the archbishop of Canterbury's office. Edmund Burke, who had used his oratorial skills to promote American interests in Parliament before the American Revolution, excoriated dissenters for their destabilizing and disruptive philosophies in his *Reflections on the Revolution in France* in 1790. Exiled American Anglicans, men such as loyalist refugee Jonathan Boucher, formed a core base within the emergent conservative movement, and they advocated for a highly imperial version of the Church of England linked to the British constitution and political stability. For those pushing back against what they saw as a rising tide of irreligion and political chaos—an easy case to make as matters deteriorated in France—the American Revolution had been a catastrophe led by rabid dissenters in a land bereft of true establishments. As Boucher wrote in 1797, if a greater effort to stop the rebellion in America had been made, then so much of what came after might have been avoided, even the "French revolution, with all those other convulsions to which it may yet give birth, would then have been nipped in the bud." For

26. *Parliamentary Register,* XXI, 557–559, 563–564. One speaker made an explicit reference to a sermon published by Joseph Priestley, in which Priestley suggested "placing, as it were, grain by grain, a train of gunpowder, to which the match would, one day, be laid to blow up that fabric which could never again be raised upon the same foundation" (568). For the discussion of the Priestley reference, see David L. Wykes, "Joseph Priestley, Minister and Teacher," in Isabel Rivers and Wykes, eds., *Joseph Priestley, Scientist, Philosopher, and Theologian* (Oxford, 2008), 42.

conservative voices, reinforcing the connections between Britain's governments and its protestant institutions was the solution. The radicalization of the two sides marked a significant departure from the dynamics of the colonial period, when dissenters and Anglicans framed their disagreements within a common commitment to Britain's mixed establishment. Each side had learned powerful lessons through the course of the American Revolution. Dissenters watched the successive disestablishments in the United States with a sense that the tide of history had turned and they were in a new era of religious liberty. Anglicans realized, in equal measure, how much damage had resulted from their church's limitations in the colonies, and they invested in a stronger, "higher" version of church authority.[27]

Conservative forces had the upper hand, and they wielded it with more strength in the years that followed. The dissenters lost all three of their bids to have the Test and Corporation Acts repealed. Somewhat parallel projects to increase the status of Scottish episcopalians also foundered. Conservative leaders encouraged King George to issue a new proclamation "for the Encouragement of Piety and Virtue, and for the preventing and punishing of Vice, Profaness and Immorality" that were the "Scandal of Our Holy Religion." Fears of irreligion, further stoked by the violent anticlericalism in France, galvanized crowds into riots directed at Joseph Priestley in Birmingham in 1791, leading the scientist-cleric to immigrate to western Pennsylvania (see Figure 19). Both the riots and the conservative turn drew their immediate causes from the revolution

27. F. C. Mather, *High Church Prophet: Bishop Samuel Horsley (1733–1806) and the Caroline Tradition in the Later Georgian Church* (Oxford, 1992), 68 ("one branch"); Jonathan Boucher, *A View of the Causes and Consequences of the American Revolution; in Thirteen Discourses . . .* (London, 1797), x ("French revolution"), xxiv–xxv (analysis of religion in the revolution); J[oseph] Priestley, *A Letter to the Right Honourable William Pitt . . .* (London, 1787); Richard Price, *The Evidence for a Future Period of Improvement in the State of Mankind . . .* (London, 1787); Edmund Burke, *Reflections on the Revolution in France . . .* (London, 1790), esp. 12–16. For discussion of these works, see Robert E. Schofield, *The Enlightened Joseph Priestley: A Study of His Life and Work from 1773 to 1804* (University Park, Pa., 2004), 268–273; and Barlow, *Citizenship and Conscience*, 239–243. For the Anglican response to the repeal effort, see Mather, *High Church Prophet*, 64–87. Using the French Revolution to frame religious reform in England is common. See, for example, Peter Benedict Nockles, *The Oxford Movement in Context, Anglican High Churchmanship, 1760–1857* (Cambridge, 1994), 63; Mather, *High Church Prophet*, 76; and Bonwick, *English Radicals*, 216. For the activism and influence of American Anglican exiles in Britain, see Walker, "The Church Militant"; Smith, "The Anglican Churches, 1783–1829," in Gregory, ed., *Oxford History of Anglicanism*, II, 73–74; Robert M. Andrews, *Lay Activism and the High Church Movement of the Late Eighteenth Century: The Life and Thought of William Stevens, 1732–1807* (Leiden, 2015), 62–63, 86–87, 248; William L. Sachs, *The Transformation of Anglicanism: From State Church to Global Communion* (Cambridge, 1993), 32–33; and Anne Y. Zimmer, *Jonathan Boucher: Loyalist in Exile* (Detroit, Mich., 1978). See also *A Collection of the Resolutions Passed at the Meetings of the Clergy of the Church of England of the Counties, Corporations, Cities, and Towns, and of the Society for Promoting Christian Knowledge; Assembled to Take into Consideration the Late Application of the Dissenters to Parliament, for the Repeal of the Corporation and Test Acts* (London, 1790).

FIGURE 19 *Doctor Phlogiston, the Priestley Politician or the Political Priest.* Joseph Priestley is depicted in this 1791 satiric print wielding his writings as burning weapons. He was forced to flee Britain that year after rioters in Birmingham targeted him and other dissenting radicals. 1873,0712.1150. © The Trustees of the British Museum. All rights reserved

in France, but that should not obscure the process set in motion by the imperial rupture over the preceding fifteen years. The unsettled nature of England's religious establishment in the early 1790s had been caused by the shocks of that earlier crisis. It had emboldened the voices of dissenters and also of those who believed a strong Britain required clear support for the Church of England. The scaffolding that had kept these forces in comparative balance for the decades before the war, in the interests of political harmony across a far-flung "protestant" empire, no longer performed that function.[28]

28. "By the King, A Proclamation; for the Encouragement of Piety and Virtue, and for the Preventing and Punishing of Vice, Profaneness and Immorality," *London Gazette,* May 29 to June 2, 1787, 262–263. For the Proclamation Society, see Joanna Innes, "Politics and Morals: The Reformation of Manners Movement in Later Eighteenth-Century England," in Eckhart Hellmuth, ed., *The Transformation of Political Culture: England and Germany in the Late Eighteenth Century* (London, 1990), 74–103; Schofield, *The Enlightened Joseph Priestley,* 276–277, 283–289; and Robert Hole, *Pulpits, Politics, and Public Order in England, 1760–1832* (Cambridge, 1989), 97–107. See also J. C. D. Clark, "Churches, Parties, and Politics," in Gregory, ed., *Oxford History of Anglicanism,* II, 298–299.

If the American Revolution raised the temperature of religious dispute in Britain, it simplified matters in the remaining empire, opening possibilities that had been foreclosed before. Nova Scotia and New Brunswick, regions that stayed within the British fold, had undergone dramatic change during the war, including substantial migration from the south and waves of revivals. Government leaders were concerned, both because of the challenges faced by Anglicans in the new provinces and because they worried that without a strong Anglican presence the region would be more prone to disloyalty. Anglicans there also wanted to enhance the church's hierarchy, in part because "the people should be attached to the State by means of its Religion," according to a petition from Anglican clergy to Governor Sir Guy Carleton. The requests met a more positive response from imperial officials, including Carleton, than similar ones had received during the colonial period. The new proposals, like their predecessors, were for a bishop that would have no political or governing authority. This "suffragan" bishop represented an innovation for the Church of England, where bishops also sat in the House of Lords, but the suffragan system also meant that the creation of a bishop for Nova Scotia did not require an act of Parliament, like the one that had been passed for the bishops of the episcopal church in the new United States. The new bishop would, in theory at least, encourage a strong and patriotic piety in those provinces, but without necessitating political action in itself. Before the Revolution, similar proposals had been thwarted by the fear of political outcry from New England and from English dissenters. Now those political problems were gone—eliminated with the loss of New England and its dissenting establishment. From the perspective of the Church of England, the war's loss could even be termed a positive development, at least in the sense that it meant fewer political compromises with dissenters.[29]

Of course, things that are theoretically possible are not always bureaucratically quick. Despite the comparative simplicity of appointing a bishop without temporal powers in a territory still under British control, the matter languished for years while those in government attended to other matters. Only in 1785,

29. Peter M. Doll, *Revolution, Religion, and National Identity: Imperial Anglicanism in British North America, 1745–1795* (Madison, N.J., 2000), 210–220 (quotation on 218); Walker, "The Church Militant," 223–224. See also Judith Fingard, "The Establishment of the First English Colonial Episcopate," *Dalhousie Review,* XLVII (1967), 475–491; and Wilson, *The Sense of the People,* 282–284. Scholars have disputed whether the Nova Scotia episcopate was primarily an act designed for political purposes or a reflection of growing "high church" Anglicanism. I would argue that such distinctions are less important than the fact that uncoupling the suffragan bishop from political function enabled a new kind of religious politics. Decreasing the institutional entanglements of the colonial period increased the political options of Anglicans. See Doll, *Revolution, Religion, and National Identity,* 210–212.

after Samuel Seabury's controversial journey to Scotland, did the appointment move forward. The Society for the Propagation of the Gospel in Foreign Parts, the traditional advocate of the Church of England in the colonies, then in the midst of refocusing its efforts on Britain's remaining empire, played a significant role. Its agents included Jonathan Boucher and John Moore, the archbishop of Canterbury. As the gears of government moved slowly into action, the Board of Trade took up the matter, and eventually the Privy Council recommended that a bishop be sent to Nova Scotia. It deemed that "such Bishop [would] have Ecclesiastical Authority and Jurisdiction in the said province and its Dependencies, without civil Authority except what may be necessary for the discharge of his Jurisdiction in Clerum," or as a clergyman. That recommendation, made in May 1787, resulted in the consecration of Charles Inglis, another American loyalist in London, as the first colonial bishop on August 9, 1787.[30]

Inglis brought with him to Canada the belief that the established church was the bedrock of political stability, a view he had reiterated often during his years observing the war from occupied New York. As the first Anglican bishop appointed to territory outside the British Isles, he preached a sermon before Nova Scotia's assembled authorities on November 25, 1787. His text was Proverbs 14:34, "Righteousness exalteth a nation; but sin is a reproach to any people." It outlined, in terms that echoed King George's recent proclamation, how "piety and virtue advance the prosperity of a nation." He reminded his audience that, "when a deep and rational sense of religion has taken possession of the heart," salutary benefits followed for all. Such a condition "would banish faction, violence and murmurings out of the state; all schisms, scandals and lukewarmness out of the church. . . . It would exalt a nation." Everyone had a part to play in this collective project, but the most important role was reserved for the legislators to whom he spoke most directly. "Nor should the civil power neglect religion, or fail to take it under its patronage and protection," the new bishop proclaimed. Laws had to protect the people from "wild and fanciful opinions" that might "shoot up" and "which assume the respectable name of religion." Inglis acknowledged the importance of the "rights of conscience," which "should ever be preserved inviolate," but he also made a clear and direct statement of the importance of religious establishment. Conscience would not suffer, he said, "by cherishing that mode of religion which is not only

30. Fingard, "The Establishment of the First English Colonial Episcopate," *Dalhousie Review*, XLVII (1967), 481–482 (quotation on 482). For the SPG's activities, see Journal of the Society for the Propagation of the Gospel in Foreign Parts, Apr. 15, 1785, MS, XXIV, 1785–1787, 74–78, Colonial Missionaries' Papers from America and the West Indies, 1701–1870, British Online Archives, https://microform.digital/boa. See also Doll, *Revolution, Religion, and National Identity*, 230–236.

true, but tends most to the general benefit." For this reason, "there is no point perhaps in which all civilized states, all legislators, ancient and modern, have more unanimously concurred, than in establishing religion, and afterwards supporting that establishment." The key to political harmony and success was a strong state church.[31]

It was an aggressive assertion in light of events of which Inglis was quite well aware: the progressive disestablishment of religion in the United States, the controversies over dissenters' rights in England, and, most importantly, the enormous and violent division that had just concluded within an empire that had been united by its shared protestantism. His response to these developments would undoubtedly have been that the failure of authorities to extend the Church of England throughout the empire at the right moment was in no small measure to blame for the imperial rupture. But any such hindsight was, of course, predicated on the Americans' rebellion and victory. A half century earlier, the empire's mixed establishment had kept religious conflicts from boiling over. Yet it had not, quite clearly, prevented anger, disloyalty, and ultimately rebellion from coalescing around nonreligious issues. There had always been Anglicans who argued for the kind of imperial church that Inglis championed. The key difference, after the war, was that influential leaders at the empire's center, men like Governor Guy Carleton and Archbishop John Moore, agreed with that point of view and (even more important) were willing to act to bring it about now that the impediments posed by the empire's mixed establishment were gone.[32]

At the same time, Inglis's view of establishment in Nova Scotia was largely aspirational because of the complexities on the ground, and Inglis knew it. The Church of England did not become the dominant religious institution in either that region or in neighboring New Brunswick. The baptist Allinite revivals that were surging in the area, the work of Black protestant leaders David George (a baptist) and Boston King (a Methodist) among the refugee African American population, and the diversity that had always existed among Nova Scotia's protestants meant that Nova Scotia would not become the kind of Anglican paradise Inglis envisioned. Instead, his new ecclesiastical see was home to a religious environment as cacophonous as any that could be found farther to the south, and he had no more power to influence it than the Episcopalian bishops in the

31. Charles Inglis, *The Bishop of Nova Scotia's Sermon before the Lieutenant Governor, Council, and House of Assembly of the Province of Nova Scotia, on Sunday, November 25, 1787* (Halifax, 1787), 5, 17, 18–19, 21, 22.

32. Doll, *Revolution, Religion, and National Identity,* 238, similarly argues for a change in circumstances after the war, but with a focus on changing arguments rather than changing institutions. When organizing Canada's government in 1790 and 1791, these issues were debated in Parliament (245–247).

United States. Though the episcopacy created by imperial administrators for Quebec in 1791 included temporal powers, there, too, it proved difficult to make them a reality. Britain's nineteenth-century religious imperialism would not be a product of the institutional Church of England, nor of the pre-Revolutionary imperial protestant system, but would result from a new mix of efforts with a new set of goals.[33]

The American Revolution forced Britain's leaders to reassess their protestant system. Without the lost American colonies, the political calculations around religious conflict changed. For both dissenters and Anglicans, there were new opportunities and perceived threats. Dissenters seized the momentum of revolution and attempted to alter their legal status in England, only to find that many Britons, in Parliament and out, responded to the loss of the colonies and the new dangers presented by events in France by doubling down on the importance of an Anglican—rather than a mixed—establishment. Anglicans, by contrast, used the momentum they gained in the empire's remaining colonies, but there they faced a different reality. In those places, Anglican hegemony was even more unlikely than in England. As important as their respective changing fortunes, however, is the changing terms of their fight. No longer bound by an imperial scaffolding that forced a measure of parity and cooperation between dominant protestant denominations, the terms of religious establishment in Britain entered an extended era of transformation.

SPLINTERING NATION FROM NATIONAL RELIGION

The story of American national religion in the years after the American Revolution was an altogether different matter than that of either American religion at the state level or of that unfolding in the British Empire. The states inherited legal-religious structures that had been formed by imperial protestantism and the British Empire still worked within that heritage after the war, even in an era of intensified contestation. But the United States, as a nation, was differ-

33. Charles Inglis to the archbishop of Canterbury, Charles and John Inglis Fonds, MG 1, vol. 479, 30–39, Provincial Archives of Nova Scotia, Halifax; Cassandra Pybus, *Epic Journeys of Freedom: Runaway Slaves of the American Revolution and Their Global Quest for Liberty* (Boston, 2006), 145–150; Neil Semple, *The Lord's Dominion: The History of Canadian Methodism* (Montreal, 1996), 32–33; G. A. Rawlyk, *The Canada Fire: Radical Evangelicalism in British North America, 1775–1812* (Kingston, Ontario, 1994), 126–132; Ann Gorman Condon, *The Loyalist Dream for New Brunswick: The Envy of the American States* (Frederickton, N.B., 1984), 184–190; Doll, *Revolution, Religion, and National Identity*, 253–260; Hilary M. Carey, *God's Empire: Religion and Colonialism in the British World, c. 1801–1908* (Cambridge, 2011), 40–71; Andrew Porter, *Religion versus Empire? British Protestant Missionaries and Overseas Expansion, 1700–1914* (Manchester, U.K., 2004), 40–45.

ent. Though the Continental Congress had collaborated with the leaders of protestant institutions to create a public religion in the early years of the war, the polity of the United States had little in the way of connections to protestant institutions, and after the war ended government and religious leaders moved further into separate spheres. Yet even as national institutions, following the path set by the Articles of Confederation, became progressively more independent of connections—rhetorical or legal—to religion, religious and political leaders nonetheless imagined into being a disembodied national religion. Their words implied institutional connections that no longer existed. They conjured memories of a protestant empire like the shadow pain of an amputated limb. The United States had no national religion capable of replicating the form and function of imperial protestantism, but that did not stop some of the nation's leaders from acting as if it did. These conflicting trajectories set the stage for contests over the religious nature of the United States in the years to come.

The tension between theory and reality in the new nation's religious arrangements predated even the signing of the peace treaty. Moments at which Congress invoked public religion declined rapidly after the war, in no small part because Congress itself was in crisis. It declared December 11, 1783, as a day of thanksgiving to mark the coming peace treaty. But by then Congress already found it difficult to muster either a quorum or the necessary unity to act. The Congress's last thanksgiving was declared for October 19, 1784, to mark the definitive news of the peace treaty. In that case, the members adjourned before finally voting on the drafted proclamation, so its official status was dubious, and there appears to have been no national observance of the day. New England states also declared a thanksgiving for that date, so it was observed in that region regardless of its formal sponsorship, but it does not seem to have garnered much notice even there. The celebration of national religion, directed by a national institution, was not a significant cultural factor in 1784. Not even Ezra Stiles noted it in his meticulous diary. After that there were no more efforts to command the apparatus of public religion in service of the nation until President George Washington declared November 26, 1789, a day of thanksgiving. Coming at the heart of the nation's founding period, the five-year gap is important. The trajectory from the heady days of national public religion in 1775 and 1776 to American religious nationalism in the early Republic was not straight, and it cratered before it recovered.[34]

A counterpoint to Congress's abandonment of public religion came from religious leaders who continued to see a providential destiny for the United States,

34. *Journals of the Continental Congress, 1774–1789 . . .*, 34 vols. (Washington, D.C., 1904–1937), XXVII, 625–630; Franklin Bowditch Dexter, ed., *The Literary Diary of Ezra Stiles, D.D., LL.D., President of Yale College*, III, *January 1, 1782–May 6, 1795* (New York, 1901), 140. For discussion

despite its troubled national government. Perhaps the most famous ode to the new nation came from Ezra Stiles, the moderate New Englander who had taken up the presidency of Yale, in an election sermon preached in Hartford on May 8, 1783. Stiles imagined a new protestant nation free of its old tethers to the British protestantism of the confessional era. The sermon championed God's providential support for the United States, building from Deuteronomy 26:19, "and to make thee high above all nations, which he hath made in praise, and in name, and in honor." The United States, by virtue of God's blessing, was destined for a providential and triumphant future. Before it could enjoy that future, however, Stiles had to separate the United States from the sacred geography of Britain's protestant empire. He compared the United States' government to China, India, Rome, and Venice, eschewing the dynamics of protestant and papist empires that shaped his childhood years. He claimed that "true liberty is preserved in the *Belgic* and *Haelvetic* republics, and among the nobles in the elective monarchy of *Poland,*" but he avoided the kind of lengthy investigation of the British constitution that would have been commonplace before the imperial rupture. In this telling, the United States took its position at the fore of a transcendent history, framed in no particular way by the narrative of the Reformation and the Glorious Revolution. As he imagined an independent United States, Stiles also took specific pains to trace its changed relationship with Britain. "Oh England!" he lamented, "how did I once love thee" and "glory in the future honor of having thee for the head of the Britannico-American empire for the many ages till the millennium—when thy great national glory should have been advanced in then becoming a member of the universal empire of the Prince of Peace." This vision was past, however, and he bid "farewell—a long farewell—to all this greatness," replacing it with dedication to a United States that God had already blessed through the successes at Lexington and Concord and the providential discovery of Benedict Arnold's treachery. This United States was truly independent of Britain's protestant empire, ready for a glorious future.[35]

---

of the timing of fast days, see Spencer McBride, *Pulpit and Nation: Clergymen and the Politics of Revolutionary America* (Charlottesville, Va., 2016), 180 n. 27; Benjamin H. Irvin, *Clothed in Robes of Sovereignty: The Continental Congress and the People Out of Doors* (New York, 2011), 116; W. DeLoss Love, Jr., *The Fast and Thanksgiving Days of New England* (Boston, 1895), 403, 506. No printed sermons preached on the October 19, 1784, national thanksgiving appear to be extant. Massachusetts declared another fast day for November 25 of the same year, for which there is an extant sermon by John Lathrop, *A Discourse on the Peace; Preached on the Day of Public Thanksgiving, November 25, 1784* (Boston, 1784). See also Robert Middlekauf, *The Glorious Cause: The American Revolution, 1763–1789* (New York, 1982), 573–575; and Irvin, *Clothed in Robes of Sovereignty*, 268–272, 278–279.

35. Ezra Stiles, *The United States Elevated to Glory and Honor . . .* (New Haven, Conn., 1783), 5, 17, 32. Although Stiles appealed to British authorities when needed, his primary concern with

But how would the independent nation ensure it achieved the divine future for which it was destined? And what *was* the new nation? Stiles did not call for the creation of a national religious system that would replicate Britain's institutionally complex "constitution in church and state." Such imaginings would have been frankly ridiculous at a moment when the United States barely had a shared government. Instead, he imagined a protestant American people, independent of any particular government arrangement, who would fulfill his vision. He drew on early modern racial theory to argue that "Heaven hath provided this country, not indeed *derelict,* but only *partially settled"* and therefore available for the descendants of Japhet, the Europeans. Indigenous Americans, whom he saw as *"Canaanites* of the expulsion of Joshua," were small in numbers, and the "European Population so surpasses them already, that of whatever origin, they will eventually be, as the most of them have already become, *servants unto Japhet.*" Furthermore, "We are increasing with great rapidity; and the *Indians,* as well as the million *Africans* in America, are decreasing *as rapidly.*" When those groups naturally disappeared, "an unrighteous SLAVERY may at length, in God's good providence, be abolished and cease in this land of LIBERTY," apparently without any effort on the part of the ascendant Europeans. By thus dismissing racial outsiders, Stiles conjured a white American people, naturally protestant and capable of being described as united despite the lack of functioning shared institutions. To solve the problem of religious divisions among American protestants, he argued that "the united states will embosom all the religious sects or denominations in christendom" but that "the united body of the *congregational, consociated* and *presbyterian* churches," the dominant groups in New England, would be first among equals. Stiles imagined the United States as a successor to protestant Britain, but one in which the uniting mechanism was no longer political compromise between protestant denominations but rather racial unity defined against the nonwhite objects of British imperial power, peoples who were now shunted to the boundaries of the protestant American people. Religio-racial peoplehood stood in place of shared religious institutions.[36]

---

the former parent state was economic. The sermon is discussed in James P. Byrd, *Sacred Scripture, Sacred War: The Bible and the American Revolution* (New York, 2013), 63–64; and Edmund S. Morgan, *The Gentle Puritan: A Life of Ezra Stiles, 1727–1795* (Williamsburg, Va., and Chapel Hill, N.C., 1962), 451–455. For scholars who have used Stiles as representative of a postwar ethos, see Albert J. Raboteau, "African Americans, Exodus, and the American Israel," in Paul E. Johnson, ed., *African American Christianity: Essays in History* (Berkeley, Calif., 1994), 11–12; and "Rev. Ezra Stiles, America Will Sustain Christian Truth, 1783," in Richard D. Brown, ed., *Major Problems in the Era of the American Revolution,* 2d ed. (Boston, 2000), 317–318.

36. Stiles, *United States Elevated,* 9, 10, 14, 54, 57. For the Japhet theory, see Colin Kidd, *The Forging of Races: Race and Scripture in the Protestant Atlantic World, 1600–2000* (Cambridge, 2006), 20–23. For the creation of a white American polity through the progress of the American

Stiles's confidence about what white American protestants would achieve evaporated when he turned to their governments, however, which were rapidly separating religious institutions from government and becoming less explicitly or structurally protestant. Here he could only encourage and admonish. Though he insisted that the Congress was the "crown and glory of our confederacy" and celebrated the constitutions of the various states, he also worried about the trend to "disunite, divide and separate" church and state. "A general spirit reigns," he lamented, "against the most liberal and generous establishments in religion"—so much so that "civil magistrates" would be left with little "more to do about religion, than to keep the civil peace among contending sects." Even further, the decline of religious tests for office, a mainstay of imperial protestantism, suggested that Americans now believed it might be "wise to consign government over into the hands of those who, *gallio* like, have no religion at all." Stiles championed the new age and yet feared the consequences of the quickly evaporating guardrails around protestantism.[37]

This was the problem the American religious leaders faced: many had given their support to the United States as it was forming, but the partnership between Congress and the religious leaders had not grown—and it would not grow in the future—beyond public religion into something more institutionally or legally tangible. Though Stiles argued for a partnership between "MOSES and AARON," between the "MAGISTRACY and PRIESTHOOD," that would preserve what he understood as religious liberty, he could not deny that the trend was against such entanglements at the national level. His triumphalist sermon thus carried with it a message of worry and a call to action. The United States might have a place in God's plan, but there was no guarantee that its "religion," devoid of any national institutional basis, would sustain it.[38]

Stiles was right to be worried about the place for Aaron—for the leaders of protestant institutions and the bodies they led—in the United States' future. The Constitutional Convention that convened in 1787 had little use for either public religion or for imagining ways that the nation's government might fabricate formal links to protestant institutions. The absence of public religion at the Constitutional Convention can only be read as a deliberate omission for a body that was conscious of the import of its task to national unity and stability.

Revolution, see Robert G. Parkinson, *The Common Cause: Creating Race and Nation in the American Revolution* (Williamsburg, Va., and Chapel Hill, N.C., 2016).

37. Stiles, *United States Elevated,* 23, 37, 70, 71. For Gallio, a judge in a case brought against the apostle Paul, see Acts 18:12–17.

38. Stiles, *United States Elevated,* 70.

That there were no clergymen as members of the delegations is less surprising than that no opening prayers were called for to solemnize the proceedings. The Convention's most logical predecessor was the first General Congress in 1774, another body that had assembled with dubious legal standing. Facing the clear threat of British repression and a strong need to unify colonists, the General Congress had turned immediately to prayer, in the oft-remembered moment when Anglican Jacob Duché had preached with such passion that he moved his audience deeply. In 1787, the delegates to the Constitutional Convention did not seek to unify the nation through the fact of their proceedings, however. They kept their discussions secret, and they aspired instead to create a stronger nation through the results of their efforts. In other words, shows of unity could wait until they were done. Public religion was thus better left to one side.[39]

The only mention of prayer in the meetings of the Constitutional Convention confirms rather than disproves the idea that the Convention's delegates actively avoided displays of religion. It came only midway through, in late June, when the men grew weary of trying to solve the problem of how to structure the new legislature. Benjamin Franklin, an unlikely advocate for religion, reminded the delegates how the Congress in 1774 had opened its sessions with prayers, and he moved that "henceforth Prayers imploring the Assistance of Heaven, and its Blessing on our Deliberations, be held in this Assembly every Morning." It was not an impromptu proposal; Franklin had written out his notes in advance. Roger Sherman, a devout delegate from Connecticut, seconded Franklin's motion, but Alexander Hamilton raised doubts. Had they prayed all along, he argued, the act might have been fine, but to resort to prayer in the middle could "lead the public to believe that the embarrassments and dissentions within the convention, had suggested this measure." It is possible that this was Franklin's goal; his proposal effectively served as a threat that the difficulties they were facing would be made public. Either way, he noted afterward that "the Convention except three or four Persons, thought Prayers unnecessary!!" The delegates, who desired neither to pray in their meetings nor to draw attention to their struggles, maneuvered away from the proposal. They protested that they had no funds to pay clergymen, suggested that a sermon might be called for on the upcoming Fourth of July holiday instead (it was not), and adjourned

39. For synthetic and concise discussions of the calling of the Constitutional Convention, see Alan Taylor, *American Revolutions: A Continental History, 1750–1804* (New York, 2016), 367–393; and Pauline Maier, *Ratification: The People Debate the Constitution, 1787–1788* (New York, 2010), 1–26. For religion and the Convention, see Edwin S. Gaustad, "Religious Tests, Constitutions, and 'Christian Nation,'" in Ronald Hoffman and Peter J. Albert, eds., *Religion in a Revolutionary Age* (Charlottesville, Va., 1994), 225; and McBride, *Pulpit and Nation*, 102.

without a vote. The delegates, both at that moment and in the text they produced, chose not to use public religion as a means to sanctify their new nation.[40]

To further prove Stiles's point that in this new era government leaders gave little thought to the religion of those in civil office, there is only one explicit reference to religion in the Federal Constitution: Article VI states that "no religious Test shall ever be required as a Qualification to any Office or public Trust under the United States." The prohibition, included with several other measures as part of the article, passed without discussion. In the context of imperial protestantism, the omission of religious tests for office at the highest level is worthy of notice. During the Glorious Revolution, Parliament had used James II's Catholicism as a justification for making William and Mary the new sovereigns. The English Bill of Rights provided specific qualifications for the crown to be protestant. "It hath been found by experience that it is inconsistent with the safety and welfare of this Protestant kingdom to be governed by a popish prince," the document stated, so "the said Lords Spiritual and Temporal and Commons" recommended that "[papists] be excluded and be for ever incapable to inherit, possess or enjoy the crown and government of this realm and Ireland and the dominions thereunto belonging." The provision was reiterated in the Act of Settlement of 1701, keeping the crown in the "Protestant Line" by transferring it to the Hanoverians on Queen Anne's death. The delegates to the Constitutional Convention, however, shared no such concerns that a Catholic (or a member of some other kind of religion) might endanger the Republic. The decision, as uncontroversial as it apparently was for the delegates, turned the United States firmly away from the religious politics of the confessional age.[41]

The choice of the framers to eliminate religious tests caused some consternation when the states came to ratify the Constitution. Though religious issues played a minor role in the process of ratification compared with debates about

40. Benjamin Franklin, "Convention Speech Proposing Prayers," June 28, 1787, franklinpapers.org; Max Farrand, ed., *The Records of the Federal Convention of 1787*, 3 vols. (New Haven, Conn., 1911), I, 450–453 (quotation on 452); Richard Beeman, *Plain, Honest Men: The Making of the American Constitution* (New York, 2009), 177–178; Lambert, *Founding Fathers*, 246–250; Fea, *Was America Founded as a Christian Nation?* 150–153.

41. U.S. Const. art. VI; Farrand, ed., *Records of the Federal Constitution*, Max II, 334–340, esp. 335; "English Bill of Rights 1689: An Act Declaring the Rights and Liberties of the Subject and Settling the Succession of the Crown," Avalon Project: Documents in Law, History, and Diplomacy, https://avalon.law.yale.edu/17th_century/england.asp; Act of Settlement, https://www.legislation.gov.uk/aep/Will3/12-13/2/contents. The Federal Constitution also includes two references to religion that were not likely thought of as such by the framers but that have received attention from Christian nationalists. One is the phrase "in the year of our lord" in the date, and the other is the provision that Sundays would not be counted in the number of days the president has to approve (or veto) a law. See Michael I. Meyerson, *Endowed by Our Creator: The Birth of Religious Freedom in America* (New Haven, Conn., 2012), 144–146.

nonreligious issues, those who believed religious character or unity ought to be central to the state viewed the decision to forbid them as an abandonment of a tested protection against corruption and tyranny. It was an ominous signal in particular to those who feared an overpowerful or corrupting central state, a threat that resonated with past worries about popery. Those in Belchertown, Massachusetts, told their delegates to the state's convention to object to the clause because "it has Ever been the Principale and Practice of the Papists to Persicute those of the Protestant Religion." They saw it as "of the highest Importance . . . that no man of the Papist Religion be Ever a President or Senator." On the other hand, Isaac Backus, a prominent baptist advocate for eliminating the state's religious establishment, embraced the Constitution's prohibitions on religious tests. He argued before the Massachusetts convention that religious tests "hath been the greatest engine of tyranny in the world." Nor did he fear the consequences of leaving protestantism without its usual protection from Catholicism. "Some serious minds discover a concern lest, if all religious tests should be excluded, the Congress would hereafter establish Popery, or some other tyrannical way of worship," he posited. He, however, found nothing to fear. "No such way of worship can be established, without any religious test." Questions about establishment of a single denomination and issues about religious tests thus intermingled. None of them, however, proved powerful enough to stop the Constitution's adoption. The primary result was thus to raise the same sorts of anxieties that Stiles had expressed, that the new nation might be structured in a way that left either religion or the nation vulnerable.[42]

As the federal government took shape, it remained unclear what kind of relationship would develop between the kind of national religion that could be described in lofty rhetoric by men like Ezra Stiles and the government that had been created. The Constitution included no place for institutional religion. Many Americans embraced the idea of a republic free of entanglements with religion of any sort, and yet there were still plenty of Americans who longed for the kind of religious community that could only be created at the national level. Trying to establish which group was more numerous, or more powerful, misses the point. They were both natural products of the Revolution.

42. For Belchertown, see John P. Kaminski et al., eds., *The Documentary History of the Ratification of the Constitution Digital Edition* (Charlottesville, Va., 2009), http://rotunda.upress.virginia.edu/founders/RNCN-02-05-02-0003-0011-0003; Maier, *Ratification,* 152–153, 220; Lambert, *Founding Fathers;* Curry, *First Freedoms,* 194–196. For Backus, see Kaminski et al., eds., *Documentary History of the Ratification of the Constitution Digital Edition,* http://rotunda.upress.virginia.edu/founders/RNCN-02-06-02-0002-0027-0001. Spencer McBride has argued that religious leaders' participation in the constitutional debates was itself a significant source of controversy; see McBride, *Pulpit and Nation,* 121–128.

The immediate results of this tension can be seen in the awkward expressions of national religion that unfolded in the First Congress as it prepared for the inauguration of the first president, George Washington. Scrambling to work out many matters of government business and ceremony before Washington arrived in New York, a congressional committee decided to elect two chaplains from different denominations, one for the House of Representatives and one for the Senate. The newly consecrated Episcopal bishop Samuel Provoost was chosen by the Senate. The next week, a committee considered the ceremonies involved in the upcoming inauguration; it sought out the best room for the gathering and then resolved that, "after the oath shall have been administered to the President, he, attended by the Vice President, and members of the Senate, and House of Representatives, [would] proceed to St. Paul's Chapel, to hear divine service, to be performed by the Chaplain of Congress, already appointed." It was a controversial choice, but on procedural and governmental grounds rather than because of an ideological rejection of any perceived mingling between church and state. An earlier committee had rejected the inclusion of services, and now it seemed possible that the ceremony might cause "dissension between the Houses," according to Pennsylvania Senator William Maclay. Moreover, the House of Representatives wanted its chaplain included, too, even though that individual had not yet been chosen (and would not be selected until after the inauguration). The worries, never a major issue, suggest that members of Congress thought public religion could be useful to the ceremony, but they lacked the tools for decisive or clear action.[43]

The inaugural ceremony on April 30, 1789, was less remarkable for its stilted use of public religion than for Washington's personal contribution to the event. After the inauguration at Federal Hall, "there was a grand procession to Saint Paul's Church, where prayers were said by the Bishop," according to Maclay. Provoost led a service using the new prayer book that the American Episcopal Church was creating, but he did not preach a sermon. Washington's deployment of religion on the occasion was not a part of the Congress's careful planning,

43. *The Debates and Proceedings in the Congress of the United States . . . [Annals of Congress]*, I (Washington, D.C., 1834), 16–29 (quotation on 25), 232–234; Edgar S. Maclay, ed., *The Journal of William Maclay: United States Senator from Pennsylvania, 1789–1791* (New York, 1890), 4 ("dissension"); Martin J. Medhurst, "From Duché to Provoost: The Birth of Inaugural Prayer," *Journal of Church and State*, XXIV (1982), 573–588 ("dissension" also on 583–584). The first chaplain for the House, William Linn, was selected on May 1 (ibid., 585). The concern for proper order among the bodies and representatives of the government is also evident in "The committees of both houses of Congress, appointed to take order for conducting the ceremonial of the formal receptions . . ." (New York, 1789), Library of Congress, https://www.loc.gov/item/rbpe.1110160k. For discussion of the process of creating a federal political culture, see Joanne B. Freeman, *Affairs of Honor: National Politics in the New Republic* (New Haven, Conn., 2001).

but it turned out to be far more powerful than anything officials had in mind. He famously added the phrase "so help me God" to the constitutional oath. It was a common phrase used during oath taking, and it also echoed the British coronation procedure. In addition, Washington's inaugural address, delivered before Congress, gave his "fervent supplications to that Almighty Being who rules over the Universe,—who presides in the councils of nations, and whose providential aids can supply every human defect, that his benediction may consecrate to the liberties and happiness of the people of the United States." He continued that he was sure he spoke for both himself and for his "fellow-citizens at large," for they, above all, were "bound to acknowledge and adore the invisible hand, which conducts the affairs of men." In the course of his speech, Washington used language associated with public religion numerous times, including references to providence, the "smiles of Heaven," the "sacred fire of liberty," the "benign Parent of the human race," and "divine blessing." By voluntarily bringing a sense of the moment's religious significance to the day, Washington balanced out the lack of formal, institutional public religion. But in doing so he also perpetuated, rather than resolved, the tension between an imagined Christian nation and the practical, legal reality, which was quite the opposite.[44]

The same confused tendencies to both employ public religion and to minimize it reappeared in the first of the two proclamations Washington issued for a day of thanksgiving (see Figure 20). At the end of September 1789, both houses of Congress were rapidly finishing up major pieces of legislation, including the Judiciary Act and the series of amendments now known as the Bill of Rights. A day after agreeing to the language of what became the First Amendment, with its explicit statement that they would "make no law respecting an establishment of religion," Congressman Elias Boudinot of New Jersey "said, he could

44. Maclay, ed., *Journal,* 9; *New-York Daily Gazette,* May 1, 1789, 426 [2]; *New-York Packet,* May 1, 1789, [2–3]; *Daily Advertiser* (New York), May 1, 1789, [2]. As discussed below, the *Daily Advertiser* included a separate note on church services before the inauguration, which apparently did not include Washington. For a description of debates about a "Christian presidency," see McBride, *Pulpit and Nation,* 148–170. For Washington, see Fea, *Was America Founded as a Christian Nation?* 171–175. Washington's first inaugural statement can be found at "Washington's Inaugural Address of 1789," Apr. 30, 1789, https://www.archives.gov/exhibits/american_originals/inaugtxt.html; Medhurst, "From Duché to Provoost," *Journal of Church and State,* XXIV (1982), 586–587. Scholars of American religious history have debated the mechanisms and details of disestablishment, as well as the creation of informal establishments by the new federal state, most obviously through education and the support of missionaries to Indigenous peoples. That history, and the questions of whether for decades or centuries religion benefited or suffered, are beyond the scope of the present project. For introductions to that literature, see Esbeck and Den Hartog, eds., *Disestablishment and Religious Dissent;* Sehat, *The Myth of American Religious Freedom;* and Green, *The Second Disestablishment.*

not think of letting the session pass over without offering an opportunity to all the citizens of the United States of joining, with one voice, in returning to Almighty God their sincere thanks for the many blessings he had poured down upon them." He proposed that a joint committee from the House and the Senate "wait upon" Washington to request a presidential proclamation. Some debate followed; the move could be seen as a "mimicking of European customs," which were shams anyhow. Another offered, "It is a religious matter, and, as such, is proscribed to us." Nonetheless, the resolution passed, and Washington officially made the proclamation on October 3. In its wording, the president made it clear that he took the step at the behest of Congress. In other ways, the proclamation resonated with the traditions of public religion stretching back for generations, including a desire "to promote the Knowledge and Practice of true Religion and Virtue." By employing an old tradition, U.S. leaders tried to harness public religion to their ends. Yet, without the structures of institutional protestantism to support them, the effort was feeble.[45] Celebrations of the first national fast day under the Federal Constitution were remarkably subdued when compared with those of 1775 or 1776, as measured by published sermons, discussions among the clergy, or notices in the newspapers.[46]

The adoption of the First Amendment to the Constitution is the end point of this story, though it in no way put a stop to controversies over connections between church and state. On one level, its prohibition of federal establishment and of federal restrictions on religious expression was hardly surprising. There had never been any institutional establishment at the national level in

45. *Debates and Proceedings in the Congress*, I, 914–915, 923–924 (House), 88 (Senate); *By the President of the United States of America: A Proclamation* (New York, 1789), https://www.loc.gov/item/rbpe.1110150m. The day established by Washington's proclamation was Thursday, November 26, 1789. See also Benjamin E. Park, *American Nationalisms: Imagining Union in the Age of Revolutions, 1783–1833* (Cambridge, 2018), 79–84; and David Waldstreicher, *In the Midst of Perpetual Fetes: The Making of American Nationalism, 1776–1820* (Williamsburg, Va., and Chapel Hill, N.C., 1997), 146–147.

46. Dexter, ed., *Literary Diary of Ezra Stiles*, III, 373; John Woodhull, *A Sermon, for the Day of Publick Thanksgiving, Appointed by the President, on Account of the Establishment of the New Constitution, etc. November 26, 1789* (Trenton, N.J., 1790); "If ever the interposition of Divine Providence . . . ," *Federal Gazette, and Philadelphia Evening Post*, Nov. 25, 1789, [3]; "New York, November 26," *New-York Daily Gazette*, Nov. 26, 1789, [3]; "This day, the 26th of November . . . ," *New-York Journal, and Weekly Register*, Nov. 26, 1789, [3]; "So far as our Information extends . . . ," *Gazette of the United States* (New York), Dec. 5, 1789, 27. See also "Federal Thanksgiving . . . ," *Massachusetts Centinel* (Boston), Nov. 25, 1789, 83; "Reflections for Thanksgiving Day," *New-York Packet*, Nov. 26, 1789, [3]; "In compliance with the recommendation . . . ," *Federal Gazette, and Philadelphia Evening Post*, Nov. 17, 1789, [2]; "Thanksgiving: Yesterday was observed . . . ," *Independent Chronicle: and the Universal Advertiser* (Boston), Nov. 27, 1789, [3]; "Yesterday, notwithstanding the inclemency of the weather . . . ," *New-York Daily Gazette*, Nov. 27, 1789, [2]; "Yesterday, the 26th inst. . . . ," *Delaware Gazette, and General Advertiser*, Nov. 28, 1789, [3]. Isaac Backus made passing reference to the "General Thanksgiving" in his journal; see William G. McLoughlin, ed., *The Diary of Isaac Backus*, III (Providence, R.I., 1979), 1282. Francis Asbury did not.

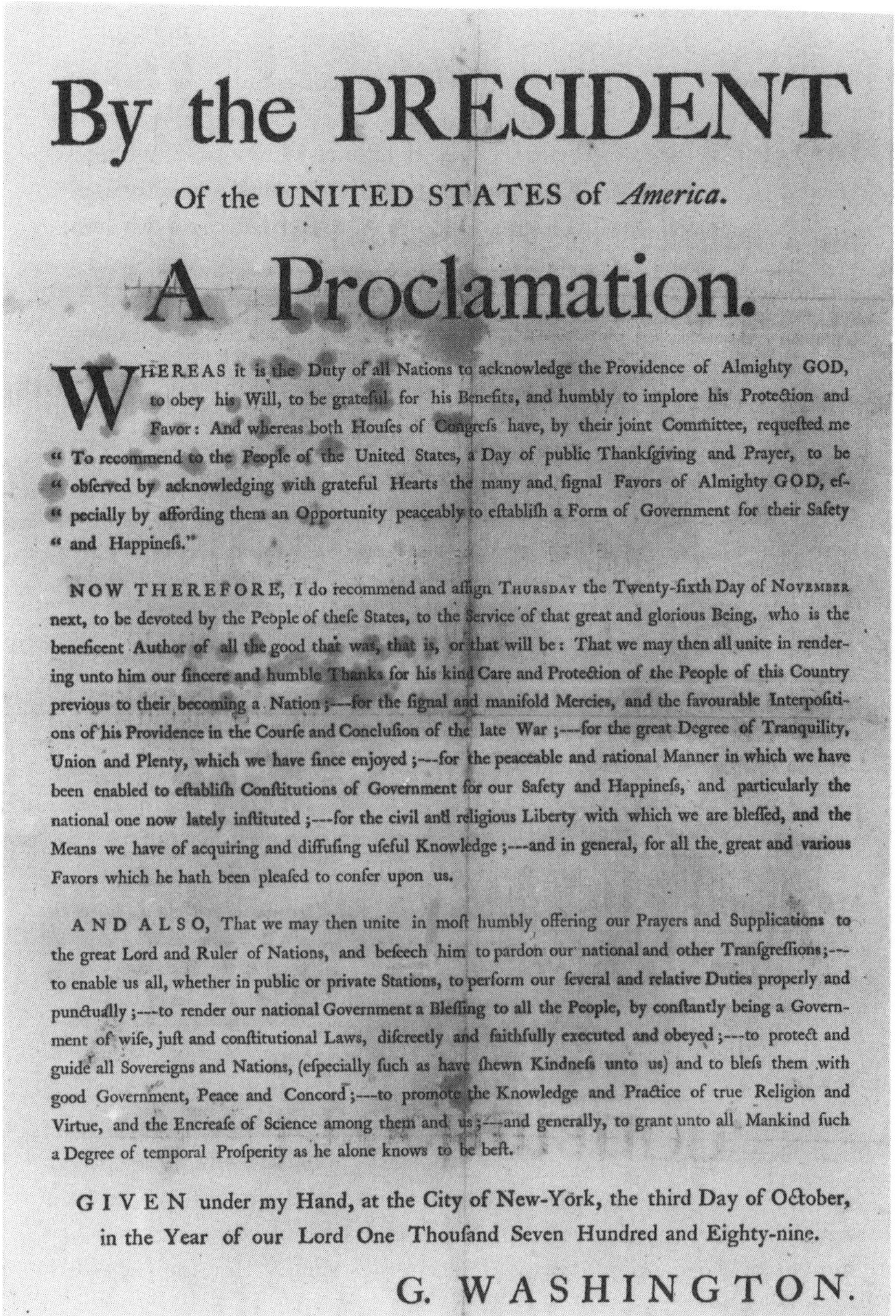

By the PRESIDENT

Of the UNITED STATES of *America*.

A Proclamation.

WHEREAS it is the Duty of all Nations to acknowledge the Providence of Almighty GOD, to obey his Will, to be grateful for his Benefits, and humbly to implore his Protection and Favor: And whereas both Houſes of Congreſs have, by their joint Committee, requeſted me "To recommend to the People of the United States, a Day of public Thankſgiving and Prayer, to be "obſerved by acknowledging with grateful Hearts the many and ſignal Favors of Almighty GOD, eſ- "pecially by affording them an Opportunity peaceably to eſtabliſh a Form of Government for their Safety "and Happineſs."

NOW THEREFORE, I do recommend and aſſign THURSDAY the Twenty-ſixth Day of NOVEMBER next, to be devoted by the People of theſe States, to the Service of that great and glorious Being, who is the beneficent Author of all the good that was, that is, or that will be: That we may then all unite in rendering unto him our ſincere and humble Thanks for his kind Care and Protection of the People of this Country previous to their becoming a Nation;---for the ſignal and manifold Mercies, and the favourable Interpoſitions of his Providence in the Courſe and Concluſion of the late War;---for the great Degree of Tranquility, Union and Plenty, which we have ſince enjoyed;---for the peaceable and rational Manner in which we have been enabled to eſtabliſh Conſtitutions of Government for our Safety and Happineſs, and particularly the national one now lately inſtituted;---for the civil and religious Liberty with which we are bleſſed, and the Means we have of acquiring and diffuſing uſeful Knowledge;---and in general, for all the great and various Favors which he hath been pleaſed to confer upon us.

AND ALSO, That we may then unite in moſt humbly offering our Prayers and Supplications to the great Lord and Ruler of Nations, and beſeech him to pardon our national and other Tranſgreſſions;---to enable us all, whether in public or private Stations, to perform our ſeveral and relative Duties properly and punctually;---to render our national Government a Bleſſing to all the People, by conſtantly being a Government of wiſe, juſt and conſtitutional Laws, diſcreetly and faithfully executed and obeyed;---to protect and guide all Sovereigns and Nations, (eſpecially ſuch as have ſhewn Kindneſs unto us) and to bleſs them with good Government, Peace and Concord;---to promote the Knowledge and Practice of true Religion and Virtue, and the Encreaſe of Science among them and us;---and generally, to grant unto all Mankind ſuch a Degree of temporal Proſperity as he alone knows to be beſt.

GIVEN under my Hand, at the City of New-York, the third Day of October, in the Year of our Lord One Thouſand Seven Hundred and Eighty-nine.

G. WASHINGTON.

FIGURE 20 *By the President of the United States of America: A Proclamation.* George Washington's Thanksgiving Proclamation, Oct. 3, 1789. Courtesy of the Library of Congress Prints and Photographs Division, Washington, D.C.

the United States. At no point had any national American government even attempted to create political unity out of denominational categories in the way that Britain had a century before. There was little impetus to do so anyway. Religious divisions were no longer the primary threat to political stability, as they had been in the seventeenth century. The American Revolution—a cataclysmic war sparked by issues of sovereignty and taxation in an empire that had been united by shared protestantism—had been enough to prove how radically the fault lines within Anglo-American society had shifted since the days of James II and the Glorious Revolution. It was, therefore, in 1791, a natural step for the United States government to formalize its lack of national establishment in the First Amendment. Yet it still bears noting that the amended Constitution foreclosed the kind of intimate relationship with national government that American protestant leaders had enjoyed for nearly a century under British rule. At the same time, as regular pronouncements from prominent clergy of the new nation's prophetic destiny suggested, that legal shift did not fully eliminate the memory of, or the desire for, a nation defined by religious unity. Looking forward into the nineteenth century, American religious history can be told as the tension between memories and assumptions formed within the scaffolding of imperial protestantism, on the one hand, and a nation with none of the apparatus to support such habits, on the other.[47]

Setting aside those later developments, the First Amendment brought closure to an earlier era. With the scaffolding of imperial protestantism from the colonial period in mind, it is possible to find its rusting and disconnected remnants in the United States of the early Republic. Protestants still dominated civic life in the United States, but the boundaries around the dominant denominations—once enforced from London in the name of imperial stability—had been cut down, enabling the rapid growth of new, often awakened, groups who thrived without the benefits of establishment and challenged the demographic primacy of episcopalians, presbyterians, and congregationalists within a generation. In place of the transatlantic competitions between Anglicans and dissenters, or between awakened protestants and their opponents, which often played out in contests over local establishments and for imperial resources, American religious leaders fought against threats of irreligion and skepticism that they feared would undermine the basis of their fragile Republic. Government leaders

47. See, for example, John Fea, *The Bible Cause: A History of the American Bible Society* (New York, 2016); Sehat, *Myth of American Religious Freedom;* Jonathan J. Den Hartog, *Patriotism and Piety: Federalist Politics and Religious Struggle in the New American Nation* (Charlottesville, Va., 2015); Philip Hamburger, *Separation of Church and State* (Cambridge, Mass., 2002); and Sassi, *A Republic of Righteousness.*

were still overwhelmingly protestants, but their protestantism was not a basis for their citizenship or their right to hold office. Anti-Catholicism lingered in the population, but the United States would never go to war explicitly to defend protestantism from the dangers of popery. Voices across the nation might call the United States a "protestant zion," as Ezra Stiles had done in 1783, or a "Christian nation." But at the national level, there was no institutional proof that it was so.[48]

The American Revolution transformed the relationship of protestant institutions to the state on both sides of the Atlantic. The parallel structures of mixed establishment that had privileged certain protestant denominations across the empire, as well as determined the boundaries of toleration, had been torn down in the new United States. In Britain and its remaining empire, the balance that had existed between dissenters and Anglicans within imperial protestantism was also disrupted, leading to new contests for political power. By the early 1790s, the Anglicans were ascendant, as Charles Inglis could tell from his new post in Nova Scotia, but those contests would continue. In the United States, the consequences were far more profound. The new American states rapidly distanced themselves from the kinds of institutional arrangements that had existed within imperial protestantism, shedding their responsibilities for adjudicating competitions between protestants and for defining what counted as a legitimate protestant group. As they did so, they embraced an understanding of religion in which an individual's faith presented no serious threat to the state, not because religion's institutions and leaders promised loyalty, but because religion was primarily a matter of thought. The national story followed different lines. The inability of any national American government to insist on institutional protestant unity dictated that there would be no national religion of the sort that had existed within imperial protestantism. Britain's protestant empire would thus have no direct successor in America. Yet this did not stop religious leaders—and even those in elected office—from acting as if such a protestant nation existed. The tension between institutional weakness and rhetorical insistence on protestant hegemony is a lasting legacy of the Revolutionary era. On both sides of the Atlantic, the connections of imperial protestantism, and the confessional age they had grown out of, were gone.

48. See, for example, Grasso, *Skepticism and American Faith;* and Porterfield, *Conceived in Doubt.*

Conclusion

"The children of God are all one household. The Atlantic flowing between prevents not our united hands and hearts from cordially meeting in this work of faith and labor of love." These words were printed by the newly founded *Connecticut Evangelical Magazine* in 1800, and they came from the pen of Thomas Haweis, a Welsh awakened Anglican and founder of the London Missionary Society. His moving assertions of common Anglo-American sentiment can too easily suggest that little had changed since the days of colonial cooperation. In fact, they were evidence of a profound transformation in the nature of Anglophone protestant community.[1]

In 1800, it was necessary to claim, to assert, and to champion transatlantic religious sentiments. In 1750, no such statements would have been necessary. The structured—institutional and governmental—connections created by the scaffolding of imperial protestantism had ensured that Anglo-American protestants collaborated. The attentions of protestants in Great Britain, seeking to promote their faith in a world where sacred history revolved around the competitions between protestant and Catholic powers, had been focused on their empire's distant American territories. They had raised funds to provide more ministers, more churches, and more books to promote protestant devotion. They had paid attention, too, to what they perceived as the spiritual needs of the Indigenous peoples and enslaved Africans within the empire's reach, while simultaneously building and sustaining structures of legitimate religion that excluded those same peoples and their voices. British colonists, and their European-descended fellows, on the western side of the Atlantic had been full partners in these projects, distributing resources, preaching to souls they thought needed saving, and buttressing Britain's protestant empire on its fringe. Though imperial protestantism was never without conflict, its proponents and advocates nevertheless built a shared edifice that connected their religious work to the empire in which they lived. They wrapped their religious communities around the geography and goals of that empire.

1. *Connecticut Evangelical Magazine,* I (July 1800–June 1801), 32. I would like to thank Brian Franklin for generously sharing this citation.

The American Revolution transformed that protestant world. It pushed the empire's protestants into separate worlds, from which they then created the new, nationally bounded religious projects supported by Haweis and the readers of the *Connecticut Evangelical Magazine*. That process was part of a thoroughgoing reorganization of the connections nurtured by Anglo-American protestants and the networks they used to structure their institutional religious lives. Whereas once a few denominations—principally the Anglicans, presbyterians, and congregationalists that were established in the empire's various sections—dominated institutional protestant life, after the war a rapidly multiplying landscape of groups, many of them stemming from awakened movements, proliferated. Before the war, the dynamics of competition between the dominant denominations had fostered transatlantic networks of Anglicans, dissenters, and awakened protestants, communities that integrated the empire's distant reaches. After its conclusion, protestants had to build new ties to distant fellows and to the mission of spreading the gospel. Awakened protestants such as Haweis took the lead in connecting groups that had so recently been at war, but their postwar vision could not, and did not seek to, re-create the colonial community that had been rooted in the eighteenth-century British Empire's boundaries and goals. They now saw a global reach for their message, and they turned their backs on what they saw as the failures of their predecessors. Meanwhile, many Americans, who had once nurtured ties to British coreligionists as Anglicans or dissenters, now chose to create a distinctively American religious world.

American independence changed the terms of competition between protestants on both sides of the Atlantic. The results of those changes can be measured in bishops. Before the war, Anglicans spent decades scheming to place a bishop in the American colonies, and dissenters remained steadfastly opposed. The war's conclusion brought an almost instant expansion in the number of bishops in the western protestant Atlantic. By 1791, three had been consecrated for the Protestant Episcopal Church of the United States by the Anglican hierarchy, and a further two had been sent to Canadian regions. A sixth, Samuel Seabury, had received consecration from Scotland's minority episcopal church. Finally, John Wesley's Methodists also created bishops, through a mix of selection and election. The changes in denominational organization and political possibilities that made such a rapid multiplication in the number of American bishops possible were a direct result of the end of the scaffolding of imperial protestantism. When Parliament no longer set the terms for protestant competition in the United States, Americans abandoned any effort to define winners and losers among the demographically dominant bodies of episcopalians, presbyterians, and congregationalists as well as the rapidly expanding methodists and baptists. Bishops no longer troubled them. In Britain, the loss of the colonies reopened and polarized older tensions, but it also enabled Anglicans to argue—successfully—that the strengthening of the Church of England in the remaining colonies, through the creation of bishops, was politically expedient.

These transformations marked the dissolution of the early modern era of empire. The contest between protestant and Catholic empires that shaped religious work in those centuries faded from the political landscape. The Americans' willingness to make common cause with the French, and the British need to rely on the resources of their empire's increasing number of Catholic subjects, forced protestant leaders to choose between their privileged positions as cultural-political brokers and their abiding anti-Catholicism. Most religious leaders in both countries continued to support government stability and policy, and the confessional era came to an end. In that context, it made perfect sense that the new United States, a polity whose leaders could imagine no form of institutional religious unity that would be effective, asserted that there would never be a national religious establishment and that no religious tests would be required for holding office. On both sides of the Atlantic, the empire's disruption turned the page between an older era and a new one, between one regime of religious community and organization, fostered by the scaffolding of imperial protestantism, and its successors, more suited for the nations, and expanding empires, of the nineteenth century.

This book has eschewed the words *politics* and *political* whenever possible. The reason is that the motivations of all its actors—imperial governments, American Revolutionaries, and religious leaders on both sides of the Atlantic—were in one way or another political because they were shaped by intersecting systems of power and influence. If one characterizes the Stamp Act protests carried out in the streets or London's Gordon Riots as politically motivated, then one must do the same for the choices of religious leaders to preach at the days of thanksgiving proclaimed for the Stamp Act's repeal or the decisions of English protestant leaders not to embrace the Protestant Association behind the Gordon Riots. To do otherwise would be to construe the term *political* as outside religion, to conjure religion as something apolitical. That was, after all, precisely the intention of the comment made in the aftermath of the Gordon Riots that "the Protestant religion had nothing to do in the late disturbances." Yet the intersection between protestant institutions and government was always political, as were the actions of the influential people who led them. The American Revolution transformed the ways in which those intersections occurred and who could participate in them. The scaffolding of imperial protestantism had linked British protestants in distant places, and, without cynicism, it had guided their sense of how to be *religious* and *protestant* into directions that supported the empire.[2]

That scaffolding set the terms through which Anglo-American religious leaders encountered the imperial crisis and the violence it brought; it determined many of their political options and also the ways they engaged the Revolutionary crisis. Often it determined when and how religious leaders spoke out. Awakened Anglican Jacob Duché most likely did not hesitate when the leaders of the First General Congress called him to pray with them in 1774, a moment that so galvanized those who heard him that he is still remembered by many as a hero of American patriotism despite his subsequent rejection of the Declaration of Independence and flight to Britain. His choice in 1774 to offer a public prayer was a natural act for a leader of the empire's largest denomination, the Church of England. Through many such examples, the scaffolding of imperial protestantism provided the tools with which the Continental Congress helped construct its war as a cause worthy of the support of Christians. Conversely, it functioned to gather the support of British protestants to their country's war effort, silencing protests and cutting off former partners in religious work. Finally, in the war's wake, when the scaffolding of imperial protestantism fully ceased to bind Anglo-American protestants into one system, those who had participated in its communities faced a different set of decisions about what it meant to be leaders of religious institutions in a reshaped political world.

While many Anglo-American religious leaders acted in this new world—participating in new waves of revival, founding denominations, and pressing for advantages in changed political landscapes—some rejected it all. Duché, who embraced the teachings of Emanuel Swedenborg late in life, distanced himself from the woes of the world and the progress of history. "How little and contemptible the Politics of a foolish world," he wrote, "how idle, how wickd, the busy, bustling, selfish Contentious, which have lately shaken two unhappy Countries." In the end, he continued, "both now sacrificed to the dirty views of their pretended Patriots on both sides—the Lust of Dominion—not the genuine Love of Liberty, has at length fully appeared to be their motives." Duché felt "favoured . . . to be torn from the Worldly Contention in which I was too much engaged—and enabled to spend my last seven years in increasing Tranquility, and Reparation for the Appearance of [Christ's] Kingdom." Duché's ambiva-

2. [Thomas Lewis O'Beirne], *Considerations of the Late Disturbances, by a Consistent Whig* (London, 1780), 6, 14–15, 29 (quotation).

lence in the new world is a reminder that the burst of energy that followed the collapse of imperial protestantism had come at a cost.[3]

After the war, greater distance emerged between the goals of state and the projects of protestant institutions. It was a moment of incredible possibility, when protestants found ways and means to influence policy, and simultaneously feared their own loss of cultural power. The best example of such religious activism is the abolition movement, which coordinated the activities of African American and Afro-British protestants, Quakers, awakened Anglicans, and religious mavericks like Granville Sharpe. Together this unwieldly body of diverse religious actors—a configuration that could in no way be explained through the institutional religious structures of the colonial era—lobbied for political changes in a fashion that would have been nearly unimaginable a half century earlier. They disregarded many of the habits that defined traditional religious bodies and thus overcame the intertwining of protestant institutions and imperial goals—including slavery—that had shaped British protestant institutions for centuries, turning religious ends to political protest.[4]

The opposite of abolitionism's energy was anxiety about the place of religious leaders in this new world. Spasms of conservative fear, exemplified by the American Illuminati crisis of 1798, attested to the worry that, in the words of Jedidiah Morse, "in proportion as the genuine effects of Christianity are diminished in any nation, either through unbelief, or the corruption of its doctrines, or the neglect of its institutions; in the same proportion will the people of that nation recede from the blessings of genuine freedom, and approximate the miseries of complete despotism." These phenomena were reverse sides of the same coin; protestant leaders and institutions, no longer so tightly linked to government, had both a far greater capacity to advocate for their aims and no guarantees that anyone would listen.[5]

3. Jacob Duché to Mary Hopkinson, May 5, 1785, Redwood Collection, AM 12905, Historical Society of Pennsylvania, Philadelphia. For Duché's turn to Swedenborgianism, see Kevin J. Dellape, *America's First Chaplain: The Life and Times of the Reverend Jacob Duché* (Bethlehem, Pa., 2013), 159.

4. The literature on abolition is immense. A good starting point is Christopher Leslie Brown, *Moral Capital: Foundations of British Abolitionism* (Williamsburg, Va., and Chapel Hill, N.C., 2006).

5. Jedidiah Morse, *A Sermon, Exhibiting the Present Dangers, and Consequent Duties of the Citizens of the United States of America, Delivered at Charlestown, April 25, 1799, the Day of the National Fast* (New York, 1799), 9. For the Illuminati crisis, see Jonathan D. Sassi, *A Republic of Righteousness: The Public Christianity of the Post-Revolutionary New England Clergy* (New York, 2001), 79–82; and Bryan Waterman, "The Bavarian Illuminati, the Early American Novel, and Histories of the Public Sphere," *William and Mary Quarterly*, 3d Ser., LXII (2005), 9–30.

Index

Act of Settlement (1701), 30, 368n. 8
Act of Toleration (1689): and legitimate religion, 29, 31, 37–38; and imperial protection, 33, 50; and church support, 58, 66; and dissenting clergy, 100–101, 112
Act of Uniformity (1662), 103
Act of Union (1707), 25, 30, 33, 45, 103, 263, 269–270
Adams, John: and colonial protests, 94, 109; and Continental Congress, 157–158; and fast-day proclamation, 178; as American diplomat, 310, 319; as president of the United States, 335
Adams, Samuel, 157, 251, 256
African-descended peoples: and empire building, 12, 78, 376; and Anglican mission work, 46–47, 80–81; and awakened protestant missions, 54–55, 115, 231; and awakened protestantism, 288–289, 297n. 13; post-Revolution diaspora of, 292, 298–300, 361; in U.S. South, 296–302; religious leadership among, 297–300; in Nova Scotia, 299, 302; and Methodists, 306, 361; and baptists, 332; in abolition movements, 333, 380; and religio-racial order, 365
Alison, Francis, 88, 179
Allen, John, 131–132
Alline, Henry, 293–295, 299–302
"Amazing Grace" (song), 1
American Methodist Episcopal Church, 222, 287, 307, 321; Christmas Conference of, 315–316
American national religion: in Revolutionary period, 17, 167, 169, 196, 239, 259; as post-Revolutionary phenomenon, 21, 205, 335–337; state separation from, 21, 337, 362–375; in colonial and Revolutionary periods, 157, 204; as separate from imperial protestantism, 198, 285, 364; as not explicitly protestant, 259, 285; collapse of, in critical period, 363; creation of, in federal period, 364–374
American Revolution: historiography of religion in, 8–10, 15–16, 83–85
André, John, 256
Anglican network, 45–48, 57, 128, 213, 216, 219, 223, 244; and dissenters, 23–27, 63, 85–86, 98–116, 119, 145, 162, 176, 351–359; and awakened protestants, 64–66; debates within, 112; protests of, against coming war, 164–167; wartime challenges of, 213–219, 229–230; in Revolutionary-era British Empire, 235–237. *See also* Bishop controversy; Networks of imperial protestantism
Anstruther, John, 279
Anti-Catholicism: and imperial protestantism, 28–29, 73–74, 262–263; in North American British colonies, 34, 42, 108, 141, 154, 166, 168, 246; and Quebec Act, 141–142; and Continental Congress, 160; and Pope's Day, 252; and slavery, 255; and Benedict Arnold, 256–259; British, 259, 278, 280, 285; and Charles Wesley, 260, 279; in Scotland, 263–272; and public pulpit, 265; in England, 274–278; and John Wesley, 276–277, 282–283; and mission projects, 329–330. *See also* Antipopery; Edinburgh riots; Glasgow riots; Gordon Riots; Quebec Act
Antigua, 233, 237
Antipopery: and imperial protestantism, 4, 28–29, 34, 37, 73–74, 87, 135, 187, 189, 199, 364, 375; and Quebec Act, 139–140, 144–146, 154; and loyalists, 166, 251–252; in British wartime public religion, 187; and French alliance, 248–259; and Scotland (1778–1779), 259–272; and England (1779–1780), 272–286; and disestablishment, 339, 352, 355, 368–369
Appleton, Nathaniel, 174
Apthorp, East, 105–106, 194
Archbishop of Canterbury: and SPG, 23, 45, 47, 105, 360; and North American

authority, 107; and charitable projects, 119, 121; silence of, on Boston Tea Party, 142; and refugee clergy, 235; and Anglican church authority, 319. *See also* Burnet, Gilbert; Cornwallis, Frederick; Moore, John; Secker, Thomas
Archbishop of York, 106, 119, 306, 219. *See also* Hay, Robert
Arnold, Benedict, 256–259, 280, 364
Articles of Confederation, 169, 201, 363
Asbury, Francis, 223, 307, 315–316
Associated Pastors of Boston, 48, 150
Associates of Dr. Bray, 47, 237
Atheism, 4, 100, 268
Auchmuty, Samuel, 125, 175–176
Avery, Benjamin, 49
Awakened network: and imperial protestantism, 6, 43, 53–57, 60–62, 65, 68–71, 86–87, 377; as network connector, 114–116; vitality of, in 1760s, 114–125; and imperial protestant tensions, 120–124; difficulties of, during war, 219–223
Awakened protestantism: definition of, 6n. 7; and imperial protestantism, 20, 53–57, 115, 124; and racial boundaries, 60n. 45; and disruptions to imperial protestantism, 63–72; postwar survival of, 222–223, 232, 240, 244; postwar growth of, 288–289, 301–302, 309, 321; and missions to African-descended peoples, 297n. 13; and postwar institutions, 330, 332–334, 374

Backus, Isaac, 50, 68–69, 290, 302, 340, 369
Bahamas, 46
Bailey, Jacob, 215
Baptism, 46–47, 290, 296, 301
Baptist Missionary Society (BMS), 328–330
Baptists: dissenting denomination of, 23, 28, 39, 48, 50–51, 58; and Rhode Island, 35; and awakening movement, 67–68, 71, 117, 287; colleges and universities founded by, 114, 224; and friction with Britain, 125, 131, 134, 166; and Continental Congress, 176–177; and pro-Revolution sermon, 181; as no longer dissenters, 211, 243; and accusations of loyalism, 213; destruction of buildings of, 226; and Ezra Stiles's vision of Christian unity, 239; in expanded definition of *protestant,* 246; postwar growth of, 289–290, 301–302, 377–378; and postwar awakening movement, 294–296; Black, 296–300, 332, 361; missionary movement of, 327–333; and Jefferson's 1802 letter, 335; and state constitutions, 340, 343, 346–347, 369
Barbados, 33, 38
Barton, Thomas, 74
Battle of Lexington and Concord, 168, 172, 177, 364
Battle of Princeton, 228–229
Battle of Saratoga, 249–250
Batwell, Daniel, 180–181, 227, 230
Beaufoy, Henry (member of Parliament), 354–355
Bell, James B., 83, 218
Bellamy, Joseph: in imperial protestantism, 54–57, 62, 69, 120, 125; and postwar awakened networks, 222, 290
Berkeley, George, Jr., 305–306
Bermuda, 233, 237, 305
Bethesda, Ga.: orphan house and college in, 55, 86, 115–116, 120–124, 231, 233–234, 296, 298, 325
Bill of Rights (England), 29, 368
Bishop controversy: and dissenting networks, 83–84, 86, 98, 98n. 17, 135, 209; and imperial establishment, 104–114, 119–120, 123
Bishop of London, 24, 27, 45, 47, 65–66, 80, 106, 111, 123, 214, 233, 304, 309, 323. *See also* Sherlock, Thomas; Terrick, Richard
Bishops' bench, 144–145, 276
Blackburne, Francis, 57, 135
"Black Regiment," 90–92
Blasphemy, 37
Board of Trade, 1, 41, 67, 76
Boston Harbor, 126, 132, 138, 156
Boston Massacre, 126
Boston Port Act. *See* Coercive Acts
Boston Tea Party, 127–138, 142, 161
Boucher, Jonathan, 88, 164–165, 216–217, 356, 360
Boudinot, Elias, 371–372
Bowie, Ralph, 282
Boyle, Robert, 323
Brainerd, David, 55, 329
British and Foreign Bible Society, 332
British constitution: and taxation, 88; and colonial protest, 92, 130; and popular rule, 139, 142, 147; and dissenting networks, 150, 355–356; and defenders of liberty, 153, 166, 187, 191, 199, 204, 364; and anti-Catholicism, 260; and protestant interest, 277
British Empire: as protestant, 3, 5, 10, 19, 44, 57, 62, 72–81, 140–141, 144–147, 188, 244, 258, 260–286; and North American

colonies, 8, 14, 86; geography of, 14; and seventeenth-century religious diversity, 27–28; as unified by protestantism, 28–34; and bi-confessional state, 30–31; mobility in, 42; and taxes, 74, 83, 88, 95; break of, with Americans, 163, 171, 179, 205, 209, 233, 287, 336–337; Roman Catholics as subjects of, 246–247 (*see also* Mixed establishment); in postwar era, 329–330. *See also* Great Britain
Brown University, 114, 213
Bryan, Andrew, 300, 302
Burgoyne, John, 224
Burnet, Gilbert (archbishop of Canterbury), 108
Burr, Aaron, Sr., 114
Burton, Daniel, 119
Butler, John, 195
Butler, Joseph, 79
Byrd, James, 165n. 48

Calvinists / Calvinism: and protestant establishment, 41, 52; and College of New Jersey, 61; in religious liberty debates, 251; rejection of, by Freewill Baptists, 295–296; and baptists, 302, 331
Cambridge University, 240
Campbell, George, 194–195
Caner, Henry, 47, 88–89
Carey, William, 328–330, 332
Caribbean, 28, 34, 47, 138, 237
Carleton, Guy (governor of Canada), 359, 361
Carroll, Charles, 255
Cathcart, Charles, ninth Lord Cathcart, 190–191
Catholic Relief Act (1788), 261–263, 278, 351
Chandler, Samuel, 61, 121
Chandler, Thomas Bradbury, 108, 111, 164–166, 216, 314
Chaplaincy: civil, 36, 90, 158–159, 174, 181, 241, 252–253, 370; military, 210–211, 218
Charles II, 52, 342
Chauncy, Charles, 7, 162, 209–210
Christ Church and Saint Peter's Church (Philadelphia), 240, 303
Christian nationalism, 7–8, 127n. 2, 158, 218, 220–221, 368n. 41
Churches: destruction of, during Revolution, 223–228
Church of England: colonial establishment of, 8–9; and Methodists, 20; and protestant establishment, 20, 27, 32, 63; as empire's dominant denomination, 20, 33–34, 205, 302; and Act of Toleration, 29–31; monarchy as head of, 36; and North American dissenters, 41, 100; and awakened networks, 54, 70, 122, 287; Wesleys' commitment to, 68, 124, 185; and public pulpit, 77, 178–181, 193–196, 214; and New England, 89; and Thirty-Nine Articles, 101, 113, 135, 261, 339; and colonial protests, 103–109, 379; and Dartmouth College, 123; and American Revolution, 135, 190–191; and Quebec Act, 140–144; and anti-dissenters, 166; wartime and postwar collapse of, 207, 302, 306, 334, 338; and American allegiance, 208, 216, 218; and wartime American Anglican persecution, 215–217; and postwar Methodism, 222; and protestant institutions, 229; and refugee American clergy, 235; and wartime antipopery, 276; pre-Revolution colonial support for, 291; postwar dismantling of, 302–321; and unity across empire, 303, 320–321; historical episcopate in, 304, 305n. 24, 306, 313; and Wesleyan ordination, 307–316; and American disestablishment, 342, 347; and postwar British dissenters, 353, 355–356, 358; in postwar British Empire, 359–362, 378. *See also* Anglican network; Archbishop of Canterbury; Bishop of London; Society for the Propagation of the Gospel in Foreign Parts
Church of Scotland: after union, 31, 33; General Assembly of, 32, 48, 102, 264; English monarch as protector of, 36; in awakening movement, 54, 57–58, 64–65, 115, 120; and anti-Catholicism, 73, 265–270; as dissenting institution, 143, 166, 190–192; and toleration within British Empire, 205, 246; and American Revolution, 212
City of London Corporation, 99
Civil religion, 73
Clergy: and institutional protestant projects, 2–3, 47; homogeneity of, 12; as leaders of protestant institutions, 12–13; dissenting, 36, 101; recognized, 38–40; Anglican, 45, 64–65; congregationalist, 66; awakened, 69; and public religion, 77–79, 149, 155–156, 169; in colonial resistance, 89–90, 93–95, 172; and public speaking, 92; subscription of, to Thirty-Nine Articles, 101, 124, 135; and Church of England during resistance, 107–108; and antipopery, 144; and Continental Congress, 159; opposition of, to Revolution, 165; and American

nationalism, 175–178; Scottish, and the Revolution, 191–192; and American Anglican collapse, 213–218; Revolutionary-era challenges of, 235–236; and postwar antipopery, 264, 267, 270, 276–277; and disestablishment, 344–347; and Constitutional Convention, 367. *See also* Bishop controversy; Consecration; Ordination
Clinton, Henry, 298
Coercive Acts, 127, 138, 142–143, 147–150, 153–156, 162, 185, 222
Coke, Thomas, 307–308, 311, 315–316
Colden, Cadwallader (lieutenant governor of New York), 164
College of New Jersey (Princeton University), 50, 61, 114, 224, 228, 324
College of Philadelphia, 121, 178, 240
College of William and Mary, 323
Committees of Correspondence, 113, 131, 155, 215; as model in Scottish protests, 272
Committees of Safety, 218
Concert for Prayer (1747), 68, 328
Confessional era, 19, 246–248, 254n. 9; end of, 274, 285, 364, 378
Congregationalists: transatlantic movement of, 2, 58, 239; and religious establishment, 6, 31, 39, 48, 287, 290, 293–295, 377; as dissenters, 23, 32, 50, 52, 210–213, 243–244, 246; in New England, 27–28, 32–34, 39, 41, 45, 49, 52, 58, 66, 68, 77, 205; mobility of, in empire, 42; and anti-Catholicism, 74; and colonial protests, 83, 215; leaders of, and civil authority, 89–90; and bishop controversy, 105; and imperial protestant institutions, 116, 292; and Quebec Act, 143; and public religion, 172, 174, 178; and Franco-American alliance, 251; and American disestablishment, 291, 343, 374; British participation of, in postwar missions, 330, 332
Connecticut: and public religion, 93–94, 134, 152; and Wheelock's Indian school, 116–117, 122; and General Association (congregational), 212, 292; and Danbury Baptists, 335
Connecticut Indian School. *See* Moor's Indian School
Consecration (episcopal), 106, 225, 303–306, 318–319, 351; of Samuel Seabury, 310–314, 317, 320; of Charles Inglis, 360; and Protestant Episcopal Church, 370, 377. *See also* Ordination
Consociated Churches of Connecticut, 211
Continental Congress: and imperial protestantism, 17–18, 169; and public religion, 157, 176–182, 196, 212, 214, 285, 363, 379; and American unification, 200–201; and Articles of Confederation, 204–206; and chaplaincy, 210; critics of, 215, 217; and American governance, 247
Cook, Joseph, 332
Cooper, Myles, 194–195, 216, 227, 230
Cooper, Samuel, 75, 132, 158, 174, 250, 254
Cornwallis, Edward (governor of Nova Scotia), 40–41
Cornwallis, Frederick (archbishop of Canterbury), 193, 235
Court of Chancery, 323
Cromwell, Oliver, 199
Cushing, Thomas, 157

Dartmouth, William Legge, earl of: and imperial protestantism, 1–2, 5, 59, 115, 117, 131–132, 164, 219, 228, 232; as secretary of state, 16, 22, 102, 148, 150, 167; fundraising efforts of, for Moor's Indian School / Dartmouth College, 122–123, 325; and response to Boston Tea Party, 137; and Coercive Acts, 141–142; and John Wesley, 185, 186n. 20
Dartmouth College, 122–123, 228, 325. *See also* Moor's Indian School
Davenport, James, 65
Davies, Samuel: as dissenter, 50–52; in awakened and dissenting networks, 61–62; in Virginia's awakening movement, 63–67; as awakened leader, 69–71; and imperial protestantism, 74, 114, 290, 324
Deane, Silas, 179, 201
De Berdt, Dennys, 50, 56, 117, 228
Declaration of Colonial Rights and Grievances, 160
Declaration of Independence, 196–198, 206, 239, 241, 244, 258, 379
Declaratory Act, 98, 103
De Lancey, James (governor of New York), 76–77
Denny, William (governor of Pennsylvania), 77
Denominations: names for, xix; and imperial protestantism, 20, 67–69; and imperial protestant networks, 57–58; and historiography on imperial protestantism, 208n. 2; growth of, in wartime United States, 211; strife between, 239; in postwar protestant order, 287–288, 301, 331, 334; and Church

of England's splintering, 302–321. *See also specific denominations*
Dickinson, John, 157, 197; Articles of Confederation and, 201–204, 342
Diet of Speyer, 11
Disestablishment: American, 20, 259, 336–337; and Articles of Confederation, 204; of congregationalists in Nova Scotia, 291, 375; legitimate religion under, 337–348, 375; in New York, 338; in Georgia, 338, 340; in Anglican colonies, 338–339; in South Carolina, 338–339, 341–342, 344; in Maryland, 338–340, 342, 345; and U.S. Constitution, 338–345, 349, 366; and clergy, 341–342, 346; and state security, 342–343, 355, 368–369; and Church of England, 342–347; in northern New England, 343; and religious liberty, 343, 354, 357, 366; in Pennsylvania, 344; and presbyterians and baptists, 344–347; discussions of, in Britain, 351–352
Dissenting network: and tensions with Anglican network, 23–27, 63, 85–86, 98–116, 119, 145, 162, 176, 351–359; in imperial protestantism, 48–58, 66; and institutional protestant projects, 61, 115, 119; and political thought, 83, 88; and mixed establishment, 101; and repeal of subscription to Thirty-Nine Articles, 101, 101n. 21; and bishop controversy, 105–106, 110, 112; and colonial protest, 128, 133, 135, 143, 147, 167–168, 190–191; and public religion, 150, 152; and North administration, 163–164; and antipopery, 166, 258, 263, 276–277; wartime collapse of, 207, 209–213, 223, 239–240, 243–244, 330–331; and chaplaincy, 210–211; and awakened protestantism, 290–291. *See also* Networks of imperial protestantism; New England Company; Protestant Dissenting Deputies; Society for Promoting Religious Knowledge among the Poor
Doddridge, Philip, 66
Drayton, William Henry, 176
Drummond, William Abernethy, 266
Duché, Jacob: support of, for British Empire, 130–131; at Continental Congress, 158–159, 177, 179, 206, 241, 367, 379; fast-day sermon of, 181; as moderate, 214; biography of, 240–241; and George Washington, 241–243; and Declaration of Independence, 258; flight of, to London, 303; postwar career of, 379–380
Dundas, Henry (lord advocate of Scotland), 262
Dunmore, John Murray, fourth earl of, 148–149
Dutch Reformed, 20, 28, 34, 39, 60, 103, 117, 166, 175, 246
Dwight, Timothy: wartime American national religion and, 198–199

East India Company, 15, 132, 237
Edinburgh riots, 271–272
Edwards, Jonathan, 52, 54–57, 68–69, 114, 290, 328
Eighty-Five Private Societies, 267, 269, 274
Eliot, Andrew, 92, 110, 226–227
Eliot, John, 52, 329
Emerson, Joseph, 97
Emerson, William, 172–174
Episcopal structure / churches: definition of, 27; and English Restoration, 28; and imperial protestantism, 28, 30, 374; and Church of England, 30, 246; and Scottish episcopalians, 31, 246, 306, 317, 357, 377; and Act of Union, 45; and colonial episcopate, 47, 164; and bishop controversy, 104–114, 130; and Anglicans in Revolutionary War, 218–219, 225–226; and postwar American episcopalians, 303–320, 323, 330, 345–347, 359, 361–362, 370, 377; and historical episcopate, 304, 305n. 24; extension of, to the United States, 305–306, 317
Equiano, Olaudah, 333
Erskine, John: and dissenting network, 54–57, 61; and awakened network, 69, 115, 119, 222, 290, 328; and Townshend Acts, 125; and American Revolution, 188, 249; and antipopery, 268–270, 281; and Dartmouth College, 325
Establishment, religious: definition of, 4–6, 5n. 6; and Glorious Revolution, 6, 20, 25, 28, 270; and Church of England, 8–9; and awakened movement, 20; and Massachusetts, 23, 34, 58, 79, 172, 174; in Scotland, 27, 36, 48, 102, 143, 192, 270, 276; and Pennsylvania, 28, 34–35; and Britain's bi-confessional state, 30; denominations of, 31, 59, 124, 142, 341; Anglican, 33, 45, 58, 67, 104, 156, 121, 222, 291, 301, 338–339; and New England, 34, 48, 52, 68, 129; and taxation, 34–35, 41, 58; local, 65, 67, 71, 338, 374; and political tyranny, 108–111; and protestantatism, 141, 281; and Quebec Act, 144, 154; and Articles of Confederation,

201–204; and Maryland, 218; and Virginia, 218; and SSPCK, 269; and South Carolina, 339, 341; postwar changes of, in U.S. states, 339–350. *See also* Disestablishment; Mixed establishment; Toleration
Evans, Caleb, 186–188, 190
Ewer, John, 105–106

Farley, Samuel, 260
Fasting, days of, 3, 75, 77, 92–95, 97, 131; as public religion, 148–157, 160, 169; and American nationalism, 171–174, 177–182, 201; and Continental Congress, 177–180, 212, 214; for British during American conflict, 193–197, 206; and southern Anglicans in wartime, 217–218 (*see* Boucher, Jonathan); and antipopery, 266; and celebration of Federal Constitution, 372
Feathers Tavern petition (1772), 101, 261, 263
Finch, Robert Pool, 194
Finley, Samuel, 115
Fiske, Nathan, 150–151
Fitch, Thomas, 93
Fithian, Philip Vickers, 211
Fletcher, John, 186, 188
Floyd, Margaret, 231
Foreign protestants, 36n. 14, 39–40, 58; in Nova Scotia, 41; SPCK and, 47
Fothergill, John, 117
France: Catholic, 5, 19, 29, 73–74, 86, 246, 258, 262; and Treaty of Alliance, 17; and British mixed establishment, 36–37, 40; and Seven Years' War, 96, 247; and Quebec Act, 139–142; support of, for Americans, 247–255, 258–260, 378; and British anti-Catholic riots, 278–279, 284, 286; comparison of, to American separation, 322, 324; influence of, on new protestant order, 331, 337, 362; and disestablishment, 341; and Revolution, 351, 356–358
Francke, August Gottlieb, 54
Francke, Gotthilf August, 88
Franco-American Treaty of Alliance (1778), 17; reasons for, 248; celebration of, 250–251; and loyalists, 251–252; and American religious leaders, 253–256; and Benedict Arnold, 258; consequences of, for American religion, 259
Franklin, Benjamin, 88, 132, 142, 162, 167, 201, 249–250, 310n. 32, 367
Frederick (Prince of Wales), 36
Freewill Baptists, 295, 302. *See also* Randel, Benjamin
French Prophets, 37–38
Fuller, Andrew, 328
Furneaux, Philip, 50, 52, 101n. 21, 112, 168

Gage, Thomas, General (governor of Massachusetts), 150, 156, 173
Galphin, George, 298
Gano, John, 175
Gaspee (ship), 131
George, David, 298–230, 302
George II, 76
George III: and establishment, 36; and transatlantic protestant fundraising, 119; and public religion and colonial protest, 178; as protestant protector, 140–142, 192, 200, 235, 252, 270, 280, 357, 360; and American Revolution, 182, 193, 206, 211, 277
Georgia: and Whitefield's orphan house and college (*see* Bethesda, Ga.), 120; and Anglican establishment, 291; and disestablishment, 338, 340
Gérard, Conrad-Alexandre (French ambassador), 252–254
Germaine, George, 237
German Lutherans, 20, 39, 76, 246
German Reformed, 39
Germans / Germany, 36, 40–41, 54, 58, 69, 117, 166
Gerry, Elbridge, 251
Gibbons, Thomas, 50, 330
Gibson, Edmund, 80–81
Gifford, Andrew, 117
Gilbert, Mary, 233–234
Gill, John, 50
Gillespie, Thomas, 56
Gillies, John, 115, 264
Glasgow riots, 270
Glorious Revolution: and religious establishment, 6, 20, 25, 28, 270; and transatlantic religious communities, 44; political allusions to, 78, 160; in protestant history, 97, 187; and Gilbert Burnet, 108; and right types of religion, 153; and colonial protests, 192, 199–200; and antipopery, 253, 368; postwar British uses of, 352, 356; distinction between U.S. settlement and, 364, 374
Gordon, Lord George, 274–284
Gordon, William: and dissenting networks, 62, 120, 137; on the colonies' break with Britain, 130–131, 224–225, 228n. 25, 232, 244, 251; sermon of, for Congress, 174
Gordon Riots, 19, 259, 272–286, 378

Gorham, Nathaniel, 322
Grant, David, 281–282
Great Britain: and transatlantic networks, 115, 128, 189–190, 194, 235, 237–238; and anti-Catholicism, 259, 278, 280, 285; and transatlantic charity, 324–327; and post-Revolutionary church establishments, 350, 356, 362
Grenada, 138–139, 261
Grenville, George, 87
Griffith, David, 218, 320
Gronniosaw, Ukawksaw, 333
Gunpowder Plot, 97
Guy Fawkes Day, 187
Gwatkin, Richard, 148–149

Habersham, James, 88–89
Hall, Robert, 328
Hamilton, Alexander, 367
Hanover, Va., Presbytery, 347
Hanoverian dynasty, 36, 58, 78–79, 141, 153–154, 200, 269, 368
Hart, Levi, 149
Hart, Oliver, 176
Harvard College, 73–74, 178, 224, 322–323; Dudleian lecture of, 73–74
Haweis, Thomas, 376–377
Hawley, Gideon, 322
Hay, George (Catholic bishop of Scotland), 266, 271
Hay, Robert (archbishop of York), 106, 119
Henry, Patrick, 87, 157, 326, 346–347
Henry VIII, 252
Herbert, George, 198
Heywood, Samuel, 353
Hilliard, Timothy, 151
Hillsborough, Wills Hill, earl of, 1, 110
Hinchcliffe, John, 262
Hoadley, Benjamin, 78
Hollis, Thomas, 49, 110
Holly, Israel, 134–136
Hooper, William, 178
Hopkins, Samuel, 54, 149
Hopkinson, Francis, 242
Howe, Admiral Richard, 167n. 50
Howe, General William, 232
Huguenots, 37, 40, 103, 117, 240
Huntingdon, Selina Hastings, countess of: and George Whitefield, 1–2, 55–56, 70, 231; in awakened networks, 54–56, 69–70, 117, 124n. 47, 222, 244, 296, 298; as patron of Occom and Whitaker, 117; and Bethesda, Ga., orphan house, 231, 234, 332; and David Margrett, 296, 332; and postwar disentanglement from the United States, 325–327
Hurd, Richard, 194–195
Hurt, John, 218
Hutchinson, Thomas (lieutenant governor of Massachusetts), 90, 150

Illuminati crisis, 380
Impartial Administration of Justice Act. *See* Coercive Acts
Imperial crisis, 17, 84–85, 126–128. *See also* Boston Tea Party; Coercive Acts; Quebec Act; Stamp Act
Imperial protestantism: definition of, 2–5, 25–26; and legitimate religion, 4–5, 10, 42, 59–60, 62, 65, 67, 90, 101–103, 203; networks of, 6, 43–44; and public religion, 13, 60, 73, 77, 79; and Ireland, 14, 219; and public pulpit, 17, 72, 74–75, 77–78, 81, 86; and Continental Congress, 17–18, 169; functioning of, 23–24, 41, 43; and Parliament, 30–32, 368; Parliament as arbiter of, 33, 36, 39, 40, 64, 86, 101, 103–107, 124, 130, 264–265, 359, 361n. 32; and slavery, 78–81, 376, 380; and Stamp Act crisis, 95, 98, 103; stability of, in imperial crisis, 98, 124–125, 128–132; uses of, during Revolutionary War, 157–161, 172–174, 177, 191–196; challenges to wartime use of, 185–190; United States' severance from, 237–238; and anti-Catholic protests, 268–269, 276–277; postwar separation from, 321–327, 377; and British postwar shifts, 351–362. *See also* Anglican network; Awakened network; Dissenting network; Networks of imperial protestantism; *specific locations*
Indigenous peoples: and empire building, 2–3, 12, 16, 129, 376; missionary endeavors of, 24, 54, 73, 78–81, 232, 322; and westward expansion, 72; and institution building, 116–117, 322–327; rejection of Christianity by, 129; American anti-Catholicism and, 255; and religio-racial protestantism, 365
Infidels / Infidelity, 4, 80, 100, 253, 266
Inglis, Charles: rebuttal of Charles Chauncy by, 106n. 25; in New York during the war, 216, 227, 230, 249; and Jacob Duché, 242; Wesley's ordination of clergy and, 314n. 35; and episcopal consecrations, 320n. 42; as bishop of Nova Scotia, 360–361, 375
Institutional religion, 12–13

Ireland: and imperial protestantism, 14, 219; immigrants from, in Canada, 41; and public religion, 76; and institutional protestant projects, 116; and wartime antipopery, 247, 262, 276; as source of British military forces, 247, 284; and baptists, 331
Irreligion, 34, 100, 106, 129, 203, 356–357, 374

Jacobites / Jacobitism, 79, 193, 246, 261
Jamaica, 299, 332
James I (James VI), 27
James II, 28, 152–153, 356, 368, 374
Jay, James, 326
Jay, John, 157, 319, 324
Jefferson, Thomas, 335, 349, 351
Jennings, Joseph, 50
Jews, 149, 179–180, 204, 355
Johnson, Samuel, 185
Johnson, Stephen, 90, 94
Johnson, William, 117
Judiciary Act (1791), 371

Keen, Robert, 56, 115, 234
King, Boston, 361
King's College, 60, 164, 216, 224, 227, 229–230
Kinnoull, Thomas Hay, ninth earl of, 268
Kirkland, Samuel, 232, 251

Laidlie, Archibald, 175
Lardner, Nathaniel, 49–50, 112
Latrobe, Benjamin, 316
Laud, William (archbishop of Canterbury), 104
Laurens, Henry, 252
Law, Edmund, 135–136
Lee, Richard Henry, 319, 326, 347
Legitimate religion: and imperial protestantism, 10, 42, 59–60, 62, 65, 67, 90, 101–103, 203; and American Revolution, 14, 24; and Continental Congress, 17, 174–175, 177, 181–182; and mixed establishment, 29–32, 36–38; and awakened protestantism, 53, 69; and public religion, 77, 79, 150–151, 205; and dissenters, 100; and institutional projects, 116–117, 119, 121, 124; and Quebec Act, 140; and antipopery, 248, 253; and postwar order, 287, 290, 297, 302, 334; under disestablishment, 337, 339–347, 375. *See also* Mixed establishment
Leven, David Leslie, sixth earl of, 268–269
Liele, George, 297–302, 332
Lindsey, Theophilus, 162–163, 263, 279
Livingstone, William, 109
Log College, 114
London Missionary Society, 332, 376
Lords of Trade. *See* Board of Trade
Louis XVI, 250, 252
Loyalists: and clergy, 90, 175, 241–243, 306, 314; as exiles, 156, 356; baptists as, 213; Anglican, 216–219, 222, 360; Wesleyans as, 222–236, 326; Black, 292, 298–300
Luther, Martin, 11

Maclay, William, 370
Madan, Martin, 117
Madison, James (episcopal bishop), 320
Madison, James (politician), 347–349
Makemie, Francis, 33–34, 38–39, 63
Manning, James, 50, 125, 213, 290
Mansfield, William Murray, first earl of, 100, 278, 313
Margrett, David, 296
Maryland: and Anglicans, 33, 38, 45, 107, 216–218; and Catholics in Revolutionary government, 255; and disestablishment, 338–340, 342, 345
Mason, Jonathan, 115
Massachusetts: General Assembly of, 23, 75; 1691 charter of, 33; Regulatory Act of, 138 (*see also* Coercive Acts); public religion and colonial protest in, 149–151, 172–174; and congregationalist establishment, 176–177, 333–335; and postwar religious establishment, 339–344, 350
Massachusetts Provincial Congress, 173–174, 215
Mauduit, Israel, 50, 61, 322
Mauduit, Jasper, 50–51, 61, 113
Mayhew, Jonathan: and colonial protests, 7, 90, 94–96; and dissenting networks, 49–50, 52, 78–79, 83–84; and Anglican missions, 105
Mennonites (Menonists), 348
Methodist Episcopal Church. *See* American Methodist Episcopal Church; Wesleyans
Methodists: awakened, 20, 303, 333; and Church of England, 222, 326; Black, 300, 306–307, 361; postwar ordinations of, 308–309, 313–314, 316, 377; and denominational fracture, 314; postwar missions of, 330
Mid-Atlantic region: religious demography of, in colonial period, 28, 34, 40, 58, 65; SPG in, 129; public religion in, 155–156; end of dissenting network in, 208, 212. *See also specific colonies or states*
Middleton, Erasmus, 275, 277n. 36

Missions: Anglican, 1; and imperial protestantism, 2–5, 23–24, 41, 43; wartime disruption of, 19, 210, 215, 222–223, 230–233, 236, 244; and dissenting network, 52, 54–55; among Indigenous and Black populations, 79–82; and postwar American and transatlantic movements, 288, 292, 295–300, 307, 317–327, 348, 377; and postwar British movements, 332–334. *See also* Baptist Missionary Society; London Missionary Society; Society for Promoting Christian Knowledge; Society for Propagating Christian Knowledge among the Indians in North-America; Society for the Propagation of the Gospel in Foreign Parts

Mixed establishment, 31–36; and imperial scaffolding, 6, 58–59, 72, 82, 85, 101, 111, 263, 375; and American disestablishment, 20, 336–337, 339, 343–344; and British bi-confessional state, 31, 34–45; and toleration, 39; and dissenting network, 48, 209; awakening movement in, 63–67, 301; and public religion, 75; and colonial protests, 126–128, 156, 161, 163, 167–168; and Quebec Act, 139–140, 145; and Continental Congress, 203; and American episcopal church, 303; and British dissenters, 353–355, 357, 361–362

Monarchy, in imperial protestantism, 30–31, 36, 252, 258, 261, 364

Moore, Benjamin, 313

Moore, John (archbishop of Canterbury), 354, 360–361

Moore, Matthew, 297–298

Moor's Indian School, 116–117

Moravians: and religious establishment, 20, 36, 39; and awakened networks, 53, 55, 58–59, 69; and ordination, 107; and public religion, 180; and postwar network collapse, 239; and Gordon Riots, 279; and missionary work, 329; and postwar protestant definitional expansion, 331

Morse, Jedidiah, 380

Moses (preacher), 296–297, 300

Mühlenberg, Henry Melchior, 76, 88

Muhlenberg, Peter Gabriel, 218

Muslims (Mahometans), 355

Nationalism, 7–8, 17, 21, 218, 238, 240, 363

Native Americans. *See* Indigenous peoples

Networks of imperial protestantism, 43–44, 59–62, 65–67; and tensions between Anglicans and dissenters, 23–27, 63, 85–86, 98–116, 119, 145, 162, 176, 351–359; and awakened network and conflict, 70–71; and Stamp Act, 87–88, 95; and awakened network's functioning in, 114–116; disruption of, by war, 239, 351, 374; postwar disintegration of, 321–327. *See also* Anglican network; Awakened network; Bishop controversy; Dissenting network

New Brunswick, 294, 322, 327, 359, 361

New England: and American religious mythology, 7; religious leaders of, and imperial conflict, 15, 83–84, 84n. 2, 94–95, 127, 133, 161; image of, as puritans or dissenters, 23, 83, 109, 166, 174, 199; and imperial protestantism, 27, 32, 34, 89, 97; religious demography of, during colonial period, 28, 41, 205; and Anglicans, 46, 215; and dissenters, 48–52, 209; and awakened protestants, 54, 57, 65, 67–68, 222; response of, to Coercive Acts, 149–156; and public religion in wartime, 172–174; and end of dissenting network, 208, 213; and anti-baptist sentiment, 213; postwar revivals in, 291–297; and postwar establishments, 343. *See also* New England Company; Society for Propagating Christian Knowledge among the Indians in North-America; *specific colonies or states*

New England Company (NEC) (Society for the Propagation of the Gospel in New England), 52, 79, 116, 232, 244, 321–323, 327

New France, 138

New Light, 70, 296, 302

Newport, R.I., 49, 94, 147, 149, 157, 179–180, 213, 226, 238

Newton, John, 1, 117, 183

New York: and imperial protestantism, 33–34, 37, 39; and public religion, 76–77, 175; Provincial Congress of, 175; and disestablishment, 338

Nonconformists, 48, 352–353. *See also* Dissenting network

North, Frederick, Lord North: on Dartmouth as secretary of state for American affairs, 1; and mixed establishment, 101; and colonial protest, 125, 138, 142, 144, 147, 163; and Revolutionary War, 182, 185, 209, 275; and Test Act, 355

Northamptonshire Association, 328

North ministry: and accusations of popery, 140; Wesley's support for, 185–186, 222; dissenters and, 187

Nova Scotia: and Church of England, 34; and imperial protestantism, 40–42; and dissenters, 48; and postwar migration, 291, 293–294, 299, 302, 359; and postwar Anglican decline, 292; Anglican bishop of, 360–361

Occom, Samson, 116–122, 243
Ohio Company, 16
Ohio Valley, 1, 122, 139
Old Light, 70
Old Side Synod of Philadelphia, 65
Old South Church, 132, 224
Olive Branch Petition, 179
Oliver, Peter, 90, 155n. 36
Ordination: and establishment, 38, 43; and awakening movement, 63–64, 295; and American Anglicans, 104; and consecration, 106, 225, 303–306, 310–311, 313–314, 317–320, 351, 360, 370–371, 377; of Sansom Occom, 116–117, 119; and Black religious leaders, 298; and baptists, 301; and American episcopalians, 304; John Wesley and, 306–309, 311, 314, 316. *See also* Bishop controversy; Consecration
Otis, James, 94
Oughton, Adolphus (military official in Scotland), 270–271
Oxford University, 123, 277n. 36, 305

Paca, William (governor of Maryland), 344
Paine, Robert Treat, 178
Paine, Thomas, 216
Paley, William, 353
Palmer, Brother, 298
Pamphlet, Gowan, 300
Parliament: and imperial conflict, 7, 15, 16, 78, 83, 103–104, 108–109, 113–114, 123, 125, 126, 128, 135, 137, 152, 156, 160, 177; and creation of imperial protestantism, 30–32, 368; as arbiter of imperial protestantism, 33, 36, 39, 40, 64, 86, 101, 103–107, 124, 130, 264–265, 359, 361n. 32; and Stamp Act, 86–89; and colonial protests, 92, 94; and Stamp Act repeal, 95–97; and bishop controversy, 104–111; and Coercive Acts, 127, 138; and Tea Act, 132; and Quebec Act, 141–143, 154, 166, 168, 247, 253; and 1774 elections, 147, 163, 166; connections of, to Church of England, 191; separation of American religious groups from, 211; and Catholic Relief, 260–263, 267, 272; and Gordon Riots, 278, 284–285; and ordination for American episcopalians, 310; and religious lobbying, 333; and American episcopalian consecration, 319–320; attempt of, to repeal Test and Corporation Acts, 354–357. *See also* North ministry
Pasche, Friedrich Wilhelm, 117
Payson, Phillips, 253
Peace of Paris (1783), 247
Pennsylvania: and imperial protestantism, 28, 34–35; and public religion, 76–77, 180; and disestablishment, 344
Peters, Richard, 111, 125
Philadelphia Bible Society, 332–333
Philadelphia Synod, 63
Piercy, Richard, 180, 231, 234
Piercy, William, 180, 231, 234
Pietists, 47, 54, 58, 69, 237
Pitt, William, first earl of Chatham, 96, 140–141
Pitt, William (the younger), 351, 354, 356
Porteous, William, 266, 270
Porteus, Beilby, 276, 282–284, 286, 333
Portugal, 322
Powder Alarm, 156–157
Pownalborough, Maine: Committee of Correspondence of, 215
Pownall, Thomas, 97
Presbyterians / presbyterianism: and establishment, 6, 10, 20, 23, 345, 377; in Scotland, 27–28, 30–31, 190, 194; and mixed establishment, 31–41, 48–50, 52, 54; and dissenting network, 56–61, 162, 166, 208, 211–213, 239, 243–244, 346; and awakening movement, 63–71, 73, 77, 176; and missions, 79; and colonial protests, 96–97, 102–104, 131, 143; and bishop controversy, 109, 113; and prewar institution building, 116–117, 119; and Continental Congress, 175, 179; and national wars and religion, 200, 205; British attacks upon, 228; and postwar institution building, 232; and antipopery, 246, 264–266, 270; and postwar protestant order, 287, 290; and ordination, 308, 313; and disestablishment, 374
Price, Richard, 52, 77, 101n. 21, 162, 186, 189–190, 209–210, 356
Priestley, Joseph, 162–163, 283–284, 356–358
Princess Mary, 182
Princeton University. *See* College of New Jersey
Privy Council, 23–24, 103, 360
Proclamation Line of 1763, 126

Protestant Association (England), 19, 274–284, 378
Protestant Dissenting Deputies: and dissenting networks, 48–49, 52, 62; in Sherriff's Cause, 99; and bishop controversy, 112; and Quebec Act, 143; and Revolutionary War, 190; and Catholic relief, 263; and Test and Corporation Acts' repeal, 351; and American disestablishment, 348
Protestant Dissenting Ministers of the Three Denominations, 48, 52, 62, 190, 263
Protestant Episcopal Church, 287, 318, 377
Protestant Interest (Scotland), 267–269, 274
Protestantism: and the protestant interest, 10–12, 29–30, 74, 97, 153, 246–247, 267, 269, 274, 277; as separate from politics, 11; definition of, and historiography, 19; and religio-racial peoplehood, 365
Provoost, Samuel, 320, 370–371
Prussia, 107, 331
Public pulpit: and toleration, 4; and imperial protestantism, 17, 72, 74–75, 77–78, 81, 86; and colonial protest, 92–97, 127, 147, 150–151, 155, 161; and awakened movement, 124; American nationalist uses of, 169, 171, 175, 200–201, 205; in Britain, 182; and postwar American Anglicans, 214; and anti-Catholicism, 265
Public religion: and imperial protestantism, 13, 60, 73, 77, 79; in American Revolution, 18; Ireland and, 76; Scotland and, 76; New York and, 76–77, 175; Pennsylvania and, 76–77, 180; legitimate religion and, 77, 79, 150–151, 205; and clergy, 77–79, 149, 155–156, 169; Massachusetts and, 149–151, 172–174; and dissenting networks, 150, 152; and Continental Congress, 157, 176–182, 196, 212, 214, 363, 379; and congregationalists, 172, 174, 178; and Catholicism, 252. *See also* American national religion; Fasting, days of; Thanksgiving, days of
Public rituals, 76, 154, 180
Public sphere, 78n. 66
Public worship, 3–4, 31, 45–47, 77, 293, 340, 342, 347
Puritans: and myth of religious freedom, 7; and British Empire, 8, 69; in North American colonies, 27, 33, 35, 83, 199; and transatlantic networks, 48, 52, 78; and "universal liberty," 109; and New England's heritage, 173–174, 319, 344; suffering of, in seventeenth century, 236
Quakers: and religious establishment, 20, 28, 39, 41; in Pennsylvania, 35; downplaying of shared protestantism by, 58–59; and public religion, 155; and dissenters, 166; and transatlantic network collapse, 239; and mission societies, 333; and abolition, 348
Quartering Act. *See* Coercive Acts
Quebec Act, 15, 138–147, 151, 154, 166–167, 169, 247, 261
Quebecois: cultivation of support from, 160, 168, 261
Queen Anne, 33, 103, 107, 368
Queen Charlotte, 142
Quincy, Josiah, 162–163

Randel, Benjamin, 294–295, 300, 302
Rankin, Thomas, 183–184, 219, 222
Reformation, 11, 27, 69, 109, 199, 252, 306, 364
Religion. *See* Civil religion; Institutional religion; Legitimate religion; Public religion; Public worship; Vital religion
Religious liberty: myth of, in America, 7; and new postwar era, 21; and Britain's mixed establishment, 35, 39; in dissenting network, 52–53; and colonial protest, 83, 94, 96, 133, 135, 148, 186–188; and bishop controversy, 83, 108; and Anglican support of Britain, 130–131, 166; and ecclesiastical tyranny, 140, 152, 154; and Quebec Act, 143, 168; and Articles of Confederation, 197, 201, 342; in postwar American nationalism, 199–204; and Catholicism, 251, 263; and American disestablishment, 337–354, 357, 366
Religious tests for officeholding, 203, 344, 355, 366–369, 378
Religious toleration. *See* Toleration
Religious Tract Society, 332
Revivals: and awakening movement, 1, 9; after the Revolution, 20, 289–301, 359, 379; and itinerancy, 43, 53; and awakened network, 55, 60, 63; threat of, to established ministers, 65–68, 70; and George Whitefield, 77, 116; and transatlantic institutional projects, 114, 120; and postwar leadership in the United States, 293–301; Black leaders of, 296–301, 361; and postwar British baptists, 328
Revolutionary War and destruction in America, 223–233
Rippon, John, 330–333
Roberdeau, Daniel, 115

Robertson, William, 191–192, 265, 270–272, 279, 286
Rodgers, John, 175, 239
Rogerenes, 37
Romaine, William, 117
Roman Catholics / Roman Catholic Church: powers of, 5, 86, 246 (*see also* France; Spain); split of, with Church of England, 27, 252; and Jesuits, 73; in Grenada and ceded territories, 138–139; in Quebec, 139–140, 142, 166, 251; toleration of, 247; and Continental Congress and public religion, 252; in Revolutionary United States, 255, 259; in England, 260–261; in Scotland, 263. *See also* Anti-Catholicism; Antipopery; Catholic Relief Act; Franco-American Treaty of Alliance
Rosbrugh (Roxburgh), John, 228
Ross, George, 46
Rowland, David S., 253
Russia, 331
Ryland, John, Jr., 328
Ryland, John, Sr., 114, 117

Saint Paul's Church (New York), 227, 370
Saint Paul's Church (Philadelphia), 70
Sandemanians, 239
Sargeant, John, 52
Savile, George (member of Parliament), 261–262, 285
Saybrook Platform, 344
Schism: avoidance of, 39, 66, 68–70, 133, 313, 316, 360; and Wesleyans, 309, 315
Scotland: and establishment, 6, 102; and creation of bi-confessional state, 27–28, 30–36; and episcopalians, 31, 246, 306, 311, 317, 357, 377; and dissenting network, 48, 115, 347, 353; and awakened network, 53–54, 56, 58; opposition of, to awakening movement, 64–65; and public religion, 76; and religion and state reinforcement, 89; and bishop controversy, 107; and institutional protestant projects, 119–122, 325; and colonial unrest, 125; and colonial protests, 161; and antipopery, 260–278, 281–282, 286; and postwar religious authority, 316–317, 360, 377; and baptists, 331. *See also* Church of Scotland; Society in Scotland for Propagating Christian Knowledge
Scott, James, 90–91
Scottish Seceders, 36
Seabury, Samuel: objections of, to Continental Congress, 165; in New York during the war, 216; consecration of, as bishop of Connecticut, 306–307, 311, 314, 317–318, 320, 360, 377
Secker, Thomas (archbishop of Canterbury): SPCKNA and, 23–24, 27, 59–60; correspondence of, in Anglican network, 47, 88; and Sheriff's Cause, 100; and bishop controversy, 105–108; Samson Occom and, 119; George Whitefield and, 121
Serle, Ambrose, 232
Seven Years' War: and Revolutionary War, 19, 109; and Quebec, 75, 261; and imperial reform, 87, 104; and Treaty of Paris, 138; and protestant interest, 153, 193, 246
Shadford, George, 222
Sharp, Granville, 317, 333, 380
Sheriff's Cause, 99, 101, 112–113
Sherlock, Thomas (bishop of London), 66
Sherman, Roger, 157, 367
Sherwood, Samuel, 152–155
Shipley, Jonathan, 128–130, 133, 135–136, 142
Skinner, John, 305
Slavery: and empire, 12, 16, 72, 84; and enslaved peoples, 46–47; and imperial protestantism, 78–81, 297n. 13, 376, 380; and *notitia,* 80; and Somerset decision, 126; in colonists' argument for liberty, 151; and protestant institutions, 189, 231; and anti-Catholicism, 255; and postwar religion, 297–300; and abolition, 317; and postwar British missionary societies, 327; and antislavery baptist politics, 332–333; and religio-racial protestant peoplehood, 365
Smith, Isaac, 322
Smith, William: and revivals, 70; and bishop controversy, 111; and Whitefield's orphanage, 121; sermon of, supporting colonial protests, 178–179, 181, 234; as moderate Anglican, 189, 214, 234, 240; letter to, from Boucher, 217; in American disestablishment discussions, 345
Society for Promoting Christian Knowledge (SPCK), 1, 47, 194, 235–237, 244, 329
Society for Promoting Religious Knowledge among the Poor (SPRKP), 55, 70
Society for Propagating Christian Knowledge among the Indians in North-America (SPCKNA), 23–24, 43, 59
Society for the Abolition of the Slave Trade, 333
Society for the Propagation of the Gospel in Foreign Parts (SPG): and Church

of England, 23, 34; secretary of, 45 (*see also* Burton, Daniel); and transatlantic networks, 45–47, 59, 292; and anti-Catholicism, 73, 329; and missions to Indigenous peoples, 79–80; and colonial protests, 105–106, 133, 135–136, 142; and John Adams, 109; and charitable endeavors, 119, 123; and Boston Tea Party, 128–130; Revolution's effects upon, 215, 227, 230, 234–236, 244; and postwar consecration of Samuel Seabury, 317
Society in Scotland for Propagating Christian Knowledge (SSPCK): and dissenting missionary network, 52, 55; and anti-Catholicism, 73, 268–269; and missions to Indigenous peoples, 79, 232; and Dartmouth College, 116, 119, 325; postwar activities of, 244
Somerset v. Stewart (1772), 126
Sophia, electress of Hanover, 30
South Carolina: and Anglican establishment, 33; and imperial protestantism, 40; and Indigenous missionizing, 80; and Provincial Congress, 176; and disestablishment, 338–339, 341–342, 344
Southern colonies / states, 9, 28, 41, 65; and Anglicans, 97, 107–108, 156, 164, 166, 205, 216–218; Revolutionary losses in, 256; and postwar growth of awakened protestants, 291, 296–302; and American religious establishment, 344; and migration, 359
Spain, 5, 73, 86, 97, 187, 199, 246, 249, 322
Stamp Act crisis: and Board of Trade, 1; repeal of, 17, 124, 137; and imperial tensions, 82, 86–89, 126, 128; religious leaders' opposition to, 83, 94, 96–97, 148, 250, 378; silence of clergy on, 89–93; and limited protest within imperial protestantism, 95; and British commitment to imperial protestantism, 98, 103; and John Adams, 109, 319; and charitable fundraising, 117
Stennet, Samuel, 50–51, 101n. 21, 117, 125
Stiles, Ezra: and dissenting networks, 49–50, 61, 88; in colonial protests, 94, 147, 149, 156–157, 168; and bishop controversy, 112; and Shipley's sermon, 130; and public ritual, 179–180; as anti-baptist, 213; on churches destroyed in Revolution, 226; and loss of transatlantic connection, 238–240, 243; as Yale president, 238, 254, 364; and Franco-American relations, 254; and national religion, 363–366, 368–369, 375
Stuart dynasty, 27, 30, 153, 277
Suffolk, Henry Howard, twelfth earl of (secretary of state), 267
Sugar Act (1764), 87
Synod of Glasgow and Ayr, 265–266
Synod of New York and Philadelphia, 70, 97, 155, 212–212, 218

Tahiti, 330
Taxation: and colonial protest, 7, 83, 86–89, 94–95, 98, 125–126, 169, 177, 185–188; and religious establishment, 34–35, 41, 58; and sermons on Boston Tea Party, 134, 138; and Continental Congress, 214; and colonies' support of Church of England, 291; and state constitutions, 339, 342–343, 345, 347
Tennent, Gilbert, 56, 69
Tennent, William, 50, 61, 176, 222, 324
Terrick, Richard (bishop of London), 47, 106, 111, 123
Test and Corporation Acts, 32, 263, 322, 351–352, 355–357
Thanksgiving, days of: as marks of government events, 75–77; and colonial protests, 93, 96, 149, 378; for royal births, 142, 149; as national public religion, 172, 174, 182, 201; postwar, 363, 371
Theology: and anti-Catholicism, 5, 140, 249, 259; as part of protestant movement, 11; and Church of England, 29; and British mixed establishment, 37, 42, 62, 65, 73, 100–101; and awakened protestants, 53, 58, 289–290, 294–295; in British imperial religion, 77, 81; and colonial protest, 94, 153–154; and dissenters, 135–136; and Church of England in postwar America, 306, 309–310; in state constitutions, 339
Thirty-Nine Articles (Church of England), 101, 113, 135, 261, 339; and efforts for repeal of, 101, 101n. 21, 135
Thornton, John, 1, 115, 137, 183, 233, 325, 342
Toleration: in British Empire, 4, 6, 30–32, 35, 41, 205, 375; Act of, 29, 33, 37–38, 50, 66, 100–101, 112, 309; and Protestant dissenters, 39, 58, 209, 353; in Virginia, 63–67; and charitable causes, 121; of Catholicism, 139–140, 247, 251; in Continental Congress, 177; as center of imperial protestantism, 200; in Articles of Confederation, 203–204; and postwar antipopery, 261–265, 277, 283, 285, 351; in state constitutions, 342–343; and noninstitutional

Christianity, 348–349. *See also* Mixed establishment
Towgood, Micaiah, 50, 83–84, 95
Townshend Acts, 98, 113, 125–126
Treaty of Paris (1763), 138
Trinity Church (New York), 216, 227
Tucker, John, 89
Tucker, Josiah, 190
Turner, Charles, 133–136

United States, religion of. *See* American national religion
United States Federal Constitution (1787), 7, 21, 335, 350, 372, 374; and religious disestablishment, 338–345, 349, 366; First Amendment of, 350, 371–372, 374; and Constitutional Convention, 366–369; and oath, 371
United States House of Representatives, 370
University of Edinburgh, 120

Virginia: and Anglican establishment, 45, 64–67, 107, 218, 291; House of Burgesses of, 65, 87, 131, 148; and Statute for Religious Freedom (1786), 338, 349, 351; and disestablishment, 338–339, 342, 345–350; General Assembly of, 346–347; and Declaration of Rights, 348
Vital religion, 56–57, 69, 124, 200, 228
Voluntary societies, 24, 44, 47, 292

Wales, 27–29, 34, 36, 76, 107, 331
Wallin, Benjamin, 68, 77
Walpole, Horace, 144
Warren Association, 296
Washington, George: and Continental Congress, 157; as Anglican, 218; appeal to, to abandon Revolution, 241–242, 303; and halting of Pope's Day celebrations, 252; and Benedict Arnold, 256; and Selena Hastings, 326; declaration by, for day of thanksgiving, 363; inauguration of, and public religion, 370–373
Watts, Isaac, 97
Weems, Mason Locke, 310
Wesley, Charles: and Methodist movement, 69, 316; as hymnist, 77; and Dartmouth College, 117; and Church of England, 124; and Revolutionary War, 183; as awakened Anglican, 260; and anti-Catholicism, 260, 279; on ordination, 311–314, 316
Wesley, John: and Church of England, 20, 68–69, 124; and Methodist movement, 20, 219, 287, 300, 303; and transatlantic protestant networks, 53–54; and Revolutionary War, 183–186; support of, for Britain against colonies, 222–223, 244; and anti-Catholicism, 276–277, 282–283; and ordination, 306–309, 311, 313–316, 321, 337; and charitable projects, 324; as institution builder, 331, 333
Wesleyans: and Church of England, 222; and awakening movement, 300, 307, 333; and postwar American growth, 306–307; and ordination, 308–309, 313–314, 316; and loyalism, 326
Western Baptist Association, 333
Westward expansion, 126, 198–199, 296
Wheatley, Phillis, 2, 333
Wheelock, Eleazar, 1, 116–124, 232, 325
Wheelock, John, 325
Whitaker, Nathanael, 116–122
White, William, 303–305, 317–318, 320, 345
Whitefield, George: as itinerant preacher, 1, 77, 294–295; in transatlantic networks, 53–56, 62–63, 69–70; and Bethesda, Ga., orphanage, 55, 115–116, 231; and Bethesda, Ga., college, 86, 115–116, 120–124, 231; in lead-up to Revolution, 88
Whitney, Peter, 150–151
Wigglesworth, Edward, 74
Wilkes, John, 141–142
William III, 29, 148, 153, 160, 163, 368
William and Mary. *See* William III
William of Orange. *See* William III
Williams, Roger, 35
Wilton, Samuel, 168
Winthrop, John, Jr., 209
Witherspoon, John: in imperial protestant networks, 61–62, 114–115, 143; and *Dominion of Providence*, 197–200, 206; and Continental Congress, 228–229; postwar fundraising trip of, for the College of New Jersey, 324
Wright, Thomas, 53, 112

Yale University, 198–199, 224, 238–239, 254, 364

Ziegenhagen, Frederick Michael, 117
Zubly, Johan Joachim, 96–97, 131–132